PRAISE FOR

Paul Theroux and *Dark Star Safari*

"Theroux, who for decades has been reporting the universe with eyes and ears so acute they seem Darwinian adaptations to the genre . . . regales us with the humor of ill humor, maintaining a tricky balance of crankiness, curiosity and charm." —***New York Times Book Review***

"If you appreciate a fine writer in his finest form, if you are curious about Africa, if you delight in eccentricity, make the trek with Theroux."
—***Chicago Sun-Times***

"A masterpiece . . . To read just a few pages is to be caught up immediately in the troubling, amazing story that is Africa's past and present—and to be captivated by the storytelling power of one of our great writers."
—***Town & Country***

"Sparkling prose . . . Even the quietest moments come alive on the page."
—***Newsday***

"Theroux remains the inveterate snoop, questioning, often provoking the people he meets. He describes them with a novelist's eye for detail."
—***Wall Street Journal***

"The next best thing to going to Africa is to read (compulsively) this account." —***Boston Herald***

"Wholly satisfying . . . Armchair travelers will wish the book went on twice as long." —***Minneapolis Star Tribune***

"Few recent books provide such a litany of Africa's ills, even as they make one fall in love with the continent." —***Washington Post***

"*Dark Star Safari* is a wonderful, powerful book, a loving letter to the continent from a writer who has discovered that he has carried something of its essence, like a talisman, through his adult life."

—***Sunday Times*** **(London)**

"Theroux keeps us rapt . . . A wistful, clear-eyed elegy for a continent."

—***MSNBC News***

"As good as his novels can be, Paul Theroux is best when he writes about travel . . . *Dark Star Safari* reveals the mystery of Africa, a continent of incredible disparity and resilience." —***Playboy***

"A book that offers insight into a part of the world largely ignored by most Americans. You won't find this trip advertised in travel brochures, but it's well worth taking vicariously." —***Atlanta Journal-Constitution***

"The inveterate, insatiable adventurer [is] at his writerly best when conveying the beauty and wonder of Africa." —***Miami Herald***

"By turns hilarious and harrowing . . . [Theroux] outdoes himself in *Dark Star Safari*." —***Austin Chronicle***

"An African journey of exquisite details . . . A marvel of observation."

—***Buffalo News***

"Entertaining, intelligent, clear-eyed . . . [Theroux] is the best of travelers: intelligent, observant, not easily conned." —***San Jose Mercury News***

"An exciting account, full of drama and, occasionally, danger [from] perhaps the finest living travel writer." —***Star-Ledger*** **(New Jersey)**

Books by Paul Theroux

Fiction

WALDO
FONG AND THE INDIANS
GIRLS AT PLAY
MURDER IN MOUNT HOLLY
JUNGLE LOVERS
SINNING WITH ANNIE
SAINT JACK
THE BLACK HOUSE
THE FAMILY ARSENAL
THE CONSUL'S FILE
A CHRISTMAS CARD
PICTURE PALACE
LONDON SNOW
WORLD'S END
THE MOSQUITO COAST
THE LONDON EMBASSY
HALF MOON STREET
O-ZONE
MY SECRET HISTORY
CHICAGO LOOP
MILLROY THE MAGICIAN
MY OTHER LIFE
KOWLOON TONG
HOTEL HONOLULU
THE STRANGER AT THE PALAZZO D'ORO

Criticism

V. S. NAIPAUL

Nonfiction

THE GREAT RAILWAY BAZAAR
THE OLD PATAGONIAN EXPRESS
THE KINGDOM BY THE SEA
SAILING THROUGH CHINA
SUNRISE WITH SEAMONSTERS
THE IMPERIAL WAY
RIDING THE IRON ROOSTER
TO THE ENDS OF THE EARTH
THE HAPPY ISLES OF OCEANIA
THE PILLARS OF HERCULES
SIR VIDIA'S SHADOW
FRESH AIR FIEND
DARK STAR SAFARI

Paul Theroux

Dark Star Safari

Overland from
Cairo to Cape Town

A MARINER BOOK
HOUGHTON MIFFLIN COMPANY
BOSTON • NEW YORK

For my mother, Anne Dittami Theroux,
on her ninety-second birthday

◇

First Mariner Books edition 2004

Visit our Web site: www.houghtonmifflinbooks.com.

ISBN-13 978-0-618-13424-3 ISBN-10 0-618-13424-7
ISBN-13 978-0-618-44687-2 (pbk.) ISBN-10 0-618-44687-7 (pbk.)

Library of Congress Cataloging-in-Publication Data
Theroux, Paul, date.
Dark star safari : overland from Cairo to
Cape Town / Paul Theroux.
p. cm.
ISBN 0-618-13424-7
ISBN 0-618-44687-7 (pbk.)
1. Africa—Description and travel. I. Title.
DT12.25 .T48 2003
916.04'329—dc21 2002032710

Printed in the United States of America

Book design by Robert Overholtzer
Maps by Jacques Chazaud

DOC 20 19 18 17 16 15 14 13 12

Contents

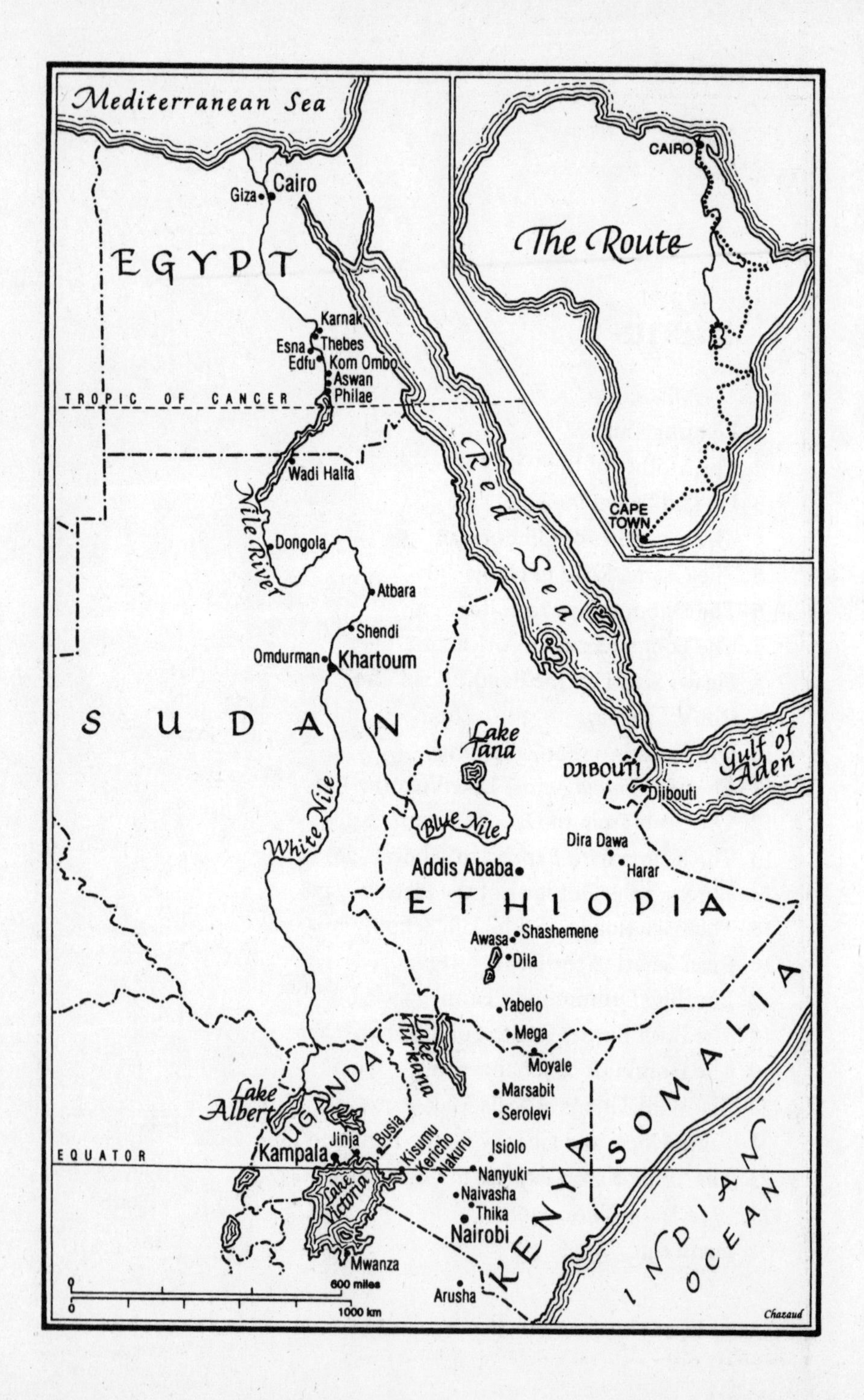

Mediterranean Sea
The Route
CAIRO
CAPE TOWN
Giza
Cairo
EGYPT
Karnak
Esna
Thebes
Edfu
Kom Ombo
Aswan
Philae
TROPIC OF CANCER
Wadi Halfa
Nile River
Dongola
Atbara
Shendi
Omdurman
Khartoum
Red Sea
SUDAN
Lake Tana
DJIBOUTI
Djibouti
Gulf of Aden
White Nile
Blue Nile
Dira Dawa
Harar
Addis Ababa
ETHIOPIA
Awasa
Shashemene
Dila
Yabelo
Mega
Moyale
Lake Turkana
SOMALIA
UGANDA
Lake Albert
Marsabit
Serolevi
Busia
Jinja
Kampala
Isiolo
EQUATOR
Kisumu
Kericho
Nakuru
Nanyuki
Lake Victoria
Naivasha
Thika
Nairobi
KENYA
INDIAN OCEAN
Mwanza
600 miles
Arusha
1000 km
Chazaud

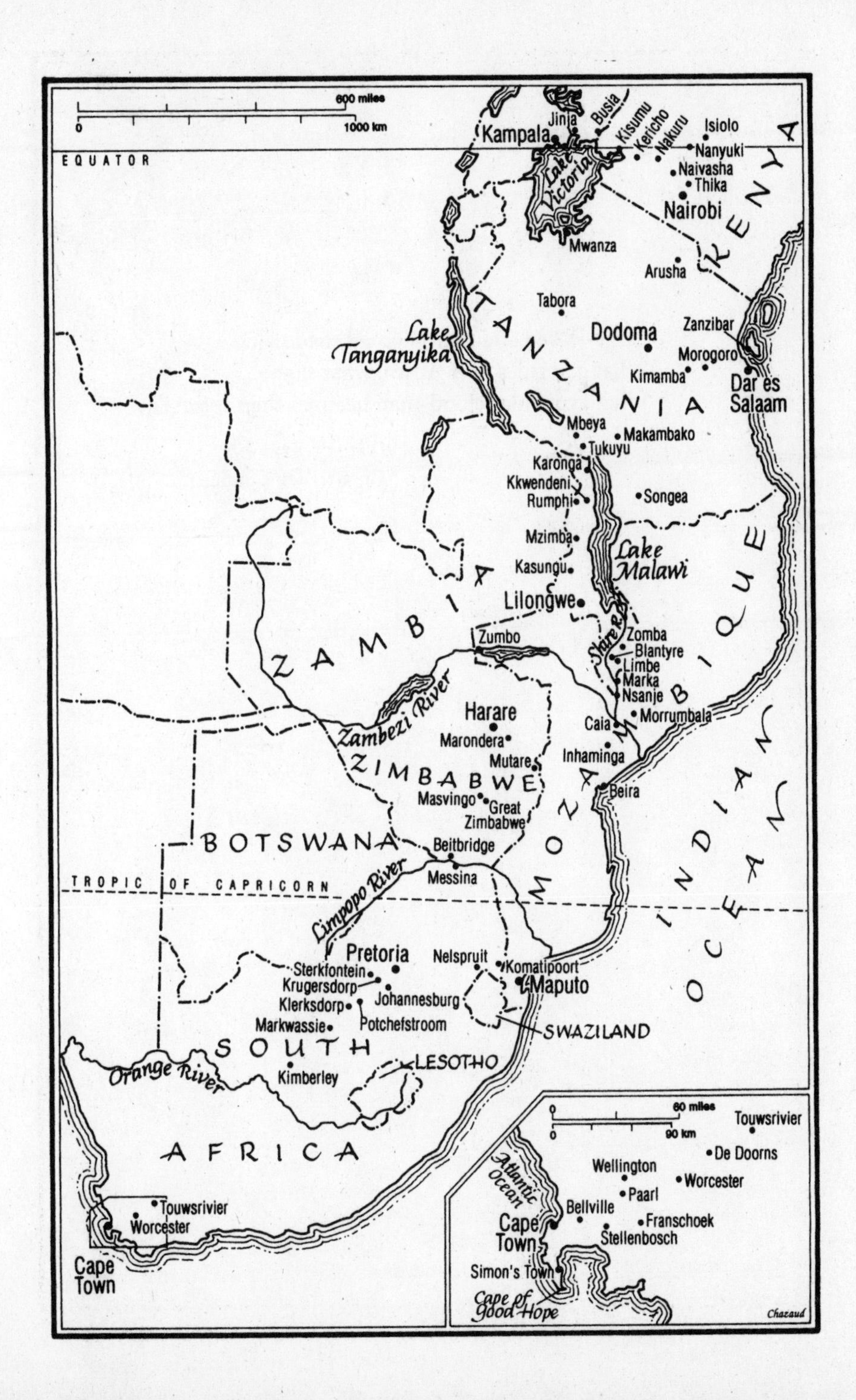

600 miles
0
1000 km
EQUATOR
Kampala
Jinja
Busia
Kisumu
Kericho
Nakuru
Isiolo
Nanyuki
Naivasha
Thika
Nairobi
KENYA
Lake Victoria
Mwanza
Arusha
Tabora
Lake Tanganyika
TANZANIA
Dodoma
Zanzibar
Morogoro
Kimamba
Dar es Salaam
Mbeya
Makambako
Tukuyu
Karonga
Kkwendeni
Rumphi
Songea
Mzimba
Kasungu
Lake Malawi
Lilongwe
ZAMBIA
Zumbo
Shire R.
Zomba
Blantyre
Limbe
Marka
Nsanje
Morrumbala
MOZAMBIQUE
Zambezi River
Harare
Marondera
Mutare
Caia
Inhaminga
ZIMBABWE
Beira
Masvingo
Great Zimbabwe
BOTSWANA
Beitbridge
Messina
TROPIC OF CAPRICORN
Limpopo River
INDIAN OCEAN
Pretoria
Nelspruit
Komatipoort
Sterkfontein
Krugersdorp
Maputo
Klerksdorp
Johannesburg
Markwassie
Potchefstroom
SWAZILAND
SOUTH
LESOTHO
Orange River
Kimberley
AFRICA
Touwsrivier
Worcester
Cape Town
60 miles
0
90 km
Touwsrivier
De Doorns
Atlantic Ocean
Wellington
Worcester
Paarl
Bellville
Franschoek
Cape Town
Stellenbosch
Simon's Town
Cape of Good Hope
Chazaud

Large-leaved and many-footed shadowing,
What god rules over Africa, what shape,
What avuncular cloud-man beamier than spears?

—WALLACE STEVENS,
"The Greenest Continent"

1 ◇◇◇

Lighting Out

ALL NEWS out of Africa is bad. It made me want to go there, though not for the horror, the hot spots, the massacre-and-earthquake stories you read in the newspaper; I wanted the pleasure of being in Africa again. Feeling that the place was so large it contained many untold tales and some hope and comedy and sweetness, too — feeling that there was more to Africa than misery and terror — I aimed to reinsert myself in the *bundu,* as we used to call the bush, and to wander the antique hinterland. There I had lived and worked, happily, almost forty years ago, in the heart of the greenest continent.

To skip ahead, I am writing this a year later, just back from Africa, having taken my long safari and been reminded that all travel is a lesson in self-preservation. I was mistaken in so much — delayed, shot at, howled at, and robbed. No massacres or earthquakes, but terrific heat and the roads were terrible, the trains were derelict, forget the telephones. Exasperated white farmers said, "It all went tits-up!" Africa is materially more decrepit than it was when I first knew it — hungrier, poorer, less educated, more pessimistic, more corrupt, and you can't tell the politicians from the witch doctors. Africans, less esteemed than ever, seemed to me the most lied-to people on earth — manipulated by their governments, burned by foreign experts, befooled by charities, and cheated at every turn. To be an African leader was to be a thief, but evangelists stole people's innocence, and self-serving aid agencies gave them false hope, which seemed worse. In reply, Africans dragged their feet or tried to emigrate, they begged, they pleaded, they demanded money and gifts with a rude, weird sense of entitlement. Not that Africa is one place. It is an assortment of motley republics and seedy chiefdoms. I got sick, I got stranded, but I was never bored. In fact, my trip was a delight and a revelation. Such a paragraph needs some explanation — at least a book. This book perhaps.

As I was saying, in those old undramatic days of my schoolteaching in the *bundu,* folks lived their lives on bush paths at the ends of unpaved roads of red clay, in villages of grass-roofed huts. They had a new national flag to replace the Union Jack, they had just gotten the vote, some had bikes, many talked about buying their first pair of shoes. They were hopeful and so was I, a teacher living near a settlement of mud huts among dusty trees and parched fields. The children shrieked at play; the women, bent double — most with infants slung on their backs — hoed patches of corn and beans; and the men sat in the shade stupefying themselves on *chibuku,* the local beer, or *kachasu,* the local gin. That was taken for the natural order in Africa: frolicking children, laboring women, idle men.

Now and then there was trouble: someone transfixed by a spear, drunken brawls, political violence, goon squads wearing the ruling-party T-shirt and raising hell. But in general the Africa I knew was sunlit and lovely, a soft green emptiness of low, flat-topped trees and dense bush, bird squawks, giggling kids, red roads, cracked and crusty brown cliffs that looked newly baked, blue remembered hills, striped and spotted animals and ones with yellow fur and fangs, and every hue of human being, from pink-faced planters in knee socks and shorts to brown Indians to Africans with black gleaming faces, and some people so dark they were purple. The predominant sound of the African bush was not the trumpeting of elephants nor the roar of lions but the coo-cooing of the turtledove.

After I left Africa, there was an eruption of news about things going wrong, acts of God, acts of tyrants, tribal warfare and plagues, floods and starvation, bad-tempered political commissars, and little teenage soldiers who were hacking people. "Long sleeves?" they teased, cutting off hands; "short sleeves" meant lopping the whole arm. One million people died, mostly Tutsis, in the Rwanda massacres of 1994. The red African roads remained, but they were now crowded with ragged, bundle-burdened, fleeing refugees.

Journalists pursued them. Goaded by their editors to feed a public hungering for proof of savagery on earth, reporters stood near starving Africans in their last shaking fuddle and intoned on the TV news for people gobbling snacks on their sofas and watching in horror. "And these people" — tight close-up of a death rattle — "these are the lucky ones."

You always think, Who says so? Had something fundamental changed since I was there? I wanted to find out. My plan was to go from Cairo to Cape Town, top to bottom, and to see everything in between.

Now African news was as awful as the rumors. The place was said to be desperate, unspeakable, violent, plague-ridden, starving, hopeless, dying on its feet. *And these are the lucky ones.* I thought, since I had plenty of time and nothing pressing, that I might connect the dots, crossing borders and seeing the hinterland rather than flitting from capital to capital, being greeted by unctuous tour guides. I had no desire to see game parks, though I supposed at some point I would. The word "safari," in Swahili, means "journey"; it has nothing to do with animals. Someone "on safari" is just away and unobtainable and out of touch.

Out of touch in Africa was where I wanted to be. The wish to disappear sends many travelers away. If you are thoroughly sick of being kept waiting at home or at work, travel is perfect: let other people wait for a change. Travel is a sort of revenge for having been put on hold, having to leave messages on answering machines, not knowing your party's extension, being kept waiting all your working life — the homebound writer's irritants. Being kept waiting is the human condition.

I thought, Let other people explain where I am. I imagined the dialogue:

"When will Paul be back?"

"We don't know."

"Where is he?"

"We're not sure."

"Can we get in touch with him?"

"No."

Travel in the African bush can also be a sort of revenge on cellular phones and fax machines, on telephones and the daily paper, on the creepier aspects of globalization that allow anyone who chooses to get his insinuating hands on you. I desired to be unobtainable. Kurtz, sick as he is, attempts to escape from Marlow's riverboat, crawling on all fours like an animal, trying to flee into the jungle. I understood that.

I was going to Africa for the best reason — in a spirit of discovery; and for the pettiest — simply to disappear, to light out, with a suggestion of *I dare you to try and find me.*

Home had become a routine, and routines make time pass quickly. I was a sitting duck in my predictable routine: people knew when to call me; they knew when I would be at my desk. I was in such regular touch it was like having a job, a mode of life I hated. I was sick of being called up and importuned, asked for favors, hit up for money. You stick around too long and people begin to impose their own deadlines on you. "I need this by the twenty-fifth" or "Please read this by Friday" or "Try to finish this over the weekend" or "Let's have a conference call on Wednesday." *Call me, fax me, e-mail me. You can get me anytime on my cell phone, here's the number.*

Being available at any time in the totally accessible world seemed to me pure horror. It made me want to find a place that was not accessible at all: no phones, no fax machines, not even mail delivery, the wonderful old world of being out of touch. In other words, gone away.

All I had to do was remove myself. I loved not having to ask permission, and in fact in my domestic life things had begun to get a little predictable, too — Mr. Paul at home every evening when Mrs. Paul came home from work. "I made spaghetti sauce . . . I seared some tuna . . . I'm scrubbing some potatoes . . ." The writer in his apron, perspiring over his béchamel sauce, always within earshot of the telephone. You have to pick it up because it is ringing in your ear.

I wanted to drop out. People said, "Get a cell phone, use FedEx, sign up for Hotmail, stop in at Internet cafés, visit my Web site . . ."

I said no thanks. The whole point of my leaving was to escape this stuff, to be out of touch. The greatest justification for travel is not self-improvement but rather performing a vanishing act, disappearing without a trace. As Huck put it, lighting out for the territory.

Africa is one of the last great places on earth a person can vanish into. I wanted that. Let them wait. I have been kept waiting far too many times for far too long.

I am outta here, I told myself. The next Web site I visit will be that of the poisonous Central African bird-eating spider.

A morbid aspect of my departure for Africa was that people began offering condolences. Say you're leaving for a dangerous place. Your friends call sympathetically, as though you've caught a serious illness that might prove fatal. Yet I found these messages unexpectedly stimulating, a heartening preview of what my own demise would be like. Lots of tears! Lots of mourners! But also, undoubtedly, many people boasting solemnly, "I told him not to do it. I was one of the last people to talk to him."

I had gotten to Lower Egypt, and was heading south, in my usual traveling mood: hoping for the picturesque, expecting misery, braced for the appalling. Happiness was unthinkable, for although happiness is desirable, it is a banal subject for travel. Therefore, Africa seemed perfect for a long journey.

2 ◇◇◇

The Mother of the World

THE WEATHER FORECAST printed in a box in the Cairo newspaper was "Dust" on the cold day in February when I arrived, a day of gritty wind and dust-browned sky. The forecast for tomorrow was the same — no temperature prediction, nothing about sunshine or clouds or rain, just the one word, "Dust." It was the sort of weather report you might expect on Mars. Nevertheless, Cairo (population sixteen million), a city of bad air and hideous traffic, was made habitable, even pleasant, by its genial populace and its big placid river, brown under a brown sky.

Tourists have been visiting Egypt for 2,500 years, and Herodotus (roughly 480–420 B.C.) was the first methodical sightseer. He was fascinated by Egyptian geography and ruins, and was also collecting information for his *History*, of which the whole of volume two is Egyptiana. Herodotus traveled as far as the First Cataract, which is Aswan. Later Greeks and Romans were tourists in Egypt, raiding tombs, stealing whatever they could carry, and leaving graffiti that are still visible today. The grander structures were also pilfered, and for 2,000 years such things — obelisks mainly — were dragged away and set up elsewhere and goggled at. Though obelisks were sacred to the sun god, no one had any idea of their meaning. The Egyptians called them *tekhenu;* the Greeks named them *obeliskos*, because they looked like small spits for kebabs.

The first stolen obelisk was set up in Rome in 10 B.C., and a dozen more followed. Felix Fabri of Ulm, a German friar, went to Egypt in 1480, taking notes throughout his trip. An obelisk he sketched in Alexandria now stands in New York's Central Park. In the same spirit of plunder and trophy hunting, Mussolini looted a fourth-century obelisk from Ethiopia, the Obelisk of Axum. This treasure now stands in front of the United Nations Food and Agriculture Organization in Rome, near Caracalla. Because the scattered wars in Europe in the seventeenth and eighteenth centuries made travel difficult, Egypt was regarded as a safe and colorful destination. Egypt stood for the Orient, for sensuality, for paganism. Egyptology did not start in earnest until the early nineteenth century, when the Rosetta stone was deciphered and at last the ruins disclosed the secrets of their script. This discovery unleashed a rage for Egyptiana, and travelers, writers, and painters flocked to the Nile Valley in search of the exotic.

Even then, Egyptian ruins had been ruins for thousands of years. The Egyptians themselves had never left, and though Arabized and Islamized, and nominally conquered by the French, the British, and the Turks, and their homeland used as a battleground in European wars, Egyptians went on farming, fishing, and living at the edges of their broken temples and tombs. They were blessed with the Nile. The ruins they regarded as a kind of quarry, a great stockpile of building materials to cannibalize for new houses and walls. Foreign soldiers had done the same, customarily garrisoning themselves in the ancient shrines, and any temple unsuitable for French or British cavalrymen was commandeered for their animals.

Throughout, as Egypt was looted and trampled and gaped at, Egyptians remained Egyptian. In pharaonic times Egyptians made a habit of repelling or subverting or enslaving anyone who ventured into their kingdom. But ever since Herodotus they have been welcoming foreigners with a mixture of banter, hearty browbeating, teasing humor, effusiveness, and the sort of insincere familiarity I associate with people trying to become intimate enough with me to pick my pocket.

"Meesta, meesta! My fren', what country you come from? America number one! My fren', you come with me . . . my house. You come. Meesta!"

In Cairo, there was a thin line between pestering and hospitality. Indeed, they often amounted to the same thing, and although there were plenty of beggars, there was little thievery. Egyptians seemed amazingly agreeable. You think they have been briefed by some government bureau to tell jokes, but no, they are just hungry, desperation making them genial and innovative. It was obvious they were hoping to make a buck, but at least they had the grace to do it with a smile.

"You don't speak Arabic today," Amir, a cab driver, said, "but you speak Arabic very good tomorrow."

Everyone in this vast, much-visited city had the patter. Amir then taught me the Arabic for "please," "thank you," and "sorry." I already knew *inshallah,* which means "God willing."

"Now teach me 'No, thank you. I have no need.'"

Amir did so, and before he dropped me off, he insisted that I hire him the next day.

"No, thank you. I have no need," I said in Arabic.

He laughed, but of course kept pestering.

"My name Guda, like same as Dutch cheese," another cab driver said. "This is not limousine — not cost one hundred pounds. Just car, black-and-white taxi only. But clean. Fast. Handsome driver."

Guda spent the entire ride nagging me to hire him for the whole day. That was the theme in Cairo. Once someone had your attention he didn't want to let go, for if he did you would slip away, forcing him to spend the day prowling for a fare. Business was slow, but I saw the spiel as another age-old artifact. Like the plaster sphinxes and the chess sets and the camel saddles sold to the tourists, the patter was another homemade curio, burnished over the centuries.

Nearer the ruins, the pyramids, and the sights they just gabbled, aiming to nail you, and they were expert, like Mohammed Kaburia, chubby, greasy-faced, wearing a made-in-China nylon jacket. It was sunset in Giza. I wanted to see the pyramids and the Sphinx in the weird dusty light.

"Only twenty for the horse — you come, my fren'," Mohammed said. "You see Safinkees! I take you into a pyramid and you see the rooms and touch the moomiya."

I fished for my twenty Egyptian pounds. We mounted the horses and were off, trotting through garbage beside ancient walls.

"You pay later. Hey, how many wives you got? I got four — two Egyptian, two English. I keep them very busy!"

"Of course."

"You are a gentleman. I can see in your face."

"Twenty pounds, right?"

"No, no, twenty American dollars. See Safinkees. You touch the moomiya! My fren' he let me. He know me. Maybe you buy picture. Papyrus. Mother-of-pearl box."

"You said twenty pounds."

"I say 'twenty.' You hear me say 'twenty'? Use Visa card!" He leaned over and whipped my pony. "Make the horse gallop. I see you next week. Ha!"

He took out a cell phone and stabbed the buttons with his stubby fingers and shouted into it, and then, "This my phone. 'Hello, hello!' Cost two thousand. Horse is five thousand. Arabian is twenty thousand, maybe thirty. Money! You give me baksheesh."

"Money, money."

"America, best country! America money, best money!"

We were still jogging along, up one muddy littered alley, down another. As dusk fell, men in gowns and women in robes walked in a stately way, in spite of the puddles, and children shrieked at me on my pony.

"You give me America money. I take you inside pyramid."

"Money, money, money, money. Please stop saying 'money.'"

Mohammed howled into his phone and dug his heels into his horse's belly and slapped the reins against his horse's flanks. He led me past a wall that formed the perimeter of the Giza pyramids and a tumbledown neighborhood of squatters and slum dwellers attached to the wall. In Egypt every wall attracts dumpers, litterers, shitters and pissers, dogs and cats, and the noisiest children.

Mohammed was manic in his banter: "America — strong country. Number-one country. My fren', baksheesh! You buy papyrus . . . you touch moomiya . . . you take picture in pyramid . . . see Safinkees."

Yakkety-yak, all for money.

And yet, in spite of his banter and his pestering and his deceits, the jaunt on horseback that early evening in Giza was gorgeous. Trotting through the back alleys that reeked of rotting food and litter, we passed basins of dirty water and buckets of garbage and chamber pots that were being emptied from upper balconies, with a squawk that might have meant "gardy loo." The smoke from fires lit in braziers, the stink of pissed-on walls, the graffiti, the dust piles, the brick shards, the dried mud, the neighborhood so decrepit and worn, so pulverized, it looked as though it had been made out of whole wheat flour and baked five thousand years ago and was now turning into crumbs. But I loved riding in the crepuscular dusk, parting the air that was penetrated with food smells and smoke and garbage, jogging through puddles with the muezzin howling, the dogs barking, the children chasing my sorry pony — the lovely evening sky showing through the dust cloud and striped bright yellow and cobalt blue. And then the pyramid, smaller than I had expected, so brown and corrugated and geometric it looked like giant origami folded from cardboard.

"Safinkees," he said, and waved his arms.

The Greek word "sphinx" is unpronounceable to Egyptians, and also inaccurate. The fanciful Greeks associated it with their own mythical creature and appropriated it, much as the Arabs have done.

"What do you call it?" I asked.

"His name Abu el-Houl," Mohammed said.

But that is no more than an Arab nickname meaning "the Father of Terror." The enigmatic creature is Ra-Herakhti, manifestation of the sun god, with a lion's body and the facial features of Khafre, who was king of Egypt at the time of its construction 4,500 years ago. *Sesheb ankh,* or "living image," is the ancient Egyptian term for such a statue.

Holding on to my saddle, I peered into the dusk at the worn-down and noseless face resting on crumbly forepaws, like a sand sculpture that had been rained on.

Because the Sphinx is the embodiment of dawn, it faces east, and so the sun was setting in the dust cloud directly behind it. You would not know its orientation from some of the paintings that have been done of it. Egyptian ruins are so atmospheric they tend to inspire the watcher to blur reality — the overexcited traveler seeing much more than is there. Hardly a painting depicts the Sphinx as it is, and even that stickler for Middle Eastern detail David Roberts gives it a yearning expression and, for effect, has it facing the wrong way. Earlier painters gave it thick lips and big staring eyes; the painter-traveler Dominique-Vivant Denon gave it a Negroid face and a wondering gaze.

"No drawing that I have seen conveys a proper idea of it," Flaubert wrote, which is probably true. When he rode out to it in 1849 he repeated the name the Arabs had told him, Abu el-Houl, the Father of Terror, and noted in his diary, "We stop before the Sphinx; it fixes us with a terrifying stare." He also said it seemed to him doglike, "pug-nosed and tattered," and Flaubert's friend Maxime du Camp claimed that it looked "like an enormous mushroom when viewed from behind." The Sphinx was the one sight on his grand tour that Mark Twain did not mock. The pages in *The Innocents Abroad* that concern the Sphinx are unique in that breezy book, and rare in Twain's work, for their descriptive flights, as he rhapsodizes, even gushes, studying the thing. "So sad, so earnest, so longing, so patient . . . It was MEMORY-RETROSPECTION wrought into visible tangible form . . . [and] reveals to one something of what he shall feel when he shall stand in the presence of God."

This is travelers' invention: I saw it, you didn't, therefore I am licensed to exaggerate. Twain tells us how he had longed to see the Sphinx, but he at least had seen a photo of it. Flaubert had seen drawings but never a photograph — there were none. In fact, Maxime du Camp claimed to be the first to take a picture of it. In his life of Flaubert, Geoffrey Wall noted that these men were probably the last Europeans to see it in this way, afresh. But photography's spoiling the visual pleasure of places is nothing compared to the way the Internet and our age of information have destroyed the pleasure of discovery in travel.

Invention in travel accords with Jorge Luis Borges's view, floated beautifully through his poem "Happiness" ("La Dicha"), that in our encounters with the world, "everything happens for the first time." Just as "whoever embraces a woman is Adam," and "whoever lights a match in the dark is inventing fire," anyone's first view of the Sphinx is new: "In the desert I saw the young Sphinx, which has just been sculpted . . . Everything happens for the first time, but in a way that is eternal."

Ruins especially lend themselves to invention; because they are incomplete, we finish them in our imagination. And although later that evening I ran into a beaky-faced man, in wilting clothes, thirtyish, fogeyish, frumpish, one of those pale bosomy academics you could easily mistake for a senile old woman, who waved his art history degree at me and said with slushy pedantry, "The Sphinx is vastly overrated," the Sphinx is a perfect object to turn into something of your very own, something grand or, in Nigel's case, something negligible.

Mohammed said, "You give me money. I show you moomiya. You touch!"

"Please stop saying 'money.'"

He laughed, he gabbled, I was not listening, I didn't really care, I was laughing myself. I felt a great happiness — the horse, the light, the decay, the ancient shapes, the children's laughter — and this day became one of the epiphanies of my traveling life.

I dismounted and, leading my horse closer to the Sphinx, was approached by a woman who asked, using gestures, if I would help her lift a heavy plastic basket. I heaved it. It was heavy, perhaps forty pounds, and Mohammed laughed at me from where he sat on his horse. The woman curtsied while I placed the big basket onto her noggin. She could not hoist it alone, but she easily carried it on her head.

Riding back to the stable, Mohammed began shouting ahead of me, louder than before.

"Look! Look! See that man!"

Someone was standing by a wall, a young man in a white robe, a tangle of turban on his head.

"He not from Egypt. He from Sudan. I know, I know, because his face. He from there."

Mohammed waved his arm, indicating far away — southerly, in a Sudanese direction.

"Black!" he howled, for blackness was a novelty in Lower Egypt, and he galloped onward. "Black!"

◈ ◈ ◈

Traveling south of Egypt, I would be entering Sudan. I did not have a Sudanese visa, and for Americans such visas were hard to come by. The reason was understandable. On the pretext that Sudan was making anti-American bombs (and, some people felt, in order to correct the negative image created by his involvement in a sex scandal, to look decisive and presidential even if it meant risking lives and flattening foreign real estate), President Clinton ordered air strikes against Sudan. He succeeded in destroying a pharmaceutical plant outside Khartoum in August 1998. This bomb crater would be on my itinerary, for after the bombs were dropped no one in the United States took much interest. Though we become hysterical at the thought that someone might bomb us, bombs that we explode elsewhere, in little countries far away, are just theater, of small consequence, another public performance of our White House, the event factory.

"I would like to see the bomb site," I was telling the Sudanese ambassador, Salih Mashamoun, in his office in Cairo. He was a pleasant, well-educated man who had been ambassador to Vietnam. He was Nubian, he said, from northern Sudan, and raised speaking Nubian.

"Is Nubian anything like Arabic?"

"Nubian has no connection with Arabic. It is the true pharaonic tongue."

He said that he regarded Nubians as the genuine Egyptians and that colonialists had confused the issue by imposing a frontier that divided Egypt and Sudan. Talking with him made me want to go to Nubia.

"There, *inshallah,* you will find pyramids and ruins that are greater than Egyptian. Nubia is the source of Egyptian culture. You must see Dongola and Meroë. The Upper Nile. The Nubian tombs."

First I needed a visa. I made repeated visits to the Sudanese embassy. The doorman got to know me, and after three visits he simply waved me through the gate and I went unaccompanied upstairs to the ambassador's office. When I put my head through the doorway the ambassador beckoned me in, urged me to sit and talk, offered me tea, and told me that Khartoum had not responded to my visa application.

"But perhaps, *inshallah,* it will be given."

"What shall I do?"

"You can reapply. Or see Mr. Qurashi. He is consul."

Qurashi Saleh Ahmed was thin, smirking, officious, always waving a cigarette, with a male secretary who constantly shouted at him. Mr. Qurashi blew smoke at him and did not respond.

"No fax from Khartoum."

"Maybe it will come tomorrow."

"*Inshallah.*"

At this early stage of my trip it was helpful to be reminded of the conflicting meanings of *inshallah,* which include "we hope" and "don't count on it."

Mr. Qurashi said, "You can reapply."

Inaction from an official in such circumstances inspires the thought, Does he want baksheesh? I hung around, wondering whether to offer a bribe and how to phrase the offer.

I took Mr. Qurashi aside and said, "Is there anything I might do to help this matter along?"

He said nothing. He happened to be reading a closely typed letter.

"Perhaps I could pay in advance?"

He was not tempted. He accepted my new application and urged me to pay another visit because phones were unreliable. "But they will be repaired, *inshallah*."

I went the next day, and the day after. The same taxi driver, Guda ("like same as Dutch cheese," I got the joke every day), said, "In my whole life I have never taken an American to this embassy. And why you want to go to Sudan?"

"To see the pyramids. To talk to the people."

"Leetle birameed! Boor beeble!"

There is no *p* in Arabic, no *v* either.

More visits followed; I wanted to give this visa my best shot. But in a narrative of this kind, such stories of delays are not interesting. The traveler awaiting a visa sits in a stinking armchair in the embassy foyer, looking at the national map and the color photographs of the national sights and the dusty national calendar. There is a framed picture of the head of state smiling insincerely, the unfamiliar national flag, cranky officials, the sounds of telephones and murmurs, the back-and-forth of harassed secretaries. In these circumstances it is easy to talk yourself out of going, for this awful building and this dreary room begin to seem like the country itself.

To pass the time in this week of waiting, I went to the Egyptian Museum; I visited the Nobel Prize winner Naguib Mahfouz, whom I had last seen in the intensive care unit of a military hospital after his stabbing by a Muslim fanatic (recently hanged); I went to a party; I got other, easier visas.

Images of the African interior, where I was headed, filled the museum. I consoled myself by strolling up and down the enormous rooms before ornate exhibits, looking at the Africa of wild animals and majestic palms and sculptural faces with the heavy-lidded Nubian gaze, vividly displayed in ancient carvings, paintings, bas-reliefs, and sculptures. Representations in gold and ebony and precious stones of lions, cheetahs, cobras, eagles, and hippos were everywhere, not as incidental decorations but as idols: the cobra god, Nether-Ankh, the bat-eared jackal Anubis, god of mummification, the sly sexual lion-headed goddess Sekhmet, lion-bodied men, alabaster cats, huge gold hawks — even the chariots and the gold beds were given an African theme in the imagery of posts with the features of hippos, and rails in the shape of leopards.

Small blue-glazed hippos, King Tut's cheetah-skin shield, the multitude of stone-carved upright cats — all of them feline gods. To me this was an African treasure house with fantastic mummifications: the mummified falcon Horus, the mummified sacred ibis, fish in mummy wrappings, and a crocodile in cloth, too, for crocs were worshiped up the Nile in Kom Ombo, where I wanted to go. The goddess of joy, Baskel the cat, mummified as a slender gauzy idol. The sentiment and craze for preservation had Egyptians mummifying their pets, their trophies, their prize catches, much as a moose hunter seeks a taxidermist and for reasons just as frivolous — a mummified Nile perch five feet long, a mummified dog with its tail jerked vertically, the skeleton of a horse.

I was reminded that from medieval times mummies were taken to Europe for use in medicine (Montaigne mentions this in his essay "On the Cannibals"), and that Othello's handkerchief, woven by an Egyptian, had magical properties, for it was "dyed in mummy."

Nothing was weirder to me than a seated baboon, also a manifestation of Thoth (as well as "god of libraries, a birdgod, moony-crowned"), this one mummified but coming apart, the wrapping over its head falling loose, its unwrapped paw extended, still furry and a little dusty, like an ape stirring in a haunted house, shedding its bandages, peeping through its blindfold, looking hairy and vindictive.

And if you were planning to worship anything, it might as well be the three-thousand-year-old stone carving, towering over me, of the goddess Tawerel, "the Great One": a pregnant hippo standing upright with its big belly ballooning out, with human arms and a lion's hind legs, associated with fertility and childbirth.

These marvels were within walking distance of the Sudanese embassy, and my desire to see others like them on the Nile and in Nubia kept me pestering Ambassador Mashamoun for a visa.

"Nothing yet, but maybe soon, *inshallah*," his excellency said. "Will you take tea?"

He was more upbeat than many others. I went to a party given by a hospitable family in the salubrious suburb of El Maadi, and at dinner an American woman on my left, hearing of my proposed trip, said, "I have never been to Africa."

"I've never been to Africa either," said an American man across the table.

"But this is Africa," I said.

"No, no. Africa is . . ." The woman made a gesture, like Mohammed Kaburia's gesture at the Nubian boy, meaning, Down there somewhere.

Without perhaps intending to be negative, the partygoers conveyed to me nothing but discouragement.

"I was in the Sudan," a man said. "Lovely people. But the roads are awful. I wonder how you'll manage."

"When were you in the Sudan?"

"Oh, this was" — and he wagged his head — "this was years ago."

An Irish diplomat said, "Your man in Kenya met with six members of the opposition in Khartoum last week, and after he left every single one of them was arrested."

The American man who had claimed Egypt wasn't Africa said, "Zambia's the place you want to avoid. Zambia's a mess. People have high walls around their houses. You can't walk the streets."

"Ethiopia — now there's a place you want to stay away from. It's still at war with Eritrea."

A Ugandan man said, "Don't go anywhere near Uganda until after the eighth of March. There's an election that day, and it will be violent."

"You heard the AIDS statistics in Kenya? AIDS is wiping out whole communities."

"Kenya's kind of funny. They hired a guy to look at corruption — Richard Leakey. He found lots of it, but when he turned in his report he was sacked."

"The thing about the roads in Tanzania is that there aren't any."

"There are no roads in the Congo either. That's why it's ungovernable. Anyway, it's really about six countries."

"The Sudan is two countries. The Muslim north, the Christian south."

"Those land seizures in Zimbabwe are horrendous. White farmers wake up in the morning and find hundreds of Africans camped in their fields saying, 'This is ours now.'"

"Did anyone read that book about the massacres in Rwanda? I tell you, I got so depressed I couldn't finish it."

"Somalia's not even a country. It has no government, just these so-called warlords, about fifty of them, all fighting it out like street gangs."

"You know about the drought in the Ogaden? Three years without rain."

Dessert was served, and there were more pronouncements of this sort, with gestures south at the big hopeless heart of the continent.

A man with a Slavic accent claimed that he had met me many years ago. He became very friendly, though he could not remember where or when we had met — Uganda perhaps, he said, in the sixties. At his matiest he confided to me: "Colonialism just slowed down a process that was inevitable. These countries are like the Africa of hundreds of years ago."

This was a crudely coded way of saying Africans were reverting to savagery. Yet in another respect what he was saying was true. After a spell of being familiar and promising, Africa had slipped into a stereotype of itself: starving people in a blighted land governed by tyrants, rumors of unspeakable atrocities, despair and darkness.

Not darkness, really, but a blankness so blank and so distant you could ascribe almost anything to it — banditry, anarchy, cannibalism, rebellion, massacre, starvation, violence, disease, division. No one could dispute what you said. In fact, the existing literature, the news, and the documentation seemed to support the notion that it was all a savage jungle. To these party guests Africa was the blankness that it had been in the nineteenth century, the sort of white space on a map that Marlow mentions at the beginning of *Heart of Darkness.* For Marlow, only the empty spaces hold any attraction, and it was Africa — "the biggest, the most blank, so to speak — that I had a hankering after." Young Marlow exactly resembles young Conrad (little Józef Korzeniowski) in this respect, in his love for "exciting spaces of white paper."

I was not dissuaded by the apparent ignorance of what these people said. Their pessimism made Africa seem contradictory, unknown, worth visiting. They were saying what everyone said all the time: Ain't Africa awful! But really they were proving that the features on the Africa map had dimmed and faded so utterly that it had gone blank. Marlow goes on to say, at about the time he set off for the Congo, that Africa "had ceased to be a blank space of delightful mystery — a white patch for a boy to dream gloriously over. It had become a place of darkness."

Blind whiteness and crepuscular darkness amount to pretty much the same thing: terra incognita. There was a kind of poetic logic, too. In *Moby-Dick* whiteness stands for wickedness. So the image I carried with me on my trip was of a burned-out wilderness, empty of significant life, having no promise. I was in a land of despair, full of predators, tumbling down the side of a dark star.

I was not dismayed. The traveler's conceit is that he is heading into the unknown. The best travel is a leap in the dark. If the destination were familiar and friendly, what would be the point of going there?

◇ ◇ ◇

Still in Lower Egypt, in the opposite, Arabesque corner of Africa from Cape Town, I had all sorts of chance encounters with black Africa, tantalizing suggestions of the bewitchment of the larger continent, the African faces that are sometimes identical to African masks.

Traipsing between my hotel in the shadow of the Sphinx and the Sudan embassy in the middle of Cairo; going to the museum, to coffee shops, to the university, where I was buying books and checking facts; on the way to the party in El Maadi and to literary gatherings, I encountered the tall, slender Sudanese, the mute watchfulness of Nubians, the big beautiful animals — lions, elephants, cheetahs — carved in bold relief on coffins and bedsteads. Sometimes it was the drumming I heard, a syncopation in the night air, or the aroma of Zanzibari cloves and Kenyan coffee, or a splintered chest in a rubbish heap, stenciled *Tea — Uganda.* Ethiopians and West Africans hawked tourist carvings in the markets of Cairo, and as the *haj* was soon to start, and Cairo was a gateway to Jidda and the holy places of Saudi Arabia, I got used to seeing the sneering small-boned people of Djibouti and Somalia, robed Muslims from Mali and Chad and Niger, Nigerian Hausas, Fang people and Dogons and Malian mullahs from Timbuktu, all in white for their pilgrimage. Representatives of the whole of Africa gathered here, as if this were the polyglot capital of a vast black empire and I was seeing examples of every animal and every kind of food and every human face.

What reassured me was the appropriateness of this African imagery in my Egyptian captivity, my prologue of waiting for a Sudanese visa. For in that self-conscious mental narrative that serves a writer as a sort of memory gimmick, seeing these features and these faces was just right as an introduction, as grace notes and little pips that would be repeated themes, struck louder as my trip progressed, went deeper, grew denser, got blacker.

◇ ◇ ◇

Needing to boost my morale with a sense of accomplishment, and to make use of my time in Cairo — Umm al-Dunya, Mother of the World — I decided to apply for other visas. I went to the Uganda embassy, still with Guda at the wheel, getting lost in the district of Dokki. "I have never taken an American to this embassy!"

The Ugandan I met, Stephen Mushana, was friendly, a youngish round-faced man in the dusty second secretary's office in Midan El Messaha. He was fluent in Arabic, having lived for five years in Cairo. His home village was in a deep valley in craggy southwestern Uganda. He was a Mukiga, a member of the Bakiga tribe, whose customs have always fascinated me: their frenzied dances, their ingenious terrace farming, their urine ceremony — a promise of polygamy performed by the groom and his brothers that assures that a widow will be guaranteed a husband, one of those surviving brothers.

"My brother died," Stephen Mushana said. "But I didn't have to marry his wife." He paused as though wondering how much more information to give me. "Well, she died a little while later."

"Sorry to hear it."

"AIDS is very bad in my country."

"It didn't exist when I lived there."

"Maybe it existed but people didn't know it."

"I left there thirty-six years ago."

"I was two years old!"

I got this all the time. The average life expectancy in Africa was so short that many diplomats were in their thirties, some were in their twenties, and they had no memory of their country as a big placid republic but only as a nest of problems. I had never seen these places at war; some of them grew up on war. There had been fighting in Uganda from the 1970s onward.

"It must have been good then."

"Very good. Very peaceful." Looking back, remembering friends and colleagues, it seemed to me a golden age.

"Do you know Aggrey Awori?"

Mushana said, "He's an old man."

Awori was my age, regarded as a miracle of longevity in an AIDS-stricken country; a Harvard graduate, class of '63, a track star. Thirty years ago he was a rising bureaucrat, friend and confidant of the pugnacious prime minister, Milton Obote, a pompous gap-toothed northerner who had placed his trust in a goofy general named Idi Amin. Awori, powerful then, had been something of a scourge and a nationalist, but he was from a tribe that straddled the Kenya border, where even the politics overlapped: Awori's brother was a minister in the Kenya government.

"Awori is running for president."

"Does he have a chance?"

Mushana shrugged. "Museveni will get another term."

"I had some good friends, really funny ones. My best friend was a guy called Apolo Nsibambi. We shared an office in the Extra-Mural Department at Makerere, and then I got a promotion — became acting director — and I was his boss! I used to tease him for calling himself Doctor — he had a Ph.D. in political science. I mocked him for wearing a tie and carrying a briefcase and being pompous. I went to his wedding. He came to my wedding. And then I completely lost touch with him. I wonder what happened to him."

"Doctor Nsibambi is the prime minister of Uganda."

◇ ◇ ◇

Perhaps the oldest inhabited street in the high-density city of Cairo — one thousand years of donkey droppings, hawkers' wagons, barrow boys, veiled women, jostling camels, hand-holding men, and hubble-bubble smokers, amid mosques and princes' palaces and a bazaar with shops selling trinkets, brass pots, and sacks of beans — is Bayna al-Qasrayn, or Between Two Palaces, or Palace Walk.

Peering through the lovely door of the mosque, I could see the faithful at prayer in the posture of submission, kneeling, bowing low, forehead thumping the carpet, like a dog hugging a football.

Raymond Stock, the biographer of Naguib Mahfouz, was my guide once again. He said, "All the goods and the glory were the lifeblood of the great city, Al-Qahirah" — Cairo — "the Victorious."

By chance I had bumped into Raymond at the Semiramis Hotel one afternoon. He was sitting with a big pink-cheeked man, very elegant in a pinstriped suit and silk tie, a matching silk hankie in his breast pocket.

"He is the son of the khedive," Raymond said, telling me his name. "He is a prince!"

The face of the big pink-cheeked man grew rosier and princelier at the mention of his pedigree, Turkish rather than Arabic, with a dash of snobbery, for the khedives were giggly Anglophiles.

"His family used to run Egypt!"

The big pink-cheeked man fluffed his silk hankie and tut-tutted. The last khedive, an Ottoman relic, was seen in Cairo in 1914, dumped by the British when Egypt became a protectorate.

"Paul's a writer," Raymond said.

The big pink-cheeked pinstriped prince smiled at my safari jacket and baggy pants and scuffed shoes.

"I've just come from the Sudanese embassy," I said, explaining the dust. "They're renovating."

"Paul's going to Africa," Raymond said.

"People keep saying that, but isn't this Africa?"

The prince's chubby cheeks went pinker and pinker with mirth. He didn't say much, but he had a way of glowing that took the place of conversation. He finished his meal, dabbed at his lips, and left, murmuring a farewell in French.

"Son of the khedive!" Raymond said.

I had last seen Raymond six years ago, when I had been traveling around the shores of the Mediterranean on my *Pillars of Hercules* trip and had docked in Alexandria, having sailed from Istanbul on a Turkish cruise ship with 450 Turks, my genial messmates Fikret, General Salih, and Onan among them.

Then, May 1994, Naguib Mahfouz was in intensive care after being stabbed in the neck by an Islamic zealot. Mahfouz was not expected to recover, yet he had. His wound had healed, he coped with the nerve damage, he was back from the brink. He had even resumed writing.

"Naguib-bey shows up some nights around Cairo. He has a sort of salon," Raymond said. "I could show you where he was born and grew up."

That was how it happened that we were strolling down Palace Walk, in the district of Gamaliyeh, which means "Place of Beauty," a noisy, cluttered, crowded suburb. Its inaccurate name was part of its charm, like calling a frozen waste Greenland or a garbage truck a honey wagon.

But the people are the interest now, not the littered streets and alleys.

We went to Judge's House Square, Midan Bayt al-Qadi, to see some beat-up and dusty trees called Pasha's beard, named for the furry shape of their blossoms — the Indian walnut, the scrupulous Raymond Stock informed me, *Albizia lebbek* — the centerpiece of "this complex, compact, and nearly self-enclosed world."

In the square we passed the mosque school of Al-Mithqal ("the Sequined One," a sort of Ottoman Sparkle Plenty), entered Harat Qirmiz (Crimson Alley), and found number eight, Mahfouz's childhood home. He was born in this ancient tenement, with its tall cracked edifice, and named after the doctor who delivered him on December 10, 1911. After growing up in that house ("He used to stare out of that window"), he wrote about his early passions — for a certain revolutionary, and Charlie Chaplin, and a neighborhood girl whom he idolized.

"Harat Qirmiz has a high stone wall," Mahfouz wrote, in Raymond's translation. "Its doors are locked upon its secrets; there is no revealing of its mysteries without seeing them from within. There one sees a quarter for the poor folk and beggars gathered in the spot for their housework and to take care of their daily needs; and one sees a paradise singing with gardens, with a hall to receive visitors, and a hareem for the ladies. And from the little high window just before the 'qabw' sometimes appears a face luminous like the moon; I see it from the window of my little house which looks out over the harah and I wander, despite my infancy, in the magic of its beauty. I hear its melodious voice while it banters greetings with my mother when she passes out of the alley, and perhaps this is what impressed on my soul the love of song. Fatimah, al Umri, the unknown dream of childhood."

He also wrote about the *afreets*, the demons, that lurked in the tunnel that linked Judge's House Square to Palace Walk. Clapping our hands to disperse the *afreets*, we crawled through the tunnel and alley, which were so littered we were knee-deep in household rubbish and garbage, more demonic to me than any *afreet*.

"I'd like to see Mahfouz again."

"He might be somewhere tonight."

Cairo had an old-fashioned literary culture, with cliques and salons. The city's most endearing characteristic was that all this socializing was accomplished through word of mouth. Raymond made a call and found out that at a certain time Mahfouz would be in a certain hotel in a certain district near the Nile.

We arrived at the place at the same time as Mahfouz, who was being guided, a burly man on each side of him, steering him to an upstairs lounge, for he is somewhat feeble, almost blind, and nearly deaf. He is sallow and diabetic, yet looked much healthier than the last time I had seen him, supine in the military hospital. Looking like a head of state, he wore a heavy overcoat because of the February chill of nighttime Cairo.

"I feel better now," he said when I complimented him on his recovery from the stab wound.

He kissed Raymond in the Egyptian way and groped for my hand and shook it. Then he seated himself on a red plush sofa and held court — silent court, for he said almost nothing. Men took turns sitting beside him, shouting into his left ear, his reasonably good ear, and because he is so deaf they seemed to rant. They monologued to Mahfouz and to the room at large, they engaged in debate, they read articles they had recently published. Mahfouz simply listened and smoked cigarettes and looked Sphinxlike.

Mahfouz held these audiences as *majlis* ceremonies, like a pasha on a divan, to lift his spirits, Raymond said. He had been very low after his stabbing and made a deliberate effort to get out of the house, as a way of sending a message to the fanatics that they had not put him out of business.

One man took a seat next to Mahfouz and shouted the contents of a whole long article he had written, rattling the pages of the morning paper while Mahfouz puffed his cigarette and sat staring through his thick lenses with a stern concentrated gaze. His expression hardly changed as he listened, and when he responded, he did so with a crooked-toothed smile of jeering triumph.

The United States and Britain had just bombed Iraq, claiming that Iraqi planes had fired on their planes in a "no-fly zone." The view of Mahfouz's audience was that although Iraq was an unfriendly country, it seemed like an Anglo-American provocation to declare portions of it forbidden zones and then arbitrarily to strafe it, inviting an attack as a pretext to justify a severe bombing. In other words, Iraq was being bombed for defending itself against the humiliation of hostile fighter planes in its skies. I refrained from saying that to call the bluff of the United States, Iraq had, early on, actually agreed in writing to the no-fly zones.

Reflecting on the bombing, Mahfouz murmured a sentence in Arabic, then laughed and lit another cigarette.

Raymond translated. "He says, 'The attack on Iraq is like the random attack in Camus's *The Stranger*.'"

The sun-dazed Meursault in that novel shoots a shadowy Arab on the beach for no logical reason.

"As usual, America is simply trying to appease Israel," one man said.

"Israel is part of America," another man said.

"Yes. We say Israel is America's fifty-first state," a woman said. "What do you think, Mr. Theroux?"

I said, and Raymond translated, "What I think is that Israel is the window through which America looks at the Middle East."

"Yes! Yes!" said the man sitting next to Mahfouz.

"And it is rather a small window," I said.

"Say some more."

"The window is too small to see every country clearly. For example, Egypt is much larger and poorer and more harmless than it appears. But Israel insists that we see every country through its own window. And by the way, it is not an American window."

While all this was translated for Mahfouz and the others, I felt that I was being drawn into a fruitless political debate. I was encouraged to elaborate, but what was the point?

"It's tribal warfare," I said. "I want to stay out of it. Anyway, what does Mahfouz think?"

"No one cares what I think," Mahfouz said, and everyone laughed, including him.

More people arrived: some writers from Alexandria, a French journalist, a German woman, and the writer Ali Salem, a big man with a melonlike paunch and a bald head that seemed like part of his elongated and satirical face.

One man leaned over and said to me, "Israel is America's baby."

I said, "Many countries are America's babies. Some good babies, some bad babies."

"We don't like to fight," he said. "Egyptians want peace."

"Ladies and gentlemen," Ali Salem said, unfolding a large newspaper page. He smacked it with the flat of his hand and sat down next to Mahfouz. "You must listen to these jewels."

Declaiming rather than reading the article, he bugged out his eyes and went on smacking the sheet of newsprint. This was an article he had written about a trial of some Islamic fundamentalists who had attacked Mahfouz's novels for their secularity. Mahfouz, who had made a career out of twitting and needling Muslims, just listened, staring into space, holding his burning cigarette sideways like a snack.

When Ali Salem finished, another man took his place by Mahfouz's good ear and began to shout into it. Mahfouz, unmoved by the man's screeching, went on puffing his cigarette.

This man was ranting about the state of writing in the Arab world. His sort of loudness seemed like self-parody, yet it was possible, even likely, that he was not being ironical.

"The Nobel Prize was given to Naguib Mahfouz, and in so doing it recognized traditional writing. When the prize was given to García Márquez, many other Latin American writers were inspired to write books and publish them. But what has happened in the Arab world? Where is Arab literature? Nothing has happened!"

Hearing his name shouted over and over, Mahfouz did not appear to be impressed. He remained impassive.

"Naguib Mahfouz won the first and last Nobel Prize for Arab literature. He won it for all Arabs. But no other Arabs will get the prize."

The shrillness of the man's voice made the speech seem like a piece of buffoonery.

"Why hasn't the rest of Arab literature achieved any recognition?" Now the man was glaring at me. "It is a conspiracy by the West!"

I had become the West. Well, I didn't mind, as long as it kept these people talking, for nothing is more revealing of a person's mind than a person's anger. Mahfouz just shrugged. He seemed a worthy laureate — dignified, prolific, rebellious in his point of view, for in this Islamic country he refused to indulge in sanctimony or religion at all, and yet he was gentle, going against the political and religious grain with grace and humor.

There were more attacks on the West — that is, on me — but when I was asked to respond, I changed the subject to Nubia. Mahfouz had set many stories in pharaonic times, so I asked him whether he felt, as some historians did, that a complex culture had risen up the Nile, from East and Central Africa through Nubia and Cush, to enrich Egypt.

Mahfouz said, "Egyptians conquered Nubia, and Nubians turned around and conquered Egypt."

"But are the Nubians the genuine pharaonic people, as is sometimes claimed?"

"Everyone asks this question, especially Nubians."

There was more talk, more shouting, everyone smoking and talking at once. "The next Arab-Israeli war will be different!" a man yelled. I crept down to the bar and drank a beer, and when I came back the gathering around Mahfouz had grown to a small crowd. I had lost my seat. Three hours of this and they were still shouting. Mahfouz went through this five nights a week and found it a tonic.

"He wants to know where you're going," Raymond said when I made my excuses and began to leave.

"To Nubia," I said.

Mahfouz said something in Arabic, and it was translated. "Nubia is 'the Gold Place.' *Nub* means 'gold.'"

◈ ◈ ◈

Before I took the train to Aswan, awaiting my Sudanese visa, I decided to boost my spirits by getting an Ethiopian visa. That would be easy, I was told, because Ethiopia was still at war with its breakaway province of Eritrea, now a sovereign state — but a battle-scarred sovereign state littered with corpses, casualties of war. No one wanted to go to Ethiopia.

Some consulates are full of atmosphere, a certain quality of dust and worn furnishings and the lingering odors of the national dish. The Ethiopian consulate in Cairo gave me that impression: faded glory, high ceilings, beat-up sofas, unswept floors, the aromas of fasting food, the fermented smell of *injera* and spiced beans, the thick nutty fragrance of Abyssinian coffee, a slight stinkiness of old-fashioned men's suits and stained neckties.

I was received warmly by the balding, thirty-four-year-old consul general, Eshete Tilohun. He was small with an impressive head, a big bulging brow like that of an extraterrestrial or a math whiz, and deep-set eyes. He told me that for seventy U.S. dollars I could have a visa that would remain valid for two years.

"Look!" he said, a cry of anguish, lifting his eyes from my passport.

A large multicolored map of Ethiopia and the surrounding countries in the Horn of Africa covered part of the far wall of his office.

"No outlet to the sea," he said in a lamenting voice. "Eritrea! Djibouti! Somalia! And we are landlocked. That is why we are poor."

"What about the war with Eritrea?"

"Not our fault," he said. "It is those people. Bring an Eritrean here and you would see the difference in culture. Ha!"

He had rubber-stamped my passport but had not filled in any of the blanks. His pen was poised, but he was still clucking over the map.

"Djibouti — so small! The soldiers of the Derg wrecked the country. Mengistu gave Djibouti away. The Eritreans made trouble. The Somalis are just bandit people."

"But things are quiet now?"

"Very quiet." His eyes bulged when he emphasized a point. I liked his passion. He seemed to care that I wanted to go to Ethiopia. He reflected, "Of course the emperor made his mistakes. The country was backward."

"In what way backward?"

"Feudal," he said, and shrugged. "But go to Tana! See churches! Go to Gonder and Tigre. The women have tattooed faces there. They are good Christians — since 34 A.D. they have been Christians. They have been Jews for longer. Go to the southwest. See the Mursi people. The naked Mursi people. Your name is?"

"Paul."

"Paul, the Mursi are the last naked people in the world."

I disputed this and told him in detail about nudist camps in such places as the United States and Europe, how the campers might play bare-assed Ping-Pong, or eat or chitchat or swim mother-naked.

"No! They go into the street like this?" Mr. Tilohun asked.

"Just around their camp," I said.

"Like the Mursi."

"For them it's not sex. It's health."

"Exactly like the Mursi! They say, 'Why do you wear these clothes?'" Mr. Tilohun tried to look shocked and indignant, but I could see he found the whole idea of public nudity extravagantly funny. "One of my friends had his picture taken with a Mursi woman. She had no clothes on at all."

Mr. Tilohun's eyes glittered at the thought of his decently clothed friend standing next to the naked woman — who, by the way, being a Mursi, might not have been wearing a dress but would have worn a saucer-sized plug in her lower lip.

"The Mursi are real Africans," Mr. Tilohun said. "And there are others. The Oromo. The Galla. The Wolayta."

"I can't wait," I said, and meant it.

At one point, speaking of my trip and the road south, Mr. Tilohun said, "There is only one road going south in Ethiopia. It is the road to Johannesburg. The longest road in Africa. You just keep going."

The weather had not changed, nor had the weather report. "Tomorrow — Dust" was the forecast, and it occurred as predicted, but more dramatically than before, a high, deep dust cloud approaching from the west, looking like a mountain range on the move, gray and dense, overwhelming the city, and at last the sun setting into it, turning into a dull disk. It was in fact a dust storm, with the appearance of fog but the texture of grit, covering everything, even the pages of the book I was reading, blurring the windows of Cairo, getting into my teeth.

One last visit to the Sudanese. Mr. Qurashi said, "Next week, *inshallah*."

Ten days earlier, on my arrival in Cairo, *inshallah* had meant "God willing" and "soon" and then "eventually" and "in the fullness of time." Later it meant "we hope" and "don't count on it." Now it meant "you wish!" "no way!" and "not bloody likely!"

3 ◈◈◈

Up and Down the Nile

THE *Philae,* a river cruiser, lay aslant of the bank, captive in her mooring lines in the winter sunshine at Aswan on the Nile — yes, *Heart of Darkness* opens something like this. I really did suspect that I might be headed to a dark place, and as with all long trips I fantasized that I might die there. Last night's rain had freshened the air and turned the riverbank to gleaming paste. Fellaheen with fishing poles stood in mud to their knees, and other muddy men were calling out, "Felucca ride! Felucca ride!"

A young man in a grubby white gown said to me, "We go. Nice felucca. We find Nubian banana."

"Nubian banana?"

"Big banana," he said, and made an unambiguous gesture near a portion of his grubby gown. "You come with me. Big banana."

He went on flattering himself until I said, "Oh, bugger off."

His sort of importuning was common in the tourist-haunted parts of Egypt, where I regularly saw visiting men and visiting women tacking in quaint feluccas at dusk toward the less-frequented parts of the Nile embankment, where, unobserved in the shadows of overhanging ferns, they would find the Nubian banana.

I had been told to board the *Philae* at noon for the scenic trip downriver to Luxor, where the boat stopped and I would continue. I planned to keep going overland, on the longest road trip of my life, over the frontier to Wadi Halfa and Upper Nubia and beyond, to Dongola and Khartoum, to Ethiopia, Kenya, Uganda, and deeper south to Malawi, via Zomba and Limbe, where I had lived so long ago, to see what had happened to Africa while I had been elsewhere.

I had come from Cairo in a sleeper on the night train. There the taxi driver had asked for fifty Egyptian pounds (about twelve dollars). I offered him thirty, assuming he would negotiate as all the others had done, but instead he became peevish and indignant and lapsed into a lofty silence, no haggling at all. At the station, which was crowded with commuters and cars, he became ridiculously attentive. He bowed to me, insisted on carrying my bag, and parted the crowd. He found the right platform for the Aswan train, even the section of track where the sleeper would stop. So I handed him fifty for the extra help he had given me. He scrupulously fished in his purse and gave me twenty pounds in change and thanked me in a sneering way. I tried to hand the money back to him. He touched his heart, waving away the tip. Wounded feelings had turned him into a paragon of virtue.

Yet I had been so touched by the trouble he had taken and his elaborate courtesies that I persisted, and it became a charade, face-saving on both our parts, as I pursued him down the high road, so to speak, insisting he accept the tip. At last I uttered the right formula, *Ashani ana* ("For my sake"), and begged him to accept, and he took it, holding the money like a trifle, his favor to me: a very clever man and a lesson to me in Egyptian pride.

Rameses I Station, usually called Cairo Railway Station, is a century old, like the railway system itself, which stretches from Alexandria, on the shores of the Mediterranean, to Aswan, on the Upper Nile, at the northern edge of Lake Nasser — the border of Sudan on the south side. It has been said that the design of the station represents the epitome of nineteenth-century Egyptian architects' desire to combine classical and Islamic building styles, in response to Khedive Ismail's plan to create a "European Cairo" — Moorish meets modern.

Kings, queens, princes, heads of state, and generals have arrived and departed here. One of Naguib Mahfouz's earliest heroes, the ultranationalist anti-British rabble-rouser Saad Zaghlul, escaped an assassination attempt at Cairo Station in 1924, on his return from one of his numerous exiles. Given Egypt's history of dramatic arrivals and departures, the station figures as a focal point and a scene of many riotous sendoffs and welcomes.

The best story about the station, told to me by a man who witnessed it unfold, does not concern a luminary but rather a person delayed in the third-class ticket line. When this fussed and furious man at last got to the window, he expressed his exasperation to the clerk, saying, "Do you know who I am?"

The clerk looked him up and down and, without missing a beat, said, "In that shabby suit, with a watermelon under your arm, and a third-class ticket to El Minya, who could you possibly be?"

Leaving the enormous sprawling dust-blown city of gridlock and gritty buildings in the sleeper to Aswan was bliss. It was quarter to eight on a chilly night. I sat down in my inexpensive first-class compartment, listened to the departure whistles, and soon we were rolling through Cairo. Within minutes we reached Giza — the ruins overwhelmed by the traffic and bright lights, the tenements and bazaar — and in less than half an hour we were in open country, with little settlements of square mud-block houses, fluorescent lights reflected in the canal beside the track, the blackness of the countryside at night, a mosque with a lighted minaret, now and then a solitary car or truck, and on one remote road about twenty men in white robes going home after prayers. In Cairo they would have been unremarkable, just part of the mob; here they looked magical, their robes seeming much whiter on the nighttime road, their procession much spookier for its orderliness, like a troupe of sorcerers.

I went into the corridor and opened the train window to see the robed men better, and there I was joined by Walter Frakes from St. Louis, an enormous man with a long mild face and a smooth baggy chin, who found his compartment small, "but what's the use of fussing?" He was traveling with his wife, Marylou, and another couple, the Norrises, Lenny and Marge, also from St. Louis. They too were heading to Aswan to meet a boat and take a river cruise.

"If I don't get a decent bed on that ship I'm going to be a wreck," Walter Frakes said. He was a gentle man in spite of his size, which I took to be close to three hundred pounds, and he was kindly and generally uncomplaining. All he said in the morning was "Didn't get a wink of sleep. Tried to. Woke up every time the train stopped. Must have stopped a hundred times. Durn."

I had woken now and then as the train had slowed at crossings or stopped at the larger stations. There were sometimes flaring lights and barking dogs, but otherwise the silence and darkness of the Nile Valley and a great emptiness: the vast and starry sky of the Egyptian desert, and the road south that ran alongside the train, the only road south, as Mr. Tilohun had said: the road to Johannesburg.

In the bright early morning I saw a sign, *Kom Ombo — 8 km.*, indicating the direction to its lovely temple with a dual dedication, to Horus, the hawk-headed god, and to Sobek, the croc-skulled deity. Another sign said *Abu Simbel Macaroni* and depicted its glutinous product in a red bowl.

Date palms in clusters, orange trees, low boxy houses, donkey carts piled high with tomatoes, the occasional camel, men in white gowns and skullcaps. Boys walked to the fields carrying farm implements, and the wide slow river and the flat bright land shimmered under the blue sky. This was new Egypt, but it was also old Egypt, for I had seen many of these images in the Cairo museum — the adzes and mattocks the boys carried I had seen looking much the same, and the heavy-browed bullocks I had seen hammered in gold or carved in stone I saw browsing by the river; the same dogs with upright tails and big ears, the same narrow cats, and had I seen a snake or a croc, it would have had its counterpart in gold on a chariot or else mummified and moldering in a museum case.

Some of those cap and gowned men were seated in groups eating pieces of the same shaped bread loaves I had seen in the museum, removed intact, solid and stale, from ancient tombs; the same fava beans that had been disinterred from crypts were being gobbled up from wagons of men selling *foul*, the stewed beans that are still an Egyptian staple. The same-shaped ewers and bowls I had seen as artifacts were visible here in the hands of women faffing around at the kitchen doors of their huts.

The Nile was near, about three hundred yards from bank to bank, slow-moving and light brown, showing clouds on its surface, with green fields on either side, some with marked-out plots and others divided into date plantations. Hawks drifted over the fields on wind currents, and in the river feluccas with sails — impossible to see these sails and not think of gulls' wings. And then, as though indicating we were approaching a populous place, there was a succession of cemeteries with great long slopes of sun-baked graves and grave markers, small rectangles set into the stony ground with raised edges, like a whole hillside of truckle beds where the dead people lay. Beyond the next hill was Aswan.

◇ ◇ ◇

This easy train trip south from Cairo to Aswan had rushed me five hundred miles into Africa, almost to the far edge of Egypt, to the shore of the lake — Lake Nasser — that borders Sudan. With a visa I could have got a ferry down the lake and nipped over the border; a boat left the Aswan High Dam every week, bringing workers to Wadi Halfa, in Nubia. But I had no visa yet.

Aswan was mainly a bazaar and a destination for tourists heading for the ruins. But it was a good-natured bazaar, divided in half: local people buying melons, grapes, fava beans, coffee, and spices, and tourists haggling over plaster images of the pyramids and the Sphinx and Nefertiti, brassware depicting King Tut's shiny face, colorful carpets, walking sticks, and T-shirts. Egyptian tourist kitsch is to my mind the ugliest in the world, and some of it ambitious, too: expensive malachite funerary urns, scale-model sarcophagi complete with model mummies, stone-carved cats and hippos.

Heavily armed policemen were all over the place. There was a reason, especially here. Temples and ruins and tourist destinations were often targeted by Muslim extremists. There were attacks inside railway trains, and many shots fired into first-class cars from beside the tracks as the Aswan train made its way south — shooting into first was the best way of hitting a tourist. There were kidnappings, too, and ransoms paid. Egypt, particularly the Nile Valley, had a reputation as a danger zone.

Metal detectors flanked the entrances of most buildings, though they were seldom used and seemed more symbolic than practical. Perhaps they didn't work. Certainly the electricity supply was unreliable, and there seemed to be a labor shortage. The armed men, with assault rifles slung at their sides, meant to reassure the tourists, simply looked sinister and added to the atmosphere of menace. The touts and curio sellers were persistent, haranguing, stalking, tugging sleeves. There was donkey shit everywhere and the sound of car horns and loud music playing at the tape-and-CD stalls, and pestering beggars, lepers, and the usual naggers outside restaurants and coffee shops snatching at passersby. The bazaar, with its density of hangers-on and hawkers, has its nearest analogue in the American shopping mall — just as diverting, as much of a time killer and a recreation. The pedestrian zone, the food court, the wedged-together shops of the mall, all have their counterparts in the Egyptian bazaar, which may be dirtier, smellier, and noisier, but is much cheaper and better humored.

My hotel was on the river within walking distance of the train station. Gull-winged feluccas on the sparkling Nile, hawks and crows overhead, breathable air, a clear sky, and hundreds of riverboats moored for the Nile cruises to Luxor. Business was poor — there were more boats than mooring places or piers, and the boats were piled up and double- and triple-parked. It was February, the low season, and because tourists confused Israeli and Palestinian violence with much more placid Egypt, they were avoiding the Nile cruises.

I had coffee, bought some amber beads in the bazaar, and did the *Al Ahram* (English edition) crossword puzzle in the sunshine, sitting on a bench.

It was then, setting down one answer (it was "aa," a Hawaiian word for a kind of cindery lava rock), that I was approached by the young man in a grubby white gown who said to me, "We go. Nice felucca. We find Nubian banana."

There were plenty of takers. Young women, singly or in pairs, being sailed by Egyptians, singly or in pairs, at sundown, had to know that they were doing something that no Egyptian woman would do without understanding that they were putting themselves completely in the hands of these young men — these priapic young men.

While watching the feluccas tacking into the darkness, into crepuscular copulations, I was approached by a big dark man.

"I am Nubian," he said. "Mohammed."

Another unambiguous flirtation, I was sure.

"You ever been to Japan?"

"Yes, I have. Several times." Thinking, An ambiguous flirtation, then.

"You like?"

"Japan? Lots of people. Very expensive. Unlike Aswan — not many people. Very cheap."

"I am a tour guide here for ten years for Japanese people," he said. "I hate Japanese people. What is in their heads? What is inside? They are . . ." He didn't finish the sentence. He winced, searching for words. "I hate to be a guide for them. Something is wrong with Japanese people."

"Maybe they are not like you," I said, trying to calm him.

"They are not like me. Not like you. Not like anyone."

"You think so?"

"I know this!"

To a Nubian like Mohammed, the Japanese were mask-faced, backward-looking, strangely attired, oddly aromatic, and inexplicable—much as a Nubian might seem to a Japanese. It was not for me to arrange for the twain to meet here in Aswan, but in fact there were a great number of Nubians here, who had been uprooted and rehoused because of the disruption of the high dam and the lake it created.

Sudan was on the other side of the lake, and there was a clear cultural and racial link with greater Nubia, the coming and going, the language most of all. No one said to me here, as people said all the time in Cairo, "This isn't Africa." This *was* Africa, and Aswan was full of relocated Nubians whose villages had been inundated by Lake Nasser.

At noon that day I boarded the *Philae*, a river cruiser with a capacity of about one hundred passengers, and there were almost that number on this down-the-Nile trip, lots of Germans, some British and Americans, Egyptians, Dutch, and one Indian family: two adults and a small, badly behaved boy, the only child on the boat, who was bored and whiny the whole trip.

Recreational history—what most sightseeing amounts to, the History Channel in 3-D—to justify the enormous buffets and fabulous dinners and drinks on the upper deck: this was the mission of the *Philae* contingent. I had been on only two other cruises in my life: the luxury *Seabourn Spirit* ("Your caviar will be sent to your suite shortly, sir") and a Turkish junket on the MV *Akdeniz*, which had delivered me to the coast of Egypt with 450 courteous Turks, who reminisced about the Ottomans and wished the khedive still had the whip hand.

Wealthy people too lazy to read love cruises for the anecdotal history and archeological chats, which they use to one-up their listeners in boasting bouts after they go home. The Nile cruise passenger is someone in the process of becoming a licensed bore. The apprenticeship is filled with exploratory questions in the realm of Egyptology rather than just the correct pronunciation of "Ptah" and "Hatshepsut."

"So the common people weren't allowed to enter the temple?" and "Which one is Horus?" and the recurring question of the tourist on the Nile: "How in heck did they manage to lift these things?"

Now and then the queries were detailed. "You mean there's more than one Ptolemy?" To which the answer was "Zayre was feefseen" — and Ptolemy the math whiz wasn't one of them.

Or: "How many centuries did you say?" And the answer: "Seerty."

The more meaningless the question, the more detailed the interrogation, and the cruise passenger would simply nod when the answer was delivered.

A woman on the *Philae*, for reasons of her own, kept asking the onboard Egyptologist, "Is that *fronic?*"

And the answer was sometimes yes and sometimes spelled out on the item in question — say, the two hieroglyphs indicated in the cartouche, *per* and *oni*, meaning "big house," "big structure," "king," or "pharaonic."

One night in Aswan I went by felucca to Elephantine Island, while in the distance, in midstream, other feluccas, Egyptians at the tiller, were steering foreign women into the darkness, and the quality of light gave the expression "being spirited away" a definite meaning. The island was a gift to Horatio, Lord Kitchener, for mercilessly putting down a rebellion in Sudan, a massacre known as the Battle of Omdurman. Kitchener turned Elephantine Island into a botanical garden, which he could view from his villa. Some of the palms, plumeria, and exotic shrubs still flourish, but what is most remarkable about the island is that from the east bank there is a view of the cliffside town and the bazaar, and from the west, across a stretch of river, just sand dunes, long monumental pistes of smoothness, suggesting depth in the way the sand lay in windswept swathes, scooped and carved, like trackless snow fields tinted pink and gold at sunset, awaiting skiers.

My felucca sailor dropped me off in the dark at the east bank, below the town where, at the edge of the bazaar, I spotted an imam in a white djellaba standing in front of his mosque. It was too dark for me to see the outlines of this place of worship. As I walked closer, I saw it was not an imam but a priest in a white cassock — what's the difference?

He was standing at the gateway of his church, inhaling the night air. Seeing me, he beckoned with a benign wave of the hand.

He was Benito Cruciani, from Macerata in Italy, and had come here to Aswan by way of Sudan, where he had stayed for nine years until he became ill and was invalided out.

"I was in Darfur," he said — a remote district in western Sudan. "The Africans used to throw stones at me. But when I said, 'I am not American, I am Italian,' they stopped."

He was a Comboni father, the order named for Daniel Comboni, whose motto "Africa or death" was prophetic, for in the event he achieved both simultaneously, dying in Sudan in 1881. Father Comboni's plan was "Save Africa through Africa," which seemed a gnomic way of expressing a missionary intention. In fact, such priests made few converts, taught by example, and were watched closely by the Muslim Brotherhood, which was less robust in Sudan than in Cairo but robust all the same. That is to say, unbelievers were now and then made an example of by being murdered.

"Your name, Cruciani, sounds like 'cross' in Italian," I said.

Yes, he said, it was a deliberate construction. Cruciani was a Florentine family associated with the Crusades, and six centuries later he was still a crusader (*crociato*), promoting Christ in an intolerant Islamic fastness.

"I want to go to Sudan. I'm still waiting for my visa. Any advice for me?"

"You are alone?"

"Yes."

"We say, 'Mountain and sea, never travel alone.'"

"A proverb?"

"Not so much a proverb as a rule you should obey."

"I don't have much choice."

"So my advice is — pray," Father Cruciani said. He then beckoned, Italian fashion, dog-paddling with one hand. "Come."

He stepped inside the church, and just as I entered I heard a booming muezzin's voice calling the faithful to pray: *"Allahu akbar!"* As this reverberated in the crypt, Father Cruciani showed me the under-altar effigy of Saint Teresa, her life-size figure in a glass coffin. While we looked at it four youths in blue-and-white school uniforms crept toward it and stuffed some notes through a slot in the coffin.

"So they will pass their exams," Father Cruciani said, and made a satirical face.

Outside I said, "No one is very upbeat about Sudan."

He said, "Wonderful people. Terrible government. The African story."

◇ ◇ ◇

In a corner of the rescued and reconstructed Temple of Isis at Philae, in the river south of Aswan, was a bull in stone, the image of the god Hapi, or Apis, surrounded by protective snakes. Apis was the sacred bull of Memphis, associated with the river and so with fertility, and worshiped as the god of the Nile. Nearby was the image of Osiris, god of the earth, in his candlepin headgear, personification of the Nile, the flooding of the river symbolizing his rebirth. Osiris's features were smashed, and so were those of Horus, its falcon face obliterated by fanatic early Christians. There were lots of Napoleonic graffiti on the walls. The Nile cruise past Egyptian ruins is an experience of obliterations and graffiti. More than one hundred and fifty years ago, the young Gustave Flaubert lamented these very things in a letter to his mother: "In the temples we read travelers' names; they strike us as petty and futile. We never write ours; there are some that must have taken three days to carve, so deeply are they cut in the stone. There are some that you keep meeting everywhere — sublime persistence of stupidity."

The human faces were scratched away, the gods' images were chipped off, the walls have been stripped and chiseled into. Though the experience of the ruins is the experience of millennia of vandalism, the proof of the strength and glory of the ruins is that they are still beautiful, even cracked and defaced and scribbled on.

The tall pink granite obelisks that you see in London and Paris and Central Park originated at the ancient quarry outside Aswan, where work in stoppage shows the famous Unfinished Obelisk. This stone pillar, eighty feet long, distinctly geometric and symmetrical, partly chopped from the granite ledge, lies half hewn and is gaped at and trodden upon by bewildered admirers.

"It was all by hand!"

"Maybe they just got sick of working on it."

"How in heck did they manage to lift these things?"

An Egyptologist was saying, "So Osiris was killed by his evil brother Seth and cut into fourteen pieces. One of them was eaten by a fish, and Isis used it to revive Osiris and give birth to Horus. Which one, do you think?"

His leer suggested the obvious answer, but speaking for the group, one passenger asked, "Any crocs in the river here?"

The answer was no, none here, none even downstream at Crocodilopolis — though one had been kept and worshiped at the temple there, as the cat — image of the goddess of joy and love — had been worshiped in the temple at Bast. The big crocs these days lazed on the banks of the White Nile, in the swampy Sudd in southern Sudan and farther upriver at the source of the Nile, Lake Albert and Lake Victoria. The crocs here had long since been made into handbags and belts.

We visited the high dam and Lake Nasser, then waited until our flight to Abu Simbel, two hundred miles south at the border of Sudan and the head of the lake, was canceled.

The pleasantest aspect of the river cruise was the combination of gourmandizing and sightseeing, gliding with the current and stopping every now and then at a resurrected ruin. I liked the ruins most for the way they were overrun by the rackety bazaar, not just curio sellers but browsing donkeys among the pillars, goats in the roadway, hawkers' stalls in the foreground and Ptolemaic colors on the sheltered upper parts of the temples, still bright after thousands of years. Kom Ombo, where the *Philae* stopped the first day, was an example of these features: the bazaar, the ruins, the chewing animals, the loud music, the double shrine to Horus and the croc god represented by mummified crocs inside the temple. Kom Ombo was not just a temple but a small town, and its name, meaning "Pile of Gold," was both flattery and mockery. The temple looked more appropriate as part of the life of the town rather than as a fenced-off museum piece. It did not gain dignity in being reconstructed; it looked false and approximated. The town itself, with its Nubian name, was ancient.

"Who lived here way back?"

"Many bibble."

The walls of the temple at Kom Ombo were Egyptology in pictures, history and culture. As a reminder of the wisdom and skill of the Egyptians, one wall depicted medical instruments: pliers, forceps, knives, hooks, suction devices, all the paraphernalia for carrying out serious surgery, possibly more surgery than was being carried out in the present-day Kom Ombo General Hospital. Childbirth was illustrated in one hieroglyph. I sketched a picture of the Eye of Horus, which in a simplified form became the symbol (℞) for a prescription. Elsewhere on the temple walls were representations of the natural world — vultures, ducks, bulls, and hawks, and farther on, warriors and a pantheon of the Egyptians' enemies, including an unmistakable Negroid head and torso, a fierce soldier with the heavy-lidded gaze of the Nubian. It was wonderful to see such assertive black faces glaring from the walls of these ancient temples, like DNA in bas-relief, proof of the power and persistence of the African.

We floated onward in the *Philae,* nibbling delicacies, sipping fine wines, leering at the honeymooners on board, dodging the boisterous little Indian boy. We came to Edfu. "The Temple of Edfu serves as a latrine for the entire village," Flaubert noted in his diary in 1850. But it was disinterred and tidied up and is said to be the best-preserved temple in Egypt.

Until the late-nineteenth century, all these temples were torsos, broken and fallen, just smashed-up carvings and fat pointless pillars scattered in the Upper Nile Valley. "There is always some temple buried to its shoulders in the sand, partially visible, like an old dug-up skeleton," Flaubert wrote. The great delineator of wrecked Egyptian sites, David Roberts, loved the ruination, and in 1840 he said the structures seemed to him more beautiful half buried and bruised. They reminded him of Piranesi etchings of the Forum in Rome.

I saw what he meant when I came across a ruin in the middle of nowhere — a brilliant image, the lovely carving fallen and forgotten in the desert, a much more dramatic subject than a rebuilt temple teeming with hot-faced and complaining tourists. Flaubert took delight in reporting how dilapidated the temples were, and because he was not in search of ruins, he preferred the oddities of the Nile journey and dallying with dancing girls and prostitutes. Twenty-seven years after Flaubert visited, another traveler reported that the two-thousand-year-old Temple of Edfu was being dug out and had begun to look like its old self, as in the festival days of Edfu's greatness, celebrating the enactment of Horus avenging his father, Osiris, by stabbing hippo-bodied Seth.

In a new interpretation of these images, Horus is seen by some astronomers as the representation of a failed star in our solar system. The Egyptians had seen this so-called brown dwarf in the skies at its perihelion, spinning around the sun beyond the known planets. That this massive phantom star, out there unseen in the wilderness of space, crucially controls our own planet is only one aspect of the dark star theory.

The Greeks learned how to make columns by studying the symmetry of Egyptian pillars like those at Edfu. If a temple is buried deeply enough and the soil is dry and no archeologist or treasure hunter disturbs it, there is a sort of preservation in that very neglect. The Temple of Horus looks whole, cathedral-like in the way the pillars soar, some friezes retaining the reddish flesh tones on human figures and bluebirds and green snakes coiled on the upper walls. At the main gateway the upright falcon Horus, its eyes the sun and moon, stands sentinel, its halo the disk of the sun god.

Some images were defaced. In the past, tourists broke off pieces of Egyptian sculpture to keep as souvenirs — Twain describes an American chipping off a chunk of the Sphinx. But in Edfu, defaced was an exact word: it told precisely what had happened to the depictions of these soldiers, workers, and striding women on the walls. It was so consistent and stylistically similar as to seem a kind of negative sculpture, the art of obliteration. As striking as the images of gods and humans and animals on this temple — and it was a theme throughout — was the vandalism: defaced human heads, scratched-out hands and feet, chopped-off legs, hacked bodies, everything representing flesh was chipped away, even the heads and hooves of animals. Headdresses, hats, and cloaks were left, so that in a particularly pretty sculpture of an elaborately dressed prince, all the finery would be intact, but the face would be scooped out and the hands scraped off.

"Done by early Christians" was the usual explanation. But it might have been done by fanatical Muslims, who abhor human images. Muslim Egyptologists denied it, and insisted that Christians — especially Christians from Ethiopia — were to blame for these amazingly methodical defacings.

"Maybe not out of anger," Fawzi, one Egyptologist, said. "Maybe because the Christians had been persecuted. Maybe to obliterate pre-Christian history."

But he admitted that no one knew. What drew me was the fact that the defacers had not wrecked the temple or gone at the wall with sledgehammers. They had poked away at the carvings with a care bordering on respect, and you had to conclude that they could not have done it in this way, removing little, leaving so much, if they had not felt a certain terror.

Whatever the reason, and as with the Napoleonic graffiti, which has acquired significance over the years, the defacings are as fascinating as the finished sculptures, giving the figures the eeriness and mystery of a mutilated corpse at a crime scene.

Syrians, Asians, and Nubians were pointed out on the temple walls, and while the Egyptologist was explaining their features and their characteristic clothes, some of the cruise passengers were becoming impatient, jostling in the little cluster of concentrating and querulous tourists to ask a supplementary question. "Which Ptolemy was that?"

At last when Fawzi was done, the question came: "What about the Jews?"

It so happened, Fawzi said, that for the length and breadth of the Nile Valley, from the Delta south to Upper Egypt and to the dark pyramids and temples of Nubia, there was no mention of the Jews, nothing of Israelites, and even when captives were shown, their religion was not indicated; they were merely a mass of undifferentiated pagan prisoners. There are potbellied hippos and bat-eared jackals, plump-lipped Nubians and Asiatics squinting across the millennia, but there are no Jews. There are whole dynasties of pharaohs depicted, but not the faintest trace of Moses on an Egyptian wall.

So he said. Yet there was a people whose generic name, "Other-siders" or "Crossers-over," occurred now and then on Egyptian tombs and temples and in papyrus scrolls. The pharaonic word for these people was *Apiru* or *Habiru,* and was derived from an Aramaic word, *ibri,* which meant "one from the other side." It is not a great phonetic leap from *Habiru* or *ibri* to "Hebrew," a crudely descriptive name (like "wetback," for Mexican) for people who had crossed the water, in this case the Red Sea. And the word for "Hebrew," in Hebrew, is *Ivri.*

Some of these migrants ("*Habiru,* in cuneiform sources") found employment doing the heavy lifting on building projects in the eastern Delta. The Egyptologist K. A. Kitchen described them, in his life of Rameses II, as "displaced, rootless people who drifted or were drafted into various callings . . . Lumped in with the Apiru generally were doubtless those who in the Bible appear as the Hebrews, and specifically the clan-groups of Israel." Those people had been resident in the eastern Delta since the time of Jacob and Joseph, when their forefathers fled to Egypt to escape famine.

That I found out later. While I listened to Fawzi's explanation, and someone saying "I guess it's all a riddle," a woman approached me and hit me on the arm.

"Hey, that's a dandy idea!" She was from Texas. I had seen her on the boat, looking unsteady. She had a new hip. New hips are common on cruise ships, and among cruise passengers chitchat about hip surgery is frequently audible.

"What is?" I said.

"Little old notebook to write stuff on."

I shut my notebook and held it like a sandwich.

"Little old pen."

I had been doodling a hieroglyph, a squatting man in a stool-shaped hat, one knee up, both arms crooked and raised above his head in a gesture of amazement, as though saying, "This is incredible!" This lovely, compact, and comic image was the hieroglyph for "one million."

The woman punched my arm again as a sort of compliment, and when she moved off, favoring one leg, I wrote, *Hey, that's a dandy idea.*

Some aspects of the touristy Nile cannot have changed much in a hundred years. Edfu had no taxis, only pony carts, and they clashed and competed for customers, the drivers yelling, flailing their whips, maneuvering their carts, scraping their wheels. There was something ancient, perhaps timeless, in the way a driver — my Mustafa, say — turned, as the pony trotted toward the temple, and demanded more money, double the price in fact, whining, "Food for my babies! Food for my horse! Give me, bleeeez!"

◇ ◇ ◇

The most idyllic stretch of the Nile that I saw, an Egyptian pastoral as serene as any watercolor, lay between Edfu and Esna. Afterward, when I thought about Egypt I always saw it as it appeared to me that hot afternoon from the deck of the *Philae.* Fifty miles of farms and plowed fields, mud houses and domed mausoleums on hilltops; fishermen in rowboats, in the stream of the river, and donkeys and camels on the banks, loping among the palms. The only sounds were the gurgle of the boat's bow wave, the whine of locusts, and the flop and splash of the fishermen's oars. The sky was cloudless and blue, the land baked the color of biscuits and with the same rough, dry texture, as though these low hills and riverbanks had just come out of the oven. The green was deep and well watered. The river was a mirror of all of this — the sky, the banks, the boats, the animals, a brimming reflection of everything near and far, an ambitious aquarelle that took in the whole visible peaceful landscape.

Esna had always been a stopping-off place, even when the temple lay buried "to its chin," as one Victorian traveler wrote. The ruination had not made it less popular. The advantage of a mostly buried temple like this was that a visitor had a close-up view of the upper parts of the huge pillars: the great sculpted capitals and the interior ceiling showing papyrus leaves and ferns, grasshoppers, the symbolic garden easily visible, with zodiac signs, an enormous scorpion, and the ram-headed god Khnum, to whom the temple was dedicated.

The young sensualist Flaubert — he was only twenty-seven — went to Esna in search of a celebrated courtesan, Kuchuk Hanem ("Little Princess"), and her famous dance, the Dance of the Bee. Esna at that time was the most vicious town in Egypt, filled with prostitutes who by law had been rounded up and rusticated there from Cairo. Flaubert found Kuchuk Hanem, and she danced naked for him among blindfolded musicians.

The Dance of the Bee has been described as "essentially a frenzied comic routine in which the dancer, attacked by the bee, has to take all her clothes off." But the word "bee" also has a distinct allusion, for it is an Arabic euphemism for the clitoris. Flaubert slept with the dancer and minutely recorded in his travel notes the particularities of each copulation, the temperature of her body parts, his own performance ("I felt like a tiger"), even the bedbugs in her bed, which he loved ("I want a touch of bitterness in everything"). In every sense of the word, he anatomized his Egyptian experience, and he became an informal guide and role model for me.

At Esna, Flaubert made two memorable entries in his diary. At the temple, while an Arab is measuring the length of one of the exposed columns for him, he notes, "a yellow cow, on the left, poked her head inside."

Without that yellow cow we see nothing; with it, the scene is vivid and complete. Leaving Kuchuk Hanem's room after the sexual encounter, he writes, "How flattering it would be to one's pride if at the moment of leaving you were sure that you left a memory behind, that she would think of you more than of the others who had been there, that you would remain in her heart!"

But that is a lament, with the foreknowledge that he will be quickly forgotten, for later he concedes that, even as he is "weaving an aesthetic around her," the courtesan — well, whore — cannot possibly be thinking of him. He concludes: "Traveling makes one modest — you see what a tiny place you occupy in the world."

After the *Philae* docked, I went ashore and walked through the little town to the enormous and now fully exposed temple. A bazaar surrounded it, with narrow lanes, screeching traders, children and animals crowding around. The temple lay in a great square pit as if quarried from the earth. The painted signs of the zodiac were beautiful, the columns massive and intact. It is a late, Roman-era temple, but the Egyptian style is that of a thousand years earlier. The worst damage is in the façade, bullet-pocked by French soldiers who took potshots at it in the 1840s, plinking away at the magnificent edifice for the sheer hell of it.

I went back to the *Philae*. I finished Flaubert and started *Heart of Darkness*, which I was to read twelve more times before I reached Cape Town. Lolling on the upper deck, I realized that the *Philae* was not the *Roi des Belges* but rather one of those ships — very few, in my experience — that I wished would keep sailing, bearing me onward to Khartoum, southward through the Sudd, into Uganda and the big lakes, pioneering a water route down to the Zambezi.

"Just yourself this evening, sir?" Ibrahim, the waiter, asked each night at dinner.

I smiled. Yes, just me and Joseph Conrad.

"Going to Cairo afterwards, sir?"

"Yes, to get a visa. Then I am heading south. To Nubia, Sudan, Ethiopia. And beyond, I hope."

"Alone, sir?"

"*Inshallah.*"

"Business or pleasure, sir?"

"Both. Neither."

"Very good, sir. An adventure for you, sir."

Ibrahim was the soul of courtesy. They all were, really, full of compliments. It is well known that the staff on cruise ships are helpful and friendly because they are hustling for tips. They smile and banter so that you will reward them. I smile, you give me money.

Tipping confounds me because it is not a reward but a travel tax, one of many, one of the more insulting. No one is spared. It does not matter that you are paying thousands to stay in the presidential suite in the best hotel: the uniformed man seeing you to the elevator, inquiring about your trip, giving you a weather report, and carrying your bags to the suite expects money for this unasked-for attention. Out front, the doorman, gasconading in gold braid, wants a tip for snatching open a cab door. The bartender wants a proportion of your bill, so does the waiter, and chambermaids sometimes leave unambiguous messages with an accompanying envelope, demanding cash. It is bad enough that people expect something extra for just doing their jobs; it is a more dismal thought that every smile has a price.

Still, on the *Philae,* the waiters had a cheerful, even celebratory way of working, as though they were acting in an Egyptian comedy. And in such a country, where a schoolteacher earned fifty dollars a month, they probably needed tips in order to get by.

Although I was alone at my table, I was one of a hundred passengers — mainly those plump, rich, amphibious-looking people for whom travel is an expensive kind of laziness, spent in the company of other idle people to whom they relate details of their previous trips. "This reminds me of parts of Brazil," and "Now that, that could be Malta." They were American, British, German, with a scattering of South Americans, and of course the gloomy Indians with the boisterous child. The Americans on board could be divided into young friends traveling happily together, contentious aged couples traveling alone, and honeymooners, three pairs, everyone's favorites.

I resisted mocking them because they were harmless and most were committed to geniality, but except for one friendly pair of honeymooners who insisted that I dine with them from time to time, I ate alone. As for the others, trying to recall them, I only see them eating — feeding time was always closely observed on shipboard, and they were at their most animated then. The table of older blond German women, exquisitely dressed; the four German men who were often curt with the waiter, and one was actually named Kurt; the young American couples, distressed by the news of the failing stock market; the hard-faced woman and her bosomy husband, each seemingly midway through a sex change; the Indian couple and their bored bratty child.

Of the Germans, the sextet of aging, occasionally exuberant blondes, like the reunion of a chorus line, interested me most, because they were traveling with a Levantine doctor. We were on the upper deck one day, having a drink, and he said to me, "My field is reconstructive surgery." I turned to the women who were talking and sunning themselves, in that odd heliotropic posture of sunbathers, canted toward the sun, grimacing and just perceptibly turning.

I was struck by their similarity — the sharp noses, the smooth cheeks, the tight eyes, the bright brittle hair — and I realized that he was traveling with his patients, all of whom were so pretty that he, not they, deserved the compliment. This peculiar revelation seemed to me a great subject for a story — say, a young man's involvement with a much older woman who looks thirty, traveling with her plastic surgeon. To calm myself with the illusion that I was working, I began writing this story. *This is my only story. Now that I am sixty I can tell it* . . . As the days and weeks passed, the story became by turns melancholy, comic, reminiscing, and consolingly erotic.

Inevitably, on the *Philae* there was one of those helpfully nosy couples who asked all the questions the rest of us did not dare to ask for fear of revealing our ignorance. "How in heck did they manage to move those things?" and "Is that fronic?" were two of their questions. The wife interrogated the women, her husband badgered the men for information.

"Do you work?" the bullying wife asked the shyest-seeming woman, one of the petite and pretty honeymooners.

"I'm a prison officer," the new bride said.

"That must be so difficult!" was the predictable rejoinder.

When the honeymooner said "Oh, no. We have some wonderful inmates," all conversation ceased.

The nosy woman's husband, an irritating old philistine who looked like Piltdown man in a golf cap, kept saying to me, "I guess I'll have to read one of your books now."

I begged him not to, in a friendly way. One thing I had learned about traveling with lots of other people was that it was usually a good idea to hold my tongue. The talkers were self-advertisers, people to avoid, along with the networkers, the salesmen, and the evangelists. The quieter ones were often worth knowing, but in any case I regarded the whole boatload as one of the sights of Egypt, like the fat stone hippos and the mummified cats and the pesky curio sellers. I guessed that after Egypt I would not see many more tourists.

None of us knew much about Egyptology, we were hazy on dates, and "My history's real shaky" was as common a remark as "How in heck did they manage to move those things?"

For me this cruise was a picnic, and I suspected my last picnic before plunging deeper in Africa. It was comfortable, undemanding travel among mostly companionable people, and if it was true that we didn't know much about Egyptian history, neither did the Egyptians. It would have been very tedious if some pedantic historian had been on board, correcting impressions and setting us straight. I preferred listening to the improvisations:

"They must have used those for climbing up the wall."

"I imagine they took baths in that thing."

"Those ruts were probably made by chariots, or wagon wheels of some kind."

"Looks like a kind of duck."

"That's definitely fronic."

Some countries are perfect for tourists. Italy is. So are Mexico and Spain. Turkey, too. Egypt, of course. Pretty big. Not too dirty. Nice food. Courteous people. Sunshine. Lots of masterpieces. Ruins all over the place. Names that ring a bell. Long, vague history. The guide says "papyrus" or "hieroglyphic" or "Tutankhamen" or "one of the Ptolemys," and you say "Yup."

What you remember most is the friendly waiter, the goofball with the cell phone on the camel, the old man pissing against the ancient wall, the look of a tray of glossy pomegranates in the market, the sacks of spices, the yellow cow ruminating in the temple, or just the colors, for the colors of Egypt are gorgeous. Edward Lear wrote in his diary on the Nile, "Egypt is at least a land to learn color in."

What was I doing? Making progress, I felt. From the shores of the Mediterranean, via the Pillars of Hercules, I was proceeding, by degrees, deeper into Africa. Travel is transition, and at its best it is a journey from home, a setting forth. I hated parachuting into a place. I needed to be able to link one place to another. One of the problems I had with travel in general was the ease and speed with which a person could be transported from the familiar to the strange, the moon shot whereby the New York office worker, say, is insinuated overnight into the middle of Africa to gape at gorillas. That was just a way of feeling foreign. The other way, going slowly, crossing national frontiers, scuttling past razor wire with my bag and my passport, was the best way of being reminded that there was a relationship between Here and There, and that a travel narrative was the story of There and Back.

Close-up: me rowing hard, sweating like a galley slave. The camera draws back, revealing that I am on a rowing machine. A wider shot: I am in an exercise room. Wider still: I am on a boat, the *Philae,* near a window. The camera rises from me rowing on my machine and focuses out the window, finding a man at his oars on a rowboat on the Nile, rowing in the same rhythm.

◇ ◇ ◇

We came to Luxor, Thebes, the Valley of the Kings, the dream of Egyptologists and fidgety tourists, for even if you know nothing, you can still gape at the beauties and listen to recited facts: that the sun is born in the morning as a beetle, the scarab; becomes the god Ra at noon; and reigns until night falls, becoming the god Atun. You can read the Profession of Sinlessness, the Negative Confession, the pharaohs listing all their good deeds on the wall of the tomb. Sun imagery blazed everywhere in the form of solar boats, sun disks on the heads of compound gods, orbs over doorways. The Egyptians saw such power in the sun they called themselves "cattle of Ra."

But I most remember the graffiti, the vandalism, the names of ancients chiseled into the tomb walls, the scrawls of the French army, of the English nineteenth-century travelers, of the crazed Copts, the defacements of the iconoclast Akhenaton, who decided to be a monotheist.

And the gravel-crunching sandals of the old German professor in the tomb of Amenkopshef, as he approached the glass case, leaned over, and said, "See the shy-eld."

A clutch of little bones and a crushed skull.

"Is a moomy."

Indeed, it was a mummified fetus.

I remember the tomb of Nefertary, the Nubian wife of Rameses II, not for the many years and many millions spent in its restoration, not for the svelte Nefertary in her see-through gown and tattooed arms (a wide-open eye on each arm), playing a board game, and not for the jet blacks, bright colors, storks, beetles, cobras, greens, reds, and yellows. What I remember is that tickets were scarce and the visit was limited to ten minutes, and among all these scenes in the depths of the tomb, the attendant approached me, whispering, "You must go now! No, okay, stay three minutes more," and putting his hand out for bak-sheesh.

At Karnak, the great city and temple complex, nothing on earth like it, all those columns, I remember mainly the images of honey bees — Nesrut Bity, King Bee, symbol of the king of Upper and Lower Egypt — painted high on a roof truss, and how the bee thoraxes and legs were defaced. Flaubert said that Karnak looked like "a house where giants live, a place where they used to serve up men roasted whole, *à la brochette,* on gold plates, like larks."

At the three-thousand-year-old Mortuary Temple of Medinet Habu, commemorating the victories of Rameses III, I watched a group of Spanish tourists do a double take — first shock, then fascination — as they passed one wall depicting hands and penises being cut off captives — the tourists peering at the great stack of dicks carved into the temple wall.

"Paynees," one man murmured softly, putting his knees together.

I remember the Rameses temples, of course, the howling statues on the plain that alarmed the Greeks, and the melancholy trunkless legs of the Rameses colossus that inspired Shelley to write "Ozymandias," one of my favorites from Poetry Corner. Flaubert camped in Luxor, too.

But as impressive as anything else in Egypt in terms of obsessive continuity over the centuries was the sight of the dark bump and bruise on the forehead of devout Muslim men, from striking their head on the mosque floor — the *alamat el-salah,* "mark of prayer," colloquially called a raisin (*zabibah*) in Egypt. It was here in Luxor in 1997 that Islamic fanatics appeared at a temple and opened fire on some tour buses. Fifty-seven tourists died in this outrage. A month after I left the Nile six German tourists were taken hostage in Luxor. The kidnapper was said to be a nutter, and the hostages were released after a week, but more incidents were expected.

One day at the Temple of Hatshepsut, a name I could utter only by slowly syllabicating it, I found myself saying, "How in heck did they manage to move those things?" I took this as a sign that it was time to move on.

Because of the terrorist threat, a convoy left Luxor for the coast every morning, thirty cars and buses led by speeding police cars across the Eastern Desert, about one hundred miles to Port Safaga and another thirty to Hurghada, on the Red Sea. For about two hours the desert was flat and featureless, then there were low hills like rubble piles and heaps of stone, and finally tumbledown mountains of brown boulders, among which Bedouin children in dark gowns scampered, herding goats.

On the barren coast of the deep-blue Red Sea the town of Hurghada sprawled, a Russian resort with all that that implied: cheap hotels, tourists in track suits, terrible food, joyless gambling halls, and hard-faced hookers. Here and there were luxuriating Romanians and budget-conscious Poles and backpackers who had lost their way. There was nothing but sunshine here, and somehow that glary light made the tacky hotels look uglier.

"In 1980 this was a Bedouin village," a local man told me.

I had found a nice hotel at the southernmost dune in the district, a place with the fetching name of Sahl Hasheesh, the epitome of splendid isolation. Though the place was arid, *hasheesh* in fact means "greenery," and *sahl* means "coast" (thus *swahili* means "coastal people").

"You can relax here," the manager said.

I thought: I don't want to relax. If I wanted to relax, I would not have come to Africa.

"You can rest."

To me, travel was not about rest and relaxation. It was action, exertion, motion, and the built-in delays were longueurs necessitated by the inevitable problem-solving of forward movement: waiting for buses and trains, enduring breakdowns that you tried to make the best of.

"You can sit on the beach. You can go for a swim."

As someone who lived half the year in Hawaii, doing such things here seemed perverse. The Red Sea in February was cold, "sand" was a euphemism for gravel and sharp stones, and the wind was strong enough to snatch at my clothes.

What about a ship? I thought. I called an American travel agency in Cairo. The agent, a vague English girl, confused by my request, said she knew nothing of ships.

"How about a Nile cruise?" she inquired.

"Did that."

"Or you could visit Cairo and see real dervishes."

"We have dervishes in Hurghada."

She couldn't help: no brochures for ships, though the Red Sea must have been full of them. I went to Port Safaga. No ships to Djibouti, only a ship full of *hajis* bound for Jidda in fanatic Arabia.

Back at Sahl Hasheesh, the kindly manager could see I was agitated.

"Just relax. Have a nice time."

"I want to be on the move."

"Where to go?" He laughed.

"Well, Cape Town eventually."

This left him puzzled. It is always a mistake to try to explain plans for the onward journey. Such plans sound meaningless because they are so presumptuous. Travel at its best is accidental, and you can't explain improvisation. One day I got sick of being becalmed in Hurghada and, more worrying, I was told that the Muslim holiday of Eid al-Adha was about to begin. This six-day Feast of the Sacrifice commemorated the Lord's providing Abraham a ram to replace Isaac on the sacrificial altar (corresponding to Genesis 22). Six days of everything closed. On an impulse I decided to call the Sudanese again.

"Your visa has been approved," a man named Adil told me.

But the border was closed. I would have to fly to Khartoum. I went into town to get a ticket. With me in line was a friendly voluble man, also buying an Egypt Air ticket. He had the squarish head of an urban Egyptian, chubby cheeks and gray eyes, and a stockiness that gave the illusion of bad posture. His name was Ihab.

"Like the captain in the novel."

"What novel? Like Ihab in Holy Koran." He wiped his sweaty hands on his shirt, darkening the smear that was already there. "My name mean 'gift.'"

"You come from Hurghada?"

"No one come from Hurghada," he said. True, the resort town had been a Bedouin village twenty years ago, but Bedouins were always on the move.

"Egypt, then?"

"I am hate Egypt."

"Why?"

"I am tell you tomorrow."

Tomorrow?

Before I left for Khartoum I called the American consul general there, whose name had been given to me. What was life like in Sudan?

"I'm not allowed to live here," he said. "I live in Cairo. I fly back and forth to Khartoum. Going back to Cairo tonight."

"I'm wondering about traveling outside Khartoum."

"I'm not allowed to travel outside Khartoum, for security reasons."

"Have American citizens been hassled in Sudan?"

"Hassled? Well, one was picked up by security police a few months ago and interrogated, and I'm afraid tortured, for three days."

"That sounds awful."

"That's the only complaint we've had, but as you can see, it's a pretty serious one. I am obliged to tell you this."

"Did they let him go?"

"Not at first. Only after they subjected him to a mock execution."

"Something I would like to avoid," I said.

4 ◇◇◇

The Dervishes of Omdurman

EVEN AS I was entering Sudanese air space, Ihab, in the seat beside me, was telling me Sudan was a country he frankly hated. I was reading the U.S. State Department's unclassified travel advisory, an amazing document:

> Travel in all parts of Sudan, particularly outside Khartoum, is potentially hazardous . . . [American] travelers in Sudan have been subjected to delays and detention by Sudan's security forces, especially when traveling outside Khartoum . . . unpredictable local driving habits . . . roadblocks . . . In addition to the ongoing civil war, heavy rains and above normal Nile River levels have caused extensive flooding throughout Sudan. Nile floods have affected Khartoum . . . Water-related diseases such as malaria, typhoid and gastroenteritis will threaten many . . . The government of Sudan's control over its police and soldiers may be limited . . .

My favorite phrase was "In addition to the ongoing civil war." I glanced beside me. "You were saying?"

Being Egyptian, Ihab mocked Sudan with affectionate gusto, in the same spirit that he jeered at Egypt. His main objection was simple: "Because beeble no free!"

"In America, beeble can kiss girl on street — no broblem. But in Egypt, in Sudan, I kiss girl and bolice come! They take me!" He sulked, thinking about it. "They make a bad bosition for me!"

"For kissing a girl?"

"Is illegal. But not in America."

"You can't kiss strangers, though," I said.

He wasn't listening. "I want go to New Jersey! I want to be New Jersey man!"

A pretty Egyptian woman, traveling with an old woman who might have been her mother, sat in the seat across the aisle.

"Egyptian woman very sexy," Ihab said in a confiding whisper, his mouth full of saliva. He shifted, canting his body toward me so the woman would not hear, and said, "She cut."

I had a good idea of what he meant, but pretended I didn't so he would have to explain. This he did, first making a specific hand gesture, inserting a clitoral thumb between two labial fingers.

"She cut here," he said, slicing at his thumb with his free hand.

"Painful," I said.

"No bain! She small — leetle. One week, one month maximum, she cut."

Infant clitoridectomies were new to me but much on the mind of feminists in the West and the women's movement in Egypt as well. I asked the obvious question: What was the point?

"Better for her — make her more sexy," Ihab said. "If she cut, she like sex all day."

This conceit, echoed by other men I met on my trip, went against all medical evidence and was a bit like saying that sex for a man was more fun when his goolies had been snipped off. I also heard the opposite and more believable reason: it dulled the woman's pleasure and made her faithful. Ihab was so rhapsodic on the subject he had begun to raise his voice, and I feared the woman might hear and be offended.

"A woman who cut like this, you touch her" — he grazed my leg with his knuckles — "she get so excited."

"Imagine that."

"American woman, no. But in Egypt, Syria, Jordan, Saudi, woman who cut, they get so excited if you just touch something." He smiled at me. "Touch feenga. Touch skeen."

He showed me his hand and made the gesture again with his fingers.

"When you blay in zees blace," he said, emphasizing his thumb, "she go crazy."

Whispering the Arabic word for the procedure, Ihab compressed himself and breathed into my ear, lest anyone hear this forbidden term, which was *khitan.*

And on leaving the plane his eyes bugged out as we followed the attractive woman and her mother. Addressing the woman's secret, he looked roused and frisky, picturing in his fevered brain the thing he could not see, saying, "Woman with *khitan,* she more sexy."

Coming from Hurghada, Ihab knew a thing or two about women, especially foreign women. In his business, which was sales and marketing, he had many sexual proposals from visiting women — all Egyptian men did. Visitors found them attractive. Well, I could vouch for that: the embankments of the Nile rang with the shrieks of Europeans being pleasured on board feluccas. Indeed, the very name "felucca" had a sexual ring to it.

Ihab had had marriage proposals, too, from Russian women.

"Give me an example."

"One woman. She want to make marry with me. But I marry already. I like my wife, I like my two kids. So why marry?"

"I agree."

"But my wife so jealous."

"Mine too, sometimes."

"Yah?" He seemed somewhat shocked. "Yours? Mine? So women are all the same?"

"I don't think so."

◇ ◇ ◇

One of the first men I met in Khartoum refuted everything Ihab said. He was a small thin man named Haroun, whom I met at the Acropole Hotel. From the outside, the Acropole was just another seedy building on a dusty back street of a hot city of broken streets and deep potholes. But the hotel had been recommended. Inside, the Acropole was clean and pleasant, with marble floors and tidy rooms, run by a courteous Greek, George Pagoulatos, whose heart was in his ancestral Cephalonia but who had been born in Khartoum. "Tell me what you want to do in the Sudan," he said, "and perhaps I can arrange it." He kept his word. Because of George, many journalists and aid workers stayed at the Acropole. He was the helpful manager of the exotic hotel in the classic movie, and for much of the time I stayed there, life at the

Acropole seemed like *Casablanca* without the alcohol. Not George's fault: because of *sharia*, Islamic law, alcohol was banned in Sudan. There were no restaurants to speak of in Khartoum, so I ate all my meals in the Acropole dining room, supervised by George's cheerful Sicilian wife.

"Take it from me," Haroun said, speaking of female circumcision. "I can tell you from experience that such women feel nothing."

"But they submit?"

"They lie there. They have no idea what is happening. You feel a little silly if you are a man. And if you are a woman, I don't know."

"So what's in it for them?"

"Nothing," he said. "Well, children."

"Egyptians are pretty jolly, though."

"They laugh, yes. Nasser said, 'Our lives are terrible, but at least we know how to laugh.'"

"They seem friendly."

"You think Egyptians are friendly?" He looked at me as though I were off my head. "Their friendliness is fake."

Haroun was as skeptical of the Palestinians as he was of the Israelis. He wasn't fond of the Iraqis, and he didn't like the Iranians. "And the Saudis are just one big corrupt family."

"Arabs," he said, and showed his yellow teeth in a cynical smile and shrugged his skinny shoulders.

"What would you call yourself?"

"I am a Catholic," he said.

He was Jordanian, with a business in Amman, and didn't have much time for the Jordanian royal family either. One group of people had his total approval: the Sudanese.

"Look how they greet each other," he said. "They embrace, they slap each other on the back, they hug and kiss. No other Arabs do that. They like each other. They are good people."

"Have you had any problems here?"

"None."

◇ ◇ ◇

Khartoum, a city of tall white-robed men in thick Aladdin-like turbans and tall veiled women in bright gowns and black gloves, was a place without rain, wide and brown like its intersecting rivers. Khartoum's tallest structures were the pencil-shaped minarets of its many mosques. The lanky shrouded inhabitants looked spectral, as people often do in glary sun-dazzled places. There was no shade except the slanting shadows of the Sudanese. Their ghostliness was made emphatic by their shrouds and cloaks. Even their heads were loosely wrapped against the sun and heat, so nothing showed except brown beaky faces.

The city lay at the confluence of two wide rivers, the Blue Nile and the White Nile, both of them very muddy, bearing silt from the south, coursing past earthen banks that were cut straight up and down because they had been chunked away by rushing water. The bushes beside both Niles were hung with rags and plastic bags, snared by branches in the flood. To the west, across an old British iron bridge, was Omdurman, where more than a century ago General Gordon had been killed and decapitated by the Mahdi, whose great-grandson, Sadig el-Mahdi, still lived in the family mansion by the river. Here the river was both Niles combined in a wide, gurgling mud current flowing north toward Cairo. To the northeast, in the industrial district of North Khartoum, Clinton's rockets had fallen in 1998.

"Five rockets, very sudden," a student in a group told me, pointing it out across the river.

As I had passed this squatting group of three young men, two things had caught my attention: they were speaking English to one another and one was carrying the Penguin paperback of *Lady Windermere's Fan*. So I said hello, and soon we were talking about the rocket attack.

"The factory made pharmaceuticals, not weapons. But it was empty. There was no night shift on Thursdays. We think the Americans knew that."

They were university students in their early twenties. I obliquely asked how they felt about Americans as a result of the bombing.

"We like Americans. It was your government that did it, not you."

This distinction between politics and people was to be made quite often by people I met on my trip. Africans in general disliked their governments so intensely, and saw them as so unrepresentative of themselves, that they were happy to give me the benefit of the doubt.

"We want to be friends," one of the others said.

That was Hassan. The others were Abdullah and Saif-Din.

"*Saif* means 'sword,' and *din* is 'faith.'"

I made a slashing gesture. "'The Sword of Islam' — meaning jihad?"

"Yes, yes, exactly!"

"Not much of that stuff in this book," I said, tapping the cover of *Lady Windermere's Fan.*

"I am reading for my English. To learn better. Very important."

Hassan said, "Very, very important."

"Crucial," I said.

They didn't know the word. We sat down on the Nile bank, across from Tuti Island. I taught them "crucial" and "vital." It is *important* to learn English. It is *vital* that we understand what is happening. It is *crucial* that we act quickly.

"But let me interrupt you, sir," Abdullah said. "What you think about Afghanistan?"

"It is vital that we understand what is happening," I said. "It is tribal warfare."

"What do Americans think about Israel and Palestine?"

"That's tribal warfare, too."

Hassan said, "You see, sir, if you kill Afghans and Palestinians, they have families and they have children and they will always hate Americans and try to kill them."

This was incontestable, but I said, "The Sudanese military is dropping bombs on Dinkas and the SPLA in the south. Won't they always hate you?"

Muslims in the north, Christians in the south in this, the largest country in Africa. Forty years of war in the southern region. A Sudanese lecturing anyone on terror was drawing a very long bow. I think they realized this. They changed the subject.

Saif-Din said, "How can we go to America?"

"Can I work and study?" Abdullah said. "Get a job to support myself while I am going to university?"

"Where can we work in America?" Hassan said. "What work can we do?"

I asked them what work they were skilled at. They said, Very little. Where had they been? Just here, they said. They had been brought up in Khartoum. They had never left Khartoum — never seen their country: the south, which was oil-rich and swampy; the north, which was desert and filled with the temples and pyramids of Cush; the western mountains of Kordofan and the Nuba people. These students were not unusual in wishing to travel or emigrate. American cities were full of people from African cities, people who had never seen their own hinterland.

In Khartoum I would not have known there was a war in the south except for the presence of so many southerners — Shilluks, Dinkas, Nuer, the tall tribal Christians who had come north to escape the fighting. Some lived in refugee camps and survived on food aid distributed by various foreign agencies that operated in Khartoum. In the mid-1960s, I had been invited by Sudanese guerrillas to write about "liberated areas." I had then been living in Uganda, which was full of Sudanese refugees, who spoke of burned villages and a blighted countryside. Forty years on, this was apparently still the case.

"Whole sections of the south are uninhabited because of land mines," a mine expert told me in Khartoum. "You go there and you don't see anyone at all."

Eighteen years in the British Army had sharpened Rae McGrath's knowledge of land mine removal. On their retirement, most ex-soldiers moved to an English village and ran the local pub, Rae said. That usually meant they became drunks, in debt to the brewery that financed them. Rae, who was forty-five and stocky, used the skills he had learned in the military in Landmine Action, an organization committed to the removal of these wicked devices, which are numerous in many parts of Africa. They were lethal and long-lived: a land mine remained dangerous for about fifty years.

"They're mainly in the countryside, because armies in Africa always fight in agricultural areas," Rae told me.

Having written a book on land mine removal, he was quick to reply and sometimes epigrammatic ("Mine-finding is a bit like Zen gardening"). Not much has been written on the subject of land mines and their simple deadly technology. Land mines were usually made of plastic and nearly undetectable. Dogs could smell explosives, so they helped, but Rae's method was to probe the earth inch by inch with a metal rod pushed into the soil at a thirty-degree angle. It was pretty safe, he said. To detonate a mine you had to stand right on top of it.

Areas of southern Sudan were full of mines, and donors were urging Rae to find them and get rid of them so they could resettle people. But removal was a slow business, and sometimes the locals were not helpful.

"This woman in Malakal says to me, 'No one was blown up by a land mine here.' But then one of the neighbors said that the woman's cow had stepped on a mine and been blown up. The woman said, 'Oh, yeah. My cow.' In a war, a cow being killed is no big deal."

Rae would be in Sudan for a year or two, dealing with land mines. At the moment, he was in a top-floor room at the Acropole, surrounded by pictures of his family. He was not alone in his charitable work. Duncan, from Save the Children, was in the hotel, and so was Issa from UNICEF, and Rick (microfinance, small-business loans), and the stout Ugandan from UNESCO, and the Dutch team who often conferred over maps, and the Bangladeshi ("But I'm an American now") who was "supervising some UN projects."

They were all aid experts, and they ranged from selfless idealists to the laziest boondogglers cashing in on a crisis. In an earlier time they would have been businessmen or soldiers or visiting politicians or academics. But this was the era of charity in Africa, where the business of philanthropy was paramount, studied as closely as the coffee harvest or a hydroelectric project. Now a complex infrastructure was devoted to what had become ineradicable miseries: famine, displacement, poverty, illiteracy, AIDS, the ravages of war. Name an African problem and an agency or a charity existed to deal with it. But that did not mean a solution was produced. Charities and aid programs seemed to turn African problems into permanent conditions that were bigger and messier.

◇ ◇ ◇

The heat in Khartoum, with its sky specks of rotating hawks, left me gasping, and the sun burning in cloudless blue onto the whitewashed buildings and the streets dazzled my eyes, for the streets were all chalky dust — just as fine, just as bright. I walked in slow motion, tramping in heavy shoes. I would have been happy for a turban and a white robe, like everyone else in this begowned population. I settled on sandals, and went to the souk to buy a pair, muttering to myself, rehearsing the Arabic for the request: *Ana awiz shapath aleila,* I need some sandals now.

On the way, glancing at people's sandals to see what styles were available, I saw a man and woman heading to the mosque — it was Friday, he was clutching a Koran, and they were both dressed up for the occasion. Without question they were husband and wife, for she was decorated with henna — a blue-black lacy pattern picked out on her feet and ankles — the privilege of a married woman.

The woman was very attractive anyway, tall and black and slender, in a gold-colored gossamer veil. Parting it with a toss of her head, she gave me a glimpse of her face. Her figure was apparent in the sinuous movement of her gown, and she wore black high-heeled shoes. The hem of her gown became entangled in one stiletto heel, and as she stooped to disengage the wisp of silken cloth from the heel point with a gloved hand, lifting her gown a bit higher, I saw the filigree of dark henna on her foot and her ankle and reaching up her leg, delicately painted, as though she were wearing the sexiest French tights. In addition to the pretty shoe and the naked foot, the principal fascination of this lovely painted leg was that it belonged to a woman who was veiled. The explicit fetishism of her feet, her only exposed flesh, left her hidden charms to the imagination. Nothing to me was more erotic.

That sight made the day seem hotter. I bought my sandals — *Souri*, the seller said, Syrian ones — and spent the rest of the day breaking them in.

Travel is wonderful for the way it gives access to the past: markets in Africa show us how we once lived and traded. The market in Khartoum was medieval, a meeting place of hawkers and travelers, street performers, hustlers, city slickers in suits, more pious ones in robes, country folk from the southern regions — and if you knew even a little of their customs, you could name them, spotting the slash marks on one tribal face, the tattoos and scarification on another, the knocked-out lower teeth or lip plugs of yet others. Many urchins snatched at passersby or sold soap and cigarettes. The Khartoum market was the heart and soul of the city, as markets have been throughout history. The bus depot was nearby, and so was the street of gold and silver merchants, the street of sandal sellers (and sellers of illegal leopard skins and snakeskin purses and slippers), the vegetable barrows, the meat stalls, and at the center the country's largest mosque. Because of this mosque and the Koran's specific injunction "Repulse not the beggar" (93:10), every panhandler and cripple in town jostled the faithful as they strode to prayers.

Groups of gowned and veiled women sat in the goldsmiths' shops choosing dangling earrings, bracelets as wide as shirt cuffs, and mesh-like necklaces and snake bangles. Gold was the only luxury. Some of these shops were no more than small booths, but you knew them by their twinkling gold and their mirrors and air conditioning.

Mahmoud Almansour was selling gold and spoke English reasonably well.

"Is because I live New York City," Mahmoud said.

"What are you doing here?"

"Just visiting family, and this" — he gestured to the gold objects in a disdainful way.

"You don't like Sudan?"

"Sudan is nice. Beeble are kind." He clawed his shaven head and yanked his beard. "But . . ."

His emigration story was interesting and perhaps typical. In 1985, aged twenty-five, he flew to Mexico City, entered on a tourist visa, and vanished. He surfaced near Tijuana and paid a man five hundred dollars to take him across the U.S. border. He was hidden inside a refrigerator truck that was loaded with fish — Mahmoud stood behind boxes of fish with three Mexicans. At the border crossing the truck driver gave them mittens and hats and turned the thermostat very low, so when U.S. Customs opened the doors frozen air billowed out in clouds.

Mahmoud was dumped outside San Diego but did not linger there. In those days, no ID was needed to buy an airplane ticket. He flew to Atlanta and, having spent all his money, picked peaches until the season ended. Then he took a bus to Virginia.

"More bicking. Bicking, bicking. I bick anything."

Living in migrant workers' quarters, eating frugally, he saved enough money to move to New York City, where he knew some Sudanese. He continued to do menial work. He applied for and was granted a Green Card, and he saved his money until he gained the confidence of a man who, for a fee, fixed him up with a job driving a cab, which became his livelihood.

"I am married to an American — black American," Mahmoud specified. "But she think, Africa dangerous! Sudan not safe! I don't care. I love New York. America is *baradise*."

He planned to leave Sudan in a few months, to return to Brooklyn. He said he felt stifled by the laws of his homeland — well, he was a hard worker, but fundamentally, and like many emigrants to the United States, no respecter of laws, so that was easy to understand. Yet it was amazing how even here in the market, Khartoum's traditional souk, there were upstairs rooms where both men and women gathered. Most of the larger coffee shops had a stairway to a hidden room, heavily curtained, fans whirring, a bit stuffy and dark, where young men and women sat at tables, whispering. No kissing, no handholding, but anyone could see that these whispers were freighted with endearments, and it was all furtive enough to seem rather pleasant.

Groups of men met in such places, too. In one of these ateliers I met two men and, this being Sudan, they invited me to join them for a cup of coffee. Dr. Sheikh ad-Din was a medical doctor, and his friend Dr. Faiz Eisa was a lawyer.

"This is not a strict country like some others," Dr. Faiz said. "There are only five aspects of *sharia* law here. Against adultery. Against alcohol. Against stealing. Against defamation. And traitors — declaring war against your own country. That is forbidden."

"But people behave," Dr. Sheikh said. "As you see."

"We don't cut people's hands off," Dr. Faiz said. "And no stoning to death."

"Hey, that's pretty enlightened," I said.

◈ ◈ ◈

The next day, I walked to the Blue Nile Sailing Club, dating from the early 1920s. This British club by the river had been established for river-related activities — sailing, rowing, sculling, with plaques displayed with the engraved names of the winners of various trophies and competitions: *1927 Blue Nile Trophy — S. L. Milligan, '43–'44 Ladies' Race — Mrs W. L. Marjoribanks,* and so forth.

The clubhouse, an old steel gunboat, the *Malik,* sat in a ditch high on the riverbank. The last surviving British gunboat from the three involved in the Battle of Omdurman, the *Malik* had first come down the Nile in many boxes in 1898, to be assembled in Khartoum and used by the attacking Lord Kitchener ("We hate him here," a Sudanese told me). The *Malik* was commanded by General Gordon's nephew, a major known by his nickname, "Monkey," who had come to Sudan to avenge his uncle's murder and to desecrate the Mahdi's tomb. Seeing these slow, hard-to-maneuver gunboats, the soldiers scornfully called the fleet "Monkey Gordon's Greyhounds." The boats were well armed, though: the *Malik* had a howitzer, two Maxim guns, two Nordenfeldt guns, and a cannon on board. These guns were used with devastating effect at Omdurman, which was not only a battle to wrest control of Sudan but also a punitive mission against the Sudanese, as revenge for the death of Gordon and the expulsion of the British thirteen years earlier.

From the wheelhouse of the *Malik*, toiling upstream, Monkey Gordon saw the Mahdi's tomb, the army's first glimpse of Omdurman. Later, in the thick of battle, the *Malik* was the gunboat that decisively cut off the dervishes, who were successfully harrying the Camel Corps. In the end, more than eight thousand Sudanese were killed, and wounded men were shot where they lay bleeding. This heartlessness on the part of the British shocked the young Winston Churchill, who was in Sudan working as a journalist.

At the close of the battle, the *Malik* was chosen to fire the victorious twenty-one-gun salute (with live ammo, no blanks were available). Then Monkey Gordon, on Kitchener's orders, took charge of demolishing the Mahdi's tomb, disinterring the corpse, desecrating it by tossing it in the river, but not before hacking off the head. A historian of the battle wrote that Lord Kitchener "toyed with the idea of mounting it in silver to serve as an inkwell or a drinking cup." Some people believe he followed through, though I was told that the head is buried in a cemetery in Wadi Halfa.

The *Malik* was made of riveted steel plates, and so it was almost indestructible. But now it was beat-up, with broken portholes, twisted rails, and scruffy, littered decks and cabins full of smashed planks. Some working sailboats and motorboats were moored at the pier nearby, but even so, this club — this broken boat — had seen better days. The Mahdi's mud forts remained on the Nile banks at Omdurman, much eroded and smoothed by high water but still showing the musket holes in the battlements.

The Sudanese are so proud of their military prowess that they can quote lines from the Kipling poem "Fuzzy-Wuzzy," written in praise of the Sudanese warriors: "the Fuzzy was the finest o' the lot," and "We sloshed you with Martinis, an' it wasn't 'ardly fair." When it came to left-handed compliments, Kipling was a born southpaw. Still, the Sudanese are proud of

> An' 'ere's to you, Fuzzy-Wuzzy, with your 'ayrick 'ead of 'air —
> You big black boundin' beggar — for you broke a British square!

In the house of the Mahdi's successor in Omdurman, there is a room amounting to a shrine to General Osman Abu Baker Digna. This turbaned, saintly-looking old man was the soldier who had impressed Kipling, for he had fought nineteen battles against the British and distinguished himself by leading charges that successfully broke the troop formation known as the square. No one, not the Indians or the Zulus or Napoleon's troops, had ever managed that military feat.

Later that day, with a man named Khalifa, who was a history buff, I went to the Khartoum Museum, which was full of pharaonic statuary. It was obvious that the border of Egypt is arbitrary, and that what we take to be Egyptian gods and temples reached deep into Africa, deeper than Nubia, more southerly than Dongola, almost to Khartoum.

Khalifa said, "The kings of Cush were forced out of Egypt by the Assyrian invasions, and they ruled at Meroë and the various towns of the Dongola Reach."

"How far is Meroë?"

"You could go there in a day."

He went on to say that as late as the sixth century A.D., the statue of Isis from Philae was carried up the Nile to bless the crops.

There were Christians nosing around the Nile Valley at that time too, Khalifa said, sent from the Eastern Roman Empire to convert the Nubians, who were still (to the horror of the Christians) worshiping Isis and Osiris. Thus it can be said that Christian missionaries have been peregrinating and proselytizing in Africa for upward of 1,400 years — and fighting a rearguard action in places like Sudan, which was Islamized in the sixteenth century.

"Islam spread in the Sudan through the Sufis," Khalifa said.

I had a nodding acquaintance with Sufism, the mystical form of Islam. Khalifa said there were many Sufis in Sudan. The authority on Sufism here, Yusef Fadal Hasan, lived in Khartoum. Hasan told me that there were all sorts of Sufi devotees, according to the mosque — some danced and drummed, others didn't drum at all, and at certain mosques the Sufis performed unique musical compositions.

"And there are dervishes," Khalifa said.

◇ ◇ ◇

Toward the end of a very hot afternoon, the sun lowering into the dust cloud raised by the day, the orb growing larger and redder as it descended, we hurried through the low stone-piled graves in the vast necropolis of Hamad el-Nil Mosque in Omdurman to see the dervishes.

I could hear chanting as we approached, and coming upon the spectacle I knew that I had never seen anything like it. A crowd of several thousand stood in a dense circle in the courtyard of the mosque, which was at the edge of the cemetery — somehow the dereliction of this mute field of corpses added to the frenzy of what I was witnessing. At the center of the circle were stamping men, some in green robes, some in white, some in green sashes and green skullcaps. Six or seven were dressed in motley — multicolored patched robes and red capes and red dunce caps — and carried sticks, some spinning on one leg and others dancing or slowly whirling.

Near the mosque stood about twenty musicians with drums and cymbals. They played loudly, in a syncopated way, while everyone chanted — dervishes, green-and-white-robed priests, and the crowd, too.

"No God but Allah! No God but Allah!"

The robed men in the center began a deliberate promenade in a great circle, led by a huge black man in green — green turban, green robe — and surrounded by the dervishes, some spinning, some hopping or dancing. Nearly everyone had a stick of some sort, and some of their gestures seemed to mimic swordplay.

The robed women had been shoved to one corner, where they chanted less demonstratively. The watching crowd of thousands danced in place, chanted, and made a continuous motion of pulling an invisible rope. This slow-motion tug of war was both graceful and weird, and the tuggers' faces shone with sweat as they mimicked this yanking.

The whooping and hollering I associated with a revivalist prayer meeting, the same goofy smiles, the same hysteria. It was a prayer meeting in every respect. They were chanting "God is great" now, faster and faster, and with this speeded-up chanting, the men walked more quickly in the great circle, raising dust.

Now I noticed crippled Sufis, men with twisted and gimpy legs, spinal curvatures, crutches and canes, and two men scrabbled on all fours. They, too, approximated dance steps, and fumbled and stumbled in the sacred circle, to the tattoo of the drums and the smashing of the tin cymbals that had the sound of pot lids.

There was at once a slower beat, and I thought the dance was ending, but the thirty or so priests and dervishes made their eccentric way in the circle, now uttering a new chant.

"Allah al-hayyu! Allah al-hayyu!" God is alive!

The dervishes, with matted locks and pointed cloth caps and wild patched clothes, looked like court jesters or fools, and they even had that self-mocking conceit in their movements. They continued circling, spinning, as a man passed the perimeter of the crowd wafting incense with a thurible, directing the thin smoke into the gleaming faces of the chanting mob.

And now, with the red sun lower, the smell of dust and incense, the heavy stamping — which reminded me of the stamping in some village exorcism — the spinning cripples, the marching priests, the rat-a-tat of the drums, and the ululations that grew to a shrill yodeling, the pace quickened again, accelerating to a frenzy.

It was, I could see, essentially a rousing singsong, and when one of the dervishes snaked out a leather coach whip and began cracking it and spinning as the mob clapped and chanted — the sunset on the mosque making a long shadow on the cemetery — the drums were never louder, nor the cymbals so insistent. I was both worried and energized, for the mob had become crazed in its ecstatic chanting of "God is alive!" There is a point at which hysteria is indistinguishable from belief.

As an unbeliever, the only one among these thousands, I had reason to be alarmed.

"They are not political," Khalifa assured me. "They are Sufis. They bother no one. They dance. They are mystical. They are good people."

Perhaps so, but in any case, this was the lovely weird essence I looked for in travel — both baffling and familiar, in the sunset and the rising dust beaten into the air by all those feet, dervishes and spectators alike. Everyone was part of it. And this was not a spectacle put on for photographers and tourists but rather a weekly rite, done for the pure joy of it.

In the gold and gore of the desert sunset the whole thing ended in exhaustion, the men embracing, the women peeping out of their veils. Then they got down on their knees and prayed in the gathering darkness, in this strange spot between the river and the desert.

5 ◇◇◇

The Osama Road to Nubia

ON MY FIRST NIGHT sleeping in the desert, a traveler in an antique land, stifling in my tent, thirsting for a drink, lying naked because of the heat, I looked through the mosquito net ceiling and saw flies gathering on the seams, their fussing, twitching bodies lit by the moon and crumbs of starlight. Yet I was happy, in spite of the dire warnings: *Travel in all parts of Sudan, particularly outside Khartoum, is potentially hazardous.*

"The mere animal pleasure of traveling in a wild unexplored country is very great," David Livingstone wrote in similar circumstances. Then the flies were gone and so was the moon, as the sky was covered by a raveled skein of clouds that grew woollier and darker until the whole night was black, starless, and thick with hot, motionless air. I breathed with difficulty, feeling that odd sense of levitation that comes from being naked, flat on one's back on a summer night. But I was just a white worm in the vastness of a dark desert.

There came a trotting sound, not one animal but lots of tiny hooves, like a multitude of gazelle fawns, so soft in their approach they were less like hoofbeats than the sound of expelled breaths, *pah-pah-pah.* They advanced on me, then up and over my tent, tapping at the loose fabric.

It was rain. *Rain?* I sat up sweating. Yes, and now it came down hard, pelting into the netting and dropping onto me. In seconds I was sluiced and soaked. I had dragged my bag into the tent so as not to attract the snakes that were numerous here. My bag was wet, and so were my folded clothes, and it was still raining.

I zipped myself out of the tent and saw Ramadan crouching with his hands on his head. He yelled when he saw me. He was a dim vision. No stars, no moon, just straight down rain clattering in the blackness.

I stood in the downpour like a monkey, licking the raindrops from my lips, wondering whether to make a run for the truck. As I considered this, the rain stopped and a chewed pie of a moon appeared.

"What was that?"

"It never rains here," Ramadan said.

"That was rain."

"Just sometimes," Ramadan said.

The night was so hot, even with this cloudburst, that after I wiped out my tent and stuck my bag in the sand, I was dry in minutes and so was my tent. It was midnight. I went back to sleep. A few hours later I heard the approaching footfalls, the pattering, the lisping, then the pelted tent, and there was another downpour, as fierce as the first. I lay and let the rain hit me. When it stopped, I was so tired I turned over and went back to sleep in the evaporating puddle inside my tent.

Dawn was cool. I woke sneezing and dragged on my clothes, but the sun stoked the heat again. We made coffee, ate some grapefruit we had bought at a market the previous day, and resumed driving north up the road.

"You know who made this road?" Ramadan said.

"Tell me."

"Osama."

"He used to live in Khartoum, right?"

"The Sudan government tell him to go away."

In spite of his hasty exit, Osama bin Laden was not reviled in Sudan. "He is a good man, a holy man, we think he is not wrong," a group of Sudanese had told me in Khartoum, challenging me to disagree with them. And I did, saying, "Osama decreed that all Americans are legitimate targets and can be killed by mujahideen. Therefore, as a target, I disagree with you."

As is well known now, Osama had gone to Afghanistan in the early 1980s, a multimillionaire of twenty-two, and had used his fortune to buy arms to oppose the Soviet invasion of Afghanistan. He had come to Sudan in 1992 after the Saudis withdrew his passport and canceled his citizenship. He lived with his wives and children in Riyadh, an upscale suburb of Khartoum, in a compound of three-story houses behind a high wall, and started a construction business, building the road to Shendi and the Port Sudan Airport on the Red Sea. He had also, people said, carried out good works — dispensed money, charity, advice — while continuing to recruit Muslim zealots for Al Qaeda, the organization he had started in the 1980s.

In Sudan, Osama had financed Somali opposition to the Americans in Mogadishu and was as successful, and as destructive, as he had been in Afghanistan. Finding him an irritant, the Sudanese government expelled him in May 1996, and he returned with his entourage to Afghanistan, where he went on hatching plots, including the U.S. embassy bombings in Nairobi and Dar es Salaam as well as the mayhem in America on September 11, 2001, which turned his public image into Dr. Evil.

Officially he had been banished from Sudan, yet he was still in the thoughts of the Sudanese, a tall gangling figure — noticeably tall, even in a country of very tall people — pious and austere, full of maxims, giving alms, defending the faith, his skinny six-five frame trembling with piety, the living embodiment of the Sword of Islam. The Muslim Brotherhood was strong in Sudan, if passive on the subject of jihad, and so was the much more militant El-Gama'a el-Islamiya, which carried out multiple murders in Egypt, including the killing of tourists.

The Khartoum papers printed reminiscences of Osama. Even his old household chef, an Egyptian named Mohammed el-Faki, gushingly recalled for one newspaper how his boss had liked fruit juice, preferred boiled black cumin to tea, and ate *kabsa*, lamb on a huge platter of rice. He was abstemious, respectful, and always carried a religious chaplet in his right hand and a cane in his left hand, sometimes using it to clout his children.

"This is a good road."

"Osama road," Ramadan said, and he laughed. He also said that he had a mind to go to Afghanistan, kill Osama, and collect the multimillion-dollar reward. "But then I cannot come back to the Sudan. Sudan people will be angry with me for killing this man. Ha!"

We kept driving, and every so often Ramadan, without slowing down, would spin the wheel and drive off the Osama road, lurching over the roadside berms and up and down the ditches. We would head fifty miles into the desert, off-road, in search of a temple or some noseless, armless statuary, the remnants of yet another hubristic Ozymandias.

◈ ◈ ◈

I liked the look of the Sudanese desert — vast, browny bright, unpeopled, lots of off-road tracks — reputedly full of beautiful ruins, rocky ridges, and extensive wadis full of herons, and oases with deep wells. "Not as hot as Khartoum," someone at the Acropole had said. George Pagoulatos had found me a truck and a driver. The driver had a tent for me. What about his tent? "This my country! These my dunes! This my sand! I sleep in the sand dunes." He actually did, on the gritty sand, in his clothes, like a cat on a mat. He was named for Ramadan, the period of fasting, and his home was in the west, Kordofan, in the Nuba Mountains.

Meeting him and his vehicle on a back street in Khartoum, I had been reassured by the sight of plastic chairs roped to the truck. They were cheap molded things, but usable. A man with the foresight to bring chairs on a camping trip in the desert could be counted on to have brought the rest of the necessaries — and this assessment proved true, for even though I didn't taste them, he also brought a jar of jam, some cans of tuna fish, and a haunch of goat.

We set off through Khartoum, then crossed the bridge to North Khartoum, where he showed me the pharmaceutical factory in the industrial area that had been blown up in 1998 — still derelict, because the owner had a lawsuit pending. Then we swung back onto the main road, the Osama road to the north, and were soon in the desert, but a peculiarly Sudanese desert: gravelly and flat but also strewn with hills formed like enormous rock piles. About thirty miles north we came upon a settlement in the middle of nowhere — people camped in mean shacks and lean-tos, fighting the heat and the wind, no trees or bush, just a few skinny goats. Ramadan called them Jaaliyeh, a clan that had come here and squatted in the hope that they would be seen as a nuisance and an obstruction and told to move.

"Because when the government wants them to move, they will ask for money."

The Sudanese government, in an expansion mode, had become well known for compensating people whom they were compelled to resettle.

Farther up the road, the boulder piles were even higher, and some could have passed for mountains — or stone skeletons of mountains — while others were perfectly pyramidal. Here and there a miragelike strip of green, low in the west, indicated the north-flowing Nile. I assumed that all the settlements would be near the Nile, but I was wrong. Some villages were a whole day's donkey ride from the river, so it was two days there and back. Some settlements were that far from the nearest town — longer on foot than by donkey. It was true that there were Sudanese here who enjoyed the congeniality of living on a grid of streets in a good-sized town with a market by the river, but there seemed to me even more people who chose to live in isolated places, huddled in huts by a few boulders, a longish walk from a water source.

A little way off the road we stopped at Wadi ben Naggar, a tiny village of goatherds and farmers but also the birthplace of Omer al-Bashir, the current president of Sudan, who had come to power in a coup.

A toothless man howled at me, and to neutralize his hostility I gave him the conventional greeting, "*Salaam aleikum*." Peace be upon you.

"You are American?"

I caught the word *Ameriki*, though Ramadan was translating, and Ramadan answered for me. The man had a grubby gown and a falling-apart turban and five days' growth of beard.

I understood this man's next howl.

"Bush *ma kwais!*" Bush is no good.

"How do I say 'I don't know'?"

"*Ana ma'arif*."

I smiled at the man and said, "*Ana ma'arif*."

The man laughed and clutched at his turban, disentangling it some more.

"Clinton *Shaytaan*."

That was pretty clear: Clinton is Satan.

"A lot of Americans would agree with you," I said.

He shook his head, smiled goofily, and gabbled a little: what was I saying? Then he said, "Bush blah-di-blah."

"He is saying you look like Bush."

"I don't think so," I said to Ramadan and to the man, still practicing my new phrase, "*Ana ma'arif*."

"Not big Bush but small Bush," Ramadan translated.

"Ask him if he wants a Stim." It was the local version of 7-Up.

The man said, Yes, indeed, he wanted one.

Giving it to him, I said, "Please stop talking about Bush."

He smiled at me — still no clue — and toasted, clinking Stim bottles: "Clinton is Satan."

We left his boisterous abuse and his unfriendly smile, looked around the village, and then drove a short distance up the road and off it, straight across the soft sand and deep ditches for about forty miles. There was no road to speak of, only hard-packed desert gravel and now and then powder-soft dunes. Up ahead I would see greenery and imagine a wooded glade, but of course the glade turned out to be a hot patch of desert with a few stands of thorn bushes and the wriggle marks of snakes.

"There was a school here once," Ramadan said.

"I want to see it."

The place was ruined and desolate, just a cluster of empty buildings, perhaps an aid donor's idea in the first place, one of those good-hearted, misguided efforts to elevate Africans in a Western way.

"What happened?"

"No water, no food, no teachers — nothing."

Sand blew through the roofless classrooms, and the place looked as useless and broken as a Cushitic ruin, but without any of the art or grace. Some hobbled, tortured-looking camels tottered near the school, their forelegs tied together so they would not stray.

Then I saw the forgotten scholars and potential school kiddies. They were at a well helping their elders, watering their goats, and the smallest of the children — no more than eight or nine — was running beside a donkey, hitting his hindquarters with a sharp stick. The donkey was pulling a frayed rope, and watching him I was surprised to see how far he pulled it, down a worn path more than half the length of a football field, zipping an immense length of it out of the well.

The well was ancient, the place was ancient: a Meroitic temple complex dating from the first century A.D. stood near here, and such temples, so far from the Nile, could be sustained only by deep and reliable wells. This one was 175 feet deep. The opening at the top was about four feet in diameter. I was spooked contemplating its deepness. A man would drop a goatskin pail into the depths of the well and then jerk the rope, bobbing the pail and filling it. He would hoist it a few feet and, satisfied that the pail was full, knot the rope to a donkey. A little boy would chase the donkey into the desert, belaboring it with a stick. There was not a shred of clothing or any item of apparatus here that was any more modern than the first-century Meroitic temple on the other side of the dune. The school must have seemed a nice idea, but nothing here could have seemed more superfluous than those classrooms.

"So you're American?" one of the men said to me in Arabic, because Ramadan had tipped him off.

"Peace be upon you."

"And peace be upon you," he replied.

"Bush is no good," another man said — the Arabic was simple enough.

"I don't know."

"Why is he saying he doesn't know?" one of the men at the well said.

Ramadan said, "Does everyone in the Sudan love President Omer?"

Yes, yes, they understood this, and laughed angrily and stamped on their little hillock for emphasis. I thought of the lovely lines of Joyce: "The movements which work revolutions in the world are born out of the dreams and visions in a peasant's heart on the hillside. For them the earth is not exploitable ground but the living mother." They loved their well. They explained the well to me, how deep it was. It had been dug ages ago. Sometimes they had to rope up and descend into its darkness to retrieve a lost pail, not a happy task.

"There are snakes in the well," one man explained. To my next obvious questions they said, "Yes, the snakes are a meter long and they bite with poison."

I walked around, looked at the goats, the camels, the toiling men and women, the children who were standing in the sun, performing this necessary and never-ending job. Then I said goodbye.

"Tell Bush we want a pump!" one man screamed in Arabic, Ramadan helpfully translating.

No, I don't think so: a pump would need gasoline, spare parts, regular maintenance. Ultimately the contraption would fail them. They were better off hauling water the ancient way, with donkeys, goatskin pails, and goatskin water containers that when filled looked like little fat goat corpses.

But I said, "The next time I see President Bush I will mention it," which when translated brought forth a howl of derision.

Two thousand years ago, Al-Naggar ("Carpenter"), this dune-haunted ruin in the desert, was a city, with cisterns and water tanks, roads and houses, sophisticated agriculture and a high degree of prosperity, artisans everywhere, and priests and devotees. It was the center of a cult of the lion god Apademak, chief deity of the Meroites, probably with good reason. There must have been many lions roaming central Sudan then — there were plenty in the south even now — and it is human nature to worship what we fear.

In form and ornament the temple complex at Al-Naggar was Egyptian, resembling many others farther down the Nile. This temple in the middle of Sudan, situated farther south even than Nubia, was like a copy of the temple at Edfu. The walls had the same symbolic figures of the king and queen holding enemy prisoners by the hair, and lions preparing to eat them. On the sides of one pylon a coiled python with a lion's head — Apademak again — rose from a lotus flower, the symbol of everlasting life. On another pylon, King Natakamani was shown worshiping the lion god.

On every surface there were bas-reliefs, some of ram-headed Amun and Khnum, and many lions, beautifully sculpted and rampant, their paws extended to snatch and gobble prisoners. The north wall showed symbols of peace and prosperity, the south wall images of chaos and war. A crocodile with its jaws tightly tied symbolized peace; armored battle elephants dragging captives depicted war.

Inside the kiosk of the temple were old pieces of graffiti (*Holroyd 1837*) and pharaonic scenes too, delicately cut into the sandstone that had been quarried from the hills that surrounded this ancient settlement. The place was known by its Arabic name, Musarrawat al-Sofra, "Yellow Drawings."

"But why these people here?" Ramadan said dismissively, meaning the Sudanese peasants at the well. "A few huts. A few goats. Two days by donkey to Shendi if they want to buy something."

A handful of Sudanese toiled with donkeys, drawing water from another well half a mile away — a well that probably dated from this Cushitic site. But what seemed like the back of beyond had once been on a trade route. It had to have been, because there was a way south in the wadi here that had produced the prizes from deeper in Africa: wood, honey, gold, and slaves. And ivory: it was said that many tusks had been dug out of the ancient storerooms on this site.

Here we camped, in the dune near the temple, just the two of us, like a pair of nineteenth-century travelers who had happened upon an ancient ruin in the desert. No fences, no signs, no commercial activity, no touts, no postcards. The locked-up quarters of the German archeologists who were cataloguing this site were over the next hill.

When we started cooking, some local men drifted over and squatted with us and shared our food. You couldn't blame them: in the odorless desert the aroma of shish kebab must have stirred appetites in the distant huts. We talked awhile, and then I sat in a plastic chair in the dark and in this peaceful place listened to bad news in the larger world on my shortwave radio.

That was the night Ramadan said, "This my country! This my desert! I sleep here on the sand!" That was the night the moon was clouded over, the night in the hot darkness when I heard the pitter-pat of tiny feet that turned out to be raindrops, the prelude to a violent downpour, and another later. In the morning I woke up sneezing, surrounded by these glorious temples, reddish gold in the sunrise.

Part of that next day I spent at another temple on a nearby hill, an Amun temple with a ramp, a walkway flanked by recumbent rams (a dozen altogether, their faces broken). Khnum was the ram god, "god of the kings, and king of the gods." The king and queen who had had this temple built were shown on the bas-reliefs with ram heads. But Egyptology seemed a discipline based largely on conjecture, the experts assigning names to eroded faces of royalty and deities and animals. So much was speculation, for the Kingdom of Cush, the Napatan and Meroitic periods, had lasted for a thousand years, until the fourth century A.D. What was known was piddling compared to what was not known. A quarter of a mile away was the Great Enclosure. It was lovely but enigmatic: carved pillars, lions, elephant sculpture, feet, legs, torsos, with the implied self-mocking command: "Look on my works, ye Mighty, and despair!"

Was this a center for training elephants for warfare — the battle elephants depicted on the temple at Al-Naggar? Some archeologists thought so. Others thought it was a religious center. It might have been used for coronation rites or some sort of royal arena: "The ruler might have had to renew publicly his or her show of strength in order to retain the throne."

The experts didn't know, so how should I? I was just a wanderer heading to Cape Town, wearing a faded shirt and flapping pants, sunburned toes showing in my Syrian sandals, and with a head cold from having been rained on: a traveler in an antique land.

The greatest part of my satisfaction was animal pleasure: the remoteness of the site, the grandeur of the surrounding mesalike mountains and rock cliffs, the sunlight and scrub, the pale camels in the distance, the big sky, the utter emptiness and silence, for round the decay of these colossal wrecks the lone and level sands stretched far away.

◇ ◇ ◇

In the remote provinces of Sudan it was necessary for foreigners to report to the local security police within twenty-four hours of arrival. These were the same police who had interrogated one American man for days before they performed a mock execution on him. The same police of which the State Department advisory had warned: "The government of Sudan's control of its police and soldiers may be limited."

True, I might be interrogated when I showed up, but if I didn't show up the consequences could be dire. There were worse things than a mock execution; there were real executions, for example.

Shendi was the nearest town. For centuries, Shendi was one of the most important markets in Africa, "the great crossroads of the Nile," Alan Moorehead wrote in *The Blue Nile*, where he devoted a detailed chapter to Shendi, noting that five thousand slaves passed through the market every year in the early nineteenth century, on their way to Egypt and Arabia. We drove across the desert to it and entered. The place was biscuit-colored and dusty, a low settlement of poor huts and small shops, the streets overrun with goats and camels. The largest house in town, a conspicuous villa, belonged to the president's brother. There were some beat-up vans and old trucks and a fleet of battered blue taxis, which Ramadan said were all Russian-built, jalopies from long ago called Volgas. This was the only town in the country where you would see such vehicles, but the engines had been replaced with newer Japanese ones, purloined from other cars. There were no trees anywhere, and not much shade.

The security office was on a side street at the edge of town, the officer in charge a stern skullcapped man with a visible prayer bump on his forehead, a facial feature I took to be a warning sign. He was with three other men who, Sudanese style, sat on chairs with their feet tucked under them. They were all watching a small TV set — more worry, a black-and-white set showing a howling placard-carrying mob, some of the slogans readable in English. They were angry Palestinians. The sound was turned up, so the only voices audible in the office were those of outraged Philistines.

I had a very bad moment just then, for in my passport were two Israeli stamps, one from the checkpoint at Allenby Bridge, where I entered from Jordan, the other at Haifa, where I departed Israel on a ferry. The instructions from the Sudanese embassy said that any passport "with Israeli markings" would be rejected. Yet I had handed in my passport and been granted the visa. If any Sudanese had seen the "Israeli markings," he had not mentioned it.

But a scowling man with a prayer bump in the desert town of Shendi might find them, and might object. He took my passport and laid it flat, and smoothed it with the heel of his hand, and began scrutinizing it. Perhaps the stamps from Kiribati, Ecuador, Albania, Malaysia, India, Hong Kong, Gibraltar, and Brazil dazzled him. Some were colorful. He glanced from time to time at the television. He wiped his mouth. I sat rigid, expecting the worst. Then, without a word, he gave me back my passport and dismissed me and went on watching the Middle Eastern mob scene.

Ramadan and I walked through the Shendi market, choosing tomatoes and basil for lunch.

"Awaya," children called out often, and less often *"Aferingi."* White man. For I was a novelty. The only other foreigners they saw were the occasional Chinese who manned the oil refinery up the road. The market was full of vegetables and fruit, spices and herbs. Lots of plump grapefruit, lots of bananas. Not many buyers circulated among the stalls, so people hectored me and thrust melons in my face and tried to sell me baskets of limes, because as an *awaya* — even better, as a *masihi,* a Christian, a believer in the messiah — I was likely to have lots of Sudanese dinars.

Ramadan and I ended up at the Shendi ferry ramp, drinking coffee with a distinctive taste.

It wasn't really coffee but an unusual brew called *jebana,* coffee husks steeped in water, with sugar and, Ramadan said, a certain *dawa* — I recognized the Swahili word for medicine — *zinjabil,* powdered ginger. It was a cultural link with the Horn of Africa, of which Sudan has many. That same drink in Yemen and the Emirates is called *qashar.*

A few miles up the riverbank was the ancient Royal Palace, hot, muddy, flyblown, and mosquito-ridden, but at least with a tree or two. I could not make heads or tails of the place. There were friezes showing animals and gods, and cartouches enclosing hieroglyphs, but this complex of crumbled foundations spoke of nothing except the visible fact that once upon a time the site had been a populous town with many avenues and buildings — one perhaps a Roman-style bath. Had the Romans come here?

Mohammed, the resident watchman and guide, was not much use.

"American?" he said in Arabic, an unmistakable word, accusing me with a brown twisted forefinger.

"American," I said.

"Bush is Satan."

"Ana ma'arif," I said.

"Clinton is Satan," Mohammed said.

"Ana ma'arif."

"Why you say you don't know?"

I just smiled at him.

"American soldiers no good. Kill people!"

We were walking from the broken steps to the broken wall and, along it, treading on Cushitic bricks. Mohammed looked tired and disgruntled. He said he had three daughters, no sons. He had no money. His grandfather had been the caretaker and guide here, so had his father. But if Mohammed knew anything technical or historical about this place, he did not reveal it to me.

Suddenly he said in halting English, "I want to go America."

"America *ma kwais,*" I said, mimicking what he had said.

"Yes, but no work here."

"You want to work in America?"

"Yes. Get job. Get dollars."

"Bush *Shaytaan,*" I said, teasing him again.

"How I can go America?" Mohammed said, kicking at the ancient bricks.

"Ana ma'arif," I said.

◈ ◈ ◈

In the most atmospheric of nineteenth-century exotic scenes, the essence of Orientalism, explorers camp at the foot of dramatic ruins: the tent beside the Sphinx's paw, the canvas shelter at the base of the pyramids, the campfire glowing near the Temple of Isis. Ideally, the whole thing is moonlit, and there are some hobbled camels nearby, looking luminous in the moonshine. No one else around, just this tableau: hardy campers, lovely ruins, big-eyed camels, a cooking fire.

This was precisely my experience that night. We camped by pyramids, and I felt as those old travelers must have — lucky, humbled, uplifted by being alone in this sacred place, a solitary meditation among marvels. These Sudanese pyramids, remnants of burials of the Kingdom of Cush, were numerous — about thirty-five of them on a sandstone ridge. They were smaller and steeper than the ones at Giza, like a mass of Art Deco salt shakers up close, and from a little distance like a row of fangs in the jawbone of the ossified ridge. Ribbed drifts of golden brown sand were heaped against the pyramids and their chapels. The sand glowed beautifully at sunset, the great dunes of it piled up and scooped out at the corners, the way snow blows and stays in improbable forms, in sculpted shapes and overhangs.

There wasn't time to look around; the sun was setting. We cooked potatoes we had bought at Shendi and made tomato and cucumber salad. I put up my tent, and Ramadan the romantic ("The sand is my pillow!") chose a sandy crease in a dune. The night was clear but the wind came up, blew sand against my tent, and covered Ramadan. The moon passed overhead, and when it dropped into the west the dark stars shone with such power their intense light pierced the nylon of my tent, and the rest of the sky was blacker without the bright pollution of the moon.

The wind died at dawn, when it became so chilly I had to wear a jacket, and in this pure light, under a clear sky, the pyramids looked uncluttered and smooth-sided, standing amid the rubble of stones and fallen bricks. The tops of nearly all the pyramids had been destroyed, and all the tombs had been torn open and robbed. Several of them, just broken tumbled blocks, had been dynamited. You could see the effect of the explosions, which had shattered the bricks in the beheading of the pyramids.

The tomb raider who carried out this destruction was an obscure Italian adventurer and treasure hunter named Giuseppe Ferlini. Only a few facts are known of this man, who vandalized the pyramids and the tombs in 1834, though his name is notorious in the Nubian Desert.

He was born in Bologna in 1800, qualified as a medical doctor, and after a spell in Albania and Egypt as a soldier of fortune, he sailed up the Nile to Khartoum. On the way he visited the more obvious ancient sites and conceived the idea that they were full of gold. Records show that he received permission from the ruler of Sudan, Ali Khurshid Pasha, to excavate sites in Meroë. Ali Khurshid was a slaver who, trading in humans (he hauled Dinka and Azande from the south, to sell on the coast), could hardly have scrupled to preserve a jumble of old stones and dented bronzes.

With a large gang of Sudanese laborers Ferlini began digging and very soon found a gold statue. This trophy inspired him to keep digging. He also used explosives. Ferlini missed some treasures — we are certain of this, because when the Germans began their careful reconstruction of these sites in 1960 they found a gilded statue of Hathor (the cow goddess), a beautiful bronze of Dionysius, and numerous other bronzes. But he must have found many similar objects. He sold them for "a small fortune," according to one historian, and did violence to the pyramids. Ferlini left Sudan soon after his destruction of the sites, disappearing down the Nile with crates of booty. He wrote nothing. He lived like a prince in Italy on the proceeds of his tomb raiding. "He gave no coherent account of what happened to the treasures."

What had he taken away? Pots and chairs, carvings, little idols in black stone, mummified cats and alabaster falcons, the contents of the burial chambers, bronzes, gold statues, and the gilded heads of gods and goddesses. What he had not taken was impossible to remove: the incised murals, the processions of lion-headed kings, the queens in horned headdresses, the lotuses, cobras, elephants, and sacred bulls. The cattle in those one-thousand-year-old bas-reliefs had the twisted horns that can be seen in today's Dinka herds in southern Sudan.

As I wandered from one blasted-and-rebuilt pyramid to another, children from a nearby village showed up with trinkets they claimed they had dug out of the rubble — amulets and carvings — and clay models of the pyramids. I gave them each a banana and off they went.

Another cluster of pyramids stood on a more southerly ridge, another citadel of reddish wind-scarred sandstone, dating from about 295–250 B.C. The landscape was either this weathered stone or smooth sand, some of it like brown sugar, the rest flat and yellow. No trees, no greenery, nothing growing, not even grass. I hiked to these other pyramids, examined them, and sketched the lions and the bulls in my notebook.

While I was doing this, three tall, white-robed Sudanese appeared, impressed and gratified that I was taking the trouble to draw pictures. They were pilgrims of a sort, the leader an older man named Kamal Mohammed Khier.

"I am not an Arab," he said by way of introduction, and as a challenge and a boast.

"But you speak Arabic."

"Yes, but it is not my language." Saying so, he sounded like Salih Mashamoun, the Sudanese diplomat I had met in Cairo. "I am a Nubian. I speak Nubian. My family is Nubian. I am from Dongola in Nubia. We were kings in this country. We ruled Egypt. We built these pyramids."

It was quite a speech and perfect for the place, the visitation by this proud son of the land. He introduced the others: his son, Hassan, and another man, Hamid.

"This man, Hamid, is a real Nubian too," Kamal said. "Not an Arab."

Kamal frowned at the pyramids. He was looking at Ferlini's damage. He said, "Look at the condition of them. The government doesn't take care of them. These are great things!"

True, the Sudanese government did very little to preserve its ancient places, but almost every site had been adopted by a foreign university — German, British, American — and was in the process of restoration. A philanthropic Englishwoman was waging a single-handed battle against neglect and erosion at a temple complex just west of these pyramids, and an elderly German named Hinkel, a self-financed enthusiast apparently, visited here once a year in his long-term project of piecing together one of the nearby structures, the Temple of the Sun.

I accompanied Kamal and the others around the rest of the pyramids. They asked how I happened to be here. I pointed out my little blue tent in the dune.

"Yes, you can be safe here," Kamal said. "In Egypt, no. In other countries people will trouble you, and this and that" — he was hacking at his head with his hand. "But here no one will bother you. You are safe in Sudan. We are all your friends."

Ramadan and I broke camp and drove through the dunes and the gravelly sand to the Temple of the Sun. An old man ran over and made me sign a logbook. He saluted me. He showed me the temple. Sand had almost covered the foundation, but that was a help, for the packed sand preserved the carvings on the friezes.

The old man sat on a rock and said it was a throne for the priest. He put his hands together and mimicked the priest's greeting the sun god: "Allah!"

Ramadan teased the old man and said he didn't know what he was talking about.

The old man laughed. "No, but Hinkel does!"

"How old are you?"

"Fifty-six or fifty-seven," the old man said doubtfully.

"No — much older! Sixty-something."

"How am I supposed to know that? I can't read," the old man said. He was laughing because there was a lot of affection in Ramadan's teasing.

Ramadan laughed with him now. "Where did you get that nice wristwatch?" he asked, and made as if to snatch it.

"Hinkel," the old man said.

"This place is a mess," Ramadan said.

"Yes!" the old man said.

"You should fix it."

"It is not my place. It belongs to the government. Let the government fix it."

We drove north after that, to Atbara, the end of the paved road, where there were no temples, but there was a cement factory and a ferry across the Nile and the last bridge — it was just ferries from here to the Egyptian border. Here we camped again, at the edge of the Nubian Desert. The next town was Dongola, and after that Wadi Halfa, the border. And so I camped another night, this one by the Nile, where I had seen few fishermen, so I asked Ramadan why. He said that the Sudanese in the north were not great fish eaters. Fish didn't keep in the heat; it was not smoked; it was regarded as a snack, not much more. Lamb and camel and goat were tastier.

The next day, seeing torn rubber all over the road, Ramadan spun the steering wheel and headed into the desert, where he spied a car that had skidded there as a result of the blown tire. No one got a simple puncture in such hot places: tires just exploded in a mass of shredded rubber.

Three men stood by the old car in the hot bright desert, the only features in the landscape. Ramadan conferred with them and the men explained their dilemma, which was obvious: a blowout, no spare tire, no traffic on the road; they needed a new tire. They got into our truck, and we drove them about fifty miles and dropped them off at a repair shop in a small town way off the road. This lengthy detour of an hour and a half was considered normal courtesy, like the rule of the sea that necessitates one ship helping another in trouble, no matter the inconvenience. And here the desert much resembled a wide sea.

The men were grateful but not effusive. They saluted us, and off we went.

"They had a problem. This is what we do. We help," Ramadan said.

We picked up more fresh food — tomatoes, onions, limes, herbs, fruit, and fresh bread — and drove west toward high, dry brown mountains of rock and rubble. Ramadan found a valley through them, where there was a village surrounded by fertile green fields, irrigated by Nile water. The farmers grew wheat, corn, sorghum, and beans. We traveled on something less than a road — a goat track, a path-notion, an idea of a trail. We kept going along it, past screeching children ("*Awaya!*" White man!) to the Sixth Cataract of the Nile.

The trees grew thicker here, and the green grass was long. The cataract was a misnomer, though. All I saw was a series of muddy rapids that were easily navigable in a small boat. We made camp in a grove of trees under which were several rope beds. We ate salad and bread while swallows, sparrows, and yellow-breasted finches flew in and out of the tree boughs. Ramadan took a bath in the river. I was going to do the same, but was too tired. I fell asleep on a rope bed on the riverbank to the sound of the thrashing rapids.

As I listened to the radio the next morning in this idyllic spot — *Japan is in its most severe recession ever, with high unemployment. The world economy is expected to be in its deepest recession since World War Two* — I thought: None of this news will affect a village like this in the slightest, for such a place is both so marginalized and so self-sufficient that nothing will change it.

As if to emphasize this, an old man approached and began babbling at me.

Ramadan said, "He is telling you he has three wives. He has fifteen babies."

He was just a grizzled figure hanging around. He had discovered that such an announcement might get a rise out of a stranger, especially a *masihi.* He explained his conjugal arrangement. Each wife had a separate room. The man alternated. He grinned at me.

"Tell him I am happy for him."

Another figure, apparently a skinny child of about seven or eight, came over.

Ramadan said, "How old is he?"

I looked more closely and saw a chinless, pinched face — dwarfish rather than young.

"He is twenty-seven," Ramadan said. "His name is Abdullah Magid."

He was tiny, with a small head and skinny arms and a small boy's body, wearing a little gown about half the size of a flour sack. He was hardly four feet tall and could not have weighed more than fifty pounds. Ramadan questioned him, and Abdullah Magid replied in a strange ducklike voice. He shook my hand and then marched up and down like a soldier, as he had been taught to do, to be cute and to earn baksheesh. Ramadan was kind to him and gave him half a grapefruit, and when he stopped performing he seemed a sweet and melancholy little fellow, whose life in this harsh climate would be short. He was the smallest man I had ever seen.

"He lives here. His mother died the day he was born. I am asking him why he doesn't get married."

Abdullah Magid said in Arabic, "The girls don't like me. I can't get married. What can I give them?"

Ramadan said, "He has nothing."

The dwarf Abdullah Magid, looked after by his grandparents, was friendly and kind. He sat on the edge of a rope bed and kicked his feet. He was too small to work, too weak to do much of anything. But he was not bullied or mocked, as vulnerable physical types are in some parts of Africa. It was obvious in the kindly behavior of the villagers that he was regarded as special, unique, perhaps even blessed.

◇ ◇ ◇

"The criterion is how you treat the weak," a man told me back in Khartoum. "The measure of civilized behavior is compassion."

The speaker was Sadiq al-Mahdi, former prime minister and great-grandson of the Mahdi ("the Rightly Guided One") who had dispatched Gordon. I had not wanted to go back to the city. I would have been happy to spend another week camping — the wind, the sandstorms, the cloudbursts at night only made the experience more vivid and memorable. But I had been granted an interview with Sadiq al-Mahdi at his Omdurman mansion.

This opportunity arose because a man on the Secretariat for Peace in Sudan, another guest at the Acropole, had mentioned my name to the former prime minister. The man claimed that it had rung a bell — a small bell, I suspected, a mere tinkle, but that was enough motivation in hospitable Sudan for someone to make a pot of *jebana* coffee and strew the cushions and put out the welcome mat.

"He is a good man, a very smart man," a trader in the Khartoum market told me. "He is head of the Umma Party."

The trader's friend said, "His father was Siddiq. His grandfather was Abdelrahman. His great-grandfather — well, you know."

The meeting was fixed for nine-thirty at night, an odd time, it seemed to me. I was usually in bed by nine or ten: in Africa, daytime was for roaming, nighttime for hunkering down — predators came out at dark. But a Sudanese explained that this late hour was a sign of respect, the last meeting of the day, promising a conversation without interruption. I was still weary from my camping trip, but I was pleased to be able to meet this eminent man. A battered taxi came for me at eight-thirty. Abdullah, the driver, cursed when he could not restart it, cursed some more after he started it, and again when we were stuck in heavy traffic on the Nile bridge: "It is old. It was built by the British. The British! No one ever fixes anything here."

Glare-lighted dust in the headlights, the loud impatient car horns, the night heat, the smell of diesel fumes. Abdullah complained the whole way about all the inefficiency and dereliction.

He said he knew the house. He took side streets to the riverbank, and after a few turns I saw men in old clothes squatting in the middle of the road — the security detail — and farther on a crude roadblock. Abdullah shouted to them. We were waved on and soon came to a high wall with a lighted archway. Abdullah parked, and he crawled into the back seat to sleep as I was escorted through a narrow door.

The garden beyond it was thick with palms and night-blooming jasmine. I was led past the lighted villa and down a gravel path to a sort of summer house woven entirely of wicker but as big as a bungalow, with walls open to the night air. Some men and women rose to greet me, among them several writers and two of Sadiq's daughters, Rabah and Hamida, both of them married and very pretty. In this culture, modesty was encouraged and staring was considered rude, so I wrung my hands and told them how grateful I was to be there.

Coughing, I explained that I had caught a cold in the desert.

"*Kafara,*" a novelist named Issa said, a Sudanese expression of commiseration, the equivalent of "God bless you."

"To delete your sin and make a better relation with Allah," Issa said.

Then, with a flourish of his full creamy robes, like a conjurer at a fancy-dress party, Sadiq al-Mahdi appeared — tall, dark, hawk-nosed, with a Vandyke beard and a pale turban. Waving his wide sleeves, he urged us to be seated. He was at once imposing and charismatic, an attentive listener and a great talker. He gave the impression of formidable strength, good humor, and a sort of ferocity that I took to be passion. His manner of holding court was to solicit opinions, to listen, and at last to say his piece.

"You have been in the Sudan a little while," he said to me, "but there are some things you must know. Just some points I would like to mention."

Sudan, the largest country in Africa, was a microcosm of Africa, he said. All the African races were represented in Sudan, and all the religions too, and three of the four major African languages were spoken here. Sudan was the meeting point of all the countries in the Nile basin, and shared a border with eight countries.

"Sudanese civilization preceded Egyptian civilization," Sadiq said. "Our history is not a branch of Egyptology but something else entirely — Sudanology, one could say."

He asked what I had seen in the north. I described my camping trip and specifically how I had been impressed by the manner in which Ramadan had helped the stranded men on the road, rescuing them, much to our inconvenience.

"A stranger is not a stranger here. He is someone you know. And this, coming to the aid of a weak person, is chivalry," he said.

"That holds the society together, I suppose."

"Yes, Sudan society is stronger than the state," he said. "Sudanese people have toppled two regimes by popular uprising. Even this present regime is being chipped away."

"How is this happening?" I asked.

"Through the strong social ties. Social ties are deeper than politics. This can be a burden, but it helps us. If we had not had such social ties we would have disintegrated."

A violent overthrow was not the Sudanese way, he said. "This country has had no political assassinations. We have a high degree of tolerance, a high degree of idealism — more than the rest of Africa. In the Sudan, enemies socialize."

Coffee was poured, glasses of juice were passed around, cakes and cookies distributed. A fan whirred in a corner, but the heat was oppressive and the aroma of the river overcame the jasmine in the garden.

"We have had the bloodiest encounters with foreigners," Sadiq said. "But, as a foreigner, you will be helped. We have no antiforeign feelings."

True, he said, the present government of Sudan had tried to cultivate antiforeign sentiment — "a very Islamized view of the world" — but it had failed.

"That ideological agenda has faded," he said. "Slogans have had a field day here. We've tried all the systems in the book — socialism, democracy, Islamic rule, military rule."

I asked, "What do you think of the present government?"

"The present regime has been very intolerant and repressive. This unrepresentative nature is now very conspicuous. But we have had thugs in government for eighty percent of our independent existence." Laughing, he said, "Before 1996, I was arrested myself!" Then he grew serious again and added, "This government declared a jihad and abused human rights in the south."

"What will happen to the war in the south?"

"We have the greatest potential for change through peaceful means," he said. "We Sudanese are war-fatigued and dictator-fatigued. Southerners don't want to fight. They are running away from the war. Even the Comboni Fathers denounced the war," he said, referring to the Italian priests whose missions were in the south and west. "The Sudanese are fed up with war."

I mentioned that I had seen the ruins left by the American bombing. I wondered aloud how he felt about relations with the United States. After all, although we had an embassy residence and a big embassy building we had no ambassador, no American staff here, and only tenuous diplomatic relations, carried out in whispers by officers who came for the day, some from Cairo and others from Nairobi.

"Clinton had something like ideological blinkers about the Sudan," Sadiq said. "He thought it should be part of the Horn of Africa, so that America could be in charge, using the Horn as a springboard."

"Somalia is not much of a springboard," I said.

Somalia was famously a fragmented, clan-ridden country we had tried to pacify and control, but one we had fled after our first casualties were inflicted by a howling populace, who hated foreigners more than they hated each other. It was a nation without a government, without a head of state, without any of the institutions of society — no courts, no police, no schools — a nation of embattled warlords and clan chiefs, and in the hinterland little more than opportunistic banditry.

"We prefer Bush's ignorance to Clinton's wrong thinking and know-it-all attitude," Sadiq said.

The talk went on until after midnight, the writers talking about their favorite Sudanese novels — one, *Dongola*, by Idris Ali, had been translated by my brother Peter. They told me about memorable trips they had taken in the country — to the south, to the west, and by train north to Wadi Halfa and Egypt. How people had been kind to women travelers, taken pity on them, and how the women in the countryside had protected them and preserved their modesty.

That was when Sadiq said, "The criterion is how you treat the weak. The measure of civilized behavior is compassion."

A Sudanese basket and a clay coffeepot were brought out and presented to me.

"When you drink, you remember us," Sadiq said.

Abdullah the taxi driver complained most of the way back through Omdurman and over the bridge. But I was smiling, vitalized by the talk and bewitched by the Nile, which was coursing from the heart of Africa, and by the sight of the moon shining on it, filling its surface with shattered oblongs of light in brilliant puddles.

6 ◇◇◇

The Djibouti Line to Harar

ONLY TWO TRAINS a week ran on the Ethiopian line to Djibouti, across the low hills east of Addis Ababa and the rubbly plain to the Ethiopian town of Dire Dawa. From there I could go by road into the mountains to the old walled city of Harar. Harar was a place I had always wanted to see, for its associations with Sir Richard Burton, the first European to visit, and the boy genius Arthur Rimbaud: after he forsook poetry and civilization Rimbaud had been a trader there off and on for ten years. In spite of his whining in letters home, he had liked Harar's remoteness and wildness. Rimbaud took a quiet pleasure in Africa's motley and unexpected satisfactions, its dusty congeniality. He was seeking relief from metropolitan phonies, literary trendspotters, hangers-on, time wasters, and ambitious importuning twits. "I'm through with those birds," he said in Africa. His mood I shared, his quest I celebrated.

Haile Selassie had an intimate connection with Harar, too, having been born there and having served as governor of Harar province before becoming Ras Tafari Makonnen, Lion of Judah, Elect of God, Power of the Trinity, and *Negusa Negast,* King of Kings — in a word, emperor. His career had been patchy. King to Ethiopians, descendent of the Queen of Sheba, mocked as "Highly Salacious" by Evelyn Waugh, he was divine to Rastafarians. Exiled in England during the Italian occupation, he returned to rule as an absolute monarch to whom his subjects bowed low for thirty years. At last he was overthrown by the Derg ("the Committee"). When I was in Harar the government revealed that the eighty-three-year-old emperor, who died in 1975, had been choked to death by the Derg's leader, Mengistu Haile Mariam, who flaunted the emperor's ring on one of his own strangling fingers.

Famous for its fierce jut-jawed hyenas and handsome conceited people, Harar I regarded as one of the great destinations in Africa. For its exoticism, its special brand of fanaticism, and its remoteness, Captain Burton had compared Harar to Timbuktu, saying that, "bigoted and barbarous" — but also unique in its languages and customs — it was the eastern African "counterpart of ill-famed Timbuctoo." At last I was near enough to go there by train.

"Maybe I should go to the station for a ticket," I said to the manager of my hotel when I arrived in Addis from Sudan — by plane, because the border was closed.

The manager was a skinny fine-featured man with popping eyes, a shabby suit, and the welcoming, almost courtly manner of his fellow countrymen, who proved to be very polite if a bit melancholy. The unsmiling Ethiopians looked brokenhearted even when they weren't.

But the manager was laughing to reassure me. "No worry. The train is not popular."

◇ ◇ ◇

My first impression of Addis Ababa: handsome people in rags, possessed of both haughtiness and destitution, a race of aristocrats who had pawned the family silver. Ethiopia was unique in black Africa for having its own script, and therefore its own written history and a powerful sense of the past. Ethiopians are aware of their ancient cultural links with India and Egypt and the religious fountainhead of the Middle East, often claiming to be among the earliest Christians. When your barbarian ancestors were running around Europe bare-assed, with bellies painted in blue woad, elaborately clothed Ethiopians were breeding livestock and using the wheel and defending their civilization against the onslaught of Islam, while piously observing the Ten Commandments.

Relatively new as a city, a brainstorm of Menelik II, who craved his own capital, Addis Ababa was a sprawling high-altitude settlement resembling a vast rusty-roofed village scattered over many hills. It was a hundred years old but had a look of timeless decrepitude. Unprepossessing from a distance, up close it was dirty and falling apart, stinking horribly of unwashed people and sick animals, every wall reeking with urine, every alley blocked with garbage. Loud music, car horns, diesel fumes, and pestering urchins with hard-luck tales and insinuating fingers and dire warnings, such as "There are bad people here."

Even at their best, African cities seemed to me miserable improvised anthills, attracting the poor and the desperate from the bush and turning them into thieves and devisers of cruel scams. Scamming is the survival mode in a city where tribal niceties do not apply and there are no sanctions except those of the police, a class of people who in Africa generally are little more than licensed thieves.

Ethiopia had just ended its border war with Eritrea. Because of the rumors of that war, and Ethiopia's neighbors of low repute — Somalia and Sudan — and the paranoia of travelers, Addis had no foreign tourists. Empty hotels were wonderful for me to behold because I never made forward plans. I just showed up and hoped.

Not many Ethiopians took the train to Dire Dawa, and certainly not onward to Djibouti. Djibouti had a bad reputation locally. It occupies one of the notches on the African coast, at the upper edge of the Horn, an age-old point of entry, and exit too — for centuries Djibouti was a slave port, then part of French Somaliland, and finally what it is today, a thorn in the side of Ethiopia, an independent republic. Its oppressive heat was not relieved by the scorching breezes off the Gulf of Aden, nor was there any terrain except the landfill look of reclaimed swamp, and the baked architecture was either Frenchified (biscuity, officious, departmental) or else Arabesque (pillared, scalloped, scowling). French soldiers still garrisoned there had made the place notorious for their enthusiasm for child prostitution.

"Twelve- and thirteen-year-old girls!" an aid worker told me. "Such scenes! The soldiers go to these terrible nightclubs and get drunk. You see them staggering around the streets. Drunkenness and prostitution — drugs, too."

On the kind of trip I was taking, the idea of witnessing such colorful depravity and dissipation seriously tempted me. But I was determined to see Harar, for I wanted to be traveling south within a few weeks, to Kenya and beyond.

The Dire Dawa train was leaving early the next morning. If I didn't take it, I would have three days to wait for another. I went to the station and bought my ticket, looked at the inside of the train — not bad, not good; most trains in Africa look as if they are on their way to Auschwitz — and the next day returned and boarded it. Apart from the departure time, there was no timetable. No one knew when we were expected to arrive in Dire Dawa. "Tomorrow," the best guess, was all right with me.

We started with a scattering of passengers, and later in the morning, after many station stops in the canyons and hills that lay east of Addis, we still had picked up only a few people. At some stations we idled for as much as an hour, and twice after dark, in the middle of nowhere (I could hear the wind rising in bare branches), the train dragged to a halt and did not move for several hours. During the day I had sat and read *First Footsteps in East Africa: An Exploration of Harar,* by Captain Burton. Night came on quickly. I slept stretched out on a wooden bench, pillowing my head on my bag and gritting my teeth, hating this trip and wishing it were over and glad that I was not going on to Djibouti. Sometime after dawn, as the heat of the day was taking hold, the sun slanting into the train, we pulled in to Dire Dawa.

"Seems a little empty."

The city looked abandoned: silent houses, empty streets.

"It's a holiday."

◈ ◈ ◈

It was normally quiet in Dire Dawa, but even quieter the day I arrived because of this Ethiopian holiday, the 105th anniversary of the Battle of Adwa.

"When we defeated Mussolini," a man named Tesfaye told me.

Not quite, so I read later. The Adwa victory, a sweet one for Ethiopians, an early anticolonial one, was accomplished in 1896, when twenty thousand Italian soldiers, hurrying into northern Ethiopia from Eritrea, met ninety thousand "perfervid, battle-hungry Ethiopians," commanded by King Menelik II and his second in command, Ras Makonnen, who in this triumph over the foreign invaders were bonded in a father-son relationship. They were distantly related in any case, but that bond assured the elevation of Ras Makonnen's eldest son, Ras Tafari — Haile Selassie I — to the throne.

Adwa was crucial in other ways. It was first of all a wipeout. Trying to group for an attack in the rocky landscape near Adwa, the Italians became lost and disoriented. The Ethiopians, outnumbering them by more than four to one, surrounded them, harried them with spears and arrows, killed more than fifteen thousand, and wounded or captured the rest. They also had rifles — two thousand of them were Remingtons that Rimbaud had sold to Menelik in Entotto in 1887. Though he did not live to see it, Arthur Rimbaud, the former poet, played a part in this historic African victory. As a battle of natives against invaders, Adwa was on a par with the Sudanese dervishes' destruction of the British square. So famous was Adwa that it inspired Marcus Garvey's Back to Africa movement, known then as "Ethiopianism," as well as the pan-African consciousness that later helped transform British, French, and Portuguese colonies into independent republics. The previous successful African campaign that had won decisive battles against any European nation had been Hannibal's.

Italy's defeat and humiliation were especially bitter, since the Fascists, swayed by the Mitty-like rule of Mussolini, saw themselves as new Roman legionnaires reestablishing a great empire. Hurt pride filled the Italians with a desire to take revenge on the Ethiopians. In this they succeeded when they invaded Ethiopia in 1935, much better armed — illegally so, with poison gas — killing tens of thousands of warriors, who were battling with the same weapons they had used forty years earlier.

The whole world united in condemning the Italian adventure. Winston Churchill summed up this contempt in a speech in London at the end of September 1935 when, as he wrote later in *The Gathering Storm,* he "tried to convey a warning to Mussolini, which I believe he read." The warning was one orotund sentence, rolling onward on the devastating sonority of its clauses: "To cast an army of nearly a quarter of a million men, embodying the flower of Italian manhood, upon a barren shore two thousand miles from home, against the good will of the whole world and without command of the sea, and then in this position embark upon what may well be a series of campaigns against a people and in regions which no conqueror in four thousand years ever thought it worthwhile to subdue, is to give hostages to fortune unparalleled in all history."

Yet this deadly absurdity was exactly what the Italians perpetrated. What Churchill did not know — what few people knew — was that the

Italians were planning to speed and simplify their campaign by using phosgene gas. Italy had signed the 1928 Geneva Protocol against employing poison gas in warfare. Yet in 1935 Mussolini urged his generals to drop phosgene bombs on the Ethiopians, to win "by whatever means" (*qualsiasi mezzo*).

The Italians began their attack by bombing Adwa, the scene of their humiliation, and drove southward. Twenty-four planes, five of them carrying gas bombs, dropped poisonous phosgene on Sasa Baneh, on Ethiopian troops in the Ogaden Desert. When atrocity stories of dubious authenticity emerged from the battlefields — how Italian captives had been crucified, decapitated, and castrated by the Africans — more gas bombs were dropped. Even shooting dumdum bullets, the news of which also outraged the Italians, the Ethiopians didn't have a chance. Haile Selassie was toppled from his throne and sent into exile. A Fascist viceroy was installed in Addis Ababa. The Italian king, Victor Emmanuel III, now styling himself emperor, had two semiprecious stones in his crown, Ethiopia and Albania.

Adwa, the Italian defeat that had provoked that second invasion, was now being celebrated in Dire Dawa, which is to say that the people of this small town were given a day off from work. But there wasn't much work in the best of times, just coffee picking and khat chewing. There were no parades. The town was deserted. Dire Dawa, Amharic for "Empty Plain" — a more appropriate name than its former one of New Harar — lay small and horizontal on the hot pale scrubland beneath the big brown hills. The town built on dust and sand was only as old as the railway, a century. It was the stopping-off place for Harar and, much more important, the point of transshipment for the khat crop from Aweyde, about twenty miles up the steep road to Harar.

The informal economy of this area of Ethiopia was based on the growing of the mildly narcotic khat (*Catha edulis*), pronounced "chat" or "jat" in Ethiopia, a bush that in leaf shape, color, and size looks like a laurel hedge. The other Ethiopian cash crop, high-grade coffee, also grown here in the hills around Harar, was in demand but negligible in profit compared to khat. This daze-producing bush was so highly prized in the nonboozing Emirates and the other states in the Persian Gulf that Dire Dawa's airport was very busy with the comings and goings of small transport planes. For the greatest buzz, khat had to be fresh when it was chewed.

For its lowness and its squareness and its stucco and its dust, Dire

Dawa looked like the sort of French colonial railway town I had seen in rural Vietnam, the sort of town on any railway line built a hundred years ago by Europeans. Indeed, this one had a European pedigree. A Swiss engineer and an adviser to King Menelik, Alfred Ilg, had planned it along with the Djibouti railway. Ilg, who also did business with Rimbaud, accused the exile of secretly having "a sunny disposition."

Alfred Ilg planned and oversaw the building of Dire Dawa in 1902 to serve the railway from Djibouti. Fifteen years later the line was extended to Addis Ababa. Dire Dawa was a Swiss-French notion of what a respectable African town ought to look like: one-story tile-roofed houses of yellow stucco, most of them cracked, a precise geometry of streets, and little plazas here and there — one honoring a dung-streaked statue, another a patriotic plaque and a dusty cannon. Dire Dawa's trees had died in the last drought, but the leafless limbs and twisted trunks remained.

At the center of town was the market, an important center of commerce, and even on this national holiday a few people were selling fruits and vegetables — bananas, lemons, potatoes, carrots, piles of leafy greens, all of the produce from higher up in the region nearer Harar. Nothing grew in the hot dusty soil of Dire Dawa.

Walking through the market, wondering how I might get a ride to Harar, I came upon a big black woman in a red dress hawking bunches of herbs. To start a conversation I asked her what they were, and she laughed and said, "No English! Galla!"

"No Galla," I said.

But as I turned to walk away she said, "*Habla Español?*"

Spanish was not a language I expected to hear from a market woman of the Galla people in northeastern Ethiopia, though now and then I met an older Ethiopian, Somali, or Sudanese who was fluent in Italian, the result of a mission school education or of being a communicant of an ethnocentric pastor, such as Father Cruciani in Aswan.

"You speak Spanish?" I asked.

"Of course," she said in that language ("*Claro*"). "I learned it from the Cubans. There were many Cuban soldiers here in the time of the Derg. I liked them, and they liked me. We had good times. That was when we had another government. The Cubans all went away."

"I suppose they left some children behind?"

"I think so. They liked us very much."

The Cuban episode occurred when Mengistu Haile Mariam took over in 1974 and declared a Marxist state, renamed streets and squares, killed Haile Selassie and his entire family, and erected ridiculous obelisks here and there, displaying the crimson star of socialism. Tens of thousands of Ethiopians were imprisoned without trial. This was also the period when Ethiopia was in the news for its terrible famine. The name Ethiopia became synonymous with tyranny and starvation. Food was airlifted by Western charities, but Ethiopia's official friends were Cuba and the Soviet Union. Cuban aid included soldiers, doctors, and nurses. All you saw then was footage of rickety children and enfeebled adults, the walking wounded — *and these are the lucky ones.*

After another famine, in 1984–85, and the pressure of opposition parties, the Derg was finally overthrown in 1991, and Mengistu hopped a plane to Zimbabwe and was allowed to reside there on condition that he keep his mouth shut. Ethiopia dropped out of the news, but life went on, the rains brought fresh harvests, war was declared on the secessionists in the province of Eritrea, a war that had ended (triumphantly for Eritrea) with a cease-fire just a few weeks before I arrived at Dire Dawa Station one very hot morning in February.

Except for the misleading road squiggles on a poor map, I had no idea where Harar was or how to get there, had no knowledge of Amharic, knew no one in the province — or indeed in the whole of Ethiopia. I was aware that Harar was more than a mile high in the Chercher Highlands. I was the classic traveler, arriving bewildered and alone in a remote place, trying to be hopeful, but thinking, What now?

I stopped several Ethiopian men and asked, "Is there a bus to Harar?"

Grinning with bad news, they said, No bus today.

Stepping into the shade, for the day was very hot and the wind off the plain scorched my face, I saw an Italian-looking woman in the modern habit of a nun (brown cowl, brown dress, serious shoes). She was carrying a bag and walking with the self-contained and single-minded directness of a punctual person determined to be on time for a meeting. Yet she smiled and paused when I said hello.

"Excuse me, do you speak English, sister?"

"Yes."

"Can you tell me the way to Harar?"

She sized me up and said, "You are alone?"

"Yes," I said.

"Then you are very lucky. Come with me, I am going to Harar," she said. "Ah, here is my driver."

Saved, I thought, perhaps because the day was auspicious, my mother's ninetieth birthday. Within a few minutes — blessing my dumb luck, blessing this samaritan — I was seated in the back of a Land Rover and being driven through the back lanes of Dire Dawa to the bumpy winding road that rose into the hills that were so dusty and windblown that the air and the sky were tawny too.

"I am Sister Alexandra," the nun said. "From Malta."

She turned out to be a great talker, sitting sideways in the front passenger seat, occasionally addressing the driver in Amharic, not looking at me, but now and then calling attention to a curious feature of Ethiopian life, such as the shepherds with their flocks of goats, or the children playing with such contentment that they wrestled and rolled in the middle of the road while the cars — ours, for example — detoured around them.

"You see, they are not afraid. They are quite free here," Sister Alexandra said, and waved to the frolicking kiddies.

She did not seem surprised that I should want to visit Harar, and she wondered whether I had been to Malta (I had, on my *Pillars of Hercules* trip). At first we made small talk, about her family, her girlhood, her law studies, her choosing to be a nun, her missionary instinct, and then I understood that she was circling around one subject, a theme she returned to from time to time, which was "I have been loved."

She was much younger than me, about forty, full of life and that Maltese vivacity that is so compulsive it is close to hysteria — I had had a glimpse of it in the way she had walked with a passionate purposefulness in Dire Dawa. Not a dry dull nun at all but a full-blooded one with a tale to tell.

"I had a fiancé, I was studying to be a lawyer," she said. "I have always been very free — my father encouraged me to believe in freedom. I was happy, I was going to go into a law partnership with my brother. I had a ring, I even had a date for the marriage."

Children were lying flat in the middle of this mountain road on a hairpin turn, tickling each other and laughing, heedless of the fact that cars were speeding past them.

"No, it is their playground!" Sister Alexandra said. I had not said anything, but she had anticipated an obvious question. Then she said,

"I began to have thoughts of being a nun. I prayed for guidance, and when I was twenty I made the decision."

"What did your family think?"

"They were shocked. Shocked!" In her solemn dramatic way she seemed to enjoy the memory.

"And your fiancé?"

"My fiancé wanted to send me to a doctor in Italy to see if I was insane." Now she smiled. "Or had a mental problem."

"I suppose he was worried."

"He was sick with worry and very disappointed. The wedding was canceled, everything called off. My family — well, you can imagine. They didn't understand. Only my father saw what was in my heart. My fiancé was desperate. I loved him but I knew I had a vocation. Before I took my final vows in Addis, he flew here to Ethiopia and pleaded with me."

"He didn't change your mind?"

"He didn't change my mind, no," Sister Alexandra said. "But he gave me a ring."

I looked at her fingers: no ring. That was understandable, for a nun had to turn her back on the world of materialism and secularity and become a bride of Christ.

"My fiancé went away. For nine years he lamented," Sister Alexandra said.

Now we were entering the heart of the highlands — very dry, rubbly, chilly, windy, with brown blocky houses, robed people walking on skinny legs or squatting in front of mats selling withered vegetables. I cracked open the window and sniffed the cool air.

"He found a woman and married her and had two children. I did not even get in touch with him. I thought about him — of course, I thought about him a great deal. But I knew he had his life and I had my life." She reflected on this. "From time to time I heard about him. Well, Malta — you have been there . . ."

"Just an island. I know islands a bit."

"Malta is a small place. No secrets, much talk," she said.

We were in a high enough elevation to feel the chill. The people here wore billowing clothes and were wrapped up well, with scarves and cloaks and headgear, pressing into the wind.

"Last May I had a phone call, a woman's voice," Sister Alexandra said. In a melodramatic mimicking of a distant voice she said, "'I know who you are. I think you should know that he has died. Thank you for respecting us.' That was all."

The windblown dust whirled around us, slashing and buffeting the Land Rover. I did not know what to say about the dead man except to inquire as to whether he had had a long illness.

"It was lung cancer — he never smoked or drank. He was only forty-seven," Sister Alexandra said.

There was no commiseration I could offer. I might have said: I too have experienced the death of loved ones, but what consolation was that to someone suffering the peculiar pain of loss? I just made noises, but as I did so I realized that she was protesting.

"No, no, he is not dead," she said. "He is still alive for me. I live with the memory of him. I even speak to him, and he guides me. Can you imagine how important it is to have been loved?"

"Well, yes," I said. "There's a nice poem about that by an English poet." I partly recited and partly paraphrased the Philip Larkin lines from "Faith Healing":

> In everyone there sleeps
> A sense of life lived according to love.
> To some it means the difference they could make
> By loving others, but across most it sweeps
> As all they might have done had they been loved.

"Recently, I heard that the woman is going to marry again," she said. "No one understood him or loved him as I did. That is why he is still alive to me."

"It's true, the dead don't seem to die, and the people we love seem to go on living within us," I said. "Or maybe that's just how we deal with grieving."

"You are a writer?" she said. "Maybe this is a story you can write."

But I said what I always say to people who offer such stories as grist for my mill: You must write it yourself, because there is more to it than you've told me, and since you know everything, it is your story, not mine.

She didn't object, she said she might, and she added, "I am a bit of a poetess. I have written some poems." She smiled the enigmatic smile of *He is not dead,* and said, "But I am a nun. If I published what I wrote it might seem strange, coming from a nun."

"I'd love to read your poems," I said, imagining something steamy and ecstatic, more John Donne than Thomas Merton, both of whom (for being poets and clergymen) I mentioned to her.

If the stereotype of the missionary is of a strong, dull, smiling person with endless patience and no libido, possessed by a conversion mania, Sister Alexandra was the opposite: tenacious, certainly, but also temperamental, opinionated, open-minded and passionate. And after I got to know her better I discovered that she was a gourmet cook. She was much loved at the convent and school, but it struck me that she would have made a wonderful wife and mother. She didn't use the word "sin." Perhaps that was why she was such a success in Harar, the only European woman resident in the province.

"These people are all horribly rich," she said as we passed Aweyde. "Pay no attention to their houses. They save their money, they don't spend it on clothes or houses."

The grubby khat-producing town on both sides of the road had a teeming market with one product for sale, the bunches of green leaves. The hills were thick with hedges and bushes of khat; everyone grew it, sold it, chewed it. The particular conditions in Aweyde were perfect. The local price per bunch was $1.20. It was three times that in Addis Ababa, and cost much more in Yemen, Oman, and the Emirates, where it was shipped from Dire Dawa in small planes. The khat flights were more reliable than the passenger flights, because the stuff lost its potency so quickly and had to be sped to the khat chewers.

"The quality comes down within a day," a trader told me.

Harar was not much farther. Small houses were more numerous, the road widened, there was a stadium, a church, a mosque, then more mosques, and ahead a walled city, the gates gaping open.

Burton wrote of Harar being a forbidden city, attempted by many travelers in vain: "The bigoted ruler and barbarous people threatened death to the Infidel who ventured within their walls; some negro Merlin having, it is said, read *Decline and Fall* in the first footsteps of the Frank." He went on to say that the English were the most reviled because "at Harar slavery still holds its headquarters, and the old Dragon well knows what to expect from the hand of St. George."

There was also a superstition among the people of Harar "that the prosperity of their city depends upon the exclusion of all travelers not of the Moslem faith."

Burton set off in 1854, and after an eventful trip from Zayla (present-day Zeila, on the Somali coast, near the border of Djibouti), he saw the city on the hill, not a lovely place at all but a walled hill town, a "pile of stones." He entered the eastern gate of Harar, palavered with various officials, and was at last admitted to an audience with the emir (who called himself Sultan), who extended his hand, "bony and yellow as a kite's claw," and invited Burton to kiss it. Burton refused, "being naturally averse to performing that operation on any but a woman's hand."

Burton stayed in Harar for ten days (but unwillingly — for six of those days he was trying to leave). My stay was slightly shorter, but only because I was headed for Cape Town by road, rail, ferry, whatever, and figured on months more of travel. People all over Ethiopia still regarded Harar as a bastion of fanaticism and rural poverty where proud, warlike Muslims lived uneasily alongside Copts. In addition, groups of hungry Somalis attached themselves to the place, and camel herders, and beggars from the hills, and a good-sized leper colony at the back of the town — not to mention hyenas, wild and ravenous, for which Harar was famous. All this had compelled my attention, and the fact that people in Addis had tried to worry me with images of Harari savagery merely roused my curiosity. I would happily have stayed in Harar longer.

The beggars were numerous just then because the *haj* period was ending and the Muslim faith enjoins its believers to give generously to the poor on such occasions. Mosques are magnets for beggars, and such a festival as this had throngs of people looking for alms. I had never seen so many derelict people with their skinny hands out, demanding charity.

The xenophobia that Burton described was still a feature of life in Harar: Hararis limited their marriage partners to other Hararis and did not mix socially with anyone else. They disliked the very presence of outsiders, observing the old belief that foreigners make Harar unsafe and unlucky. It was not unusual for a person — usually aged and toothless and wild looking — to rush from a doorway and howl at me. Invariably, when I made eye contact with a Harari I saw distrust and menace, and usually the person seemed to mutter something against me.

"Oh, the things they say to *faranjis*," an Ethiopian woman told me, rolling her eyes at the memory of the remarks, "and especially to *faranji* women."

"For example?"

"I could not repeat such things."

A Belgian aid worker told me, "Some people spit on me at the market for no other reason than I am a *faranji*."

This is an interesting word. Burton said, "I heard frequently muttered by the red-headed spearmen the ominous term '*Faranj*,'" and he went on to say that the Bedouin "apply this term to all but themselves." In Burton's time, even Indian traders were called *faranji* if they happened to be wearing baggy trousers (*shalwar*).

The word is derived from "Frank" — the Franks were a Germanic tribe who peregrinated western Europe in the third and fourth centuries. But the name, of which "French" is a cognate, probably gained currency during the Crusades of the twelfth century, when Europeans plundered Islamic holy sites and massacred Muslims in the name of God. In the Levant, a Frank was any Westerner. "Immense crowds collected to witness the strange Frank and his doings," wrote Edward Lear about himself in his Albanian journal in 1848. A form of *faranji*, the word *afrangi* is regarded as obsolete in Egypt, though it is occasionally used today, especially in combination (a *kabinet afrangi* is a Western-style toilet). I heard it now and then in Sudan. The word has traveled east, to India and as far as Southeast Asia, where pale-skinned foreigners in Thailand are known as *farangs*, and in Malaysia as *feringhi*.

Almost the entire time I spent in Harar, I was followed by children chanting, "*Faranji! Faranji! Faranji!*" Sometimes older people bellowed it at me, and now and then, while I was driving slowly down the road, a crazed-looking Harari would rush from his doorstep to the window of the car and stand spitting and screaming the word into my face.

Meanwhile, I was a guest at the Ras Hotel, where Sister Alexandra directed me. Fifteen dollars a night included breakfast, and there was always Ethiopian cuisine ("national food") on the menu. The Coptic season of Lent was in full swing. Copts were as fastidious in observing their Christian holidays as Muslims were Ramadan and Eid — in fact, they seemed to vie with each other in the strictness of their pieties, "I am holier than thou" the subtext of their senseless mortifications and stern fasting rituals.

"A dreary, Coptic-flavored brew of the more absurd ideas of old Christian and Jewish priests, all this spiced with local abominations" is Vladimir Nabokov's bluff characterization of the Abyssinian Church, in one of the extensive appendixes to his four-volume translation of *Eugene Onegin.* Though modern scholars have disputed the location, Nabokov claimed that Pushkin's maternal great-grandfather was born in Abyssinia, probably in Tigre. Breezily sketching the progress of Christianity in the region, Nabokov goes on:

> The Gospel was introduced there about A.D. 327 by Frumentius (c. 290–c. 350), a native of Phoenicia, who was consecrated bishop of Aksum by Athanasius of Alexandra . . . Jesuit missionaries affronted the nameless dangers of a fabulous land for the holy joys of distributing images of their fair idols and of secretly rebaptizing native children under the pious disguise of medical care. In modern times, Russians have been pleasantly surprised at finding a kind of natural Greek-Orthodox tang to certain old eremitic practices still persisting in Ethiopia; and Protestant missionaries have been suspected by the natives of paganism because of their indifference to pictures of female saints and winged boys.

During the month-long Lent, Copts drank no milk, ate no meat or fish, only "fasting food" — mashed vegetables — mounded on *injera,* a layer of gray, spongy bread made from fermented grain and spread over a whole large platter. "Like a crepe or a pancake," people said, but no: it is cool, moist, and rubbery, less like a crepe than an old damp bathmat. Spicy sauces called *wot* were placed on the *injera* at intervals, with pulped beans, lentils, cabbage, potatoes, carrots, tomatoes, or, in nonfasting months, fish or meat. In Harar the *injera* was made from millet and was sweet, not fermented, but even so, it looked and had the mouth-feel of an overripe bathmat.

I was so contented in Harar — cheap hotel, good weather, unusual sights, unworkable telephones — I sketched out the erotic story I had conceived on the Nile about the young man, the older woman, and her enigmatic doctor. And I began writing, to console myself in my solitude and to ease the passing of time.

One morning I bumped into Nyali Tafara at the main gate of the city. "I am born and bred in Harar." He was unemployed. Most men in Harar were unemployed, he said. He had been to Addis many times, but had never set eyes on Djibouti, an easier trip, six hours up the line. He was a Christian and fasting his heart out. He said local history was his favorite subject.

Harar was the setting of a strange little tale, like something out of Borges's *Ficciones* that might have been called "The Exile."

Since aloneness is the human condition, a stark example of the perfect stranger was the white man in black Africa, alone in his post, odd man out. The whitest of these would be the celebrated poet living in obscurity in a walled town, among black illiterates and philistines whose respect he had to earn as a man. He was a solitary entrepreneur in a society of organized slavers. His head teemed with surreal imagery and cynical retorts, though he seldom spoke his own language except under his breath.

To the Africans, this original was just another sickly *faranji* in a shabby suit, wandering the reeking market, watching the lepers crouched for alms by the mosque, the alleys piled with goat shit, the flyblown camel haunches hanging in the butchery.

Even the fox-faced village woman in the gauzy headdress that he took as his mistress did not know his history. Not that he knew hers, either: they were opposites, black and white, yet they rubbed along. Perhaps his traveling with her (occasionally to Aden) seemed the proof that he loved her. She was photographed by an Italian adventurer, and she described the life she had led with the *faranji:* his silences, his questions, his maps, his stash of coins, the letters he wrote, his passion for photography, his books, how he hated interruptions and any talk of his past. She had no idea where he was from. He said he loved the desert. She did not know that he had predicted his whole strange existence years earlier in wild, premonitory, dreamlike poems.

The nineteen-year-old poet who wrote "it is necessary to be completely modern" was now almost thirty, prematurely gray, and noting with stabbing pen strokes in a company ledger the weight of elephant tusks and coffee sacks to be taken by camel train to the coast. His unexpected enthusiasms set him apart as much as his color — his facility in Arabic, his knowledge of the Koran, his skill as a photographer; he crossed the dangerous Danakil region, explored the empty Ogaden Desert, reported on its spidery routes and its few oases. After one arduous trip he wrote, "I am used to everything. I fear nothing."

The price of rifles was something else he studied. The Arabs in Harar were never so curious. *Faranjis* came and went but this one stayed off and on for ten years, living in modest houses. He hated the food. No one knew what was in his heart, nor heard his muttered ironies, nor understood his gift for concealment. He denied his wealth, claiming he was cheated, while chinking tall stacks of thick silver Maria Theresa dollars and rustling banknotes from the king.

Later, Menelik's emissaries sought him out, pleading for guns and ammunition, which he brought in caravans from the coast. He knew Makonnen, the father of Haile Selassie. The king bargained with him personally and helped make him rich.

His worst day went like this: On a visit to Aden he was confronted by his employer, a Frenchman he despised. The man was gloating with astonishing news. A traveling French journalist had told him that he recognized the name of his employee. The obscure trader had been a boy genius in France and was famous as a decadent poet. This revelation was like a horrible joke, the diligent and dull and rather sulky middleman being the toast of literary Paris. Absinthe, drunkenness, buggery, free verse! The employer needled him for the travesty of it. The sour coffee merchant in the African outpost a poet! At last the boss had something on him.

The exile denied it. "I is someone else," he had also once written, loving its enigma. But exile was a condition in which wordplay was frivolity. Finally he admitted who he had once been, and said it was "absurd" and "I'm through with all that."

You go to the ends of the earth to begin a new life, and think you have succeeded, and then the past breaks in, as it does to the fugitive in disguise spotted by an old enemy. He had been happy in his anonymity, just a white man in the bush. He was naked now.

Thus, Rimbaud in Harar.

I said to Nyali Tafara, "I want to see Rimbaud's house."

"The real house or the other one?"

"Both."

In fact, none of the many houses Rimbaud occupied in Harar now exist. The house advertised as Rimbaud's was built after his death, a three-story Indian trader's villa, mostly of wood, Islamic gingerbread in style, with colored glass windowpanes and shutters and wide verandas. As Rimbaud's latest and best biographer, Graham Robb, has demonstrated, Rimbaud's irony and self-mockery and deliberate deceptions created the myth of Rimbaud as a ruin, a bankrupt, a desperate failure, a discontented exile.

In fact, he was a resourceful traveler, an imaginative trader, a courageous explorer (his report on his discoveries in the Ogaden was published by the Société de Géographie in Paris), an accomplished linguist (he spoke Arabic and Amharic), and something of a botanist and an ethnographer. He enjoyed living in Harar. He was a clever businessman, and though he had given up poetry he planned to write a book about Abyssinia. Posterity, unsmiling as always, took his mordant wit, sarcasm, and self-mockery literally. Robb's description of him is apt: "a contented misanthrope."

In one of my favorite self-portraits, Rimbaud, grimly jeering at his life, wrote home:

> I still get very bored. In fact, I've never known anyone who gets as bored as I do. It's a wretched life anyway, don't you think — no family, no intellectual activity, lost among negroes who try to exploit you and make it impossible to settle business quickly? Forced to speak their gibberish, to eat their filthy food and suffer a thousand aggravations caused by their idleness, treachery and stupidity!
>
> And there's something even sadder than that — it's the fear of gradually turning into an idiot oneself, stranded as one is, far from intelligent company.

Though he denied it, he was the happy captain of the drunken boat. Like many of us, he made a meal of his suffering — complained even as he was rather enjoying it, thrived on adversity, and grumbled dishonestly about savagery and bad food, discomfort and poverty. Contemporary accounts prove that he lived well in Harar, made money, and felt at home in the town.

It was impossible for me to imagine Rimbaud in this villa, yet various French cultural agencies had raised money to beautify the supposed Rimbaud residence. Around 1900 the building housed a French school, and the young Haile Selassie had conjugated irregular verbs in its classroom. Now the building was devoted to the memory of Arthur Rimbaud, patron saint of all of us travelers who have echoed his unanswerable question, first uttered by him in Harar: What am I doing here?

Many of the photographs in the house had been taken by Rimbaud himself and were the more evocative for being crude blurred snapshots, like mug shots of a castaway — Rimbaud squinting in the sunshine, Rimbaud in his white suit, Rimbaud looking ill, scenes of huts and mobs in the 1880s that looked the same as the huts and mobs out the window this morning. Rimbaud had sent the snapshots home to his sister and mother. In these pictures he is no longer the anarchic youth deliberating "encrapulating" himself (as he put it) but a self-mocking Frenchman in his mid-thirties, referring to "the filthy water I use for my washing" and writing "This is only to remind you of my face."

Banners with quotations from *The Drunken Boat* (*Le Bateau ivre*), which he wrote at the age of sixteen, and *A Season in Hell* (*Une Saison en enfer*) decorated the walls. Although both works were written by the time he was nineteen, when he abandoned poetry for good, they were appropriate to the pitching and tossing of his life in Aden and Harar.

"I drifted on a river I could not control," he had written as a sixteen-year-old in *The Drunken Boat,* and in a later stanza the line "I've seen what men have only dreamed they saw." In *A Season in Hell,* the section "Bad Blood," he wrote, "The best thing is to quit this continent where madness prowls . . . I will enter the true kingdom of the sons of Ham."

These precocious insights were also prescient, for many Ethiopians are described as Hamitic, and in Africa Rimbaud's life imitated his art. The hallucinatory imagery of Rimbaud's greatest poems, written in his youth, became the startling features of the landscapes of his life in Yemen and Abyssinia. As a youth in Charleville he produced poems of genius, seeking exoticism in his imagination; in Africa, wishing for the exotic, he took up with an Abyssinian woman, led camel caravans for weeks across the Danakil Desert, traded with the king of Shoa, and in his most heroic venture was the first European to explore and write about the unknown Ogaden region.

Another house, much meaner than this trader's villa, was the real Rimbaud house, Nyali said. He told me that his father and grandfather had called it Rimbaud's house. Hawks drifted over it, as hawks drifted all over Harar. The town's skies were filled with raptors, as its night-time streets were stalked by predatory hyenas. They probably were not hawks but black kites, for the true hawks and harriers were found in the bush.

This "real" house was on one of the main squares near the west gate of the town, a small two-story stone-and-stucco building with a porch and two blue-painted windows above it and a sign in Amharic lettered in that ancient script: *Wossen Saget Bar.* I went inside and was stared at by drunken Hararis — or perhaps not Hararis, since these Muslims would not be drinking alcohol, but drunks all the same. The place had low ceilings and the darkness and dampness of a thick-walled shop house.

Going in I was pestered by beggars, and leaving I was screamed at in the square by grinning boys. Hurrying away from them, I was attacked by a black kite — that is, a kite swooped down and snatched at my cap, grazing my scalp with its talons. The grinning boys screamed at me again and called attention to my alarm, for the kite had been on my head just moments before and I was even more the butt of their joke. "*Faranji!*" the boys cried. Though the teenage boys tended to jeer and the men sometimes howled at me, I received many searching looks from women huddled in doorways.

"One day at school I was eating a piece of meat," Nyali said. "A hawk came down and took it, and did this" — took part of his thumb, the scar furrow still obvious twenty-five years later.

From a high place in town, a cobblestone lane, Nyali pointed east and said, "That is Somalia, those hills" — brown hills on the horizon. "That road is the way to Hargeysa. Somalis bring salt here." The salt caravans that Burton mentioned, which were as old as this town, a thousand years of caravans from the coast. "They trade the salt for khat and bring it back to Somalia."

There were other trade goods, too. Indians had come selling cloth, and guns had always been in demand, and these days drugs and elephant tusks. Harar was one of the centers of the illegal ivory trade in Ethiopia.

The markets had a medieval look, filled with tribal people from the countryside: the Oromo, the Hararis who were also called the Adere, the Galla, each identifiable by the color of their robes or their coiffure or the style of their jewelry. Mostly women, lovely women — Burton had remarked on their beauty; Rimbaud's common-law wife had been from the Argoba tribe nearby — they thronged the market square with their donkeys and goats and children. The stalls, covered with tents and awnings, were stacked with spices and beans, the coffee husks that were steeped to make the strong brew I had tasted in Sudan, and piles of salt, mounds of tomatoes and peppers, pumpkins and melons, beautiful leather-covered baskets unique to Harar, and tables of assorted beads. The most common spice was fenugreek (*abish* in Amharic, *hulbut* in Harari), which was an ingredient in many Harari dishes. There were bunches of khat and big enamel basins of tobacco flakes.

"*Tumbaco,* we call it," Nyali said. "Or *timbo.*"

Bundles of firewood sold for the Ethiopian equivalent of a dollar, which seemed expensive given the fact that the bundles were not large and a bundle probably would not last more than a few days. Camel meat was also high-priced, more than a dollar a pound, but to sweeten the deal the butchers hacked a few fist-sized pieces from the hump and threw that in for free. The camel's hump is pure fat, as smooth and white as cheese.

"Muslims eat camel, we eat goat," Nyali said.

Near a mosque called Sheik Abbas, Nyali took me to a passageway so narrow that two people could not pass each other in it without squeezing together. Because of this, the passage was known as Reconciliation Alley (Magera Wageri).

"God sends people here who are quarreling, and they meet, and when they try to pass, they reconcile."

It was a nice story, but the narrow alleys and passageways beside the ancient stone-and-stucco houses ran with wastewater, another medieval aspect of the city — open drains where garbage, mud, and shit mingled and you had to tread carefully. Burton mentions this too: "The streets are narrow lanes . . . strewed with gigantic rubbish heaps, upon which repose packs of mangy or one-eyed dogs." European visitors are shocked, but Europe was once exactly like this.

Nyali said, "When it rains, this will go."

"When will it rain here?"

"Maybe in May."

Today was the fourth of March.

The following morning at six I was woken by the slapping and scuffing of sandals on the road, the sound of tramping feet, and I looked out the window and saw thousands of people hurrying by. They were the faithful coming from the stadium, where they had assembled for prayers to mark the end of the *haj* period. This festival perhaps explained why the Hararis had been so irritable, for I knew from experience that observances that required extensive fasting and prayers seemed to make the believers peevish.

"Today we eat!" was a greeting in Harar to signify the feast day. The townspeople were in a good mood, the men in clean robes, the women in beautiful gowns and shawls, dressed up in their finery, wearing bangles and earrings. Some had come from the distant countryside, riding for two or three hours to be here among the celebrants, promenading and gaping, shy girls in groups and loud boasting boys. Everyone was eating or carrying food, boys hurrying with tin trays of sticky buns or grapes or melons or tureens of meat stew.

Food everywhere. I was reminded of the feast in Flaubert's *Salammbô,* a novel I had read on the Nile: "Antelopes with their horns, peacocks with their feathers, whole sheep cooked in sweet wine, haunches of she-camels and buffaloes, hedgehogs in garum, fried grasshoppers and preserved dormice . . . great lumps of fat floated in saffron."

Knowing the Koran was on their side, and taking advantage of the good feeling on the feast day, the beggars were also in their element, beseeching and nagging and demanding. They were old and young, blind, crippled, limbless women and children, war-wounded, fingerless lepers, screeching for alms like a procession of tax collectors, making their way through the narrow passageways, exacting a duty from everyone they met. I started to count them, but when I got to a hundred I gave up.

Many lepers had gathered outside the east gate of the walled town. It was the Erar gate — the various names that Burton scrupulously noted for the five gates are still in use. Just beyond the gate was a leper settlement called Gende Feron — Feron Village — after the French doctor who organized it and tended to the sick in the 1940s, though it had obviously been established as a district for outcasts long before. The settlement might have existed in ancient times, since it lay outside the town's walls.

About one thousand people lived in the leper village, mostly the old and the afflicted. In Africa, the superstitions applied to lepers — sufferers of Hansen's disease — have kept such people out of the mainstream of society. The disease is not very infectious, is easily treatable, and quite curable, yet in Ethiopia, for example, there was more talk of leprosy than of AIDS — and Ethiopia had perhaps the second- or third-highest HIV numbers in Africa (8 percent of the populace; South Africa had 10 percent), with a quarter of a million AIDS-related deaths in the year 2000. While there were many prostitutes within the walls of Harar, no one ventured into the leper village by the east gate.

The clusters of mud huts and shacks in the leper village were made of scrap wood, with goats tethered nearby and women cooking over smoky fires. But one part of the place was new — recent, anyway, even if it did appear rundown. A German aid agency had built a series of duplexes, two-story condos with balconies and stairs — the only stairs of that sort I had seen in the whole of Harar. Most of these dwellings looked empty, some looked ill used or vandalized. I asked about them — their newness, their neglect.

"The people here hate them," a man told me. "At first they would not live in them."

"But they're new, and they're stronger than mud huts," I said, baiting him, for I could see they were unsuitable.

"They are too tall. There is no space. They cannot bring their donkeys and goats inside."

"Why would they want to do that?"

"To protect them from the hyenas."

The conceit among donors is that the poor or the sick or the hungry will take anything they are given. But even the poor can be particular, and the sick have priorities, and the famine victim has a traditional diet. The Germans had built houses that did not resemble any others in Harar, did not allow for the safety of the animals, and had the wrong proportions. So they were rejected by the lepers, who chose to live more securely, with greater privacy, and — as they must have seen it — more dignity in their mud huts by the road. The German buildings, expensive and new but badly maintained, were the only real slum in Harar.

Walking back through the city, I looked at the house Haile Selassie lived in when he had been governor. It was an old Indian trader's villa, once elegant, now in disrepair, occupied by a traditional healer, Sheik Haji Bushma. He was sitting cross-legged on a carpet, in a haze of incense fumes, chewing khat. His mouth was stuffed with a green wad of it, and his lips and tongue were slick with a greenish scum.

"I cure asthma, cancer, leprosy, with the help of God and some medicine," he said.

I talked to him a little and he gave me some khat leaves, the first I had chewed. The leaves had a sharp tang that, when I got a cud of them going, also dulled my taste buds. Burton said that khat had the "singular properties of enlivening the imagination, clearing the ideas, cheering the heart, diminishing sleep, and taking the place of food."

It also killed conversation. After Sheik Haji Bushma told me his line of work, he sat and chewed like a ruminant, smiling at me occasionally and poking more leaves into his mouth from the bunch he held in his hand.

One of his serving boys gave me another bunch and I went on chewing and swallowing. I had to chew for about ten or fifteen minutes before I got a buzz. This, I felt, was an accomplishment — try anything twice was my motto — but before I could get comfortable, the doorway darkened and I realized that Sheik Bushma was receiving a patient. I gave him some baksheesh and left.

The next day I visited to the convent school to see Sister Alexandra, with some other nuns and a Red Cross worker, Christine Escurriola. Sister Alexandra had made spaghetti sauce with fresh tomatoes from her garden, and grilled fish and made salad.

"This is to give you a variation from the *injera* at the Ras Hotel," Sister Alexandra said.

Christine's job was to drive to the various prisons in the province to make sure prisoners were not being tortured or mistreated. Many were political prisoners.

"For some, there is no reason to be in prison at all — maybe they have an enemy in the police," Christine said. "For others it's a bad joke. Someone can get six years because he gave a glass of water to the wrong soldier."

As for culture shock, she said she had not gotten it here, though she got it badly when she went home to Switzerland and people talked about electric dishwashers and children's shoes.

"And here people have nothing," Sister Alexandra said.

Christine had served as a Red Cross staffer in Colombia, India, Yugoslavia, and Kuwait, and "I would like to go to Iraq for my next assignment." Christine was cheerful about the discomforts. Sometimes in Harar there was no electricity or water. In the countryside where she visited prisons, the hotels were dismal. Often there was no water, and three Red Cross women had to sleep together in the one bed.

"I am trying to picture it," I said. But I saw the picture vividly.

"If one person is clean and the others are dirty, it's a problem,"

Christine said. "But when we're all dirty, it's fine. If no one has washed, we all smell the same."

Even knowing that these women were agents of virtue, Red Cross workers concerned with human rights in remote Ethiopian prisons, Christine's revelation filled my susceptible brain with the delightful image of three untidy girls, the Three Graces, tousled and playful, with sticky fingers and smudged faces, snuggling in an Ethiopian bed, the powerfully erotic tableau of disheveled nymphs frolicking at nightfall.

"It is very bad to be out at night," she said. Thieves and bandits prowled at night in Harar.

"And," Sister Alexandra said, filling my plate with another helping of spaghetti, "of course, the hyenas."

◈ ◈ ◈

Everyone mentioned the hyenas in Harar. Burton anatomized them in *First Footsteps.* "This animal . . . prowls about the camps all night, dogs travellers and devours anything he can find, at times pulling down children and camels, and when violently pressed by hunger, men." People still talked about them for the sense of color and danger they gave to the town. In an era of vanishing wildlife, the African hyena flourishes as a successful hunter and member of a pack. They were unusual in Harar in possessing no fear of humans. Indeed, after dark they tended to skulk behind people walking in the streets.

Around the time I was in Harar I heard that a small boy dawdling behind his father in the town one night was pounced on and killed by a hyena. The boy died the next day. That was considered a somewhat rare event, since hyena attacks do not always end in death. But outside town — about fifteen miles east in Babille, on the road to Jijiga, the Somali direction — attacks were a weekly occurrence. Hararis claimed not to be frightened of hyenas, and many khat chewers sat out at night on mats, stuffing their mouths, diverted by the sight of hyenas coming and going and in their foraging similarly chewing.

One day, as I talked to Abdul Hakim Mohammed, who was a prince (his daughters were *gisti,* princesses, and he was a direct descendent of the emir of Harar), he mentioned hyenas and the hyena men. "We had saints — *walia,* holy men. They made porridge and put it out for the hyenas on a certain day. The hyenas knew the day, and they showed up then. Each hyena had a name — there were many."

Later, I discovered that Hyena Porridge Day was on the seventh day of Muharram, before the Muslim festival of Ashura. Predictions for the coming year are made on the basis of how much porridge the hyenas ate.

I said, "So Harar is famous for its hyenas."

"More famous for religion," Abdul Hakim Mohammed said. "We were like missionaries, teaching the Koran." He thought a moment. "What is written and thought is that we are xenophobians."

The Harar tradition, he suggested, was to propitiate the hyenas. This was the self-appointed task of Harar's hyena man, Yusof, who gathered scraps of meat and bones from butcher shops during the day, and at dusk brought his sack of scraps and a stool to a spot just outside town and fed the creatures.

"We have a belief that if we feed the hyenas they will not trouble the town," a Harari told me.

I found Yusof one night by the dark city wall, under a dead tree, watching the dusty fields beyond. He was very serious and untalkative, holding a hunk of camel meat in his lap, a bloodstained burlap bag beside him.

In the distance the hyenas were gathering, trotting with their characteristic bobbing gait, chattering excitedly, fighting as they approached, nipping each other on the neck or backside. I had counted eleven of them when I saw another pack approach through an adjoining field, eight or ten of them.

"They each have names," my Harari taxi driver told me.

A big hyena was sidling up to Yusof.

"What's that one's name?"

My question was relayed to Yusof, who muttered a reply and held the camel meat in front of the hyena's face, refusing to drop it, forcing the animal to take it from his hand. This the hyena did, opening its mouth wide and snarling and tearing the meat from Yusof's fingers.

"He is called the Runner."

The hyenas were moving in circles, battling for dominance. Yusof tossed the meat and bones a few feet away, and the animals fought over them. Now and then he held some meat in a forked stick and fed them that way. He put a raw steak in his mouth and leaned toward the hyenas.

Outside this area of circling scavengers dozens more had gathered and were fighting each other, growling and chattering and moving with their strange lame-looking leg motion. Hyenas that had gotten something to eat were chewing, and their chewing was loudly audible, for hyenas eat everything, including the bones, masticating them with the snap and crunch of a wood chipper.

"If you give me money I'll turn on my headlights," the taxi driver said.

I gladly handed him some money and was rewarded by the sight of a wild-eyed hyena, frightened and hungry, gnashing its teeth and then, in the bright beams of the headlights, using its toothy jaws to tear the protruding piece of meat from Yusof's mouth.

The next day, with children and some adults howling "*Faranji!*" at me, I left Harar. I didn't take the word personally; they were mocking me as they would any foreigner. I was certainly better off than the Harari woman cowering in a doorway who was being beaten by a man with a heavy stick just inside Harar's main gate. She screeched as the robed and turbaned older man, with a grizzled beard, whacked her across her body using the thick part of the stick. A woman squatting near her made a face and leaned away, so as not to be hit by mistake. No one else took any notice. When he was through, the man was a little puffed from his exertion — whaling on someone with a stick is heavy work. The woman howled and bowed down, holding her head, and the man walked away swinging his stick, in the manner of a husband who has just done his duty.

Men are beasts all over the world; that could have happened anywhere. But the lepers, hyenas, ivory tusks, and garbage; the complaining donkeys, the open drains in the cobbled alleys, and the tang of spices; the butcher covered with blood, raising his cleaver to split a furry hump and reveal the smooth cheese of camel fat — and smiling crookedly to offer the fat as a gift; the moans of people's prayers, the dark-eyed invitation to a shadowy hut, and the howls of "Foreigner!" — all these explained why Rimbaud had been so happy here. He had liked Africa for being the anti-Europe, the anti-West, which it is, sometimes defiantly, sometimes lazily. I liked it for those reasons, too, for there was nothing of home here. Being in Africa was like being on a dark star.

7 ◇◇◇

The Longest Road in Africa

BACK IN ADDIS, I tried to plot a trip by road to the Kenyan border and beyond. Not difficult to plot — there was only one road — but in these uncertain times no reliable information. The farther you got from an African capital, the worse the roads. Everyone knew that, but harder information was unobtainable, and the more you inquired the vaguer people became. In such circumstances the cliché "terra incognita" was something real and descriptive. The border was distant; distant places were unknown; the unknown was dangerous.

Border towns in African countries were awful places, known for riffraff and refugees and people sleeping rough, famous for smugglers and backhanders, notorious for bribery and delay, nitpicking officialdom, squeezing policemen, pestering moneychangers, the greatest risks, and the crummiest hotels. There was either a new national language on the other side of the border or the same tribal language straddling it — and a nasty border dispute because the dotted line ran through a divided people. Roadside customs and immigration barriers were horrible bottlenecks, usually at one end of a bridge on the bank of a muddy river. People told me, Don't go.

Some buses went to the southern towns of Dila and Mega, and occasional vehicles to the frontier town of Moyale, but Moyale was the edge of the known world for Ethiopians. None of them ever went to Kenya — why would they? The north of Kenya was waterless desert and rutted roads and quarrelsome tribes, a border dispute among the gun-toting Borena people, and worst of all, the troops of roaming, heavily armed Somalis known as shifta. Just dropping the word "shifta" into a proposed itinerary was enough to make traveling Africans go in the opposite direction.

On what was now the longest road in Africa, some of it purely theoretical, from Cairo to Cape Town, there had once been a plan for a great transcontinental railway. Apart from his dream of diamonds and conquest, Cecil Rhodes's imperial vision for Africa was of a railway line that would run from South Africa to Egypt, taking in Nairobi and Addis Ababa, Khartoum and Nubia. "Your hinterland is there" is the inscription under his bronze figure, pointing north on a pedestal in Cape Town. Sections of the northerly running railway line were built in Rhodes's lifetime (a short lifetime: he died at the age of forty-nine). Later, track was laid to the Copper Belt in Northern Rhodesia (now Zambia) as far as the Congo border. The Germans built a railway across their colony of German East Africa (later British Tanganyika, later still independent Tanzania). The Tanzanians, under the leadership of the muddled Maoist Julius Nyerere, soon had a line south from Dar es Salaam into Zambia, entirely the work of Mao-sponsored Chinese railway men, chanting the Great Helmsman's Thoughts as they hammered spikes and fastened rails. This was 1967, at the beginning of the Great Proletarian Cultural Revolution, which Tanzania too embraced in a superficial and self-destructive way.

By zigging and zagging and taking a ferry across Lake Victoria, it was possible for a solo traveler like me, with a bag and a map, to go by rail from Cape Town to Nairobi. But north of Nairobi the tarred road gives way to mud, the buses stop running at Isiolo, and after that it is just a rocky road, hyenas, and colorful Rendille tribesmen, wearing armlets and loincloths, carrying spears and sabers, and forever fussing over their elaborate hairdos. As soon as the road surface turned bad the bandits appeared, shifta carrying AK-47s, classic highwaymen. The road from Nairobi to the border was reputed to be the emptiest in Africa. That was where I was headed.

No one had any information about that road in Addis, and there wasn't much available about southern Ethiopia either. People would say they had been to a certain town in the south and then, when I questioned them further, they would go blank. Even the Kenyans went blank. Visa requirements had changed. I would need one. I went to the Kenyan embassy and was told by a sulky Kikuyu woman at a desk that I would have to wait three or four days for the visa.

"Why can't I have it today or tomorrow?"

In a scolding tone she said, "Mr. Ochieng, the visa officer, must not be distubbed."

"And why is that?"

"He is busy wucking."

"But I am busy too," I said mildly, "and I want to visit your wonderful country."

"You will have to wait." She picked up a telephone and flicked her fingers at me in a bugger-off gesture.

But I did not leave. I buttonholed diplomats and inquired about the road. Of the three officers at the embassy I spoke to, none had gone by land from Addis to Nairobi across the common border.

A Kenyan man in a three-piece suit seemed insulted that I should suggest it. "We fly," he said.

One Kenyan woman confided that she disliked Ethiopians. "They are proud," she said. She meant racist. To annoy other Africans, Ethiopians sometimes said, "We are not Africans."

◇ ◇ ◇

With time to spare in Addis, I looked around. No tourists in the country meant that the antiques shops were full of merchandise, both treasures and fakes, in the form of old Amharic Bibles made by scribes and monks (with hand-painted plates), silver crosses that looked like giant latchkeys, paintings on cloth stolen from churches, icons, chaplets, Korans, amber beads, Venetian beads, ivory bangles and armlets, spoons of horn and iron, and wooden and leather artifacts from every tribe in the country: elaborate stools, milk jugs, spears, shields, Konso funeral posts depicting the lately departed with a carved penis protruding from the forehead, Mursi lip plugs, penis sheaths, and cache-sexes — little metal aprons that Nuer women wore at their waist for modesty's sake.

An Asiatic man screaming at an Ethiopian woman in a curio shop one day caught my attention. The woman apparently owned the shop, or at least worked there.

"You give me for four hundred birr!" The man was moon-faced, and his tone of voice was harsh and bullying. He wore a white shirt and tie and looked fairly respectable, which made his anger all the more disconcerting.

"No. Six hundred birr. Last price." The woman turned away.

Shaking with rage, the Asiatic man said, "No! Four hundred! I come back! You give me!"

I listened with interest, for one of the curiosities of travel is hearing two nonnative speakers of English venting at each other in English. The dispute went back and forth for a little while longer, the man growing shriller and a pinkness blooming in his cheeks as he became enraged and incoherent. Finally, wordless, he left in a minivan with some other grim-faced Asiatics.

Four hundred Ethiopian birr was $47, six hundred birr was $72.

The shop was empty. I said to the woman, "I'll give you six hundred. That seems reasonable."

"It is a good price. Best price. I sell him some before for five hundred, but it low quality. This maximum quality."

"What is?"

"Ivory." She looked closely at me. "You give me six hundred?"

"New ivory or old?"

"New! Tusks! Big ones!"

Any trade in ivory was illegal, and so I pursued the subject. Ivory from poached elephants was available in large quantities, so I had heard. I had seen chunks of it in shops, but I never saw whole tusks and didn't know the market price. Indeed, though I had been told the trade flourished in Harar and elsewhere, I had no idea I could simply walk into a little store in Addis Ababa and say, How about some elephant tusks, please?

"How many tusks do you have?" I asked.

"How many you want?"

"Let's say quite a few."

"I have much. Fifty, sixty. Each tusk ten kilo, average. When you buy?"

Imagining a half ton of ivory stacked on the ground, something that would satisfy the greed of Mister Kurtz, I said, "Would these be Ethiopian elephants?"

"Ethiopian." *Ityopian,* she said, the usual pronunciation of the Greek word meaning "the Burned Ones."

The Ethiopian elephant, *Loxodonta africana orleansi,* is a severely endangered species — so endangered that an elephant sanctuary had been established in Babille, near Harar, to protect the creatures. Keeping the elephants in this special area made it easier for poachers, and this place (as well as Kenya) was the source of the ivory.

"So, when you come back? You come today?"

I havered and said, "I have a little problem. I'm sending the ivory to the USA, and that's illegal."

"No problem. You got friends?"

"What kind of friends?"

"Embassy friends. Diplomat people. They buy it," she said. "That man you see shouting? He someone in Korean embassy."

"So embassy people buy ivory?"

"Yah. Chinese. Japanese. They buy it."

"I see. They put it in the diplomatic bag and ship it home?"

"Yah. No one look."

"The American embassy might not want to ship a thousand pounds of elephant tusks in the diplomatic bag."

"Yes, you ask them, you ask them," the woman said, now getting a bit impatient with my questions.

Just to satisfy myself I looked around Addis and asked for elephant ivory at two other shops. The only quibble was: How much do you want? Four years before, the price had been two hundred birr ($23) a kilo. Now elephant tusks were harder to find and in great demand, so the price had risen. And a day would come, not far off perhaps, when there would be no more elephants, although no shortage of devious diplomats, stuffing diplomatic pouches with contraband.

◇ ◇ ◇

"No, I don't think we can help you send any elephant tusks back to the States," the information officer at the U.S. embassy in Addis said. He chuckled glumly and made a note to alert CITES — the Convention on International Trade in Endangered Species. He was Karl Nelson, who had served in the Peace Corps in the early to mid-sixties in the Philippines; at that time I had been a Peace Corps volunteer in Malawi.

"How was Malawi?" Karl asked me.

"It was heaven."

"I loved the Philippines, too," Karl said. He had been a teacher, married a Filipina, taught on the Pacific island of Yap for eleven years, wandered the world a bit, and then joined the Foreign Service. He was exactly my age, and our lives had been somewhat parallel. He said, "I joined late. I didn't make anything of my life." But he was wrong: he had a happy family, he loved his wife, he had raised five sturdy, successful children.

"You say you've just come from the Sudan?" Karl said. "And I know you've written about India and Singapore."

"I lived in Singapore for three dreadful years."

"You'll appreciate this, then," he said. "A Sudanese, an Indian, and a Singaporean were asked, 'In your opinion, what is the nutritional value of beef?' The Sudanese said, 'What is nutritional value?' The Indian said, 'What is beef?' And the Singaporean said, 'What is an opinion?'"

I laughed and realized I was in the company of a man whose manner of discourse was jokes and anecdotes. When his turn came in a political discussion with a bunch of bores, he would say, "Bush walks into a delicatessen and says, 'I'll have a sandwich.' Fella says, 'What do you want on that?' Bush says . . ." And Karl would make his point. They were jokes with a point, but gentle and usually deflationary, intended to demonstrate the absurdity of the proposition being debated.

"You're going to Nairobi by road?" he said, and laughed his wheezy laugh. "Well, of course you are. Flying there would be too simple for you. It'll take a week or more. You'll have a terrible time. You'll have some great stuff for your book."

"My idea is to get to the border. African borders are full of revelations. Have you been to the Ethiopian border at Moyale?"

"No. So please write your book, and then I can read about it." He added, "Did you know, in any group of half a dozen Ethiopians, five of them will have been in prison?"

"Is this a joke?"

"This is an invitation," Karl said. "I want to introduce you to some people."

We had lunch at his house on a back street of Addis, a bungalow behind a high wall, with a flower garden and birdhouses and a dovecote. Five Ethiopians and two Filipina doctors, who were also Catholic nuns. The nuns were in Addis for a few days, friends of Karl's wife, who was in the Philippines. The Ethiopians lived in a remote part of the country where there was a large Muslim population, and their mission was providing medical treatment to Muslim women, an altruistic and thankless task that, judging from their uncomplaining dispositions, they performed cheerfully.

One of the Ethiopians was a woman who had worked at the embassy for many years. She said, in a tone of resignation, "Women have no status here. They are pushed aside and beaten."

The four men were all writers, editors, and journalists. Each of them had been in prison. One had been jailed under three successive regimes, a total of twelve years. "I was even in the emperor's prison — the palace jail." It was something of an accomplishment to have annoyed both Haile Selassie and the Derg, the monarchists and the Marxists. Another man had been in prison for most of the Derg years. The two other men told the same story. None of these men had ever been formally charged or brought to trial, just tossed in jail and left to rot.

Ethiopians are vague on Western — that is, Gregorian — calendar dates because their own calendar is seven years behind the Western one (and, likewise, the Jewish one is 3,760 years ahead, and the Muslim one 581 years behind). Whenever I asked an Ethiopian the date of something that had happened in the past, he would begin to count on his fingers. To the best of his calculations, Nebiy Makonnen, an ex-prisoner of about fifty, had languished in the Central Prison from 1977 until 1987.

"It was politics. I was on the wrong side." Nebiy laughed at the very idea of an indictment or a trial. He had simply been picked up one day and thrown in the slammer, where — he was a man who was used to reading and writing — there were no books, nothing to write with, nothing to write on.

"I would go crazy in jail," I said.

"You would learn patience," he said.

"That's true!" the other ex-prisoners said.

"One day, after I had been there about a year, a man was brought in by the guards," Nebiy said. "He had been searched, but somehow they had missed the book he was carrying. It was *Gone With the Wind*. We were so happy! We were all educated men. We took turns reading it — of course, we had to share it. There were three hundred fifty men in my section, and so we were allowed to have the book for one hour at a time. That was the best part of the day in Central Prison — reading *Gone With the Wind.*

"I decided to translate it. I had no paper, so for paper I smoothed out the foil from cigarette packs and used the back side of it, where there was paper to write on. A pen was smuggled in. I wrote very small. And I was entertainment officer, so every night I read some of my translation to the other prisoners.

"But still I had to share the book — I could only have it for one hour. The translation took two years. I wrote it on three thousand sheets of cigarette foil. One by one, I folded these up and put them back into cigarette packs, and when the prisoners were released they took them out of prison, tucked in their shirt pockets."

Nebiy remained in prison for ten years. On his release, he looked for the three thousand pieces of foil that contained his translation of *Gone With the Wind.* Locating and then gathering them took him two more years. At last he published his translation of the novel, and this is the one that Ethiopians read.

"What's your favorite part of the book?" I asked.

"I don't know. I read it over and over for six years. I know the book by heart."

At the end of Evelyn Waugh's *A Handful of Dust,* the captive Tony Last is condemned to sit in a jungle clearing and read the works of Dickens, over and over, to his crazed captor, Mr. Todd. It is improbable, so it is funny. Nebiy Makonnen's story was much better and its hilarity more horrible for being true — six years squinting at Scarlett O'Hara in an Ethiopian jail.

After that, whenever I met an Ethiopian man over thirty or so I asked whether he had been in prison, and the answer was usually yes.

Wubishet Dilnessahu had done seven years. He was now a businessman living in California, and was back in Addis Ababa for only a few days, to pursue a lawsuit. A man of seventy-seven, of a good family, he had been one of Emperor Haile Selassie's ministers, concerned with cultural matters. He saw the emperor every day. He did not have to kowtow, as I had been told, but had to show respect. "I bowed very low, of course," Wubishet said.

After the Derg takeover, Haile Selassie was strangled — Wubishet said that Mengistu himself had choked the emperor to death; this information had just been revealed. At the time (August 1975) it was reported in the newspaper that the cause of death was "circulatory failure." The body was put in a hole at Menelik Palace and a structure (perhaps a latrine) built over it. In the early 1990s, the body was disinterred and the emperor's remains kept in a crypt in a church in Addis. In November 2000, in an elaborate ceremony, the emperor was at last given a solemn burial in Holy Trinity Cathedral.

"The Russians told us, 'We killed our king. If you kill yours there will be less trouble,'" Wubishet said.

A few days after the emperor was arrested, Wubishet was clapped in irons, charged with "helping the former regime," and taken to the Fourth Division Military Camp, where he was locked in a barrackslike hut with 120 other men. He showed me the prison, which is still a prison, and was that week bursting with political prisoners — university students who had recently been rounded up during a demonstration against government policies. Hundreds had been arrested, many were injured, and forty of the students had been killed by police truncheons and gunfire.

"You see the tin roof? The long building on the right? That was my prison building," Wubishet said. There were eight other buildings just like it, looking like chicken coops, and they had also been full of prisoners. None of the men were charged; there were no trials. Most of the prisoners had no idea why they were there. "Many of the young men in there could not read or write, so we started a school. We taught literacy. And we just waited."

"Did they allow visits from friends or family?"

Wubishet laughed in the dark, contemptuous way of the Ethiopian conditioned to be cynical after a lifetime of national catastrophes.

"In seven years I saw my family once, for fifteen minutes."

The royal apartments where Wubishet had worked for the emperor still stood. We went there in a taxi, for the palace Gannah Le'ul — Princely Heaven — the emperor's residence, built around 1900 by Haile Selassie's father, Ras Makonnen, had been occupied variously by Makonnen, by the Italian viceroys, including the Count of Aosta, by the Italian army, by one brief usurper (a rule of three days in 1960), by Haile Selassie, and now by the administrators of the University of Addis Ababa. It had been Wubishet's own idea to convey the palace building to the university, which was in need of space. At first Wubishet had been too timid to suggest the idea to the emperor, but finally blurted it out. The emperor said nothing. "But he summoned me in the night and said okay. I was so nervous and excited I could not sleep."

Although this building still looked like a royal residence, if a seedy one, with high doors and ornate trim and two baroque statues in front, there was a Fascist relic in the forecourt. This bizarre monument was a staircase of mildewed cement — fifteen steps representing the years that had elapsed since Mussolini entered Rome in 1922. The sculpture still stood after sixty-five years of war, monarchy, dictatorship, socialism, anarchy, and political asininity. A Fascist staircase, leading nowhere.

As Wubishet had worked in the emperor's office, I asked him if he had been aware of Haile Selassie's relationship with Rastafarians. The word had been coined in homage to the emperor's birth name, Ras Tafari.

"I know about the devotion these people have for him, but the emperor didn't think about them very much," Wubishet said. For example, the emperor never mentioned Rastas in conversation. Wubishet said he knew nothing about Shashemene, the Rasta town on the road south of Addis, and was not even aware of the established fact that the emperor had given land to the Rastas. "Of course, he was a proud man and enjoyed respect, but the way they treated him was embarrassing for him."

"But he went to Jamaica and saw them there," I said.

"They made him very embarrassed. They were kneeling! They thought he was God." Wubishet flapped his hand, dismissing the whole movement in a gesture. "You see, Ethiopians are Christians," he said. "We don't worship human beings. Even a simple Ethiopian wouldn't do it. They would think it's stupid."

"But you bowed very low to the emperor," I said.

I liked his answer to this. He said, "That shows respect. That's not worship. Worship is the forehead striking the ground. The emperor was a very small man, so you needed to bow extra low."

◇ ◇ ◇

As the days passed, Addis Ababa did not become more beautiful but it began to fascinate me for being a city of people with vivid personal stories, like Wubishet's prison tale and Nebiy's *Gone With the Wind* saga. There were many others — for example, the story of Ali's revenge.

I met Ali by chance. He had also done time in prison but it was a long, horrible story, he said. I said I had plenty of time and was eager to hear it. Ali thought he might be able to help me get a lift to the Kenya border, to Moyale at least, with some traders he knew. Ali was a broker and general factotum, dealing in cars, horses, souvenirs, even ivory. "If you hide the ivory right," he said, "you can get it into the U.S." He had been to the United States many times, and held a multiple-entry visa, but had no desire to live there. America was too expensive, he didn't like the routines, and anyway his whole family was here.

Ali had gray eyes and chipmunk cheeks and an air of circumspection about him that sometimes seemed like weariness and sometimes wiliness. He chain-smoked, rebuking himself each time he lit up. He had that special entrepreneurial sense that is able to single out a person in serious need. He saw that urgency in me — I was in need of a ride south. Of course he could supply it — he could supply anything — and the only question was how much would I be willing to pay? How much could he make on the deal?

Ali had time to kill, and so did I.

"These Kenyans!" With the businessman's disgust for bureaucracy and profitless delay he said, "They could just stamp the passport and take your money. But they make you wait."

He discovered my liking for Ethiopian food — national food, as everyone called it. And so, over several meals at Ethiopian restaurants in Addis — the most pleasant a ramshackle wooden villa called Finfine — he told me his prison story, which was different from any other I had heard and not political at all.

It had started with an innocent question from me. I had mentioned that on this long trip I missed my family, my wife and children, and feeling sentimental, I asked about his family.

Ali winced and his face darkened, a memory passing over it, and then he shook his head and said nothing — an awkward moment. Stammering self-consciously, I tried to change the subject, but he interrupted and said, "I am divorced."

That didn't seem so bad. There was no stigma about divorce in Islam, at least for a man. In the Muslim world a woman's life was over when she got dumped; there was no second act. A man just moved on, usually acquiring another wife.

"The person I trusted most in my life, the only one I cared about, lied to me," Ali said. "I ended up in jail, but God saved me, or else I would still be in jail today, or maybe dead."

We had finished eating and were drinking fragrant Ethiopian coffee under the arbor outside in the Finfine's garden. Perhaps because this was the fourth or fifth meal I'd had with Ali, and because he had found some traders who were going south — because we were on the verge of striking a deal — he now trusted me enough to tell the story. As he said, it was the worst thing that had happened to him in his life, so he told it almost without prodding from me.

"The first time I heard about it I was confused," he went on. "There was a story that my wife had been seen with another man. I asked some questions. He was a colonel in the army. This was during the Derg, when the army was in power. They were very strong. A trader like me was nothing. Just hearing that her man was a soldier made me think, *What?* So I asked her directly.

"She said: 'There was nothing. I did nothing. Yes, I was with him, but he forced me. He was a soldier. What could I do?'

"I have four children. I don't want them to be upset and to know that their mother was in this position, so I said nothing. I wasn't happy, though. I didn't like the story. I lived for a while with my mind uneasy. Then one day I had to drive to Lalibela to buy some things for my business."

Lalibela was the remote location of about a dozen twelfth-century Coptic churches that had been carved in volcanic rock, the ones you see all the time on *Visit Ethiopia* posters. The town was in the Lasta Mountains, three hundred miles or more from Addis. Lalibela was a serious trip of three or four days.

"I set off," Ali said, "but when I called ahead I was told by my friend Kamal that the goods were not ready. Bad, eh? So I decided to turn around and go south instead, with Kamal, and pick up some things.

"We were about forty-five kilometers from Addis, going through the town of Debre Zeyit, when I slowed down for the goats and heavy traffic and saw, off the road, my Peugeot car, a brown one, parked near a building. Why did I see it so clearly? I think God wanted it.

"'That's my car.'

"'That's not your car,' Kamal said. 'What would your car be doing here?'

"The building was a hotel, not a very nice one, but with a fence around it and a caretaker man at the car park. I said to him, 'Did you see a fat woman with this car?'"

I made an effort not to smile at Ali's description of his wife.

"The caretaker man said no. I gave him some money. He said, 'Yes. They are in room nine.'

"We go to the room, the three of us, me and Kamal and the caretaker. I knock on the door. I instruct the caretaker man what to say. He say, 'Please open. It's about your car.'

"The door opens. I have my gun drawn — yes, I have a gun, but I did not show it to the caretaker man before. We rush in, Kamal and me. They are naked. I punch my wife in the face, Kamal fights the soldier, and they are soon on the floor. The soldier is screaming and crying, 'Don't kill me! Don't kill me!'"

Ali smiled for the first time, remembering a detail. "The soldier's mustache is going like this" — he moved his upper lip, nervously twitching it in a rabbity way. The soldier was trapped, begging for his life. He was bollocky naked.

"I say, 'Stand up!' To my wife, too. They have no clothes. Seeing my wife, I feel a little sorry — her face bleeding from how I punched her, and she try to cover her body. She is crying and pleading. I give her a dress to wrap around, and then Kamal and I tie their hands like this."

Ali stood up and demonstrated how he had tied up his wife and her lover. He placed them back to back and tied their wrists tightly and then their arms. With her hands bound, Ali's wife could not keep the dress wrapped around her, so she was as naked as the soldier now.

"We pushed them out of the room to the car park and then down the street. It was hard for them to walk like that, so it was slow, and people saw them. They were laughing. I still had my gun pointed on them. Children were gathering around — many children, and a whole crowd of people.

"Down the side of the road — a busy road, buses, taxis, cars, and many people — everyone looking at the naked ones. We keep pushing them until we come to a big stone, a flat one. I say, 'Sit there, don't move. I am calling the police.' To the children and the people I say, 'Don't help them. They are bad. The police will come. If you help these two people you will have a problem.'

"They were laughing anyway, and I knew they wouldn't help. I didn't call the police. I went away, taking the man's clothes with me. It was his uniform and his identification. Kamal drove the Peugeot. I went to the army base and asked to see the general. I gave the soldier's clothes and everything to the general. I said, 'This is what your colonel did.' The general shook my hand. He thanked me. He said, 'You did the right thing. The colonel deserved it.'"

I wanted to know what happened to Ali's wife and her lover. Ali welcomed the question.

"They stayed on the rock by the side of the road until six-thirty at night — maybe six hours or more. People laughing at them, a big crowd. The two nakeds — man and woman. Then, when it was getting dark, an army truck passed on the road and saw him. 'Colonel!' and 'What-what.' The truck stopped and the soldiers untied them and put the colonel on the truck with my wife, gave them some clothes, and took them away.

"I left her. Left the house. I say, 'This is my children's house. They must go on living here. It belongs to them.' I got another place to stay. All I left with was two suitcases — my whole life in them. Nothing else. I went and started all over again. I said, 'God saved me.'"

Was the story over? Ali was still gray-faced and reflective — and hadn't he said something about prison?

"Yes," he said, "three months later I was arrested for 'attempting killing,' because I had a gun and threatened the soldier. I went to court. There was a judge. I was sent to prison for two months."

This was the only ex-prisoner I met in Ethiopia who had actually been charged with a crime and given a trial. It was also the shortest prison sentence I had heard about.

"Then God saved me again," Ali said, a little more intensely. "I was walking in the street in Addis and I saw them in the street, my wife and the soldier, holding hands.

"I decided to kill her. I went to my brother's house, where I was keeping my gun, because I had nowhere to lock it where I was staying. My brother was not there. He had gone away and no one had the key.

"For three days I tried to get the key. I wanted my gun — I was planning how I would kill her. Then my brother returned with the key. He opened the safe and gave me the gun."

Ali massaged his scalp, remembering, but saying nothing.

I said, "What did you do?"

"Nothing. You see, time had passed. I said to myself, 'So what? Why kill her? Let her live — it will be worse for her. She has lost everything.' God saved me."

After that, having unburdened himself with this story, having heard nothing from me of my life, he said that he felt he knew me well, and it was as though we had known each other for a long time. I could see that he meant it and was moved by this feeling.

I told him what I felt about time exposing the truth — that time did not heal wounds, but that the passing years gave us a vantage point from which to see the reality of things. I added that it was no fun to grow old, but that the compensation for it was that time turned your mental shit-detector into a highly calibrated instrument.

Ali said, "Now I know that no one is virtuous. Women will sleep with anyone. Why do they throw everything away? Why do they do these things?"

"Because men do them."

But he was baffled to think that a woman would behave so badly, that she would not do exactly as she was told. It was strange to him, this realization that someone so low and so despised had a mind of her own, an imagination, and the ability to devise elaborate stratagems for deceit and pleasure.

◇ ◇ ◇

Through Ali I met old Tadelle and young Wolde, man and boy, who were driving to the southern region to pick up spears and shields, beads and bracelets, milk jugs from the Borena people, ivory bangles from the Oromo, carvings from the Konso, and whatever baskets and knickknacks they could find. They were traders.

"If you go with someone else, they might rob you," Ali said. "There are bad people on the road, bad people in the buses. Tadelle is a good driver and has a strong vehicle. Wolde is a good boy. They know the places to stay. You will be safe."

In Africa when someone said "There are bad people there," as it was said often, I tended to listen. I was sure Ali got a cut of the money, for I paid him and he paid them, but the price was fair. Besides, this was a way of going the whole way to the Kenya frontier. The day I got my Kenya visa — four days after I applied — we set off in a southerly direction on the longest road in Africa.

The potholed roads in Addis prepared me for much worse ones out of town. Addis lies at 8,500 feet — I gasped for breath after I had rushed across a road to dodge a speeding car — and so our progress took us through rounded hills and crowded settlements, into dry valleys and the highlands again. Besides the goats and donkeys, the farting motor scooters and beat-up cars, I saw a skinny athlete in bright red shorts, a yellow jersey, and Reeboks, running fast, weaving in and out of traffic, a marathoner in training. He was one of many. Apart from the emperor, the best-known Ethiopian is the 10,000-meter gold medalist Haile Gabre Selassie (no relation), who was born near here. These south-central highlands are the home of many long-distance runners, with great legs and powerful lungs. Their speed has freed them from the hard life they would have faced as farmers and herdsmen, for there is no work here, and for the past thirty years there has been nothing in Ethiopia but uncertain harvests and war and political terror.

Tadelle said that he had been down this road many times. In fact, he had been to Kenya.

"Tell me about it."

Haltingly, for his English was poor, Tadelle said that he had sneaked into Kenya twice and made his way to refugee camps. It was his dearest wish to leave Ethiopia for good and to emigrate. "Anywhere — I go to any country!" He hated life in Ethiopia. He said it would never get better, and anywhere in the world would be better than life here. America would be just about perfect.

But the United Nations interviewers at the camps in Nairobi and Mombasa said he was not a genuine refugee. "I say, 'I no like Ethiopian government. I hate zat — all of zat.'" But they sent him back to Ethiopia.

"I go again sometime," Tadelle said.

About three hours south of Addis we came to Shashemene.

"This bad place," Tadelle said. "Very bad place. Too much thief. They are all termites."

"Let's stop," I said. Shashemene was part of my plan.

◈ ◈ ◈

If Ethiopia was the spiritual home of the Rastafarians, Shashemene was its capital, not Addis — though Addis, too, was full of un-Ethiopian-looking black men in bulgy bobble hats of multicolored wool, the Rasta banner of red, yellow, and green, which were also the colors of the Ethiopian flag. Haile Selassie had granted some acreage in Shashemene to these devotees, to satisfy their desire to return to Africa and have a place to settle. Ethiopians described the Rastas as impious and faintly ludicrous. The Muslims called them infidels, the Copts claimed they were misguided Christians. No one took them seriously, and many Ethiopians stared at them, sometimes giggling at the Rasta get-up and the "African" affectations: beaded bracelets, horn necklaces, and woven shoulder bags. The dreadlocks were weird to Ethiopians, not African at all, and not the cultural statement Rastas regarded them, but just the epitome of a bad hair day.

As soon as we entered the outskirts of Shashemene, I saw those dreadlocks and those colors and those men, very skinny ones, striding along the roadside.

Tadelle and I had agreed that in return for my paying for passage I could stop wherever I wanted, within reason. Our aim was to get to the border in three or four days. Tadelle and Wolde drove into town looking for a place to stay while I nosed around, searching for a Rastafarian to talk to.

Through a succession of chance meetings and introductions I met Gladstone Robinson, one of the earliest pioneers, virtually the first Rastafarian to settle for good in Ethiopia. He was seventy-one, the father of eleven children; his youngest, a one-year-old, was crawling out of his hut. His radiant and smiling young wife — "She's twenty-three," Gladstone said — was heavily pregnant, so he would soon be father to an even dozen.

Gladstone was friendly, funny and alert, youthful in spite of his age, with a jazz musician's easy smile and silences. He was slender but supple, with a knotted stringy beard and gray dreadlocks drooping from beneath his wool hat. His hut was a simple cement shed, two rooms. The room we sat in was stacked with files and strewn with papers. Some old photos hung on the wall, among them the requisite pictures of Haile Selassie and Bob Marley. A bulging paper bag sat on the table.

"You want some herb? You smoke?"

"Oh, right, flame a jay for me."

He laughed and fossicked in the bag. Pork and milk are abominations for Rastafarians, but marijuana is sacred, which perhaps explains their lean physique and their torpid smile. In general it was a sect of very skinny, spaced-out men and hardworking, clearheaded women.

Although Gladstone expertly rolled a doobie, he was so busy answering my questions he did not fire it up.

"My father was a Bado" — a Barbadian, he explained — "and my mother was a Cherokee Indian. But Rastas come from all over. See that picture?"

A blurred snapshot of a group of men standing shoulder to shoulder in a tropical setting hung on the wall in a chipped frame.

"Those are black Jews from Monserrat. They came over in the 1980s."

"Did you say Jews?"

"Indeed, I did. By the way, there are lots of black Jews in America. We are the true Israelites, not those so-called Jews you get in Israel. They are not true Jews. True Jews are the children of Solomon. We are, and the Falashas. The Falashas carry the ancestry of the father, not the mother."

I had seen Falashas in Jerusalem. These Ethiopian Jews, who dated their faith from ancient times, had emigrated to Israel, regarding it as a homeland and a refuge. In the event they were a melancholy bunch, sidelined by the Hasidim, squinted at by tourists, unskilled except as farm laborers yet seldom seen on kibbutzim. The irony was that West Indian Rastafarians were arriving in Ethiopia as the Falashas were leaving for Israel.

"The Falasha high priests were sent with Menelik to Solomon," Gladstone said. "The key is the Ark of the Covenant — the Ark is at Axum. Whoever has the Ark of the Covenant has God's blessing. We say that Jesus came as a lamb to the slaughter, but Haile Selassie came as a conquering lion."

"What I am wondering is" — because Gladstone was confusing me with unrelated scriptural snippets and vague historical allusions — "how is it that you happened to come here?"

"Tell you how it all began," Gladstone said. "When Haile Selassie was crowned, the words describing him showed his true lineage from the house of David. His kingship was accepted by seventy-two countries."

"What's the connection with Jamaica?"

"He went there. The hardest-praying people are the Jamaicans, and they saw who he truly was."

Envoys will come from Egypt, they had read in Psalms 68:31. *Ethiopia will stretch out her hands to God.*

Marcus Garvey, who initiated the Back to Africa movement, had predicted that a savior would come, Gladstone said. Garvey was a Jamaican, gifted in oratory and an able organizer. He was also an entrepreneur, the founder of the Black Star shipping line. The Universal Negro Improvement Association, which Garvey started in 1914, had been an inspiration to blacks in America and the Caribbean. "Ethiopia, Thou Land of Our Fathers" was Garvey's hymn. Garvey was Moses, Haile Selassie the Messiah, even if he didn't know it. Eventually, Garvey became critical of the emperor and his autocratic rule, but he never wavered in his belief that, for the blacks in the West, Ethiopia represented hope and a homeland.

Gladstone showed me a copy of the August 1970 issue of *Africa Opinion,* with a cover picture of Marcus Garvey and a piece inside about settlers in Shashemene — Gladstone himself was mentioned by name in the article.

"I was chairman of the Ethiopian World Federation," Gladstone said. "Here is our constitution."

He passed me a photocopy of a typewritten document. I glanced at the opening: "Ethiopian World Federation — 25 August 1937, New York City. We, the Black Peoples of the World, in order to effect Unity, Solidarity, Liberty, Freedom, and Self-Determination, do hereby affirm . . ."

"I was in the United States Army, trained as a pharmacist," Gladstone said, folding the constitution. "During the Korean War I was in Japan, at the Tokyo General Dispensary, with the U.S. Medical Corps. But I dreamed of Africa.

"After I joined the Ethiopian World Federation, I was put in charge of repatriation." He said, "We had three options: integration, separation, repatriation. Integration is living together. Separation is the Nation of Islam — and maybe some southern states set aside for blacks, some northern ones for whites. Repatriation was coming back to Africa."

"When did you first come here?" I asked.

"'Sixty-four," he said, and picked up an old school notebook, opening it to a page of neat penmanship. Pasted on the facing page were some yellowed newspaper clippings.

I read: "June 16, 1964. The two delegates of the African Repatriation Commission left the BOAC terminal at John F. Kennedy Airport, Gladstone Robinson and Noel Scott."

"That's my diary of the whole trip. I came here with the first twelve. There are only four left. Brother Wolfe, Brother Waugh, Sister Clark, and me, Brother Robinson."

There were about fifty Rastafarian families settled now, a hundred or so children, and many people kept a place in Shashemene as a second home, coming and going. Some blacks had come and not liked it; for others it was a refuge, Gladstone said. All this time he was shuffling snapshots: Gladstone in his pharmacy in Addis Ababa, Gladstone in a laboratory smock, Gladstone in glasses, Gladstone in dreadlocks, Gladstone posing with tourists, Gladstone in robes, Gladstone in a suit, Gladstone with some of his many children.

"My daughter, she's a New York City cop. Graduated from John Jay. She wears dreads. She went to court when they said she had to cut them off. Rastas were defending her — Rasta lawyers. She's been here to Shashemene."

"You're happy here, Gladstone?"

"I am happy. You have to go home — a tree grows better in its own soil. Those first people each got twenty-five acres. We didn't know what to do with all that land!"

"What did you do with it?"

"Built a school, and farmed, and opened up some pharmacies. I was doing all right."

"Did the Derg bother you?"

"The Derg closed me down. Took my land. That was terrible. I worked for two years with Russian and Cuban doctors at the hospital here. They were surgeons. That was okay, but one day the soldiers came and beat up the Ethiopian doctor. They said he had guns."

"Weren't you scared?"

"Sure was. I said to myself, 'Let Uncle Sam kick my butt, I am getting out of here.' Went back to New York until it was over."

Gladstone, the most genial Rastafarian I met in Shashemene, introduced me to some more immigrants from Jamaica. He said I should understand that there were many black West Indians and Americans who had come for reasons other than Rastafarianism. "We have Bobo Shanti and Nyabinghi, Ethiopian World Federation, Independents, and Twelve Tribes."

Desmond and Patrick, both Jamaicans, were members of the Twelve Tribes. Desmond was fifty and rather haggard, but talkative and open. He had been in Ethiopia for twenty-five years. He came "because this is a place of refuge," and stayed on through the worst years of the Derg, "when Mengistu was dragging young boys out of the villages and making them fight."

Patrick was young and very intense, wearing a jacket of Rasta colors, fluent and apparently knowledgeable. While Desmond, in his beret and shabby velvet jacket, was happy to put his feet up and smoke a joint, Patrick — who did not smoke herb — was just visiting, but he planned to buy a house and move here with his large family.

"I come and go, but I tell you this is my home. Jamaica is not my home. My roots are here. I am African," Patrick said. "We were taken as slaves from here, and now I am back. We are the Twelve Tribes of Israel." He raised a slender finger to make his point. "But we are not Israelis, making ethnic distinctions and coming from wherever and pretending we are people of the desert. We are really African. We want no special favors — just a home here."

"What place does Haile Selassie occupy in your theology?"

"His Majesty," Patrick said, correcting me, "is a direct descendant of the house of David. Look at the Bible — it's all there, the short version. King of Kings, Ras Tafari."

Much is made by Rastafarians of the titles Ras Tafari assumed when he became emperor. His coronation was mocked by Evelyn Waugh in his travel book *Remote People*, but it marked the beginning of Haile Selassie as a symbol of redemption to blacks in Jamaica and elsewhere. The emperor himself seemed to claim a strong biblical link. On Megabit 25, 1922 (corresponding to April 3, 1930), Ras Tafari issued a proclamation saying that His Majesty King Tafari Makonnen would be emperor, crowned His Imperial Majesty Haile Selassie I, King of Kings, Conquering Lion of the Tribe of Judah, Elect of God, Emperor of Ethiopia. His Majesty ended the proclamation, "Trader, trade! Farmer, plough! I shall govern you by the law and ordinance that has come to me, handed down by my fathers."

Because Haile Selassie was styled the Lion of Judah and claimed

Solomon as an ancestor, he inserted himself into the Bible. The Ethiopian monarchy traces its origins to Menelik I, who was the son of the Queen of Sheba and Solomon. It's all there in Kings and Chronicles, as the Rastafarians say. Well, not exactly. What is clear in scripture is only the visit of Sheba to Solomon. A subsequent visit to Solomon, and the birth of Sheba's son Menelik, are related in the Ethiopian epic *Kebra Nagast,* described by Nicholas Clapp, in *Sheba,* as "a document claimed to have been discovered in the library of Constantinople's cathedral of Santa Sofia in the third century A.D. but it is more likely a fourteenth-century compilation of Ethiopian oral history." Clapp's entire book, his sound scholarship and wide travel, is the history of this shadowy queen who flits in and out of the Bible. His conclusion is that she could be any one of eleven historical or mythological figures. And by the way, she was not named Sheba. This enigmatic woman was the unnamed queen of a country called Sheba, or Saba.

Patrick said, "His Majesty is a spiritual descendant, not a god. We don't worship him, but we see that His Majesty has many of the qualities of Jesus."

"For example?"

"For example, the Italians tried to take over this country many times. They were terrible, but His Majesty did not condemn them. He forgave them. He was merciful. It is the mercy that is written in the Bible. He is that man who was foretold. What month were you born?"

I told him April. He said, "There is one tribe for each month. April is Reuben. Very important for the eyes. Your sign is silver."

Why did this man's zealotry make me so uneasy? He seemed a kind fellow; he specifically said he accepted everyone, "even white people"; he was a musician. He said, "Some of our message is in our music." But he did not listen; he was a true believer. His zealotry worried me because it was zealotry. Zealots never listen.

Desmond, older, rather easygoing, was admiring of him, and said Patrick fasted on the Sabbath, read the Bible, did not smoke herb. "He is young, he is pure."

"Read the Bible," Patrick said. "A chapter a day keep the devil away."

"Me, I smoke ganja," Desmond said. "We grow it but" — with a hand gesture — "under, you see what I'm saying, because the government don't like it and some Ethiopians make trouble for us."

Desmond told me of his conversion. "We had a prophet in Jamaica,

Gyad" — but he might have been saying "God" the Jamaican way — "who said, 'His Majesty will leave the scene of action.' Those were his words. He prophesied that His Majesty will pass on.

"I came here immediately after that, with my wife. We had four children. My wife, now, she didn't like it. I said, 'Go! I can find another wife but I can't find another Ethiopia.' I take an Ethiopian wife and have four more children."

Seeing me, correctly, as a profound skeptic, Patrick explained that I should pay close attention to world events. The catastrophes worldwide were signs of an end time.

"The millennium came and went," I said.

"The millennium hasn't come yet," he said. "The Ethiopian calendar is behind by seven years and eight months, so the millennium is coming in about six years. You will see. The earth was destroyed by water. It will be fire next time. The Rift Valley will be spared — it will be the safest place in the world when the fire comes. You can come and be a refugee here. Bring your family."

I thanked him, and walking out to the main road I reflected on how Africa, being incomplete and so empty, was a place for people to create personal myths and indulge themselves in fantasies of atonement and redemption, melodramas of suffering, of strength — binding up wounds, feeding the hungry, looking after refugees, driving expensive Land Rovers, even living out a whole cosmology of creation and destruction, rewriting the Bible as an African epic of survival.

That night at a grim hotel in Shashemene, Tadelle seemed resentful that we had to stay and was in a bad mood. He saw some Rastas loping along, bulgy-hatted.

"Why these people come here?" he said. "Where is the country of Jamaica? They have no work there?"

◇ ◇ ◇

The next day, driving south, Tadelle told me he hated Ethiopia. He hated the army. "They are all termites." Where had he learned this expression? He said it a lot. Politicians were termites, soldiers were termites, policemen were termites.

He wanted to leave so badly he could not understand why anyone would willingly come to Ethiopia to live. He was saying this as we drove through the pretty town of Awasa and along its lakeshore, where we stopped for lunch and I went bird-watching and saw herons and hornbills. In the afternoon, still heading south, I could see mountains and the empty plain ahead, as green as AstroTurf, with a suggestion of more lakes and more mountains beyond them, and fertile valleys bursting with pineapple fields. Boys were selling the fruit by the side of the road. We stopped and I bought eight for the equivalent of a dollar. I learned the Amharic word for pineapple: *ananas,* as in Italian and Spanish. On we went down the twisting road to Dila.

Late afternoon was the time to stop. It was not a good idea to travel at dusk, and it was unthinkable to travel after dark. Dila was huddled on the main road in a coffee-growing area, a crowded market town in the Mendebo Mountains. There was not much in the market except little piles of fruit, no food in the shops, only soap, shirts, and Chinese goods that were all infringements of copyright: "Lax" soap and fake Nike, Reebok and Gap merchandise.

Wolde followed me around the dusty lanes as I went in search of a hat. The temperature was in the nineties, the sky cloudless, the sun unremitting. The heat in such a place persisted until midnight. Oromo women in orange robes and beads squatted by the roadside howling at passersby, howling at me, too, as their children pestered me for money.

A useful word in Amharic was *yellem,* meaning "there is nothing" or simply "forget it." Wolde laughed at the effect it had on the importuning Oromo.

I said, "We're going to stay here?"

Tadelle smiled apologetically. The hotel, the Get Smart, was awful, but it was the only place to stay. We were not welcomed.

"We have no room," the clerk said.

"Maybe you could check."

With a desultory fuss, the clerk flipped the pages of a scrappy school exercise book that was the hotel's guest register.

"No room with water."

"That's fine." More than fine, I thought, since the water would be corrosive.

He kept on flipping pages. "Okay, room with water, in the back."

The room was dirty, very hot, and vile smelling, much worse than the one in Shashemene, but at the Ethiopian equivalent of $2.50 an excellent value. After I had drunk three bottles of beer and written my notes on a wobbly table, I felt optimistic and happy, for here I was in a flophouse in a remote town in southern Ethiopia, within striking distance (about 250 miles) of the Kenyan border. With luck we might be there tomorrow.

A young Japanese man sat among some Ethiopians in the dining room of the Get Smart, eating national food. I joined him, and on the assumption that vegetables were less likely to be tainted, I ordered "fasting food" — it was all they had anyway. I sat at the common table, and we shredded the *injera* bathmat and squelched the vegetables.

The man was Daisuko Obayashi, sent here by NEC of Japan to install a telecommunications system. He had been in Dila for two months. He spoke no Amharic, and his English was rudimentary. He had been in rural Tanzania for two years, but preferred Ethiopia.

"Sometimes Ethiopian people they buy me drink, but two year in Tanzania no one buy me drink."

He said he did not speak Swahili. Hearing that I lived in Hawaii, he said he did not want to visit the islands. "Too many Japanese people there."

After ten minutes of this irritating small talk I thought: The only English speaker in Dila, and he's a fathead.

He said, "In Tanzania, I go to disco and girls say they want to have sex with me. But I say no, because of AIDS. Almost three years — no sex! Ha! Ha!"

Perhaps that forced celibacy explained his tetchy demeanor, so I turned my attention to Tadelle and Wolde.

"What do you think of this place?"

"Is mess," Tadelle said. Tadelle was from Tigre, as was Mengistu, and so he missed the days of the Derg, which everyone else deplored for the years of famine, bankruptcy, mass murder, terror, and arbitrary imprisonment. Mengistu had built schools and hospitals, Tadelle said, especially in Tigre.

"I sink zat Mengistu was good. Za Derg was good. Yes, some people was killed. But it was za soldiers and smaller people who did it."

"But there's democracy now," I said, to needle him: the present government persecuted any group that dissented, and had turned the Ethiopian police into junkyard dogs.

"Za democracy we have is bad. Za government is just termites."

Lying in my small hot room at the Get Smart that night, I twiddled the knobs on my shortwave radio and listened in the darkness to the news. Wall Street was in trouble: *The Dow went south again for the third straight day . . . Tech stocks deep in negative territory . . . The Nasdaq hit a five-year low . . . No sign of an uptick . . . Fears grew for a recession . . .*

But in Dila it made no difference.

◈ ◈ ◈

In the morning, I asked the Get Smart clerk for coffee. This was, after all, a coffee-growing region.

"Is finished."

"Any fruit?" It was a fruit-growing region, too.

"Is finished."

"How about Ambo?" Ambo was Ethiopian bottled water.

The Get Smart clerk smiled: *finished.*

We ate some of the pineapples we had with us and set off for Yabelo and Mega and the border town of Moyale.

Steering around the deep potholes on the road south of Dila, we entered long valleys, some of them green and cultivated, others no more than dust bowls. We came to the ramshackle town of Agera Maryam. "They have food here," Tadelle said, driving into a walled compound. A sad, sweet-faced woman brought us some evil-looking goat meat and cold pasta. I ate some of the pasta, Wolde scarfed the goat, and Tadelle said, "Za people here are thieves. I must watch za car or zey will steal from it."

The table covering at the eating place was a week-old Ethiopian English-language newspaper in which there was an alarming item reporting that this southern region was being ravaged by outbreaks of meningitis. It did not specify which form. Ethiopia (and Sudan) is in the African "meningitis belt." There is even a "meningitis season" — these very months. I made a mental note to buy some cans of food, but there were no cans. All I could find in the way of packaged food were some boxes of stale cookies, made in Abu Dhabi.

We drove onward through a wide mountain valley, down an empty road past the town of Yabelo. The people in this area wore traditional dress, tunics and beads, the men carried spears, and the women toiled on paths with bundles of wood on their heads. Very young herdboys bullied goats with their crooks. The landscape had become hotter and dryer, and in one sunstruck place a small boy had pressed himself against a tree for the relief of a little patch of shade.

"The women very pretty here," Tadelle said, slowing down.

But he was slowing down for roadkill — fifty-nine hooded vultures surrounded a dead hyena on the road, flapping their ragged wings and tearing at the animal's flesh, while other scavenging birds, kites and marabou storks, kept their distance. In the fields beyond were wild camels, or at least roaming ones, unsaddled, unhobbled, plodding toward the hills.

This was the region of the Wolayta people, who lived in beehive huts that were topped with bald ostrich eggs, a token of fertility. Clusters of these huts lay along the road. The women *were* beautiful, with long braided hair and bright cloaks, and some of them were heavily burdened with bundles of firewood. Men in fields were using yoked oxen and wooden plows shaped like wishbones, and all the boys striding with spears.

The town names were large on the map, but the towns themselves were tiny. Mega was just a wide place in the road. There was nothing to eat here, but being among so many hungry people had killed my appetite. In Ethiopia I ate one meal a day, *injera* and vegetable glop, or pasta, a dish that was a leftover of the Italian occupation.

Tadelle said, "There was a war here in 1983" — no sign of it, though, except for some wrecked vehicles on the low bare hills. The war had come and gone, people had died, life resumed, nothing had changed, still the plow and the herd of goats and the cooking fire and the bare buttocks — the African story.

I walked from shop to shop, making notes on what was for sale: cheap Chinese clothes, aluminum pots, knives, enamel basins — no food. Since I was the only *faranji* in town, I attracted attention, and boys began following me.

"Please give me one birr. I am poor and I am a schoolboy."

They took turns begging. I said no, to discourage them from pestering *faranjis. Is this the right thing to do?* I wrote in my diary that night. *I don't know.* Everywhere I went, from Cairo to Cape Town, people — kids mostly — had their hand out: "Meesta, meesta." These kids in Mega I gave some of the Abu Dhabi cookies before shooing them away.

Tadelle said it was too hot to continue for now. We would stay in

Mega for a few hours and set off again for Moyale later in the afternoon. We sat in the shade, Tadelle genially complaining about Ethiopian politicians ("Zey are termites"), and we were joined by some girls from a shop who brought us bottled water. To kill time, I demonstrated the blades of my Swiss Army knife.

"One month's salary," Tadelle said when I answered his question about the price of it — fifty dollars, I had said. But most Ethiopians earned nothing at all.

We ate some more pineapple, and the girls asked for pieces.

"*Sebat birr,*" I said, and they laughed because that's what they had charged me for the bottled water.

I loved watching the pretty girls gorging themselves on the fruit, the pulp on their fingers, the juice on their lips and running down their chins.

Tadelle said to me, "Instead of Kenya, come wiz Wolde and me and we travel togezzer. We teach you Amharic. We have good times. We go in za bush."

He explained this in Tigrinya to Wolde, who smiled and said "*Isshi*" — an emphatic yes.

I was tempted, and would have liked nothing better, but whenever I looked at the map of Africa I was reminded of the trip I had set for myself, what a long road it was to Cape Town. If Tadelle and Wolde had been going south, I would have gone with them, but they were traveling west to Konso and Jinka and the Omo River, regions of buttock-naked people and lovely handmade ornaments.

On the last leg to Moyale, a gun-toting soldier in camouflage fatigues — sticking out in the brown grass by the roadside — waved his weapon at us. Tadelle stopped, and after a laconic conversation the soldier got into the back seat with Wolde. Only a hitchhiker, but an armed one. I could tell from Tadelle's demeanor that he hated the man and was thinking: Termite.

The soldier had some information, but it was bad news. "The Oromo were fighting the Somalis here last week," he said.

Nearer Moyale, the soldier muttered something and Tadelle slowed down. After the soldier got out, Tadelle said, "I don't trust zis man."

Somalis were everywhere — women with bundles, men driving goats ahead of them.

"Any trouble here, Tadelle?"

"Zey are poor people," he said.

We had come to a very infertile and inhospitable landscape: no trees and lots of idle squatting people. Some had the look of refugees with scruffy-looking bundles, others were just chancers and riffraff, urchins, the detribalized, the lost, the Artful Dodgers who gravitate to national frontiers. We were at the brow of a hill. Below was a dry riverbed and a cleared area — no man's land — and beyond it Kenya, looking even dryer than the Ethiopian side.

"Zey are all thieves and termites — be careful," Tadelle said.

He found a parking place while I went to the border post, an empty one-story building standing in a patch of waste ground. I was told that the border would be open at six the next morning. No information was available about onward transport in Kenya. I returned to the vehicle. Tadelle said angrily that someone had kicked off half his front bumper and stolen it.

Just then a white Land Rover went by. An idealistic slogan relating to hunger in Africa was lettered on the door, two *faranjis* inside.

"Could you give me a lift across the border?" I asked them.

"This isn't a taxi," one of the men said — a West Country accent.

"I was looking for a place to stay on the other side."

"We don't run a guest house," the other one said — a Londoner.

They drove away, leaving me by the side of the road. That was to be fairly typical of my experience with aid workers in rural Africa: they were, in general, oafish self-dramatizing prigs, and often complete bastards.

I walked back to Tadelle's vehicle and saw that Wolde was crying.

"What's wrong with Wolde?"

"Wolde is so sad to see you go."

Wolde hid his face in his hands and sobbed. I was touched and a bit confused. He did not speak English, but Tadelle had a habit of translating our conversations for him, so he had shared everything we had discussed on the long road.

We found a hotel, the worst one yet but the best in Moyale, the Ysosadayo, three dollars a night for a mosquito-haunted room in the block behind it, pasta for a dollar, beer fifty cents, electricity that came and went. The hot, airless room smelled of cockroaches and dust; the bed was as hard and stinky as a prison cot. I gave ten dollars each in birr to Tadelle and Wolde and then walked around Moyale, asking questions. Within an hour, I found out that cattle trucks left the Kenya side for Marsabit at seven in the morning, that they took eight hours to reach Marsabit; no, they took ten hours to Marsabit; no, twelve. No, it was two days to Nairobi, or three, or if the truck broke down ("they always break down"), four days.

The longest road in Africa ran ever onward to the horizon, into the big bare country of hot hills in the distance, beyond the steel pipe that served as a customs and immigration barrier. Wherever I walked, I was followed and pestered for money in the insolent way of people who have nothing to lose. But the *faranjis* who came here were vagabonds themselves, and so no one was surprised when I said "*Yellem*" — there is nothing for you. There was no running water in Moyale. The Ysosadayo had a cistern; the shops got by with buckets. The principal activity on the long north–south road was carrying water, young boys and girls whacking donkeys on the hindquarters, each donkey loaded with four eight-gallon tins of water, back and forth across the border — for the water came from a well on the Kenyan side. In the no man's land between the two countries a crazy man in rags with matted hair lived in a little lean-to.

Wolde was still upset when I saw him again, but he was wearing a new shirt. He was friendly, helpful, not hustling for a tip but naturally good-hearted. I greatly regretted this parting, and felt that I could go far with them — our little team. They were game for adventure and would be loyal, Tadelle a good driver, the middle-aged pessimist ("I hate zis country, zey are all termites"), and Wolde the youthful optimist, eager to please. We could go to the ends of the earth — though we were probably already there, for that was not a bad description of Moyale.

Tadelle had bought a new jacket, two shirts, a pair of shoes, and khaki trousers, and he still had change from the ten dollars I had given him. The clothes had been smuggled from the Kenya side to the Moyale market.

"I like clothes," Tadelle said with feeling. He had changed into his new clothes and wore his jacket in spite of the heat. It was in the nineties, well after sundown.

He and Wolde wore their new clothes around Moyale, looking quite different from anyone else in town.

Dinner — cold pasta, warm beer — was a somber affair. Wolde was still snuffling with grief, and Tadelle was quietly uttering treasonous remarks. Then the lights failed and there was silence.

At last, in the darkness, Tadelle said, "My name mean 'gift.'"

"That's a nice name."

"Zere was one man," he said. "Adam."

"Yes," I said.

"He have children."

"Yes. They found the bones in Ethiopia." The Lucy skeleton, bow-legged and tiny and apelike — I had seen it in the museum.

"According to air conditioning," Tadelle said, meaning weather and climate, "za children were different colors."

"Yes," I said.

"I am black, you are red."

"Yes."

At the far end of the table, in the shadows, Wolde began quietly to sob.

"But we are bruzzers."

8 ◇◇◇

Figawi Safari on the Bandit Road

ONLY CATTLE TRUCKS went south, in a straggling convoy of ten vehicles or so. "Because of the shifta." The name was derived from a raiding, plundering, bloodthirsty Somali clan, the Mshifta, but now shifta meant any roaming bandit in the great desert that extended from Somalia to Sudan and took in the whole of northern Kenya. The shifta tended to raid remote settlements and ambush isolated people and vehicles on the road. There were only a few roads and there were many shifta.

Buses did not operate on this north–south road. There were no place names on my map, just Marsabit, in the middle of the Dida Galgalu Desert — Samburu land — a day's drive south. I was reassured by the fact that the trucks were full of cattle and not people, for in these parts cattle were valuable and people's lives not worth much at all. Even when tribesmen were shot here on this border, no one troubled to file a report. They only said, "The Borena are fighting," or the Oromo, or the Somalis, or the shifta. No one knew the body count. If cattle had been slaughtered or rustled, the exact number would have been known and lamented.

Each truck held twenty head of cattle. I paid three dollars to ride in the cab with the driver and three women, two infants, and a bronchitic boy, a tubercular child of six or seven whom I caught drinking out of my water bottle. The women, one of whom was nursing a baby, were veiled and, being married, wore henna on their hands and feet. The lovely lacy floral designs seized my attention, even at seven on this hot morning in this stifling cab.

"Do not leave your seat, *bwana*, someone will steal it," said the tout who had taken my money.

Such a surprise that, having traveled only half a mile across the border, everyone here spoke Swahili.

After a great deal of shouting and quarreling and a fight — a man had been thrown off the back for not paying up; he was defending his dignity by slapping at the men who had tossed him aside — we set off down the bad road south, into the heat and dust. The animals shuddered and trembled, and on the worst stretches of road some of them fell down and were trampled and trapped by the others. The road deteriorated into a rutted, rock-strewn track as soon as we left the border. There were three keepers among the cattle, who attacked the fallen animals, twisting their tails and smashing them in the face with sticks to get them upright. All the cattle were going to a slaughterhouse in Nairobi, and they were a melancholy sight, these animals, for they had rather benign faces and trusting eyes, and dumb and docile they were off to be butchered. In the absence of refrigerated trucks they had to be taken alive to be killed and drained of their blood, by the halal method stipulated by the Muslim faith.

The driver, Mustafa, was a grumpy chain-smoking young man who apparently spoke only Swahili. "*Wewe, muzungu,*" he said to me when he wanted my attention. "You, white man." This overfamiliar form of address was extremely rude, but he was used to dealing with oafish, budget-conscious backpackers. He clearly hated his job, and you couldn't blame him — the cab jammed with people, the truck bed filled with animals, and more men seated on the upper rungs, squatting on the cab roof, and hanging from the sides, many of them chewing khat to stay serene.

I had seen poor roads on this trip, but this one was spectacularly bad, worse than the no-road route through the Sudanese desert. This was a narrow track of deep, wheel-swallowing potholes and sudden ruts, hard steep waves of them that made the truck jiggle and jump. But the worst of it were the loose boulders. Broken and very sharp, they were so large they sent the truck in a toppling motion as it climbed them and plunged, throwing the cattle to the floor. Although still early morning, the day was very hot, there was no shade, and the land stretched ahead, white and dazzling, like an alkali desert. We were traveling at about ten miles an hour and had two hundred miles ahead of us.

African children seldom cry — almost a miracle the way they are as patient as their parents — but the ones in the cab were screaming.

Because of the fighting in the area — yes, as the soldier had said, the Oromo had attacked some police posts — we had to stop at frequent checkpoints. Being African checkpoints, each one was a financial opportunity for the armed men who controlled it, so every roadblock was a shakedown. Mustafa palmed money to the men and drove on, grumbling.

I missed the congenial company of Tadelle and Wolde, missed the much better roads and greenery of Ethiopia, missed the Ethiopian courtesies. I consoled myself with the thought that I had successfully made the transition into Kenyan territory. I was proceeding south according to plan.

At midmorning we stopped at a group of tin-roofed sheds by the roadside.

"*Chakula*," Mustafa said. Food.

Platters of fatty goat meat and lumps of gray coarse porridge the Kenyans call *ugali* were set on a table in dirty enamel bowls. The Africans, men first, pushed toward the food-splashed table and fell on it, snatching food and stuffing their mouths. I bought Mustafa a Coke to ingratiate myself and asked him when we might get to Marsabit.

He shrugged, swigged the Coke, and said, "*Si jui*" — I dunno.

The other Africans were breezy, too, even insolent, lots of *Wewe, muzungu,* and one man chewing a bone poked his goat-greased finger at me: "*Wewe, mzee.*"

"Hey, you old man," eh? This can be a term of affection or respect, as it was when Jomo Kenyatta's title was *Mzee,* emphasizing that he was an elder and a leader. But it was pretty clear to me that I was being mocked as an oldster.

"*Hapana mzee*" — Not old — I said in kitchen Swahili. Kitchen Swahili was all these northerners spoke, for they were Borena and Samburu people mainly, desert dwellers without a common language. Swahili was grammatical and subtle only on the coast and in the few cities.

"*Mimi vijana*," the man said, asserting his youth.

Another man, with no fingers on his right hand, hitting a goat bone with his left fist, seemed to be narrating in his language, Borena, that he was eating the best part, the marrow, which he smacked onto the table in a glutinous lump. He smeared it with his fingers and ate it greedily.

Outside, some of the other trucks in the convoy had also stopped here, and soldiers traveling with them asked me if there was trouble (*shauri*) where I had come from.

"There is war in Ethiopia? You have seen?"

These ignorant inhabitants, traveling on a hideous road in an overheated desert, in a neglected province of one of the most corrupt and distressed and crime-ridden countries in Africa, regarded sunny, threadbare, but dignified Ethiopia as a war zone.

When we set off again I noticed that one of the soldiers had climbed onto the back of Mustafa's truck. I was not sure whether I was concerned or relieved that we were traveling with a soldier carrying a high-caliber rifle.

The settlements visible in the desert were all Borena or Borena subtribes — the Mbuji people, the Ledile, the Gabra. They were all handsome men and attractive women, who lived sparely among their diminishing flocks of goats. Even though they were herding the creatures over this vast desert, there was not much grazing available. No rain had fallen for three years, and the people were being forced to eat their animals, which were their wealth. When we passed a mission station I saw Ledile people, just sitting, looking gaunt.

Besides the herds there was little else to eat; hardly any wildlife survived here. I saw some of the small deer called dik-diks and, of course, birds: kites, hawks, pigeons, and where there were thorn trees weaverbirds darted around their many nests.

The road extended straight ahead — rocky, rubbly, pitted with holes — to the distant horizon, cutting between two lakes. The lakes were magnificent, shimmering in the sunlight, flat expanses of water mirroring the sky and lending a coolness to the landscape, which invited the traveler and promised relief. But the lakes were mirages; only the rubbly road was real.

We were going so slowly that when a rear tire blew at two o'clock I heard not only the blowout like a pistol shot but the hissing as the air streamed out. Mustafa brought the truck to a halt and got out, cursing.

It was the inside tire — there were eight on the rear axles, two sets of four, to support the heavy weight of the cattle. A small rusty jack was dragged out and assembled, and slowly the truck was raised, the wheels taken off, the blown tire examined. It was not just a hole in the tube but a rent in the tire that was so large the African examining it could put his whole arm through it.

That was to be expected here — by me, anyway. Apparently not by Mustafa and the others, for they had no spare. They shook out junk from a burlap sack — tubes, patches, big crowbars, flat pieces of iron, tubes of glue, and something that looked like an antique foot-driven bellows — and began amateurishly to whack the wheel, as though they had never been in this fix before. Their iron tools bent as they tried to pry the tire from the rim.

They took turns fighting the tire and failing, while the rest of us stood in the intense desert sun. There was no shade, no relief from the blinding light and heat. Several men crawled into the semidarkness under the jacked-up truck and went to sleep.

Mustafa, who rarely spoke and did so only in Swahili, offered his opinion in English, saying to me, "Thees focking bad road."

I thought: This is not good — a breakdown in the desert, in a place where no one cares whether I live or die. I am stranded among the most incompetent and unresourceful mechanics I have ever seen.

An hour of this and then a loaded cattle truck rumbled past us, not stopping, obviously not giving a shit about the fix we were in. But this truck reminded me that we were supposed to be traveling in a convoy. I also thought: I should have bailed and gone with them. I walked a short distance from our dilemma and searched the horizon for another truck. After twenty minutes or so I saw clouds of rising dust: a truck.

I stood in the road and waved at the approaching truck — another cattle hauler — and when it slowed I climbed up to the cab, which was crammed with women and children, and asked for a ride.

"You can come," the driver said, "but you must ride on top."

I got my bag from Mustafa's truck and threw it up to the men riding on top, then hurried after it, for the truck had not really stopped but continued to roll past Mustafa's stranded vehicle and the assembled klutzes who were fiddling with the patches — one slapping an enormous chunk of rubber against the hole in the tire as a possible fix. It was likely that they would be there tomorrow, among dying cattle, still faffing with the flat tire.

I saw them recede into the distance. Balanced on the frame over the cab, I held on to the pipe railing in the hot wind and choking dust. The truck swayed, very unstable because of the high center of gravity and the weight of the cattle.

Yet I was calm, even happy. I wrapped my jacket around me to protect me from the dust and watched the suffering cattle. Weak from thirst, tottering from the movement of the truck, slumping to their knees and now and then knocked to the truck bed, they were getting smacked in the chops and their tails twisted. I could hear their pained mooing over the chunking of the wheels on the road.

Deep in the desert were the camel trains of the Borena, pure panic cloaked in beauty, the yellow-robed women walking ahead, the men guiding the camels. It was a lovely sight, yet it was a matter of life or death, illustrating the desperate need for water. No rain, no nearby wells, so the camel train had to travel a great distance and return laden with jerry cans and drums of water. The camels were covered in heavy tin containers, slopping the animals' shanks.

I had to hold on to stay upright. The road was not only rocky but here it ceased to be straight. It wound between huge humps, too small to be hills, but obstructions all the same. We slowed down. I could not see ahead. I was relieved that now I did not have to cling so tightly.

Then I heard a loud bang and thought, Oh, no, a blowout. But another bang followed it, and the men on top pushed past me to dive into the mass of groaning cattle.

I got a glimpse of two men in dusty robes, their faces hidden by bands of cloth, standing in the road with rifles held upright, firing into the air.

Two things happened then. First, and startlingly, the man crouched beside me, a soldier, lifted his rifle and began firing directly at the men, both of whom ducked behind boulders. Second, the truck accelerated, moving so fast that it pitched and rolled down the narrow defile between the humpy hills, like a toppling yacht traveling down the face of a wave.

At the same time I dived down from the top bars of the truck with the other men and dangled behind the metal sides (thinking, Is this steel bulletproof?) and over the staggering cattle. We went from five to twenty-five miles an hour, not great acceleration, perhaps, but enough to drag us out of range of the armed men and to demonstrate our resolve to get away.

The men were shifta, classic highwaymen positioned in a perfect place. The truck had slowed to a crawl in a spot that was squeezed between two hiding places, and the men had stepped out and fired in the air to get our attention. Perhaps they had not counted on being fired upon; more likely they were surprised by the driver's stamping on the gas and getting us out of there.

The soldier clinging to the bars beside me on our truck shook his head and laughed.

I said, "Shifta?"

"Yah." He smiled at my grim face.

I said, *"Sitaki kufa."* I don't want to die.

He said in English, "They do not want your life, *bwana.* They want your shoes."

Many times after that, in my meandering through Africa, I mumbled these words, an epitaph of underdevelopment, desperation in a single sentence. What use is your life to them? It is nothing. But your shoes — ah, they are a different matter. They are worth something, much more than your watch (they had the sun) or your pen (they were illiterate) or your bag (they had nothing to put in it). These were men who needed footwear, for they were forever walking.

When we were under way again the truck moved with greater urgency, the cattle falling faster than ever on top of each other, the ragged cowboys manhandling them. But soon we came to a checkpoint and had to stop. Four soldiers manned this checkpoint, deliberately dawdling, demanding to see my passport ("*Wewe, muzungu*"), and being officious.

This checkpoint reassured me; it seemed as though it might serve as a barrier to keep the bandits at bay. The other passengers who had been riding on top seemed to think so, too. They resumed their seats, the road improved, and we were moving quickly now toward higher ground, the hills ahead, and the setting sun. The greenery was not a mirage but rather the natural foliage of the town of Marsabit.

The truck came to a halt in the market of this small dirty settlement. I lowered myself to the ground and realized that I was trembling, with a hint of that hysterical happiness that takes hold when you have just had a close call, the giddy certainty that you have survived.

I walked around and found a place to stay, the Jey-Jey, a hotel run by a genial Muslim, who also called me *mzee.* Was it my impending birthday that made this word a particular irritation? Another three-dollar room. I had a shower in the communal washhouse, then walked to the market, drank a Tusker beer, and talked to some locals, boasting, "I got shot at!" No one was surprised or impressed. They shrugged: "It's the shifta road."

Back at the Jey-Jey, I met a man who had just arrived, having been at the rear of the convoy. He was an exhausted-looking Englishman — sweaty, dirty, unshaven, pissed off, red-eyed, laboring with a heavy duffle bag.

"How's it going?"

"We got shot at!" he shouted.

"So did we," I said, "back where the road winds between those mounds."

"We must have been right behind you," he said in a strong Lancashire accent. "But they got nowt. I fucking floored it, and the soldiers up top were shooting to kill."

He was Ben Barker, driver of a truck carrying paying passengers on an overland trip. After dinner we found his brother Abel, who was one of his mechanics, and went for a beer in the Marsabit market. Ben described his route. He had fixed up an old diesel truck and started from his home in Grange-over-Sands, traveled east via Turkey, then through Syria, Jordan, Egypt, and Sudan — a barge across Lake Nasser. He too was headed to Cape Town. He had seven backpackers on board and was happy, for a small fee, to include me as far as Nairobi.

"I don't mind the driving," Ben said. "The worst of this sort of traveling is when the people in the truck get all south-faced and whingey. 'And why can't we see the crocodiles, then?' 'Why are we driving today?' 'Can't we bloody stop for a while?'"

Scruffy though it was, Marsabit was an oasis in the middle of widely scattered villages of pastoralists whose animals were in bad shape because of the successive droughts, and agriculturalists whose gardens were weedy and stunted. Because of this, Marsabit was the haunt of aid workers and agents of virtue, many of whose spiffy white Land Rovers were parked at the Jey-Jey.

The model had been described by Mister Kurtz in *Heart of Darkness:* "Each station should be like a beacon on the road towards better things, a center for trade of course, but also for humanizing, improving, instructing." This was, of course, before disillusionment set in and Kurtz became a cannibal chieftain.

A similar scheme had been mooted fifty years earlier than Kurtz's by Mrs. Jellyby in *Bleak House*, who was "devoted to the subject of Africa" and whose obsession, to the utter neglect of her distressed family in London, was an "African project." Her plan involved "the general cultivation of the coffee berry — *and* the natives — and the happy settlement on the banks of the African rivers, of our superabundant home population . . . educating the natives of Borrioboola-Gha on the left bank of the Niger."

Fiona and Rachel worked for a British charity. What Kurtz was trying to accomplish on the Congo, and Mrs. Jellyby on the Niger, they were attempting in the region of Marsabit. They were on their weekly trip up from the south. They were in their mid-twenties, damp-faced from the heat and their long drive. They had a driver, however, and a high-tech vehicle that was worth a fortune. Am I imagining that the logo on the side showed a weeping continent and the slogan *Shed Tears for Africa*?

"We have a wet feeding tomorrow," Fiona said.

Rachel said, "Ninety underweight children, some of them malnourished, infants up to four-year-olds."

"What is a wet feeding?"

"That's porridge. Unimix for nutrition — maize, beans, oil, some sugar and fat. Americans call it Corn-Soy Blend."

"You are going to a village to dump Unimix in a trough for people to eat."

"I wouldn't put it that way," Fiona said.

I said, "We used to say, 'Give people seeds and let them grow their own food.'"

"The rains have been unreliable," Rachel said.

"Maybe they should relocate. If they relocated they might find work, and they might plant gardens if you weren't feeding them."

"We save lives, not livelihoods," Fiona said, and it sounded like a phrase from a brochure that might have been drafted by Mrs. Jellyby.

I said, "Or family planning advice — you could give them that."

"We don't discuss family planning," Rachel said. "We feed children under five and lactating mothers. Why are you looking at me like that?"

"I don't know," I said. "Something about 'supervising a wet feeding.' It sounds like something you'd do in a game park."

They were insulted, and I was sorry I'd said it like that, because they were obviously hardworking and determined. They had come a long way to dish up porridge for some ashen-faced tots in the north Kenyan desert.

I said, "In a game park, in a bad year, the rangers might spread some bales of alfalfa near a water hole to help the hippos make it through the season."

They looked at me, unhappy to be challenged.

I said, "And what would happen if you just sent the food?"

"Their parents would steal it and let the kids die."

In other words, natural selection. It was why the Samburu were so tough: the strongest survived, weak children died. Children died all the time in Africa, and yet even with AIDS and infant mortality the population growth was the highest in the world. But it had been high in Victorian England as well. In Thomas Hardy's novel *Jude the Obscure,* the doomed and starving village children leave a note: "Because we are too menny."

Fiona and Rachel were good-hearted and earnest in their mission. But it fascinated me that in order to feed these "underweight children" they had to battle the parents, who wanted (and who could blame them?) to snatch the food from the children's mouths. Or was this overdramatizing the situation, for there was often a tone of melodrama among relief workers, charity in Africa frequently being a form of theater.

"How long will you be doing this?"

"I'm leaving next week," Fiona said.

"I've got a month more," Rachel said.

"So it's possible that these people you've been feeding with Unimix will be left in the lurch after you go."

"The whole scheme comes up for review in a few months," Fiona said, turning bureaucratic.

To satisfy myself, I visited Marsabit's secondary school the next morning and met one of the head teachers, Mr. Maina, who had lived in Marsabit his whole life, except for the years he had spent getting his education degree. He denied that anyone in the district was without food. He emphasized that there was more food than ever because of the government's indifference to traditional cash crops.

"The farmers in Kenya are very demoralized, because the government does not support them," Mr. Maina said. "In so many places the farmers have torn up their coffee bushes to grow cabbages and maize for subsistence."

"Why doesn't the government care?"

"Why should they care? They get money from the World Bank and the IMF and America and Germany and everyone else."

In a word, Kenya's government too was dependent on its own version of Unimix, in the form of donor-country money. It was a proven fact that this money went into the pockets of politicians. At that moment, Dr. Richard Leakey, a white Kenyan, headed a commission to uncover corruption in Kenya. But within weeks of uncovering a great deal of corruption, Leakey was removed from his post and fighting a corruption charge himself, leveled against him by the Kenyan government.

◇ ◇ ◇

Besides Ben and Abel Barker on the overland Africa truck, there was Mick, a Yorkshireman, who as chief mechanic quietly boasted of having a complete welding kit, a spare engine, and a generator. The seven paying passengers were seriously shaken, the effect of having been attacked and shot at by shifta the day before. One, Jade, from New Zealand, was asthmatic, and the stress was giving her symptoms of suffocation — or was that caused by dust blowing through the open truck? Another, a Canadian of about twenty — an immigrant from Ukraine — welcomed me aboard, then gave me an insane grin.

"Yeah, this is a good day to die," he said as I swung myself onto the truck. He said this often; he had no other conversation. Not so much a victim of post-traumatic stress as a natural pain in the ass.

And there were two soldiers, a smiling one who never spoke and a cross, talkative one named Andrew, who grumbled from the moment we left Marsabit. The sight of Samburu tribesmen on the road — in bright togas, with earrings and beads, carrying rifles and walking sticks — roused him to fury.

"They are all shifta," Andrew said. "Him and him. And over there, all of them. The government supplies them with guns because the people demand it. 'We want to protect our cattle.' But they use the guns to attack people on this road. Forty people have been killed in the past two months."

We were in scrubby desert, as desolate and dry and vast as the day before, and the road was just as bad. I was sitting in the truck with the shell-shocked backpackers: gasping Jade, two girls named Rebecca and Laura with earphones on their heads, listening to Tracy Chapman, Mick's girlfriend, Judy (Mick was in the cab with Ben), Abel stretched out on a bench, and the Canadian grinning at the road ahead, murmuring "This is a good day to die."

Besides the Samburu, Rendille people also inhabited this area. The Rendille were so ornamented and colorful they often appeared on postcards. *Kenyan Warriors in Traditional Costume*, the cards said. They wore stiff beaded visors on their brows and tight braided locks smeared with red ocher and shaking at the back of their heads; they bristled with elaborate necklaces, gorgets of red and white beads, armlets, bracelets, anklets. Part of their attire were weapons: throwing clubs shaped like maracas jammed into their beaded belts, and knives with decorative sheaths. They carried spears and wore bright red sarongs. They were the personification of adornment, and you could spot one of these Rendille warriors a mile away in the Dida Galgalu Desert, which was perhaps the whole point.

Two of them waved us down on the road in the middle of nowhere. We picked them up, but their Swahili was so rudimentary the soldiers could not converse with them. One said "Laisamis" — the soldiers recognized the name as a mission thirty miles away. They sat, saying nothing, but allowed themselves to be photographed by Rebecca.

Laisamis, a Catholic mission, was also a desert settlement of Rendille people. There were no trees, there was no shade, yet it was market day, hundreds of gaily dressed people squatting in the dust among a large church, a small school, a bore hole, and many scattered, crudely built huts. Rendille ornamentation was limited to the person; the huts were simply rounded masses of twigs and thatch, inhabited by people in brilliant plumage. A line from Conrad came to mind: "There was no joy in the brilliance of sunshine."

Jade, the asthmatic, begged to stay awhile in Laisamis, saying that she was having trouble breathing. She looked very ill, her eyes sunken and red, her face pale, and during her worst attacks her lips turned blue. The back of the truck in the heat and blowing dust of the Dida Galgalu Desert was no place for an asthmatic, and Jade was clearly suffering but did not complain. While Ben tried to get her electric nebulizer working — he said he might be an hour — I went bird watching in a grove of thorn trees at the edge of the desert. Apart from the hawks and the vultures, I saw a grackle-sized bird, red and black and brilliant green, a lovely bird with a lovely name, the superb starling.

An off-duty Kenyan policeman named Mark strolled over to the truck and said he needed a lift. Ben obliged him, because although he was in street clothes he had his pistol with him, and another weapon was useful on this road of ambush-minded shifta. Mark was a Samburu.

"After you are circumcised, you make the choice to go to school or look after the animals," Mark said. "If you look after the animals, you dress as these men do. We call them *limooli*" — that was how he wrote it, but he pronounced it *mowlé*. "My brother is one. The Rendille copied this from us."

"My asthma's playing up again," Jade said. She was fighting for breath and apologetic and looked awful, but she had a support group of sympathetic women in the truck — Sarah, Laura, Judy, and Rebecca, who attended her with medicine and atomizers. The shifta ambush had bonded them. Sarah, who was nineteen and about to enter an English university, had sobbed with fear after the gunshots.

In the early afternoon, riding down the road, there was a terrific bang, so sharp, so loud, we all dived to the floor. The two soldiers snatched their rifles and looked for shifta as Ben drove on. But there were no more bangs. In fact, the truck was slowing down.

"We blew a tire," Mick said, sticking his head out of the cab.

"Yesterday we thought it was a tire," Judy said. "But it was shooting."

No one regretted hitting the deck. It served as emergency drill.

"Yeah, this is a good day to die," the Canadian said.

We limped four miles to a cluster of huts, so few of them they were hardly worthy of the name of a village. The place was called Serolevi. It existed because there was a barrier in the road, and being a military checkpoint it had a name. This was in the heart of Samburu land, in the desert of scrubby bushes and dead thorn trees and overdressed and overornamented Samburu herdboys. No shade, nowhere to sit, just dust and gravel, a handful of lost-looking people and some indolent policemen.

Mick and Abel jacked up the truck, Ben supervising. The tire was changed in half an hour. This speed was in great contrast to the cackhanded incompetence shown by Mustafa and his men the day before. While they worked, I looked around the settlement and thought: God, what an awful place. There was a shop — a shed with one shelf, and on the shelf raw blocks of soap, rice, maize flour, dry crackers, and Kasuku Brand fat. *Kasuku* is Swahili for "parrot," so I made a predictable joke about parrot fat, and the woman shop owner sighed with boredom.

"Those mountains ahead," Ben said as we were loading the tools. "Isiolo is behind them."

Isiolo was our objective, the edge of the desert, a decent sized town with food and water.

"Archer's Post is before that," Andrew, the soldier, said. "That is the worst place for shifta."

It was the thing I hated hearing from an African: There are bad people ahead.

I asked if I could ride in the cab. Ben said "Fine" and we set off again, Mick at the side window, me in the middle. The road was so bumpy, with long deep holes that made the truck thump and roll, that both Mick and I braced ourselves, our feet against the dashboard.

On an especially bad stretch of road the truck rose and fell heavily, the chassis banging hard with the sound of a hammer on an anvil. Ben came alert at the wheel, his head cocked, and said, "Shit."

Mick said, "What?"

"She's listing. Fuck." We rolled to a halt and Ben got out to examine the undercarriage, then delivered the news. "We knackered a spring. Three big leaves. Chassis's resting on the axle. Shit. Fuck. I was afraid of that. Shit." He put the truck into gear and began making a U-turn. "I was dreading this road ever since we left Cairo."

"So was I," I said.

"Why didn't you take the flipping plane?"

"Because I wanted to see what was on this dreaded road."

"A thousand miles of hassle," Ben said.

But Mick was thinking about the broken spring. He said, "Got to weld the leaves. Maybe chain her up, or summat."

We drove back very slowly to Serolevi, the settlement that had made my heart sink. Our escort soldiers became agitated, even the one who was normally calm. "We fix and go," the irritable one said. Ben did not even bother replying. The damage was serious. Even I could see the smashed spring and the body of the heavy truck threatening to snap the axle.

Mick jacked up the truck and set out the tools — generator, welding gear, steel boxes, basins of socket wrenches and spares, extra spring leaves. As the sun descended toward the desert horizon, he and Abel took turns trying to dislodge the broken springs. When dusk fell, they had still made little headway.

Ben said to me, "Fancy spending a night in the desert?"

"We must leave right now," the agitated soldier said. "These people will take advantage of us."

Yanking on a broken spring leaf with a crowbar, Ben, unperturbed, said, "Oh, aye."

Counting the soldiers, there were twelve of us, and darkness would soon be upon us — hunger, too. Bored already with sitting, I said I would put myself in charge of the evening meal. There were chickens running around; there was rice in the shop. The friendliest person in the village was a Kikuyu woman named Helen, who wore a green dress and said, "I am a missionary of the Full Gospel Church. I am bringing Jesus here."

"Are these your chickens?"

She said they were, and that for 1,700 shillings, about $20, she would kill three chickens and make enough potato stew and chapatis to feed the twelve of us and some of her family.

Darkness had fallen. Helen began to stoke three cooking fires, and over by the truck the welding had begun, Mick squinting through a small piece of smoked glass because his welding mask was broken. The bright sparks of the welding attracted people from huts at the edge of Serolevi, who sat and watched the action.

I helped Helen peel potatoes. I was impressed by her cooking skill and appalled by the disorder, for she squatted in a mass of chicken feathers and eviscerated birds and potato peels, hot coals and pots of sloshing water. But this was the Serolevi method: smoky fires, dented stew pots, scorched meat.

I sent a small boy to the shop for a bottle of beer and then sat on a log, peeling potatoes and swigging beer and feeling an obscure sense of contentment.

"Beer is bad," Helen said, giggling.

"Beer is not mentioned in the Bible," I said. "Jesus drank wine. He also made wine. Preferred it to water. Changed water into wine at the wedding feast at Cana. His own mother requested it. Where does it say that alcohol is bad?"

"In Galatians."

"Where Paul condemns drunkenness and reveling?" I said, "Helen, I wouldn't have thought a warm bottle of Tusker outside a mud hut in Samburu land constituted drunken reveling. What?"

Helen saw the joke and laughed, but she said, "You will not be saved."

"A man asked Jesus, 'Good master, how shall I find the Kingdom of Heaven?' Jesus said, 'Love thy neighbor. Obey the commandments.'"

"John says you must be born again. You're a good peeler," she said, hoisting the potatoes.

She was good-natured and quick and thirty-two years old — the average life expectancy in Kenya was just over forty. She was not married.

"You haven't met Mr. Right."

"Jesus is Mr. Right." She was slapping dough now, clapping it between her hands, making chapatis.

Feeling fortunate, I laughed, drank another Tusker, and thought: I love this place, I love sitting in the pink afterglow of sunset, peeling spuds and talking about salvation. The heat of the day had gone, the air was mild, and there were children everywhere, fooling, fussing, teasing each other among the flaring fires and the aromatic steam of chicken and potatoes.

Darkness lay around us. The only points of light were the cooking fires and the blinding blue arc of the welding torch. Then the torch died: the generator was out of gasoline, and the welding could not be completed until more gasoline was brought from Archer's Post. We might be stuck here for a few more days. I did not care. Others found it appalling.

This dire news seemed to bring on Jade's serious asthma attack. She said she could not breathe. She was made comfortable by the helpful backpackers, and soon a Land Rover full of robed Somalis arrived at the checkpoint. Jade begged them to take her; "I need to get to a hospital." They stuffed her in the back of their vehicle with Laura and sped south into the darkness.

The rest of us had dinner. The local headman, a young man named Chief George, joined us, and so did a few others who had been hanging around looking hungry. There were fifteen of us altogether. I helped Helen dish up the food.

Scooping with a bent spoon, I said, "This may be one of the few occasions when you've been waited on by a member of the American Academy of Arts and Letters."

Hearing "American," Chief George said, "I hear some American people are poor. We do not think of whites as poor. Also that some cannot speak English. How can this be in America?"

He claimed that Samburu herdsmen could walk forty miles a day, and that women could walk faster and farther than men. He said, "Women have a better rhythm. Men walk fast, then have to rest. Women don't rest."

That night, I lay and drowsed on a padded shelf of the open jacked-up truck. The dry air was dead still and odorless. No water meant no insects. Silence and darkness and no one stirring. The almost full moon, deep orange from the risen dust, appeared late, casting a glow on the desert around us.

In the morning, the Canadian backpacker saw me and said, "This is a good day to die." He looked around Serolevi, the dead thorn trees, the scattered children, our damaged truck. "Yeah."

"I don't think so."

"Do I get the prize for being the craziest guy on the truck?" he asked.

"Yes."

"Know where we are? Figawi. For 'where the fuck are we?'"

"The figawi safari."

"Yeah. Looks like we're stuck today, too. Want to smoke some herb?"

All he did was gabble. Meanwhile, Abel had hitched a ride to Archer's Post to buy more gasoline for the generator. The night had been benign, but daylight was a reminder that there was no shade here, nowhere to sit except on the log in front of Helen's hut. By midmorning no vehicles had passed in either direction and the temperature was back in the nineties.

What I had taken to be an improvised squatter settlement near an army checkpoint was in fact a village of several hundred Samburus. It was the checkpoint that was improvised. The schoolhouse was empty, unused — "no money for teachers" — but there was a bar, a tin-roofed shack where men drank beer throughout the day, starting at eight in the morning and fighting over space at the small pool table. On the side of the bar was a sign in Swahili and English:

MINISTRY OF HEALTH, UNFPA — UN POPULATION FUND.
PROTECT YOURSELF AND YOUR FRIENDS. USE A CONDOM.
HELP YOURSELF BELOW.

But the tin dispenser was empty.

Boys ornamented in the traditional *limooli* fashion — spears, skirts, beads — tended goats in nearby fields, and now and then children appeared with buckets of water. I borrowed a plastic basin from Helen and followed these water carriers to the bore hole, which was a standpipe beyond the abandoned schoolhouse. Water dribbled out of the pipe. I put down my basin and watched the water slowly piddling and calculated that it would take the best part of an hour to fill a bucket.

When I had a few quarts I went into a field and washed my face and dumped the rest on my head, marveling at the heat of the sun beating on my wet hair. Then I found another log to sit on and began to read. I felt only mildly inconvenienced, because I had no deadline to meet: no one was expecting me. Most of all I felt privileged that I was now in a Samburu village in the middle of the northern Kenya desert, living in perfect safety, talking to local people, and observing a way of life that was not discernible from the road.

That day, few vehicles went past the checkpoint. The bishop of Marsabit, a voluble Italian named Father Ravisi, sailed through, stopping briefly to hug the villagers and joke with them in Swahili.

"I had a parish in New Jersey for twenty years," he said. Now his parish was one of the biggest and wildest in Africa.

The welding seemed to be going very slowly, though Mick was still kneeling, pinching a small piece of smoked glass in front of one eye, and torching a leaf. The only person who seriously minded the delay was the grumpier of the two soldiers. I realized that his complaining had its origin in fear: fear of a late start, fear of being ambushed, fear of the darkness that allowed shifta to approach.

I was chatting with a policeman at the checkpoint when a white Land Rover — another aid group's vehicle, a medical-charity logo on the side — drove up and came to a halt. The man and woman inside showed their passports. Americans.

"Are you going south?" I asked.

They said they were, and had begun to inch forward as the barrier was lifted.

"I'm with that big truck," I said quickly. "We have a broken spring. Could you give me a lift to Archer's Post or Isiolo?"

"We don't have space," the man said, not making eye contact.

"Yes you do — the whole back seat."

"Sorry."

He was moving but I was walking beside him, my hand on his open window.

I said, "All right, don't help me. We'll get the truck fixed. But it's a long, empty road to Isiolo, and if we see you broken down or in trouble by the side of the road, fuck you, we're going right past you."

This propelled him faster, so I let go. After the dust settled I could hear the zapping of Mick's welding torch and men shouting drunkenly in the bar and children playing. In the truck I found a book about the IRA, *Killing Rage* by Eamon Collins, a former IRA hit man. The book was a memoir but confessional in its truthfulness, full of violence motivated by the sort of tribalism that would not have been out of place in Samburu land. After assisting in many murders, some of them innocent victims — the wrong man or unlucky bystanders — Collins dropped out and went into hiding, where remorsefully he wrote this account of his homicidal pettiness.

Mark, the Samburu policeman who was hitching a ride with us, told me that he wasn't happy traveling with soldiers. "Because if the shifta see them, they know they have to fight," he said. "They will shoot our tires or the radiator. They might shoot the driver. They shot one last week. If they are really hungry, they will shoot us."

"They do not want your life, they want your shoes. That's what I was told."

"If you don't give them your shoes, they will take your life."

This was all unsettling, because being stranded here at Serolevi, we had been left behind by the convoy that was headed to Nairobi. When we finally did set off, we would be going alone, a big lumbering target on an empty road.

Under a tree, with nothing to do, I asked Mark about female circumcision among the Samburu.

"Yes, it is the tradition, everyone does it — the Borena, the Rendille, the Meru. But I have never seen it, because women circumcise women and men circumcise men," he said. "The clitoris is cut off. Completely off."

"Painful," I said.

"Of course painful — she gets no medicine. But she must not show pain. She lies there. She says nothing. It is done so she will not feel pleasure with sex. Otherwise she will need men. But this way her husband can go away and she will remain faithful always."

"At what age?"

"Can be any age. It must be before she is married. If she is to be married at sixteen, it is done then. Or at twenty."

"But she might be having sex before then."

"Of course she is having sex before then. She is having sex from an early age. But" — he gestured for my attention to make sure I understood — "only with her age group."

He explained that there was no sanction against a boy or girl of twelve having sex, or a pair of fourteen-year-olds playing at it, or two fifteen-year-olds. But an older man was forbidden to engage in sex with a young girl unless he had marriage in mind. Within the same age group almost anything was permitted.

"There are risks, though," Mark said. "If the girl becomes pregnant and has a child, she will not find anyone to marry her. A man wants someone fresh, and his own child. The father of the child will deny he is the father if he does not want to marry. She might become a man's second wife, or else not get married at all, just raise her child alone."

"Will she be conspicuous in the village?"

"Yes, because when a woman is circumcised and married she wears different clothes, to show everyone she is a married woman."

This folklore and the IRA book were so depressing I went to Helen's house and planned another meal. This time I did not argue about the Bible. Instead, I let Helen teach me some gospel hymns in Samburu. Helen clapped her hands and sang in a joyous way:

Marango pa nana!
Shumata tengopai!
Na ti lytorian — ni!

[This world is not my home!
My home is in heaven!
Where God is!]

With that promise you were conditioned to brush off the years of drought, the poor harvests, the abandoned schoolhouse, the damaged bore hole with its trickle of water, the awful bar with drunken men, the clitoridectomy, and Kenya's horrible AIDS statistics: they were mere blips in the vale of tears on the way to heaven.

The welding was finished, but there comes a point in all African journeys, usually late in the day, when it is wiser to hunker down with the other prey than stir and tempt the predators, virtually all of whom roam at night. This is as true in the bush as it is in any African city. And so we had another night in Serolevi, another meal, more starlight, and early the following morning we set off for Isiolo, at the edge of the desert.

We did not make it. On a particularly bad stretch of road, where we were expecting shifta, there was a loud bang, and we fell to the floor again. Again it was a blown tire. This did not stop us, but it slowed us, and from the way the vehicle listed it was obvious the welded spring had lost its bounce and was settling onto the axle. We crept along, the chassis banging.

Letting go of the anxiety from the fix we were in — it was clear we would be stranded again soon, so why worry? — I looked at the scenery. No landscape since I had left Cairo had been as beautiful as this desert land of northern Kenya. It had hardly been settled; it was nominally Kenya but it was off the map, its unearthly appearance making it seem enchanted.

We were on a high plain, and although the land was mostly flat and gravelly, there were sudden and stupendous erupted mountains all around it at a distance. Some of them were huge, five- or six-thousand-foot-high bread loaves — tall steep mounds of smooth stone with rounded summits and very little vegetation. They were unlike anything I had ever seen before and suggested the surface of another planet, the dark star of Africa.

Several hours passed as we rolled slowly along, the bruised vehicle on the bad road. The road was famous for bandits, yet it was noon and so hot that nothing stirred, not even dik-diks or camels. For much of that day we had traveled through a land without people. The Canadian man was gabbling. I knew what he was saying, so I turned away and lifted my eyes to the hills.

Archer's Post was a small smudge far away. Seeing it, I reassured myself that if we broke down right here in this wadi I would grab my bag and hike the rest of the way: the distance was walkable. But that was not necessary. The truck was lopsided from the cracked spring and the blown tire flapped, yet we made it to the main street — the only street — in Archer's Post. There, with Ben's news that it might be another night of repair work, and that asthmatic Jade had to be rescued from the hospital, and with the Canadian's grinning — a self-appointed bore with one remark — I made the decision to bail out. I would abandon the congeniality of this overland trip and take my chances with the next bus to Isiolo, if there was a bus. Group tours were not for me.

"Cheerio, mate," Ben called out, waving symbolically with a monkey wrench.

I said goodbye to them all and hoisted my bag onto my shoulder and walked away from the truck. I had seen items in travel magazines all the time advertising "Overland Africa — Experience the Adventure." Now I knew what the adventure entailed. If you are on such a group tour, you are the human cargo, one of a truckload of young people, many of them good-hearted, some of them very silly, sitting on a bench on the truck bed, earphones clamped tight, eating dust, listening to your Enya tape. You might get held up by shifta, you will certainly be held up by flat tires, you will seldom wash. No one calls out "Are we there yet?" because no one except the driver has the slightest idea of the route or the difficulty. We had crossed the wide Dida Galgalu Desert, and north of Marsabit the Ngaso Plain. We had climbed to the Kaisut Plateau and been stranded for two days in Serolevi, on the Losai Reserve, and had traversed the foot of the desert mountain Olkanjo. If you had asked any of them where we had traveled, the answer would have been "Was that where Kevin barfed?" or "Was that where Jade gagged?" or "Was that where the road sucked?" After months of trucking in Africa everyone on board has the dull torpid smile and brain-damaged look of a cultist.

"Aren't you a little old for this, Dad?" my children say when I relate a travel experience that involves the back of a truck. My answer is: Not really. It is not the truck that makes me feel old; big efficient trucks overcome obstacles that baffle little cars. It is the passengers who make me feel — not old, not fogeyish, but out of place. I had been grateful for the ride, grateful to Ben and Mick for their ingenuity and patience. I was also grateful to leave, even if leaving meant wandering down the main street of Archer's Post, a tiny dust-blown town in the middle of nowhere.

Seeing me, teenage boys left their perches at the shops and followed, pestering, asking me where I was going, where I was from. They were used to foreigners in Archer's Post — the Samburu Game Reserve was west of here, and I saw game lodges advertised on signposts at the edge of town. Tourists were sped here in minibuses, fresh from the plane, dressed in expensive safari clothes with pith helmets and khaki jackets. Their trousers had eleven pockets, their sleeves were trimmed in leather and amply gusseted.

When the pestering boys had surrounded me and were making a nuisance of themselves ("*Wewe, muzungu*"), and I was on the point of shouting at them, a jeep approached. I raised my hand for it to stop. It did so: a miracle.

Saved again by another nun, Sister Matilda, with a familiar accent.

"Yes, I am from Sardinia. Get in — we can talk."

And, recalling Italy, we traveled south to Isiolo. It was only an hour away by this fast car, but we had not gone far when the unfamiliar smell of rain-soaked fields rose to cool the air. The fields were green, the road muddy in places. I had not seen mud since Addis Ababa. There were pastures, corn fields, homesteads, wooded valleys, and hills scored with the furrows of cultivation. Tufted green copses graced the banks of little creeks.

"Did you have any trouble on the road?" Sister Matilda asked.

"We were shot at by shifta around Marsabit. Several trucks were attacked. Was it in the newspaper?"

"No." She laughed. "Shot at — that is not news in Kenya!"

Obviously not, for that day's Nairobi *Nation* was for sale in Isiolo, and near dusk, traveling to Nanyuki in a *matatu* — a speeding minivan with bald tires, jammed to capacity with ripe, perspiring Kenyans — I read the news: "47 Shot Dead in Village Attack." Six hundred members of the Pokot tribe had taken revenge on a village in western Kenya, torching three hundred huts, stealing hundreds of cattle, and killing teachers, students, women, and children as young as three months. In another story a fourteen-year-old boy was killed in crossfire between cops and robbers in the town of Kisii. Yet another related the theft of four million shillings in an armed robbery: "The police collected AK-47 cartridges at the scene." There was a vivid and grisly story of a riot at a soccer match, and an update on Kenya's AIDS epidemic.

Compared to this, potshots at southbound trucks on the Marsabit road were not news at all, and anyway, the desert between the Ethiopian border and Nanyuki did not exist in the minds of most Kenyans.

"The north is not Kenya," an African told me in Nanyuki. "It is not

Somalia or Ethiopia. It is another country. The Kenya government does nothing for it. It is a place run by foreigners — they manage everything, the schools, hospitals, churches. They are run by charities and aid agencies and NGOs, not by us."

He was not angry or cynical or even grateful; he was speaking the plain truth.

The Sportsman's Arms Hotel in Nanyuki was hosting a conference on camel health. British soldiers from the nearby army post played pool and howled at each other in the upstairs bar while Africans chuckled into cell phones in the lobby. Chuckling was all I ever saw African cell-phone users do. On the road near the hotel, prostitutes in tight dresses walked up and down in stiletto heels — the wrong footwear for a muddy road, but what the hell, this was civilization.

9 ◈◈◈

Rift Valley Days

In the East African bush, apart from the ritual warnings of hungry armed shifta, no one seemed to worry much about crime. Cattle rustling was the exception, of course, but it posed no risk to the sort of traveler I was: a dusty note-taking fugitive with a small bag, an evasive manner, and no time constraints. I knew I was out of the bush and near an African town or city when the crime warnings became numerous and specific, and always illustrated by a grim story. Nothing was grimmer or more graphic than an African warning.

The nearer I got to Nairobi, the worse the warnings. I was in Nanyuki when people told me of the many dangers. If you are involved in a carjacking, surrender your car: a woman was killed, stabbed in the eye, by carjackers just last week. Hand over your wallet to robbers without hesitation: a man was slashed to death by muggers yesterday, literally disarmed, his limbs lopped off with *pangas* — machetes. Don't be misled into thinking that crime happens only at night, I was cautioned: seven armed men robbed a perfume shop at midday on Kenyatta Avenue in Nairobi this week. If you do go out at night, you will definitely be robbed, I was assured. "There is a one hundred percent chance of it. I am one hundred percent sure." Don't resist, give them what they want, and you will live.

I was still in cool, green Nanyuki, lying in the morning shadow of the seventeen-thousand-foot Batian Peak of Mount Kenya, graced with scoopings of snow, an ice field, and — wonderful on the Equator — a number of visible glaciers.

A man of the Meru people said to me, "Spirits live there. The mountain is sacred to us. We go to the mountain to pray."

But even Mount Kenya was being robbed. That same week, a deal was made by some Kenyan politicians to sell off hundreds of square miles of protected land in the ancient forest on the mountainside to loggers and developers.

I traveled to Nairobi in an overcrowded Peugeot taxi, nine of us crushed into a five-seater, and so I spent the entire trip, two hours long, in the arms of a man named Kamali. He was a professional guide. He had in his bag a new book about lions by a British author, Elizabeth Laird, with a handwritten dedication: *To Kamali, who told me stories about lions I shall remember for the rest of my life.*

"Kamali" was a nickname. It meant vervet monkey, a name he had been given by some people in the west of Kenya for his cleverness and good humor. He was knowledgeable about the north and the behavior of animals and the minutiae of conducting a safari.

Kenya had been put on the map by hunters and by people who wrote about hunting. Hemingway's name comes quickly to mind, and so does Karen Blixen's, but much earlier there was the Tarzan-like figure of Colonel Patterson and his *Man-Eaters of Tsavo.* What all such books about Kenya have in common is an obsession with animals and a lazy sentimentality about servants and gun bearers. No crime, no politics, no agents of virtue appear in these books. Hemingway's Kenya might never have existed — at this distance in time it seems the private fantasy of a wealthy writer bent on proving his manhood, with the hunting safari as one of the more offensive kinds of tourist one-upmanship.

"There is no hunting anymore," Kamali said. "I'm so glad."

I looked out the window for anything familiar. I had spent years in the late sixties going back and forth between Uganda and Kenya, but now I saw nothing that I recognized except signboards lettered with place names. It was clear to me on my way to Nairobi that the Kenya I had known was gone. I didn't mind; perhaps the newness would make this trip all the more memorable.

Our overstuffed Peugeot was going eighty. I said to Kamali, "Mind asking the driver to slow down?"

"Pole-pole, bwana," Kamali said, leaning forward.

Insulted by this suggestion, the driver went faster and more recklessly. Because so many of the roads were better than before, people drove faster and there were more fatal accidents. "Many Dead in Bus Plunge Horror" is a standing headline in Kenya.

"That was a mistake. I should have said nothing," Kamali said.

Police roadblocks — there were eight or ten on this road — did nothing to deter the man from speeding. The car was in bad shape, obviously, and overcrowded. At one roadblock the policeman glared at us and cowed the driver. After he had detained us for a few minutes, he waved us on.

"Look — the slums," Kamali said as we entered the outskirts of Nairobi. "They worry me the most."

We were hardly past Thika, which had once been the countryside, written about in an amiable way as a rural idyll by Elspeth Huxley, who had grown up there. Now it was a congested maze of improvised houses and streets thick with lurking kids and traffic and an odor of decrepitude: sewage, garbage, open drains, the stink of citified Africa.

Going slowly our car was surrounded by ragged children pleading for money and trying to insert their hands through the half-open windows.

"Be careful when you see *totos* like this," Kamali said. "Sometimes they can take their own feces in their hand and put it on you, to make you give them something."

Giving you shit in the most literal sense.

Traffic was being held up by a crowd of people rushing across the road and by curious onlookers in cars, slowing down to gawk at something.

"Look, see the thief," Kamali said.

It was a sight of old Africa, a naked man running alone down an embankment and splashing across a filthy creek, pursued by a mob.

"They have taken his clothes. He is trying to get away in the dirty water of the river."

But he was surrounded. People lined both banks of the creek, holding sticks and boulders, laughing excitedly at the man, who was so panicked he did not even think to cover his private parts but just ran, his arms pumping, splashing in the disgusting muck.

I had forgotten how cheerful, even jubilant, such murderous crowds in Africa could be, particularly these spontaneous mobs in pursuit of a weak marked man trying in vain to flee — a thief, a political outcast, a member of a despised tribe. The isolation of such prey vitalized the pursuers and made them shout with joy as they went after him, the toughest men swaggering at the front, the older men cheering them on, the women ululating, the small children screeching and jumping up and down at the sight of all this motion. The vigor, the macabre good humor of the chase, and the idea of certain death were intoxicants. Years before, I had seen similar mobs in Malawi and Uganda, always a large number of excited people persecuting one or two victims. Then, what had frightened me most was the mob's sense of fun. Fun was still a factor in massacre. Perhaps the reason was simple: weak, idle people, suddenly granted power and the opportunity blamelessly to beat someone to death, are given a snorting animal energy and become joyous in their triumph.

The laughing crowd surged toward the naked man, swinging sticks.

"They will kill him," Kamali said.

Then the traffic began to move.

Once, even in my memory of it, Nairobi had been a quiet market town of low shop houses and long verandas, two main streets and auction halls, where farmers came to sell their harvest of coffee or tea. It was overnight by train to the coast — because of the danger of bilharzia tainting freshwater lakes and rivers, Mombasa-by-the-sea was the only safe place to swim. In the opposite direction, it was overnight by train to Kampala. The Uganda line through the highlands was bordered by farms.

The White Highlands had been aptly named: Indians and Africans were forbidden to raise cash crops by the British colonial government. Indians were shopkeepers, Africans were farm laborers, or else they lived in villages and worked the land. The few tourists who visited were timid sightseers or just as timid hunters, taken in hand by white guides and brought within range of wild game. Apart from that, Kenya worked on the old colonial system of landowners and businessmen being squeezed by greedy politicians, and the rest of the population were little more than drudges and whipped serfs.

Not much had changed after independence. Jomo Kenyatta's face hung in a framed portrait in every shop where Queen Elizabeth's had been. Some schools were built, some streets renamed. But educated people are a liability in a dictatorship: all the schools were underfunded, and few of them succeeded. A great deal of foreign money was given to the government, and most of it ended up in the pockets of politicians, some of whom were assassinated. It is almost impossible to exaggerate the fatness of corrupt African politicians.

Just after Christmas in 1963, on my way to Nyasaland to be a Peace Corps teacher, I saw Jomo Kenyatta on Kenyan television. Independence had been declared two weeks before. Slightly drunk, corpulent, and looking jovial, he slurringly wished everyone a happy new year. I walked down a shady road to the Nairobi library. Two Englishwomen were at the checkout desk, stamping library cards. At the Anglican church, an Englishwoman was polishing the brasses. Stories of scandals and steamy romances among the white settlers circulated. I took this for provincial boasting, the way Englishmen in rural places habitually gloated about how drunk they had been the night before at the pub. For such drinkers there was nothing to talk about except drunkenness.

I suspected even then that I was looking at a British colony that had hardly changed in a hundred years. Nairobi had been modeled on an English county town, but with so much cheap labor available it ran more smoothly.

Kenya did not explode at independence. It did not even change much at first, and it was only superficially modernized. It merely got bigger, messier, poorer, with more squatters in the country, more slums in the city. More schools, too, but inferior ones that would not alter the social structure, because power was in the hands of a small number of businessmen and politicians. That has remained the case. Jomo Kenyatta died in 1978 and Daniel arap Moi became president. We used to joke about his saying *"L'état c'est Moi,"* but the expression accurately described his rule. Thirty years later, Moi was still president, and an obnoxious president at that.

The Nairobi I entered in that overcrowded taxi, at the end of my long road trip from Ethiopia, was a somewhat recognizable version of the small market town I had seen almost forty years before. It was still at heart a provincial place, with the same people in charge, but it was huge and dangerous and ugly.

The worst part of Nairobi — everyone said so — was the district where I arrived: the bus and taxi depot. The neighborhood was old-fashioned in that way: the floating world of travelers arriving and departing, mobbed with jostling youths and hucksters and stallholders, people selling drinks and trays of food and bunches of sunglasses. Prime pickpocket territory, for it was so crowded, so crammed with urchins snatching and begging, as well as the blind, the leprous, the maimed. I was reminded again that medieval cities were all like this. African cities recapitulate the sort of street life that had vanished from European cities — a motley liveliness that lends color and vitality to old folktales and much of early English literature. An obvious example was Dickens's London, an improvised city populated by hangers-on, hustlers, and newly arrived bumpkins — like Nairobi today.

Visitors to Kenya en route to game parks are whisked from the airport to their hotel and seldom see the desperation of Nairobi, which is not the dark side, or a patch of urban blight, but the mood of the place itself.

My idea was to walk fast and look busy and not dress like a soldier or a tourist — no khakis, no camera, no short pants, no wallet, no valuables, just a cheap watch and loose change, for it was a rapacious and hungry and scavenging society. I left all my valuables padlocked in my bag. Women worked or cruised as prostitutes, but men and boys stood around in large groups, nothing to do, yakking among themselves or staring at passersby as if to assess what article worn by that person was worth snatching. On the busiest intersections street kids twitched, hunger in their skinny faces, and seized on strangers, obvious travelers, single women, old folks, and foreigners, and followed them, threatening and pleading.

Even the wild birds were at it. Marabou storks, big untidy long-legged birds with dirty feathers and large muck-slobbered beaks, perched in the trees on the main roads where people sold food. The food sellers made such a mess that the storks had given up scavenging in game parks, where the pickings were uncertain, and had become permanent residents, hovering constantly, unafraid of humans, like the so-called beggar bears at the fringes of American forests which raided garbage cans and trash barrels. Kites and hawks swooped down and made off with students' lunches, and what they dropped the rats ate. Bold mangy rats scuttled in Nairobi's gutters and drains.

Deforestation, dramatic in Kenya, was also a result of scavenging. Hearing an account of my trip through the desert, a diplomat said to me, "Right, it hasn't rained in the north for three years. Whose fault is that? They cut down the trees for fuel, they sold them to loggers, they destroyed the watershed. And they're still doing it."

After making some choice robbery notes in my diary, I went to buy the Nairobi paper so I could read it over a cup of coffee and do the crossword. The news was that a German film crew on location had lost all their cameras and sound equipment in a theft from their hotel in Nyeri.

"Dar is better," an Indian named Shah told me. "Indian women wear gold bangles there. Not here."

Women confident enough to walk down the street wearing jewelry was one test of an African city's safety.

Shah said that his father had come to Kenya in the 1940s, looking for work. He became a dealer in secondhand goods, buying from the white Kenyans, selling to the Africans. "He bought anything." In the 1950s, with the Emergency and the terror of the Mau-Mau, white Kenyans started to sell their farms and move out; many went to South Africa. The senior Mr. Shah bought their furniture and their family silver, picture frames, leather Gladstone bags, and crystal inkpots — "anything old." The secondhand dealer of the fifties and sixties had, without realizing it, started a profitable antiques business, and this his son inherited. His son needed the business, for it was impossible to go back to India.

"There is no one left, we have nothing there, even the family house is gone," the younger Mr. Shah said. "I have no family in India. I don't even go there. My brother is in Australia. I would like to go, but my shop is full of inventory."

He worried for his children, who were terrified of the Nairobi streets. "My boy is sixteen. He is home all the time, afraid to go out. He has not been out alone at all. He has no idea how to shop, to buy the simplest things. He says, 'Dad, let's get some shoes,' when he wants shoes. But you see, he must learn how to get out from under the umbrella. For him it is like house arrest."

A similar term was used by another Indian in Nairobi, but he was a recent arrival. He had been in Kenya for six years, running a restaurant.

He said to me, "I am alone here. My family is in India. If they were here, they would not be able to go out. I go to India once a year. I am here to work. I don't speak Swahili. Why should I keep my family here in a house prison?"

Because of all the stories of mayhem in Nairobi I seldom went out after dark. Instead of doing my note-taking in the morning, I wrote my notes at night in my hotel room. On the nights when I was caught up and had time on my hands, I continued my erotic story of the man about to have a big birthday and his recalling the steamy relationship with an older German woman. The setting was Sicily in the early sixties, a decaying palazzo — autoerotic writing counted as escapist entertainment, perhaps, but it was preferable to being robbed.

Even the wariest people were robbed. In September 1998, after the U.S. embassy bombing in Nairobi, three of the FBI men who had come to sift evidence were traveling down Kenyatta Avenue, one of the main streets. Their car collided with a taxi. They got out to examine the damage and were quickly surrounded by the usual Nairobi crowd — urchins, idlers, the homeless, the scavengers, the opportunists.

Without their realizing it, the FBI men were relieved of their wallets and pistols. Slapping their pockets, very angry at the theft, they faced a laughing mob, and the newspapers the next day mocked them for their stupidity.

Cynicism had been rare and unwelcome at the time of independence, but my oldest, most idealistic African friends in Kenya were cynical now. One praised the opposition leader, Mwai Kibaki.

"He is unusual in Kenya in that he has gotten to where he is by being reasonable," my friend said. "He is one of the very few politicians in Kenya who do not see killing people as necessary for political power."

A student of one of my African friends said to me, "You think it's just poor people who turn to crime, but no, many of the people I graduated from university with are still looking for work. There is no work. So they become thieves. Boys with good degrees! One boy who graduated with a business degree was involved in a car hijacking. Another tried to rob a wealthy Asian man — he was caught and is now in jail."

"Is this what we call white-collar crime?" I asked.

"No. It is guns and robbery. Many of the robberies are committed by well-educated people."

"Most of the people in this country have nothing," another African friend said to me.

"How are things going to improve?"

"Some people say the next election might make things better," he said. "Donor countries tell us that if all state-owned utilities and industries are turned over to the private sector, it will be the answer." He smiled at me. "But it isn't the answer."

"So what is the answer?" I asked.

He smiled. "Maybe no answer."

Maybe no answer. The whites, teachers, diplomats, and agents of virtue I met at dinner parties had pretty much the same things on their minds as their counterparts had in the 1960s. They discussed relief projects and scholarships and agricultural schemes, refugee camps, emergency food programs, technical assistance. They were newcomers. They did not realize that for forty years people had been saying the same things, and the result after four decades was a lower standard of living, a higher rate of illiteracy, overpopulation, and much more disease.

Foreigners working for development agencies did not stay long, so they never discovered the full extent of their failure. Africans saw them come and go, which is why Africans were so fatalistic. *Maybe no answer,* as my friend said with a rueful smile.

Kenya's reputation was so bad that some foreigners treated it as a throwback, satirizing it as a cannibal kingdom. Around the time I was in Kenya, the mayor of Toronto, Mel Lastman, was offered a trip to Mombasa, a chance for him to speak to the Association of National Olympic Committees of Africa, to solicit support for Toronto as an Olympic venue in 2008. He did so.

The Canadian mayor explained, "Why the hell do I want to go to Mombasa? . . . I just see myself in a pot of boiling water with all these natives dancing around me."

Germans still vacationed in Mombasa and Malindi, where Kenyan hotel managers routinely spoke German; tourists had never ceased to go on safaris; game viewing was popular, and bird watchers went to Lake Baringo and saw more birds in two days than they were likely to see in an entire lifetime back home. Despite the elephant killing and the smuggling of ivory and the poaching of lions and leopards for their claws and skins, there were lots of animals in Kenya's game parks. This abundance of game was due partly to the earlier policies of the ubiquitous Richard Leakey, who advocated that park rangers shoot poachers on sight.

Tourist Kenya — predictable, programmed, day-trippers kitted out in safari garb, gaping from Land Rovers — did not interest me. Tourists yawned at the animals and the animals yawned back. And the Kenya of big game hunters and the sentimental memoirists from Hemingway and Isak Dinesen to the mythomaniacs of the present day, such as *I Dreamed of Africa*'s Kuki Gallmann, made me laugh. If the self-important romanticizing of *Out of Africa* was at one end of the shelf, the other end was crowded with safari books such as Ilka Chase's *Elephants Arrive at Half-Past Five.* You would think from their writing that Kenya was just farms and devoted servants and the high-priced rooms at Gallmann's luxury safari camp. Of the even more expensive rooms at the Mount Kenya Safari Club, outside Nanyuki, one guest commented in a travel magazine afterward that they were "so luxurious you forget you're in the wilderness," oblivious of the fact that Nanyuki is not in the wilderness.

The orbit of big-game viewing and beer drinking on the coast was a world apart from the life of Kenya. Even when I lived and worked in Africa, I regarded safari people as fantasists, heading into the tamest bush in zebra-striped minibuses with hampers of gourmet food. Nor did these credulous people take the slightest interest in the schools where I taught. Now and then a news item noted that a famous person had come to Uganda or Kenya to hunt. In the late sixties, one of Nixon's cabinet members, Maurice Stans, visited Uganda with a high-powered rifle, in search of the shy and elusive bongo, a large-boned antelope, which was hunted with dogs. It was the stag-at-bay method: the dogs pursued the bongo, and when the bongo was trapped, its head down and trying to gore the mutts, he was shot through the brain or the heart. Stans bagged one or two. Now there are no bongos left in Uganda. Though Maurice Stans is dead, his species is not in the least endangered, while the poor bongo has just about been eliminated in the rest of Africa.

"Kenya is much more than animals," an African said to me one night at a Nairobi party. He introduced himself as Wahome Mutahi, and went on, "I would say that the small things that people do here are more significant than any animal."

Wahome had been a political prisoner. "I was tortured, too," he said, smiling. "My story is too long to tell here." I made a point of seeing him the next day. One of the many African ex-prisoners I met on my trip, Wahome was a journalist and novelist, widely read in East Africa. He had an oblique manner and a self-mocking smile, always speaking of himself and Kenya's contradictions with amused wonderment. His writing style was the same — understated and bravely ironical. In his fifties when I met him, he had been young enough at independence to witness every folly and false promise. He was a real endangered specimen, an intelligent homegrown opponent of the brutal regime who still lived and worked in his native land.

"There is less debate, less intellectual activity than you saw in your time," he said over lunch at the New Stanley Hotel.

I had stayed at the New Stanley thirty-eight years before, when it was new, when the white hunters drank at the Long Bar inside and the tourists fussed at the Thorn Tree Café out front. At that time the predators had been in the bush; now they were in the Nairobi streets and in the Kenyan government.

"There was a coup attempt in '82, which failed," Wahome went on. "After that there was a clampdown on intellectual activity. I was arrested in August 1986, and jailed."

"You were charged — you got a trial?"

"I was charged with neglecting to report a felony. So I was guilty of sedition. They said that my crime was that I knew people who were publishing seditious material — that is, material critical of the government."

"Was that true?"

"No, I didn't know anyone. I was just a journalist on the *Nation*, just writing."

"But you confessed?"

"Yes" — he smiled — "but it wasn't simple." He put his knife and fork down and leaned forward. "The Special Branch came to my house at night, looking for me. I was at a bar at the time. When I was told of the visit I disappeared for a few days. They found me some days later at my office at the *Nation*, at about ten on a Sunday morning, and they took me to Nyayo House to interrogate me."

Nyayo is a nice word. It means "footsteps" in Swahili. On his becoming president in 1978, Daniel arap Moi had said he would walk in Jomo Kenyatta's footsteps. Nyayo became a byword for tradition and respect. Nyayo House was an office building for the police, respectable looking aboveground and barbaric in the basement, for down there were the interrogation center, the cells, and, as Wahome found out, the torture chambers.

"I was held there for thirty days, but the first days were the worst. They interrogated me in Nyayo. They said, 'We're not holding you for an ordinary crime. We know you're in an organized movement.'

"I said, 'If you have evidence against me, take me to court.'

"That made them very angry. They stopped talking to me. They stripped me naked and beat me — three men with pieces of wood. They demanded that I confess. Then they stood me in my cell and sprayed me with water. My cell was about the size of a mattress. They soaked me — water was everywhere. Then they locked the door and left me."

In Wahome's novel *Three Days on the Cross*, just such a scene is described. The accused prisoner, Chipota, is beaten until he is bloody, then a hose "like a cannon" is turned on him with such force it knocks the wind out of him. He turns away from it. The hose is aimed at the ceiling, the walls, and the cell is flooded. "The door had a raised floor frame, so that water could not flow out." Chipota realizes that the cell was specially designed to be used for this diabolical water torture.

Wahome said, "They left me. I couldn't tell day from night. I was still naked and really cold, standing in the water in the darkness. The water was dripping on me from the ceiling. I don't know how much time passed, maybe twelve or fifteen hours.

"The door suddenly opened and a man said, '*Una kitu ya kuambia wazee?*' Have you anything to tell the elders?"

"Elders" (*wazee*, plural of *mzee*) was another nice word for torturers.

"I said no. They left me again for a long time, and then the door opened. The same question — *Una kitu . . . ?* — and I said no.

"I came to a situation where I was living in a nightmare. I had nightmares all the time — dreaming of flying and cycling, but always crash-landing. Dreams about food, but torture dreams. I hallucinated. I saw food on the patches of the floor. I saw a sausage through the wall and tried to break through the cement to get it."

Such nightmares occur in the novel, based on his experience. The worst ones in the book are of rape and beatings and violent crash-landings, but the nightmares are preferable to the reality of imprisonment. Wahome wrote of Chipota, "Then a flash of light and he woke up from the nightmare to realize that he was still within the walls of the cell . . . He wished he could go back to the nightmare."

Craving to be returned to the nightmare was exactly how Wahome had felt, he told me. He was desolated to awaken from a bad dream to see himself ankle deep in water and shivering, pissing and shitting in the water, not able to either stand or sit.

I said, "Where did the Kenyans learn this torture technique?"

"Maybe from Romania. They were friendly to us then."

"What about your family? Did they know where you were?"

"They had no idea. I was thirty-five at the time, with two young children. They didn't know I was in the middle of Nairobi, in a dark torture cell at Nyayo House. After five or six days I got to recognize daytime from the noise above me."

"Weren't you tempted to confess?" I asked.

Again Wahome smiled the crooked smile and said, "Before I was arrested I had been amazed by all the people who had confessed to crimes. I had no idea why they said they were guilty — I knew they weren't, but they said they were. Now I knew. I was in the dark, in water. My feet were rotting. I was on the point of breakdown. I thought of suicide. When a week passed they must have thought I was dying, because they put me in a dry cell."

But the interrogation continued. He was blindfolded and taken to the twenty-second floor of Nyayo House and locked in a room with his interrogator, always the same man, always the same questions: "When did you join MwaKenya?" MwaKenya was an underground movement opposing the government. "Who recruited you? What books have you read?"

He denied being a member of any underground movement. When he said he had read *Mother* by Maxim Gorki, the interrogator ("He was very moody") screamed, "That's a recruitment manual!"

This went on for an hour or so, and then he was returned to his cell in the basement. But he knew he was weakening, and he still felt suicidal. It was not limbo, he assured me, but "a hell of suspense."

He said that his happiest time was when he was given a chance to wash the prisoners' dinner plates. "That was my highest moment. There was a mirror in the room. I looked at my face. The washing took no more than five or ten minutes, but I loved it. I was doing something. That was great."

Wahome realized that the suspense was weakening him and that he would have preferred to serve a specific sentence rather than suffer not knowing when his confinement would end.

He said, "I told them this. They gave me three options — various crimes I could confess to. I chose the third, sedition, because the sentence was the shortest. So they photographed me."

He paused in this awful story and shook his head, remembering a detail — a Kafkaesque moment in a Kafka-like story.

"I was smiling when they took my picture," he said, flashing me the same smile. "I was happy."

He was taken to court in the evening, so as not to attract attention. His family still had no idea where he was. He had no lawyer. He was in handcuffs in the dock.

"The prosecuting attorney was Bernard Chunga," Wahome said. "You might see his name in the paper. He is now chief justice — he was rewarded. He spoke as though he knew my crime.

"'The accused is an intelligent man. He knew a crime was being committed and he chose not to report the offense to the lawful authority,' — blah blah blah. The judge, H. H. Buch, was a *Muhindi*" — an Indian. "The whole trial took about seven minutes. But I was happy! I was given fifteen months. It was something definite, not torture anymore."

He said that this sort of arrest was very common in Kenya into the early 1990s. Altogether, Wahome was in three prisons, all of them in rural areas, with nearby villages and wild game, the colorful Kenya of the tourist trade and picture postcards of smiling, highly ornamented tribespeople.

He was in solitary confinement most of the time, denied paper and pencils. He found a copy of *The Rainbow* by D. H. Lawrence and read it ten or twelve times. "Funnily enough, I can't remember a thing about it." He found another book, *Spanish Made Easy*. In the short periods in the exercise yard he taught the other prisoners some Spanish, but the guards suspected they were being whispered about, and the book was confiscated. Wahome passed the time daydreaming. He contracted malaria and seemed to suffer a weekly attack of fever.

On his release, he went home and back to his job on the newspaper. "I didn't hate my captors. I thought, They should feel ashamed." He was not alone in his experience, or even in his book. Many Kenyans have been imprisoned on trumped-up charges, many have written similar accounts of detention and torture. Books such as *Detained,* by Ngugi wa Thiong'o, had helped prepare him; Koestler's *Darkness at Noon,* which Wahome read later, he loved for its accurate depiction of the details of prison life.

"I went on writing. The government wanted to break me. I wanted to prove they were wrong. Prison was a sort of baptism for me, but for others I knew it was horrible. They never recovered. They were traumatized. Even now they are broken. But I wanted to survive. It was difficult. When I got out, my friends were afraid of me."

"But those policemen and interrogators must still be around," I said.

"Yes," Wahome said. That ironic smile again. "A few years ago I was sitting on a bus. I looked across the aisle and saw the man who had interrogated me: 'Who recruited you?' It was him! When he saw me he pretended to be asleep."

"Weren't you angry?"

"No. I was scared. I was paranoid. I got off the bus."

The torturer homeward bound, jogging along on the city bus with the other commuters, became for me one of the enduring images of urban Kenya.

Wahome Mutahi, whom I saw as a hero, not a victim, became my friend, my *rafiki.* Walking around Nairobi, he talked about the past and his family, he showed me the good bookstores and coffee shops, the streets to avoid, what remained of the old market town. We looked at the bombed-out U.S. embassy — most of the area, near the railway station, was still wrecked. Wahome advised me on buying the things I would need for my onward journey to western Kenya and the Uganda border. In one bookstore I bought him a copy of *The Mosquito Coast* and he bought me his prison book. He inscribed his *To Bwana Theroux,* and we said *kwaheri* — farewell — and promised to stay in touch.

A few days later, reading the *Nation,* I saw the name of the man who had prosecuted Wahome after his confession under torture. Chief Justice Bernard Chunga, now dispensing sanctimony, "appealed to organizations caring for juveniles to ensure that they handled them in accordance with international standards."

High-mindedness was a theme in Kenyan speeches that month, because the U.S. ambassador, Johnnie Carson, had delivered a stern warning in a pep talk to Kenyan businessmen that their nation was in danger of losing its preferential trade status. To help feeble African economies, the U.S. Congress had passed the African Growth and Opportunity Act, which provides a visa system for these countries to ship goods to the United States without having to observe quotas. The charitable idea was intended to encourage local industries, but all it did was encourage local criminality. In Kenya this bypass had become a huge moneymaking scam. After paying some backhanders to high-ranking Kenyans, Chinese and Indian clothing manufacturers were labeling their goods "Made in Kenya" and transshipping them to the States through Kenya.

"The signs are not positive," Ambassador Carson said, referring to the textile scams. He went on to say that unless Kenya curbed corruption, respected the rule of law and human rights, and pursued sound economic policies, this preferential deal would end. The diplomat's scolding and finger-wagging were quite different from the patronizing noises about negritude Kenyans had heard from past ambassadors. But this was a different Kenya, a different Nairobi, crime-ridden and corrupt. I did not long for the past; I longed for the hinterland again, the simpler, happier bush.

◇ ◇ ◇

It was easy enough to leave Nairobi. Rail service to Kampala had been suspended, but there were plenty of buses to the border. They left in the early morning from the neighborhood that was associated with danger — especially dangerous in the predawn darkness when the buses left. I was warned: "Take a taxi." I followed the advice, took a taxi for three blocks with a driver named Bildad, who went on warning me, filling me with dread, until just before the bus left.

It set off in darkness, and at sunup I was traveling through the Great Rift Valley among small farms. The valley that had once been a vast, green, empty, curved expanse, deepening to the northwest, with yellow flat-topped forests of thorn trees, and beneath them antelope or bushbuck nibbling grass, was now overgrazed and deforested and filled with mobs of idle people and masses of ugly huts.

Longonot Crater, a dark burned-out volcano, was a reminder that the whole of the Rift Valley was a series of fault lines, stretching in an irregular rent from the Dead Sea to the Shire River valley in Mozambique. The Rift was created during an intense epoch of volcanism that had torn open the heart of Africa with massive eruptions and lava flows. One controversial theory held that the two different climate zones created by the Rift Valley had influenced human evolution: the tropical forests to the west had become a home for apes, while hominids had had to adapt to the openness of the eastern savanna. In any case, the oldest hominid fossils in the world had been found in this eastern portion of the Rift.

Mount Lengai in Rwanda was still erupting and displacing villagers. Kilimanjaro was dormant, and so were the Mountains of the Moon in Uganda and the twenty-mile-wide caldera that was the Ngorongoro Crater in Tanzania. Some of the titanic cracks opened by the eruptions had filled with water and become Lake Victoria, Lake Tanzania, Lake Malawi. Most of what was visible as landscape — the high Mau Escarpment just west of Longonot, for example — was the result of those early volcanoes and the plate shift.

The town of Naivasha looked quiet enough, pretty and purple with its jacarandas in bloom and a thickness of petals on its streets. Like many places in Kenya, Naivasha had a murky past and a just as murky present. Everyone in Nairobi knew the story of Father Kaiser, a Catholic priest from Minnesota who had served in a church near Naivasha. He had been a missionary in Kenya for more than thirty years and, alarmed by growing ethnic and tribal hatred, he began to collect information on specific acts of violence, which he suspected were politically inspired. No one else was keeping a record — not the police and certainly not the government, which denied the accusations, denied even that AIDS was a problem in Kenya. Father Kaiser, now scorned as a scaremonger but in fact a serious threat to the government's credibility, had a growing file on the crimes of rape and murder.

Knowing that the police would be indifferent, because a politician was involved, two young girls came to Father Kaiser in great distress and reported that they had been raped by a government minister. The minister was well known, a member of the ruling party, KANU — Kenyatta's party, Moi's party, the party that had ruled Kenya for forty years and was still in power.

Father Kaiser went to various high officials and raised the matter of the rapes as well as details of other crimes. He was at first rebuffed and then came under pressure to cease publicizing the facts. When he kept at it, he was refused a work permit and told to leave the country. He resisted, calling attention to the high crime rate and especially the government denials. In August 2000, Father Kaiser's corpse was found by the side of the road. He had been murdered. When I passed the scene the murderer was still at large, and the accused rapist still sat in his ministerial chair in Moi's cabinet.

"Kenya has a stable government," an agent of a prestigious London-based safari company insisted when, inquiring about game viewing, I raised my doubts about security. She denied the government was corrupt and unreliable, and warned me not of crime but of her company's safari prices. "I must tell you we are incredibly high-end. We tailor each safari to the client, designing the safaris to the client's comfort and interests."

"Authoritarian" is not the same as "stable," but anyway the safari client is mainly interested in big game, not politics. It is possible, using helicopters and armed guards and tight security, to assure a client's safety in Kenya. And the client must not stray from the narrow itinerary.

I mentioned to a white Kenyan that I had traveled south by road from the Ethiopian border to Marsabit and Isiolo. He was a tough man who had traveled throughout Kenya. He had one of the most powerful Land Rovers I had ever seen — the newest model, with a BMW engine. He had never taken that road.

He said, "No one goes on that road."

The shallow and corrosive soda lakes near Naivasha and Nakuru were justifiably famous for their flamingos. Lesser flamingos flocked to Lake Nakuru, greater flamingos to Lake Natron. I could see big pink patches on Lake Elmenteita, thousands of the birds. They stood in the shallows, heads down, swinging their graceful necks, feeding by dragging their beaks through the lake, sluicing the water, straining the food.

Tourists would see only those lovely birds and know nothing of Father Kaiser or the dark forces in Kenya that had undone him.

The bus stopped at Nakuru, for food and drink, for the revolting toilets. Nakuru had grown from a small market town with an agreeable climate to an enormous unplanned settlement of tin-roofed huts, with a newer community of the sort of tidy high-priced houses that have only just started to appear within commuting distance of Nairobi. For "middle management," I was told: Africans who had jobs with banks, insurance companies, car dealerships, import-export firms, and foreign charities. Old sun-faded signs were visible on the façades of some defunct colonial-era general stores, advertising patent medicine and cattle feed, and across one wall, *U-Like-Me Porridge Oats.*

Hawkers — coastal people mostly, Africans in skullcaps and djellabas — pushed trays of sunglasses and cheap watches at the circulating passengers. Improvised stalls offered ice cream and fruit, hot dogs and fried chicken.

Half the bus passengers were African, little families that looked Ugandan; the other half were Indian, bigger families in the back, and boisterous because they were in a group — carping men, silent women, squawking girls and boorish boys with baseball caps on backward. The African woman seated in front of me was reading Wayne Dyer's *Your Sacred Self,* the chapter entitled, "Making the Decision to Be Free."

In an earlier time — the sixties, say, years I could verify — a drive to Nakuru and Kericho and Kisumu, where we were headed, would have been a spin in the countryside. Narrow roads, almost no traffic, Africans on bikes, cattle grazing on hillsides, now and then a farmhouse, the occasional herd of antelope. A green and empty land under a big sky. Places that had been little towns and truck stops were now large, sprawling settlements; the sparsely inhabited bush had become populous and noticeably nasty.

That was the way of the world, but it seemed an African peculiarity that whenever a town or city grew bigger it got uglier, messier, more dangerous, an effect of bad planning, underfunding, and graft. And a feature of every settlement was the sight of African men standing under trees, congregating in the shade. They were not waiting for buses; they were killing time because they had no jobs. They must have had gardens — most people did — but the farm work of planting and hoeing was presumably done by their womenfolk. In Kenya, whenever I saw a well-formed tree near a village or town, I saw men under it, doing nothing, looking phlegmatic and abstracted.

Even the most prosperous towns in this part of Kenya had the bright signboards and relief agencies, the offices and supply depots — people doling out advice and food and condoms. The merchandise of the gang of virtue. This was true in Kericho, its large leafy tea estates softening its green hills and valleys. Maybe such places attracted missionaries and aid workers because they were so pleasant to live in. Maybe communications were better here than in the remote bush. Whenever I saw a town that looked tidy and habitable I saw the evidence of foreign charities: Oxfam, Project Hope, the Hunger Project, Food for Africa, SOS Children's Village, Caritas, and many others, with saintly names and a new white Land Rover or Land Cruiser parked in front.

As this was a coffee-growing area, any one of these vehicles could have belonged to the satirical figure of Dickens's Mrs. Jellyby and her African project. She had said, "We hope by this time next year to have from a hundred and fifty to two hundred healthy families cultivating coffee and educating the natives of Borrioboola-Gha."

Mine is not a complaint, merely an observation, because hearing horror stories about uneducated starving Africans, most Americans or Europeans become indignant and say, "Why doesn't someone do something about it?" Much was apparently being done — more than I had ever imagined. Since the Kenya government cared so little about the well-being of its people, concerns such as health and education had been taken up by sympathetic foreigners. The charities were well established. Between the Bata shoe store and the local Indian shop, you would find the office of World Vision or Save the Children — "Blurred Vision" and "Shave the Children" to the cynics. These organizations had grown out of disaster relief agencies but had become multinational institutions, permanent fixtures of welfare and services.

I wondered, really wondered, why this was all a foreign effort, why Africans were not involved in helping themselves. And also, since I had been a volunteer teacher myself, why, after forty years, had so little progress been made?

An entire library of worthy books describe at best the uselessness, at worst the serious harm, brought about by aid agencies. Some of the books are personal accounts, others are scientific and scholarly. The findings are the same.

"Aid is not help" and "aid does not work" are two of the conclusions reached by Graham Hancock in his *Lords of Poverty: The Power, Pres-*

tige, and Corruption of the International Aid Business (1989), a well-researched account of wasted money. Much of Hancock's scorn is reserved for the dubious activities of the World Bank. "Aid projects are an end in themselves," Michael Maren writes in *The Road to Hell: The Ravaging Effects of Foreign Aid and International Charity* (1997). One of Maren's targets is Save the Children, which he sees as a monumental boondoggle. Both writers report from experience, having spent many years in Third World countries on aid projects.

While these writers are kinder to volunteers in disaster relief than to highly paid bureaucrats in institutional charities, both of them also assert that all aid is self-serving, large-scale famines are welcomed as a "growth opportunity," and the advertising to stimulate donations for charities is little more than "hunger porn."

"Here is a rule of thumb that you can safely apply wherever you may wander in the Third World," Hancock writes. "If a project is funded by foreigners it will typically also be designed by foreigners and implemented by foreigners using foreign equipment procured in foreign markets."

As proof of that rule of thumb, the most salutary and least cited book about development in Africa is an Italian study, *Guidelines for the Application of Labor-Intensive Technologies* (1994). Revolutionary in its simplicity, it advocates the use of African labor to solve African problems. After describing the many social and economic advantages of employing local people, who would work with their hands to build dams, roads, sewer systems, and watercourses, the authors, Sergio Polizzotti and Daniele Fanciullacci, discuss the constraints imposed by donors. Donors specify that purchases of machinery have to be made in the donor country, or that bids be restricted to firms in the donor country, or that a time limit be placed on the scheme, which "encourages the tendency towards large contracts and heavy spending on equipment." Labor-intensive projects are few in Africa because so much donor aid is self-interested.

◇ ◇ ◇

Passing enormous smooth boulders as big as three-story houses, we came to Kisumu. Kisumu was a port on the Winam Gulf of Lake Victoria, a railhead, a ferry terminus. But the train was defunct and the ferry was so irregular and in such bad repair it was useless. I had thought I might stay here a few days and take a ferry to Uganda, but that was out of the question.

Kisumu was now just a bus stop. In its market the usual children hawked boxes of tea and containers of milk, women roasted ears of corn, and people sold huge heaps of old shoes and secondhand clothes. Even Africans found the secondhand clothes at such markets inexpensive. Most of the clothing used to belong to you — the old dresses and T-shirts and shorts and neckties and ragged sweaters and blankets you put in a box and handed in at the church for collection by the Salvation Army, Blankets for Africa, or whatever. You thought they would be doled out to needy people, but no, they are sorted into bundles: socks, shoes, slacks, blouses, skirts, and so forth. These bundles are sold cheaply to market traders, who become the distributors, stacking them in their stalls and reselling them.

When my own clothes got ragged I too bought clothes in the market. It was my way of not looking like a tourist or a soldier. I became fond of my secondhand shirts, one of which was bright red and lettered *Top Notch Plumbing.*

I spent the day in Kisumu, strolling around because I had been cramped in the bus seat. I walked to the old jetty, where there was no ferry, and to the railway station, where there was no train. The market was full of charity merchandise: nothing made in Kenya, no textiles, only a few clay pots.

Leaving Kisumu on the afternoon bus to the border, I saw a booming Kenyan industry: just outside town, shop after shop of woodworkers, all of them making coffins — the freshly cut raw wood, reddish in the dampness, the men sawing it and nailing together the long boxes, everyone hard at work. The finished coffins were stacked or standing upright, lots of them. This was the busiest local industry I had seen in the whole of Kenya: the coffin makers and their lugubrious product, a perfect image for a country that seemed terminally ill.

I made a note of those coffins and sketched pictures of their shapes and sizes. But I also noted that, sitting in these buses, watching Africa go by, getting off whenever I liked, I was traveling happily, in a state of great contentment, following the honks of the geese — on this particular day the Egyptian goose, *Alopochen aegyptiaca,* prettily named but wild geese all the same.

10 ◈◈◈

Old Friends in Bat Valley

PAPYRUS GREW in thick leafy clumps, as fresh as salad, by the lakeshore just inside the Uganda border. The tall graceful stalks swayed, the feathery heads nodded as my bus passed by, traveling west on a back road from the border town of Busia. I had not seen papyrus growing anywhere in Kenya, even on the Kisumu edge of Lake Victoria, but as soon as I crossed into Uganda I saw rafts of the tall, delicately tufted plant in the swampland by the lake. It was like further proof that Uganda is the source of the Nile. Downstream in Egypt where real papyrus no longer existed, I had seen images of the lovely plant picked out in bright vegetable dye on the walls of pharaonic tombs and on the tops of columns at Karnak. Anything that linked Egypt to the heart of Africa interested me: papyrus, lotuses, crocs, hippos, crested cranes, baboons, lions, elephants and their ivory, even the images of slaves, and the river water itself.

"How did you first come here?" I used to ask old-timers and elderly missionaries in the sixties. Many would say, "Down the Nile." That meant: by boat and train through Egypt, by train to Khartoum, by paddle steamer from Khartoum to Juba, and then fifty-eight miles by road to Uganda.

I had come by "chicken bus" — the buses that were full of Africans and their produce, including trussed-up chickens and infants so swaddled they looked mummified. One chicken bus had dropped me at the Kenya border. Good-humored hawkers and touts, moneychangers, and beggars descended on me. They followed me, running, across no man's land, a hot stony half-mile without any shade, until they were turned back at the chainlink fence and razor wire on the Uganda side. Something was revealed about a person's nature by the way he tried to run — more revealing when he ran toward you than when he tried to run away.

At the Uganda checkpoint I went through the same formalities again, a crowd shoving one another to get into a small shed, for their passports to be stamped, and outside more moneychangers and beggars. I bought a newspaper and read about bomb outrages that had occurred in Kampala the previous day: "election violence." On the next bus, on the far side, I reflected that a person who has not crossed an African border on foot has not really entered the country, for the airport in the capital is no more than a confidence trick; the distant border, what appears to be the edge, is the country's central reality.

Right from the frontier, Uganda seemed a tidier, better-governed place than Kenya, and it was visibly more fertile, palmier, lusher, with rice paddies being planted and tended, and banana trees — all sorts of bananas. Ugandans say there are sixty varieties, for they are one of the staples here. This southeastern part of the country was green and low-lying and swampy, the big lake seeping into the hinterland.

The roads were in better shape, and so were the houses, old and new, than the ones on the Kenyan side — more reminders that Kenya was on the way down and perhaps Uganda was on the way up. Sugar cane was being grown in the fields here, as in the past, on estates that had always been owned by Indians. Given the world price of sugar, and most other commodities, this was somewhat surprising. Certainly farmers in Africa were earning less for growing coffee, tea, cotton, sugar, and tobacco, and in some places were going back to subsistence farming, letting the cash crops die and planting corn for their own use.

Late in the afternoon my bus passed the town of Jinja, where at Owen Falls Lake Victoria flows north — the Victoria Nile — to Lake Kyoga and onward to Murchison Falls and Lake Albert, into the Albert Nile. This simple progression perplexed ancient speculators such as Ptolemy and the European explorers in Africa until the expedition of 1857–58, when Sir Richard Burton and John Speke crossed from the east coast to survey the lake region of the interior. While Burton lay ill in what is now Tabora, in Tanzania, it was Speke who traveled to the southern edge of the great lake, to get a glimpse. He had no idea of the lake's true size, but from what he was told by Arabs, he surmised that at its northern shore was an outflow, the headwaters of the Nile. Burton challenged him on this, and denounced him for his haste, for being too impatient to navigate the lake. Speke was defensive but insecure; he had a fragile disposition anyway (he was later to kill himself). Yet Speke's intuition was correct: Lake Victoria was later proven to be the Nile's source.

This familiar landscape gave me a soothing sense of homecoming, almost nostalgia. I was still traveling in a state of contentment, wary as always, but with a feeling of relative safety. I stood out as a *muzungu*, of course, but an older one in secondhand clothes, wearing a cheap watch and a faded hat. My sports jacket was badly torn: battery acid had burned large holes in it on one of my truck rides. Tatters in Africa are like camouflage, and mine made me less conspicuous. African markets were wonderful places for finding people to patch clothes: I could get the coat mended in Kampala. That simple mission made me happier. And I had the Rimbaudesque thrill that no one on earth knew where I was. I had successfully disappeared into the southeastern bush of Uganda, a place I knew fairly well. I loved bumping along in this bus alone, in a crimson Ugandan sunset that would go dark in about thirty minutes, as night dropped like a blanket on the bush.

I was also excited to be here because it was a return to my youth, or young adulthood. I had last been in Uganda thirty-four years before. I wondered whether, with a special birthday looming, at the back of my mind was a plan to return to a specific time in my life when I had been supremely happy. It was 1967. I had been in love with a woman who loved me, was planning to be married, and in those same months seeing my first book published. I knew that I was young and appreciated, living a life I had chosen.

I decided to avoid any birthday celebration. I was so self-conscious of my age that I often asked Africans to guess how old I was, hoping — perhaps knowing in advance — they would give me a low figure. They always did. Few people were elderly in Africa. Forty was considered old, a man of fifty was at death's door, sixty-year-olds were just crocks or crones. Despite my years I was healthy, and being agile and resilient I found traveling in Africa a pleasure. I did not seem old here, did not feel it, did not look it to Africans, and so it was a great place to be, another African fantasy, an adventure in rejuvenation.

"You are forty-something," Kamal had guessed in Addis. The highest number I got was fifty-two. Little did they know how much they flattered my vanity. But no one was vain about longevity in Africa, because the notion of longevity hardly existed. No one lived long and so age didn't matter, and perhaps that accounted for the casual way Africans regarded time. In Africa no one's lifetime was long enough to accomplish anything substantial, or to see any task of value completed. Two generations in the West equaled three generations in African time, telescoped by early marriage, early childbearing, and early death.

In southeastern Uganda I wrote in my diary: *I do not want to be young again. I am happy being what I am. This contentment is very helpful on a trip as long and difficult as this.*

It had taken me years to summon up the resolve to return to Africa, because in all travel one's mood is crucial. I had been happy and hopeful here. I began to see that Africa had aged the ways Africans themselves had aged — old at forty: most Kenyans and Ugandans I had met so far were too young to remember the period of independence. I had procrastinated about returning because I had suspected that the Africa I had known had disappeared, had become anarchic and violent. This seemed to be borne out by the headlines in Uganda that week about the bombs ("grenades") that had gone off at Kampala's main market. Two people had been killed, ten injured — postelection violence was the repeated explanation, the opposition being blamed. But that disruption went with the territory. It was politics, as Africans said. And I was just an anonymous man in old clothes on a corner seat in a chicken bus, reading about it in the local newspaper.

What all older people know, what had taken me almost sixty years to learn, is that an aged face is misleading. I did not want to be the classic bore, the reminiscing geezer, yet I now knew: the old are not as frail as you think, and they are insulted to be regarded as feeble. They are full of ideas, hidden powers, even sexual energy. Don't be fooled by the thin hair and battered features and skepticism. The older traveler knows it best: in our hearts we are youthful, and we are insulted to be treated as old men and burdens, for we have come to know that the years have made us more powerful and streetwise. Years are not an affliction. Old age is strength.

Jinja had once been full of Indian shops selling cloth, kitchenware, and food, and several shops specialized in Indian sweets: syrupy globs of gulabjam and sticky yellow laddu. There were no Indians now, no sweetshops, no panwallahs. Some of the shops were boarded up, others were run by Africans. At the bus depot in Jinja I met a pair of nervous young Americans, backpackers wearing L. L. Bean shorts and Orvis hats, sticky sun cream on their noses, the girl gulping trail mix, the boy with his thumb in a Lonely Planet guide to East Africa, looking a bit too conspicuous.

The boy said to me, "Don't you think we'll be safer staying here until things quiet down in Kampala?"

"Then you'll be in Jinja for years," I said. "Things haven't been quiet in Kampala since 1962. Get on the bus, you'll be fine."

But they didn't, they stayed. If, as they said, they weren't leaving until Kampala settled down, they might still be in Jinja now.

When I told Africans where I had come from and how slowly I had traveled, they said, "So you must be retired."

"No, no, no," I said, overreacting, because I despised the word and equated it with surrender. "I'm traveling, I'm working."

That wasn't it, either: not business, not pleasure, not work, not retirement, but the process of life, how I chose to pass the time.

Nearer Kampala, the bush was denser and the towns better defined, with clearer perimeters — regulated subdivisions rather than the straggly squatter camps that passed for suburbs in Kenya. There were signs in Uganda, too, that people were house-proud: the huts and bungalows were painted and fenced in, with vegetable or flower gardens. Among them were tall native trees standing singly or in clusters, the last remnants of the old-growth forests, the habitat that had supported troops of monkeys and dangling orchids. What I remembered most clearly about this Jinja road was that on portions of it, for reasons no one could explain, butterflies settled in long fluffy tracts. There might be eighty feet of road carpeted by white butterflies, so many of them that if you drove too fast your tires lost their grip, and some people lost their lives, skidding on butterflies.

At the edge of Kampala was a sports arena, Mandela National Stadium. In my time it would have been named Obote Stadium or Amin Stadium. In Kenya it would have been Moi Stadium. African politicians habitually bestowed their own names on roads, schools, and arenas; they put their faces on the currency, full-faced on the notes, in lumpy profile on the coins. The political health of a country was easily assessed by looking at the money and the names of streets. In the worst places you saw the same name and face everywhere, that of the president-for-life.

There had been an election in Uganda the week before I arrived. The posters and banners of the various parties still hung outside shops. I recognized some of the candidates — I personally knew two of them, for they had been ambitious ranters even in my time. The incumbent, Yoweri Museveni, had won, and though one of the losers, a man named Kizza Besigye, disputed the result, it was generally felt that the election had been fair. Yet grenades were still being lobbed into markets in different parts of the country and cars torched willy-nilly.

When I finally arrived in Kampala, the news was that the loser, Besigye, who was contesting the results of the election, had gone to Entebbe Airport for a flight to South Africa to give a lecture. He had been prevented from boarding the plane. He was told that he could not leave the country "while the explosions are being investigated."

"I am not happy about the election," a Ugandan told me. "There was intimidation and fraud. The results were *bichupali*" — a local word, not Swahili, meaning "counterfeit."

"What do you think?"

"It was rigged. We have no work. In fact, the truth will emerge."

Being a Ugandan, he said *reedged* and *wuck* and *een fukt* and *troof* and *emudge.*

Hearing this manner of speaking, the Ugandan way, also made me feel at home.

As a twenty-something I had spent many evenings drinking beer on the veranda of the Speke Hotel. I had never stayed there — my home was across town, near Bat Valley. So on my return the Speke became my home in Kampala. One of its many attractions for me now was that its phones had not been upgraded in forty years: it was impossible to call the United States, nor could anyone call me. At a better-class hotel I sent a fax to my wife to reassure her I was muddling along, and reading it she thought: Poor Paulie, all alone.

On my way back to the Speke that night I realized that I was walking through an African city in safety. This I liked: a nocturnal ramble was a novelty. I walked for an hour, all over town, even to the bombed market, and finally to an Indian restaurant. No hassles, lots of people on the street.

Many of the people were out collecting grasshoppers that had gathered under the streetlights. This I remembered from way back, grasshopper season, when families shook bed sheets under the lamps and picked the insects out of them and popped them into jars to take home and fry. The grasshoppers arrived with the rains.

"We like the *senene*," a young African man said. He was strolling with two other men and we stopped to talk.

"Locusts, right?" I said.

"No, no," he said, as though I had maligned them. "Not locusts. They do no damage."

"How do you catch them in the village or in the bush?"

"Very hard there," one of the other men said. "Not enough light."

So this urban illumination was a splendid feature of the donor aid that had allowed Uganda to light its city streets. Never mind the traffic — there were few cars on the roads at night anyway. But the modernity of city lights, a multimillion-dollar aid project, made it possible for Ugandans to harvest edible grasshoppers on the bright night streets.

"They're tasty, right?"

"So tasty!" the first African said.

"How tasty?"

"Better than white ants."

This I found so funny I exploded with laughter.

He said, "But that is the only other food you could compare them with."

True, they were both insects, and the preparation was exactly the same. They were stripped of their wings and legs, deep-fried in fat, and sold by the greasy scoopful out of big sacks in the market as a nutty delicacy.

Among the whirling grasshoppers and the grasshopper gatherers and the shoeshine boys and the strollers were a multitude of prostitutes, and they were insectile, too. They lingered in the street, they stood under trees, they sat on low walls, they leaned against cars. They were most of them very young and well dressed and looked demure, even sweet, and as I approached they hissed at me and made kissing sounds, as you would call a cat. "Want a date?" "Want a massage?" And some of the most innocent looking pushed their glazed faces at me and whispered softly, "Want a fuck?"

One of the youngest tagged along and pleaded with me to take her. She mentioned a small sum of money. She was seventeen at most, wearing a glittery red dress with sequins and high heels — the sort of girl I might have met at a university party thirty-five years before, someone's daughter, someone's girlfriend, perhaps a high school student, spirited and pretty. This one's English was reasonably good. "Let's go dancing," I might have said. But I said no, and when she hung on, promising pleasure, I said I was tired, but in fact I was flusterfied.

"Tomorrow then," she said, and reached into her expensive handbag and took out a business card. "Call me on my mobile phone."

"From an economic point of view, going into prostitution is a rational decision for an African woman," Michael Maren writes in *The Road to Hell.* "It's one of the rare avenues open for her to make real money. The sex industry is one of the few points where the local economy and the expatriate economy intersect." In this country, people sold much more than she ever had, and did a roaring trade, as Stephen Dedalus remarked: "Fear not them that sell the body but have not power to buy the soul."

My own feeling was that prostitutes were an inevitable adjunct to the aid business, camp followers in the most traditional meaning of that old expression. They traipsed after the army of foreign charities. Wherever the expatriate economy was strong in African countries — the aid-heavy economies in Addis, Nairobi, Kampala, Lilongwe, and Maputo — there was prostitution, usually pretty girls dressed in a peculiarly Western fashion to attract expatriates — the bankers, the aid experts, the charity bureaucrats. There was no mystery to this. The prostitutes followed the money.

So that night in Kampala, as on many nights on my long safari, I stayed in my room and advanced my lengthening story of the young man and the older woman in summery Sicily.

Kampala in the rainy season had always been lovely, because it was a small city of wooded hills, and every street had been lined with flowering trees — tulip trees and flamboyants and jacarandas. Many of the trees had been cut down to widen the roads for new high-rise buildings, and what trees remained were the roosts of scavenging, garbage-eating marabou storks. The storks also stood on the street, pilfering in Dumpsters or loitering on curbs or strutting in twos and threes, somewhat resembling indignant Africans themselves in these postures.

In the days that followed my arrival I left messages with some of my old African friends and colleagues and then walked around, trying to get my bearings. Kampala was no longer a city of Indian shops. The shops remained, but very few were run by Indians. Some were derelict, some were managed by Africans. The city was much larger, and the new buildings were tall but graceless. The older buildings had not been maintained and looked blighted, haunted relics of an earlier time. It seemed to me that the new buildings would go this way too, fall into disrepair and not crumble but remain, defaced and unusable, while still newer ones were built. This seemed a pattern in the African city, the unnecessary obsolescence of buildings. Nothing was fixed or kept in good repair; the concept of stewardship or maintenance hardly existed. In Kampala, the big, elegant Grindlay's Bank had become a horror, the National Theater had become a seedy monstrosity, the railway station was uncared for. Lacking a center, the city seemed to lack a purpose.

"Every one of those new buildings involved a huge number of kickbacks," a Ugandan insider told me, asking not to be named.

Nothing is more distinctive than a movie theater, for it has the type of architecture that advertises itself, with a big brow of a marquee, a wide entrance, a long flight of steps, an open lobby, and a façade designed to display movie posters. In Kampala, the Odeon, the Delite, the Norman, and the Neeta, where I had seen the early James Bond movies, *What's New Pussycat?*, and *Midnight Cowboy*, were closed. A newer, multiscreen theater had taken their place, but it was a flat-faced building of plastic and aluminum and was already falling into disrepair. The old Kampala movie theaters helped me get my bearings, though. Inside this big tumbledown city was a smaller, more familiar one.

With so many of the trees cut down, the city looked balder and uglier. Toward Makerere University, the last half-mile of Kampala road had been lined by trees — very tall ones, dark with foliage, and during the daylight hours even darker because of the bats. It was the district of Wandegeya, called Bat Valley, which was near where I had lived. It was the location I would give to a taxi driver: "Drive me to Bat Valley."

The odd place was a landmark, something that made Kampala special and the university area a little more African, for the university was adjacent to Bat Valley.

All day long, tens of thousands of small bats hung in the branches of these trees, twittering and squealing, sometimes dropping and circling to a new branch, and these idly squabbling peeps and squeals filled the air. Newcomers mistook them for birds, and if I pointed them out they'd say, "Sparrows?" and smile. But when I said, "Look closely," and they saw the huge confusion of bats, a whole tall grove of roadside trees black with them, the newcomers would wince in disgust.

At dusk, as though at a signal, the bats took off, great swirling whorls of them, like sky-darkening clouds of gnats or blowflies. Then the abandoned trees looked lacy, with the last of the sun shining through the boughs as it did not do during the day. Bats this size, none of them bigger than a human hand, went into the swampier outskirts of the city in search of insects. By dawn they were back in the trees, drizzling shit and twittering like sparrows.

I walked along the road, looking up. The trees were gone. Huts, shanties, and sheds had taken their place. No trees, no bats. Bat Valley was gone.

Hardly any trees, but many shacks. I kept walking, past the rotary, which was full of idle taxis and shops. Little shops run by African women were the visible economy now. Inside the gates of Makerere was a mosque, painted green. The sloping landscaped front lawn of a university was the last place you expected to see a mosque with its minaret. But there it was, a gift of Muammar Qaddafi, I was told. Africans refused nothing. A road, a dorm, a school, a bank, a bridge, a cultural center, a dispensary — all were accepted. But acceptance did not mean the things were needed, nor that they would be used or kept in repair. Even this mosque, which was clearly an eyesore, was falling into ruin.

Makerere University had been my place of employment for four years, from 1965 to 1968. After the expatriates went home I ran the Extra-Mural Department. I became a husband, a householder, and a father in Kampala — my first son was born in Mulago Hospital. I was encouraged in my writing in Uganda and began a thirty-year friendship with V. S. Naipaul, who had been sent to Makerere on a fellowship from the Farfield Foundation. (Innocent times: some years later the Farfield was revealed as a front for the CIA.) Uganda had been the making of me.

After a series of disruptions — the early signs of the coming of crazed, monstrous Idi Amin — I had left in a hurry. I had not been back until now, this hot afternoon thirty-four years later. I had wanted to return, for the passage of time is marvelous, and I see something dreamlike, even prophetic, in the effects of time. Aging can be startling, too: the sapling grown into a great oak, the vast edifice made into a ruin, the ironwork — like this elegant Makerere perimeter fence — rusted and broken. Places can become haunted looking or can astonish you with their modernity.

Uganda had a good reputation now, yet nothing I saw there surprised me with its newness; everything was on the wane. I did not lament this, nor was I impressed by a new hospital donated by the Swedes or the Japanese, a new school funded by the Canadians, the Baptist clinic, the flour mill that was signposted *A Gift of the American People.* These were like inspired Christmas presents, the sort that stop running when the batteries die or that break and aren't fixed. The projects would become wrecks, every one of them, because they carried with them the seeds of their destruction. And when they stopped running, no one would be sorry. That's what happened in Africa: things fell apart.

The ruin seemed like part of the plan. It had been the idea of the British Colonial Office to establish a university here. The Makerere motto was *Pro futuro aedificamus* — We build for the future. What a nice idea! But it is a rarefied humanistic notion of the West, not an African tradition. Change and decay and renewal were the African cycle: a mud hut was built; it fell down; a new one replaced it. The Uganda of the university was a country with a subsistence economy — a hand-to-mouth method, but a way of life that had enabled people to get through dreadful times. When the university was closed and became rundown under Idi Amin, when the structures of government no longer existed, when the markets were empty and fuel was in short supply and anarchy seized Uganda, it was the traditional economy that kept Ugandans fed. As the university, a useless compound, became ruinous, Ugandans fled and saved themselves in their mud huts, in the ancient refuge of their villages.

The one-story building where I had worked, the Adult Studies Centre, was in poor shape and had not been improved in more than three decades. It was being used by the law faculty.

"Most of the new buildings you see have been put up in the past ten years," a law lecturer told me. He was John Ntambirweke, a man in his late forties, I guessed, a big strong fellow who was pleasantly self-possessed and opinionated. Suitably enough, this man was occupying my former office. He offered to show me around the campus, and we got into his car. The old neglected buildings outnumbered the bright new ones. It was obvious that after all the political turmoil in the country, the university had not yet recovered to the point where it had been thirty-four years before.

I missed the trees. Why was it that I remembered the trees more clearly than the buildings? As we passed by the crumbling main building and the cracked windows of the library, I asked John Ntambirweke about the recent election.

"An election is not the only indicator of democracy," he said as he negotiated the obstacles in this derelict ivory tower. "Democracy means much more — after all, the Romans had elections. Was Rome a democracy? We need a wider definition. We need more institutions, not one thing but many, so that people can be free."

"They are free, aren't they? But they're hungry."

"The people here need to be granted some political space," he said.

That seemed an appropriate term for Africans who were always lumped together.

"What I really object to is an intelligent man like Nsibambi, the prime minister, explaining in so many words that we require a one-party system. That we Africans are not clever enough or mature enough to think for ourselves. That we are somehow less than other people — inferior to people who have a real opposition."

"There were several opposition parties fighting the election," I said. "They lost, right?"

"The election doesn't prove anything."

"Some African countries don't even have them," I said.

"We need them, but we need more than that," he said. "I am really disappointed with the level of political debate in this country."

"Haven't people in Uganda been saying that since 1962? I used to hear it all the time."

"It's worse now," he said. "We are treated as though we are unworthy, not capable of making choices and distinctions. It's insulting."

"What do people in Uganda say when you mention these things? Or maybe you don't mention these things."

"I do — all the time. I write them. I say them on the radio. I was saying them last Thursday on the radio, just after the election. These days we are free to say anything."

"That's great," I said.

"But it doesn't do any good," he said. "They will just say, 'Oh, there he goes again, that's John, complaining as usual.'"

"That's better than being locked up, which was the traditional response here."

"No one is going to lock me up for saying these things," he said, but with an air of resignation at how ineffectual his opinions were.

John told me that for shooting his mouth off he had had to flee to Kenya after the fall of Amin, when Obote regained power. Realizing that his life was in danger, he had gone to Canada to study and teach. He returned to Uganda with the new regime as a consultant in legal affairs and as an adviser to the revived East African Community, an association for the development of trade and communications.

He had traveled to most of the countries in Africa. His opinions on the other countries were trenchant, too.

"Kenya is another story," he said. "They had white settlers who were tough and who were determined to dominate. But here we just had a few — those tea planters around Fort Portal. They were nobodies. I've been looking at the records. If a white district commissioner offended one of our kings in some way, he could be immediately transferred. The white officials had to learn how to get along with Ugandan chiefs and kings. This policy lasted until independence. We were not colonized in Uganda. This was a protectorate. Our kings continued into independence."

"That's fine," I said, "but if the chiefs and kings had that much power, then maybe that's a Ugandan problem — authority figures become very bossy."

"Maybe. But it wasn't the case in Kenya. And there's the racial thing," he said. "I travel a lot with other Africans. And I notice that Kenyans, Zimbabweans, and Zambians have a strange way of dealing with white people. They behave oddly when they're around them."

"Really?"

He laughed and said, "Yes. When we're traveling in Britain or America, these other Africans detect slights, or they imagine reactions that I don't see. They are very uneasy around white people, but this is not the case among Ugandans."

I told him I was glad to hear him say that, because it was how I had felt in Uganda; it was one of the reasons I had liked living here. People looked me straight in the eye. Then racism crept into the political rhetoric, and I became just a *muzungu* from *Wazungu*land, someone to blame, and at last I had found Africa an easy place to leave.

John and I had come to the end of the Makerere campus tour. In spite of some new buildings, it looked a ghostly and decrepit place. Music blared from the dorm windows, many of which were broken. My old house had become a horror of rotted window sashes and splintered doors and scorched walls. The campus roads were full of potholes. The library — always a good gauge of the health of a university — was in very poor shape, unmaintained, with few users in sight and many empty shelves.

I said, "The prime minister you mentioned, Apolo Nsibambi, was a friend of mine. We taught together."

"He lives near here, because his wife is in the university administration."

After John Ntambirweke dropped me off I went to Apolo's house, a stucco bungalow with a well-tended flower garden. I rang the bell, and the door was answered by a woman housekeeper who told me the master was not at home. I left a *Remember me?* note and asked him to call me.

I sent similar notes and left messages with other old friends, who were now political advisers, commissars, consultants, and members of parliament. Several had been presidential candidates, and the wife of one of them had been a teaching colleague. Everyone knew them. In Africa, everyone my age knew everyone else.

I went back to the library and looked around. What few books remained on the shelves were dusty and torn. I guessed the books had been stolen. There were no new books. What had been the best library in East Africa was now just a shell. The trees around it had been cut down. Only the fact that the buildings had been well made so many years ago had kept them from falling down altogether, but anyone could see that the campus was a disgrace.

Descending the grassy hill toward the faculty housing, I remembered how just here, one hot noon in 1966, by a shaggy-bark eucalyptus tree, I was taking a walk with Vidia Naipaul, who said he hated living in Africa. He became ugly-faced with fury. He said, "The weak and oppressed. They're terrible, man. They've got to be kicked." He kicked a stone, very hard. "That's the only thing Africans understand!"

Naipaul often ranted in Uganda, but he wasn't confidently angry, he was afraid, for the source of his rage was insecurity. Africans looked at him and saw a *Muhindi,* an Indian. As time passed, Naipaul became more narrowly Indian in his attitudes and prejudices. Subsequently, everything he wrote about Africa was informed by the fear that he had known as an isolated Hindu child in black Trinidad. The childhood fear he brought to Africa became terror in his Uganda months, horror on his Congo trip, and as a face-saver he transformed his timid emotions into contempt when he wrote about Africa. *In a Free State* and *A Bend in the River* are veiled attacks on Africans and Africa by an outsider who feels weak. Rigid with a Trinidadian Indian's fear of the bush, he never understood that the bush is benign. Africa frightened him so badly he cursed it, wishing it ill until the curse became a dismissive mantra that ignorant readers could applaud: "Africa has no future."

Leaving Makerere later that day in a taxi, I asked the driver who he had voted for in the recent election. He laughed and said, "These elections are held mainly to impress donor countries — to prove that we are doing the right thing. But it was a rigged election, and we voters are not impressed."

I asked someone in the know about this. He said it was true, that in order to run for election a candidate had to give money to voters. The equivalent of about a dollar each would do, but the most successful candidates gave out pots and pans, lengths of cloth, and shirts ("not T-shirts"). Mobilizers wanted free bikes. "All elections in Uganda involve giving out money and gifts."

I had time on my hands. I got a tailor under a tree to mend my tattered canvas sports jacket. The result was wonderful: a mass of beautifully stitched patches and a new green lining. As a favor to a friend, I gave a talk to about thirty university students, many of whom, having written poems and stories, said they craved careers as full-time writers.

I wanted to go to the bush. The day I planned to take a bus to the western province, to Kabila, to see the chimps in the primate reserve, there was trouble. A news item appeared saying that an attack from the bush in a small town near Kabila had left eleven people dead ("hacked to death") and fifty cars torched. The government claimed that the opposition might have had a hand in it, but most people felt that it was a group calling itself the African Defense Force, an antigovernment organization. A few days later, a vanload of students on a game-viewing drive at Murchison Falls Park were fired upon by another antigovernment group, the Lord's Resistance Army; ten students were killed. This sort of thing seemed to be fairly common, armed men appearing from the bush and committing acts of mayhem. So I didn't go.

I stayed in Kampala, looking for the past. Even with grenades being lobbed occasionally into the central market, the city seemed quiet. "The economy is improving. It's back to where it was in 1970," an economist told me. That was around the time I had left. What kept Uganda together to a large extent was churchgoing and religious tolerance. The country had a large Muslim population — minarets spiking up everywhere, and muezzins wailing. The Church of Uganda was Anglican, with a well-attended red brick cathedral on one of Kampala's hills. Its bells were audible every Sunday. In the 1880s one of Uganda's kings, Mtesa I, had disapproved of his subjects' becoming Catholic converts and made a bonfire of a number of them. This martyrdom and their subsequent sainthood had given Ugandan Catholicism a tremendous boost, even before the pope visited.

"We must preach harmony and reconciliation," a priest was saying in his sermon, amplified on the sidewalk one Sunday. He talked about the election, how winners "were jubilating, even as others were mourning." He finished movingly with, "Love one another."

It was a mild evening, and all the strollers were within earshot of the sermon. Some of them were urchins and prostitutes and schoolgirls hustling for money. Some were selling newspapers. Others were hawking sunglasses and cigarette lighters. It was impossible to tell whether any of these people understood what was being said.

Why were there so many prostitutes in this part of town? In the past they had hung around bars and nightclubs. But these women and girls were on the street, lounging on low walls, leaning against trees. There was shade here, it was quiet, and there were three hotels in the area. I guessed that there were customers here, the aid people, the visiting bureaucrats, the foreigners. But the women also solicited passing cars driven by Africans. In my day, not many Africans owned cars, so these hookers were one of the features of the new economy.

Some prostitutes sat in the veranda café of my hotel, sizing up any man who passed by with that lingering gaze and familiar smile that is common to prostitutes and car salesmen — the lock of eye contact. They even had the same pitch: "What can I do for you?," which meant, "What can you do for me?"

What these women wanted was a drink, so they would not seem so conspicuous. By buying them beer, I got acquainted with three of them, who always sat together speaking Swahili — Clementine from the Congo, Angelique from Rwanda, Fifi from Burundi.

Fifi had arrived in Kampala from Bujumbura only the week before. "Because there was trouble," she explained. "There's a lot of fighting in Burundi right now."

She had taken three buses and had come via Kigali, in Rwanda.

"Rwanda is — ha!" Angelique threw up her hands in despair.

"But it was worse before?" I said. I was thinking of the gruesome descriptions of massacre in the book *We Wish to Inform You That We Will All Be Killed Tomorrow with Our Families.* Even if you didn't agree with the author's historical premise, that Belgian colonialism had imposed tribal distinctions and a class system in the Watutsi and Bahutu society, the book was excellent, if upsetting, reportage.

"Much worse before," Angelique said. "I mean, my family was killed."

She was the youngest of the three, hardly more than seventeen. The eldest was Clementine, from Bukavu, in the Congo. Her ambition was to go to America.

"*Ku fanya nini?*" I said. To do what? I asked in Swahili because it was a delicate question, given the sort of work she normally did.

"*Ku fanya une salon de coiffure,*" Clementine said, and explained, "I can do hair well. Look at Angelique's hair. So pretty!"

Swahili, not French, was their common language. Their English was fine, but embarrassed questions they asked in Swahili.

"*Mimi na sakia njaa,*" Fifi said to me, pouting a little. She was hungry.

I bought them fried potatoes, three plates of them, and it was obvious that what they really wanted was not a chance to perform oral sex on a strange man, or ten dollars for a massage, or a quickie in the back seat of an African bureaucrat's car, but a big plate of French fries and a beer. And perhaps a ticket to America. Anyway, they were ravenously hungry and did not hide it.

"So you're traveling?" Clementine asked.

I said yes, that I had just come from Kenya.

"We hear that Nairobi is very dangerous."

This from a Congolese who had lived in one of the most anarchic parts of the eastern Congo and who traveled through the massacres of Rwanda. I mentioned this.

"Yes, but there are good places, too," Clementine said. "Let's all go to the Congo together and we'll show you the good places."

We planned the Congo trip. I would hire a Land Rover and buy some food and cases of beer. We would need presents to give away to people. Good shoes, raincoats, maybe some medicine, and money of course — American dollars would be best. We would head southwest, cross through Rwanda into the border town of Goma, and then wander through the Congo, wherever the roads took us.

"The roads are very bad, but we don't care!" Angelique said.

"We will give you massages for nothing — three girls, all together. How you like that?" Clementine said.

"I like it very much."

"We go now?" she said, pointing upstairs.

"*Wewe napenda wazee?*" I said. You like old men?

She said, "You're not old. Maybe — what? — forty or so?"

That was another welcome touch. I was fascinated by them — by their travel, their resilience, even their glamour. These girls in tight satin dresses, upswept hairdos, and stiletto heels came from dark and dangerous villages in the dead center of Africa and had reinvented themselves as sex goddesses. But I was not interested in anything more than their stories. Though the rule in Uganda was "no condom, no sex," they were following a risky profession in an AIDS-ridden city, competing with hundreds, perhaps thousands of other women. I had to admire their resourcefulness. Now and then I heard of American or European women's groups that went to Nairobi and Kampala to encourage prostitutes to get off the streets, to retrain them — to "empower" them, the agents of virtue explained. The prostitutes I met would have laughed at such a proposition.

"So?" Clementine was smiling. "We go to your room?"

But I went to my room alone and scribbled.

For my onward journey, I was trying to arrange passage on a boat across Lake Victoria. In my comings and goings I often bumped into Clementine, Angelique, and Fifi at the hotel, and I usually stopped to buy them a drink or some food. I even asked them what work they liked doing, what they wanted for themselves. Hairdressing loomed large in their ambitions, but mostly they wanted money.

Clementine said, "I want just one man, someone to look after me. If he is good to me, I will be good to him. What about you?"

Yet, as always, I slept alone in my narrow bed.

◈ ◈ ◈

Repeated trips to the office of the Board of East African Railways convinced me that if I persevered I might get a berth on a ferry. Several ferries a week ran from Port Bell in Uganda to Mwanza, the port town on the opposite side of the lake, in Tanzania. But for the past three months, passengers had been forbidden to ride on the Lake Victoria ferries.

"Why is that so?"

"Ebola virus," the secretary to the board chairman told me. "There was an outbreak in Uganda two months ago, and so the Tanzanians took steps."

There had also been a tragic ferry sinking. In 1996, the MV *Bukoba* went down in the southern end of the lake, and more than one thousand passengers drowned. Because of the liability and the high cost of insurance, very few passengers were carried across the lake these days. This was all news to me: where had it been reported? The sinking of the *Bukoba* was one of those African catastrophes that hardly rated a mention in the world press.

"Maybe I should write a letter."

I asked for paper and sat in the office writing a florid pleading letter to the chairman. After two more visits, a letter from the chairman awaited me, stating that if I accepted the liability (Ebola? a sinking?), an exception would be made in my case. I could ride on one of the ferries. They would let me know which one I might take. This was somewhat indefinite, but having secured permission I felt I had achieved a victory.

"How will I know when a ferry is leaving?"

"You must come here every day to check."

◇ ◇ ◇

"The prime minister left a message for you, Mr. Thorax," the desk clerk said one day. This was Apolo Nsibambi, my old friend and colleague, who had risen in the world.

I called him back and he said I should come to his office the next day. He said it was a waste of his time to give me directions.

"The prime minister's office! Everyone knows where the prime minister's office is. Ask any taxi driver!"

The same bluster — he hadn't changed. From the beginning, when he joined my department as a lecturer in 1966, I had found him interesting. He had just come from Chicago, where he had earned a Ph.D. in political science. On first meeting him, I asked him how he had liked Chicago. He said, "Immensely." Some months later he said he had had several run-ins with the Chicago police, what is now known as racial profiling.

"Each time it was the same. I would be walking home late at night after studying at the library. A police car would pull up to the curb and a white policeman would say, 'Get over here, nigger. Where are you going?'"

"What did you do?" I asked.

"I said, 'Officer, I am not a nigger. Do not call me a nigger. I am Ugandan, an African. I am a student here and I am doing nothing wrong.'" And then his voice became shrill: "'I am not a nigger!'"

Saying that he was an African usually worked. One policeman had even apologized, saying, "Sorry, we didn't know you were an African. We thought you were a nigger."

Apolo was more than a Ugandan; he was something of an aristocrat, from a distinguished family. One of his grandmothers had been a princess, so he was related to the king, the Kabaka. The Kingdom of Buganda, ruled by the Kabakas, was centuries old and still powerful. The Kabaka known as King Freddy was overthrown in 1966. From our offices at the Adult Studies Centre we could see smoke rising from the siege: Idi Amin and his men firing on the palace. That week, the man who would be king, Ronald Mutebi — the present Kabaka — hid at Apolo's house for safety.

"I decided to be a commoner," Apolo said. "My children are commoners — free to marry whom they like."

The Eton of Uganda is King's College, Budo. Apolo's grandfather had been head prefect at King's, his father had been head prefect, Apolo himself had been head prefect. His father, Semyoni — a version of Simeon — had been a major landowner. In a mood of religious fervor in 1922, somewhat in the spirit of Tolstoy in old age, Semyoni divested himself of his land, abandoned his political beliefs, and started a religious revival called the Balokole movement.

Apolo called the revivalists "spiritual purists," explaining that "they believed in putting things right, and repentance, and being 'saved.' They were not fundamentalists. It was a movement within the Church of Uganda."

The first time I had met Apolo's father, he had been lying on a sofa, suffering a spell of illness. From this supine position his first words to me were "Are you saved?" I told him I didn't know. That made him laugh. He said sharply, "Then the answer is no. If you don't know, it means you are not saved!"

Apolo, my age exactly, had gotten married the same year as I had; we had gone to each other's wedding and were in all respects contemporaries. I left, he stayed. Idi Amin took over: nine years of horror. Apolo fathered four children. The 1980s were a decade of adjustment — Apolo had been a university lecturer. In the nineties he had become a government minister, Public Services and Education, and now he was prime minister. He was as well known for his reforms as he was for his patrician ways. "I saw him in New York last year," a mutual friend told me. "He had a man to carry his briefcase. I asked him why. He said, 'Because I am premier.'"

He was also a famous tease, and his affectation of pomposity made him more devastating as a needler. On seeing me after thirty years his first words were "Ah, Paul. You are in deep trouble in Uganda. You made love to my cousin. Why didn't you marry her? You were vibrant! I shall fine you ten thousand shillings for not marrying her." He made a gesture suggesting gross indecency. "You used to do this to her."

"I never knew your cousin, Apolo."

"You also did this to her," he said, flailing his arms and contorting his body. This was an odd sight, for he was full-figured, in a pinstriped suit and natty tie and affecting a plummy accent.

"Never," I said.

"You did. She was quite fond of Europeans, actually."

"What's her name?"

"You know her name. It will appear on the charge sheet when I fine you the money. Ah, you were so busy in that area."

"What area?"

"The ladies," he said, and at that moment he was buzzed and he took a call. Immediately he began abusing the person at the other end in the same plummy voice: "Tell me why this man wrote a stupid letter to me . . . But you are in charge of this man . . . What I resent is that I am regarded as a bulldozer — please let me finish. I despise him, and in fact we had a clash before . . . I want action — I don't want to hear that I am doing your work for you."

There were eight trays on his desk, labeled *Very Urgent, Urgent, Normal, Ministers, Chief Justice, Speaker, Vice President, President.* Each tray was filled with memos and papers. *Very Urgent* was overflowing.

Apolo was still shouting into the phone. "He deliberately distorted what I said. Why does he personalize the debate? I had said, 'You are a good man, but you are autocratic and overbearing.' He said I am the same! Impossible! The idiot wrote 'grieved.' But I didn't say that. I said 'aggrieved' . . . No, no, no! Why not say, 'Those people have created a culture of defeat'?"

"I am a technocratic premier," he said to me after he slammed the phone down. "What does that mean? It means — write this down, Paul — I have no electoral pressure."

He saw that I was taking notes while he had been denouncing the person at the other end of the phone. He had always been something of a monologist, and I think he took to the idea that his words were being recorded, if only in a notebook on my knee.

"Under our constitution, if you are president or minister, you are an ex-officio MP under Article Seventy-seven."

I must have stopped writing — anyway, was this interesting? — because he said, "Paul, write that down, 'Article Seventy-seven.' And consider the pressure on an MP. Pressure from constituents. Making payments for them."

"What sort of payments?"

"Buying coffins for them, paying school fees, what and what! They demand one's time. They invade one's house."

He was pacing now, like a statesman, in front of his enormous desk and a large map of Uganda and all those trays — *Very Urgent, Urgent,* and so forth — his right hand grasping one lapel, his other gesturing.

"As I see it, Paul, the crisis of governance is that ministers are overloaded and laboring under excessive pressure, parliamentary business, constituency work, and cabinet affairs. One of the functions that has suffered in parliament is attendance. We sometimes don't have a quorum."

His phone buzzed again. Another call being returned from a newspaper.

"Your reporter distorted what I said. I said the candidates 'conceded.' I did not thank them for conceding. Then I open the paper today and what do I see on page five? 'The prime minister commended those who accepted defeat.' I did not. Your reporter made several other mistakes, relating to the constitution."

Apolo listed the mistakes and then hung up, nodding approvingly that I had been taking notes — I felt that in note-taking I had been making him self-conscious and verbose. But perhaps not, since he had always been verbose.

"They are mesmerized by my understanding of the constitution," he said. "My wife says, 'Apolo is unelectable.' It's probably true! If people are foolish, I tell them they are foolish."

I wrote this down, and the phone rang again. Another ministry, Apolo shouting the other person down.

"My response to the Ministry of Health is, do they really need nine billion shillings to buy drugs? If so, why did we name the department 'microfinance'? What I am saying to you is that the emperor is naked in some respects . . . Yes, I whispered to him about that . . . Please listen to me. We have a saying, 'When you wrestle someone to the ground you don't then bite him.'"

Before he could talk to me again, there was another call, from someone in his own party.

"This proves what I have always said," Apolo crowed after listening for a few seconds. "Traditionally, the Muganda looks to the chief to tell him how to vote. For the first time, democratization has reached the countryside. This is good, because Buganda has been lagging behind. They must be accountable! Unless we fulfill Article Two-forty-six we will perish!"

He hung up and turned to me again.

"You see? I am a technocratic premier," he said. "I run the state in a specialized manner."

"Apolo," I said, "people say that this is turning into a one-party system. What do you say to that?"

"Ours is not a one-party system but a movement, unique in Africa," he replied. "In a one-party system you sack the man who does not toe the party line. In a movement you try to find a consensus."

"How do you manage that?"

"Ha! The elites here are very poor at bargaining. The British concluded that in the 1950s, and I can confirm it."

"In Buganda?" I said, thinking of the kingdom, not the country.

"You-you-*you*-ganda," he said. "Do you remember Obote's way of running the country?"

"Obote was selfish and single-minded," I said.

"I like your statement. Yes. He was that. Museveni has much more confidence. He listens. As for the multiparty system, Article Seventy-four states that during the fourth term of parliament — Paul, it is very important for you to quote our constitution. Please write this. Clause Three states that in three years this must take place. But the issue is not to be too legalistic. Better to bargain politically and attain a sustainable consensus."

He was still pacing, monologuing, stabbing his finger at the map of Uganda. He took more calls. He sipped a can of Coke. He was told that an aunt had died in France. He arranged for the body to be transported to Uganda.

"Yes, we will identify it. Yes, we will have a funeral on the twenty-eighth. Yes, we will cry." And he hung up.

Like everyone else, he said that the Idi Amin years were the worst he had known. "Too horrible for words," he said. "The soldiers took my derelict car. They seemed to be very pleased when they saw that a university professor was living in such reduced circumstances."

He teased his secretaries, he took another call, he drank another Coke, he waved his copy of the Uganda constitution, which he had had a hand in drafting. It was as annotated and thumbed as a sacred text. We talked about the need for political parties and moral authority and the necessity for public debate. It was the same sort of conversation we had had in the Makerere Staff Club over bottles of Bell beer in 1966.

"Whom do you want to meet? What do you want? What can I do for you?" he said. "I must go to parliament. You see how busy my day is."

I said, "Do you remember the story you told me about being in Chicago when you were a student — how the police stopped you and called you a nigger?"

He laughed and said, "Oh, yes. The Chicago police were quite racist in the sixties. It's a lively city. I get back there occasionally."

Then he was off to parliament, and I was off to the Railway Board.

"No ferry tonight. Maybe tomorrow."

There was none the next day, which gave me time to see several more of my old friends. Like Apolo, they were pillars of society, still married to the same spouses after thirty-odd years. The four of them had produced twenty-four children. They were plumper, grayer, and like Apolo they were great talkers. In African terms they had defied the odds, for all were around sixty, the age of a respected elder in Africa. They had survived and flourished in a country that had known regicide, two revolutions, a coup d'état, AIDS, and Idi Amin. My old friends were people of accomplishment. The one woman, Thelma Awori, was a former ambassador married to a presidential candidate who had come in third in the recent election; another, Jassy Kwesiga, was running a think tank; a third was a presidential adviser, who had refused an ambassadorial post on the grounds that "I am not good ambassador material — I told the president, and it's true." That was Chango Machyo, who had been a Maoist in the 1960s and was still a radical, the scourge of "imperialists," "neocolonialists," and "the black bourgeoisie."

"You mentioned my tribe in one of your books," Jassy Kwesiga said, as a form of greeting.

Yes, the Bachiga of southwest Uganda and their curious marriage rite, which included the groom's brothers and the bride in the urine ceremony. I could not hear the name of the tribe without thinking of the piddle-widdle of this messy rite.

Kwesiga had spent several decades as a university lecturer. His wife was a university dean, his children were successful, and he was fat and happy. We reminisced about our lives as young men in Uganda in the sixties, when our haunts had been the White Nile Club, the Gardenia, the Susanna Club, the New Life, and City Bar. Like many others, he was nostalgic for the earlier, more orderly time, when the country was still intact, before any political violence, before AIDS, an age of innocence.

"The sixties were wonderful," he said. "We were the elite without realizing it. The seventies were a disaster with Idi Amin. People disappeared — for so many reasons. It is a period to forget. Things are improving. Democracy is a process. The process is democratization. Democratic growth has its own momentum. What are you writing, *bwana?*"

"Nothing yet. Just traveling."

"People on the outside just write bad news — the disasters, Ebola virus, AIDS, bombs. And they ask the wrong questions."

"What should they ask?"

"The question should be, How did anyone survive?"

"I think I know the answer," I said. "Because it's a subsistence economy, and survival is something that Africans have learned."

"Yes. Years and years of just getting by," he said in a tone of regret, almost sorrow, and in that same tone he went on. "I've traveled too, you know. I went to Beijing some years ago. I thought I was going to a city where people were poor and miserable. It was amazing. I was on the thirty-third floor of a hotel that was beautiful, and the city was incredible. How did this happen?"

He was remembering our colleague Chango Machyo and his office copies of *Peking Review* and *China Reconstructs.* We lived vicariously through Mao's Great Proletarian Cultural Revolution this way, the whole of socialist Africa did. The Chinese in those magazines planted rice, harvested beans, and made pig iron. Their motto was: Serve the people. They wore cloth slippers and faded blue jackets and looked like geeks. Now they were a billion grinning plutocrats in neckties.

He meant: Why can't Africans do the same?

I said, "Do you want to live in China?"

"Never," he said.

"Then maybe what you see in Uganda is more or less what you asked for."

In a reversal of fortune, the now prosperous People's Republic was investing in Uganda's peasantry, because of Uganda's large cotton crop. A Chinese factory had recently opened in the northern town of Lira, for milling the cotton and making clothes to sell locally and for export. More joint ventures were planned. What China had failed to accomplish in East Africa through Maoism it might yet succeed at through venture capitalism.

A sign of Kwesiga's confidence in the country was that he had encouraged his five children to live and work in Uganda — some had married, none had left the country. My friend Chango Machyo, the Maoist, had nine children. All of them were working in Uganda. The proof of your political faith was the way you guided your children. A loving parent did not willingly sacrifice children to muddled thinking or a doomed economy.

Thelma was a Liberian, American educated, married to a Ugandan, who had lived and worked in Uganda for thirty-five years. I knew the others by their tribal affiliation. Apolo was a Muganda, Kwesiga a Muchiga, Chango a Musamia.

Chango's office was in the presidential compound on Kololo Hill, a number of mud-spattered stucco buildings behind a tall fence. His title was National Political Commissar, a vague position, but since Chango had always been an ideologue, the president must have found him a useful mentor. He looked battered and ill when I saw him, and a little unsteady. He apologized, saying that he had malaria that week and felt dizzy. I said we could meet another day.

"No. It's good to see you after so long. What do you think of the country now?"

"More people. Fewer trees."

"That's right. And no Indians."

"Is that good?"

"Very good. They were exploiting us and sucking our blood."

Even malaria had no effect on his Maoist rhetoric. We talked about the president, Yoweri Museveni.

Chango said, "Don't you remember him? He was one of our students at Ntare when we gave those weekend courses."

Ntare was a school near the rural town of Mbarara. In the sixties, we younger lecturers in the Extra-Mural Department went out to country areas and organized classes in English and political science. As for Mbarara, all I remembered was a mass of students of the pastoral Banyankole tribe taking notes in the classrooms, their cattle lowing and browsing under the windows.

"I didn't remember him either," Chango said. "But he remembered me. Times were so bad under Amin I went to Nairobi. Museveni was there. He saw me. 'Mr. Machyo!' I said, 'Eh, eh, what are you doing?' He was a soldier. He was named after his father's battalion, the Seventh. He said he had a plan. He had trained with the FRELIMO in Mozambique. I went to Dar es Salaam with him, but I missed my family. Then, after Amin, after the anarchy, after the guerrilla war against Obote, and Museveni took over in 1986, he sent for me. He made me minister of water and then minister of rehabilitation — we gave out blankets. Later I became national political commissar."

"You were always a political commissar."

"Yes, I haven't changed. I am still saying the same things."

"'Neocolonialism.' 'The proletariat.' 'Imperialism.' 'Black bourgeoisie.' 'Bloodsuckers.'"

"They have it in Kenya," Chango said. "The African bourgeoisie inherited settler farms. They took over white hotels. Just so they could make big profits. That type of African is no good for Africa. At the bourgeois level it is a struggle for power."

I told him that it seemed to me that Uganda was still recovering from the anarchy of the Idi Amin years. Chango said that was partly true. He had lost his job at the university, like many others. He had gone back to his village near the eastern town of Mbale.

"Life in Uganda was terrible under Amin," he said. "There was always shooting. For years there was a curfew, from six P.M. to six A.M. If you were caught outside you would be shot. People were fearing. If you saw a soldier you got very worried, because a soldier could do anything to you. Many people were taken away. Me, myself, I was taken but released."

"How did you live?"

"I had nothing. Times were very bad. I resumed my old job as a surveyor — yes, I am a trained surveyor — but there was no work."

"Weren't you safer in Mbale than you would have been in Kampala?"

"No. One day I was in a coffee shop in Mbale and a soldier came in. People were greeting him, but I had a bad feeling. I left the place. As soon as I got home I heard shooting from the direction of the coffee shop. What happened was this. Two men were coming down the road. The soldier said, 'Watch this.' And he shot them both for no reason. After that I went to Nairobi."

Hearing this, it occurred to me that all this talk of "it was a time to forget" and "look to the future" was perhaps a mistake. Students had asked me, "How can we become better-known writers?" But the real question should have been, "What should we be writing?" And the answer was: About those lost years. Because of the shame and humiliation and defeat, no one liked talking about the Amin years, yet it seemed that the best use of someone's writing skills would be to compile an oral history of that cruel time.

My old friend Thelma Awori had a horror story. Her husband, Aggrey, had been head of Uganda Television in 1971 when Amin was in power. Soldiers came to his office and took him by force. One wanted to shoot him on the spot, but another said, "Not here — take him away." They took him outside and put him against a tree. A soldier drew a bead on him, but just before the man fired, Aggrey dropped to the ground.

A soldier passing by recognized him and said, "Don't shoot him." The other soldiers were insistent, and an argument ensued. "Let's take him to Amin," one said. And so Amin decided Aggrey's fate: he was released. Aggrey fled the country and taught school in Kenya until it was safe to return home. He had been unsuccessful in his run for president, but he was still a member of parliament.

"And our children are here," Thelma said. "We wanted them here. We said, 'Come back and get your foot in the door. Get a decent job. Try to be part of the process.'"

They had five children, mostly American educated like their parents — Thelma was a Radcliffe graduate, Aggrey had gone to Harvard. One of their daughters had a master's degree from Wharton.

Thelma said, "She was on Wall Street. Aggrey insisted that she come back. She is earning less money by far, and she couldn't believe how inefficient things were here. But she says, 'If I weren't here, they wouldn't do things right.'"

Everyone was talking openly about the country's problems — Uganda had not changed in that respect. But Uganda, even in its apparent recovery, was a welfare case. More than half of its budget came from donor countries. AIDS had peaked in 1992 at 30 percent and through intense education had decreased: now 10 percent of the population was infected. The disease had killed off the better part of a generation. It was a nation of two million orphans.

"I'm paid to be optimistic," an American diplomat said to me in Kampala shortly before I left. "I mean, you have to be optimistic to work in places like this. But if I weren't being paid for that, I would despair of what Africans have made of their countries — the deforestation, the disorder, AIDS — God."

He asked what I thought, for I had seen before and after.

I said, "People I know — very smart people — want their children to stay here, not to emigrate. Speaking as a parent, that's a good sign."

I had nothing else to go on, but that was something: the belief that their children had a future here was a measure of confidence and a way of saying that the country had a future.

In Kampala, I had begun to live a tranquil life, not as a traveler but as a resident of a place I had begun to enjoy anew. I saw old friends, had leisurely meals, went for walks, went bird watching on the lakeshore. Most nights I worked on my long erotic story.

My kind of travel was sometimes expensive because it was improvised and always involved last-minute plans. But this two-week residence in Kampala cost me very little, and sleeping in the same bed night after night, and writing a story, restored my energy. Some days I did nothing more than stroll, watching children playing with homemade toys, hoops made of plastic, little vehicles of twisted wire, pull toys, and sometimes live insects — rhino beetles — flying on pieces of string.

One of my strolls was always to the Railway Board, to find out about a ferry. I left it to the afternoon one day. And that day the chairman's secretary stood up at her desk and pointed to the door.

She said, "Go to Port Bell right now. Bring Chairman Sentongo letter. Bring you passport. Bring you cloves. The ferry leaving just now!"

11 ◇◇◇

The MV *Umoja* Across Lake Victoria

For three hours at the Port Bell ferry pier I watched weaverbirds building nests in the papyrus stalks by the lake's edge. I was due to sail on the ferry *Kabalega.* "Soon, soon," a dock official said. "They are welding the ship." A fish eagle swooped. A man casting a net came up after many tries with some tiny fish. Another hour passed. Near some sunken boats ten or twelve boys fished for tilapia with bamboo poles. This was not recreation, it was their next meal. Another hour.

I walked up and down, thinking how every book I had ever read about Africa contained long passages and sometimes many pages about enforced delay. "We remained in the chief's compound for many days, awaiting his permission to return to the coast" is a sentence that occurs in many books of African exploration. Burton's African travel writing contains shouts of complaint against delays; so does Livingstone's and everyone else's. David Livingstone, who believed that "constipation is sure to bring on fever," ordered his men to go on long bush marches because such exertion was efficacious for their bowels. "[In Africa] with the change of climate there is often a peculiar condition of the bowels which makes the individual imagine all manner of things in others." For Livingstone delay spelled constipation. *Heart of Darkness* is a book of dramatic and maddening delays.

Even the narration is obstructive; halting and deliberately tangential. Delay is now and then a form of suspense that makes you concentrate, but more often it is a nuisance that drives you nuts. And who wants to hear about it? This paragraph is already too long.

It sometimes seems as though Africa is a place you go to wait. Many Africans I met said the same thing, but uncomplainingly, for most lived their lives with a fatalistic patience. Outsiders see Africa as a continent delayed — economies in suspension, societies up in the air, politics and human rights put on hold, communities throttled or stopped. "Not yet," voices of authority have cautioned Africans throughout the years of colonization and independence. But African time was not the same as American time. One generation in the West was two generations in Africa, where teenagers were parents and thirty-year-olds had one foot in the grave. As African time passed, I surmised that the pace of Western countries was insane, that the speed of modern technology accomplished nothing, and that because Africa was going its own way at its own pace for its own reasons, it was a refuge and a resting place, the last territory to light out for. I surmised this, yet I did not always feel it; I am impatient by nature.

"When will this welding be finished?" I asked, and was told: "Not welding, *bwana.* They are fixing the engine."

"How long have they been working on it?"

"For some days."

Night had fallen. Glaring overhead lights had come on, making it impossible to see anything. It was now more than five hours since I had arrived, breathless, at the pier, imagining that I was about to board a departing ferry. Mr. Joseph said, "Don't worry, sir." The customs agent said, "We will take care of you." These men were also teasing each other, greeting and bantering like big fat boys, as men do in such jobs that involve long delays — on docks and in depots and loading bays. But I believed them. I took comfort in their reassurance.

In the moonless lakeshore night the mud stink rose like part of the darkness, and so did the mosquitoes and lake flies. Two more hours passed.

"How long does it take to get to the other side of the lake?" I asked the customs agent.

He said, "Me, myself I cannot know, sir. I have never been there in my life."

Mr. Joseph was listening. He shook his head, laughed to express incomprehension, and said, "To sleep on water. Eh! Eh! I have never done it. It must be very strange."

Seven hours after arriving at the pier, Captain Opio of the *Kabalega* said to me, "It seems we will not leave tonight."

"Really?" My heart sank.

"Really," he said solemnly. "Therefore, let me introduce you to Captain Mansawawa of the *Umoja*."

"Are you leaving tonight, Captain?"

"Yes, when the freight cars arrive from Kampala to be loaded."

That was a detail. The important thing with a ferry, or any ship, was to get on board, secure a berth, and get your feet under the table in the galley. Then a delay did not matter: you just went to bed, and if the vessel was still at the pier tomorrow, you read a book. This was preferable to sitting on a bench at the customhouse or pacing on the pier for seven hours.

"May I come with you?"

"*Karibu,*" the captain said. Welcome. His saying it in Swahili made the word seem more sincere.

Captain Mansawawa was a serious and hardworking man from Musoma, on the lake, who also spoke Chichewa. I had learned this Bantu language in the Peace Corps in order to teach in Malawi. The captain had learned it as master of the passenger ship *Ilala,* which sailed on Lake Nyasa.

"You are our guest," the captain said, climbing up the gangway. "This is Alex. First engineer."

A man in a skullcap stood at the top of the stairs, smiling, one eye fixed on me, his other eye drifting off. His lazy eye made him look lost and lovable. He said "*Karibu*" too, and he pulled my bag out of my hands. He shook my hand and said, "You take my cabin. It is forward."

He hurried to the bow and unlocked the cabin door with a brass plate attached that read *First Engineer.* He did not open the door at once. He looked at me with one eye and gave me instructions.

"We must first put off all lights. This one and this one." He flicked off the lights on the deck. "There are sea flies. They like the lights. But they don't bite."

He opened the door quickly, pushed me in, squirmed inside himself, and slammed the door. We were in darkness.

"Don't be fearing," he said, switching the cabin light on.

The room was filled with whirling gnat-sized insects, clouds of them circling the light and smacking the cabin screens. Dead insects littered the bed. Alex swept them from the yellow sheet and the gray pillow.

"*Doodoos*," I said, the generic term for small insects.

"These *doodoos* will not bother you," Alex said, sweeping more of them aside with his hand and stuffing my bag on a shelf. His squiffy eyes made him seem more efficient, able to scrutinize two sides of the cabin at the same time.

"So they don't bite?"

"No. We eat them," he said, and smacked his lips. "They are very sweet."

"The *doodoos* don't bite you, but you bite the *doodoos?*"

He laughed and said, "Yes! Yes!" and then, "This is your cabin."

"Where will you sleep?"

"Somewhere!" He bowed and left.

This was perfect for an aptly named ferry — *umoja* is the Swahili word for unity or oneness. Never mind that the cabin was rusty and bad smelling, the bedding unwashed, and the sea flies a bother. This was harmony, privacy, and the sort of seedy comfort I craved. The cabin was large, with an armchair and a lamp. There was a stopped clock on the wall, and last year's calendar — a picture of rhinos. A table was set against the hull. In the drawer was a rubber stamp that said *1st Engineer, M.V. Umoja.* I shared a cold-water shower with the adjoining cabin. I could read, I could write, I could listen to my radio. I did not care if this crossing of the lake took two days or twenty.

A half-hour later, I was writing my notes — *To sleep on water. Eh! Eh! It must be very strange* — when there was a knock at the door, Alex calling me to the galley. The deck hands and the second engineer joined us, along with the captain, for the freight cars had not yet arrived from Kampala.

"You like *nyama ya kuku?*" the captain said, placing a chicken leg on my plate. Alex heaped some rice beside it, with a lump of mashed avocado.

"You have pili-pili sauce?" I asked.

"Too much," Alex said, knowing that he was making a joke.

"You have beer?"

"For you, yes."

"I'm in heaven," I said, and toasted them. They were on duty and couldn't drink alcohol.

"You are welcome, Mr. Paul."

Alex was of the Sukuma tribe. The WaSukuma lived at the southern end of the lakeshore in what was known as Greater Unyamwezi. These people were on my mind. In Nairobi I had seen a giant wooden marionette in a shop, a doll about five feet high with a plump torso and conical breasts and a spooky staring face. It was old and beautifully made, with articulated arms and legs. It weighed about forty pounds. "From the Sukuma people," the Indian shop owner said. He had bought it from a bush trader in Tanzania, and I bought it from him. When I returned home, I would notify him and he would send it to me.

"They use them in the villages," Alex said.

He called it a *vinyago vibubwa* (a large doll), a benevolent figure that was paraded around the village at harvest time. He was pleased to talk about it but had the East African city dweller's self-conscious tendency to dissociate himself from any sort of superstitious ritual.

"Just in the bush," he said. "The far bush."

It occurred to me, sitting there, that no one at the dock or on the ferry had asked to see my passport. No one had looked at my letter authorizing my trip. There was no mention of money, no one had asked for references or a ticket. I had merely been introduced. It was just "Climb aboard," as the driver of the cattle truck had said to me north of Marsabit, on the shifta road before we were ambushed.

The crew were all Tanzanians, friendly and solicitous. They had been in Port Bell for several days, loading the ferry. They were sensationally grease-stained as a result, which made the hand-washing ceremony at mealtimes something to behold: everyone at the table leaned aside and took turns with the basin and the soap while someone else poured water from the pitcher. Lots of scrubbing, for ferry loading was filthy work. No matter how grubby an eater might be, he had to have clean hands.

"I like coming here," the captain said in Swahili. "Uganda is our friend. Kenyans are also our friends, but the Kenya police are always looking for *rushwa*."

That was a new word to me.

"Baksheesh," the captain explained. "Extra money. Kenya is a bad place."

When the meal ended, the hour was late. Still we had not left the port, but so what? I went to my cabin and finished my notes, brushing sea flies off the bright page with one hand, writing with the other. Then I lay in my bunk and listened to my shortwave radio. News from home, disaster euphemisms from stock market analysts: "The market is in a long drought mode" and "The market is in a rinse cycle," meaningless here on the shore of Lake Victoria. Sea flies settled on my face. I clawed them off. I heard the lurch and rumble of freight cars shunted on board — there were rails set in the deck. With the shouting of deck hands, the ferry responded to the weight of the new cargo and steadied itself.

I was already dozing, tasting sea flies each time I yawned. The ferry shuddered when its engines revved, but I was asleep by the time we set sail. About an hour and a half out of Port Bell we crossed the Equator.

I woke several times in the night, though from odd dreams — the dreams you have in a strange bed — not from the movement of the ship. The *Umoja* stayed on an even keel, plowing across the calm lake, with only a slight chop from the southeast wind. The temperature was pleasant — cool fresh air drifting through the porthole — the engines droned deep in the body of the vessel, and the hull vibrated in a massaging motion that soothed me.

When I woke I could not see land anywhere: we were at sea. Lake Victoria is the largest body of water in Africa, 27,000 square miles. A whole intact people, the Sese islanders, occupied a distinct archipelago in the north of the lake. The lake was full of fish, but also full of crocs, bilharzia, pirates, and primitive craft. Victoria had not been properly surveyed since colonial times, and only old charts were in use. So there were many uncharted rocks and other hazards.

Clouds of sea flies blew across the deck as I went outside. They smacked me in the face and got in my eyes. To the west was a smudge and when we came closer I could see that it was an island, flat and forested.

"Goziba Island," Alex said.

"Who lives there?"

"Everyone. Ugandans, Kenyans, Tanzanians, Congolese, Rwandans, and more. They come in dugouts or motorboats or dhows. It is nice! No police, no government people. No taxes. Just in the middle of nowhere."

The detailed chart in the wheelhouse showed the lake to be dotted with many such islands, around the edge, in the middle, some regulated and named, others nameless, open to whatever squatters could paddle to them. Dugouts were frequently overturned by crocodiles and the paddlers devoured. Sigulu Island, in the northeast of the lake, recorded forty-three deaths from crocs in a recent six-month period. The intense crocodile activity seemed to emphasize the free-for-all that was the general rule on Lake Vic.

Breakfast was *ugali,* African porridge, a pasty gruel, served with sweet tea. I was reminded that the Africa I knew had never been a gourmet experience, but most of the food was palatable. Places might be famous for particular produce, like southern Ethiopia and its pineapples, Kenyan oranges, Ugandan bananas. The Tanzanian side of this lake was renowned for its mangos, said to be the best in the world. The lakeside avocados were also plump and tasty. Avocados were in season, so we feasted on those.

The chief engineer was at breakfast, reading the latest issue of *Shipping News and Ship Repair.* It was a British publication, from the Royal Institute of Naval Architects.

I said, "Maybe you should have let the engineers on the *Kabalega* read that."

The chief engineer looked up and said, "There is nothing practical in here that will help them. They have a problem of water contaminating their fuel line. They haven't located the source of it."

I thought again of the captain's act of kindness. And that if these men had not helped me and taken me aboard, I would still be on that pier at Port Bell, cooling my heels. And who was I? Just another scruffy airplane-hating *muzungu* who wanted to go by boat to Mwanza. Here as elsewhere, I was the only *muzungu* traveler. The others didn't take buses, feared Sudan and Ethiopia, stuck to selected routes, and traveled in groups to look at animals. As a rule, they stayed a great distance from the locals. Yet, though I was solitary, all I heard was *karibu, karibu,* welcome, welcome, and "Take more *ugali?*"

The chief engineer was John Kataraihya, a man in his early forties. Like most of the other crew members he had grown up on the lakeshore. He had studied naval engineering and engine repair in Belgium. He was a bright, friendly man with a steady gaze, intelligent and quietly confident in his opinions. He had seen a good deal of the world. He preferred Lake Victoria.

"The Belgians have many problems," he said, and I laughed to hear him generalize about Belgians the way Belgians themselves generalized about Africans.

In an ironic turnabout, John had spent a lot of time in the city Marlow specifically disparages in *Heart of Darkness.* Brussels, he says, is "a city that always makes me think of a whited sepulchre," for it is in the company office of that city that he gets his orders to go up the Congo River. The seemingly civilized company in the orderly city sends out King Leopold's brutal directives. Marlow also notices German East Africa on a wall map, "a purple patch, to show where the jolly pioneers of progress drink the jolly lager-beer." German East Africa had become Tanganyika and then Tanzania.

"But the Belgians have one big thing that makes them unhappy," John said, folding his copy of *Shipping News and Ship Repair.* "The main problem with Belgians is they can't get along with each other. The Flemish-speaking ones hate the French-speaking ones. It's a kind of racism, you can say. Or similar." As though referring to a benighted settlement in the bush, he added, "Antwerp is bad in that respect."

Most of the time he had been studying naval engineering, but he had also traveled — tentatively at first, and then, as his French improved, farther and farther afield. He had seen most of Belgium and its neighboring countries. "Even some small villages, I can say, very tiny ones," he said, which put me in mind of obscure Bombo and Bundibugyo in Uganda and the huddled community on Goziba Island.

"Any problems traveling?"

"For myself, I had a few problems," John said of his peregrinations in Belgium. "If they think you are a Congolese — one of their former people — they can treat you very badly and they insult you."

"That's not friendly. No *karibu.*"

He laughed. "I said, 'I am from Tanzania!' and that was okay with them. They said, 'So you're from Nairobi?' Ha!"

The idea that after almost a hundred years of colonial rule in Africa these ignoramuses still had no idea of the difference between Kenya and Tanzania made him erupt in mocking laughter.

This was a good subject for chitchat in the *Umoja* galley with John and some of the crew. I had recently read and greatly liked *King Leopold's Ghost,* Adam Hochschild's history of this bizarre period of colonialist Africa. The book detailed the savageries of imperialism, the pathology of megalomania and rule through intimidation, as well as the idealistic reaction to it, the origin of the modern human rights movement. The Belgians had inspired Vachel Lindsay's poem "The Congo," part of which went:

> Listen to the yell of Leopold's ghost
> Burning in Hell for his hand-maimed host.
> Hear how the demons chuckle and yell
> Cutting his hands off, down in Hell.

I said it was odd that Belgians were rude to the Congolese, since it was the Belgians who had plundered their country, first in search of ivory, then of rubber, and then of diamonds and chrome and gold. Mostly slave labor had been used, whole villages were turned out to find ivory or collect rubber, and the punishment for slacking was death or the lopping off of hands. Decades of this, an enormous colony bled of its wealth. As the indignant Irishman in the pub in Joyce's *Ulysses* puts it, "Raping the women and girls and flogging the natives on the belly to squeeze all the red rubber they can out of them."

I said, "The whole of the Congo belonged to the Belgian king. It was his private property. The Congo was the king's own *shamba*."

This interested the men at the table, and it was an amazing fact. The Congo was not a Belgian colony but, for twenty-three years starting in 1885, King Leopold's private domain. The horror of it had outraged Joseph Conrad on his trip upriver to Stanleyville and had inspired *Heart of Darkness*.

"The whole Congo, his *shamba?*" one of the crewmen said.

Sneering, John said, "In Belgium, they name big streets after Leopold!"

The crew of the *Umoja* were attentive listeners. They understood the contradictions of the period Hochschild had called "one of the silences of history." They responded with shrewd questions, and at last when duty called them to their stations on the ferry, they said they wanted to read the book.

"Come, I'll show you the engine room," John said.

Heat and noise rose from the narrow stairwell as we climbed down slippery treads. The lower levels we reached by iron ladder, and the noise from the pounding engines was so loud I could barely hear what

John was saying. He was explaining that the ferry was British built, first launched in 1962. Neither its diesel engines nor its Caterpillar generators nor its boilers had been changed in forty years. The company that had built the ferry was no longer in business; the diesel engines were obsolete.

Over the deafening noise in the engine room, John shouted, "Very hard to get spare parts. Two engines — so we can always make it. Sometimes we have a steering problem."

He handed me a pair of earmuffs, the sort you see clamped on the heads of cannoneers, to block the engines' roar. And he led me on into the heat.

One of the oddest sights I was privileged to observe in my many months of travel from Cairo to Cape Town I glimpsed belowdecks in the engine room of the *Umoja.* At the lowest depth of the engine room, amid the most deafening noise, the worst heat, the hottest pipes — most of them unlagged, some of them spitting jets of steam from their iron elbows — a young African crewman was sitting at a wet wooden table doing complex mathematical equations. He seemed at first glance to be naked. His thumb was stuck in a book of logarithmic tables, and a textbook was open in front of him. The sheet of paper he used was covered with algebraic equations, numbers and letters, from top to bottom. To me the heat and noise were terrifying in their intensity. But the young man was serene, and he worked with the stub of a pencil, wearing nothing but undershorts, with pink rubber plugs in his ears.

He was so engrossed in his work, which seemed like school homework, he did not greet us. Only when I lifted the book cover to read the title did he look up and smile, but then he went back to his work. The book was *Principles of Diesel and High-Compression Engines.*

"English is the language of the imperialists," Tanzanian officials had often said in the past. One of the stated policies instituted by the much-loved first president of Tanzania, *Mwalimu* ("Teacher") Julius Nyerere, was the translation, at great expense, of all school textbooks into Swahili. To prove it could be done, he personally translated Shakespeare's *Julius Caesar* into this coastal idiom. It struck me here in the engine room of the *Umoja* that it might be a little time before *Principles of Diesel and High-Compression Engines* was available in Swahili.

Conversation in this noise was impossible. I took a piece of paper and wrote, *What is he doing?*

John nodded and took the paper and pen. He wrote, *He is studying.*

What for? I wrote in reply.

Perspiring in the heat, his jaw fixed — for he was not wearing earmuffs — John wrote, *To boost up his academic qualifications for his employment.*

In the din, we sat down in a caged control room and had a cup of hot coffee out of a thermos. Once, I removed my earmuffs, but the engine howl was unbearable. John laughed at my reaction, which was like being hammered on the head. He did not seem to mind it, but perhaps many years of this noise had rendered him partly deaf. I also noticed that the engine room was very tidy and efficient, much more orderly and better maintained than the upper decks of the ferry. Pointing to dials, he showed me the boiler pressure, the fuel levels, the temperature, and the fact that we were proceeding at between eleven and twelve knots, a pretty good clip.

After twenty minutes or so of drinking coffee in the boiler room I could not take any more of this. I signaled that I was going topside. There, in the cool air and sunshine, we were still at sea, no land in sight.

"You don't take passengers anymore?" I said.

John said, "This is designated a cargo vessel. If we take more than six people, we are regarded as a passenger vessel and therefore must enforce very careful safety regulations. Number of life jackets. Lifeboats. Give lifeboat drill."

"Because the *Bukoba* sank?"

"Yes. We will pass it. It was sailing to Mwanza."

Later I read that Lake Victoria had never been properly surveyed, and that all the available data on hazards were collected in 1954 by the British colonial government. The information about landmarks and warnings was now out-of-date. The only people qualified to pilot a large vessel on Lake Victoria were those with local knowledge and experience.

John and the captain had worked together on the *Umoja* since the late seventies. At that time it was a Tanzanian military vessel. "During the war against Idi Amin we made trips bringing many soldiers. Five thousand of them, standing like this" — John tightened his face and stood rigid to show how tightly packed the men were. "We took them to Jinja Port and they hid when they went ashore."

"What do you bring into Uganda now?" I asked.

"I don't know. It is all in freight cars and sealed and packed up," John said. "Out of Uganda we take coffee and tea. We ourselves produce cotton, coffee, tea, cashews, and the cloves in Zanzibar."

"What about cloth?"

"We have only one textile factory now," John said. "We sell our cotton, we don't make it into cloth."

Forty years of independent rule and foreign investment, forty years of mind-deadening political rhetoric about *ujamaa* ("familyhood") and "African socialism," forty years of nationalization and industrialization and neutrality, and that vast fertile country of twenty million people had achieved a condition of near bankruptcy and had one factory.

Strangely, I felt I had encountered one of Tanzania's successes, the ferry *Umoja*, which had been faithfully crossing and recrossing the lake for the same four decades, in war and peace, carrying citizens and soldiers, cows, cash crops, the necessities for Uganda to function and for Tanzania to make money. The ferry had been a steady earner, and it was staffed by a serious and dedicated crew, one of whom was belowdecks in his undershorts, boosting up his academic qualifications.

In the southeast corner of the lake we passed a chain of islands. I went to the bridge to use the captain's binoculars and to check the names of them. The largest one was Ukerewe, and the land distantly behind it was the shoreline of Tanzania.

Ukerewe was the name by which the entire lake had been known by the Arabs whom Burton and Speke met on their 1858 expedition. At Kazeh (Tabora), the widely traveled Arab slaver Snay bin Amir said it was "fifteen or sixteen marches" to Ukerewe, but dangerous because of the unfriendly people. If the folks were unfriendly, it might have been because of their unwillingness to become enslaved and marched in chains to a coastal slave port with the melancholy name Bagamoyo, meaning "I Leave My Heart Behind."

Arab traders from Zanzibar and Aden had been in this area for more than a century before Europeans penetrated it. The Arabs trafficked in slaves, but also in ivory and honey, as they did farther south on the Zambezi. They plundered, of course, but they never controlled this distant savanna. They had made themselves unwelcome through their slave trading, so they had to stick to the safest routes, in many cases counting on Africans themselves to supply them with slaves or ivory, in return for trade goods.

The most startling sign of this old occupation by Arabs and coastal people was the many dhows I saw on the lake — dhows of considerable size, thirty feet and more, most of them under sail, others with the rigging down, carrying fishermen. This slow but stable boat with its lateen sail, the very emblem of Arab seamanship, was still nodding across the lake, which was the heart of Africa.

In the late afternoon I could see Mwanza clearly, and the coast around it, the headlands, and little islands. Every feature of land was composed of smooth tumbled boulders, many of them huge, two- and three-story boulders that dwarfed the huts and made every other dwelling look like a dollhouse. At first glance the shore looked like Stonington, Maine, with palms instead of spruce trees: piled rocks, a rocky shore, rounded boulders, and small low wooden houses set close to the ground.

I was at the rail with Alex, the first engineer, and watching the shore I saw a speedboat go by, a white plastic noisy one, bow upraised, going fast.

"*Muzungu,*" Alex said.

Another speedboat followed.

"*Muzungu,*" Alex said.

Maybe missionaries, maybe traders, maybe farmers, maybe doctors or agents of virtue. No one knew. They were just white men in loud white boats.

Pointing to the headland, Alex said, "Those rocks we call Bismarck Rocks. After the Englishman who found them."

Or maybe Otto von Bismarck, who once ruled this distant outpost of Teutonism, along with Samoa and New Guinea and the Cameroons.

Not long after drawing near the port of Mwanza, we circled awhile and then hovered, making little forward progress. A Kenyan ferry, the MV *Uhuru,* was unloading freight cars and loose cargo. This work was proceeding very slowly.

Most of the crew, including Alex, were at their posts — in the engine room, on deck, at the lines. So I went to the galley and found the captain eating.

"Don't worry, *mzee*," the captain said. "We will be docking soon."

I joined him in the usual *Umoja* meal: rice, vegetables, a withered chicken part, the whole of it reddened with gouts of pili-pili sauce.

"Thanks so much for having me as a passenger," I said. "I like this ferry. Everyone is helpful and very friendly."

"They are good," the captain said.

"And friendly," I repeated, wishing to stress my gratitude.

I was alone, the only alien, a nonpaying passenger, the idlest person on board. They had no idea who I was or where I was going, and I was being treated like an esteemed guest. How could I not be grateful?

"They are friendly," the captain said carefully. "But I am not too friendly with them."

He was still eating, but I could see he was making a subtle point, one that he wanted me to understand, a sort of leadership issue.

"For me, too friendly is harmful," the captain said.

We did not dock, we did not anchor, we only hovered. The *Uhuru* kept unloading. The shoreline was littered with wrecked and scuttled boats. I went to the aft deck, found a barrel to sit on, and listened to my radio. I found the BBC, a program about an Azerbaijani novel called *Ali and Nino.* I had written an introduction to this novel and had contributed to the program — my two cents' worth had been recorded, but so long before that I had forgotten about it. So I listened to snippets of my own voice coming from London, and another hour passed on Lake Victoria.

"Don't worry, *mzee*," the captain said.

"I am not worried," I said, wanting to add, And I am not a *mzee* either.

What did I care if this ferry docked now or tonight, or tomorrow, or next week? The only plan I had was to find the railway station in Mwanza and take a train to the coast, to Dar es Salaam, where no one was expecting me. In the meantime, I was happy here on the *Umoja.* I did not seriously want to leave this vessel.

As darkness fell, many things happened quickly. The Kenyan ferry swung away from the pier and the *Umoja* took its place, the captain and Alex working together, one on the bridge, the other in the engine room, a tricky maneuver. Just as we docked, the temperature went up, for without the lake breeze, the air was sultry.

I was in no hurry to leave, but the rest of the crew were scurrying — they were in their home port and eager to get to their villages and wives and children. They could not go ashore until the ferry was unloaded, and so they saw me off.

"*Kwaheri, mzee!*" they called out as I stepped off the loading flap onto Tanzanian soil. Farewell, old man.

12 ◇◇◇

The Bush Train to Dar es Salaam

"ANY GUNS?" the Tanzanian customs inspector asked me in the little shed in Mwanza, poking my bag. Never mind his dirty clothes, you guessed he was an official from all the ballpoints leaking ink in his shirt pocket.

Though there was a pie slice of Tanzania lying in Lake Victoria, the southern shore of the lake was the enforceable border.

"No guns."

"You can go."

I walked through the crowd of people who were welcoming the ferry — the ferry's irregular arrival being one of the highlights of life in Mwanza. Walking toward town I could understand why. The place was just ruined and empty shops and an unpaved main street that was almost impassable because of its entrenched corrugations. Old buses swayed, almost toppling as their wheels descended into deep potholes. This was another haunted border post, a dismal and interesting one, that the safari-going tourists who flew into the international airport at Arusha would never see. They would see only some slavering animals and colorful natives.

In Mwanza, the natives were not colorful, merely numerous and ragged, and so many of them had attached themselves to me that when the first taxi came by, I flagged it down and got in.

"What day does the train go to Dar es Salaam?" I asked.

"Today night," the driver said.

"What time?"

"Maybe one hour."

We went down the lumpy road to the railway station, which was crowded with food sellers and people carrying plastic-wrapped bales of their belongings. This bustle looked odd — the dressed-up people, some of them running — for it was drama in a place where drama and urgency were in short supply.

I roused the stationmaster, who was eating peanuts in his office with the peanut seller, a crouching woman holding a big tin tray of them.

"Is it too late to get a ticket on this train?"

"We have space for you, *bwana,*" he said.

He went to get me a ticket, and the peanut seller shook her tray of peanuts and said, "*Njugu? Njugu?*"

Within an hour of arriving in Mwanza, *Farewell, old man!* still ringing in my ears, I was on the train, in a little two-berth compartment but apparently alone, with bottles of water from the drink seller who hawked them by the track.

"Are you comfortable?" the stationmaster said, stopping by my compartment to solicit a tip.

"Yes, thank you," I said, handing him some unearned income. "When will we get to Dar?"

"Sometime on Sunday," he said, and went on his way.

It was now Friday night, but so what? I had a berth and a window on Africa in a railway car full of Africans. In a short time we would be in the bush, traveling east through the middle of Tanzania.

Because of the bright lights of the station yard, people were attracted to the place, and they sat and chatted. A large gathering of children were kicking a soccer ball under the lights. It wasn't a proper game, but it was such hearty playing, with laughter and shouts, that it held my attention. Africa was full of skinny energetic children, and their game usually involved kicking a ball. These children did not have a round rubber ball but rather a misshapen cloth ball stuffed with rags. The field was not flat and smooth — it was a succession of dirt piles and humps, very stony. The children played barefoot, probably twenty or more, not teams but a free-for-all.

Watching them play and call to each other on this hot night, raising dust in the lights of the station yard, I was impressed by their exertion and heartened by their high spirits. The playing field was a wasteland, and part of it lay in darkness. The children ran in and out of the shadows, screeching. The dark didn't matter, the bumpy field didn't matter, nor did the squashed ball. By any reckoning, these children were playing and laughing in one of the more desperate provinces of a semi-derelict country. Even after the engine whistle blew and we started to draw out of Mwanza, I heard their tinkling laughter and then remembered why I had been so fascinated by this happy sight, which also made me feel lonely.

I was reminded of the end of Saki's novel *The Unbearable Bassington,* where there is just such a scene — children playing excitedly, observed by a solitary man, Comus Bassington. That setting was Africa, too, a place much like Mwanza, a "heat-blistered, fever-scourged wilderness, where men lived like groundbait and died like flies. Demons one might believe in, if one did not hold one's imagination in healthy check, but a kindly all-managing God, never."

Bassington is so lonely and miserable he cannot bear to look upon the happy scene. "Those wild young human kittens represented the joy of life; he was the outsider, the lonely alien, watching something in which he could not join, a happiness in which he had no part or lot . . . [and] in his unutterable loneliness he bowed his head on his arms, that he might not see this joyous scrambling frolic on yonder hillside."

There was enough moon for me to see that the landscape outside Mwanza was as bouldery as the lakeshore. But this was a flat plain with interruptions of boulder piles, some as high as hills, others as smooth as burial mounds.

The villages were no more than mud huts with oil lamps flickering inside, but for all their simplicity they had a wholeness that was lacking in Uganda's villages. The villages of Uganda showed signs of having been attacked, abandoned, repossessed, rebuilt, improved, and battered again, the result of war, expulsion, violent change. Its battle scars made Uganda seem a strong country. In Tanzania there was no such graphic evidence of the past, but only decline — simple linear decrepitude, and in some villages collapse.

Very quickly — twenty miles or less — we were in the bush: the grassy plains with low trees, the great African emptiness, as empty as

Lake Victoria had looked, and just as oceanic under the watery glow of the moon.

When clouds covered the moon I looked around the train and found a dining car and some Africans inside, already drunk. The attendant asked me in Swahili if I was hungry, and to tempt me he showed me some heaped plates, saying "*Chakula, chakula.*" Food, food.

To the novice, this was "mystery meat." But I knew better. One dish was obviously a purple amblongus pie, the others were a stack of crumbobblious cutlets and some gosky patties, all of which I recognized from "The Book of Nonsense Cookery" by Edward Lear. The cutlets were done to perfection, the recipe having been closely followed ("When the whole is thus minced, brush it up hastily with a new clothes brush"). The attendant kept waving them in my face, yet I declined.

"Just a beer," I said.

I took it back to my compartment. On the way I spotted two aliens, the only other ones on the train. They were pale and blotchy and sunburned, a young man and woman, probably in their twenties, though their bulk made them seem older. They were, it turned out, the sort of podgy, cookie-munching, Christ-bitten evangelists who pop up in places like Mwanza with nothing but a Bible and a rucksack and the requisite provisions: cookies and cake and a hymn book in Swahili. I discovered this because the train windows were open for any available breeze, and once when the train slowed down I heard my name: *Paul.*

Good God, had they seen me? Were they going to mention that their parents liked my books and what an amazing coincidence it was that they were meeting me on a train?

No, for the man was saying, in a pedantic way, his mouth filled with cookies, "Paul tells us in Galatians . . ."

The sky at the western horizon began to glow with slow explosions. The bursts of light widened from the ground up on a jagged stalk of fire, traveling into clouds that swelled hugely as they were illuminated, going from black to bright. The light was more sudden than fireworks, closer in violence and scale to a big battle — one in which the bombers and combatants were too small to see, though their bombs were overwhelmingly hot and powerful. It was an African thunderstorm twenty or thirty miles away. Now and then the whole sky of blackish clouds was convulsed by a bolt of lightning that lingered as a penetrating flash. In that flash I could see the land clearly — could see that it was empty, the storm doing nothing but showing it as empty and indestructible.

"Another direction he gives in Galatians," the man was saying again, and the sky was foaming with fire, and just a chuckle of thunder, the storm was so distant.

Look for the truth in nature, I wanted to say to those cookie-eating missionaries in the next compartment; nothing is complete, everything is imperfect, nothing lasts. Go to bed.

◇ ◇ ◇

Before dawn we arrived at the town of Tabora. We were still there three hours later. The missionaries had left the train, most of the other people had left the train, but in the meantime it had filled up with new passengers. An African joined me in my compartment, assigned to the upper berth.

The train was the only practical way in or out of Tabora. The railway was the link between this good-sized if ruinous town and the capital, eight hundred miles away. Decades of neglect had left Tanzania's roads in a deplorable state, many of them unusable. The exceptions, as always, were the tourist routes. A safari geek wearing whipcord jodhpurs and a pith helmet, jogging along in a Land Rover on the way to Ngorongoro Crater to gape at warthogs, might marvel at Tanzania's modernity — great hotels, excellent roads, robust wildlife. But a Sukuma fisherman intending to sell his catch down the line in Shinyanga, just sixty miles away, would be hard pressed to find a passable road, much less a vehicle, and his attainment of Tabora would be out of the question, except on this bush train.

Tanzania had reached a dead end on the socialist path, and as an economic failure in both industry and agriculture, the country was advertising itself as a superior collection of game parks, inviting foreigners to take pictures of its endangered species and to spend money. Great tracts of bush on a principal migratory route for game, at Loliondo, near the Kenya border, had been leased to a nob in the United Arab Emirates to use as a private unregulated hunting reserve for the very rich who wanted to kill leopards. The locals, Masai warriors, were guides and scrubbers in the game lodge, who resented the intrusion and claimed that when the game was thin in Loliondo, the hunters shot animals in Serengeti National Park.

Tanzania was a tourist destination. The comrades, the Maoists, the ideologues, the revolutionaries, the sloganeering Fidelistas, were now hustling for jobs in hotels and taking tourists for game drives. And if as a Tanzanian your village was not near any lions or elephants — and Tabora wasn't — you were out of luck, and had to put up with crummy schools and bad roads and this amazingly casual railway, once called the Central Line, which had been built almost a hundred years ago by the Germans.

The man in the upper berth introduced himself as Julius, named after the father of his country, Julius Nyerere. He was an educated man in his mid-forties, well-spoken and considerate — he always left the compartment to smoke a cigarette, for example. Julius worked for the Land Use Department, helping farmers make money by growing viable crops. This was a serious subject in Tabora. He was on his way to a staff meeting in Dar es Salaam, leaving home a week early to be sure of being in Dar on time.

"The local cash crop is tobacco for cigarettes," Julius said. "There was once a tobacco cooperative. The government bought the crop. The price was all right."

"So what happened?"

"The managers were corrupt. They mismanaged the cooperatives. The cooperatives failed, so the industries were privatized."

He spoke without passion, in a chastened, almost defeated tone. The dogmatic, motto-chanting Tanzanians had been humbled. No one talked of imperialism and neocolonialism now, nor of the evils of capitalism — though they could have, for even capitalism had failed in Tanzania.

"In Tabora there are many small tobacco farms — an acre or half an acre," Julius said. "Two years ago private companies bought the crop. The prices were good, per kilo of flue-cured tobacco. But this year the price is one quarter of what it was. The farmers — well, we call them peasants — they are struggling. They can't make ends meet."

I said, "In Kenya the coffee growers are planting maize."

"Here too," Julius said. "Many have turned to just growing food for themselves, maize and beans and onions."

After all this time, the return to subsistence farming. This way of life in Africa was familiar to me. The strong impression I had was not that the places I knew were worse off, but that they had not changed at all. After forty years of experimenting with various ideologies and industries they were back to farming by hand and pounding maize into flour, living on porridge and beans. Nothing was new except that there were many more people, grubbier buildings, more litter, fewer trees, more poachers, less game.

During the long delay I got off the train and looked around Tabora. The shelves in the shops were bare, though there was produce in the market — women selling bananas and tomatoes and bunches of dusty onions.

We finally left Tabora in midmorning, in the heat, and headed into green wooded bush of flitting birds and emptiness. It was so little changed from the old unexplored Africa of the nineteenth century that Burton and Speke, who had walked through here from the coast 150 years ago, would easily have recognized it. It was the Arab trade route, the slave route.

Julius said to me, "Why don't you go to Arusha and see the animals — lions and elephants?"

That was what visitors did, flying into the international airport that had been built for their convenience, near the animals. But the rest of the vast country had no connection with that, and was in a sense still undeveloped, even undiscovered. The irony was that Arusha in 1967 was the site of the national assertion of self-determination, an eloquent document by the president announcing that Tanzania would be self-sufficient. This so-called Arusha Declaration pledged that the government would eradicate "all types of exploitation" so as to "prevent the accumulation of wealth which is inconsistent with the existence of a classless society." Now the question, here and elsewhere, was not exploitation or class or wealth, but how to get a meal.

Zimbabwe was in the radio news — white farms being invaded by Africans demanding land. President Mugabe was siding with the Africans who were breaking the laws of trespass, and in some cases murdering the white farmers. I shared this news with Julius.

"Mugabe wants to last a few more years," Julius said. "So he makes speeches about land. Yes, they will take that land away from those white farmers. It happened here in Tanzania. Some land will go to rich

Africans. The rest will be subdivided among the peasants — small plots. They will grow whatever they want, and they will end up where we are now, just peasants struggling on small farms, growing maize and beans to feed their families."

I often heard pitiless assessments like this from Africans on trains or people in villages, but never such trenchant good sense from African politicians or from foreign agents of virtue.

Because of the season and this equatorial spot, at noon the sun was directly overhead. We stopped at the station of Kazi-Kazi, a tin-roofed shed. The dense bush lay all around, the head-high grass and bunches of yellow wildflowers. Beyond this was an immense flat plain.

The starkness of it all was a wonder. I had come this way in the 1960s and even then had probably seen the old station, the rusty roof, the posts and pylons, the tree clumps, the baled thorn branches used as a fence, the twiggy whips like barbed wire. This halt could not have changed in forty years, for that matter not since the railway was built — a hundred years. Although it was unimproved, it was not very deteriorated. Farther down the line, at the halt at Kilaraka, a small boy hurried down the dusty path from a cluster of mud huts carrying a bowl of boiled eggs, hoping to sell some for a few pennies to the passengers. Just as he reached the train, the whistle blew and we were on our way, leaving him howling.

We were in the Wagogo Plains, the wild heart of Tanzania: no roads, no towns, only this railway. What animals existed here were hunted — poached for food by the Wagogo, who were pastoralists. Had they been as colorful as the Masai, whom they somewhat resembled with their earlobe plugs and lethal-looking spears, more attention might have been paid to them. The Wagogo sharpened their front teeth into points, and they wore beads, but still no one paid them any heed. They might have prospered on their own, but because of drought, dwindling herds, and neglect, they were about as well off as they were when Sir Richard Burton passed through in the 1850s. He had stopped briefly to investigate the Wagogo's sexual habits, with his customary thoroughness, questioning the women, measuring the men. The women were "well disposed towards strangers with fair complexions," and one man, "when quiescent, numbered nearly six inches."

The Rift Valley lay ahead, a visible dip in the great green plain, shallower and less dramatic than in Kenya, but more wooded, forested in places, another sight of old Africa and its seemingly limitless savanna. By the tracks were purple wildflowers and darting swallows, and in the distance only bush. At long intervals there would be the sort of specimen tree — a mango or a baobab — that indicated a Wagogo village. But the villages were hardly that — no more than five huts in a circle, just the number that could fit in the shade of a few trees.

There were Wagogo at all the small stations, at Itigi and Saranda, some begging, others hawking food and artifacts. They smiled, showing their sharpened teeth, and since I was the only *muzungu* on this train, they clustered around my car, offering carved wooden mortars and pestles, woven reed mats, paddles and wooden spoons and baskets. Cooked food, too: chicken and flyblown fish.

The afternoon heat was in the nineties, the sun burning in a cloudless sky. This was something of a disappointment to the local people, who needed rain for their newly planted maize, so the sunshine seemed like a blight — people tried to hide from it, but it was not easy.

At one small halt in this great sun-baked emptiness a single tree grew, a mango of modest size but leafy with dense boughs. There was a circle of shade beneath it. Within that circle were thirty people, pressed against one another to keep in the shade, watched by a miserable goat tethered in the sunshine. What looked like a group game was obviously an afternoon routine of survival. As interesting to me as this packed-together mob of villagers around the lone tree trunk was the idea that no one in this hot exposed place had thought to plant more mango trees for the shade they offered. It was simple enough to plant a tree — this mango itself contained a thousand seeds — yet no one had planted one, or if anyone had, the tree had been cut down. The sight of these Africans in this tiny place in central Tanzania struggling to keep within a patch of shade stayed with me as a vivid instance of forward planning, or rather the lack of it.

Beyond this place were the sort of boulders I had seen near Mwanza, but bigger and gray-toned and rounded, looking from a distance like a herd of elephants, great gray elephant-assed boulders, so many of them browsing on a hillside that they obscured the hills: hills like gray elephants.

The only signs of humans were the wrecked and twisted railway cars tipped off the track with the rusty rails from some long-ago train wreck. I was rereading *Heart of Darkness* and was reminded of this when I read: "I came upon a boiler wallowing in the grass . . . [and] an undersized railway-truck lying there on its back with its wheels in the air. One was off. The thing looked as dead as the carcass of some animal. I came upon more pieces of decaying machinery, a stack of rusty rails." Broken or scuttled machinery by the roadside is a common sight in Africa. Not one to lament, not any longer, anyway for me.

One of the themes in *Heart of Darkness*—harped on rather than suggested—is cannibalism. Africans are casually referred to as "cannibals" by Marlow. Even Kurtz, the idealist turned bogeyman, developed a taste for human flesh and kept human skulls as household accessories, which is reason enough for his last words to be "The horror! The horror!" The heavy hints of anthropophagy are a bit of stage-managing on Conrad's part. Though mutilation and amputation and massacre by Belgians had been customary, cannibalism had never been institutionalized by Africans in the Congo (as it had been in, say, Fiji). The suggestion of flesh eating was just another racist dig, like that of the Toronto mayor refusing to go to Kenya "because I don't want to end up in a cooking pot." There are similar gibes in *Heart of Darkness.*

More prosaically observed in the book, and so more horrible, were the unsensational examples of ruin and exploitation—roads leading nowhere, collapsed huts, pointless effort, broken machinery, rusty metal. Details like these, which were intended to appall the reader in 1902, were the simple facts of everyday life in Africa a century later. Years ago I might have said that such ruin represented failed hopes, but now I knew they were not African hopes.

This railway line built by the Germans linked Dar to Kigoma on Lake Tanganyika. The idea, like most colonial ideas, was to plunder the country more efficiently. The British had built the spur to Mwanza. Since then, not a single foot of track had been added and no improvements had been made. Dodoma, where we arrived in the early evening, was a good example of the colonial period being the high-water mark of railway technology in central Tanzania. The station was a hundred years old and, though ramshackle, still functioning.

Never mind, Dodoma (like Tabora and Dilla, Marsabit and Nanyuki) was the kind of place I could have lived in quite happily—doing something worthy, of course, like teaching in the local school or getting the local people as interested in beekeeping (another forgotten skill in East Africa) as their ancestors had been. People would say of me, in a praising way, as they always said of such do-gooders: "He devoted his life to Africa." But that was not it at all, for it was just a version of Rimbaud in Harar: the exile, a selfish beast with modest fantasies of power, secretly enjoying a life of beer drinking and scribbling and occasional mythomania in a nice climate, where there were no interruptions such as unwelcome letters or faxes or cell phones. It was an eccentric ideal, life lived off the map.

Dodoma was also where the east-west railway crossed the Great North Road, which penetrated the Masai Steppe. If the railway was in poor shape, this major highway was much worse, a road to avoid for its potholes and, in this season, its mud. Black clouds were gathering around Dodoma, teasing its farmers with thunder. Bolts of lightning exploded inside the dark clouds, illuminating them for a few seconds, making them seem blacker.

Seeing me scribbling, Julius said, "What are you writing?"

"Just a report," I said.

He would understand that. He would not understand that I was writing an erotic story that was becoming a novella in my notebook.

When I was not doing that, I was staring out the window, making notes, listening to the radio. I bought bananas and boiled eggs from hawkers by the tracks, and sometimes risked the crumbobblious cutlets in the dining car. If the train stopped for a while, I got out and paced and bought a coconut. I had spent some time talking to the stationmaster at Dodoma, who was doing his best with antiquated switching equipment.

Later in the day I discovered that Julius had been summoned from our compartment to deal with a drama.

"It was very bad," he said.

"What's the story?"

He did not say anything at first. Then there was another commotion, in the passageway of the sleeping car. A group of big boys slouched past, followed by the stern conductor. The boys were the ragged drunken youths I had seen in the dining car — the reason I usually stayed away from the dining car.

"Those three boys," Julius said, lowering his voice. "They trapped a girl in the toilet. She went in, and when she tried to come out they entered and trapped her."

"What did they want?"

"They were going to rape her, but she screamed and someone heard. The conductor called me because I know her. She was very worried — she is still worried. I will tell the police."

I expected more trouble but there was none, only silence, a conspicuous silence. Around midnight we came to a dead stop. Instead of entering Morogoro, the next-to-last town on the line, we halted at the little town of Kimamba and moved no farther. We were still there seven hours later, in the hot, humid morning in sticky air that was filled with mosquitoes.

I heard the word *shauri* mumbled — a problem, a fuss. Then someone in the corridor said, "A derailment."

The townsfolk of Kimamba gathered on the embankment to stare at the stopped train. Though it was an unscheduled stop, some enterprising people sold bananas and tea, but most just gaped. From a distant mosque a muezzin began wailing.

Beneath distressed façades on the main street of abandoned shops I could read faded signs, one about tractors, another saying *New Planters Hotel*. After I peered at Kimamba for a long while it was possible to discern that it had once been a real town, possibly important, with something resembling a local economy. It was now like an ancient ruin.

Julius, the expert in land use, said, "They used to grow sisal here."

Sisal was the vital fiber in all the rope in the world, until nylon came along. Julius explained that sisal had been grown here by European and Indian planters on large estates. There were no smallholders. Sisal production peaked in Tanzania in the mid-sixties and during this boom the estates were nationalized by a government eager to cash in. The expatriate planters were booted out of the country. Then the bottom fell out of the sisal market. Production dropped to a quarter of what it had been, and in the nineties it was less than a tenth. At this point the government cut its losses and sold off the sisal estates to private individuals. Sisal growing was now back to where it had been forty years earlier, but the market for it hardly existed anymore. Terrible Tanzanian economics once again.

Sisal growing is not very difficult. The plant can endure drought and heavy rain and poor husbandry. It is troubled by few pests and diseases and is fireproof except after repeated burnings. It can be planted in alternating rows with food crops. It was a wonderful cash crop and is still grown in Brazil, Mexico, China, and the Philippines, all by smallholders. But — no one knew why — it had been a failure in Tanzania.

"Maybe bad management," Julius said. "The people are just growing food for themselves."

I said, "That's not a bad idea, is it? If they had been growing sisal, they would have used the money to buy food."

The people would survive somehow. In such circumstances it was the government that was left in the lurch, with no income, no exports, no hard currency.

I sat by the tracks and listened to the radio: foot and mouth disease was destroying British cattle; there was war in Macedonia, death in Chechnya, Borneo, Israel, and Afghanistan; Wall Street was racking up steep losses and "tech stocks haven't found the bottom yet."

Kimamba was hot, dirty, and poor, but it was able to feed itself. And it was seizing an opportunity today with the stopped train, selling the passengers food and drinks.

Seeing me, a young boy with a big tin teapot, hot milk, and teacups stopped by.

"Good morning, sah."

"What's your name?"

"My name is Wycliffe."

"What's the problem, Wycliffe?"

"The problem, sah, it is money."

As the hours passed we made a mess of our portion of track in Kimamba. The toilets dumped sewage onto the ground, passengers tossed banana peels, waste paper, tin cans, and plastic bottles out the windows. Along with this littering was loudness: the rap music that was played now and then in the dining car was being played now. The Kimamba folk came closer to listen. Drunken Africans in the train became boisterous. This I did not like at all.

Looking for information about the derailment, I ran into an African named Weston, who said he was an accountant. He was going to Dar es Salaam to conduct an audit of someone's books. He said that Tanzania was in a bad way.

"We are poorer than Malawi. We have no economy. We have nothing," he said. "But it was worse before liberalization."

Liberalization was when the Tanzanian government dumped all the money-losing industries, selling them to the private sector. Now they had more or less what they had had before independence: creaky trains, simple agriculture, and a certain number of lions and elephants and quite a few gnus.

Many blasts of the train whistle shattered the silence in Kimamba and cut through the rap music. A few more blasts and the passengers leaped aboard. We left Kimamba around noontime, just as abruptly as we had stopped there in the middle of the night.

We rattled into a wilderness of stunted trees and grassy plains and absolutely no people. Settlements like Kimamba were like flat little islands in a green sea. A few hours later we were among green hills, the hills like high islands in the same sea. The town of Morogoro was in those hills. I wanted to stop there, because it was a road junction: I could go south from there and avoid the urban sprawl of Dar es Salaam. But I had a problem. Because the immigration office had been closed in Mwanza, the official had given me a four-day visa. I could buy a visa extension only in Dar, and would have to do it tomorrow.

After all the thunder and the portents of rain en route, the weather finally hit as we approached the coast. We were in a hot wet flatland of boggy earth and even boggier rice fields. The planting season had just begun here, with the onset of the rains.

Julius joined me at the window.

I remembered something I had wanted to ask him. "Ever heard of Kwanza?"

"As you know, it means 'first,'" he said, pronouncing it *fust.*

"Yes. But I am thinking of Kwanza the festival."

"There is no festival. *Kwanza* means 'first.'" He rapped the wall of the coach. "*Gari a kwanza.*"

"First-class carriage," I said.

"That is correct."

But it was a euphemism. Almost three days out of Mwanza the train was very grubby. The staff cleaned all the sinks with strong disinfectant, knowing that most of the men lazily used the sinks in their compartments as urinals. Before eating, you washed your hands with a pitcher and basin, the waiter handing over a crumb of soap. But you couldn't bathe. No showers made this hot train reek of unwashed humanity. The toilets were vile. The dining car was filthy—not that there was any food left after the delays. I liked riding this train because it crossed a part of Tanzania where roads were impassable. A little activity with a broom, a mop, a scrub brush, and the trip would have been agreeable. Delays did not bother me. I had no deadline, nor anyone to meet me. But the filth, the dirt, the litter, the shit, and the drunks made this side of travel in Africa hard to bear.

Perhaps it was remarkable that the train ran at all. Yet how else, except for flying, would these thousand or so Tanzanians be able to travel from Mwanza or Tabora? The train was a necessity. The pressure of numbers and the poor maintenance made smooth running impossible, but there was no excuse for the filth.

The low steep hills indicated we were near the coast. In the hillsides were sharply defined cave entrances.

"Kaolin," Julius said. The hills were a source of the stuff, and the caves — he said — dated from German times. Kaolin was once a Tanzanian export. Roofing tiles, bricks, and pots were made from this useful clay. "But these days people sneak in and steal it."

Another defunct industry, like the sisal and the tobacco and the rice and the cotton and the apiaries in Tabora, started by Peace Corps volunteers, which had produced high-quality honey. The volunteers had gone home.

"What happened to the beehives after that?"

"They just failed."

Dar es Salaam started miles from the coast, with scrappy rice fields and scattered villages and mud houses with pretensions, the buildings clustered closer and closer. Cement-block houses, square one-story affairs, pressed in, became linked in an outer shantytown, poor sheds and too many people jammed together, everything sitting in puddles.

Yet life went on. In the middle of this muddy slum, in the drizzling rain, a man was propped up, washing his feet with a bucket and scrub brush. People hacked at the earth with mattocks, preparing small plots for planting. Some women stirred soot-blackened pots over smoky fires — cooking outdoors in the rain. Maize stalks sprouted by the track, someone's garden. The passing scene began to resemble a slum picture by Hogarth, down to the Hogarthian details: people drinking and fighting, lazing around, emptying chamber pots, a man pissing against a post, a child crying, no one even looking up. At one level crossing an overexcited boy jumped up and down in a mud puddle, screaming at the train.

I was in no hurry, I wasn't due anywhere, yet whenever I arrived in an African city, I wanted to leave.

◇ ◇ ◇

Urban life is nasty all over the world, but it is nastiest in Africa — better a year in Tabora than a day in Nairobi. None of the African cities I had so far seen, from Cairo southward, seemed fit for human habitation, though there was never a shortage of foreigners to sing the praises of these snake pits — how you could use cell phones, send faxes, log onto the Internet, buy pizzas, and call home — naming the very things I wanted to avoid.

One day, in an African newspaper I read: "In the year 2005, 75 percent of the people in Africa will be living in urban areas." This was only a few years away. It made me glad I was taking my trip now, because African cities became more awful — more desperate and dangerous — as they grew larger. They did not become denser, they simply sprawled more, became gigantic villages. In such cities, women still lugged water from standpipes and cooked over wood fires and washed clothes in filthy creeks, and people shat in open latrines. "Citified" in Africa meant bigger and dirtier.

Like the person so poor and downtrodden he loses self-respect and any sense of shame, African cities did not even pretend to be anything except large slums. Once, each city had a distinct look: Nairobi had a stucco and tile-roof style of architecture, Kampala had its harmonious hills, Dar es Salaam was coastal colonial, with thick-walled buildings designed to be cool in the heat. Such particularities gave a city atmosphere and an appearance of order in which hope was not wholly absent.

Now, one city was much like another, because a slum is a slum. Improvisation had taken the place of planning. Cheap new buildings were put up because the older buildings were regarded as too expensive to renovate. And because no building was properly maintained, every structure in an African city was in a state of deterioration. I had a list of Dar es Salaam hotels I might stay in. I mentioned one to a taxi driver. He said, "Finished." I said another name. "Bunt by fire." Another: "*Shenzi*" (dirty). Another: "Closed down." Another: "Not wucking."

Tanzanians began most assertions with, "The problem, you see . . ." To any observation or chance remark, Tanzanians I met would respond by apportioning blame. Yet they had had a fairly peaceful time of it — no war, no revolution, no coups d'état, no martial law. Once or twice in forty years Tanzanians had even voted in free elections.

You could not spend a more wasted day than in an office of the Tanzanian government, as I discovered in Dar es Salaam. This waste of time suggested what might be wrong. Tanzanians complained of unemployment — in the capital almost half the adults had no jobs. But those with jobs did next to nothing, if the Office of Immigration was anything to go by. I had my passport, my fifty U.S. dollars in cash, my filled-out application for a tourist visa, and I stood the requisite hour in line. I was no one special. Everyone else in line was encountering the same obstacles in the open-plan office of twenty employees: apathy, then rudeness, and finally hostility.

The crowd I was among just watched and waited. The office was dirty, the desks messy: one civil servant was eating a hunk of cake; another one, a woman with curlers in her hair, was reading the morning paper at her desk; yet another, a man, simply stared into space, drumming his fingers. I tried to detach my personal urgency from this charade (in fact, I needed this visa and my passport to buy a train ticket) and watched as though it were a comic documentary. "You come back later," a surly woman said. But I wanted to monitor my application as it proceeded through all the stages, moving from desk to desk, getting cake crumbs on it from the gobbling man, tea stains from the fingers of the cup sipper. Six people examined and initialed my form. And then it was put in a tray, where it remained for twenty minutes. It was then handed through a slot in the wall, a side office.

If I had complained, they would have replied, with justification, "What's the hurry?" "Who are you?" "What does it matter?" "Why should we care?" Nothing had ever worked in Tanzania. All Tanzanians had ever known was failure, empty political rhetoric, broken promises. True, the unemployed in Dar es Salaam looked desperate, but the workers, too, looked cheated, envious, and angry.

Following my passport, I sneaked over to the side office door and opened it, apologizing — pretending to have entered the wrong office — and saw the visa officer in a white shirt and blue necktie with a tin tray on his desk, a hunk of bread in his hand, tucking into a big bowl of meat stew, slopping gobs of gravy on the stack of visa forms.

"Sorry," I said, and hurried outside to laugh.

There I found Christopher Njau. He was twenty-two, university educated, unemployed, trying to get a passport.

"The problem, you see," he began, as soon as I remarked that I had spent two and a half hours and fifty dollars to wait for a tourist visa — this in a country that was begging tourists to visit. "The World Bank won't give us money."

"I don't see the connection between this inefficient office and a World Bank loan."

"Also," Njau said, "there is too much of corruption here."

"Should I have offered a bribe?"

He shrugged. "Nationalizing the banks was a mistake. Also, we have overpopulation."

"So what's the answer?"

"I want to leave," he said. "That's why I am here. I need a passport to leave — but already it has been months."

"Where would you like to go?"

"My sister is in Texas. She is studying. She has her own car! With a car she can drive to work and also study."

He shook his head in disbelief. It seemed almost unimaginable that his sister, a woman of twenty-four, would own a car. I found it much harder to imagine that she had actually been to this office and gotten a passport.

Later that day I picked up my visa and bought my train ticket. An ordinary ticket from Dar es Salaam to the middle of Zambia was twenty dollars; first class was fifty-five. In first class you shared a compartment with three other people — not my idea of first class, but it would do.

With time to kill, I took the ferry to Zanzibar. Zanzibar remained mostly intact, an island smelling of cloves, its whitewashed houses fronted with decorated parapets and screened verandas. There were apartment blocks, too, as ugly as anything in Romania, and perhaps built by the Romanians, among Tanzania's earlier well-wishers.

There were dhows at the Zanzibar waterfront, and boats, and traders, stallholders, fruit sellers, and the usual medieval touch: on this day a boy about to walk on a high rope strung between two trees. He had attracted fifty or sixty spectators, Zanzibari boys with nothing to do but be entertained by the patter of the acrobat's buildup — he made much of the fact that he had no safety net.

"I might fall! I might die!"

Dazzling white as it loomed from the sea, Zanzibar was an island of smelly alleys and sulky Muslims. I looked around the bazaar and found a grouchy Indian merchant.

"Business is down."

"When was it up?"

"'Sixty-something."

"How much are these sandals?"

They were stiff, antique, made of silver. They were a bride's silver slippers, to be worn on her wedding night as she went scuff-scuff in the semidarkness to the bed where her groom awaited his triumph, her defloration.

"I must weigh them."

I laughed at the thought that these pretty objects were being sold by weight.

"Silver is two-twenty a gram," he said, naming a price in shillings.

I calculated the price to be $120. We haggled for a while and then I gave him $100 in cash, and he wrapped the slippers in old newspaper and snapped a rubber band around them. While doing this, he said that his grandfather had come to Zanzibar in 1885. His whole family was here.

"We want to leave, but how?"

"You mean go to India?"

"Not India. I have never been to India."

"You mean America?"

"Yes. I want America."

"Have you ever been there?"

"No."

Over the next two days I bought supplies for the train trip south. It was impossible to be in Dar es Salaam and not meet foreigners attempting to solve Tanzania's problems. What struck me was the modest size of the efforts. No one was handing out large amounts of money anymore. This was mainly "microfinance," a popular term for a popular activity. One American man I met was doling out loans of $200 to $500, to be repaid in a relatively short time.

"I say to them, 'Don't think about another donor. We're going to get you on your feet. We're the last donor you will ever need.'"

"Do you believe that?"

He laughed and said that Africans were "grant-savvy." They were so used to getting grants, they were aware that the money would dry up in three to five years and assumed that they would have to look elsewhere for more money for their plans: small-scale milk processing, retail shops, women's marketing projects.

"Maybe we're wasting our money, but it's not much money," the American said.

One day in a coffee shop I overheard an American preacher who was meeting some Africans, two men and two women, who were petitioning for grants of money. They said they needed the money soon. The preacher said that while they might be in a hurry, he was not. The preacher was seventy perhaps, with bushy white eyebrows that gave him a severely owlish gaze.

"I am here to look at the situation," the preacher said. "Yes, we have resources, but they are coming to us through God's concern and God's love."

One of the African men mentioned a school that needed cash right now.

The preacher bore down on him, saying, "One thing we insist upon is, no government involvement at all."

"Just guidance only," the African man said.

"We take our guidance from the Bible."

"Partnering," one of the women said, just putting a word in, but wincing when the preacher spoke up.

"We will consider partners, but only faith-based partners, who share our principles," he said.

The second woman mentioned money again.

"Submit your forms so I can study them," the preacher said, and then after he told them what a very great privilege it was for him to interact with them, he led them in a solemn prayer, his head bowed. The Africans watched with pleading eyes, thinking (as I thought), We're never going to see this guy's money.

So many donors had been burned in Tanzania that some grants were hard to come by — so people told me. Tanzanians might insist that the need for money was urgent, but donors could point out the visible fact that the enormous amounts that had been handed out in the past had done little good.

It was easier to emigrate. "I want to go to South Africa," a young man said to me in the market, before his unsuccessful attempt to beg money from me. "Many people I know have gone there. My friends just want to leave Tanzania. There is nothing here."

"How do they get to South Africa?" I asked.

"The train from here to Zambia, then the bus."

"How's the train?"

He made a face, wrinkled his nose, perhaps intending to discourage me. But I was not discouraged. I wanted to leave, too.

13 ◈◈◈

The Kilimanjaro Express to Mbeya

THE TAZARA RAILWAY, a gift from the Chinese, had been inspired by the Great Proletarian Cultural Revolution. Its construction by Chinese workers — engineers, grunt laborers, and Red Guards — had occupied the whole of China's disastrous decade, 1966 to 1976. The Chinese intention, a worthy one, was to liberate both Tanzania and Zambia from their dependence on "imperialist," white-dominated South Africa as a supply line. The building of the railway was also intended to demonstrate what willing hands could accomplish when hardworking peasants became rustless screws in the revolutionary machine (as the Maoist saying went). Unfortunately, there were no revolutionary peasants, only pissed-off peanut farmers getting shortchanged in the Tanzanian heartland, but the Red Guards seemed not to have noticed that. The railway was completed ahead of schedule and was, by any reckoning, a magnificent Chinese achievement.

As a way of showing their thanks to China, Tanzanian bureaucrats parroted Maoist slogans for years afterward, called each other "comrade," and affected Mao suits. In the mid-eighties the Chinese pronounced the Cultural Revolution a horrible mistake. This revision did not reach Dar es Salaam. Long after the Chinese ceased to regard Mao as the Great Helmsman, and saw his platitudes as embarrassing, and adopted neckties and sunglasses along with the new line "To get rich is glorious," Africans were chanting "Serve the people," though it was the last thing anyone in Tanzania wanted to do. They were still pissed-off peanut farmers.

The Tazara Railway went into decline the moment it was finished, though over the years there were spells — convulsions, really — during which attempts were made to repair it. Some years it was unridable. Foreigners were banned from it for a while. At least now it was running, and it had been renamed the Kilimanjaro Express, though it had no connection with the mountain. "It's always late," I was warned in Dar. As if I cared.

The main station itself was an indicator of how little trouble anyone took to maintain the Tazara Railway. The Dar es Salaam terminus was the sort of building in which I had spent a great deal of time buying tickets and eating noodles while riding various Iron Roosters through China. Large, stark, like a Marxist mausoleum, no waiting rooms, no annexes, it was entirely open, Chinese style, designed to make it easy for police to manage crowds and keep everyone visible. "Nowhere to hide" was the subtext of Chinese urban planning. This station was from a standard Chinese blueprint, and would have suited the center of Datong — an identical station could be found in most Chinese cities. Though it seemed out of place here, it was no odder than the colonial structures: the old German office buildings or the British clubs in the center of Dar, or the Arabesque architecture of Zanzibar.

Assuming there would be delays, breakdowns, and shortages, I brought a box of food and enough bottles of water to last four days. The two-day trip to Mbeya usually took three. At Mbeya I intended to go by bus to Malawi. Altogether, I was pleased with my overland African effort. I had not left the ground since my Sudan Air flight to Addis Ababa.

Three Africans awaited me in the compartment: Michel, a Congolese; Phiri, a Zambian; and a Zanzibari named Ali.

Ali said, "You are going to Malawi? Malawians make good houseboys. They are educated. They speak English. We ourselves prefer to sell things."

Phiri, a fifty-three-year-old railwayman nearing retirement, agreed with this. He added, "And they like working for white people."

I had the feeling this was criticism rather than praise.

We left at eleven in the morning. About twenty miles south of Dar we came to a tunnel, the first tunnel I had seen in East Africa — a long one, cut under a big hill, because the point about Chinese railway building was that obstacles were blasted through and the tracks laid straight.

On the other side of the tunnel was the bush, nothing but deep grass and flat-topped trees, everything green from the recent heavy rain. Yet the day was sunny and warm. Though Michel, the Congolese man, did little else but sleep — he was a heavy fellow with a sick mother in Lubumbashi — the others were chatty and informative.

Three hours after we set off, speeding south, we came to a halt. "There is something wrong. We should not be stopping here." Four hours later we were still there. "See what I mean?" It seemed there was a problem with the track. "The heat of the sun has caused the iron rail to expand and buckle. We must wait until it cools." This was an unconvincing explanation.

Killing time, two Africans, a pair of muscular boys, were standing on their heads beside the track. They dropped to their knees and did backflips. Then one climbed onto the other's shoulders and somersaulted to the embankment. It was unusual in the East African bush to see such strong Africans with well-developed muscles. They told me they were professional acrobats.

"We are going to Botswana," one said. "There is no work here for acrobats."

A young blond woman sat by the track reading a thick, torn paperback, one I recognized.

"What do you think of that book?"

"Fantastic. It's about this bloke in Africa, shagging all these African women."

"But it's a novel."

"Reckon so."

"Funnily enough, I wrote it."

"Get out! Did you?" She had a lovely smile and her accent had a soft South African slant. She called out, "Conor, come here!"

A young energetic man hurried over and confronted me, saying, "Kelli, is this bloke touching you up?"

Then he laughed — accusing me of fondling his wife was his matey way of greeting me. He was Irish, his wife was from Cape Town, and both now lived and worked in San Francisco.

They were on their way to South Africa, they said, traveling in the next carriage. Because many of the passengers had spilled out onto the line, I could size them up. A good number were Africans returning home, but there was a scattering of European backpackers, some aid workers, a shocked-looking Finnish woman, a white missionary couple traveling with small barefoot children, some Indian families, and many Tanzanians heading out of the country to seek their fortune.

"They're waiting for the track to cool," Conor said. "Do you fucking believe it?"

Yet as dusk gathered and the air grew cool, the train whistle blew and off we went.

Sunset is breathtaking but so brief in East Africa it seems fast-forwarded: the sun descends into the risen dust of day, the clouds above it blaze, and the whole western sky becomes a canopy as hot pink as molten gold, fringed with orange and purply blue, with beaky faces and filigree, a scattering of mashed hyacinths, a shattered syllabub, a melting light show. Or it may be corporeal, incarnadine, a great bleeding liver slab of sky that slips into separate slices, discoloring, drying into crisp fritters and fragments of friable light before being spun into cotton and vanishing. You can only look at parts of the sunset, because the whole is too wide. This magic enchants for a matter of minutes, and the best of it lasts seconds before darkness falls.

The sun was gone but the sky was alight, the backcloth of the heavens the color of Tanzania's unique gem, the bluey lavender tanzanite, with strands of yellow, braids of thick golden sky illuminating the bush.

I peered into shadows by the track, and what I took to be a tall slender tree was a giraffe, and just as I saw it I heard the Swahili word from the corridor, *twiga*. There were two more loping among the trees. We were passing a wilderness area where animals were gathering at waterholes in the fading light — warthogs, a couple of elephants, some bushbuck, so beautiful painted in the unexpected afterglow of the sunset, purples and yellows, mauve warthogs, golden elephants.

Then night fell, the animals dissolved into darkness, and there was silence except for the frogs' *gleep-gleep*.

Wandering through the train later that night, I came upon a lounge car. Loud American rap music was being played — angry obscenities, accusations, incomprehensible slang. The place was full of drunken shouting Africans. One stuck his sweaty face into mine and demanded that I buy him a beer. "*Kesho, kesho,*" I said. Tomorrow, tomorrow. My saying it that way took the edge off the confrontation.

I was about to leave when I saw Conor and Kelli drinking Tuskers at the far end. They invited me to join them and their friend, the Finnish woman, who still seemed shocked. She was pretty, but her pinched expression of worry made her beauty look somewhat alarming.

"This is Ursula," Kelli said. "Paul's a writer. His *Secret History* book's all about this guy shagging African girls."

Ursula winced. It was a sensitive topic. She was working on an AIDS project in Zambia, heading back there, but not for long.

"Before I left Finland I understood the problem of AIDS in Zambia and I thought I had some good solutions," Ursula said. She rocked back and forth slightly as she spoke, another cause for concern, but somehow part of her faintly singsong Finnish accent. "After I got to Zambia I realized that it's more complicated than I thought. Now I don't understand the problem so clearly. It is all so complicated, and I don't know about any solution."

"What did you find out in Zambia that you didn't know before?" I asked.

"The behavior," she said, and rolled her eyes. "There is so much sex. It is all sex. And so young!"

"How young?"

"As if you don't know," Kelli said, teasing me.

"Ten years old is common," Ursula said.

"But with their own age group," I said, repeating what I had learned in the Chalbi Desert from the Samburu man.

"Not with their age group. Anyone with anyone," Ursula said.

Conor said, "Sounds like fun — just joking!"

Ursula shook her head. "It is horrible. There is no sex education. No one will talk about sex, but everyone does it. No one will talk about AIDS, and everyone is infected. We were sent an anti-AIDS film and we showed it. But people in the villages said it was shameful — too indecent — and so it was withdrawn. What could we do?"

"Did you talk to them about it?"

"I tried to."

"And what happened?"

"They wanted to have sex with me."

Conor covered his face and howled into his hands.

"The men follow me. They call me *muzungu*. I hate that. Always calling out to me, '*Muzungu! Muzungu!*'"

"Racial profiling," Conor said, trying to lighten the mood. "Shouldn't stand for it, if I was you, not a bit of it."

But Ursula did not smile. For her it was more than outraged decency — it was despair, a recognition of futility, a kind of grief even, along with anger.

"They ask me for money all the time. 'You give me money' — just me, because I am white."

She was trembling and silent after that, sitting barracked by the hideous rap music and the yelling drunks.

Conor and Kelli had just come from what they had hoped would be a tour of the game parks. It had not been a success.

"I wanted to leave Arusha almost as soon as I got there," Kelli said. "Some people saw a thief and chased him. 'Thief! Thief!' They caught him and knocked him down, and *right there* they beat him to death. It made me sick."

I told them how I had seen the same thing my first day in Nairobi, a suspected thief being chased into a muddy creek.

"So what do you reckon?" Conor said to no one in particular.

"I am going home to Finland," Ursula said. She stopped rocking and sat back in her chair and hugged herself into a ball.

The three Africans were snoring when I got back to my compartment. I crawled into my lower berth and let the movement of the train put me to sleep. With the shutters down and the door locked to keep thieves at bay, the small space was stifling, and the heat and strangeness gave me disturbing dreams of dangerous stinking machinery that woke me with their violence, cog wheels flying apart, bolts becoming projectiles.

The heat and smell were just as strong outside. We traveled in swampland by the Kilombero River for most of the night, but by morning we were in upland, where it was chilly. About an hour after sunrise we came to a station, Makambako, where a great many passengers got out to catch buses for the distant south Tanzanian town of Songea.

The train did not move for an hour. Phiri, the railwayman, spoke to one of the crew and confirmed that the delay was caused by a problem on the line.

Remembering that I had had no dinner the night before, I went to a shop with a sign saying *Station Canteen* and looked for some safe food. I bought a hard-boiled egg, two chapatis, and a cup of hot tea. While I was eating, Conor entered the shop.

"He's actually putting that stuff in his gob," he said, mocking me. "Hey, there's supposed to be a three-hour delay. Want to go for a walk?"

We walked half a mile into Makambako, which was not a town at all but a collection of hovels on a stretch of paved road where idle people sat or stood. Boys called out in jeering voices and pretended that they were going to throw stones at us. Thirty years before, the party line was: *This railway will open up this province to progress. People will want to live here. The train will give everyone access to markets. They'll grow crops. Schools will spring up. Life will change and people's lives will be better.* As Livingstone had called the Zambezi "God's Highway," this railway line was "the People's Highway."

It hadn't happened. I had traveled this way before, in 1965, by road, and it had looked much the same. What had changed? There was now a makeshift market, women squatting by the road. There was a gas station, but it was derelict, empty, and few manmade objects are uglier than an abandoned gas station. What had been mud huts before were now shanties made of scrap lumber. The boys were ragged and insolent. Grown men, doing nothing, stood in the street talking, killing time. The old women selling fruit and peanuts bowed their heads against the cold gritty wind that tore at broken thorn scrub.

We bought some bananas and peanuts, and I found a week-old newspaper. I read the headlines to Conor: "Desire for More Beautiful Buttocks Leads to Death" and "Wife (10 Years Old) Admitted to Mental Ward in Dar."

"But that's the one that scares me," Conor said, pointing to "U.S. Stock Market in Renewed Plunge."

This piece helped me add to my collection of market metaphors: "The market is flushing itself out" and "We are seeing the unwinding of a bubble situation."

As Conor was Irish, I asked him if he had heard of Eamon Collins's *Killing Rage*, the remorseful book I had read in northern Kenya about an Irishman's life as a hit man for the IRA.

"Oh, sure. Great book. Pity about Eamon, though."

"What happened?"

"He was murdered in front of his family a couple of months back by an IRA hit squad. For writing the book."

And the gunmen, the Irish generally, would cluck about savagery in Africa.

I sat on the platform among the delayed passengers. No one seemed to mind the waiting. If you learned anything on a trip such as this, it was that in East Africa haste was a foreign concept. Though there were a number of words for urgency in Swahili — *lazima, juhudi, shidda, haraka* — none had Bantu roots; all were based on loan words from Arabic. In East African culture, hurrying had a negative connotation, illustrated in the rhyming maxim *Haraka, haraka haina baraka* — Hurry, hurry makes bad luck. Of course, some Africans were driven mad by the lack of urgency and tried to emigrate. But usually such complacency made people patient and accounted for the utter indifference to things going wrong. In a place where time seemed to matter so little, there existed a sort of nihilism that was also a form of serenity and a survival skill.

A man with a runny nose was selling oranges, handing the snot-smeared fruit to customers. Another man carried a small rack of Chinese-made bras and panties. Boys followed him, giggling at the merchandise. The missionary children, pink-cheeked and frisky, ran barefoot in the fields next to the platform, in the dirt and dog shit, while their parents cheered them on. I did not feel it was my place to warn them of hookworm. The station building, another Chinese design, was empty, the ticket booth vandalized, the floor littered and unswept.

The two acrobats did handstands, to the delight of the local people. They were from Zanzibar, one of them told me. They were looking forward to their gig in Botswana.

"Mr. Morris invited us."

"For a show?"

"Something like that. Our contract is for three years."

They were very happy to be leaving and about to take up a real job.

A young man headed to the Congo to buy artifacts said that it wasn't much trouble to get to Lubumbashi — he would catch a bus from northern Zambia. He said he knew nothing about masks or fetishes, but that he was meeting a Luba man in Katanga who knew all the tribes. This was the greatest time to be buying old Congolese carvings and antiques, he said. Villages were selling their best items.

"Museum quality!"

I laughed at this trader's expression.

"Because they are poor. They sell everything."

As the morning wore on, the sun became hotter. The surrounding countryside was bush, but the settlement of Makambako was a blight. I wondered whether, with so much empty land and wilderness around, a littered town seemed of no importance.

Around noon the whistle blew and we were off again, jouncing and shaking into the bush on rails that seemed unfastened. We crossed a great sloping plain, green hills in the distance. Some gardens nearby were planted with sunflowers and corn, but farther into the plain there were no people, nothing was planted, only the trackless bush of southwest Tanzania, fat baobabs and woods so dense in places there were many signs of game — hoof prints at the muddy shores of water holes, battered trees with broken limbs and chewed bark, the signs of hungry elephants.

Several more breakdowns immobilized the train. The Africans in my compartment yawned and slept. I went to the dining car and stood, marveling at the filth of it.

"What do you want, *bwana?*"

"I want a smoked turkey sandwich on a seeded roll, with a slice of provolone cheese, lettuce and tomato, a little mustard — no mayo. A glass of freshly squeezed juice and a cup of coffee."

He laughed because it meant nothing. I was just gabbling. But hadn't he asked me what I wanted?

"What have you got?"

"Rice and stew."

My stash of food was gone, so I sat by the window eating the rice and stew, bewitched by the beautiful landscape, the long enormous valleys, the rim of mountains and hills.

A small village near the settlement of Chimala made me wonder: how is this grass-roofed village today different from the grass-roofed village that stood here in, say, 1850, before European missionaries and improvers got anywhere near this region? It was a fair question. There was even an answer. In many respects it was the same grass-roofed village — the hut design, the cooking fire, the wooden mortar and pestle, the crude axes and knives, the baskets and bowls, the texture of life was much the same. That accounted for its persistence. The inhabitants had worked their little plots and fed themselves, but had lain mute and overlooked through a century and a half of exploitation, colonialism, and independence. They were probably Christians now, and wished for things like bikes and radios, but there were no signs of such contraptions, and any prospect for change seemed unlikely.

Save them, agents of virtue said of such people, yet farmers like these had saved themselves. Subsistence farming was not a sad thing to me anymore. And if this every-man-for-himself attitude was hard on the debt-ridden Tanzanian government, that was tough luck for the bureaucrats who had wasted donor money and planned the economy so badly. The people in this tiny village clearly had the skills to survive and perhaps prevail. At the rate we were going, laboring toward Mbeya, they would outlast the Kilimanjaro Express.

◈ ◈ ◈

At a distance, the small hillside town of Mbeya looked pretty, the approach to it through deep green coffee plantations and plowed fields. Visiting the town in 1960, Evelyn Waugh wrote, "Mbeya is a little English garden-suburb with no particular reason for existence . . . a collection of red roofs among conifers and eucalyptus trees." Five years later, when I passed through, it was still small and orderly, its prosperity based on its coffee crop.

Nearing Mbeya today, I saw a ruined town of ramshackle houses, broken streets, and paltry shops. Most of the shops sold identical merchandise: dusty envelopes and ballpoint pens, Chinese clothes and sports shoes. The radio ripoff brands were "Philibs" and "Naiwa" and "Sunny" — very subtle, and I knew them to be junk, for I had bought a "Sunny" in Egypt and it broke. More melancholy shops sold cast-off books, which comprised a sort of library of Tanzanian political wrong turns: *One Party Democracy, Which Way Africa?, The Speeches of Mwalimu Nyerere, The Tanzanian Road to Development, Marxism in Africa,* and so forth. I stood and read a chapter in one of the books, entitled "Elections in Ugogo Land," by an old colleague from Makerere, a cheery Irishman who was so persecuted and paranoid under Idi Amin that he went haywire, became a Muslim, and renounced his Wagogo scholarship.

I had said goodbye to my friends on the Kilimanjaro Express and decided to stay a few days in Mbeya, because it was a place I had visited thirty-five years before. I wanted to see what time had done to it. I had seen from the moment I laid eyes on it that time had not improved it, though time had certainly changed it. Instead of the garden suburb with conifers, Mbeya was now big and bare and rundown and creepy looking. It was still full of gloomy Indians. One Indian family was selling electric stoves, clothes irons, toasters, and the like.

"But who has electricity?" one of the Indians said to me. The irons that were in demand were the old-fashioned hollow ones that you filled with hot coals.

"I was sent from Dar to improve things," a younger Indian man said. "But things are still bad. Business is terrible."

"What's your most popular item?"

"Pots. Metal pots. That's the only thing Africans can buy. Who has money? They have no money."

I said I was heading for Malawi.

"Malawi is just as bad. He goes that side," the first Indian said, pointing to the younger man.

"It is dead city," the younger man said.

"What city? Lilongwe?"

"Whole of Malawi — dead city."

This corner of Tanzania I considered one of the remoter inhabited parts of Africa. It was not wilderness, but it was bush, far from the capital and too near to Zambia and Malawi to invite investment. The southeast corner of the Congo was just over the nearby range of hills; that proximity was another liability. In the 1930s Mbeya had been established as a provincial capital, but now it was off the map and on the wane, attracting smugglers and aimless people like me, just passing through.

Mbeya, as a habitable ruin, attracted foreign charities. This I found depressing rather than hopeful, for they had been at it for decades and the situation was more pathetic than ever. There were many aid workers in the town, looking busy and deeply suspicious, always traveling in pairs in the manner of cultists and Mormon evangelists, never sharing. They seemed to represent a new breed of priesthood, but they were the most circumspect, evasive, and unforthcoming people, like the most bureaucratic social workers, which in a sense they were, either scolding or silent.

As a breed, the agents of virtue avoided intimacy with outsiders, especially the likes of me, unattached wanderers whom they seemed to regard as dangerous to their mission. They must have seen into my heart, for at this point in my trip I seriously questioned their mission. They hardly made eye contact. This English habit of averting the gaze was inspired by the fear that any show of friendliness meant they might be obligated to make a gesture — offer a ride, a favor. They had brand-new vehicles, always white Land Rovers or white Toyota Land Cruisers, and they drove them with ministerial haughtiness.

Those vehicles were sometimes being washed and polished by Africans in the parking lot of the Mount Livingstone Hotel, where I was staying. It was a dismal hotel, empty and clammy, and dead except for a dark room which at six in the evening filled with drunken African men. The reason for the darkness was that most light bulbs were missing from their fixtures.

The aid workers had the best rooms, but they kept to themselves. I tried to approach them, to get any information I could about the road to Malawi, but they shied away with that squinting expression that seemed to say, Am I wearing something of yours?

"I'm here for a conference," one said before backing away.

"Malawi's not in my area," another informed me. "Excuse me, I've got a series of meetings."

"There's a panel this afternoon" was another line I heard.

Yet another: "We're holding a workshop."

I had begun to cotton to the view set out in the antidonor books, *The Lords of Poverty* and *The Road to Hell,* that foreign aid has been destructive to Africa — has actually caused harm. Another vocal advocate of this theory was an African economist, George B. N. Ayittey, who in two books, *Africa Betrayed* and *Africa in Chaos,* documented the decline in African fortunes as a result of donor aid.

It is for someone else, not me, to evaluate the success or failure of charitable efforts in Africa. Offhand, I would say the whole push has been misguided, because it has gone on too long with negligible results. If anyone had asked me to explain, my reasoning would have been: Where are the Africans in all this? In my view, aid is a failure if in forty years of charity the only people still dishing up the food and doling out the money are foreigners. No Africans are involved — there is not even a concept of African volunteerism or labor-intensive projects. If all you have done is spend money and have not inspired anyone, you can teach the sharpest lesson by turning your back and going home.

It was what Africans did. The most imaginative solution Africans had to their plight was simply to leave — to bail out, escape, run, bolt — go to Britain or America and abandon their homelands. That was the lesson of the Kilimanjaro Express — half the African passengers on it were fleeing, intending to emigrate.

In a town like Mbeya I understood the sense of futility. Perhaps that was why I liked rural Africa so much and avoided towns, because in villages I saw self-sufficiency and sustainable agriculture. In the towns and cities, not the villages, I felt the full weight of all the broken promises and thwarted hope and cynicism. And all the lame explanations: "The coffee price is down . . . The floods hurt the maize harvest . . . The cooperative was nationalized . . . The managers were stealing the funds . . . They closed the factory . . . The problem, you see, is no money."

In such towns I felt: no achievements, no successes, the place is only bigger and darker and worse. I began to fantasize that the Africa I traveled through was often like a parallel universe, the dark star image in my mind, in which everyone existed as a sort of shadow counterpart of someone in the brighter world.

The foreign clothes were like proof of this shadow existence. Most people did not wear the new Chinese-made clothes from the shops, but rather the hand-me-downs from the market. These secondhand clothes had been donated by well-meaning people in clothing drives at their churches or the school Clothes for Africa Day or the People in Need Fund Drive that requested "any usable articles of clothing." In Africa, these clothes are sorted into large bales: trousers, dresses, T-shirts, socks, ties, jeans, and so forth, and the bales are sold cheaply to people who hawk them in markets. This helped fuel my fantasy. I saw Africans wearing T-shirts saying *Springfield Little League* and *St. Mary's Youth Services* and *Gonzaga* and *Jackman Auto Co.* and *Notre Dame College Summer Hockey, Wilcox, Sask.*, and I imagined the wearers to be the doppelgängers of the folks in that other world.

I had stopped in Mbeya to see how things were going in the years I had been away. The answer was that things were going very badly but that no one seemed to mind. Time to leave.

There was a bus from Mbeya to Malawi. A boy sold me a ticket.

Later, when I went to catch the bus, I was told that it wasn't running that day, and it might not be running tomorrow, and I could not have a refund, because the money I had paid had been sent to the main office in Dar es Salaam.

"The problem, you see," someone started to say.

Hearing that, I walked away.

The boy who cheated me tagged along and asked me to give him more money. He said, "Buy me a soda. I am hungry. I have had nothing to eat today."

"Don't you have a mother?"

"Yes."

"Then go find her and ask her to feed you. I am trying to get to Malawi and this ticket you sold me is worthless."

Thinking some Indian traders might be going to the Malawi border, I found a shop where two Indians were grading long yellow sticks of raw unwrapped laundry soap. They knew nothing about Malawi except that smugglers occasionally came from that direction. The two men did not speak Swahili. Amazingly, they were not from Mbeya — a newcomer, Prasad, and Shiva, an old-timer, were expatriates from Bombay.

"Soap is an easy business," Shiva said. "We make it in Dar, from palm oil and caustic soda. We sell it by the stick or by the cake. We cut it, see. No one else in the world uses this soap, no one buys it like this. We sell it in villages, but business is flat."

"No purchasing power," Prasad said.

"Nothing has happened in Tanzania. Nothing. Nothing. And in ten more years, nothing."

"There was a textile factory here, run by an Indian chap who was born here. It was very successful. Nyerere nationalized it and put in African managers. They stole. It failed. It was shut. In 1987 the factory was sold — to an Indian! The machines were still good. It is working now."

"Africans are bad managers. The workers are lazy. Lazy! Lazy! Even my people — lazy! I have to kick! Kick! Kick!" He was kicking air as he repeated this, looking and sounding like V. S. Naipaul on his first visit to Africa. *Kick them — it's all they understand.*

Shiva seemed hysterical. I had obviously touched a nerve, raising the subject of Africans. He was reminded that he hated Africans, yet he liked being in Mbeya.

"This is like a vacation to me," Prasad said. "It is peaceful here — no trouble. My children can walk in the streets. Vegetables are very good and cheap. The rice is fine — they grow it here. In Bombay I spend so much time in traffic, hours every day. Here I can drive the whole town in fifteen minutes."

"The soap business is so simple," Shiva said. "Anyone with a little common sense could do my job. Anyone. It is so simple I am ashamed. But not one African can do it. Who can we hire? The Africans can't even sell one stick of soap."

"They don't care, because what do they need? A little food, some clothes, and — what? They don't think about tomorrow. They don't have to. Food is cheap. Life is cheap. They don't think ahead. Next year is — what? Next year is nothing to them."

For years I had heard Indians uttering these ignorant platitudes. They were still saying them! The difference now was that these men were strangers. They were like the first Indians ever to come to East Africa to trade or build railways a century before, imported as coolies from impoverished villages in Gujarat and Kutch, like the Indian railway navvies in *The Man-Eaters of Tsavo* that Patterson calls *baboos.* And like those bewildered precolonial souls, these soap sellers had no idea how to get to the neighboring countries, did not speak the language, knew no Africans, lived in a darkness, and of course were intending, in the fullness of time, to leave.

Seeing my patience as a form of desperate fatalism, I spent another day in Mbeya and then made an effort to move on. There was no bus, but I could get a minibus, a rusty stinking *matatu,* to the border.

Seeing me with my bag, recognizing an opportunity, some boys gathered around me, though I tried to back away.

"Yes, that *matatu* goes to the border, but when you get to the border you might be harmed."

"Why would anyone harm me?"

"There are bad people there."

The direst warning — yet what choice did I have?

No vehicle was leaving until noon. Rain began to fall. I walked away, the boys following me, trying to cadge money and, I felt, trying to distract me so they could steal my bag. I walked from the bus station to town and back again. Then I boarded a filthy dangerous-looking *matatu* and inserted myself among the sixteen squashed passengers, who smelled horribly, and I thought, I am out of my mind.

The routine was: the driver speeded, swerved, stopped, dropped one person, picked up two, sped away leaning on his horn. Whenever he stopped there was a petty quarrel, someone with no money, someone asking him to wait, some yelling in Swahili, "Hey, I'm walking here!" Women pressed themselves against the minibus, offering peanuts and fruit. What dismayed me most was that it was now raining very hard. I had a poncho, but that wasn't it — the road was slick, our tires were bald, the man's driving was amateurish.

On that same stretch of road, exactly one week later in a similar rainstorm, two vehicles collided head-on, a minibus in which eighteen people died — all the passengers — and a bigger bus, fourteen passengers dead, many injured. The driver of the speeding minibus had skidded trying to avoid hitting a cow, then overturned and rammed the big bus.

According to the paper I read, a busy man appeared at the scene of the accident and began picking up "heads and other body parts of the 32 victims." He described himself as "a traditional healer." Villagers who had heard the crash and come to gape asked him what he was doing. "The man explained that he had cast a spell the previous day for the accident to happen, so that he could get body parts to use for his treatments."

Hearing this, the villagers beat him to death on the spot.

We arrived at the town of Tukuyu. Everyone got out of the minibus — seventeen people, big and small. The driver said, "We go no farther."

I was glad to leave this deathtrap. I found Tukuyu on my map. "Meesta, meesta, you want taxi?" The usual punks, two of them in a battered car. We agreed on a price to cross the border. "We take you to Karonga." That seemed so good it made me doubtful. We drove thirty miles in silence. Near the border, a scene of disorder and mud, more fruit sellers, and people in shanties, the punks pulled off the road (as I had guessed they might) and demanded more money. "We need to buy petrol."

"Let's discuss it over there," I said. I got out and started walking.

They sauntered after me. They waited while I got my passport stamped at the Tanzania border post, then demanded more money. The rain let up while I walked down the road toward the Malawi side, followed by urchins. I suppose I should have felt dismayed — it was late in the day, I was being nagged by kids and moneychangers and shouted at by the punks in the taxi who had put the squeeze on me.

Yet I was pleased. Mbeya was behind me, I had not gotten stuck in Tukuyu, and I had circumvented the curse of *There are bad people there.* The border ahead looked lovely. I could see beyond a range of mountains, the Republic of Malawi a much flatter landscape in the distance. The Tanzanian boys were still pestering me, but I picked up my pace and walked past the final gate, one they could not cross, leaving them behind, clinging to the fence. Just before dusk, the sun came out and flashed — a whole gold bar pressed against the earth — and then liquefied and slipped, and I followed the last of the light into Malawi.

14 ◇◇◇

Through the Outposts of the Plateau

I CROSSED THE BORDER, three or four footsteps, striding into a different country, glad to be home again in slaphappy Malawi, land of prostrate forests and dusty roads and even dustier faces, the eighth-poorest country in the world. The amount you paid for one meal in a good American restaurant, a single Malawian earned in an entire year. Here in Malawi, called Nyasaland when I had first arrived, I had spent my two Peace Corps years trying to be a teacher in a schoolhouse at the foot of a hill in the southern province. Here, also, I had encountered my first dictator, had my first dose of the clap, and had a gun shoved in my face by an idiot soldier enraged by my color — three somewhat related events that inspired in me feelings of fear and disgust. But I had been happy here too, and perhaps for similar reasons, since the horror of near-death experiences can swell our capacity for love and fill us with a zest for life.

Malawi time was an hour earlier than Tanzania, yet it was night at the border. No one else was immigrating. I was alone in the office, a small building on the dark road leading into a forest. All these elements created the strong impression that I was entering the country by the back door.

I greeted the officials in their own language, using the polite form of address, the formal "you," and filled out my application form. Under

"Occupation" I wrote "Teacher," though I wanted to write "Provocateur." I paid my visa fee and got my passport stamped. As I was headed out the door into the country itself, a small man sitting at a bare wooden table said, "Yellow fever certificate, please."

Amazingly, I had one. I handed it over.

"Out-of-date," the man said. "It expired last year. Good for ten years only."

"I didn't know that."

"You should read the certificate." The tiny nondescript man, speaking to me sharply in this way, acquired distinct features — became a skinny, cold-eyed, rat-faced predator in a sweaty shirt, with flecks of lint in his hair. "Also, your vaccination is out-of-date."

"Do you have yellow fever in Karonga? Because that's where I'm going."

"Yes, we have yellow fever," he said, turning his fangy face on me. "We have cholera. We have smallpox. We have malaria. Polio, too. We have many illnesses."

"Ntenda kwambiri — pepani!" I said. Lots of sickness — sorry!

"This is very serious. Come with me."

As soon as he uttered them, I knew that the actual meaning of these words was "Bribe me." He believed he had the advantage: the border had just closed, the office was empty except for a few officers, the road was dark, and we were at the remotest, northernmost point of this elongated land. The first time I had entered the country, in December 1963, the African immigration officer had smiled and welcomed me and thanked me in advance for being a teacher in Malawi.

"In here," the rat-faced man said, ordering me. He opened the door to a small shabby office. The building was so badly made, so temporary looking, that the walls did not reach to the ceiling. I could hear mutterings from other rooms. I sat on a plastic chair, while he took his place behind a desk, under a portrait of the president of Malawi, Bakili Muluzi, a gap-toothed fatty in glasses. This politician's first act in office was to put his unappealing face on all the national currency, his chubby profile on coins, full faced on the notes. The act had since been rescinded, but the money still circulated, and his intimidating portrait hung on every shop wall in the country. One of Muluzi's objections to his predecessor in office was that the man had created a cult of personality.

Smiling at the bribe-minded man behind the desk, I thought, You will get nothing from me, buster.

"This is very serious," he said, fingering an official form that was perhaps a deportation order.

"I will get a revaccination in Karonga. Also a yellow fever shot."

"Not possible in Karonga. There is no hospital."

"In Lilongwe, then."

"The prophylaxis, so to say, does not take effect for ten days. What if you fell ill? That would be serious."

I hated his pomposity, and every time he used the word "serious," it sounded insistently extortionate. I decided not to speak to him in English.

"*Ndithu, bambo. Ndadwala ndikupita ku chipatala,*" I said in Chichewa. Definitely, sir. If I got sick, I would go to the hospital.

He said, "I would be very sorry if you fell ill."

"*Pepani, pepani sapolitsa chironda.*" It was an old Malawi saw: Saying "Sorry, sorry" doesn't heal the wound.

He didn't react to that jape. He said, "The road is very bad because of rain. You might not reach up to Lilongwe for many days."

"*Mvula! Matope! Nzeru za kale, anthu anasema 'Walila mvula, malila matope!'*" Rain! Mud! Long ago, the wisdom was "Ask for rain and you're asking for mud!"

My yakking clearly irritated him, but he was intent on delaying me and not dissuaded from circling around a bribery demand. Now he dangled my passport at me. "You must understand, this is serious. Your certificate is out-of-date. It has failed."

"Like you'd say of a bow: *Uta wabwino wanga wagwa.*" My good bow has failed.

Finishing this alliteration, for it was a magnificently alliterative language, I heard an African yodeling in Chichewa from the other side of the transom: "Eh! Eh! What is this I hear? A white man speaking this language. Where is this white man?"

The door opened and a stout bald man in a policeman's uniform entered, laughing and reaching to shake my hand. We exchanged polite greetings in Chichewa. He asked me my name, my country, and welcomed me.

"I want to go to America," he said in his language, and then, "Where did you learn to speak Chichewa?"

"I was a teacher a long time ago at Soche Hill."

"Please, be a teacher again here. We need you, father."

While the policeman clutched my hand in his two hands, to show respect, I said, "I want to help. But I have a problem."

"What is the problem?" he said, raising his voice and leaning to look at the small scruffy man at the desk.

But the scruffy man's head was down and he was writing fast, completing the form he had waved at me. He said in a breathless, furtive way, "I am allowing you entry on humanitarian grounds."

The policeman accompanied me to the gate, saying, "Did you have a problem in there?"

I reminded him of another bit of Malawi wisdom: "Two buttocks cannot avoid friction." *(Matako alaabili tabuli kucumbana.)*

"You must stay," he said, laughing. "Our schools are bad these days. We want teachers."

"I am not a teacher now. I am a *mlendo.*" It was a nice all-purpose word meaning traveler, wanderer, stranger, guest.

I found a minibus parked on the dark road near some fruit and drink stalls. The vehicle reeked of diesel oil and chicken blood in the evening heat, and was half filled with passengers. I stood near it, listening to the racket of the nighttime insects. The market was ramshackle and dirty, run by grannies and very ragged boys. A man was roasting corncobs on a smoky fire. A short distance away, glowing in moonlight, was a huge cactus like a saguaro with upraised arms.

"When is this bus going to Karonga?" I asked.

"We don't know."

I did not mind. I was forgiving and patient, because I was where I wanted to be. I was not spooked by the darkness and this empty road, the disorderly market, the rotting garbage, the blowing smoke, the rags, the stinks; I was reassured. For one thing, it seemed that nothing had changed: the simplest country I had ever known was still simple.

After a while, the driver got in, and after many tries with the key and several denunciations, he started the engine, and off we went.

In the fifty miles to Karonga in the battered bus, I made a mental list headed, "You Know You're in Malawi When . . ."

the first seven shops you pass are coffin makers' shops

an old man on the road is wearing a women's fur-trimmed pink housecoat from the 1950s

the rear rack of a bike is stacked with ten uncured cow hides a roadblock is a bamboo pole across two barrels, and the official manning it is wearing a T-shirt lettered *Winnipeg Blue Bombers*

two policemen stop your minibus for no reason and at gunpoint force the fourteen passengers to pile out in the dark (and they looked at my passport for quite a long time)

the smooth tarred road abruptly becomes a rutted muddy track that is barely passable

people start sentences with "But we are suffering, sir"

people say, apropos of nothing, "The day the old woman disappears is when the hyena shits gray hair"

on the day the minister of finance announces his national austerity plan, it is revealed that thirty-eight Mercedes-Benzes have just been ordered from Germany.

In the cool wet air, over muddy broken roads, past huts and hovels lit by kerosene lamps, we traveled slowly, stopped by armed policemen at some roadblocks and by insolent youths at others. We were in darkness. In some places, people squatted in the road, awaiting any vehicle to take them into Karonga. This seemed the height of desperation; it was after eight P.M., two hours after sunset, and hardly anyone drove at night. But we picked them up and they got in blinking, pulling sacks and children after them.

The teenager collecting the fares had been calling me *muzungu* since the border. At first I ignored him, because it was insulting and beneath my notice, but the punk kept it up, asking me in Chichewa, "White man, where are you going?"

The correct form of address was *bambo* (father) or *bwana* (sir) or even *achimwene* (brother). In the past, no Malawian would have dreamed of speaking to a stranger in such a rude way.

Finally, when he persisted — this was in the darkness of the crowded, smelly minibus on the rutted road — I faced him and said, "Do you want me to call you 'dark man'?" (*muntu muda* — the adjective covered dark, black, brown, and blue).

He went silent and sulked. The minibus labored onward. I was still facing him.

"*Kodi. Dzina lanu ndani?*" Excuse me. What's your name?

"Simon," he said.

"Good. Don't call me 'white man' and I won't call you 'dark man.' My name is Paul."

"Mr. Paul, where are you going?" he said in a chastened voice.

I had no idea where I was going. We entered the small, shadowy town of Karonga, where the main street was in even worse condition than the road from the border: deep ruts, potholes, and wide mud puddles. The light of fluorescent bulbs that served as street lamps showed that most of the shops were shut.

"Drop me at the hotel," I said, assuming there was a hotel.

From the ripe smell and rising damp I knew we were headed to the shore of Lake Malawi, and there they dropped me off at a bleak set of buildings made of cinderblocks with a sign saying *Marina Hotel.* As soon as I got out of the bus, rain began to fall, not heavy but spattery, like a noisy warning, smacking the big leaves of the trees overhead and making a crashing sound on the lake.

I was led to a room in a thatch-roofed hut that was full of mosquitoes. This was one of the "deluxe suites," fifteen dollars a night, including breakfast. I put down my bag, sprayed myself with insect repellent, and went to find some food. I could not remember whether I had eaten anything that day — maybe some bananas or peanuts. In Tanzania, as in Ethiopia, the people looked so desperate I had no appetite.

There was a restaurant and bar at the Marina, and though it was a stormy night there was loud music and drunken Malawians, some of them singing, others staggering, perhaps dancing. The rain came down hard now, lashing the awnings, wetting the tables, flooding the driveway. Two men with the hardy sunburned look of safari guides shoved out a chair and asked me to join them.

One said, "This rain is nothing. Last night was a torrent. It was the hardest rain I've ever seen in my life." He was raising his voice to be heard over the falling rain.

"What are you doing here?" I asked.

"Driving to Kenya," the other man, who was younger, said. "You alone?"

"Yes. I just came from the border," I said. "Actually, I'm on my way from Cairo. I passed through Kenya. You know Moyale?"

The younger man said, "I was born in Kenya and lived there my whole life and I've never been to Moyale."

That made me feel that I had accomplished something. And I was right about their having the look of safari guides, because they ran an upmarket company called Royal African Safaris. The name called to mind the sort of luxury safari where the clients wore pith helmets and khakis and camped in elegant tents by water holes in the bush, a different Africa from the one I traveled through.

The younger man was David Penrose; his partner, huge and weather-beaten and white-haired, was Jonny Baxendale. They both looked jovial and dauntless and reliable. We drank beer and ate fish and chips as the rain grew louder. They had worked on the film *Out of Africa*. David lived in Nanyuki, Jonny in Karen, which he said was safe now: "We chased the rascals out." They admitted that Nairobi was in deep decline, people moving to the outskirts. "But our business is in the bush."

They were driving north, having just bought a new Land Rover in South Africa. They had driven through Zimbabwe and Zambia.

"You're going to like South Africa. Cape Town is great," David said. "You'd think you were in Europe."

"What do you make of Malawi?" I asked.

"It's okay," Jonny said. "We've just come over the plateau. It's dead empty. There's some game. It's Africa, all right."

As we talked and drank beer, the wind became stronger and drove the rain onto the veranda where we were sitting. We moved farther in and were preparing to move inside when, with an uprush of wind and drenching rain, the lights went out, the music stopped, and the Africans began shouting. We sat in the howling gale in complete darkness.

"We've got to make an early start," David said after a while, standing up.

We shook hands and parted. The bartender gave me a lantern and pointed me in the direction of my hut.

The hut's interior was damp and buggy, but there was a mosquito net knotted over the bed. I undid it, tucked it in, slipped inside, and there I lay, listening to the radio — news of an attempted coup in the capital, Lilongwe. This might have been alarming, but I guessed it was the usual ruse, a pretext to arrest members of the opposition and an inspiration for the police to squeeze travelers at roadblocks.

Twiddling knobs, I found a station playing country music of the type that had always been popular in Malawi — Jim Reeves, Hank Williams, and Flatt and Scruggs, good old songs. Then a preacher came on and began talking about sinners and said, "Welcome to World Harvest Radio, Christian country music." I was like the Mexican heathens in the Paul Bowles short story "Pastor Dow at Tacaté," who are so enthralled by the pastor's playing "Fascinatin' Rhythm" on his wind-up record player in the chapel that they stick around for the sermon.

I switched off the radio and I lay in the dark, listening to the rain and marveling that I had made it to Malawi alone on the long safari. I was eager to spend my big birthday here, and even had a plan. I had asked the U.S. embassies in Uganda and Kenya to send an e-mail to the embassy in Lilongwe, saying that I was available to speak at any school or college in the country or to meet aspiring African writers. I would also visit my old school, maybe bring some textbooks, and I would volunteer to spend a week teaching, to show my gratitude to Malawi after so many years: the long-lost son returning to give something back on his birthday. I wanted to signify my return in some way, with a gesture.

The morning in Karonga was golden after the rain, with sharp colors: glittering lake, pure blue sky without a scrap of cloud, thick green foliage, black mud. Some trees still dripped. The heat and dampness were heavy against my body. A delivery man at the hotel gave me a lift back to the main road so I could look for a ride south.

Karonga's main street was a shock to me. The shops that had been in darkness, that I had taken to be shut the night before, were hollow-eyed and abandoned. This was the first big difference I noticed — the closed-down shops, which had been Indian shops. The second were the coffin makers. Coffin making in Africa is a common outdoor business, with men working at sawhorses under trees. The high incidence of death from AIDS accounted for the coffin making.

Indians had been officially hectored in the sixties. The first president, Hastings Banda, had come to Karonga in 1965 and singled them out, berated them, accusing Indian traders of taking advantage of Africans. "Africans should be running these businesses," he howled. But many of the Indians stayed. In the 1970s the president returned to Karonga and denounced the Indians again. This time the Indians got the message: nearly all left, and those few that hesitated saw their shops burned down by Banda's Israeli-trained Young Pioneers. Eventually, the remaining Indians either left Karonga for cities in the south or emigrated. Banda had gone to other rural towns and given the same speech, provoking the same result.

The shock to me was not that all the Indians were gone but that no one had come to take their place; that the shops were in ruins, still with the names of Ismailis and Gujaratis on them. The empty shops and the coffin makers gave Karonga the look of a city hit by plague, which in a sense was just what had happened.

At Karonga's main market I found a minibus going south and jammed myself in with twenty-one others, adults and children, steaming, aromatic. And when the driver began to go much too fast I wondered again: Why am I risking my life in an overcrowded and unsafe jalopy being driven by an incompetent boy?

The answer was simple: there was no other way. I could have flown, of course. There was an airstrip in Karonga and a weekly plane, but that was for missionaries and politicians and agents of virtue, and the tourists who wanted to parachute into Karonga to see Lake Malawi.

I promised myself on the road out of Karonga that after this Africa trip I would never take another chicken bus, minibus, or *matatu,* and no more cattle trucks or overcrowded taxis. If I was spared on this journey, I would not put my life in the hands of an idiot driver in a deathtrap.

The cracked windows were jammed shut, the damp passengers pressed together. "A symphony of smells fuses the mass of huddled human forms. Sour reek of armpits, nozzled oranges, melting breast ointments, mastick water, the breath of suppers of sulphurous garlic, foul phosphorescent farts, opoponax, the frank sweat of marriageable and married womankind, the soapy stink of men." James Joyce anatomizing the malodorous upper gallery of the opera house in Trieste seemed proof of a common humanity in body odor. But the strong human reek on African buses was a smell of mortality that seemed to me like a whiff of death.

The bad road was a help to safety, for on most parts of it there was no way to speed. The potholes were so numerous and so deep the driver had to slow down and steer around them, as in an obstacle course; or else he plunged into them, going dumpty-dumpty-dumpty, in and out of the holes, causing some of the children on board to puke on their chins. The driver went much too fast on the smooth parts of the road, but his speed sent us careering into stretches of mud. Twice we became mired, and a few male passengers got out and pushed. Not me. I walked ahead through the mud with some other, older men until the minibus caught up with us elders.

I walked thinking, What has changed? The road had always been bad. The lakeshore had always been thinly populated by Tumbuka-speaking fishing families in thatched huts, using dugout canoes and nets they spread on bushes to dry. They smoked the little fish, *kapenta,* and the plumper *chambo* on grills made of tree branches. Rice was grown here in lakeside paddies that were easily flooded. I saw the fishermen and dugouts and drying racks and rice fields and thought, Anyone who had snapped a picture of this lakeside forty years ago would have been able to take the same picture today.

On one of the muddy stretches we passed a small, somewhat misshapen man, perhaps a dwarf, certainly a hunchback, and the boys in the minibus yelled out the window, mocking him for his deformity.

The hunchback screamed at them, "You've got trouble!"

"You've got bigger trouble!" one of the boys called out, and everyone laughed.

I had caught the word *mabvuto,* trouble, and the man next to me told me what had been said in Tumbuka. People walking by the road shouted at us so often that I asked the same man why this was so.

He said, "Because they are forced to walk, they are mocking us."

"And you mock them, too."

"Just to make a joke."

The Malawi joke, shouted from the bus, was *Keep walking, sucker!*

The lake was beautiful, with golden mountains on the Mozambique side, and on our side an escarpment leading to the Nyika Plateau — glittering water and great heights and the natural beauty of Africa. That was half the story. The other half was this miserable bus and the stinking hostile boys in it mocking the heavily laden women and the deformed man.

We came to Chilumba, a fishing village, where a man was frying cut-up potatoes in fat. The potatoes were crusted lumps, the fat looked like motor oil. I bought some and ate them while we waited for passengers and, still hungry, ate a couple of bananas.

We climbed the escarpment on a treacherous road of hairpin bends, many of them with hastily — and badly — cleared landslides. We passed some disused coal mines and reached the settlement of Livingstonia, the earliest mission in the country. The mission had once been a brick church and bungalows, a hospital and huts, a high cool place where expats could grow Brussels sprouts and chrysanthemums.

Now it sprawled more and had lost many trees, the school looked neglected, but it was much the same as it had been.

Beyond Livingstonia the plateau rolled on, green, unpeopled. We stopped often, because a minibus made its greatest profit by traveling overstuffed, picking up whoever signaled for it to stop, along with their produce and livestock. When I thought the sorry vehicle could not take any more passengers, the ticket taker slid the door aside and hung on as the bus sped with the door open, some passengers hanging out.

The towns of Rumphi and Ekwendeni — places I had once known pretty well — had also lost their Indian shops and not replaced them with African shops. This interested me: the ruined and abandoned shops with faded signs painted *Patel Bros, Bombay Bazaar,* and *Alibhai Merchandise Mart* — the roofs caved in, the windows broken, many of them vandalized with graffiti. In front of them, on the grass verge by the storm drain and the roadside ditch, were African women displaying soap and salt and matches and cooking oil on a small square of cloth. The commercial life of these towns in the northern province had declined from main streets of busy shops to simple open-air markets of hawkers and fruit sellers sitting in the mud.

Six hours after leaving Karonga we came to the town of Mzuzu, at the edge of the Viphya Plateau. I knew some people here, so I decided to stay in a hotel and look them up. The person I most wanted to see was Margaret, the widow of one of my first friends in Malawi, Sir Martin Roseveare.

On his retirement from the British civil service in 1962, Sir Martin had come to Nyasaland to run a teachers' college. He was a good-humored pipe-smoking gentleman who in his late sixties was a hearty field hockey player. He was also a stickler for detail. The frugality that World War II had imposed on the British people had made many of them misers and cheese-parers but had inspired in others an incomparable ingenuity, turning them into inventors and self-helpers. Wartime deprivation had brought out Sir Martin's resourcefulness. He first devised the fraud-proof ration book, and was awarded a knighthood for his effort. He also took an interest in education, gardening, and sports. These enthusiasms he carried to Malawi. And he was of the old breed, an educator, not an evangelist, someone who had come to Africa to serve, to call it home, and to die in the bush.

His wife, Lady Margaret, was the same: sporty, intelligent, resourceful, and able to mend the water-driven stirrup pump that generated their electricity. I would sometimes see her bent over a greasy machine — tweed skirt, hair in a bun, argyle socks and muddy sandals, waving a socket wrench and saying, "Crikey!"

Sir Martin had died in his nineties, Lady Margaret lived on, and in her widowhood she ran Viphya Secondary School. I had always seen these people as admirable, even as role models, vigorous retirees I might emulate in my own later years. They gave me the ambition, one I nursed for a long time, of returning to Africa, perhaps in my mid-sixties, and doing as they had done. Of course, I would go on writing, but I would justify my presence in this country by starting a school or whipping a school into shape. To devote the rest of my life to seeing my self-financed school producing bright, well-educated students seemed perfect. I did not intend a deliberate martyrdom or even much of a sacrifice, for I liked the remoteness, the vegetable growing, the rusticity, the Tolstoyan pedagogy. Living in this positive purposeful way would be so healthy as to be life lengthening. I would be a pink-cheeked bore in baggy shorts, doing some writing, a beekeeper in the *bundu*, running a school of overachievers, imagining the gossip:

Whatever happened to Paul?

He's somewhere in Central Africa. Just upped and left. Been there for years.

"Lady Margaret, she is dead," a girl told me at the school. The place was looking rundown in a way that would not have pleased its scrupulous late headmistress.

She had passed away two years before, at the age of eighty-seven.

"Where is she buried?"

The girl shrugged — no idea. The Roseveares were not proselytizers but they were churchgoers, so I went to the Anglican church in Mzuzu and asked the African vicar if he had known them. "Vicar general," he said, correcting me. Yes, he had known them. They were wonderful, he said. They had helped build the church. They were buried right here.

Their graves were rectangular slabs set side by side in the muddy churchyard, Lady Margaret's unmarked, Sir Martin's inscribed *Beloved by All.* The graves were overgrown with weeds and looked not just neglected but forgotten.

As serious gardeners, haters of disorder, they would have been dismayed at the sight of this tangle of weeds. So I knelt and, as a form of veneration, weeded their graves for old times' sake.

Later, walking through Mzuzu to my hotel, I stopped in a bar to drink a beer, knowing that inevitably an African would join me, ask me for a drink, and tell me a story.

His name was Mkosi. "We are Angoni, the Zulus from South Africa who came here," he said.

"So how are things, Mkosi?"

"We are just suffering, sir."

"And why is that?"

"For myself, sir, my wife is going about with a soldier. I found a letter she wrote to him. 'I love you, my dearest darling.' I showed her the letter. She cheeked me. 'How can I love you? You have no money. I can't love someone who is poor. You are poor.'"

"Good riddance to her," I said.

Two of Mkosi's friends came over, looking for free drinks. But I decided to leave. They followed me outside, wanting to talk. Since I had seen obvious prostitutes in the bar, I brought up the subject of AIDS. They said that people died all the time in Malawi — how could anyone say for sure the cause was AIDS?

"If you went home with one of those women, would you use a condom?"

One said energetically, with gestures, "We are Malawians — we like skeen-to-skeen," and the others laughed.

"Condoms are rubber," another said. "Rubber has so many tiny holes in it. The germs can go through it, and even air, it can go through."

A taxi was parked at the curb.

"If rubber leaks, why isn't that tire flat?" I said.

They hung around arguing, and talking about the upcoming tobacco auctions, but when they saw that I was not going to give them any money, they drifted away.

The next day I looked for a car or bus going south. There were many vehicles in Mzuzu. The most expensive of them, of course, were the white four-wheel drives displaying the doorside logos of charities, every one that I had ever heard of and some new ones: People to People, Mission Against Ignorance and Poverty, the Food Project, Action Aid, Poverty Crusade, and more.

I was not surprised when they refused to give me a lift — I knew from experience that they were the last people to offer travelers assistance. Still, I was annoyed. I analyzed my annoyance. It was that the vehicles were often driven by Africans, the white people riding as passengers in what resembled ministerial seats. They had CD players, usually with music playing loudly, and now and then I saw the whole deal: an African or a white person driving in his white Save the Children vehicle one-handed, talking on a cell phone with music playing — the happiest person in the country. For every agent of virtue I saw slogging his or her guts out in the field, I saw two of them joyriding.

This visible bliss on wheels, courtesy of the First World saps who had been guilt-tripped out of their money, was only one of my objections, and the pettiest. A more substantial one was the notion that after decades of charitable diligence, there were more charities in Malawi than ever. Charities and NGOs were now part of the Malawi economy, surely one of the larger parts. They were troughs into which many people were unsuccessfully trying to insert their snouts. I was not shocked when I later learned that the hotshots who doled out aid in some African countries demanded sex from famine victims in return for the food parcels.

Some minibuses were going to Lilongwe, but they looked dangerous — overcrowded, bald tires, doors mended with baling wire, people riding on the roof, drivers with glazed ganja eyes. I looked for something a bit bigger and safer, but saw nothing — only the deathtraps and the superb Land Rovers of the charities. "Maybe there's a big bus this afternoon," a man told me.

I went back to the hotel and reflected on the past few weeks. I had been three days on the bush train from Mwanza; abused by the immigration people in Dar es Salaam; bewildered by the dreadful train to Mbeya, a filthy town where I had been overcharged at the hotel and cheated out of my bus fare; delayed by a bus that didn't show up. Then the struggle to the Tanzanian border — where punks had tried to shake me down and the health officer wanted a bribe — before the nighttime trip through the roadblocks to Karonga, and at last the long slow ride across the plateau to drizzly Mzuzu.

Now I was within striking distance of the capital, Lilongwe. Knowing that I would be arriving there in the next few days, I decided to call the U.S. embassy there. I had volunteered to give lectures anytime, anyplace, to talk to students, to be a Peace Corps helper all over again. My goodwill message had been sent to Lilongwe, or so I hoped.

I called the embassy's public affairs office from my hotel in Mzuzu and was greeted by a gloomy, somewhat impatient woman. "Yes, yes, I know who you are. The e-mails came a few weeks ago."

"About those lectures —"

Cutting me off, in fact snapping at me, the officer said, "I haven't arranged anything for you."

"Nothing?"

"You wouldn't believe the week I had," she said.

Had she, like me, been abused, terrified, stranded, harassed, cheated, bitten, flooded, insulted, exhausted, robbed, lied to, browbeaten, poisoned, stunk up, and starved?

To avoid howling at her, I put the phone down. I was discouraged at first, for she had only a lazy reply to my offer of help. But in a kinder moment I thought: in a culture where foreigners constantly showed up, offering themselves and their time and even material help, charity was nothing special — in fact, in Malawi it was another necessary routine, not philanthropic but a permanent drip feed, part of a system of handouts.

In offering to teach or give lectures, who was I but just another agent of virtue being reminded by a harassed official that she was far busier than I. Overpaid, officious, disingenuous, blame-shifting and offhand as she was, this embassy hack was also probably right in saying, Take a number, sonny. Get in line. There's plenty of people like you.

◇ ◇ ◇

Morning on the Viphya Plateau: drizzling rain, blackish trees in heavy fog, slick muddy roads, Africans tugging plastic bags on their heads to keep dry. At six-thirty in the street outside the Mzuzu bus terminal, sheltered by the twig roof of a banana stand, balancing on a boulder to keep her feet dry, was a white woman of about sixty, very thin, very pale in the darkness of the wet morning, searching wide-eyed through the mountain mist for the Lilongwe bus.

She boarded the bus and we sat side by side in the front, the rain slopping on the windshield as we crossed the plateau. The bus was old but wide enough and high enough to impart a sense of safety. Every passenger had a seat, the driver was a cautious middle-aged man, and he used his brakes and his directional signals.

The woman beside me was Una Brownly, a nurse from Livingstonia mission. She and her husband, Don, had been in Africa for twenty-seven years. Don, a doctor, had stayed behind at the mission because of the large number of patients. Una had two weeks home leave. She had taken the bus from Livingstonia the day before — all day to Mzuzu. A night in a dirty hotel in Mzuzu. Another bus today — all day to Lilongwe. A day in Lilongwe to wait for the London flight. It would take another day for her to get home to Ulster, a four-day trip to have a week at home, before turning around and taking the reverse sequence of planes and buses. A plane from Mzuzu and a connecting flight to London were out of the question — too expensive. Una was not being funded by an international NGO — no white Land Rover, no cell phone, no CD player. She and her husband were medical missionaries, living on money collected by her church back home. They were not well paid, not even by Malawi standards. Many African doctors had been asked to work in Livingstonia; they knew the long history of the hospital and the dire need for medical officers. They all turned the job down.

"There isn't a surgeon north of Lilongwe," Una said.

Forty years after independence and still the northern half of the country lacked a surgeon to perform the more complex operations that her husband was not trained for.

"The government doesn't pay its doctors enough," she said. "They leave the country and go where the pay is better."

"What about your pay?"

She said, "African doctors don't work for what we're paid."

I began to understand the futility of charity in Africa. It was generally fueled by the best of motives, but its worst aspect was that it was noninspirational. Aliens had been helping for so long and were so deeply entrenched that Africans lost interest — if indeed they had ever had it — in doing the same sort of work themselves. Not only was there no spirit of volunteerism, there was no desire to replace aid workers in paying jobs. Yet many Africans were unemployed, doing nothing but sitting under trees.

"Does the Malawi government help fund your hospital?"

"Not at all. They don't even run their own hospitals."

"How did things get this bad?"

"I don't know," she said. "There's corruption, of course. All the ministers want a cut of whatever aid is given. But I don't think about politics. What's the point? And there's lots of aid. Some people think that's the problem. There are some doctors here — Elspeth and Michael King — who wrote a book arguing that Africa is backward because of aid."

"What do you think?"

My soliciting her opinion on this subject seemed to amuse Una, for it is a characteristic of the long-term expatriate health workers in Africa that they do their jobs without complaint or cynicism. Anyone preoccupied with the contradictions and the daily repetition of the myth of Sisyphus would find such work intolerable, and complaints just tedious if not demoralizing.

"There's always strings attached to aid," she said. "That's no bad thing, but in many cases there's no local input. The donor determines what is needed, and the local people adapt their project to get the money."

Cross-purposes was the kindest interpretation, scamming the more brutal one. I asked, "Why are the roads in the north so bad?"

"That escarpment road is a hundred years old. It has been beautiful, but did you see all the landslides?" she said. "In the past they cleared the landslides manually — it took a lot of people, but labor is cheap. And doing it by hand kept the storm drains open. For the past few years they've been using donor bulldozers to clear the rock slides. They bulldoze them to the side, blocking the drains. So when the rain comes it washes the road away and creates a torrent — another landslide."

So the solution of donor bulldozers had made the problem worse and put many manual laborers out of work.

"The government had been paying five men to maintain the road. Then they stopped paying them. The road has been deteriorating ever since."

"The school in Livingstonia looked in pretty poor shape," I said.

"They need twenty-four teachers to run it. There are only fourteen at the school. The English chap is leaving, so in a month they will have only thirteen teachers for about six hundred students. Teachers' salaries are so low, you see."

I said, "I'm wondering why a foreign teacher should go to Livingstonia to teach if Malawians are not willing to make the sacrifice."

With the sweetest smile Una dismissed the question as much too logical.

"What sort of vehicle do you have at Livingstonia?" I asked, thinking of the white charities dispensing Land Rovers everywhere.

"An ambulance, but it's nine years old and it's off the road at the moment for repairs," she said. "Rather a sad story, I'm afraid. We were in Lilongwe a month ago buying parts for it, and tools, and a roll of material for school uniforms. We had tied them securely in the back of a pickup truck, but just as we got in and started to pull away some boys jumped on the truck and cut the ropes and stole everything."

There was theft and vandalism everywhere, she said. A boy in Lilongwe had yanked a gold chain from her neck. She had shouted "Thief! Thief!" but men sitting in cars nearby watched as the boy ran away. The Livingstonia boat was damaged by vandals, so the two clinics on the lakeshore that could be reached only by water were out of luck.

"My husband's very good at fixing things, though." When he wasn't operating on patients, Don patched boats and repaired motors. And it turned out that he had known those two other do-it-yourselfers, the Roseveares.

We talked about AIDS. Una said, "There must be a great deal in the country because we're seeing many cases, and we're in a very rural area." Hospital workers themselves were being infected, and two of the Livingstonia clinical workers were HIV positive. (In January 2002 the World Health Organization reported that 60 percent of the patients in Malawi hospitals suffered from AIDS, and that as a result of the AIDS epidemic there were two million orphans in Malawi.)

"We have no means to treat AIDS patients — no medicines. They die at home. We had a man who had a severe hernia. We operated on him but he didn't improve. We tested him. He was positive. He went home and died."

"Why do so many people have AIDS here? Is it just because they don't use condoms?"

"I asked that question some years ago," she said. "There has to be blood-to-blood contact, but many Africans have had the other STDs, and its those that create the possibility of infection. But we see so many other ailments. Lots of malnourished children. Lots of anemia. It's the malaria — it destroys the red blood cells."

We had crossed the forest of the plateau, the dense pinewoods that had been planted fifty or sixty years before as a source of paper pulp. The project hadn't worked — too costly to transport the logs, too expensive to manage, and so the trees were being cut down for fuel and charcoal. Past the forest, we came to a moorland and the outposts of the plateau, sodden and isolated villages, huts with roofs of black-rotted thatch. Then we descended through the rain and mist to flatter land, great expanses with the bouldery hills I had seen in Tanzania and Kenya — Rift Valley features, remnants of the age of volcanism. Some egg-shaped boulders were the size of small mountains.

At Mzimba, where we stopped to refuel, I looked around the market. There was hardly anything to eat for sale, only some dirt-caked roots and wilted greens.

"It's the time of year," Una said. "The crops aren't ready. Last season's food's been eaten. And, you know, children in Africa aren't a priority. We see children in advanced stages of malnutrition — bellies distended, skin peeling off. Some of the children are dead by the time they get to us."

Since this mission nurse of long experience was such a fund of information, I asked her about simple hygiene. Why were buses and *matatus* and enclosed places so much smellier than they had seemed long ago? Was I more fastidious now as an older, fussier man? Asking her this, I struck a nerve.

"Oh, the smell!" she said. "In church when they are all together — the smell in church!" She shut her eyes and smiled in horror. "But you see, there is no hot water for washing. And they don't wash sick people — they think it's bad for the patient, that washing will make them cold and more ill."

At Kasungu we stopped for passengers and I got out to stretch my legs. The rain was coming down so hard I had to take shelter inside the depot, where I complained about the rain.

"That is because you are a European," said a man in the garage where I was sheltering, looking out at the downpour. "I am an African. We like rain. We don't like the sun as Europeans do. Europeans lie down in the sun almost naked. Africans — do you ever see them do that? Eh! No! The sun makes us hot. But the rain is good. It gives us a good temperature. It makes the crops to grow. Unfortunately, now we have floods and the maize cobs are rotting in the fields."

This seemed to me a pretty fair assessment of cultural difference.

Back on the bus, I said to Una, "It's such an uphill battle. Do you ever ask yourself, What's the point?"

"We do what we can," she said. "And you know that Livingstonia is very beautiful. The lake is lovely. The people have good hearts."

"But so little has changed. This is practically the same country I left thirty-five years ago. Maybe worse. The government doesn't even care enough to help you."

This was too broad a subject. With what seemed like hesitation but was actually a statement of fortitude, she said, "It's — just — light a little candle."

We passed grass huts, small tobacco farms, some of which were being harvested, and soggy fields. Not much traffic, though many ragged people were tramping down the road.

"My husband is sixty-four. He's going to retire sometime soon. The government has no plan to replace him. They probably won't send anyone." She looked grim, saying this. "If we're not here, there'll be no one."

"What'll happen then?"

"They'll die," she said softly. "They'll just die."

We were in open country, nothing in the distance but bush, and clouds pressing on the horizon, everything green. I had been nagging about the problems, but Una the optimist had reminded me that Livingstonia was lovely. This sloping bush was lovely, too — empty Africa, green from the long rains.

But she was pondering her absence, because after a lengthy pause she spoke again. "That's what happened before. They just died."

She went back to watching the road ahead, for we had entered the outer villages of Lilongwe district, the tumbled huts, some mud-walled, others simple shacks. I admired this woman, for her humility especially. One of her greatest virtues was that she was unaware of how virtuous she was. She had not uttered a single word of sanctimony. She had no idea that I was a writer. Her sympathy was tempered by realism, yet she had not complained of her fate. No Malawian nurse or doctor would have gone near this public bus, nor taken the three-day road trip from Livingstonia to Lilongwe.

Medical and teaching skills were not lacking in Africa, even in distressed countries like Malawi. But the will to use them was often nonexistent. The question was, should outsiders go on doing jobs and taking risks that Africans refused?

◇ ◇ ◇

I decided to stay in Lilongwe for a week before heading farther south. I needed a rest from my incessant travel, and I had to remind my family that I was still alive. I chose a hotel on the main street. Third World luxury resorts are one aberration — Malawi had a few on the lake. And Third World luxury hotels are another, just as awful, because they attract economists, UN people, refugee experts, heads of charities, visiting opportunists, and politicians. Malawi had the worst and most expensive hotels I encountered on my whole trip, and all charged two daily rates: a low one for Africans, an exorbitant one for foreigners. They were most of them state-owned, run by South African management companies.

"What is this?" I said at the Lilongwe Hotel, pointing to a 10 percent addition on a bill.

"Service charge."

"Where is the service? There is no one to carry bags, no one sweeps the floors, the room isn't clean, the toilet is broken. You know what I mean? No service, so why the charge?"

"It is the name. 'Service charge.' Ten percent, plus-plus."

The charities and foreign donors had had a questionable effect on the poverty and misery in the country, but they were positively destructive when it came to hotels, because they were expense-accounters for whom money was no object. Those of us who were budget-conscious and aimless wanderers were punished for their profligacy. But I stayed at the bad expensive hotel; I had no choice. Lying in bed in that hotel, I rehearsed the writing of this paragraph, and during the day, in the week I spent in Lilongwe, I busied myself writing my erotic novella.

Lilongwe was two towns. One was the old market town of shops and gas stations and crowds of idle ragged boys; the other was the adjacent, much newer town, the nation's capital, of wide streets, government offices, the presidential palace, official residences, mansions, and embassies. Soldiers and policemen stood guard all over the streets of the capital, but in slummy Lilongwe's Old Town, everyone complained of crime, especially the Indian shopkeepers.

Chased from the rural areas by Hastings Banda's party thugs, Indians had come to old commercial Lilongwe, where life was safer and they were for a time lost in the shuffle. One feature of Banda's dictatorial rule was that political violence was common but that civilian crime — car theft, burglary, rape, murder — was comparatively rare. This had changed, in fact reversed — rape and murder were now more common than political terror.

Banda was gone now, after thirty-four years in power, and his name had been removed from the national stadium and the roads and schools and hospitals. Under the new president, Bakili Muluzi, the man who had put his chubby face on the money, the streets were unsafe and house break-ins were frequent. Muluzi had been seen as a populist, the anti-Banda; now he was turning into a despot. He was a Muslim in a mostly Christian country, and one of his ardent foreign supporters was the Libyan government of Muammar Qaddafi. The Malawi proverb explaining someone like Muluzi was "Raise a python and he will swallow you."

"We could sleep at night in our homes before," a man named Salim told me. He ran a restaurant. He had joined me at a table while I ate one of his samosas. "We can't feel safe now. Not now. There are thieves."

"I used to live here," I said.

"What do you think?" he said, challenging me.

"You tell me, Salim."

"It is worse, worse, worse. And not getting better. Getting much worse!"

But, being watchful, I walked the streets of Lilongwe and explored the market, an enormous emporium of secondhand clothes, here as elsewhere being retailed by hustlers who had gotten them from charities. There was so little traffic that people habitually walked in the middle of the street. I was warned by Indians of theft, but I was poorly dressed, and though I had valuables in my bag (cash, passport, artifacts) I carried nothing that was worth stealing. Most of my clothes had come from secondhand markets like these.

Even the prostitutes avoided me, unless I bought them drinks, which I did out of pure loneliness, like one of those geezers you see on back streets at odd hours feeding stray cats, a displacement activity this much resembled. All the talk of AIDS kept me detumescent. Usually, I sat alone under the trees at the bar next to the Hotel Lilongwe. Sometimes I joined a table of loitering girls and talked to them. They were nicely dressed and even demure.

"We are schoolgirls. We are all cousins."

"I am studying secretarial."

"Myself, I am studying business."

"Me, I am working for the Anything Goes shop."

They were in their mid- to late teens, not married, no children, and didn't drink beer, only soft drinks. They giggled and murmured and meowed. They told me about themselves, asked me questions, teased me.

"You are not old — what? — forty or forty-five."

"Have another Coke, dear!"

There were Christmas lights tangled in the tree branches, the music was mellow, the place was not rowdy. For an abused traveler who had been catching buses, trucks, and trains through the whole of the Great Rift Valley from Ethiopia to Malawi, it was a novelty and a pleasure just to stay in one place and eat regular meals, take baths, have my laundry done, hold meaningless conversations, write my novella, and do the *New York Times* crossword, faxed from home.

"What are you doing, Mr. Paul?"

"Just a puzzle. Filling in words. Ah, the clue is 'Forbidden tea.'"

They leaned over, smelling of perfume and face powder and hair oil, the bodices of their crunchy dresses like the prom gowns of my youth, pressed against me.

"I guess that's 'taboo oolong.' It fits."

When I had finished and was tucking the folded puzzle into my pocket, one of the girls would lean over and whisper with warm breaths, her lips grazing my ear, "I want to give you a massage, Mr. Paul. Please take me. I am good."

But I went chastely to my room and lay there alone on my damp mildewed bed, staring at the stains like faces on the ceiling and thinking: What went wrong here?

The newspapers ran headlines such as "A New Journey from Poverty to Prosperity" (reporting a speech by the minister of agriculture),

"Fresh Start in the Ag Sector" (an American-funded project for tobacco farmers to switch to growing pigeon peas and soybeans), and "Tobacco Auction Projections Raise Hopes" (a week later the auction prices were a fifth of what they had been the year before). I thought, What gives?

Still smarting from having been rebuffed as a volunteer speaker, I asked to see the American ambassador. The usual form in a book such as this, answering the question of attribution, is to describe the man as "informed sources" or "a high-level Western diplomat" or "someone I happened to meet." But the meeting was so brief and so anodyne it needs no camouflage, and his being a diplomat made me smile as I was talking with him.

I had the impression the ambassador did not like me any more than the embassy woman, apparently his ally, who had said to me, "You wouldn't believe the week I had." He was about my age, rather benign on the whole but visibly seeming to suppress a mood of fuss and fret. Was it my faded American thrift-shop clothes from the African market? More likely it was my wild-eyed frustration, my reckless criticism, my incautious gibes, but I was road weary from my dark star safari, and Africa's fortunes had become my obsessive subject. In other countries I was a detached observer, but, absurd as it seemed, I took the Malawi situation personally.

I said, "I used to teach here. I know the country pretty well. I even speak the local language. I offered to give some lectures here, but your public affairs officer wasn't interested and didn't do anything to help me."

The ambassador was not provoked.

I said, "I suppose you get lots of offers like that."

The ambassador sipped his drink and pushed a saucer of peanuts at me as though to mollify me.

I said, "Nothing has *improved* in this country, for goodness sake. I mean, name one thing."

The ambassador said, "There is no political terror. There was before."

I said, "I've been frisked and delayed at twenty roadblocks from Karonga to here."

The ambassador said, "I'm planning to make a trip to the north."

I said, "The roads are terrible. We had to push the bus."

The ambassador said, "The roads are much better than they were."

I yawned and rounded my arm and wagged some peanuts in my hand.

The ambassador said, "My last post was the Congo. In the Congo there aren't any roads."

I said, "What good are roads if there are no motor vehicles?"

The ambassador said, "There are buses."

I said, "Ever take one?" That was a low blow, so I added, "And tobacco is the cash crop. Tobacco!"

The ambassador said, "Tobacco can now be grown by smallholders. It was a government monopoly before."

I said, "It's a declining commodity."

The ambassador said, "Coffee production is increasing."

I said, "The price is down. Coffee is another money loser."

The ambassador said, "This is all anecdotal, of course. But I feel some changes for the better are in the air."

I said, "Well, as a diplomat you're paid to be an optimist."

The ambassador scowled into his drink for my presumptuous remark. He did not like that imputation at all.

I said, "Honestly, I am really depressed here. Nothing works, the schools are awful, the infant mortality rate is the highest in the world. I think the government wants to have bad schools, because ignorant people are easier to govern."

The ambassador said, "The government is committed to improving the schools. But teachers are poorly paid."

I said, "So what? No one ever became a teacher to get rich."

The ambassador said, "And there are some exciting new developments in telecommunications in Malawi. Cell phone technology. Next year, perhaps."

His ghastly credulous phrase "next year" made me laugh as much as his mention of cell phones. "We hope by this time next year," Mrs. Jellyby says of her African project for the natives of Borrioboola-Gha, and Dickens is making satire of the phrase. But the ambassador bore a greater resemblance to Mrs. Jellyby's fellow philanthropist, Mr. Quale ("with large shining knobs for temples"), whose project was "for teaching the coffee colonists to teach the natives to turn piano-forte legs and establish an export trade." Makework schemes and cottage industries started by present-day Jellybys and Quales were common in

Africa. A hundred and fifty years ago, what had seemed an insanely mocking idea to Charles Dickens was considered a solemn hope for Malawi now.

I said, "Ha! Cell phones! They'll play with them like people in a cargo cult! They'll treat them like toys!"

A bald man can express frustration with his entire head. My friskiness tried the ambassador's patience, but even with his scalp creased with anger he remained polite and positive. I had to admire his equanimity, yet I could see he was dying for me to leave. He did not refill my drink. This is an effective suggestion that one's time is up. When it was conveyed to me through meaningful silences that the meeting was over, we strolled through his garden, admiring his palm trees, and off I went, back to my hotel room to brood.

The next day I called the president of the University of Malawi, a man I knew — he had been a fellow teacher long ago. He said he was glad to hear from me.

"I'm just passing through," I said. I did not mention my birthday promise to myself, to spend a week or so teaching, helping out, doing something useful. "I want to offer my services — give a lecture at the university or do some teaching at Soche Hill."

"That's excellent. Come to Zomba. I'll arrange something. And welcome home, *achimwene*."

Achimwene was the fondest word for brother.

15 ◈◈◈

The Back Road to Soche Hill School

"YOUR MOTHER is your mother, even if one of her legs is too short," Malawians say, another old saw, and this was also their offhand way of forgiving their country its lapses.

Most people didn't complain. Some people even boasted — "Better roads," many people said. Well, maybe so here in the south, but Malawi was so poor only the politicians had proper cars. They drove Mercedes-Benzes on these good roads while everyone else walked or rode bikes or herded their animals. Children used the main roads for playing games — the pavement was good for bouncing balls or tugging their homemade wire toys. As for buses, most of them were such a misery the good roads made little difference. I was so demoralized by my various bus trips from the far north, I had rented a car in Lilongwe. It was the first and last time on my trip that I did so. Now I was the driver being hassled by police at the roadblocks.

"Open the boot, *bwana*," ordered a heavily armed policeman at a barrier.

"What are you looking for?"

"Drugs and guns."

"Do you ever find any of that stuff?" I asked.

Two of the policeman's helpers were rifling through my bag in the trunk, one inhaling deeply like a sniffer dog smelling for ganja, or *chamba* as it was known in Malawi, a very inexpensive item that was widely available.

"Before this day ends we will find some," the policeman said.

Apart from the roadblocks, the two-hundred-mile trip to Zomba was a pleasure. I drove slowly, loving the freedom of my own car and the starkness of the weirdly shaped mountains, each one of them standing alone on the green plain. I came to see them as specifically African, as unique as the animals that grazed beneath them. These Rift Valley boulders were scorched gray mountains, as though shot from the cannon's mouth of a volcanic crater during some fiery epoch of prehistory. Smooth and solitary, not quite buttes, not quite mesas, some of them were egg-shaped and some like exotic fruit. I was reminded of how I had felt when I had first seen them, the deep impression they had left that I was in a special place, the dark star of Africa, and that traveling across other continents, I never saw anything like them.

Paved roads ran where there had once been only rutted red clay tracks. The train line to Balaka that I had taken in 1964 to a Mua leprosarium by the lake was defunct, and so was the leper colony. The ferry at Liwonde across the Shire River, brimming and brown in flood, had been replaced by a bridge. All this was progress, but on these new thoroughfares the Africans, buttocks showing through their tattered clothes, still walked barefoot.

I traveled idly, stopping often to look at birds or talk to farmers, so I did not arrive in the hill town of Zomba until after dark. The main street was unlit, people flitting and stumbling in the dark. I had instructions to proceed to the Zomba Club and there to call my friend, who would meet me and guide me to his hard-to-find house high on the steep side of the plateau.

Zomba had been the capital of Malawi's British incarnation, the little tea-growing protectorate of Nyasaland. The still-small town was a collection of tin-roofed red brick buildings clustered together at the edge of Zomba Plateau. From the main road, the plateau looked like an ironing board draped in a green sheet, and was high enough to be seen from a great distance — one of the peaks was well over six thousand feet. The craggy sides were misty and parts of the plateau wild enough to support hyena packs, small bushbucks, and troops of monkeys and baboons. All the features of British rule had been imposed on the lower slopes in Zomba: the red brick governor general's house, the red brick Anglican church, the red brick civil servants' bungalows, the red brick club. The tin roofs of these buildings were now rusted the same hue as the bricks.

The Zomba Gymkhana Club had been the settlers' meeting place and social center in British times, but, absurdly, membership had been restricted according to pigmentation, whites predominating, a few Indians, some golden-skinned mixed-race people known then as "coloureds." Even in the years just after Malawi's independence, the club was nearly all white — horsy men and women, cricketers and rugger hearties. No footballers: kicking a soccer ball was regarded as an African sport.

Back then, I was not a member of any club, but was sometimes an unwilling party to rants by beer-swilling Brits wearing club blazers and cardigans ("This is my U.K. woolly"): "Let Africans in here and they'll be tearing up the billiard table and getting drunk and bringing their snotty little piccanins in the bar. There'll be some African woman nursing her baby in the games room." This was considered rude and racist, yet in its offensive way it was fairly prescient, for the rowdy teenagers at the billiard table were stabbing their cues at the torn felt, the bar was full of drunks (no children, though, and no one used the crude word "piccanins" anymore), and a woman was breastfeeding her baby under the dartboard. Yet if the fabric of the place had deteriorated, the atmosphere was about the same as before.

Some relics remained: the sets of kudu and springbok horns mounted high on the wall, the glass cases of dusty fishing flies, all neatly tied and categorized in rows, the biggest for salmon, the tiny midges for smaller fish. The calendar was months out-of-date, the portraits were gone, the floor was unswept, and the overbright lights made the interior seem harsher and dirtier.

I sat drinking a beer, noting these observations, waiting for my friend to arrive.

Soon he came and greeted me warmly in two languages. He was David Rubadiri, whom I had first met in 1963, when he had been headmaster of my school, Soche Hill — *Sochay* was the correct way of saying it. The shortage of college graduates at independence meant that Rubadiri was plucked from the school and put into the diplomatic service. Hastings Banda appointed him Malawi's ambassador to

Washington. There, Rubadiri prospered until three or four months after independence, when there was a sudden power struggle. The cabinet ministers denounced Banda as a despot, attacked him verbally, and held a vote of no confidence in parliament. From a distance, Rubadiri joined in, but Banda survived what became an attempted coup d'état, and he turned on his accusers. Those who had opposed him either left the country or fought in the guerrilla underground. Banda remained in power for the next thirty years.

Rubadiri was disgraced politically for taking sides, and lost his job in the coup attempt. He went to Uganda to teach at Makerere. After it became known that I assisted him — I delivered him his car, driving it through the bush, two thousand miles to Uganda — I was accused of aiding the rebels and branded a revolutionary. I was deported from Malawi late in 1965, ejected from the Peace Corps ("You have jeopardized the whole program!"), and with Rubadiri's help was hired at Makerere. One week I was a schoolteacher, the following week a university professor. The combination of physical risk, social activism, revolutionary fervor, Third World politics, and naiveté characterized this drama of the 1960s. (The whole grim story of my involvement is described in my essay "The Killing of Hastings Banda," in *Sunrise with Seamonsters.*)

So our careers, Rubadiri's and mine, had become intertwined. We had been friends for thirty-eight years. His fortunes had risen again with the change of government in Malawi. In the mid-1990s he was appointed Malawi's ambassador to the United Nations, and after four or five years was made vice chancellor of the University of Malawi. He had two wives and nine children and was now almost seventy, grizzled and dignified and venerable, like General Othello, a role he had played in a college production while studying in England. After a few drinks Rubadiri sometimes raised his hand, cocked an eyebrow, and said in a deep smoky voice,

> Soft you; a word or two before you go.
> I have done the state some service . . .

It was wonderful to see him again in the Zomba Gymkhana Club, still alive, a survivor from the distant past. Following his car along the narrow switchback road rising beside the Zomba Plateau — guard dogs and night watchmen darting out of the darkness — I had a glimpse of officialdom at home. These former residences of British bureaucrats were now the houses of African bureaucrats. Rubadiri's had been the British high commissioner's house, a sprawling one-story colonial mansion (tin roof, brick and stucco walls) set into a steep slope atop a terraced garden.

Only one of his wives was in residence, Gertrude, whom I had known as an intelligent and sensible person. She greeted me, welcomed me, and made me feel at home.

"Dinner is in one hour."

"Time for you to talk to some students," Rubadiri said.

We went downhill to the University Club, a glorified bar from the 1920s, and I spoke to a group of students and teachers — another pep talk. One man I recognized almost immediately as an old student of mine, the same chubby face and big head on narrow shoulders, the same solemn heavy-lidded eyes that made him look ironic. His hair was gray but otherwise he was Sam Mpechetula, now wearing shoes. I had last seen him when he was a barefoot fifteen-year-old in gray shorts. He was now fifty-two, in a jacket and necktie.

Sam said he happened to be in Zomba and had heard I was speaking, so he showed up. He was married, a father of four, and a teacher at Bunda College, outside Lilongwe. So at least I could say that one of my students had taken my place as an English teacher in a Malawi classroom. That had been one of my more modest goals.

"Do you remember much about our school?" I asked.

"It was a good school — the best. They were the best days of my life," he said. "The Peace Corps guys were wonderful. They brought blue jeans and long hair to Malawi."

"What a legacy," I said, because Rubadiri was listening.

Sam said, "They talked to Africans. Do you know, before they came, white people didn't talk to us."

Rubadiri said, "You remember this man, eh?"

"Oh, yes. When he was declared PI we were sad."

PI was Prohibited Immigrant. My reward for helping Rubadiri.

"Around that time Jack Mapanje also taught us. You remember him?"

Another political casualty. Jack Mapanje was jailed for ten years for writing poems deemed by the Malawi government to be subversive.

Sam brought me up to date on the students I had taught. Many were dead, some had left the country, but a number were working in useful jobs in different parts of the country. A high proportion of these former students were working women.

Later that night, after dinner, I was reminded again of the strength and clear-sightedness of Malawian women when David Rubadiri went to bed and his wife stayed up, drinking tea and monologuing. Gertrude was a short, solid woman with a full face and powerful arms. She sat deep in the cushions of a sofa, leaning slightly forward, looking alert. She was intelligent and, for her generation, highly educated, having gone to Fort Hare University in South Africa. Robert Mugabe, later a guerrilla fighter and the erratic president of Zimbabwe, had been one of her classmates. We talked about him a little because that month he was harassing white farmers in Zimbabwe so severely, people were warning me to stay away from that country.

"Mugabe was so studious. We called him 'bookworm.'"

Fearful of offering an insult, for I was a houseguest, I at first tentatively suggested that on my return to Malawi I was seeing a country greatly reduced. Gertrude seized on this, for she too had been away for a long time — perhaps twenty-five years.

"Things are worse," Gertrude said decisively. "When I came back in 1994 I was surprised. The poverty here really shocked me. I could not believe the people could be so poor. I saw a boy with some small money in his hand trying to buy some soap. He needed one kwacha" — less than two cents — "but didn't have it, and so he went away. The people were dressed in rags. The streets were littered with rubbish."

"I've noticed that myself," I said.

"But do you know? Within two weeks I had stopped seeing it."

"What else shocked you when you came back?"

"The way the young people spoke in the house really bothered me. Some of them were my own nephews. If I asked a question, they would answer with a question, sometimes saying '*Si chapita?*' [So what?] That is not traditional at all — it shows no respect. I might ask for sugar and the child would just shrug and sit there and say '*Si watha?*' [Isn't it all gone?] Shocking!

"And the way people gossip. Well, you know this has always been an envious society. Someone comes from abroad with a Ph.D. and we say it stands for 'pull him down.' They gossip about the person and say he or she is proud. I was at a funeral recently and heard people gossiping. Can you imagine — at a funeral?

"We have become so dirty, throwing garbage on the street. Also personally — people are less clean in their personal habits. You notice it on buses. The smell. And you see how people push? They never did that before. It is not part of our culture to be in a crowd or to press against each other. Our culture determines that we need space. A servant gives you space — he stands aside. People do the same with each other. So it is unnatural to be pushed and pressed, yet it happens all the time. No one respects old people. No one gives me a seat. Maybe I am saying that because I am old!

"What went wrong? Is it because of all those years of Banda's rule, telling people what to do, to be tidy, to be respectful? And now they say, 'The old man is gone. Now I can be messy, to make up for all those years.'

"The foreign charities here are doing our work for us — so many of them! What progress are they making? Will we have them forever? There were not so many before. Why do we still need them after so long? David says I am a pessimist, but to tell the truth I am a bit ashamed."

I went to bed thinking, So I'm not imagining this.

I set off the next morning to revisit my school, forty-five miles down the back road from Zomba to Soche Hill.

Some trips mean so much to us that we rehearse them over and over in our heads, not to prepare ourselves but in anticipation, for the delicious foretaste. I had been imagining this return trip down the narrow track to Soche Hill for many years. It was a homecoming in a more profound sense than my going back to Medford, Massachusetts, where I had grown up. In Medford, I was one of many people struggling to leave, to start my life; but in Malawi, at Soche Hill School, I was alone, making my life.

In Africa for the first time, I got a glimpse of the pattern my life would take — that it would be dominated by writing and solitariness and risk, and already in my early twenties I tasted those ambiguous pleasures. I had learned what many others had discovered before me — that Africa, for all its perils, represented wilderness and possibility. Not only did I have the freedom to write in Africa, I had something new to write about.

The African world I got to know was not the narrow existence of the tourist or big-game hunter, not the rarefied and hobnobbing experience of the diplomat, but the more revealing progress of an ambitious exile in the bush. I had no money and no status. In Malawi I began identifying with Rimbaud and Graham Greene, and it was in Africa that I began my lifelong dislike of Ernest Hemingway, from his shotguns to his mannered prose. Ernest was both a tourist and a big-game hunter. The Hemingway vision of Africa begins and ends with the killing of large animals, so that their heads may be displayed to impress visitors with your prowess. That kind of safari is easily come by. You pay your money and you are shown elephants and leopards. You talk to servile Africans, who are generic natives, little more than obedient Oompa Loompas. The human side of Africa is an afternoon visit to a colorful village. This is why, of all the sorts of travel available in Africa, the easiest to find and the most misleading is the Hemingway experience. In some respects the feed-the-people obsession that fuels some charities is related to this, for I seldom saw relief workers who did not in some way remind me of people herding animals and throwing food to them, much as rangers did to the animals in drought-stricken game parks.

The schoolteaching experience in Africa, harder to come by, takes less money but more humility. I had been lucky. Fearing the draft, I had joined the Peace Corps, in one of the earliest waves of volunteers, and been sent to Nyasaland, an African country not yet independent. I experienced the last gasp of British colonialism, the in-between period of uncertain changeover, and the hopeful assertion of black rule. That was lucky, too, for I saw this process at close quarters, and African rule, necessary as it was, was also a tyranny in Malawi from day one.

Schoolteaching was perfect for understanding how people lived and what they wanted for themselves. And my work justified my existence in Africa. I had never wanted to be a tourist. I wished to be far away, as remote as possible, among people I could talk to. I achieved that in Malawi. What I loved most about Africa was that it seemed unfinished, and was still somewhat unknown and undiscovered, lying mostly mute but imposing, like the giant obelisk in the quarry at Aswan. The beautiful flawed thing lay trapped in rock, but if erected it would have risen 150 feet. It was for me the very symbol of the Africa I knew.

What I liked then was what I liked now, village life and tenacious people, saddleback mountains of stone and flat plains where anthills rose higher than any hut. The road from Zomba had everything: vistas almost to Mozambique, the savanna of scattered trees, small villages, roadside stands where people sold potatoes and sugar cane — famine food, for the maize was not yet harvested. I liked the sweet somnolence of rural Africa, which I always regarded with a sense of safety.

Instead of driving straight to the school, I stopped at the nearby town of Limbe, which began abruptly, the edge of the town slummy, with outdoor businesses — bicycle menders, car repairers, coffin makers — and the rest of it chaotic, litter and mobs, small businesses and shop houses, and a proliferation of bars and dubious-looking clinics. I drove around looking for landmarks and found a bar where I used to drink, the Coconut Grove; and the Limbe Market; and the Rainbow Theater, where we had to stand for "God Save the Queen," which was played before every movie until independence.

The countryside seemed emptier than before, the town was much fuller — larger and meaner looking. I parked my car and went into a bank to get a cash advance on my credit card.

The clerk said, "This transaction will take three days."

An African behind me in line sighed on my behalf and said, "That should take no more than an hour. That's disgusting."

I abandoned the thought of getting money and talked to the man instead. He was a Malawian, Dr. Jonathan Banda, a political science teacher at Georgetown. He had left Malawi while quite young, in 1974, had traveled and studied in various countries, and had finished his Ph.D. in the United States. He had just come back to Malawi and was disappointed by what he saw.

"It is dirty — it's awful," he said.

We were standing on the main street of Limbe amid the crowds. Jonathan Banda was hardly forty, and having lived so long abroad he was better fed, and so bigger and stronger than any of his fellow Malawians. He had the look of an athlete, the same confidence that is also a sort of muscularity and an upright, assertive way of standing, and his posture matched his skeptical smile.

"The people are greedy and materialistic," he went on. "They're lazy, too. They show no respect. They push and shove. They are awful to each other."

"What are you doing here?"

"Seeing my family, but also I wanted to come back to teach. I was recently interviewed by the university."

I listened closely — after all, I was staying at the house of the university's vice chancellor.

"So what happened?"

"I was questioned by a panel of officials. They asked me about my political views. Can you imagine? If I were teaching science or geography, no problem. But my field is political science. I said, 'I have no specific party affiliation.'"

"What did they say to that?"

"They didn't like it. I said, 'I want to teach my students to make up their own minds, to form political ideas of their own. That's what matters most to me.' They looked at each other and one said, 'We can't pay you much.'"

"I'm sure it would be less than Georgetown," I said.

"I don't care. I said to them, 'That's fine with me. I am here to learn.'"

But Dr. Jonathan Banda didn't get the job. He was sure the reasons for his being turned down were political. He said that if he had praised the government and the ruling party, they would have hired him.

Thinking of what the ambassador had told me, I said, "A diplomat told me there is no political terror here anymore. Is that true?"

"Maybe not, but there is political pressure of a very insidious sort."

He seemed so outspoken I asked him the questions about charities and aid agencies that had been nagging at me. The agents of virtue in white Land Rovers — what were they changing?

"Not much, because all aid is political," he said. "When this country became independent it had very few institutions. It still doesn't have many. The donors aren't contributing to development. They maintain the status quo. Politicians love that, because they hate change. The tyrants love aid. Aid helps them stay in power and contributes to underdevelopment. It's not social or cultural and it certainly isn't economic. Aid is one of the main reasons for underdevelopment in Africa."

"You said it, I didn't," I said. "There's an awful lot of aid agencies here."

"All those vehicles, everywhere you look," he said, which is precisely what I had felt.

"So how will things change for the better?"

He said, "Change will involve all the old men dying off. Or it might take another forty years."

"What if all the donors just went away?"

"That might work."

I wished him luck and walked up the main street to confirm an old memory, to see if the Malawi Censorship Board was doing business as usual. Indeed, it was still a government office, in its own substantial building at the east end of town. The offices were heavily staffed, all the names listed on a board in the lobby: Executive Director, Assistant Director, Accountant, Typing Pool, Screening Room Technician, and so forth — about thirty people altogether.

I knocked on a door at random and found an African man in a pinstriped suit sitting at a desk, a Bible open at his elbow — but otherwise a tidy desk.

"Excuse me, do you have an updated list?" Not sure of what I was asking for, I was deliberately vague.

"I can sell you this," he said, and handed me a pamphlet titled *Catalogue of Banned Publications, Cinematograph Pictures and Records, with Supplement,* dated 1991. "Please give me five kwacha."

He straightened his tie. Then he opened a ledger labeled *Accounts Section Censorship Board* and laboriously filled out a lengthy receipt in triplicate, stamped it, and tore out a copy for me. All this work for about seven cents.

"Don't you have anything more recent than 1991?"

"I will check. What is your interest?"

"I want to write something about censorship," I said. "I'm studying the problem."

"Please wait here. I will need your name."

I wrote my name on a piece of paper, and he took it and left the room. While he was gone I looked around — lots of uplifting mottoes on the office walls, a portrait of President Muluzi, some religious tracts on a bookshelf. The man's Bible was open to the Book of Ezekiel, the hellfire chapters of punishment, "threats against sinners," in its denunciations a sort of mission statement for the Malawi Censorship Board, but containing a great deal of explicit imagery that might have been deemed unfit for Malawian readers. Ezekiel 23:20 "Oholibah . . . surpassed her sister in lust . . . and played the whore over and over again. She was infatuated with their male prostitutes, whose members were like those of donkeys and whose seed came in floods like that of stallions."

The paradox was that this Malawi catalogue of banned books

would have constituted a first-year college reading list in any enlightened country. Flipping through the pamphlet, I saw that it contained novels by John Updike, Graham Greene, Bernard Malamud, Norman Mailer, Yukio Mishima, D. H. Lawrence, James Baldwin, Kurt Vonnegut, Vladimir Nabokov, and George Orwell. *Animal Farm* was banned, as well as — more predictably — many books with titles such as *Promiscuous Pauline* and *School Girl Sex*. Salman Rushdie's name was on the list — the president was a Muslim, which could explain it; and so was my name — after all these years, my novel *Jungle Lovers*, set in Malawi, was still banned.

The censorship officer had not yet returned. It seemed to me that the wisest thing to do would be to leave before they linked my name with that of the pernicious author on the list. I tiptoed out of the office, saw that the hall was empty, all the office doors shut, and hurried away as storm clouds gathered over the nearby hills.

In a fine, chilly, drifting mist, known in Malawi as *chiperoni*, I drove out of Limbe by a familiar route: uphill through a forest that had once been much larger, past a village that had once been much smaller, on a paved road that had once been a muddy track. My hopes were raised by this narrow but good back road that ascended to the lower slopes of Soche Hill, for I assumed that this improved road implied that the school too had been improved.

I was wrong. The school was almost unrecognizable. What had been a group of school buildings in a large grove of trees was a compound of battered buildings in a muddy open field. The trees had been cut down, the grass was chest high. At first glance the place was so poorly maintained as to seem abandoned: broken windows, doors ajar, mildewed walls, gashes in the roofs, and only a few people standing around, empty-handed, doing nothing but gaping at me.

I walked to the house I had once lived in. Now battered, it had once lain behind hedges in a bower of blossoming shrubs, but the shrubbery was gone, replaced by a small scrappy garden of withered maize and cassava in one corner. Tall elephant grass — symbol of the bush — had almost overwhelmed it. The tall grass now pressed against the house. The building was scorched and patched — one sooty wall where the boiler fire was fed — and the veranda roof broken. Mats lay in the driveway, mounds of white flour drying on it — except that falling rain had begun to turn it to paste. Faggots of firewood had been thrown in a higgledy-piggledy stack outside the kitchen.

To someone unfamiliar with Africa, the house was the very picture of disorder. I knew better. A transformation had occurred: an English chalet-bungalow had been turned into a serviceable African hut, not a very colorful hut, even an unlovely hut. But it was not for me to blame the occupants for finding other uses for the driveway, or chopping down the trees for firewood, or slashing the hedges, or growing cassava where I had grown petunias. I did regret that the paint had peeled from the trim and the eaves, that the wood had rotted and the brickwork had cracked and the windows had slipped from their frames. Village huts were kept in better repair. It would not be long before this badly maintained dwelling would fall down.

"Yes, you are looking for someone?"

The occupant of what had been my house stepped out, barefoot, in stained trousers and an undershirt, dabbing at the floury scraps on his cheeks. He had been eating.

"No. Just passing by," I said. "I used to live here. In the sixties."

"A long time ago!" he said.

That remark fascinated me, for it did not seem long at all to me, and in the heart of ancient, changeless Africa it seemed like nothing. But it was before he was born. The man did not introduce himself or welcome me, which was unusually inhospitable here. He didn't ask why I might have lived in the house or what I had done there all those years ago. He licked food from his lips and folded his arms. He was a village man eating a village meal in his village hut, and I was an interruption, from another planet.

"It's a very old house," he said. He turned to examine it.

"Not really."

"Built around independence time," he said, as though pegging it to some remote period in the past.

Independence was 1964. In a place where people married young, bore children young, and died young, that was two generations, far off to him in African time.

The old Roseveare homestead next door, much larger, was in worse shape. To those two meticulous English green-fingered gardeners, unweeded plants were a nightmare. But this was transformation, too. There was a solid maize crop growing where their roses and lupines had been. This vividly illustrated African life, which was the story not of adaptation but of survival.

"The Roseveares used to live there."

"Myself, I am not knowing them."

"Sir Martin Roseveare founded this school. He and his wife taught here for many years."

The man shrugged: not a clue.

"They are dead now."

"Oh, sorry." But he seemed more suspicious than sorry, as though I were spinning a yarn to catch him off-guard and perhaps rob him.

"You're a teacher?"

"Communications and whatnot," he said.

"Thanks. I must be going."

"Bye-bye, mister."

More rain-stained mildewed walls and sagging roofs, more broken windows and cracked verandas up the road at the other teachers' houses. The rain came down steadily now, but the drizzle and the mud and the dripping trees and the green slime on the brick walls were appropriate to the melancholy I felt.

I met two people standing in the wet road, chatting together. They introduced themselves as Anne Holt, from Fife in Scotland, and Jackson Yekha, a Malawian — new teachers here.

"I've read some of your books," Anne said. "I didn't know you'd taught here."

"It was a while ago. Ever hear of the Roseveares? They actually started the school. They lived over there."

Nothing, no memory of them, and I began to think that the weeds that covered their graves in Mzuzu were an accurate reflection of how much their decades of work and sacrifice mattered. It was as if they had never existed or were just ghostly figures. What they had helped create was almost gone, so in a sense they might never have come, though they still haunted the school.

I was a specter, too: a wraith from the past, knocking on broken windows with my bony fingers, pressing my skull against the glass and looking death's-head toothy, and saying, *Remember me?* I was so obscure and insubstantial a spook I was hardly visible to these people, but I saw them clearly as a repetition, another cycle, a sadder incarnation than before. Anne Holt was twenty-two, as I had been here at Soche Hill, and so as a ghost I was visiting and haunting my earlier self and seeing myself as I had been: thin, pale, standing on a wet road in the bush, with a foxed and mildewed textbook in my hand.

As we talked the rain turned very heavy, smacking the leaves overhead and threatening to drench us. We sheltered in the nearest house, that of Jackson Yekha. It so happened that Jackson's house was also the first house in Malawi I had ever occupied. While my house was being finished, I stayed in this one, belonging to a hardworking Scottish teacher from the island of South Uist. He was John MacKinnon, a stalwart at the school and another forgotten man. The same dining table that had once held sauce bottles and the mustard pot and a sticky jar of Branston Pickle was now dusted with the talcum of maize flour from *nsima* spills. This house too had become bushlike and cluttered and scorched: bungalow into hut.

Sitting there listening to the rain hammering the roof, it was Jackson Yekha, not I, who bemoaned the poverty and disorder in the country.

I said, "When I was here, people used to say, 'In five or ten years things will improve.'"

I didn't have to finish the thought, for Jackson said, "Things are terrible. What can we do to change?"

I said, "First you have to decide what's important to you. What do you want?"

"I want things to be better. Houses. Money. The life."

"What's stopping you?"

"The government is not helping us."

"Maybe the government wants to prevent things from becoming better."

I sketched out my theory that some governments in Africa depended on underdevelopment to survive — bad schools, poor communications, a feeble press, and ragged people. The leaders needed poverty to obtain foreign aid, needed an uneducated and passive populace to keep themselves in office for decades. A great education system in an open society would produce rivals, competitors, and an effective opposition to people who wanted only to cling to power. It was heresy to say such things here, but this was how it seemed to me.

"That's so depressing," Anne said. "But no one wants to be a teacher. A primary school teacher only makes two thousand kwacha a month. The college level is about five thousand kwacha."

These figures represented around $27 to $67 — very low. The average annual per capita income in Malawi was $200.

"The NGOs pull out the teachers," Jackson said. "They offer them better pay and conditions."

The foreign charities and virtue activists, aiming to improve matters, co-opted underpaid teachers, turned them into food distributors, and left the schools understaffed.

Seeing that the rain had let up, I asked Anne to show me around the school. In the main office, I met the principal.

Anne said, "This is Mr. Theroux. He used to teach here."

The principal shortened his neck like a startled turtle and glanced at me. He said, "That's interesting," and returned to his reading. He read using his fingers, like a blind man at braille.

The library, a substantial building, had been the heart of the school. It had never been difficult to get crates of new books from overseas agencies. My memory of the Soche library was of an open-plan room divided with many high bookcases and filled shelves — ten thousand books, a table of magazines, a reference section with encyclopedias.

The library was in almost total darkness. One light burned. Nearly all the shelves were empty. The light fixtures were empty, too.

"It's a little dark in here."

"You should have seen it before," Anne said. "At least we've got that one light. We've asked the ministry countless times to send us fluorescent bulbs, but they don't even reply to our letters."

"You're asking for bulbs and they won't give them to you?" I said. "I think they're sending you a message that they don't care."

"Aye, possibly."

"This used to be one of the best schools in the country."

"Aye, it's sad, I agree."

"What happened to the books?"

"Students stole them."

"Good God."

"We're trying to work out a new system. When we get it up and running we'll be able to prevent a lot of the theft."

I thought: I will never send another book to this country. I also thought: If you're an African student and you need money, it made a certain criminal sense to steal books and sell them. It was a justifiable form of poaching, like a villager snaring a warthog, disapproved of by the authorities but perhaps necessary. There was no tribal sanction against poaching when it concerned survival.

Leaving the library I felt as though I were emerging from a dark hole of ignorance and plunder. We walked to the classrooms, which were as seedy as everything else, but in some respects worse, for the verandas had not been swept and the grass had not been cut, and there was litter on the paths. What was the excuse for that?

"There's a serious money shortage in this country," Anne said.

"That's probably true," I said. "But how much does a broom cost? The students could sweep this place and cut the grass. I don't think it's a money problem. I think it's something more serious. No one cares. You're here to do the work, and you're willing, so why should anyone help?"

"I'm not just teaching," she said. "I'm learning a lot."

"Absolutely. That's a good reason to be here," I said. "That's why I liked being here."

We walked through the building to the schoolyard, where several students lingered, watching us. Morning assembly was held here, a bigger space than I had known, but now paved with cinders and bordered by more unswept and damp-stained classroom blocks. A stout, confident-looking woman in a green dress stepped out of a classroom, where she had obviously been eating, for she was licking her fingers. The headmistress.

"This is Mr. Theroux. He used to teach here."

"Thank you. That's interesting."

With her fingers in her mouth, the headmistress returned to the classroom, to her meal.

Anne and I walked onto the assembly ground. I looked around the dismal school and thought how I had longed to return here. I had planned to spend a week helping, perhaps teaching, reliving my days as a volunteer. This was my Africa. *You're planting a seed!* some people had said. But the seed had not sprouted, and now it was decayed and probably moribund.

Perhaps reading my thoughts, Anne said, "I have my doubts sometimes. I say to my mother, 'What if we just upped and left? All of us. Every last one.'"

"What do you think would happen?"

"Then the people here would have to think for themselves. They'd have to decide what's best for them — what they want. No one would influence them. Maybe they would say they wanted education — and they'd have to do the teaching. They'd have to do what we're doing."

"For your measly salary."

"Right," she said. "Or maybe they'd decide that they wouldn't want a change. They might allow things to stay as they are. Lots of the people in villages are fine. They're not miserable."

These perceptive comments from someone who was willing to work — the person I had been — gave me hope. Not enough Africans saw the problems as clearly.

I wanted to see some African volunteers caring for the place — sweeping the floors, cutting the grass, washing windows, gluing the spines back onto the few remaining books, scrubbing the slime off the classroom walls. Or, if that was not their choice, I wanted to see them torch the place and burn it to the ground and dance around the flames, then plow everything under and plant food crops. Until either of those things happened, I would not be back. I felt no desire to linger, and certainly none to work here. I wished Anne Holt lots of luck and left the place in her hands, feeling that I would never return, that this was my last safari to Soche Hill.

I did not know the answer; I didn't even know the question. A kind of clarity came to me: I saw the pointlessness, almost the triviality, of my staying and attempting to teach. That effort would have been something purely to please myself. I did not feel despair at having been prevented from doing it, but rather a solemn sense that since only Africans could define their problems, only Africans could fix them.

Maybe none of these flawed schools were problems at all but only foreign institutions like foreign contraptions — like the big metal containers that were sent full of machinery or computers that were distributed and used for a while and then broke and were never fixed. I saw them all over Africa, the castoff containers at the edge of town. Whatever their contents might have been, what remained as the most valuable object was the metal container itself. The empty things became sturdy dwellings, and there were always people or animals living in them, like credulous corrupted tribesmen in a cargo cult.

On my way back to Zomba, I drove to Blantyre (named for David Livingstone's birthplace in Scotland) and stopped at a shop on a side street, Supreme Furnishers, to see another of my former students, Steve Kamwendo. Steve was now a branch manager, aged fifty-one, a father of six, a big healthy man with the powerful features and chiefly presence of Vernon Jordan. Steve hugged me and said he was glad to see me. I told him where I had been. His face fell.

"You went to Soche?" he said. "Did you shed tears?"

That summed it up. To anyone who felt I had been too hard on my old school, I could send them to Steve, who lamented that Soche Hill was in a bad way, that crime was terrible and life in general very hard. His own business was good. Malawi-made furniture, and bedsteads and lamps from South Africa and Zimbabwe were popular, because furniture imported from outside Africa was so expensive.

"Your old students are doing well, but the country is not doing well. People are different — much poorer, not respectful."

"What about your kids, Steve?"

"They are in America. Four of them are in college in Indiana. One is graduating in June."

By any standard, Steve's was a success story. All his savings went toward educating his children elsewhere, and though he was gloomy about Malawi's prospects, he was encouraging his children to return to the country to work.

"It's up to them now," I said.

I returned to Zomba sooner than I had expected, with an unanswered question in my mind. Why were the schools so underfunded?

"I can tell you that," Gertrude Rubadiri said, her feet squarely on the ground as usual. "The money was taken."

It seemed that two million American dollars, earmarked for education from a European donor country, had recently been embezzled by the finance minister and two other politicians in a scam that involved the creation of fictional schools and fictional teachers. More money was unaccounted for. The men were in jail awaiting trial, but the money was gone and would never be found.

So there was a good reason for the broken windows and dead lights and unpainted walls at Soche Hill and every other school in the country. A large and essential part of the education budget had been stolen by the government official to whom it had been entrusted.

The next day the Rubadiris invited some friends for dinner. One man, very fat and self-possessed, had been a Malawi ambassador in Europe and was now a bureaucrat living in Zomba.

"You have seen so much of the country, Paul. So tell us, what do you think?"

"The visitor usually brings a sharp knife," someone said — another proverb. The stranger was known for having the keenest insights.

I did not know where to begin. For some reason I kept seeing in my mind the main road through the northern towns, the outposts of the plateaus — Karonga, Livingstonia, Rumphi, Ekwendeni, Mzuzu — the empty Indian shops, the women squatting on the ground selling bananas and peanuts. I mentioned this vision of rural decline — but I didn't say "decline," I said "change."

"The Indians were chased away," the former ambassador said. "It wasn't a law, it wasn't gazetted. But that is a detail. As soon as the president made the speech against the Indians — mid-seventies, about — they closed their shops. The Indians went to the U.K. or South Africa."

I knew this, but I wanted to hear him say it. I asked, "What was the motive behind the president's speech?"

"We wanted Africans to be given a chance to run the shops. So that Africans could go into business. The shops were handed over. I bought one myself."

"With what result?"

"Ha-ha! Not much! It didn't work. They all got finished!"

He was saying: We kicked out the Indians, we took over their shops, we failed — so what? End of story. He even tried to change the subject, but I was interested and asked him to describe the failure in more detail.

"Well, as you know, Indians are good at business," he said. Then, laughing in dismay as if he had just dropped a slice of bread butter-side down, "What do we know about these things? We had no capital. The shops failed — almost all of them. Ha! They were abandoned, as you saw. And the rest were turned into *chibuku* bars." Beer bars.

The result in the rural areas: no shops at all, and twenty-seven years later, still no shops. So the whole scheme had backfired. When I pointed this out, one of the other African guests began, perversely, denigrating the Indians for their business acumen in a mocking voice.

"They sit there, you see, and they have these little pieces of paper, and have these columns of numbers." He spoke pompously about the Indians as though describing demented obsessive children with broken toys. "And one Indian is running the calculator, and another is counting the sacks of flour and the tins of condensed milk. One two three. One two three."

What this educated African with his plummy voice intended as mockery — the apparent absurdity of all this counting — was the description of people doing a simple inventory of goods in a shop.

I said, "But that's how a shop is run. That's normal business. You make a list of what you've sold, so you know what stuff to reorder."

"Indians know no other life!" he said. "Just this rather secluded life — all numbers and money and goods on shelves. One two three."

"Recordkeeping is the nature of small business, isn't it?" I resented his belittling the shopkeeper, yet I kept calm so as to draw him out. "The profit margins are so small."

"But we Africans are not raised in this way," he said, nodding to the others for approval. "What do we care about shops and counting? We have a much freer existence. We have no interest in this — shops are not our strong point."

"Why close the shops, then?"

That stumped him, but not for long.

"Maybe something can be done with them. Selling is not our heritage. We are not business people."

"Women are selling soap and matches and cooking oil."

"But not in shops."

"No, they're sitting in the mud in Mzuzu," I said, feeling agitated.

"I'll tell you why these shops didn't work out," the former ambassador said. "When Africans run businesses, their families come and stay with them and eat all their food — just live off them. As soon as an African succeeds in something, he has his family cadging from him. Not so?"

"That is true, brother," another guest said.

"And we are not cut out for this shopkeeping and bookkeeping and" — the former ambassador winked at me — "number crunching."

I had never heard such bullshit. Well, perhaps I had and not recognized it. The man was saying: This is all too much for us. We cannot learn how to do business. We must be given money, we must be given sinecures, because we don't know how to make a profit.

I said, "If you're no good at bookkeeping and keeping track of expenses, why do you expect donor countries to go on giving you money?"

This was a bit too blunt, and it had the effect of ending this particular discussion.

As if to explain my irritation, David Rubadiri said, "Paul has had a very powerful experience returning to his old school. That is why he was such a good teacher. It meant so much to him."

Feeling patronized, I said, "No lights. The place is falling down. They stole the books. I know what you're going to say, but hey, why doesn't anyone sweep the dirty floor?"

"There is a panel studying the education system."

Oh, bollocks, I thought, and drank another beer and sat back in my chair while they talked about other things.

I did not hear what they were saying. I heard rats scurrying and squabbling in the space above the wooden ceiling of the old colonial house. The open window admitted gossamer-winged dragonflies and diaphanous yellow moths and big bumbling beetles.

The stout man was staring at me. I was at a loss for words. Finally I said, "Which country were you ambassador in?"

"Germany. Four years."

"Lovely museums," I said.

"I only went to a museum once," he said. "They gave a dinner at the museum — inside, you see. Tables and chairs set up where the pictures were. We ate and looked at the pictures. It was very nice. I didn't go to any other museums."

"Lovely music," I said.

"I learned a bit about classical music. Up to then my favorite music was pata-pata." That was South African shantytown jive. "But I still love pata-pata. It's my Mozart."

"Did you travel much in Germany?"

"Ah, I was in Berlin, at that hotel, the Adlon. So beautiful. It costs three hundred dollars a night."

I resisted the gibe that the Mount Soche, a mediocre and pretentious hotel in Blantyre, cost $250 a night, because it was where all the economists and aid people and political observers on junkets stayed.

The former ambassador said, "One night, I was having a drink in the bar of the Adlon — my wife was with Mrs. President when our president was visiting Germany. I looked up and saw James Bond — that chap, what's his name, Pierce Brosnan. I went up to him. 'Hello. I want a few words with you.' He said, 'Yes?' I was actually talking to him! Oh, he was so nice. I had nothing to write on, so he signed the menu. My daughter was very cross. 'Why didn't you take me to see him, Papa?' Yes, that James Bond chap, I was talking to him. In Berlin!"

After the dinner party broke up and the guests left, I sat with David

Rubadiri, feeling so irritable I thought I was experiencing the symptoms of an illness. I drank some more beer. The loud thumps and scrabbling of the rats in the space above the wooden ceiling had died down, had become scratchings and squealings. The glider-winged dragonflies still drifted through the windows and seemed as large and nimble as swallows.

I did not dare approach the subject of how appalled I felt that so much effort had been wasted here, for Rubadiri was being friendly. In his expansive mood he was a romantic. He had lived through the worst years of Malawi, he had occupied high positions, he had been an exile, and he was now powerful again, running the national university, though it was millions in debt and so behind in paying salaries that all classes had been canceled. Students were threatening to hold demonstrations in Zomba.

"Your children are doing so well," he said. "When I was in London one of them had his own TV show and the other had just published a novel. Clever chaps."

"Thanks," I said. Though I was flattered, I found it hard to say more. Dizziness and nausea made me laconic. My feeling of annoyance had turned into physical discomfort. I wondered if I had eaten something foul. "Yes, Marcel and Louis are good boys. They work very hard."

"What I would like," David said in an emphatic way, a little theatrical in his demand, "what I would like very much indeed is for one of your children to come here for a spell."

After what I had seen since entering Malawi through Karonga weeks before, I found the idea shocking and unacceptable, like Almighty God instructing Abraham to sacrifice Isaac. Shock gave way to incredulity and bewilderment.

"What would either of my sons do here, for goodness sake?"

"He would work, he would teach, he would be a source of ideas and inspiration." It was the old song, but just a song.

Smiling angrily, and bent slightly because my guts ached, I said, "But you've had plenty of those people. Years of those people. Years and years."

"I want your son."

What he meant as praise, and perhaps flattery, offended me. In his insistence he sounded like one of Herod's hatchet men just before the Slaughter of the Innocents. *I want your son.*

Why were these murderous biblical metaphors occurring to me? Perhaps because Malawians were such a churchgoing bunch.

"How many children do you have, David?"

"As you know, nine."

"How many of them are teaching here?"

"One is in Reno, one in Baltimore, one in London, one in Kampala, another . . ." He stopped himself and looked tetchy. "Why are you inquiring?"

"Because you're doing what everyone does — you're asking me to hand over one of my kids to teach in Malawi. But Marcel taught in India, and Louis was a teacher in Zimbabwe. They've had that experience. Have yours?"

I was a bit too shrill in my reply. He took it well, but he saw me as unwilling, someone no longer persuaded by the cause. He suspected that I had turned into Mister Kurtz. He was wrong. I was passionate about the cause. But I had had an epiphany: though my children would be enriched by the experience of working in Africa, nothing at all would change as a result of their being here. I thought of what my friend in Uganda had said about her American-educated children: "We wanted them here. We said, 'Come back and get your foot in the door. Get a decent job. Try to be part of the process.'"

Still trying to control my indignation, I said as quietly as I could, "What about your kids? This is their country. They could make a difference. They are the only people — the only possible people — who will ever make a difference here."

That was my Malawi epiphany. Only Africans were capable of making a difference in Africa. Everyone else, donors and volunteers and bankers, however idealistic, were simply agents of subversion.

In my room that night I was struck down — cramps, nausea, griping guts, evil gurgling in the knotted tubes of my intestines. The *chimbudzi* was down the corridor. I visited the little room every hour throughout the night. In the morning I was still weak and felt sick, for the first time since Cairo. I drowsed and slept late. No one was around the house when I woke. I rehydrated myself with a mixture of sugar and salt in water, took some pills, and drove away, downhill, past people — I almost wrote "ragged," I almost wrote "barefoot," I almost wrote "trudging." But no, just Malawians walking along the road, people I could not help.

In Blantyre, I checked into a hotel and stayed in my room, medicating myself. I lay doubled-up for a few days and then strayed into town. What I had not noticed on my previous visit was the great number of shops and churches run by Christian evangelists — Jimmy Swaggart Ministries among them. The education system was appalling, but there was no shortage of dreary hymn-singing pietists and preachers who promised people food if they handed over their souls.

"Be sure you give the poor the aid they most need," Thoreau wrote in *Walden.* "There are a thousand hacking at the branches of evil to one who is striking at the root, and it may be that he who bestows the largest amount of time and money on the needy is doing the most by his mode of life to produce that misery which he strives in vain to relieve."

I realized I was somewhat out of sympathy with this new Malawi when I saw a man on the sidewalk lying in wait for me.

Seeing me, the man smiled and frolicked ahead, flapping his arms to get my attention. He capered some more, then crouched in front of me, blocking my path, and said, "I am hungry. Give me money."

I said no, and stepped over him, and kept walking.

16 ◇◇◇

River Safari to the Coast

POSSESSED by another yearning to light out for the territory — another territory — I fell ill. Sickness of the sort I suffered is so common among travelers there is no point reporting the particulars. My ailment's effect on me was to make me idle. My ailment's effect on others was to make them active and pestiferous. The Africans who seemed to understand that I was weak pursued me, the way predators harry slower or uncertain prey animals, and they demanded money, as though knowing that I was too weak to refuse them. Seeing me hollow-eyed and scuffing along the crowded streets of Blantyre, they nagged me. I walked slowly. Boys tagged along, snatching and calling out, "*Muzungu! Muzungu!*"

A man accosted me outside a shop. He said, "Please give me money for food."

I said in his language, "Why are you asking me for money for nothing? Why don't you ask me for work?"

This perplexed him and threw him off his spiel.

"Don't you want to work? If you work you'll have money every week."

He knelt — got down on his ragged knees — and implored me for money. This abasement must have worked well for him before, because he did it without hesitation. He even gripped my ankles as he begged.

"Get up," I said. "You're a man. Get off your knees. Stand up like a man and ask me for work."

"I'm hungry," he said.

"I'm sick, can't you tell?" I said. "Why don't you give me money for being sick?"

My unexpected aggression and strange demand seemed to frighten him, and it surprised me too, for I had not planned on saying any of that. He walked quickly away.

In my weakened state I felt irritable and contrary and persecuted. Blantyre had once been a mixed community: Greek bakers, Italian tea planters, many mixed-race families, and not just generic Indians but enclaves of Ismailis, Sikhs, Gujaratis. Even the worst of them had played a part in making society in Malawi work — the friction had been necessary, the challenges had made people think harder, the pluralism had forced people to become considerate. But all these exotic-looking people had been driven out. There were no racial differences now, except for the agents of virtue, all white, all short-timers. The workings of society were in the hands of charities, which ran orphanages, staffed hospitals, performed triage in the pathetic education system. They were saving lives — you couldn't fault them, but in general I despaired at the very sight of aid workers. They were no more than a maintenance crew on a power trip, who had turned Malawians into beggars and whiners, and development into a study in futility.

The news in the paper was that the maize harvest was a failure. A famine was expected for the coming year.

◇ ◇ ◇

One day I woke up well. Having no desire to stay any longer in Malawi and discuss what went wrong, I decided to leave. I was now strong enough to depart by an unusual route, through the bush to light out for the territory south, an almost unknown land.

It was the ultimate safari, one of my own devising, down the Shire River and into Mozambique to the Zambezi. Downstream at Caia I could go by road west to Beira, on the Mozambican coast, then travel inland on the direct road to Harare. I justified the detour by telling myself that I would compare it with a previous trip I had taken on this same route. But in fact this, the most roundabout way of getting to Zimbabwe, was a jaunt, a lark, an antidote to all the miserable buses and all the dishonest blamers.

Having sworn off risky minibuses, I dickered with a taxi driver to take me down the muddy and weirdly ferric-colored road to Nsanje, the southernmost settlement in Malawi. Once known as Port Herald, Nsanje was so buggy and malarial it had been Malawi's Siberia for decades, a penal colony for political dissidents. Undesirables were sent to the southern region to rot.

But Nsanje was one of those distant rural places that retained the look and feel of old Africa. Not populous, inhabited by the Sena people, who were despised for being unmodern and remote in their low-lying swampy land, Nsanje was wild enough to have its own game park, the Mwabvi Game Reserve. Nsanje was also on a wide navigable river. When David Livingstone had first come to this area he had traveled along the Zambezi and up one of its larger tributaries, the Shire, to Nsanje and the labyrinthine Elephant Marsh and into the highlands. On the way, he made the observation that cotton would be an ideal crop here. One hundred fifty years later, cotton was still grown around Nsanje. The crop was not in great demand.

My driver's name was Hudson. He repeated what the papers had said, that the southern region was due for a famine, because of the heavy rain that had come before the maize crop had been harvested.

The rain had been torrential in the south. The growing cycle had been skewed. The government gave out free seeds (ten kilos per family, courtesy of donor countries), enough for an acre. This in itself was a problem, for it suggested to me that small-scale sustainable agriculture was not the norm. Anyone who grows crops with unmodified seeds can set aside one field as seed corn. But because they were using hybrid seeds (big plants, but sterile seeds), the farmers could not create seeds for the following year. Instead, they waited for them to be doled out. Without free seeds every year these people would starve.

Normally, fields were dug in September, the ground hoed and prepared in October, dry-planted in November, then the farmers prayed for rain. The maize stalks that matured in February were left in the field to dry, and in April the ears were picked. The cobs were stripped of their kernels and bagged for milling into flour. June, July, and August were months of abundance. Malawi's Independence Day was in July, when people had plenty of free time and enough to eat. At the first independence celebration, Hastings Banda had stood in the National Stadium and led the thousands of Malawians present in the robust hymn, significant in that month, "Bringing In the Sheaves."

The average family of four or five people required twelve bags of maize (one bag equaled fifty kilograms). These were kept in a silo (*nkokwe*) outside the hut. Rats, rotting, and importuning relatives diminished the hoard. To make flour for *nsima* — a blob of steamed white dough, served with stew, that I had been eating ever since Karonga — to create this Malawi staple, the kernels were pounded in mortars or ground in a communal mill. Of all the activities in Central Africa, the maize-growing cycle was the most vital, the only important work, the difference between life and death. Anything that interrupted it — war, political trouble, spoiled seeds, flood, drought, or wildfires — spelled doom.

This season the rains had been late. Some seeds had not germinated. Many had sprouted and produced a crop. But the rain was still falling in March, and the ripe ungathered maize began to rot in the fields. Much of the south had been flooded. The harvest would be small. Because of this shortfall, in Nsanje and elsewhere, famine was a certainty.

"These people will get hungry," Hudson said, looking at the wet fields and blackened corn stalks, the decayed stubble, the rotted stooks, the soaked slumping thatch on the huts.

Ten months later, the situation was dire. Maize was so scarce that South Africa sent a shipment of 150,000 metric tons, and more was ordered from Uganda, which had a surplus. But since the price per bag had tripled, the maize was unaffordable. Malawi newspapers reported people eating boiled cassava leaves, digging for wild roots, and eating earthworms.

"A bit farther," I said when we got to Nsanje. "I want to go to Marka."

"You know this place?"

I did. I had come here in the 1990s to research a story about the Zambezi River. I had had my own kayak then, but I found out that I could hire a dugout canoe for the downriver trip; that with an early start it was two nights to the Zambezi, another night at Caia, and then about twelve hours by road to the coast. I had the essential equipment: a raincoat, a down-filled sleeping bag that could be compressed to the size of a football, and bug spray. I also had cash to buy food.

Hudson dropped me off at the compound of the headman of Marka village, whom I had dealt with before. A group of women with children bandaged to their backs sat in a circle, sorting beans in tin basins, picking out stones and chatting. I greeted them with the usual formulas, the equivalents of "May I enter?" and "May I have permission to speak?"

They welcomed me and offered a wobbly stool.

"I am looking for Chief Nyachikadza," I said.

He wasn't there, and that was bad news: from their euphemisms and circumspect manner I feared he might be ill or possibly dead. In a village such as Marka, in the Lower River District of Malawi, no one is dead. If people appear to vanish from their corporeal existence, it is just a ducking out before returning as spirits, sometimes troubling the order of daily life, sometimes acting to smooth its course.

The women directed me to the chief's son, Karsten, whom I knew from my previous visit. Karsten lived elsewhere on the river, but he happened to be in Marka, delivering goods in his dugout canoe.

"Delivering" could mean anything in Marka. The place was so far off the map there was hardly any law enforcement. There were police in Nsanje, and they had a motorboat, but the river was too wide and too long for any of them to monitor the comings and goings of dugouts. So smuggling was common. Sugar and cotton were smuggled out to Mozambique, and other items — tin pots, enamel plates, knives and machetes — were smuggled into Malawi.

The Lower River was a forgotten province, inhabited by the despised and dendrophobic Sena people. The Shire Valley was neglected by the Malawi government; and farther downstream, where the river entered Mozambique, it was neglected by that government, too. Who could blame these people living on its banks for finding illegal ways of fending for themselves? No one looked after them. The region, like many border areas in Africa, was undefined. The Sena people lived on both sides, and the river made it even more ambiguous — not Malawi, not Mozambique, but miles and miles of moving water, something fluid, a river in Africa.

Even the riverbanks had no definition, for at the muddy margins of the river were vast swathes of reeds that obscured the bank, and in places dense stretches of water hyacinths — very pretty but a nuisance to the paddlers in the dugout canoes.

The women who had mentioned Karsten ordered a young boy to take me to him. We walked through the village of mud huts — their walls eroded by the rain — and down to the landing. About twenty dugouts were lined up on the foreshore.

Some men were unloading plastic sacks from an oversize dugout —

cloudy-clear plastic sacks that allowed me to see that the cargo was plastic sandals. I presumed that they had come upriver from a dropoff spot in Mozambique. The sacks were being heaped on wooden pallets to keep them out of the mud.

A fisherman was untangling his nets. His catch, a bucket thrashing with big fish, lay next to him. Another man was scooping water from a dugout using a plastic gallon jug, cut off to serve as a bailer. I thought I recognized Karsten Nyachikadza in a group of men who were standing near the unloaded sacks of sandals.

A heavy smoker of *chamba,* Karsten was in his mid-thirties — short, thin-faced, small-boned, but even with his scrawny physique he was unexpectedly strong and tenacious. He had a hard stroke and he could paddle all day. His habit was to rise early, before dawn, and push his boat out and keep at it, not stopping to eat though sometimes pausing to roll a joint. He ate fruit — oranges, bananas, tangerines, whatever was in season — and at the end of the day made a proper meal of *nsima* and stewed greens and smoked fish.

Even glassy-eyed from the dope he seemed to remember me. He turned from the group and shook my hand and called out something to the others, explaining who I was and laughing at the memory of that previous trip.

"I want to go to Caia in your boat," I said.

He smiled. His expression said, *Sure.* He hung on to my hand as though to seal the agreement. His was a paddler's hand, scaly, with a muscly palm, and pads so hardened with calluses they seemed abrasive.

"When?"

"How about tomorrow?"

"Tonight we go to my house. Sleep there. Start tomorrow morning for Caia."

He was more eager to leave than I was, which pleased me. But there were preparations to make.

"What about food? I want to bring bottled water. We'll need *ufa*" — flour for *nsima.*

"The shop in the market has tins. Give me money. I will buy flour."

We went together, walking through the village to the shop. For me, this was one of the most pleasant aspects of a trip — stocking up on the necessaries, filling a box with solid food and extras like cookies and canned cheese. Because bottled water was in short supply, I bought a case of Fanta and a case of beer. An African shop like this was just right for such food and the basics for survival — matches, candles, rope. I wanted to buy pots and spoons and camping paraphernalia, but Karsten said he had everything we needed. The plastic tarp he had for covering his contraband we could use as a tent if it rained.

On the way back to the landing (young boys following us, carrying the food boxes on their heads), we agreed on a price for renting the dugout — a hundred dollars in small bills. Karsten said we would need another paddler — his friend, Wilson Matenge. But by the time Wilson was found, the sun had dropped behind the trees and daylight was slipping away. It was too late to go to Karsten's. I did not mind travelling in the dusk, but just at dark the mosquitoes came out in clouds. I wanted to find a hut to sleep in, and a smoky fire; to cover myself with bug spray and go to sleep early.

Village dogs barked all night outside the shed I had been assigned, probably because hyenas were lurking. It was still dark when I heard Karsten's footfalls and his wide-awake voice: "We go now."

◈ ◈ ◈

Dawn, too, was mosquito time on the Shire River. As we set off they whined around my head in bunches, as thick and busy as blackflies in Maine. But I was well sprayed, and as soon as the sun came up the mosquitoes dispersed. The dugout had been hollowed from an enormous log, about seventeen feet from tip to tip, and so wide it plowed through the marsh to the main stream. Karsten paddled in the stern and steered, Wilson and I took turns paddling in the bow.

The entry to the landing was a narrow lane of open water through the matted thickness of closely packed leaves and flowers of the hyacinths. Much of the time I sat on a stool amidships, like Stanley in the *Lady Alice,* or else crouched in the bow. As master of this vessel, Karsten was reluctant to surrender his paddle. Even Wilson was happiest when paddling, and I supposed he wanted to humor me by giving me a chance. But it passed the time for me to paddle, and by midmorning we had made it through the hyacinths and the twisting waterway through the marsh grass. We were now in the swift main stream of the Shire, riding the current south.

The recent rain had muddied the river and deepened it, but though it brimmed against some of the banks, it hadn't spilled over and flooded the plains and gardens. We moved steadily with the flow and at times we used the paddles just to steer, the current speeding us.

People on the banks called out to us, and they must have been asking where we were going, because Karsten yelled, "Zambezi!"

In places the river twisted into bewildering marshland, dividing into many separate streams, softening, losing its riverine look and becoming slow water in a mass of spongy reeds. The Shire ceased to be a river at the Ndinde Marsh, which was so dense with high grass and reeds we could not see ahead of us, so choked with hyacinths that our progress was slowed to hard paddling. In this marsh we could navigate only by occasionally going upstream, fighting the current. I thought that perhaps Karsten's *chamba* intake had destroyed his judgment, but after an hour in the marsh we emerged, with a view of Mozambique.

I could see no villages, but here and there were clusters of huts set back from the river's edge. Karsten stopped at one village and bought mangoes, and at another he bought dried fish. The people knew him, which encouraged my confidence in him, for he could know these half-hidden places only by being intensely knowledgeable about navigating the river.

A muddy embankment was the Mozambique border. There was no indication it was a frontier, but there were wrecked vehicles and boats on the muddy banks, always signs of civilization. The riverside settlement of Megaza consisted of two wrecked riverboats, a rusted truck chassis, a slippery ramp, some sheds that sold the usual — oil, candles, matches, crackers, raw soap, cigarettes — and idle skinny Africans sitting under another wrecked truck for the shade. The place had everything except Mister Kurtz and his human skulls. Under a mango tree a man sat at a table, the Mozambican immigration officer. We pulled our dugout up the bank, and Wilson made a fire while Karsten went in search of water.

I sat under the mango tree with the immigration official as he thumbed through my passport, which he finally stamped. Then I walked up the road to see what else was here. I noticed the immigration officer was following me. I let him catch up. We walked together in silence. Ahead were three wooden buildings. One was a government office — a single room. One was an abandoned shop — I peered in and saw empty shelves and a long bench. I liked the width of the bench. The third building was a bar — just a counter, warm beer on shelves, and Portuguese music blaring from a radio.

"You buy me *kachasu?*" the immigration man said.

It was Malawi gin, made from bananas. I bought two. We drank. I said, "I want to sleep next door tonight, okay?"

He shrugged, not saying yes or no. I bought him another glass, and when I started to walk away he said, "Come. You can sleep."

Boiling the flour with water in a blackened pot, Karsten had mixed up some *nsima.* He mashed the dried fish with greens. I opened a can of stew, heated it on the fire, and ate that with the *nsima.* We squatted around the smoky fire and talked.

"How far can we get tomorrow? Maybe the Zambezi?"

He made an equivocating face and said, "*Mphepho*" — wind.

If there was a headwind, we probably would not make it as far as the Zambezi, he said. The dugout rode so high in the water that the wind affected us more than other, shallow-hulled craft.

It was hardly seven-thirty when we turned in. I reclined on my bench in the shed up the road, and though I could hear the idiot music coming from the bar, I fell into a sleep so deep I did not awaken until Karsten came for me in the darkness of early morning.

We slid into the river and paddled in the predawn silence for almost an hour. The sun came up — no warning, a flicker, the whole sky lighted and then the powerful heat and blaze of the quickly risen sun. Ahead I could see a single loaf-shaped mountain, Morrumbala. My map showed a town nearby called Morrumbala, but there was no sign of that, only this beautiful rounded thing rising four thousand feet from the flat marshy land by the river. There was not another hill or high spot anywhere.

We toiled toward it all that hot morning. When Livingstone had come through here in 1859 he urged some of his crew to climb it. The Zambezi and the Shire had allowed Livingstone to penetrate the African interior with all its marvels — Lakes Shirwa and Nyasa, the country we know today as Malawi, the labyrinthine marsh on the Shire with its abundant elephants, and the mountain Morrumbala, or "the Lofty Watchtower." But for Livingstone it was a horrible trip on a riverboat that had too deep a draft for this river, making it slow going through the sandbanks and the marsh. He had gone at a time of widespread famine, and the river was full of crocs. The verdict of one of Livingstone's men was that the Shire was "a river of death."

As a monumental land feature, sculpted like a citadel, Morrumbala had been regarded as a prize from the earliest days of Portuguese exploration. In the 1640s this general area was the haunt of Portuguese *sertanejos* — literally, backwoodsmen — each of whom chose a region to rule. All were colonists from the mother country, but while some were aristocrats, others were criminals. They were conquistadors, united in their greed and in their delusions of grandeur, for they made themselves into provincial potentates, lived like little kings, created retinues, cultivated courtiers, and owned and traded in slaves.

From the seventeenth to the nineteenth century *sertanejos* inhabited the Mozambican hinterland, turning featureless bush into a number of rural kingdoms, where they amassed silver and gold and ivory. (Conrad's Kurtz is a Belgian version of a *sertanejo.*) In his doublet and hose, carrying an arquebus, the wild-eyed Portuguese backwoodsman is colorful in a contemptible way and an illustration of Sir Richard Burton's remark, "There is a time to leave the Dark Continent and that is when the *idée fixe* begins to develop itself. 'Madness comes from Africa.'"

In the mid-seventeenth century the immediate area of Morrumbala was held by a self-appointed lord of the manor, a backwoodsman named Sisnanda Dias Bayão, who settled in Sena, not far away. The Africans farther up the Shire and in Sena land were mostly not warlike or well armed, so Bayão had an easy time suppressing them, enslaving them, and putting them to work searching for silver and gold. There was a gold rush of brief duration in this area in Bayão's time, all those years ago. When the colonial government objected to Bayão's methods and pursued him, he holed up on the mountain. At the same time, because of its gullies and caves, the wooded slopes of Morrumbala became a favorite route for escaped slaves. Morrumbala as a refuge persisted to the present day. The mountain was a favorite hiding place for fleeing soldiers in the vicious guerrilla wars, twenty-five years of them, fought in the Mozambique bush in the twentieth century.

The wind picked up in the afternoon, riffling the river, pushing our boat sideways. To steel himself, Karsten paused in his paddling, fired up a doobie, and with wild staring eyes headed downriver again.

As with the last time I had come here, for many miles downstream we could see Morrumbala. For its isolation and its solitary strangeness — no one on it or around it — I regarded Morrumbala as an inspiration. I fastened my attention on it and delighted in it. Its shape was more that of a mesa than a mountain. There were abandoned farms and fruit orchards at the top, we were told by Africans in passing dugouts. How had the Portuguese gotten up and down the mountain, I wondered.

"They were carried by Africans," Wilson said.

I could just imagine a pink Portuguese planter in a palanquin, fanning himself as he was being trundled by four Africans up the steep mountainside. Shells of houses and plantations, remnants of the Portuguese colonial presence, were visible in many places on the riverbanks. They had the melancholy look of ruins in a wilderness, mute but solid signs of a lost world. The river itself was swampy in some places and just marsh in others — a series of divided streams running through dense reeds. "A swampy plain sacred to buffaloes and water buck and mosquitoes," a traveler, one of Livingstone's companions, wrote in 1863. "We almost despair of finding the waters of the Shire in the various currents that mingle there."

Karsten was never in any doubt of the stream. He had paddled the river so often that he had come to know the backwaters and the wrong turns. We came to a village. I thought Karsten was intending to buy fish or fruit, so I rested on my paddle. But he grabbed the food box and swung it to the bank.

"What's happening?"

"We sleep here."

There were at least two hours of daylight left, and the wind was not bad. I could see a gentle bend in the river beckoning, a stillness and gilded look in the reach. Why not go a few more miles?

He pointed to the bend in the river. "Bad people there." His saying this in English made them seem more dangerous.

That simple statement was all it took to persuade me to leap ashore and claw my way up the steep bank and through a crowd of women and children. A cluster of huts stood on higher ground a little distance away.

They watched us laboring with our boxes and bundles, and I knew they were not idle spectators. Anything we did not want — bits of plastic or paper, tin cans, anything reusable — they were ready to seize. A little while later, after we started a fire, a woman crouched next to me as I opened a can of beans. She said, "*Wanga*" — That's mine — meaning the can, when it was empty.

Many people were watching me, children sitting in a semicircle, tall skinny girls standing behind them, ten or a dozen women and a few men standing at a little distance, perhaps thirty people altogether, observing Karsten, Wilson, and me as we steamed *nsima* and slopped food out of cans. They had enough to eat themselves — this was not a place deprived of food, but a village where the men fished and the women tilled the fields. Watching us was their evening entertainment.

I became aware of a ripple of laughter that ran through the watchers and I turned to see a small ugly man tottering toward me. From his hideous face, bumpy with boils and growths and seeping wounds, and his withered fingers, I took him to be a leper. But he might also have been an epileptic, because the fresh bruises and his smashed nose were injuries I associated with grand mal sufferers who repeatedly fall down during seizures.

Anyway, for his deformities he must have been considered the village fool — blameless, an object of scorn, teased but also a teaser when he found someone weirder looking than himself. This would be me, the *muzungu* who had wandered into his village.

He took to poking his finger in my plate of *nsima* and pretending to snatch my food. His finger was truly disgusting. His face was stained and gleaming from the leaking wounds, his eyes were crazed, his hands were scaly, leprous, and very dirty. When he opened his mouth to laugh I could see his teeth were broken.

His antics roused the watching villagers to laugh, some in mockery, others in embarrassment, for they were unsure of how I would react to this teasing. But I could see that the little battered man, miserable in his disfigurement and probably simple-minded, was like the Fool in a Shakespeare play, the court jester who is licensed to do or say anything he likes.

"This man is stupid," Karsten said, on my behalf using an unequivocal Chichewa word, *wopusa.*

But I beckoned the man over, and when I gestured I saw a kind of fear come into his eyes. The watching people laughed as the man wobbled toward me on his twisted feet.

I said, "*Mukufuna mankhwala?*" Do you want medicine? I gave him some chocolate cookies I had bought in the little shop in Marka village.

Needing to protect his cookies from the villagers, he ran away. Then we ate in peace, though we were watched the whole time. All the while the children crept closer, nearer to our dying fire.

At last, hoarse with shyness, one of them said, "We want medicine, too."

I gave them cookies and sent them away. Karsten handed the pots and plates to a woman to wash in the river, and he lay back and fired up a postprandial joint.

Since we were going to sleep in the open, the only question I had in my mind was whether there were hyenas in the area. Hyenas root among rubbish, and though they stay out of huts, they have been known to nibble human feet protruding from hut doors, and in some instances to chew the face of the person sleeping nearest the entrance.

"*Palibe mafisi*," Wilson said. No hyenas. But I wanted to hear it from a villager, so when the woman came back with the washed plates, I asked her. I liked her reply, which sounded poetic.

"No hyenas, lots of ghosts." *(Palibe mafisi, alipo mfiti.)*

Curious to ask Karsten a political question, I said, "Do you ever think about the president?"

"No. Because he never thinks about me," he said.

Urging Karsten to pile wood on the fire to keep the snakes away, I sprayed my head and hands and zipped myself into my sleeping bag and went to sleep.

Hyenas and snakes were not the problem. The most dangerous aspects of the river were almost invisible: the wind, the mosquitoes that carry malaria, the biting tsetse flies, and the innocent-looking fruit of a riverside plant called buffalo beans, which causes painful welts on the skin. There were also spiders, scorpions, and in some places big wet frogs that positioned themselves near anyone sleeping in the open and then jumped with a gulp in a great smothering flop onto your face.

We left before dawn, slipping away into the still water, as we had done the day before. I asked Karsten if we would get to the Zambezi today. Maybe, he grunted. *Kapena.* He seemed intent on his paddling, and so I joined him and Wilson, using a board for a paddle, the three of us propelling the dugout forward in silence. It was only after sunup that I remembered what he had said the day before, of the stretch we had traveled: *Bad people there.*

In midmorning, while I sat eating a mango, Karsten said, "There are some hippos coming."

We rounded a bend and there they were, snuffling and looking fierce. Next to humans, they were the most territorial of river critters. I tried to think of the wild animals I had seen since I had left Cairo, but all I came up with were the hyenas in Harar, various antelope in Ethiopia and Kenya, the flamingos in Lake Elmenteita, and the game I had seen from the train in Tanzania. These were my first hippos in months. Hippo meat was sold in Zambezi markets in Mozambique, so Karsten said. Given the rate of deforestation and the growth in population, it was predicted by environmentalists that the day was not far off when the bigger game would be poached out of existence.

Around noon we came to a ferry landing, where a barge was approaching from the east bank, bringing a pickup truck across the river. The white man at the wheel of the vehicle that rolled onto the landing was a South African farmer, growing red peppers on an estate he had bought cheaply from a Portuguese who had bolted. He said he enjoyed living in the remote Mozambican bush.

"South Africa used to be like this," he said. "I don't like what's happening down there."

He had an African foreman to translate work orders for him and to manage the workers, but he seemed completely out of his element — a plump sunburned man in a floppy hat and shorts. The variety of red pepper he grew he sold to a Dutch pharmaceutical firm — the pepper was used in some sort of medicine.

"Aren't you afraid of people coming out of the bush and trespassing or breaking in?"

He thrust out his chest, made a fist, and said with growly authority, "They should be afraid of me."

Karsten and Wilson wandered toward me obliquely to ask for money to buy soft drinks being sold out of a burlap bag — soaked to cool them — by a woman sitting on a crate. I gave them some Malawi money and they walked away. They were very skinny, very ragged, barefoot, bushy-haired.

"Those your chaps?"

It was a significant question, the moment when one *muzungu* sized up another's workers. "My Africans are better than your Africans" was a serious colonial boast. The Africans in the white farmer's pickup truck were dressed in sturdy overalls and floppy-brimmed bush hats. Most wore shoes, one wore rubber boots. By Mozambique standards they were well dressed.

Karsten's and Wilson's clothes were purely symbolic: Karsten's ripped T-shirt and split shorts, Wilson's long-sleeve white shirt draped over his shoulders in ribbons. His shorts, too, were split.

"Yup. Those are my guys," I said. And I thought: In countries where all the crooked politicians wear pinstriped suits, the best people are bare-assed.

Farther downstream, as the river became wider, showing shallows and mudbanks, we saw more hippos. There were herons, too, and hawks and cormorants, and in the clay banks were the riverside nests of white-fronted and carmine bee-eaters.

Karsten said the Zambezi was not far off. Yet nothing was visible ahead except bush, some of it marshland, and where there were huts they lay in small circular compounds. We never passed a cluster of huts without hearing the thudding of a mortar in a pestle — a woman laboring to make flour, sometimes two of them, taking turns raising the heavy pestle. Men fished with throw nets or with boxlike traps woven from reeds. In some trees there were logs, hoisted there to serve as beehives. Livingstone had noticed these cultural features on the Zambezi and on this river, too.

Honey was prized by the Arabs who had come here in the seventeenth and eighteenth centuries, looking for slaves and ivory, and slavers still operated in Livingstone's time. Livingstone said he was here commanding his steamboat, the *Ma Robert*, with the intention of saving souls for Jesus and eliminating the slave trade. But the real intention of this strange depressive man was to open Africa to commerce. The Zambezi he called "God's Highway." He had a negligible impact on the slave trade, the trackless bush of Zambezia was proof that commerce had been a failure, and Livingstone's total number of converts to Christianity was just one man, who later lapsed.

"Zambezi," Karsten said.

God's Highway was in view, a sun-dazzled sheet of water half a mile wide, carrying whole trees and big boughs and enormous logs in its muddy current, debris from the heart of Africa, beautiful flotsam.

I caught a few words of a story that Karsten was telling Wilson — "Indian" and "fish" and "money" — and as we paddled across the Zambezi, our dugout pulled sideways by the power of the stream, he told me the story.

Farther up the Zambezi, on the Zambian side, he said, lived Indian traders who made a practice of abducting very young African girls from villages. The Indians killed the girls and cut out their hearts. Using the fresh hearts of these African virgins as bait on large hooks, they were able to catch certain Zambezi fish that were stuffed full of diamonds.

"That is why the Indians have so much money," Karsten said.

I was so glad to be heading down the Zambezi, I told them both it was a delightful story. In the late 1990s, I had read of riots in Zambia against Indians who were accused of trading illegally in human body parts. The rumor then was that they were killing Africans and disemboweling them, selling their hearts, lungs, and kidneys to Western hospitals, to make money in the organ donor business. Even some Westerners believed this improbable story to be true.

The land beside the river was featureless and flat, a grassy floodplain with a low forest in the distance. We paddled among floating trees and logs in the middle of the river where the current was strongest, eddies giving the water the cloudy, muddy bubbles you see on the surface of a chocolate milk shake. The wide river moved slowly and we had to go on paddling, yet the current helped enough so that I was able to sit back from time to time and reflect.

I was happy. The riverside villages were sorry looking but self-sufficient. No one in the government either helped them or meddled with them. I had sometimes been uneasy about stopping at one of these places, but on the river, borne onward by the muddy water, watched by fishermen and herons and pods of hippos (only their bulging eyes and nostrils showing), protected by Karsten and Wilson, I was the nearest thing on earth to Huckleberry Finn. I had fulfilled one of my fondest yearnings at the outset of my trip, for this was the territory I had lit out for, and cruising down this empty river in a hollow log was pure Huck Finn pleasure.

About two hours after turning from the Shire River into the Zambezi, I heard a loud chugging, the working engine of a tublike vessel making its way from a landing on the north side of the river.

The engine noise was the barge at Caia, big enough to serve as a drive-on ferry for trailer trucks. A British aid group called the Mariners had cobbled together this barge from twelve Uniflote pontoons and the reassembled parts of eight junked engines. This barge-ferry was the only way a wheeled vehicle could travel the hundreds of miles from southern to northern Mozambique.

Caia was a settlement of shacks, drink shops, and squatting Mozambicans. I hopped ashore and held the boat for Karsten, but Karsten stuck out his arm to shake my hand.

"We are going back," he said.

Just turning around, hurrying upstream to the Shire, and heading home. He still had time to get back to the confluence of the Shire and the Zambezi, but it would be upstream from then on. Karsten was looking at the ragged men and boys on shore — they were pestering him, asking him where he had come from — and I knew he was thinking: There are bad people here. Anyone could see that a ferry landing on a wide river would attract the opportunists, the predators, the homeless riffraff, and the lost souls. Instead of helping him land, I palmed some money as a tip and slipped it to him so that the watchers wouldn't see, then I shoved the dugout back into the current.

Meanwhile, the ferry had docked, its lines were secured, and a big topheavy truck of fat sacks was being driven up the embankment, heading toward a lineup of other trucks. With boys tagging along, offering to carry my bag, I went to where the trucks were parked — four of them now. A group of men sat on a restaurant veranda, drinking and eating.

"Okay, meesta," one of them said, laughing at the approach of a *muzungu.*

"*Bom dia,*" I said, and asked whether any of them were going to Beira.

"We are all going," another man said. He was sitting with a spoon in his hand over a bowl of chicken and rice.

"Can you take me?"

Instead of replying he made a motion with his head, and I took this to mean yes. His name was João. I bought two beers, gave him one, and sat down with him. We bargained a little over the price, for I had vowed that for the sake of my family I would not ride on top of any more trucks. After a while he wiped his face on his shirt, paid his bill, and we left, four of us in the cab, about fifteen Africans clinging to the bags of beans on top. Beira was two hundred miles away, on a soft road of sand and mud that led along the old Portuguese railway line. Railways and roads had connected all the provinces in Mozambique. In colonial times there had been a plan to build a railway bridge across the Zambezi at Caia. Part of the foundation had been set into the embankments, but the idea was premature and perhaps grandiose. Even in Caia and its outskirts there were tipped-over railway cars and rusted broken locomotives.

This hinterland had only recently opened. For twenty-five years, two guerrilla actions, one after the other, turned the interior of Mozambique into a war zone. First came FRELIMO's decade-long struggle against the Portuguese. After independence in 1974 an anti-FRELIMO movement called RENAMO was formed, supported mainly by white South Africans and an assortment of right-wing well-wishers in Portugal and the United States. In the RENAMO war millions of people were either killed or displaced, bridges were blown up, communications shattered, roads closed, towns and villages depopulated by massacres. Because of this civil war, the Mozambique Zambezi, from Zumbo to the delta in the Indian Ocean, and the main tributary, the Shire River, were inaccessible to outsiders as well as to many Mozambicans. Throughout the war, the Mozambique bush was a heart of darkness, just as dangerous and confused and hard to penetrate.

It was just after four, so we had about two hours of daylight. In those two hours I saw that every bridge along the road had been destroyed, blown up or burned; every railway track had been twisted apart; and all the old colonial buildings were roofless ruins.

In the middle of nowhere we made a pit stop. Seeing me heading off the road to relieve myself, João said "No!" and waved me to the edge of the truck. He pointed into the woods and said, "Land mines."

It was the conventional wisdom in rural Mozambique that you were not to stray off any main road, nor were you to deviate from any path, for only the well-trodden ways were sure to be free of the mines that had been set and hidden by all those different soldiers, all those well-armed factions.

Darkness fell. We traveled the wet, mushy one-lane road in a tunnel of our own orange headlights. We came to Inhaminga. In Portuguese times Inhaminga had been a good-sized railway town, with a wide main street of two-story shop houses and large villas enclosed by garden walls. But guerrilla conflict and neglect had turned Inhaminga into a ruined settlement of collapsed buildings and rusted machinery and broken rolling stock. Seeing me in the cab of the truck, youths screamed at me.

"White people never come here," João explained.

"How odd."

We arrived at the coast, the edge of Beira, in the early hours of the morning. Since leaving Blantyre, in Malawi, I had not seen an electric light, a telephone, a paved road, or piped water. I did not lament this. I found it restful, for Mozambique was not a country in decline — this part of it, anyway, could not fall any further. Some months before the people had experienced the worst that nature could throw their way — deep, devastating floods — and had survived. As everyone said, the worst aspect of the floods was not the destruction of crops and huts but the uprooting of the land mines, for these explosive devices had floated and moved into different and unknown positions.

The town of Beira was also a ruin. João dropped me off at a hotel on a side street. I slept until midmorning and then went for a walk among abandoned buildings on streets where grass had sprouted. The most interesting building I saw in Beira was the one that had been the Grand Hotel, a huge skeletal structure facing the Indian Ocean. The whole place, a big decrepit gambling resort, had been taken over by plunderers and invaders. These homeless people were living in the guest rooms and had cooking fires going on the balconies and had rigged up tents on the verandas. Some were emptying buckets of shit over the rails; their laundry hung limp on strung-up lines. The building was a vast crumbling pile of broken stucco and rusted railings, filled with ragged squatters. Smoke issued from most of the rooms. I supposed that for some people this looked like the past, but to me it had the haunted look of a desperate distant future, an intimation of how the world would end, the Third World luxury resorts turned into squatters' camps.

In the market, looking for a long-distance bus to Harare, I wandered into a parking lot of battered taxis. A man leaning against an old car said he would drive me the 160 miles to the Mozambique-Zimbabwe border at Machipanda for a reasonable price. He would show me the sights along the way. I said that was fine with me if we could leave soon. We left an hour later. About halfway into the trip he pulled off the road at a junction. An arrow indicated *Nova Vanduzi.* I said, "I don't see anything." Putting on his surliest face, he replied that if I did not pay him more money, he would not take me to Machipanda. I argued for a while, then agreed, but still he whined at me for more money all the way to Machipanda, while I wearily complained to him that I was often the victim of my own trusting nature.

17 ◇◇◇

Invading Drummond's Farm

ZIMBABWE had a fearsome reputation for political mayhem at the time I walked across the eastern border from Mozambique into Mashonaland and caught a bus to the capital. Everything was wrong in the country, so I heard, and it was growing worse: dangerous, disrupted, dispirited, bankrupt. But I couldn't wait to see such extreme strife for myself — the journalistic exaggeration, the possible drama of it, *these are the lucky ones.* Strife makes people talkative, and this is a gift to anyone who wants to write about it. The admonishment "Stay away from farms," in a U.S. embassy advisory on Zimbabwe, made me want to stay on a farm. I had no names, no contacts, just the idle wanderer's distinct confidence that having arrived here I was available for some sort of enlightenment; that I would meet the right people, that I would be fine. I had no idea at that early stage how any of this was going to happen, for I didn't have a friend in the whole country.

Don't go, some people said. But they had warned me about going to Sudan and I had loved that big dusty place. Sitting on the Harare bus, traveling the road through Zimbabwe's eastern highlands, the farming country from Mutare to Marondera, I had an intimation of distress and made a note at the back of the book I was reading: *Not many cars.* It was a beautiful land of tilled fields and browsing cattle and farmhouses, yet it seemed oddly empty, as though a plague had struck. Much of what I saw could have been the set of *Invasion of the Body*

Snatchers, for here and there were perambulating Africans, and I got glimpses of Spam-colored settlers. Apart from these few individuals the place seemed curiously unpeopled and inert.

The book in my lap, which I'd bought in Mutare, helped me understand a little of what was happening. It was *African Tears: The Zimbabwe Land Invasions,* written by Catherine Buckle, a woman who had been robbed in installments. Her Marondera farm had been snatched from her in piecemeal and violent intrusions over a six-month period.

"It's a one-man problem," many white Zimbabweans explained to me. Depending on whom I talked to, they said variously, "The president is out of his mind" or "He's lost it" or "He's off his chump." Even the kindly winner of the Nobel Peace Prize, the Reverend Desmond Tutu, had said, "The man is bonkers."

The Robert Mugabe rumors, which I dutifully collected, depicted the poor thing as demented as a result of having been tortured in a white-run prison: long periods in solitary, lots of abuse, cattle prods electrifying his privates, and the ultimate insult — his goolies had been crimped. Another rumor had him in an advanced stage of syphilis; his brain was on fire. "He was trained by the Chinese, you know," many people said. And: "We knew something was up when he started calling himself 'comrade.'" He had reverted, too — did not make a decision without consulting his witch doctors. His disgust with gays was well known: "They are dogs and should be treated like dogs." He had banned the standard school exams in Zimbabwe, "to break with the colonial past." Some rumors were fairly simple: he had a lifelong hatred of whites, and it was his ambition to drive them out of the country. Of the British prime minister he said, "I don't want him sticking his pink nose in our affairs." Noting all this, I kept thinking of what Gertrude Rubadiri had told me: "We called him 'bookworm.'" Really, there was no deadlier combination than bookworm and megalomaniac. It was, for example, the crazed condition of many novelists and travelers.

The long lines I saw at gas stations told part of the story: Zimbabwe had a gasoline shortage. The new $500 million Harare International Airport had run out of aviation fuel. No hard currency meant a severe reduction in imported goods. There had been food riots in Harare. The opposition parties had been persecuted by the ruling party's goon squads. The unemployment figure had risen to 75 percent, and visitor numbers had dropped by 70 percent. The irrationality of the president was so well known his accusations had ceased to be quoted in the world's press, except for his maddest utterances, such as "I have a degree in violence." Foreign journalists had been attacked, some seriously injured, and others had been deported for trying to cover stories of intimidation and disruption. Fearing the same fate, under "Occupation" on my entry visa application I wrote "Geography teacher."

Zimbabwe had been for years one of the great African destinations, for it had the Zambezi, river rafting, bungee jumping off Victoria Falls Bridge, and so many wild animals that big-game hunting was freely available. Gun-toting hunters banged away at the Big Five: elephants, rhinos, leopards, lions, and buffalo. A Zimbabwean guide told me that some foreign hunters were very fussy and would decline to shoot an elephant if the animal's tusks were four feet instead of five feet long. Zimbabwe was perhaps the only country in Africa where you could legally buy those elephant-foot wastebaskets that gave environmentalists the horrors. Huge, newly chopped-off ivory tusks were also available in Harare shops, and so were the skins of lions and leopards, crocodile belts, elephant- or hippo-hide wallets, and such curiosities as a yard-long giraffe femur with an African landscape scratched on its shank, like scrimshaw.

But tourists and curio collectors and travelers were staying away. The problem was land invasions. The president had actively encouraged veterans of the independence struggle — "landless peasants" — to invade, occupy, and squat in the fields of white farmers and to take their land by force. Many black Zimbabweans had done so to white Zimbabweans, some of them violently. Eight white farmers had been murdered by these intruders, none of whom had been prosecuted — indeed, they were congratulated for achieving their objective, having seized the whites' land and become landowners and gentry themselves. When a High Court judge questioned the legality of the farm invasions he was attacked by the government, and he eventually resigned. As for the stolen farms, in some cases the government had failed to supply the invaders with free maize seed, fertilizer, and tractors, and so they had left the land and returned to city life. Almost two thousand properties had been invaded and occupied; more were promised, so the threat was real.

Whenever a local paper wrote critically of the land invasions, the journalist on the story was arrested or harassed. Foreign journalists were thrown out of the country and their work permits revoked. The editor of the independent *Daily News* and two of his reporters were charged with "criminal defamation" after reporting a well-sourced story about kickbacks connected with the new airport. The briber, the son of a former Saudi oil minister, had whined publicly that he had not received a fair return for his $3 million payoff.

The editor had been the target of an assassination attempt. Zimbabweans said that the proof that it had been government-inspired was its cackhandedness. That it had been botched was certain evidence of the regime's connivance, since it could not do anything right. Another paper, the *Independent*, was being sued for "contempt of parliament" for its verbatim reporting of an incriminating parliamentary debate. A bill had been passed stipulating that music, drama, news, and current affairs programming on Zimbabwe radio and TV had to be purely Zimbabwean, "in order to foster a sense of Zimbabwean national identity and values." Since Zimbabweans had already established themselves as some of the greatest innovators in African music, and its musicians played to large crowds in the United States and Europe, the intention of the bill was to make white Zimbabweans nervous.

"Everything Mugabe says and does is intended to drive the whites away," a white Zimbabwean told me. I replied that it seemed to me that black Zimbabweans were enduring an equally bad time, with such high unemployment, high inflation, unstable currency, and an economy in ruins. Blacks were being driven away too — many had fled to South Africa.

◇ ◇ ◇

But Harare did not look like a ruin. Even in its bankruptcy, Harare was to my mind the most pleasant African city I had seen so far — the safest, the tidiest, the least polluted, the most orderly. After traffic-clogged Cairo, overheated Khartoum, crumbling tin-roofed Addis, crime-ridden Nairobi, disorderly Kampala, demoralized Dar es Salaam, ragged Lilongwe, desperate Blantyre, and battle-scarred and bombed-out Beira, Harare looked pretty and clean, the picture of tranquility, the countryside an Eden.

Much of Harare's apparent peacefulness was due to the extreme tension in the city, for its order was also a sort of lifelessness, the unnatural silence of someone holding his breath. I had the premonition that something was about to happen, within months or a year perhaps, and this was a prelude of silence and inaction before an enormous collapse, a violent election, social disorder, even civil war. It was wrong to mistake this calm for obedience and belief, since it was more likely the natural reserve of people who had already been through serious upheavals. British rule had ended abruptly when a white minority proclaimed a unilateral declaration of independence in 1965. Britain imposed sanctions thereafter, and a ten-year guerrilla war ended with the black majority taking power in 1980, and then began twenty years of Comrade Bob.

Years of sanctions had made Zimbabweans resilient and self-sufficient. Zimbabwe was at its core an independent and proud place, a country that had a manufacturing industry. There was hardly any gasoline or diesel fuel for sale, but most other necessities were available. Even in these hard times, Zimbabweans were still making things — paper products, clothing, household furniture, shoes; they had dairies, bakeries, breweries, meat-processing plants, and canneries. There were many good hotels, though most of them were empty.

Zimbabweans, black and white, grumbled openly. This was new to me. Tanzanians and Malawians had seemed more supine and oblique; they had surrendered and, having abandoned any hope of things improving, were reduced to unapologetic beggary that contained a subtext of entitlement: *My country has failed me, therefore you must help.* Some exasperated Zimbabweans talked of leaving. The man who had sold me my bus ticket asked me where I was from, and responded promptly, "I want to go to America." Another said, "Three years ago this was a good place, but, ah, not anymore." An African woman tapped her head and said in that accent peculiar to black Zimbabwe, "You will be laining a loat" — learning a lot.

Malawi had lowered my spirits. My interlude on the Shire and Zambezi rivers had lifted my mood. In central Mozambique's blighted bush and decayed coastal city my guard had been up. Now, in Harare, I could indulge my passion for walking, for it was a city of sidewalks and parks. I felt stimulated, sensing that I was witnessing something that did not yet have a name; yet its very absence of drama signaled the suspenseful onset of a period of historic change. Something radical was going to happen, no one knew what. At this point, catastrophe was just a warning odor, a tang of bitterness in the air, the sort of whiff that made people put on a listening face and wrinkle their nose and say, "Do you smell something?"

I walked, I began eating good meals — a great novelty on this trip. In the market, I stopped in shops to look at merchandise and note the prices. And at every opportunity I encouraged people to talk about what was happening here. The fuel shortage was on most people's minds, and inflation was at 65 percent and salaries were staying low. A recent strike by government workers had been broken up by police, and many strikers had been injured. For most black Zimbabweans the issue was money, the collapsing economy; for most white Zimbabweans the issue was security, for the lawlessness of the farm invasions made all whites, even the urban business people, feel insecure.

Soon after I arrived, a morning headline in the *Daily News* was "Government to Acquire 95 More Commercial Farms." The text explained that this was not a business deal — no money was changing hands. This was "compulsory acquisition as part of the ongoing land reform and resettlement program." These 95 farms brought to 3,023 the number of commercial farms singled out by the government as ripe for invasion in the past three years. The names of the farms were listed.

The leader of the militant War Veterans Association was an angry AIDS-stricken doctor named Chenjerai Hunzvi, who had nicknamed himself "Hitler." Well-documented stories had appeared in Zimbabwe newspapers stating that Hitler Hunzvi's suburban medical office was used for viciously torturing men who refused to support him. Hunzvi threatened whites and sent gangs to their farms. Hunzvi's bluster was the irrationality of someone who knows he is doomed, raving in his ill health, yet Mugabe's government backed him up in his reckless threats.

So, because he was a white Zimbabwean (and there were many), a farmer who had already been up for hours at his chores would go back to his house for breakfast and, finding his name in the morning paper, expect a mob of veterans to be camping on his land before lunchtime. If he was lucky, they would demand a portion of his property; if he was unlucky, they would threaten him with weapons and tell him to leave, screaming (as many of the farm invaders did), "This is my farm now!"

This is precisely what happened to Catherine and Ian Buckle, as recounted in Mrs. Buckle's *African Tears,* which had just appeared in bookstores. One day in March 2000, three dozen men invaded their farm, singing songs and shouting "*Hondo*" — the Shona word for "war" and also a popular song by the Zimbabwean singer-composer Thomas Mapfumo. The Buckles had owned the farm for ten years and had been assured on buying it that it was not designated on the government list for resettlement. But that was a detail; events moved quickly. A man introduced himself: "I am the one sleeping on your farm." The reason for his salutation was that he needed the Buckles' help. Would they give him a ride into town so he could get some money to pay the other men who were illegally squatting with him? A week or so after that, a Zimbabwe flag was hoisted on the property. An African beer hall was built, and soon there were drunks on the farm, and a larger squatter camp, and more singing on the premises.

Neighboring farms were occupied. Farmers who resisted were attacked. A number of them were murdered. The Buckles appealed to the government to help them stop the illegal occupation of their land. Nothing was done. No police were sent, though more war vets showed up and demanded that the Buckles loan them their farm truck so they could go to political rallies to denounce white farmers.

At last the leader of a drunken gang appeared and chanted, "This is my fields! This is my cows! This is my grass! This is my farm!" He ordered Mrs. Buckle to leave her house. "This is my house!" The Buckles resisted his intimidation. Soon after, the defiant group of war vets started a grass fire on the property, and when it overwhelmed the farm and threatened the house, the Buckles' will was broken. A malevolent man emerged from the smoke and said fiercely, "*Siya*" — Leave. And so, six months after the first threat the Buckles departed, fearing for their lives, losing everything.

In his introduction to *African Tears,* Trevor Ncube, editor in chief of the Zimbabwe *Independent,* described the story as "one family's struggle against state-sponsored terror."

All this news was fairly fresh. Less than a year after the Buckles were forced off their farm, I had passed near it, outside Marondera.

And then I was in Harare, on my walking tour. On a side street, in a shop that sold African artifacts, I was examining some objects that looked old — that is, worn by common use. Any carving that had acquired a patina or was rubbed smooth by years of handling or had the smoky smell of use attracted me. Cooking implements — bowls, spoons, stirrers — interested me, and so did wooden tools — clubs, hatchets, digging sticks, stools. I happened to be holding a carved wooden slingshot. Turned upside down, it was a figure with a head and wide-apart legs.

"What's the story with this?" I asked the woman at the counter. "Is this old?"

She said, "See how it's blackened? It's been scorched in a fire to harden the wood. It's Chokwe, I think." She thought a moment and added, "But I go on the assumption that nothing is old."

That wise and honest statement from a dealer in artifacts made me trust her. She was a woman of about sixty, white-haired, plainspoken, African-born of English parents. Her son was a farmer, and of course worried about his fate, but he had not been invaded. We talked some more. I said I wanted to meet a farmer whose land had been invaded.

"I know one. He's rather outspoken. He might talk to you. He's got a mobile phone in his truck."

She picked up her phone and called him, explaining my request in a few sentences. Then she listened closely, thanked him, and hung up.

"He's rather busy, but he'll be at this coffee shop later this morning." She wrote the name of the coffee shop on a piece of paper. "He said you're welcome to join him."

That was how I met Peter Drummond, a tall white-haired man in his mid-fifties, his weather-beaten face softened by his blue ironic eyes. He had been aged by military service and farm work and political harassment, which was a condition of being a white farmer in Zimbabwe. He was gentle but very tough and full of plans. He had a habit of prefacing a remark by saying, "This is a very funny story," and then relating something horrific, involving machine guns and blood. "Very funny" usually meant a narrow escape.

He owned a seven-thousand-acre farm outside the town of Norton, which was about fifty miles west of Harare. He grew maize for seed, grew vegetables, raised cattle and pigs, and had a dairy; two of his sons helped him. Peter himself ran the chicken operation. Every week he imported 23,000 day-old chicks from the United States, and these he reared for local consumption, slaughtering them, freezing some, selling others fresh. He trucked 4,300 dressed birds, some fresh, some frozen, into Harare every day, and supplied markets, shops, hotels, and restaurants. Like many other big farmers he was helping to feed Zimbabwe, but he was not finding it easy.

What concerned Drummond was the war veterans trespassing on his land — the disruption, the violent threats, the drunkenness, their cutting down his trees, killing his animals, frightening his family. And because of the diesel fuel shortage, he could not operate many of his tractors. This season, a great deal of his land had gone unplowed and unplanted. Weeds grew where there should have been crops.

"The funny thing is that I was on Japanese TV talking about the situation," he said. "I was pretty frank. The afternoon of the day it aired, I got a death threat."

"Verbal or in writing?"

"Phone rang. African voice. 'You've been pushing the MDC'" — the opposition, the Movement for Democratic Change. "'We're going to kill you.'"

The Movement for Democratic Change and its leader, Morgan Tsvangirai, criticized the government for its policy of sanctioning the illegal farm invasions and turning a blind eye to the violence. The government's ruling party reacted by accusing the MDC of being in cahoots with the white farmers and by refusing to allow the MDC to use rural sports stadiums for political rallies. The reporting of any criticisms was suppressed.

"So I made a tape of all the news that was appearing on the BBC, Sky News, South African News, and CNN," Drummond said. "I had about twenty minutes of it, showing what the foreign correspondents were saying about Zimbabwe. And I played the tape to my workers — I've got about two hundred of them. I said, 'You look at this. It's what the foreign press is saying. I'm not saying a word. If I get involved, I might get killed.'"

He had bought his first farm in 1975, during the struggle. "I didn't have much money, but lots of farmers were being killed, so farms were cheap. I bought a three-thousand-acre farm on the never-never." He worked the land and assumed he would be there for some time. "But we were attacked in 1979 by a group of fifteen men. It's quite a funny story."

It was a terrifying story. He was woken by the sound of gunfire, thirty shots, an entire magazine of an AK-47 fired into his cook's house. "Missed him! Providential, I say!" Drummond had an AK himself. He crept out of the house, which was surrounded by a barrier wall. "That was to protect us from rockets. They were using Russian RPG-7 rockets, which explode after they penetrate a wall. That way, they would explode after the first wall and leave the house intact." He took a brick out of the barrier wall and emptied a magazine at the intruders. "Two of my men started shooting. Everyone was shooting." The fifteen attackers fled. And when a farmers' rescue team hurried to help, they found an arms cache on his property — weapons, explosives, and land mines, enough for the all-out assault that was thwarted.

"Like I say, this is quite a funny story," he repeated. "My boys were five, four, and one. My wife went to wake them up. My son Garth said, 'What's all the noise?' 'It's nothing,' my wife says. Garth turns over and says, 'Dad will shoot them.' He was so calm. We were all calm."

He sold that farm and bought another, sharing pastures with a friend on a large piece of adjacent land. These two farms were sold to the government for resettlement.

"We had reassurances from the government that when we bought again there would be no more resettlement issues — no invasions."

With the proceeds of the sale Drummond bought the land he presently farmed, the seven-thousand-acre Hunyani Estate. He planted trees and built a house to live in and a machine shop and the chicken operation. He plowed, he introduced cattle, and in one section some wild game — eland and impala. All this investment meant he had to borrow heavily. He was paying off a housing loan as well as a half-million-dollar overdraft at the bank.

"Then we were invaded," he said, smiling grimly. "It's quite funny, really. The guy's not really a war veteran. He was a driver during the struggle. Just looking for free land."

All this time, sitting in the coffee shop, I was scribbling in the little notebook on my knee.

Drummond said, "Aren't you hungry?"

I said I was.

"Come to lunch," he said. "I'm meeting my family in about ten minutes in a restaurant near here. It's pretty good food. I sell them their chickens."

Ten minutes later I was sitting at a big table eating roast chicken with the Drummond family — Peter, his wife, Lindsay, two of his four boys, Troy and Garth, and Garth's girlfriend, Lauren.

To be so suddenly and casually gathered into the bosom of this generous family on a hot day in Harare was one of the tenderest episodes of my trip. The hospitality of farmers in the bush of southern Africa is well known, but this was more than hospitality. I was a stranger, and sharing a meal is peacemaking, so including me at their table represented a profound ceremony of acceptance and goodwill.

"This is kind of a family council," Drummond said.

The specific purpose of this gathering, their deciding how to spend their spring vacation, made the meal even more significant. They talked about what they might do: go camping in the bush, visit Lake Kariba in the north, drive to the coast of Mozambique for a swimming holiday, stay on the farm together. "We have to do it cheap. We have no money." The discussion went round and round, and to a loner on a safari through Africa, this cozy manifestation of family life was like heaven.

After they settled on the trip to Mozambique, Peter Drummond said to his son Garth, "I told Paul about the time we were attacked by those fifteen guys."

"And you weren't scared," I said.

Garth said, "I was never scared."

Lindsay said, "We never made the war an issue. I just said, 'If there's trouble, get under your beds.'"

"Still, ten percent of the white farmers were killed and, of the rest, half of them left the country," Lauren said.

Lauren was a woman in her mid-twenties, attractive and forthright, brought up on a farm in rural Zimbabwe.

"My father's farm was occupied by invaders," she told me. "It was called Chipadzi Farm. My father had owned it for years. A local chap was Chief Chipadzi. One day he came to my father and said, 'This is my farm.' Just claimed it as his own. The government was against us. What could we do? My father and mother emigrated to Australia — Toowoomba, west of Brisbane. But they're not farming anymore."

"What happened to Chipadzi Farm?"

Drummond said, "That's rather a funny story. Tell him, Lauren."

"We went by it not long ago. There's a little planting, not much. Small patches of maize here and there. Just subsistence."

They were back to hoes and hand weeding. But her father's mechanized farm had produced enough maize to feed a thousand people.

"The trouble these days is that we don't have decent weapons,"

Drummond said. "We used to have AKs and backup from the security forces. But if we have a problem now, the police don't help us."

"We've had war vets with AKs walking around our garden," Lindsay said. "I see them all the time. Trying to frighten us. I felt more secure before, during the struggle."

"I've got five big combretum trees," Drummond said. "They're indigenous — very pretty. I love those trees. Well, one Sunday we were coming home from church and saw a war vet there, just a local drunk. He had cut down one of my trees. It left a big gap. It was to send a message, see. But that made me angrier than almost anything I could think of. Came to my house and cut down my own tree!"

The drunk had another annoying habit. Whenever he needed money, he met with local Africans and sold them parcels of Drummond's farm.

"They pitch up all the time, showing me pieces of paper that say that they now own some of my land," Drummond said. "You should come out and see them. It's really quite funny."

"I'd love to invade your farm," I said, and we agreed on a day.

◇ ◇ ◇

Since tourists and white hunters and even overland travelers were avoiding Zimbabwe, I was curious to know what the minister of tourism was doing to counter the impression that the country was a black hole. Impersonating a harmless journalist, I asked to see the man who held this post, and to my surprise he agreed to see me. This was Edward Chindori-Chininga, member of parliament and minister for environment and tourism.

When I went to the ministry, a secretary greeted me and asked me to wait — "the minister is running late." I sat on the leather sofa in his outer office, put my head back, and went to sleep. I awoke refreshed a half-hour later, ready to meet the man.

The minister was young and fat, around thirty, and personable, wearing a tight dark suit and a silk tie. He was from Kanyemba, in the northeast corner of Zimbabwe, on the Zambezi.

"Don't the two-toed Vadoma people live up there?" I asked.

He said that was correct but had nothing to add to what I already knew: a genetic trait in the hobbling, limping tribe produced people with strange split-apart feet, literally cleft-footed.

The minister himself was a member of the Shona tribe and was quick to point out that the Shona were losing their cultural values and traditional beliefs. "People say our beliefs are devilish or what-what. But you can't run away from your good culture."

"Give me an example of your good culture."

"The belief that no family can exist without respect for ancestors."

"But I believe that myself," I said.

"I see how you people in the United States mourn your dead."

"Of course we do. Everyone in the world mourns their dead," I said.

"And they must always be consulted, because ancestors control and influence our day-to-day life."

"I don't know about 'influence.'"

"Seriously influence," the minister said. "If there is a problem in a family here — a boy in prison or a girl unhappy — we consult our ancestors and find we can heal the problem. If something is wrong, I myself go to my home village and see my *mondhoro*" — the healer, but the Shona word also meant "lion."

This healer was the repository of all local history and especially knew the lineage of everyone in the village. The minister emphasized that the *mondhoro* had no books, nothing written: the history was all in his head. Hearing of a person's difficulty, he could relate it to something that had happened in the past — a long-dead ancestor who was exerting a malign influence on the present. I liked this belief for its completeness and for its insistence that no one died: the dead were ever present.

"We also have animals who help us," the minister said. "Every African in Zimbabwe has a link with an animal. When people meet here they often ask, 'What is your totem?'"

So I asked him, "What is your totem?"

"A certain mouse," the minister said. "It is the one animal I cannot eat. For some people it is an eland, or a zebra, or an elephant. Mine is a specific mouse, *nhika* — I don't know the name in English. It is very tiny. It has a white patch on its head. Some people, they eat it, but not myself, no."

I mentioned to him that buses in Zimbabwe sometimes had an animal painted on the back.

"Those are totems," he said. "So you see, our people are respectful of animals because of their totems."

"How do you explain all the poaching, then?"

"People are hungry. The economy is way down, in a bad situation," the minister said, and then he became cheerful. "There are benefits, though. The situation shows us that we need to be self-reliant. No one outside Zimbabwe will necessarily come to our rescue. We will have to learn to help ourselves."

In great contrast to Malawi, Tanzania, and Kenya, Zimbabwe was not a destination for the white Land Rover and the charitable effort and the foreign agent of virtue. There was little for the Hunger Project or Save the Children to do, since there was no starvation and the children were generally in good shape. The country's patchy history as British-ruled Southern Rhodesia, the renegade white-ruled Republic of Rhodesia, and finally Zimbabwe had already forced people to learn important lessons in self-help. But the minister's hint of the pariah status of Mugabe's government I saw as my chance to bring up the subject of the war veterans and the farm invasions. I said, "Doesn't this situation worry you?"

"It is complicated. Everything has been mixed up together." He clawed at the back of his neck and went on gabbling, embarrassed by my direct question. "Yes, some land has been taken away and some farms have been resettled by so-called invaders. But the people who have taken the land are being productive. It is not what the papers are saying. People reporting should see for themselves."

"I'm going to look. I've heard that the seized farms are a lot less productive and that there's a maize shortage," I said. "But even so, taking the land by force is illegal, isn't it?"

"Maybe you could say we need a level of political maturity," the minister said, with what I felt was unusual candor. "Competing parties have to speak to each other. We have to see that the country is more important than our philosophies. And maybe you can help us."

I leaned forward and said, "What would you like me to do?"

"You can portray the positive aspects of life here," the minister said. "You can dispel the image of instability."

"I'll do what I can, sir," I said, and then with gusto he went back to discussing the ambiguous prohibitions of the Shona people.

◈ ◈ ◈

The day that I drove out to Peter Drummond's farm I heard on the radio that the British government had stopped aid to Zimbabwe and canceled a large loan, because of the "resettlements" — farm invasions. Two reasons for the British move were mentioned: the land was not being given to the poor, and none of this was being done legally. That news had Chenjerai "Hitler" Hunzvi screaming denunciations of the British.

"You can see for yourself," Peter Drummond said. He had picked me up at my hotel. "Talk to the squatters. Talk to my people. Talk to anyone you like. Stay on the farm."

I told him the conciliatory remarks the minister had made about the need for political maturity in Zimbabwe and for the different parties to speak to each other.

"Maybe he was telling you what you wanted to hear," Drummond said. "But also there are a lot of reasonable people in the government. I'm sure you've heard that it's a one-man problem."

"Everyone says it."

"He hates us."

In that year's Independence Day speech, President Mugabe referred to whites in Zimbabwe as snakes: "The snake we thought was dead is coming back again. The whites are coming back!" And the Movement for Democratic Change he saw as a "puppet" of the whites, who were antigovernment.

The white farmers generally were so accustomed to adversity that simple-minded abuse — being called snakes — just made them shrug.

Outside Harare the road straightened, became narrower, closely fenced, with plowed fields on either side and regular stands of trees, which marked the presence of farmhouses. After twenty miles we were in open country, grazing land and in places tall maize stalks drying and turning brown, awaiting the harvest.

"How's business?"

Drummond chuckled. He said, "Could be better. There are the thefts, of course. We discovered that between November and March several of the workers have been stealing chickens. Quite a few. So for three months we lost all our profit. Also, because it was an inside job, the thefts buggered our books."

"What happened to the thieves?"

"They still work for me. I couldn't sack them because they're politically connected — there would have been trouble. The police wouldn't have been helpful either."

Thefts by employees were not unusual, he said. Old-timers stole diesel fuel, maize bags routinely disappeared from trucks on the way to market, tools were pinched. So many chickens had been stolen that the bookkeeping and delivery figures were skewed, and for three months Drummond could not service his bank loan.

"It's pretty funny," he said. Then he gestured out the window and said, "My estate starts about here."

We drove for miles after that. Drummond explained that he had recently learned that a mining company had been given permission from the government to look for minerals on his land. The miners had discovered a vast platinum deposit beneath an extensive dike on his property. The bad news was that although he owned the diesel fuel, the stony fields, the pigpens, and the chicken houses that were being raided, the platinum deposit was not his.

"I don't own what's under my land. That belongs to the government. They can do whatever they like with it."

Drummond's house was on a little hill, a *kopje,* at the end of a dusty track. On the way, we passed some of his workers — men repairing fences, cutting grass, tinkering with the plumbing at water troughs. Drummond spoke to them in Shona and the patois known in Zimbabwe as Chilapalapa.

The house he had built for himself was made of bricks he had fired in his own kiln, and thatched with grass that had been cut on his own land. The mortar was made from mixing the clay from anthills with sand. It was not large, a squarish house with a sitting room upstairs in what would have been the attic, several rooms cluttered with books and files, much of it decorated with African handicrafts. Nearby were stables, workers' houses, clumps of banana trees, and a lovely rose garden. The compound was simple and comfortable while retaining the look of a headquarters. Drummond's great regret was that he had not put a fireplace in the house.

"It can get cold here. We have frost in June."

His estate lay on the shore of a large lake, Manyame (formerly Lake Robertson). After he had taken me around some of his land, I had the impression that his farm was more than a simple settlement; it resembled a small town, with the same solid infrastructure. It had good roads, a gas station, a fuel depot, a substantial machine shop, a garage, a main road, a piggery, sheep and lambs in the fields, a chicken factory, cattle grazing, lots of crops, and plenty of water. The various operations were located on different parts of the land, requiring a great deal of driving. He had two hundred workers and, including dependents, there were four hundred people altogether on the property, in a workers' village of substantial huts.

I remarked on the self-sufficiency of the place and its orderly appearance. I was impressed by the way he recycled the chicken byproducts, using the manure and the plucked feathers to fertilize the crops.

He dismissed my praise. He said any look of prosperity was illusory, and that ever since diesel fuel had been rationed he had had to cut back on his operation. "What you see is a farm working at half its capacity."

At the chicken station he said, "A woman came here not long ago and told me she wanted some of my land. The Zimbabwean women are keen and they have a good work ethic. She said she wanted to build a house here" — he indicated a field near a warehouse. "She planned to hook up her electricity to my line there. That way, she'd have lights and I would be paying her electric bill for the rest of her life. Good arrangement, eh?"

"Was she a war vet?"

"That's what I asked her!" He laughed, remembering the woman. "She said, 'In a way.' I said, 'Where were you fighting?'"

"You talk to Africans about these things?"

"Oh, sure. I tell them I was fighting for my side," he said. "I ask them where they were fighting. I tease them a little. They can take it. As ex-soldiers, we have a lot in common. That war is history. It's over. It was foolish for us to think that a small number of whites could govern millions of Africans."

"Do you get into the specifics of the war?"

"Yeah. I often say, 'Oh, you were in that sector? I was in that sector, too. I was probably shooting at you.'"

"What kind of a reaction do you get?"

"A good one," Drummond said. "We often talk about the people who didn't fight — the informers. I say, 'Oh, you had information from whites? What did you think of that?' They say, 'We just used them.' No fondness for them, see. I say, 'Well, we had African informers. We just used them, too.'" Drummond looked at me to make his point. "The informers weren't fighting. I can't talk to an informer. But a fighter — that's another story."

Back in the car, driving around his estate, he must have been ruminating on this and wanting me to understand, because out of the blue he said with emphasis, "A certain bond exists between ex-fighters — the soldiers. We each had our own side, but we shared a common experience."

That night in his farmhouse, poring over a map of his estate, he told me of various plans he had to keep the place viable. One was to subdivide a portion of the land and sell off parcels to Zimbabweans, who would become smallholders, growers of flowers or vegetables, making the farm a sort of cooperative. The idea was not to hand the parcels out to invaders and squatters but to sell each one with a legal title.

"Or maybe time-share cottages," Drummond said, sketching a corner with his finger. "And this whole area could be retirement homes." He indicated some water holes and said, "Perfect for campgrounds. Already this area attracts eland, kudu, and impala. We could put up a huge fence and manage some of the estate as a game reserve."

I looked at the map and imagined the cottages, the bungalows, the tents, the long-horned animals.

"Or maybe I'll go to Australia," Drummond said. "But I really want to stay here. The trouble is, I have this debt. Inflation is sixty-five percent, I get my chicks from the U.S. and have to pay in U.S. dollars, and the Zim dollar is falling."

The night was cold and clear, the bright moon reflected on the lake. Except for the barking dogs — a big Labrador retriever and a frisky Jack Russell terrier — there was silence. Whenever the dogs yapped I thought we were being invaded, and I imagined war vets, thieves, opportunists, predators.

"I'll just check those dogs," Drummond said. Perhaps he was anxious, too.

Still, I preferred this farm to Harare, to being in a hotel, a town, or a city. I kept thinking how much like old Russia this was — old America, too. And how the stories I liked best had seldom been tales of the city but nearly always the gothic fictions and tragicomedies of rural life: Olive Schreiner's *The Story of an African Farm*, Etienne Leroux's Welgevonden trilogy, Doris Lessing's *The Grass Is Singing* (set near Drummond's farm), Chekhov's provincial dramas, books by writers of the American South — Faulkner and Flannery O'Connor, the best work of Mark Twain, all of their comic gloom and isolation summed up in Gogol's evocative title *Evenings on a Farm near Dikanka*.

Morning at Drummond's farm was clear and bright, the cold dew sparkling on the long grass. I had been woken by the dogs and by Drummond's comings and goings. At breakfast he said he was off with two of his men to Karoi, about 120 miles north, to build a classroom as payment in kind for his daughter Misty's school fees.

His parting words were "My son Troy will be over to take you around. Talk to anyone you like."

Troy was twenty-six, an Olympic windsurfer who had recently represented Zimbabwe in an international tournament in New Caledonia, in the western Pacific, earning a respectable place. He was modest, soft-spoken, easygoing, and knowledgeable about modern farm methods. He and his brother Shane supervised the seed maize, the pigs, the horses, and the vehicles. He had farmed the tobacco, but "my father doesn't smoke, tobacco's against his philosophy, so we phased it out."

He said, "My father said to show you anything you wanted to see."

"I'd like to talk to the invaders."

"We can do that."

"But don't tell me anything in advance. I want to get acquainted myself."

Laughing, Troy said, "They're friendly blokes anyway."

We drove across the estate, and again I was reminded of the size and complexity of the place, which seemed bigger than a town now and more like a whole county.

The first invader was not at home. Stakes had been pounded into the ground to mark his fields — quite an irony, too, since the stakes were also a warning to possible intruders on the land he had seized. I saw no crops. The hut was a shanty, the improvements derisory.

"Not much action here," I said.

We took another road and after fifteen minutes or so turned onto a narrow track. At the margin of the track was a field planted with maize that looked just sprouted, though this was nearly the harvest season. Nothing was pickable.

"That's not a crop," I said. "There's nothing to eat here."

Obeying my request not to tell me anything, Troy shrugged.

In the distance, in front of four round, well-made huts with conical roofs, was a skinny tortoise-faced man in a dirty T-shirt waving his arms.

"That's another one," Troy said.

Attempting to ingratiate myself, I greeted the African in Chichewa. I wasn't surprised that he answered me, since Chichewa was widely spoken outside Malawi. But he said that he had learned it in Zambia, where he had lived for twenty-one years. His mother was a Zambian. His name was Reywa, and he had a large family, all of them living with him on the land he had seized from the Drummond family.

"What were you doing in Zambia?" I asked him in English.

"I was a driver."

"Are you a war vet?"

"No. No fighting. I am landless."

"I thought only war vets could invade the land."

"A war vet said I could come here," Reywa said.

I said to Troy, "He's just a guy who wants land."

Troy said, "Right."

"Reywa, your garden isn't doing too well."

He started to scream at me, his tightened face even more tortoise-like. "Garden is nothing! Because I planted too late! The government promised seed, fertilizer, use of a tractor. But they didn't give me. I just waited for them until it was too late. They didn't help me!" He was whining and moaning. "I did this all myself by hand — yes, myself!"

"But there's nothing to eat here."

"Near the anthill some maize is bigger." He indicated a mound about forty yards off with tall plants on its dome. "I have some pumpkin blossoms to eat, some small tomatoes." He turned to Troy and said, "I need a fence. The animals will come here and eat my plants. Tell your father he must put up a fence or else."

"Or else what?" I asked.

His beaky face became agitated and he said, "Or else there will be war! Because I must have a fence." He kicked at the edge of his garden in frustration. He said, "Next year will be better. The government will help me."

"What if they don't help you?"

"Then Mr. Drummond will help me."

"Why should Mr. Drummond help you? After all, you invaded his land."

"Because I was landless."

"Now you have land."

"What good is land if I don't have a tractor? Mr. Drummond has a tractor. He must help me. He will plow for me."

"Why should he do that for you?"

"He has money!" Reywa screamed. "I am poor!"

"He owes twenty-two million dollars to the bank," I said.

"I don't care. If Mr. Drummond does not plow for me, then" — Reywa paused and scowled at Troy, conveying a message — "then we do not understand each other."

Having invaded the land and staked his claim and put up four big huts, he now wanted free seed, free fertilizer, and the fields plowed at his bidding, his victim working the tractor. It was like a thief who, having stolen a coat, insisted that his victim have the coat dry-cleaned and tailored to fit. Reywa was very cross in anticipation of any delay in these demands being met.

We sat in front of the largest hut and I sketched a hypothetical episode. Reywa had seized a large piece of Mr. Drummond's land — too large for him to plant it all, that was obvious. What if, I said, someone came along and saw that little work had been done on the farthest acres — for "neglected land" was one of the conditions that sanctioned a farm invasion. What would happen if someone wanted to squat and build a little hut on that corner of his land? What would Reywa do to an invader on his farm?

Almost before I finished speaking, Reywa was frowning with aggression and hyperventilating through flared nostrils. "No! No! I have nothing! I would chase them away!"

He saw no contradiction; the thought of someone taking even a small part of his land just enraged him. He got up and began to pace. He shook his fist and then pointed to his stunted maize.

"It almost happened. A stupid war vet from here needed some money, so he sold some of my land. People came! They said, 'This is our land.'"

"What did you do, Reywa?"

He clamped his teeth and said, "I send them away!"

So what I had given as a grotesque hypothesis of ingratitude had actually taken place.

Troy said, "You want to see the others?"

I said no. I didn't have the stomach for this absurdity. I hung around and looked at Troy's horse and then at a 1962 Land Cruiser he was restoring to its original luster. "Notice the bullet holes in the door? They're from the struggle."

Later on, near the lake, I chatted with an African who owned a fishing cooperative. He was Joseph, a Malawian, who said the farm invasions were "a disaster." I asked him what he thought of his homeland, Malawi. "Hopeless," he said. He added that he seldom went home, because it so happened that he was successful in his fishing business.

"If I go back to Malawi my relatives will borrow money and eat my food and make me poor."

Joseph explained that protecting what you had achieved was a serious problem in this part of Africa. He was not speaking of the white farmers whose land had been invaded, but he could have been. If someone had money or land or food, onlookers were attracted, feeling they were entitled, and everyone tried to take something.

Later that day, Troy drove me back to Harare. He pointed out various farms that had been invaded. He indicated something else — how Africans took shortcuts through fields of maize on the white farms, both as a convenience and as an insult. These tracks ran willy-nilly through otherwise neat rows of maize.

Seeing an African man and woman hitchhiking, Troy slowed and asked them where they were going. "Harare," the man said. Troy said they could get into the truck. This was the countryside, where it was common to pick up hitchhikers or people waiting at bus stops.

I said, "If I were hitchhiking here, would an African pick me up?"

"Probably," he said. "But they'd expect you to pay them something. They know we never ask. But they always demand money from each other."

Like his father, he spoke without bitterness. Then we jogged along the country road in silence, in sunshine, under a big blue African sky, until the people in the back rapped on the window, asking to be dropped off.

I stayed in Harare a few more days, fascinated by the apparent order — children in school uniforms, solemn policemen directing very little traffic, big empty department stores, flower sellers, coffee shops, street sweepers, and a serenity that I now realized was extreme tension.

One of the Americans I met in Harare was a former journalist who owned a house in the suburbs. He had no plans to leave. He said, "This is the best city in Africa. This is a wonderful country. It's going through a bad patch at the moment." Another man was a diplomat. He said, "I want to stay here, to see how things turn out."

18 ◇◇◇

The Bush Border Bus to South Africa

SOUTHWARD one hot morning down the hot straight road out of Harare — a farm fence on either side, past the grazing land of white-owned cattle ranches with names like Broad Acres and Sunset, a sentry at every gate, a raptor on most telephone poles, always a watching hawk here — to South Africa. What a pleasure it was to leave Harare on a sunny day, sitting in an upholstered seat on this long-distance bush bus, on the road that began in Cairo.

Low white farm buildings were dwarfed by bougainvillea as high as apple trees. Rivulets and little streams, and the land so flat and rural I might have been on a back road in Ohio. But every now and then there was an emphatic reminder of Africa: a bungalow-sized anthill, an African in a blue suit and porkpie hat pedaling a bike, a fat-bellied zebra and a skinny horse grazing side by side, an ostrich under a tree, glaring in disapproval, a monkey picking his teeth on a fence post, and the distinct signs of farm invasions — crude huts, the Zimbabwe flag, stacks of gum tree poles for another hut, and in large farm fields small circumscribed maize patches where there should have been a whole hillside of stalks. In the bright dusty town of Dryton twenty-two cars were lined up at a gas station because of the shortage of fuel.

The pious voice of the driver animated the bus's loudspeaker: "With the help of Almighty Goad we will be guided on our jinny and shall be safe in His divine hayns."

Had I chuckled? Perhaps. All I ever thought of when on an African bus was the standing headline "Many Dead in Bus Plunge Horror." Whatever noise I had made provoked the man sitting next to me, who was fingering a devotional pamphlet, to lift his face near mine.

"Are you a Christian?" he asked.

This impertinence I found to be a frequent inquiry in Africa.

"Let's say I have a lot of questions."

"I was like you once," he said.

Where do people learn to talk like this? I could see that he believed himself to be, as the man said, in sole possession of the truth. The odd thing was that I happened to be working on my erotic story of the young man and the older woman, started in Egypt and now more than half completed in a notebook. I smiled at the evangelist, indicated my work, and went on writing, the notebook on my knee.

In that somber starry light was a specter handing me a wine glass, and still she wore her lace gloves. I drank and touched her hand and was surprised by the warmth of the lace, how her flesh had heated her gloves, and when I reached to touch her breasts I was surprised by the way in which her body had heated her silk chemise, her gown, her sleeves . . .

The land was dry, the grass a dusty green that turned it silver in the sun. One hour passed, and another, and a third, all of unvarying pretty pastures. Every so often the sign of a farm — a hot straight road running at right angles to this main road — white dust, the soft talcum of the deep countryside, two parallel wheel tracks disappearing into the distance.

The African man next to me was smiling the triumphant patronizing smile of the true believer.

"What sort of questions?" he asked.

"Like, do you eat crows?" I said, and I quoted Deuteronomy, chapter and verse, and added a few more inedible abominations of the Mosaic law that most people in Zimbabwe would have been delighted to eat in a stew with their evening sadza porridge.

The man equivocated.

I said, "How do you interpret chapter ten in the Acts of the Apostles, when Peter has the vision of the unclean animals in the house of Cornelius?"

"I asked you a simple question and you are asking me ones that are not simple."

"Here is a simple one," I said. "Jesus was born two thousand years ago. What happened to the millions of people who were born before Jesus? Were they saved?"

"They are damned for worshiping false idols," he said.

"I see. What is your name?"

"Washington," he said.

"Washington, what is your tribe?"

"I am Shona."

"Excellent." I said that since the minister of tourism had given me to believe that a person was enlightened and calmed by consulting a traditional healer, a *mondhoro*, what did Washington, as a Shona, think of that?

"Spirit worship is pagan and *mondhoros* are responsible for the deaths of many children."

He explained that the *mondhoro* could diagnose a problem, but often the solution required sacrificing a young boy or girl. Ritual slaughter was as common as brewing beer or finding a certain herb to undo a curse.

"The child is then strangled."

"Don't look at me," I said. "Many people in your government, including your president, believe that *mondhoros* must be consulted."

"Then they are wrong," he said. "If you trust in Almighty God you will be saved."

"And if Almighty God had been an immense duck capable of emitting an eternal quack, we would all have been born web-footed, each as infallible as the pope. And we would never have had to learn to swim," I said, somewhat misquoting Henry James's father.

But it did the trick. Washington saw that he was wasting his time with me. He went back to his devotions, and I wrote a bit more of my story. Then I looked out the window at the rocks resembling ruins, tumbled temples on the summits of small rounded hills, the litter of boulders looking like broken-apart foundations, reminiscent of the monumental boulders on the plains near Mwanza in far-off Tanzania by the lakeshore. Yet these rocks were even more forceful reminders of the stately piled-up stones in Great Zimbabwe, which was just over the next hill, near the town of Masvingo.

When we came to Masvingo, I thought of lingering and visiting the ruins. But it was against my temperament to go sightseeing, and

Washington got off the bus here, which was an inducement for me to stay on.

Masvingo was a lovely country town. I thought that I could live here, and quickly realized that I actually did live in a small country town just like it. Masvingo had been Fort Victoria, the site of the first white settlers' fort, and then a farming town. The name had changed but the town had not, for here was the Victoria Hotel and the dry-goods shop and the Indian clothing store, Zubair for Flair, and the bottle store and the ironmonger's. The street, like all old main streets in Zimbabwe, was wide enough to allow an ox wagon to make a U-turn.

The scheduled stop in Masvingo turned into a delay, but that was fine with me. I was able to see that the other passengers on the bus were all-sorts: white families, black families, Indian women in a group, six white girls in gym slips traveling as part of a school soccer team, African men in suits and ties, others dressed like me. Although the vehicle resembled a Greyhound bus and the passengers looked like the people you might find on a long-distance Greyhound — the decent, the hard-pressed, the marginal, the weird, the aromatic — I still felt that I was on another planet, one that bore a striking similarity to the planet Earth but was in fact a dark star.

We spent a good part of the afternoon in Masvingo. I went for a walk up the main street, wondering at its emptiness until I remembered it was Sunday. We set off again into the stillness and green hills of Matabeleland and were at Beitbridge at dusk, another river marking the border, this one the Limpopo, South Africa's border.

◈ ◈ ◈

In the darkness, after all the slow lines and the fussing with passports and the interrogations, the trip became hallucinatory. Beyond the Limpopo was a tall steel fence topped with razor wire, and the bright searchlights playing on it gave it the look of an armed camp or a jail we were being bused into along a fortified bridge. No other border crossing in Africa was as menacing or efficient as this — like a nightmare of being whisked into prison, dreary and dark except for the occasional blinding lights, many sentry posts and roadblocks on a short stretch of road. At the last roadblock a white soldier boarded the bus and reexamined every passenger's entry stamp — politely, but strangely goose-eyed and carrying an automatic rifle.

At the town of Messina a young African girl got on and sat beside me, jostling the notebook on my knee.

"What are you writing?"

"Just a letter," I said, but it was my erotic story. "How long to Jo'burg?"

"Twelve hours," she said. "But more for me. I am going to Maseru."

Maseru, in Lesotho, was her home. Her name was Thulo, she was a Suthu. She said, "My country makes nothing. Nothing. Nothing."

She went to sleep briefly, and when she woke we talked a little about Lesotho, how it sometimes snowed there.

"I want to leave Lesotho — leave South Africa," she said. "Not emigrate, just get away. You know? Just get away from the Third World for a while."

After that, flashes of light indicated settlements — no other place I had seen on my trip was so well lit at night as this introduction to South Africa. No other country had been so electrified. The light was interruptive and disturbing, for it gave bright, not quite right glimpses of prosperity — tall power lines and large houses and used-car lots with shiny vehicles and the sinister order of urban life. Then more lights, more fences, illuminated windows. So much electric light seemed nightmarish after the darkness my eyes were accustomed to, for the glare conveyed a sense of distortion and bigness. And really there was not much modernity here at all, for this Northern Transvaal — the market towns of Louis Trichardt and Bandelierkop, the hills of Soutpansberg — was lightly settled, all of it farming country.

Around midnight, during a long delay in the town of Pietersberg, I walked around in the cold and saw some people in the street, even women selling bananas and oranges, much as their counterparts did in rural Malawi. But these women were selling them in front of the Big Bite convenience store, which was still open and smelling of warm meat pies and carbolic soap and disinfectant. People in this town were swathed in sweaters and shawls and leggings and aprons and turbans, which they would peel off, unlayering themselves as the day grew warmer. But in the dark, plumped up and wrapped in all these woolens, they also looked like creatures in a dream, especially the ones wandering into the bright empty main street.

I was lulled to sleep on the highway traversing Springbok Flats and the hundreds of miles of booming Afrikaner place names — Potgietersrus, Vanalphensvlei, Naboomspruit, Warmbad, and Nylstroom. That last place, with its "Nile" prefix, was significantly named by the trekking Boers in the 1840s who were guided by the Holy Bible. The river they encountered here, the Mokalakwena, flowed north, which could mean only one thing. It had to be the Nile, flowing into the unmapped heart of Africa and eventually through Egypt. Thus their logical name for the village on its banks, Nylstroom, the Nile Stream.

Now and then I woke in my seat and through glazed eyes saw bright raised-up motorway signs, and after so many months of bush the very look of these signs — Days Inn, IBM, Xerox, DHL — spooked me, for in a dream the scariest things are the most familiar.

The lights woke Thulo. She said, "I just had a dream that I would marry someone from the Philippines. I think I probably will."

But she had a boyfriend. He was in Zimbabwe. "He wants to be a personal trainer." She had a seven-year-old daughter. "She's living with my mother."

I dozed, I woke. Lights blazed beside the highway.

"Pretoria," Thulo said. "They say Indians never sleep. They just stay awake, doing business night and day. That's why they are rich."

When I dozed and woke again, Thulo said, "It's nice. But I want to leave the Third World." She said it as if it were a trip she would be taking in a rocket ship to another planet.

Around four-thirty in the morning of this night of blazing imagery and strange dreams, like a psychedelic journey fueled by acid or ayahuasca, we entered the outskirts of Johannesburg. The road glittered black and our vehicle was alone on the broad empty highway, as though making a grand entrance into a nightmare city, the packed Zimbabwean bus speeding under the dazzling lights, and the driver on the loudspeaker again thanking God for delivering us safely.

"Jo'burg is so dangerous," Thulo said.

We entered a tunnel, a covered garage, a lighted empty station. Everyone on the bus looked alarmed, piling out with gray worried faces and claiming bags and shuffling in the cold of the station platform. They did not linger, and before I could say goodbye Thulo was gone. There was light in the station, darkness outside, and no taxis. After almost twenty hours sitting upright on the bus, I felt sick with fatigue.

Thinking it better to take my chances in daylight in this city of low repute, I sat down, holding my bag between my knees, and drowsed until the sun came up.

At dawn, to kill a little more time in Park Station, I bought a *Star*, one of the daily newspapers. This was unwise, probably the worst thing I could have done as a stranger to the city — surely the most unsettling. The front page was filled with sordid political stories, and a lengthy feature was devoted to Johannesburg prostitution, one of the growth areas in the country's shaky economy. The story was surprisingly upbeat, the women speaking in a positive way about their jobs as hookers. "With this job I will never be retrenched [laid off]," and "No need for a CV or a formal education," and "You can drink on the job," and "You can work your own chosen hours."

As if in support of this career choice, half a page of classifieds in the *Star* were explicit ads for prostitutes, escorts, brothels, promises of threesomes, Greek, bondage, punishment, pleasure, gays, black, Malay, Indians, Chinese, "Zulu," white, "European," and whole columns headed "Horny College Girls" and "Bored Housewives." I supposed it to be a mark of successful urbanization, if not civilization, that so many diverse sexual tastes were catered to. And by the way, these humid classifieds also seemed to represent the epitome of multiracialism.

The inside pages — much more worrying for their being inside — were all crime stories. In the worst one, four tied-up and blindfolded people, two men and two women, were found "shot execution-style" in a van outside Johannesburg. No clues, no identities, no leads. "The motive is thought to be robbery." In a second story, "another witness" in an upcoming murder trial was found dead; eight witnesses altogether had been killed, leaving no one to testify. And there were assorted instances of racial vendettas, road rage, carjackings, farm invasions, poisonings, and deliberately scalded tots. An astonishing number were muggings, maimings, and robberies with gratuitous violence. In the quaintest story a man had been assaulted — one eye poked out, his throat slashed, and his penis chopped off. "Police suspect that his genitals — which are still missing — will be used for *muti* [medicine] by an *inganga* [witch doctor]."

The morning newspaper, especially that report of forcible organ donation, made me cautious about leaving Park Station. What I read seemed to support the startling statistics most visitors find out soon after they arrive in the country: there are twenty thousand murders a year in South Africa and fifty-two thousand reported rapes, almost a quarter of the rapes against small children and even infants. The most grotesque explanation for the child rapes was the vicious folklore that having sex with a virgin was a cure for AIDS. Some of the same people who praised South Africa as the richest and most successful country on the continent said it was also a jungle.

Still I paced, and procrastinated, and sat restlessly on a molded plastic chair. I was not emboldened to leave the station until the sun was shining on everyone equally. Only then did I feel I was entering South Africa.

19 ◇◇◇

The Hominids of Johannesburg

"THESE PEOPLE!" the taxi driver screamed as I got into his car, around seven-thirty, having hurried from the entrance of Park Station in Johannesburg. The station had an imposing carved frieze on its façade — granite elephants and lions and native trees and iconic African scenes. This was an appropriate backdrop, for I felt smaller and more disoriented here in this huge city than I had in the Elephant Marsh of the Lower Shire River in southern Malawi, athwart a dugout canoe and slapping my paddle at the water hyacinths. The city was gray, and the only humans I saw were sleeping rough all over the sidewalk and on the grass outside the station, in the manner of critters in the bush.

The driver's name was Norman. He looked to be a Khoikhoin — light brown, small head, tiny chin, daintily slant-eyed. The Khoikhoin were better known as Hottentots, a rude name bestowed on them by Afrikaners who, hearing the clicks in their subtle language, nailed them as stammerers.

Norman was still cursing "those people": the ones in the tents, lean-tos, plastic huts, ingenious humpies, sheds of scrap lumber; the people lying jumbled croclike in the grass, others lying singly or with their backs against light poles — the vagrants, the drunks, the desperate, the sinister, the bewildered, the uncaring, the lost, cluttering the station entrance.

"They smell, they make messes, they make shit, they fight, they won't go away. And the government does nothing, so it will get worse. I hate it."

He said he was from Soweto, he was indignant and angry.

"People like you will stay away. Our business will suffer."

"Who are they?" I asked.

"Other people," he said, meaning not South Africans. "In Yeoville and Hillbrow there are too many *tsotsis*" — rascals. "Congolese and Nigerians. Why do they come to Janiceburg? They just only make trouble."

But he became cheery as he drove on. I asked him why.

"The end of the world is coming. Another end of the world. The Waist is finished."

"You think?"

"I know."

He was, of course, a Jehovah's Witness. He claimed the large amount of crime and violence was a sign. He saw explicit indications of Doomsday all over South Africa.

"You might well be right, Norman," I said.

It so happened that at a stoplight there was a gaunt greasy-haired beggar standing in the middle of the road holding a sign: *No home — No work — No food — Please help.* The people sleeping rough at the station had not been actively begging, and so the first South African beggar I saw was an able-bodied white man.

My hotel in Braamfontein was not far from Park Station, within walking distance in fact, in a neighborhood reputed to be dangerous. But what did "dangerous" mean in a city where people were mugged and their cars swiped by hijackers in the driveways of their own gated communities? The exchange rate made everything a bargain. I had a bath, ate breakfast, and went for a walk, feeling happy.

I was happy most of all because I was alive. Before I had set out, I'd had a premonition that I would die in some sort of road accident en route ("Globetrotter Lost in Bus Plunge Horror"). As this had not happened, I could now apportion my time and make onward plans. I had never known from week to week how long my travel would take, but South Africa was a land of railways and reliable train timetables. I was encouraged to think that I might eat well here. I had not had many good meals since leaving Cairo, but the breakfast I'd just had and a glimpse of the dinner menu made me hopeful for more. Also, having arrived in South Africa I was able to begin pondering my trip, and it seemed to me a safari that had been worth taking, the ideal picnic.

Lastly, I was happy because my birthday was the day after tomorrow. I considered my birthday a national holiday, a day to devote myself to pleasure and reflection, on which I would do no work. And because I was among people who didn't know it was my birthday, I would have no one here forcing jollification on me and making facetious remarks involving the word "sexagenarian."

Another satisfaction about being in South Africa was that the country had been written about by many gifted people, among them Nadine Gordimer. I had known Nadine since the 1970s, when she made annual visits to New York and London. Unlike many other South African writers and activists, she had resisted fleeing into exile. By staying put in Johannesburg, where she had lived her whole life, she had become one of the most reliable witnesses to the seismic South African transformation. She was that wonderful thing, the national writer who transcended nationality by being true to her art, like Borges in Argentina, R. K. Narayan in India, Jorge Amado in Brazil, V. S. Pritchett in England, Shusaku Endo in Japan, Naguib Mahfouz in Egypt, and Yasar Kemal in Turkey. They were writers I had sought out as a traveler.

Months before, I had warned Nadine that I was heading for South Africa and was looking forward to seeing her in Johannesburg. She was a writer who belonged to the world, but true to her home and her disposition, she had made South Africa her subject, had anatomized its problems and its people. The complex country became human and comprehensible in her prose. Among the few books I had held on to was one by Mahfouz, whom I had met in Cairo, the gnomic *Echoes of an Autobiography*. Nadine had written an introduction to it, as a friend and fellow Nobel laureate. Seeing her here would be pleasant and symmetrical, another way of joining two distant corners of Africa.

The truth of Gordimer's writing was apparent to me from my first days in Johannesburg, for her fiction was full of immigrants — from remote villages, from distant countries — Portuguese, Arabs, Lithuanians, Russians, Greeks, English, Hindus, Jews, Hereros, Swazis, and Khoikhoin. Johannesburg was full of immigrants, too, wanderers like the earliest hominids, another native species. I was not in the city long before I met a Lithuanian, a Bulgarian, a Portuguese, a Senegalese holy man, a Congolese trader. I quickly learned that everyone in South Africa had a story, usually a pretty good one.

After a few days I became attuned to the accent, which in its twanging and swallowed way seemed both assertive and friendly. Johannesburg was "Janiceburg" or "Jozi," busy was "buzzy," congested "congisted," West "Waist," and said "sid." There was no shortage of glottal stops, and a distinct Scottishness crept into some expressions; for example, a military buildup was a "mulatree buldup." Nearly everyone had a tendency to use Afrikaans words in ordinary speech, such as *dorp, bakkie, takkies, naartjies,* and *dagga.* These words had percolated throughout Central Africa long ago, and I knew from having lived in Malawi that they meant town, pickup truck, sneakers, tangerines, and marijuana. If there was a pronunciation problem, it was that for *dagga* or Gauteng (the province that includes Johannesburg) you needed to use the soft, deep, throat-clearing, gargled *g* of Hollanders.

Voetsek meant "bugger off" all over southern Africa, and was regarded as impolite. Forbidden words sometimes slipped into conversation. *Kaffer* was the worst, *koelie* ("coolie" for Indian) not far behind, and so was *bushies* (for "coloureds," mixed-race people). *Piccanin* was one vulgar word for African children, but there were others. When a white High Court judge, perhaps believing himself to be affectionate, described some African children with the diminutive *klein kaffertjies* ("little niggerlings"), he was suspended from his judicial duties. Afrikaans was nothing if not picturesque, though some slang words had etymologies that needed explanation, such as *moffie,* for homosexual, which derived from *mofskaap,* a castrated sheep.

"I don't call them kaffirs, I call them crows," a white seventy-two-year-old janitor said in a newspaper story about racism in Pretoria *(Ek noem hulle nie kaffers nie, ek noem hulle kraaie),* laughing at his waggishness. One headline read "Unlikely Romance in Conservative Town Has Rightwingers Reeling." In this story, when Ethel Dorfling, a white thirty-year-old full-figured mother of four, disappeared and set up house with Clyde Le Batie, a black forty-two-year-old full-figured detergent salesman, none of her friends would speak to her except to call her a *kafferboetie,* the equivalent of "nigger lover." A joshing term, from Yiddish, for a very young wife or a heavily made-up floozy was *kugel,* a type of sweet dish.

Moving his vowels, someone would say, "Ah thoat ah'd osk for an expinsive gless of shirry." That was clear enough, once you got used to the cadence. But the newer, more despised immigrants tended to stick with the accents they had brought with them.

"It is a nice place, South Africa, but I don't like the people," the man from Senegal told me.

This tall thin man in a multicolored Rasta bonnet called himself El Hadji and believed he was of Ethiopian ancestry. "Look at my face. You find us everywhere in Africa. *Nous avons des boeufs.* We traveled with our cattle for hundreds and thousands of years." He sold artifacts. I was always looking for unusual carvings and fetish objects. He had some, but instead of describing them, he grumbled about South Africans.

"Which people don't you like?"

"All the people — black, white — all. It's their history, maybe. They fight, they hate each other. They hate us, they call us foreigners. It is such a problem. But I like the country." Flourishing a fetish, pinching its head, he added, "And the business is okay."

He had come in the early nineties when Nelson Mandela, having recently been released, encouraged diverse people to emigrate to South Africa and help build a new nation. This open-door policy had been criticized and curtailed, but many people I met had arrived when the policy had been instituted, just ten years before.

Edward, a Lithuanian, was one. He was skinny, pasty-faced, agitated, only thirty or so but with thinning hair and that squinting adversarial manner of eastern Europeans, raised in an authoritarian system, untrusting and humorless. He had been brought to South Africa by his fleeing parents when he was a twenty-year-old civil engineering student in Vilnius. "But engineering wasn't me. I was bored." His parents hated working for peanuts, hated having to wait to buy the simplest material things, hated the feeling of confinement and destitution that came with the departure of the Soviets. I listened hard but heard no patriotic Lithuanian noises.

"In Lithuania they have nothing. You wait twenty years for a car. Life in Lithuania is terrible. I go once a year to visit friends. They make nothing. They just buy and sell. What kind of business is that? Here, everything is simple."

I said, "But this is Africa. It's so far from Lithuania. You could have gone to Britain."

"The weather sucks there."

Sniffing at Britain's quality of life, the climate-conscious Lithuanian émigrés had landed in Johannesburg.

"My father is Jewish, my mother is Lithuanian," Edward said. "I would not go to Israel with all their problems, but even if I could, they wouldn't want me. In Israel I'm a Lithuanian, everywhere else I'm a Jew. Jewishness comes from your mother. Ha! My mother is nothing!"

I still didn't understand why his family had chosen South Africa. He explained that it would have taken ten years to get a U.S. visa, but they found it very easy to secure visas and work permits for South Africa. "And here, if you work, you can make money. You can buy things. I want to own things."

"Such as?"

"Clothes. A car. A stereo."

South Africa, for many people a wilderness of wild animals and high desert and nationalistic Africans, represented to Edward the Lithuanian a modern world of accessible material culture. As others traveled to South Africa to see gnus, he had come for the stereo systems. A hominid in search of glittery objects.

"I do day trading on the stock market in the day. I drive a cab at night. Okay, the market is down right now, but for three years we made money. The Nasdaq people who are complaining should shut up — they made a lot of money."

Edward, who was unmarried, said he had no African friends and did not speak Afrikaans or any African language. There are eleven official languages in South Africa.

The Bulgarian whom I met in Johannesburg — Dave, an electronics expert — was in his mid-thirties and small and pale; and he too had Edward's look of suspicion. He had come from Sofia in 1991 and had a similar story to tell: two jobs, his main one fixing and reconditioning electronic contraptions, like TVs and VCRs. He spoke only English and Bulgar, had not been outside Johannesburg, and knew no Africans well. His two kids went to a private school in which there were a few African students. He said with satisfaction, "The school fees keep most blacks out."

Like Edward, he liked the South African weather, but he wasn't happy about the economy.

"It's going to get worse here, sure," Dave said. "I think I have a hundred thousand in U.S. dollars — my flat, my car, my things. When the rand gets to ten to the dollar, I will go away. I don't know where. Not Canada — I don't like the weather. Maybe the States, if I can live in California."

He had no notion of South African history, not even recent history. He shook his head doubtfully when I talked about it. When I mentioned that the fiercest and most successful of the South African political activists had been Communists, he began to rave.

"Ha! They must have had mental instability!" Dave said. "If you live in a democratic country and you are a Communist, there is something wrong with your mind. You have to be crazy."

I said, "But this wasn't a democratic country before 1994. That's when they had their first free election."

"It was all right before — everyone says so."

That cynical view, that apartheid was preferable to a multiracial society, was still held by some skeptics, even Africans. But on the whole they tended to be marginalized people: the Boers, the Khoikhoin, the "coloureds," or migrants from nearby countries.

One Suthu named Solly, from Lesotho, said, "My parents came here from Maseru. My father worked on farms. Sometimes he had work, sometimes none. He went from farm to farm. It was not an easy life, but it was better than this."

I questioned this: the life of a migrant farm laborer under apartheid was better than that of a worker with a secure job in free South Africa?

"It was better," Solly said in a don't-argue-with-me tone. "There is too much crime. I see it every day. I would like to go, but where? The white government was better!"

"In what way?"

"Not as much crime. Not as much litter," Solly said. "I am not saying this because you have a white face. It is true — the white government was better. Now I don't know what to do."

Speaking to people at random, I was constantly meeting strangers and émigrés, people who regarded Johannesburg with a mixture of disgust and wonderment. Nearly all of them had come to make money, and now that the work had begun to dry up, they were seriously questioning whether to stay. But even to many of the whites who were old-timers, living here seemed to them like being in a foreign country. I had the notion that for many whites, black South Africa was a foreign land that they had only recently begun to inhabit, and it took some getting used to.

"We're economic prisoners," one white man told me. He owned his own small business. "We can't afford to go anywhere else."

When I pressed him, though, he said that he really didn't want to go anywhere else. He was shocked, he said, by how little the white government had done over many decades to educate Africans. Like everyone else, he said crime was South Africa's worst problem. And the police were part of the problem.

"During the apartheid era the police were horrible," he said. "They arrested people for no reason — for being in a white area, for not having an ID card. They killed people, they tortured people, they were unfair. No one respected them. Now this whole past of theirs has come back to bite them on the ass."

One of my taxi drivers was a Portuguese man who had fled to Spain from Portugal in the 1960s, to Mozambique from Spain in the 1970s, then to South Africa from Mozambique in the 1980s. He had run out of countries to flee to. "Because of the EU, Portugal is full of foreigners." He said he thought South Africa had become a dismal place.

I said, "This isn't a Third World country."

"Not yet," he said, and winked at me in the rearview mirror.

We were rolling down a tree-lined street in a pretty part of Johannesburg known as Parktown West. The garden walls were whitewashed and high, concealing each premises, and inside the walls big solid houses loomed. On most gates, along with the house number, was the name of an alarm company and the words "Armed Response." It could have been Bel-Air or Malibu.

"But if you live on this street, you never have worries," the driver said.

◇ ◇ ◇

That was presumptuous, because Nadine Gordimer lived here, and she had known plenty of anxiety in her seventy-seven years in South Africa. She was a Johannesburger to her fingertips, having been born in Springs, a mining town only twenty-five miles from this pretty house in Parktown. She was of Latvian descent, through her father, who had left Riga and come to South Africa at the age of thirteen, alone, to escape czarist pogroms in an earlier wave of immigration. That boy, her father, had come to find his brother. He had no trade. He became a watch mender, he went from town to town in the Transvaal tinkering with watches. Later he set up a business selling watches, and ultimately trinkets, gewgaws, wedding rings, and jewelry, in the gold-mining town of Springs. Nadine had written about her father in "My Father Leaves Home," a story in the collection *Jump*.

I had valued her writing from my first reading, but I had discovered her only in the 1960s, and she had been writing since the late forties. She started to write at the age of fifteen; as a twenty-four-year-old she began publishing in *The New Yorker*. Her first story, "A Watcher of the Dead" is a beautifully observed tale of the conflict between the impulses of a daughter's love and the demands of ritual, in this case a Jewish funeral in Johannesburg.

Very early in her writing career, Nadine had marked out her emotional territory — the passionate relations between men and women; and her geography — settlers' South Africa, Mozambique, and Rhodesia, as well as the much more foreign and forbidden territory of the African village and the black township. She had never ceased to be political in a wide sense. In her first collection of stories, *The Soft Voice of the Serpent* (1952), that territory was represented: the lovers traveling on the road to Lourenço Marques in "The End of the Tunnel," the mismatched couple in "The Train from Rhodesia," the woman in "The Defeated" who begins her story, "My mother did not want me to go near the Concession stores because they smelled, and were dirty, and the natives spat tuberculosis germs into the dust. She said it was no place for little girls." In this story, the little girl goes to the African store and discovers vitality and sadness.

So, from the first — and life was wickedly divided in the early years of the apartheid era — Nadine wrote of race relations, and her black characters were as carefully delineated as her white ones. One of the hallmarks of her prose has always been its intense physicality — the pleasures of sex, of food, of sunshine, or the opposite of these, frustration, hunger, bad weather.

It seemed puzzling to me to reflect that I had never been in Johannesburg before, for the city seemed so familiar. There was a reason. The voices, the faces, the smells, the slur and twang of speech, the dissonant combination of sunshine and strife, the sense of place in

Nadine's work, had made Johannesburg seem like a city I was returning to, as Mahfouz's work had done for me in Egypt. For an author, there is no greater achievement than this, the successful re-creation in prose of the texture and emotions of a real place, making the reading of the work like a travel experience, containing many of the pleasures of a visit. How nice it would be, I thought, if someone reading the narrative of my African trip felt the same, that it was the next best thing to being there — or even better, because reading about being shot at and poisoned and insulted was in general less upsetting than the real thing.

Blossom-filled jacaranda trees hung over Nadine's garden, and big scallop-leafed monstera vines clung to their trunks. Her garden wall was softened with bougainvillea and thorny whips of rose bushes. The bedding plants were velvety violets and spongy primroses. Nadine's work was also full of closely observed flora.

I had called the day before and invited her to dinner — she could choose the restaurant. My idea was to enjoy a pleasant meal with a good friend as a secret celebration of my birthday. I went to the iron gate at the driveway and got barked at by a big brown dog until an African woman at the kitchen door howled at the dog to shut up. An African man in a white shirt and blue pants swung the gate open for me. Something possessed me to thank him in Chichewa, which was widely spoken in southern Africa because of the wandering Malawians looking for work.

"*Zikomo, bambo.*" Thank you, father.

We talked a bit and I asked him his name.

His name was Albino. He was from Mozambique.

The house was servant-tidy, mopped and spare and shadowy. As I was led from one room to another through narrow corridors, past the kitchen with its tableau of elderly servants (old women sitting, old man standing), I could just make out African masks and baskets and a hat rack piled with wide-brimmed hats.

Then I was propelled through a door, as if onstage, into the sitting room, which was well lighted and hung with family photos and lovely paintings, and Nadine was standing there, very straight, rather small, with piercing eyes. She kissed me, welcoming me with the first good hug — she was strong for her size — I had had since leaving home.

"That looks familiar," I said as we kissed, for I saw just behind her head, over the fireplace, a framed picture, three vividly drawn figures, heads and shoulders, and you knew it had to be a Daumier, the way you knew a certain paragraph had to be a Gordimer.

Turning to size up the room, looking for a place to sit, I saw a brilliantly colored picture, a lithograph of Napoleon flanked by a lancer and an Arab sheik.

"Toulouse-Lautrec," Nadine said. "Isn't Napoleon handsome? I always think he looks like Marlon Brando."

That was when I saw the other person in the room — motionless, seated with a blanket over his knees, so quiet I had missed him. He was hooked up to a breathing machine, tubes to his nostrils, and he was smiling — apparently had been smiling the whole time at the apparition of a big, badly dressed American ogling his paintings. He was Reinhold Cassirer, bright and friendly and clearly frail. He was ninety-three years old and ailing, but fully alert, with good color, and even sitting in his wheelchair I could see that he was a tall man.

"He came from Cairo — on the bus!" Nadine said sharply to her husband.

Reinhold smiled at me, raised one hand in salute, and murmured, "Good, good, good."

He had a beautiful smile, the sort of smile that indicates great generosity and a capacity for pleasure. He sat in the center of the room seeming to enjoy the warmth, the light, the talk. He hated the confinement of his sickroom and the ministrations of his nurse. What he liked best, Nadine told me later, was what he had liked best throughout their marriage, drinking a predinner whiskey at the end of the working day.

A young African arrived, Raks Seakhoa, a poet and former political prisoner.

I said, "I want to hear about your imprisonment. I've been meeting ex-convicts all along my route."

"Paul came from Cairo — on the bus!"

"I'll be glad to tell you about it. I served five years on Robben Island."

"With Mandela?"

"Yes. We passed notes secretly, on philosophical subjects."

Nadine said smartly, "Isn't it your birthday?"

I tried not to look deflated. I said, "How did you know?"

"Someone saw it on the Internet."

"Oh, God, the world of useless information."

Raks Seakhoa said, "It's my birthday, too."

The rumbling of my secret seemed less awkward then, for someone who shares your birthday shares much more, a certain kinship and characteristics. Raks was turning forty-two. He looked older — another former prisoner whose time in jail had added years to his life, made him gaunt, grayed his hair. I liked the thought that we two Arieses were brothers under the skin, but he had suffered in his life, and my life had been a picnic.

Another guest entered, hugged Reinhold, hugged Nadine, hugged Raks, and was introduced to me as Maureen Isaacson, the literary editor of the Johannesburg *Sunday Independent.*

"Happy birthday," she said.

"He came from Cairo — on the bus!"

We drove to the restaurant in two cars; I went with Maureen, Nadine with Raks. Maureen carefully locked each door before we set off, and said, "I've had robbery attempts. But I refuse to be intimidated by the violence, so I'm vigilant."

"What happened?"

"People trying to get into my car on the Queen Elizabeth Bridge — one bloke taps at the windscreen and distracts me while another snatches at the back door. Pretty soon I'm surrounded by these men, six or eight of them."

"God. What did you do?"

"I screamed at them. 'Fuck off!'" Maureen said, sounding fierce. She added quietly, "Now I lock everything."

The restaurant — ornate, furnished with antiques, very large — was almost empty, a consequence of the crime in the city center after dark, the muggings and carjackings. Of perhaps thirty other tables, only one was occupied. The owners warmly welcomed Nadine. She commiserated with them about the crime that kept their restaurant empty. Then she introduced me.

"Paul came on the bus — from Cairo!"

Over dinner, Nadine said she was weary from spending the day reading the galley proofs of her new novel, *The Pickup.* "The American proofreaders often try to correct my English," she said. "They follow the rules. I don't. I like my sentences."

I mentioned that I kept meeting Johannesburgers who had amazing tales to tell. She said this was a characteristic of South Africans generally; their lives were full of events. My mention of the recent immigrants stirred memories of her father, his arrival here as a thirteen-year-old.

"Imagine my father," she said, and let her voice trail off.

Her mother had been English, from a Jewish family long established in London. Nadine smiled at the memory of her piano-playing mother turning up her nose at her husband's origins, and in a shocked accent of mimicry said, "They slept round the stove."

There is a pitiless description of her parents in her story "My Father Leaves Home": "In the quarrels between husband and wife, she saw them [the relatives] as ignorant and dirty; she must have read something somewhere that served as a taunt: you slept like animals round a stove, stinking of garlic, you bathed once a week. The children knew how low it was to be unwashed. And whipped into anger, he knew the lowest category of all in her country, this country. *You speak to me as if I was a kaffir.*"

"Sounds like Mrs. Morel in *Sons and Lovers.* 'I was cut out for better things than this.'"

"Yes. That was my mother. Mrs. Morel."

"I don't think I could bear to reread that novel again. What do you reread?"

"Everything. All the time. I want to reread Dostoyevsky."

I asked, "What should I read to understand South Africa better?"

"There are so many good South African writers," Nadine said, and she encouraged Raks and Maureen to help make a reading list for me. They suggested, among others, *The Peasants' Revolt* by Govan Mbeki, Hugh Lewin's *Bandiet, Ways of Dying* by Zakes Mda, *The Soft Vengeance of a Freedom Fighter* by Albie Sachs, and poems by Don Mattera and Jeremy Cronin.

"And Raks, too. I wish he would write more," Maureen said.

Just then Raks's cell phone rang, and when Nadine loudly sighed at the silly noise, Raks left the table to talk.

"I'm glad I read your book about Naipaul," Nadine said. "The reviews put me off. It's about you, not him — and unsparing about you. It's such a good book. I cheered for you at the end. 'He's free,' I thought."

"Naipaul always wears such a gloomy face," Maureen said. "But isn't *A House for Mr. Biswas* wonderful?"

"Vidia hates it when people mention only that one book."

Nadine said, "The book of mine that everyone mentions is *July's People*."

"Patrick White complained that everyone praised *Voss*, which is a great book."

Nadine agreed, and said that she admired White's *A Fringe of Leaves* ("I want to reread it"). Her generous praise for her contemporaries was not the usual writer's characteristic.

I said, "Will it annoy you if I ask you about *July's People*?"

She laughed, and I said that the reason people liked the book was because it represented their secret fears — having to flee a political cataclysm, losing your home, becoming a fugitive in your own country, finding that the world had been turned upside down. This was the ultimate white South African nightmare, becoming totally dependent on your black servants, reduced to living in a simple remote village.

"I was writing about the present," Nadine said, meaning the years of its composition, between 1976 and 1980. "It was a very bad time here. Everything was happening. I put all that into the book."

She said that by the time she finished *July's People* she was committed to staying in South Africa. "I felt we had been through it all." But there had been a period when she had thought seriously about leaving, in the late 1960s when she had been writing *A Guest of Honor*. "We traveled around. We had friends in Zimbabwe and Zambia. I felt I might consider one of those places. I'm an African. That's Africa." She needed to be near South Africa.

"Or so I thought," she added. "I looked closely at my friends. They were mostly white, mostly expatriates, they had loyalties elsewhere. So what life would it have been for me? I would have been a nice white woman who was interested in Africans, but living in this world of expatriates. I couldn't do it. And so I stopped thinking of leaving."

I said, "Were you a member of a political party?"

She smiled at the question. "I suppose I could have joined the Liberal Party, but they were so weak. And whom did they represent? I thought hard about the South African Communist Party. But it was too late for me. I should have joined earlier. Yet I have the greatest respect for the Communists here. We would never have achieved our freedom without them."

Raks returned to the table, and talked about what it was like to be hearing about the political struggle while serving time on Robben Island as a political prisoner. The news from the outside world came in whispers and scribbled messages, for newspapers were forbidden.

Nadine had been ruminating. She said, "I didn't leave. I stayed. I saw everything. The people who left — well, you can't blame the Africans. Life was awful for them. But the others — the whites, the writers" — she shook her head — "after they left, what did they write?"

Maureen said, "I feel sorry for anyone who left, who missed it. All those years. And it went on for so long — beyond Mandela's release."

I said, "Isn't it still going on?"

"Yes it is. You can write about it," Nadine said.

Afterward, driving Nadine's car — Nadine navigating — I asked about Reinhold's health. She said it was terrible but that she felt lucky in having had such a happy marriage. "Reinie smoked a lot," she said. "Smoking is nice. Did you ever smoke *dagga?*" She lamented that the center of Johannesburg was so empty. We talked about our children. And at last we said goodbye. She wished me a happy birthday once more and said, "Travel well. Travel safely."

It is all right to be Steppenwolf, or the Lone Ranger, or Rimbaud, or even me. You visit a place and peer at it closely and then move on, making a virtue of disconnection. But such an evening as this, after months of solitary travel, reminded me that a meal with friends was a mood improver, and that a birthday need not be an ordeal. I had been self-conscious, though. One of Nadine's many strengths was that she noticed everything. The best writers were scrupulous, pitiless observers. And since a birthday is an occasion for a summing up, the annual balance sheet, I was sure that she had seen, in my patched Ugandan jacket, my baggy pants, my scuffed shoes, my tattoos, my thinning hair, how I had changed in the twenty years since I had last seen her. I couldn't complain: that was life. And yet, alert, bright, fully engaged, and funny, she had not changed at all.

The next day, Raks Seakhoa invited me to a poetry reading at the Windybrow Theater. "Take a taxi." The theater was in one of the most dangerous areas of Johannesburg. I almost didn't go at all, because leaving my hotel I met a man who said that the big event that night was a soccer match between the two best teams in South Africa, the Chiefs and the Pirates. As a visitor, I was duty bound to see these great local athletes. He said, "You can buy tickets at the stadium."

But I met Raks instead, in the arts center that had once been the mansion of a Johannesburg millionaire (cupola, mullioned windows, porches, wood paneling), and after the poetry reading, plucking at his pebble glasses, Raks told me his story. He had been arrested at the age of eighteen in a township outside Johannesburg. He was charged with sabotage and belonging to an unlawful organization. While in police custody he had been tortured. This was in the late 1970s.

"They wanted me to tell them about the ANC" — the African National Congress — "but I didn't know much," Raks said. "The black consciousness movement was what animated me."

"What about the charge of sabotage?"

"We were in various actions," he said blandly. "But the police were vicious. At first they just hit us. No questions, just *whack*. We were beaten really hard. It went on for two or three weeks. We were put into sacks and thrown into the river. We thought we would drown — we knew people who had died."

"Didn't they interrogate you?"

"After that, yes. But the beatings went on. They wanted to know who our friends were — the details. 'Who are the Communists?' That kind of thing."

Raks spoke with feeling but without much anger, as though it had all happened long ago in another galaxy, far away. He was quite well dressed, wearing a jacket and tie, as he had been at the birthday dinner, but there was something about him — an intimation of frailty — that was disturbing.

"They stopped beating us when they realized that we had nothing to tell them," Raks said. "Then we went to trial. It was a short trial. Torture was not mentioned, nothing of our treatment came out. We were sentenced. I got five years. In those days you did every day of your sentence."

"Tell me about Robben Island."

Robben Island, in the sea just a mile off Cape Town, was now a popular tourist attraction, though a sobering one. Visitors were taken out in boats, and former political prisoners served as guides.

"I served my whole sentence there, from 1979 to 1984," Raks said. "It was cold and uncomfortable and impossible to escape from. As I told you, we saw Nelson Mandela. We passed notes, scribbling on pieces of paper and smuggling them back and forth."

Books, paper, and pencils were forbidden, and confiscated if they were found. Even Mandela, the future president, was trifled with — his books and writing materials were taken from him. In place of study or self-improvement or any intellectual activity there was manual labor.

"We did road repairs," Raks said, for the island had once had a community on it — houses, roads, churches, a leper settlement. "Most days we dragged seaweed out of the ocean, ten-foot lengths of kelp. The seaweed was sold to Taiwan and Korea."

That was an interesting detail: the Chinese and the Koreans enjoying the delicacy of Cape Town seaweed with their noodles by wringing the sweat from the faces of these slave laborers. But there were no recriminations against them. Raks had no hard words for Margaret Thatcher or Dick Cheney, who had both publicly declared Mandela a terrorist; no bitterness against the Belgians who bought diamonds, and the Israelis who traded in guns and food with a racist government that was committed to torturing, imprisoning, and killing some Africans and creating ghettos for others; and only laughter for the Japanese who got themselves officially declared white, in part so that they could trade with the white supremacist government, but mainly so that they could play golf at whites-only country clubs.

Raks said, "When I got out I was deported to Bophuthatswana."

Bophuthatswana had been a Bantustan, a small deprived ghetto of bad land and poor houses where "separate development" was to take place. Bantustans had since been dismantled, the fences taken down, and were now a source of labor and of emigrants to the shantytowns outside the major cities.

That was Raks's story. He had disliked telling it. Listening to him, I saw something familiar in his limp posture and sad expression. It was the ravaged look of someone who had had a near-death experience that had gone on far too long: years in a cage. I had seen that same look in the Ethiopians who had been locked up in Central Prison in Addis, in my friends in Uganda who had suffered through Amin's tyranny, in Wahome Mutahi, who had been subjected to water torture in Nairobi. It was the look not of a broken spirit but of a fractured body, a premature aging. They had a sort of sidelong mode of delivery, hating to look back. No, their spirit had not been broken, but their health had been shattered.

Going home that night, I noticed a great fuss in the streets. The taxi driver was excited, his blood was up, his radio was chattering. I suspected a riot or some kind of civil disorder, for there were helicopters going *thunk-thunk-thunk* overhead and ambulance sirens blared.

"Trouble at the Pirates football game," the driver said.

"What kind of trouble?"

"Stampede," he said.

Latecomers to the game, fifteen thousand of them, had been trapped and crushed in a tunnel at the stadium entrance. There had been nowhere for them to go, for there were sixty thousand people inside the stadium. Forty-three people had been killed and hundreds injured. With the first screams and the confusion, the game had been stopped and then abandoned.

"Someone told me to go to that game."

"Would have been a great game. But the stampede. Ach. Was terrible, man."

◈ ◈ ◈

Through a friend I met Mike Kirkinis, a guide to fossil sites. I liked him immediately. He was energetic and an optimist and he worked hard. He was no snob. He said, "Africans in Jo'burg tell me that they're from the bush, that their grandparents herded goats. I say, 'Hey, what a coincidence! My grandfather herded goats in Cyprus.' It's true. It helps to remember where you came from."

Mike, in his early forties, owned a helicopter. He ran tours out to the archeological sites of Sterkfontein and Swartkrans, places that bristled with the bones of hominids, the richest fossil sites in the world and South Africa's first World Heritage Sites. I agreed to go out with Mike one Sunday morning.

"I'll bring my girlfriend. We can have a picnic."

His girlfriend, Sybilla, was a German veterinarian. She was six foot one and very beautiful. She owned a rottweiler. As a vet, she specialized in the health of elephants. The previous year, while on an expedition in Mali "darting" elephants and treating them, an elephant that had been insufficiently tranquilized rose unexpectedly, tossed Sybilla to the ground, and trampled her, smashing her pelvis and her legs. Mike flew to Bamako and helped her, and over the course of the year she healed. You would not have known she had come close to being destroyed by big elephant feet unless you gave way to temptation, as I did, and gazed intently at her legs. The tiny scars and stitches did not detract from their beauty but only reminded me of her strength and courage. She had long silken hair and flinty blue eyes. She flew the chopper expertly.

"She intimidates people," Mike said.

I said, "Not me. I mean, if you wanted to go to the ends of the earth, she's the one to go with."

When we were aloft, Mike explained that what I was seeing below was the ridge on which Johannesburg sat — the Witwatersrand, the "White Water Ridge" — clearly upraised because (so he said) an asteroid had hit the planet right here a few billion years ago and rearranged the landscape, displacing the inland sea by pushing the gold-bearing reef, the great lip of rock, nearer to the surface. The gold, discovered in 1886, was the making of Johannesburg. (Diamonds had been found in great quantities in Kimberly about twenty years earlier.)

Flying in this helicopter was a guilty pleasure, because although I bemoaned air travel, I loved flying low over the Johannesburg suburbs, looking at the mansions, the evidence of white flight from the city, and black flight, too. From aloft I could see clusters of condominiums and gated communities, stately homes with swimming pools and horse paddocks, the adjacent slums, the squatter settlements — everything was visible. Flying with Mike was a language lesson, too: the parkland, the drifts, the *vlei* (marshland), the *kloofs* (ravines), the *kopjes* (little hills), the narrow tracks (*spoor*) across the veld, a large *wildtuin* (game reserve), the *snelweg* (highway), the *vrymaak* (freeway). Also the variously named detritus from the gold mines, for they created enormous rubble and sludge — the mine dumps and slime dams.

We saw busloads of tourists at Sterkfontein, so we landed at Swartkrans, and no one else was there.

"The oldest bones on earth have been found here," Mike said, and led us through the cave system, down a narrow path. White bones like fragments of flint and chalk protruded from the walls. Looking closely, I could easily discern molars, vertebrae, long hollow limb bones, canine teeth, and chunks of skull. Every vertical surface was covered with bits of smashed bone.

At the base of the cave, Mike said, "This site contains evidence of the first controlled use of fire by early man anywhere in the world. That was probably the single major pivotal point in human evolution — a million years ago. Imagine what a difference fire made. It gave humans the ability to master their environment and to become the most destructive species in the history of the planet."

The remains of prehistoric handmade bone tools had also been found in the cave, as well as evidence that the humans there had been the prey of large animals. The site at Swartkrans had been excavated since the 1930s, Mike said, and two types of early hominids coexisted here almost two million years ago, *Homo erectus* and *Homo robustus*. The cave had been continuously occupied for those two million years. Besides early humans, animals had also used it as a lair. It had served as a shelter for African pastoralists for hundreds of years. During the Boer War it was used by Boer soldiers. And more recently such caves served as hideouts for African guerrillas in the struggle to overthrow the white government.

With Sybilla working the controls, we flew into a remote gully and had a picnic by a cold spring, among twittering birds and ocher butterflies and watching hawks.

"Humans evolved here," Mike said. "Right here where we're sitting. We've found stone tools and bones and everything else. Africa was perfect for evolution. But you want to know something?"

Sybilla had been combing her long hair by the spring. She looked up at Mike, and I too tore my attention away from the comb tugs fluttering Sybilla's hair and gave him my full attention.

"Probably none of those bones are those of our direct ancestors."

"I thought that was Adam and Eve in the cave back there."

"What are you doing tomorrow?" Mike asked. "There's a guy you have to meet. He's got this amazing theory."

◇ ◇ ◇

The man to whom Mike introduced me, in a sushi bar in an upscale Johannesburg shopping mall, was Professor Lee Berger. He was head of the Paleoanthropological Unit for Research and Exploration at the University of the Witwatersrand. A paleoanthropologist studies ancient humans, but Professor Berger has said that this science of taking the widest view of history is "one of the greatest privileges . . . of being human." It was a vast search into our own elusive ancestry.

A genial American from Georgia in his late thirties, Berger had published a book in 2000 elaborating his research, *In the Footsteps of Eve.* His theory was that humankind's direct ancestor was probably not among any of the bones or fossil forms that had been dug up in Africa or anywhere else. Yes, humanoid species had been found, and the forms were more related to us than to chimps. But while the finds were extraordinarily close, they were not a direct link to us. Our actual ancestor had not been found.

I said, "What about these people who report startling findings? 'The ancestor of man.' There was one just this year."

"Kenyanthropus," Professor Berger said. He was smiling. "Imagine naming a new genus, just like that. And so quickly — three weeks between the submission of the research findings and the acceptance."

"So you don't buy it?"

He said, "Paleoanthropologists are competing for money and grants, so they tend to make earthshaking pronouncements about finding our ancestors. If you need money for research, it helps to make headlines."

Lee Berger's forthrightness and skepticism, his insistence on presenting fossils in the right context, his habit of doubting and demanding proof, had earned him many admirers and some enemies. Because paleoanthropology involved so much interpretation and "emotional resonance," rivalries were inevitable and competition among scientists and fossil hunters was intense. He said that the Leakeys, competitive within their own family, had not found "Adam" in Olduvai Gorge, and for him the 3.2-million-year-old Lucy skeleton that I had seen in Addis Ababa was not "Eve" but rather a three-foot-tall bipedal ape with a chimplike jaw.

"She's in our family tree. We were an ape until two million years ago. We became *erectus* — had skills, learned to control fire, learned hunting, got weapons. But the Lucy fossil is probably a dead end."

"Family tree" was not an expression Berger used much, and in fact he said that such a concept misrepresented the progress of our origins. The notion of a tree was too simple for being so linear, for the pattern of our ancestry more likely resembled a "complex bush."

Disputing fossil finds had given him some predictable supporters, among them creationists, who believed literally in Adam and Eve, and the Flood, and Lot's wife turning into a pillar of salt. Taking Professor Berger's words out of context, creationists cited his work as evidence that Darwin and his heresies were nothing but a low trick in getting God out of America's schools.

It was understandable that little was known about our distant ancestors, he said. "The study of human origins is only thirty or forty years old. That's all. Before then it was like stamp collecting."

Berger had come to South Africa via Kenya in the 1980s. He had worked with Richard Leakey on a dig at Lake Turkana, in northwestern Kenya. At that time, South Africa awaited discovery. Because of the Nationalist Party, which came to power in 1948, and the academic boycott that was called because of the white supremacist policies of that party, there was no digging at all in South Africa for forty years — no work in paleoanthropology and no finds from 1948 until 1989. Just as bad, a great deal of fossil material that had been found earlier was useless because it was undated.

"It's not like Europe, where they have lake sites. Lake sites are easily datable. We didn't have volcanism. No geochemical signals. No one here knew exactly what they had found."

In 1990, when Berger seriously started looking for fossils, there were only five established early hominid sites in South Africa. "But there were dozens of caves, dozens and dozens," he said. "I began by walking in the bush around Krugersdorp" — Swartkrans is near there — "and I'd see a cave and we'd dig and find fossils. There were fossils everywhere. We started digging in Gladysville, and two weeks later we found fossils of hominids. In some caves we found hominids that had been preyed upon by saber-toothed cats — no, not the other way around."

Talking about Africa and the larger meaning of the fossils, Berger lost his circumspection and spoke of "the incredible binding power of fossils," how they brought people together. The lesson of evolution in Africa, he said, was not tribalism and division, but cooperation. "Every critical event in the development of *Homo sapiens* has come out of Africa."

In *In the Footsteps of Eve* he had written: "Humanity is a product of Africa. We are what we are today because we've been shaped by our environment — and it was the African environment that hosted almost every major evolutionary change we've experienced on our journey towards being human."

"The morphology of the face, how we lost our canines, the very definitions of our humanity," he said. "We are defined by peacefulness and cooperation. Those qualities developed here in Africa."

There were four of us seated at the sushi bar — Lee Berger had brought a friend, and Mike Kirkinis had brought me.

"Look at us," Berger said. "You couldn't take four of any other mammalian species and sit down as we are doing here. This is the proof that we are the cooperative species."

Picking up a spicy tuna hand roll, Mike said, "So maybe there's hope for the world?"

"We are undoubtedly a peaceful species. We developed a pedomorphic face — childlike, nonthreatening. Go ahead, Paul, threaten me with your face."

I attempted a fierce face.

Berger crowed to the table, "See, he didn't show his teeth! Other mammals express threat by showing their teeth, but humans don't. Warfare is symbolic — it was, anyway, until this century. The idea of mass slaughter is pretty recent."

A recurrent event in history that has always fascinated me is first contact. The most vivid examples come from travel — the age of exploration and discovery. Usually, first contact is construed as Columbus meeting his first Arawak and calling him an Indian; but consider the reverse: the Arawak meeting a fat little Italian clutching a copy of Marco Polo's *Travels* on the deck of a caravel. In the year of contact, 1778, the Hawaiians believed Captain Cook to be the god Lono. The Aztecs in 1517 took the Spaniards to be avatars of Quetzalcoatl, the plumed serpent, god of learning and of wind. The polar Inuit assumed that they were the only people in the world, so in 1821 when they met their first white stranger, the explorer Sir William Parry, they said to him, "Are you from the sun or the moon?"

And as recently as the 1930s, Australian gold prospectors and New Guinea highlanders met for the first time. The grasping, world-weary Aussies took the highlanders to be savages, while the highlanders, assuming that the Aussies were the ghosts of their own dead ancestors back on a visit, felt a kinship and gave them food, thinking, They are like people you see in a dream. But the Australians were looking for gold and killed the highlanders, who were uncooperative.

We talked about this, appropriately, four strangers discussing the elements of meeting, the hope implied in our amiable lunch. First contact was a vivid and recurrent event for everyone — bumping into a stranger on the subway, finding yourself with a fellow rider in an elevator, knocking elbows with your seatmate on a plane — at a bus stop, at a checkout counter, on a beach, in a church or a movie theater, wherever we were thrown together and had to deal with it. As a traveler, first contact was the story of my life, and was a motif of my African trip — the safari that had taken me through the Sudan desert, on a cattle truck on the Ethiopian border, on a steamer on Lake Victoria or in a dugout on the Zambezi, at a lunch table or a farm in Harare, and right here in the sushi bar.

"All the evidence in first contact proves that we are a peaceful species," Berger said, summing it up. "The aggression comes later."

Africa, ancient in human terms, was the best place for studying our ancestry, he said. Humankind had been able to develop here without leaving, had roamed over this enormous fruitful place with its good climate and shelter. Africa had everything, Europe not much, which was why humans had lived in Africa for 160,000 years before anyone remotely human existed in Europe.

"We are a coastal species — we lived, historically, with access to the sea," Berger said. "That's especially true in Africa. We were able to conquer the marine environment. When we ran out of animals to kill, we turned to the sea. There's never a lean season if you know how to fish."

One theory he had discussed in his book was that the larger brain size of early humans was attributable to the protein-rich marine diet available on the African coast.

I said, "But what about the people who have always been living in the African forests — in the jungle, even in the deserts."

"People in the forest were historically sidelined," he said. "Look at the Pygmies in the Ituri Forest. Also the desert-dwelling Arabs, the Khoikhoin, and certain native Americans. The people who lived away from the watercourses were people who became marginalized."

He had painted a bright persuasive picture: we humans were peaceable, resourceful, cooperative. But there was a dark side. Not long after that lunch, a Johannesburg psychologist described South Africa as "a society that has come out of an abyss."

The man was Saths Cooper, a close colleague of Steve Biko, the activist who had been murdered by South African police in 1977. Cooper's political activism had earned him a jail term of nine years, more than five of them spent on Robben Island. He was now a doctor. He chaired the Statutory Professional Board for Psychology at the Health Professions Council of South Africa. He said, "We have not come to actual grips with the depth of depravity that occurred."

At its high-minded best, South Africa was a society concerned with justice, dealing with its murderous past in a noble way, through the Truth and Reconciliation Commission, and trying to get a handle on its conflict-ridden present. Capital punishment had been eliminated, mercy and forgiveness was the text of every sermon and of most political speeches. Yet there was something akin to savagery suggested in the crime figures — fifty-five murders a day, a rape every twenty-three seconds. These were just the reported incidents; the actual numbers were higher. The society that existed in South Africa — probably the most open on the continent — had a free press, virtually no censorship, no political terror, and had produced a distinguished literature in two languages. Its very openness ensured that every lapse, every crime, every transgression was scrutinized in detail.

At a popular level, a shopping-mall culture had begun to develop at the edge of its cities, partly as a response to the insecurity and high crime in city centers but also because there were enough consumers with money to spend on new clothes and restaurants. The suburbs of Rosebank and Sandton were multiracial and generally safe, and their malls were palmy and serene.

I took heart from the words of a wise paleoanthropologist who knew his hominids: *Here we are, four strangers together, sitting at the same table. We are peaceful. We are the cooperative species.* That was hopeful, and the fact that he was saying this in the clean and safe food court of an African shopping mall was hopeful, too.

20 ◇◇◇

The Wild Things at Mala Mala

THE BIG FURRY reason that most people are drawn to Africa is the possibility of viewing dangerous animals from the comfort and safety of a Land Rover, wearing a silly hat and carrying a scorecard. At the end of the day, the score has to show the Big Five. I could tick off only one of these, a tottering *tembo* I had accidentally glimpsed from the train in Tanzania. Much as I despaired of tourism in Africa and mocked the voyeurism that amounted to pestering animals in the bush, my idea was to satisfy myself that my own improvised safari would also include a week of peering at the wild creatures Africa was famous for.

I had seen so few — some jaw-snapping hyenas in Harar, shy gazelles in Kenya, several loping giraffes and the trudging elephant from the windows of the Kilimanjaro Express, mottled hippos in the Shire River, an ostrich glaring at me in Zimbabwe, dik-diks and baboons here and there, birds everywhere. No rhinos, no leopards, no herds of anything. I could relate to animals in their awkwardness, for they looked like loners in the bush, and all of them were more or less fleeing. The gazelles had fled with sharply lifted knees as in a steeplechase.

The most dangerous creatures I had seen so far in Africa had been the shifta bandits firing their rifles over the truck I was riding in just north of Marsabit: wild men. The most exotic were the Ugandan hookers in their nighttime plumage, hissing at me from the roadside trees in Kampala: wild women.

A year or so before my African trip, tourists on a gorilla safari had been massacred on the Uganda-Rwanda border. Not content with leaving the pathetically diminished number of poor beasts alone, and aiming to intrude on their shrinking habitat so that they could boast of having had the ultimate primate experience of paddling paws and pinching fingers with a six-hundred-pound silverback gorilla and his mates in the dripping seclusion of the bewildered apes' bower, a dozen trekkers panted into the high Bwindi Impenetrable Forest in Uganda and were mauled — not by apes but by gun-toting Hutu rebels. Eight tourists were murdered; the other captives managed to escape. While tittering insincerely that Africa was full of dangerous and unpredictable animals, most foreign visitors were more preoccupied by the thought of dangerous and unpredictable Africans. By comparison, the Big Five were rather sedate and safe and standoffish.

Tourists in Africa were whisked to a game park, and within a few days could boast of having bagged photos of the Big Five without a single horror story. At the end of the safari the foreign travelers, sounding like the rambling, overprivileged fatheads of a century earlier, would rate their trip, as I was to read later in *Condé Nast Traveler* (January 2002): "[African staff] try to make you happy"; "[They] do everything — you really feel pampered"; "[They] wake you gently with a small breakfast treat at bedside"; "[African] waiters are willing to set up a picnic wherever you like"; "No bugs to contend with." And, of a lodge in Tanzania's Ngorongoro Crater, "After the guided safaris and cultural tours, have your butler draw you a bath."

This was the tidier, deep-pockets-in-the-safari-suit, small-bore-in-Africa safari, the romancers' one of deluxe howdahs on elephant expeditions in the Okavango, picnic hampers in Amboseli ("Pass The Gentleman's Relish, Nigel"), and luxurious tents in Masai Mara Reserve and the Serengeti. It was the "Yes, *bwana*" Africa of escapists and honeymooners and so-called "consumer travelers" in designer khaki. This Africa, in which Hemingway's gun bearers had morphed into Jeeves-like butlers and game spotters, was available to anyone who, like Ernie, had lots of money and no interest in Africans. In a moment of candor, in a travel essay written in the seventies, Martha Gellhorn, the penultimate of Hemingway's four wives and a sometime Kenya resident, confessed her indifference to Africans. Writing breezily in *Travels with Myself and Another*, unaware of giving offense, she said how her love for Africa's natural world "did not extend to mankind in Africa or its differing ways of life."

The safari-as-charade included charter flights, obsequious Africans, gourmet food, bush jackets by Harrods' Field Sports Department, pith helmets by Holland & Holland, five-hundred-dollar boots by Gokey ("guaranteed to be snakeproof"), and the Elephant Cloth Bushveld Shirt by Orvis, this last item pitched with a colorful flourish:

> Our African Train Safari will take you from Pretoria to Victoria Falls in 9 days, stopping along the way for hunts in the "Bushveld" country, with more than a hundred beaters driving the guinea fowl and francolin over the line to you. In the desert, you'll shoot Namaqua sandgrouse from traditional stone butts, where 1,000 or more birds fly to water holes in the early morning. This shirt is designed for that kind of adventure.
>
> — from the spring 2002 catalogue

This was a far cry from my safari-as-struggle, including public transport, fungal infections, petty extortion, mocking lepers, dreary bedrooms, bad food, exploding bowels, fleeing animals, rotting schoolrooms, meaningless delays, and blunt threats: "There are bad people there" and "Give me money!" Consumer travelers raved about flying into Malawi to spend a few days in a lakeside resort, but in Malawi I had been appalled — as a Bible-pious Malawian might put it — at "the years that the locust hath eaten" (Joel 2:25).

Although I hated nuisances, I did not mind hardships. And if I had endured some miseries, I had also discovered some splendors, enjoyed some adventures, and found friends. I had crossed many borders, picnicked by the Sixth Cataract of the Nile, navigated Lake Victoria, paddled on the Mozambique Zambezi, and spent a day with my old friend the prime minister of Uganda. En route, whenever someone asked me to sum up my safari I just stammered and went mute, for it was less a trip than an experience of vanishing, a long period in my life spent alone, improvising my way through the greenest continent. I was proud that I could not say, "Africa's great!" "Our servants were neat!" "I got a facial in our game lodge and Wendy got a pedicure!" "We had eland bourguignon!" "There was, like, a riot in the capital and we didn't even know it!" or "My butler drew me a bath."

Yet I was so immersed in my trip I hardly questioned it. After a week in Johannesburg I had the appetite for much more. Looking at the map of Africa I saw that I was not very far from Cape Town, so I took a detour in the other direction.

Mala Mala, a game reserve that adjoined Kruger National Park, was highly recommended to me by a trusted friend. It was north of the fruit-growing *dorp* of Nelspruit, about three hundred miles east of Johannesburg, so near to the Mozambique border that Mozambican elephants wandered over to chew the trees. One of Mala Mala's virtues as a game reserve was that it was located on a twenty-mile stretch of a good-sized river, far from any village or the intrusion of poachers: big game were happiest among plentiful greenery, near a safe year-round water source.

On my way to Nelspruit I met Hansie, who was half Boer and half English. He seemed slow to answer my questions, rather absent-minded or at a loss for words. He said, "Sometimes my brain works faster than my tongue." I asked him a little about himself and understood fairly quickly the reason for his vagueness and stunned way of speaking. He had been in the South African army, fighting the bush war for five years, and had had a harrowing time.

"I was in the Koevoet," he said, and explained that the word meant "Crowbar" in Afrikaans. "It was the military branch of the intelligence service. I was only eighteen."

"How did you happen to join?"

"I don't know why. I guess because everyone was joining. But it was a tough group," Hansie said. "Our commander flew to America and went through Navy SEAL training, then went to Britain and was put through the SAS course. He adapted those courses for our training."

"What a grind that must have been," I said, thinking of the physical demands of such training. "What was the worst of it?"

"The worst? Ach, well, I wasn't prepared for killing people — I mean, killing that many people. The actual killing was the one thing we couldn't train for, see."

He had misunderstood me. I thought we had been talking about long marches or swimming underwater, the physical effort of commando training.

"But it was either them or us," he said, still talking quietly. "Ach, we had to or we'd get it in the neck. We were in Namibia, fighting SWAPO guerrillas." The South-West Africa People's Organization provided

Namibia with its first president, Sam Nujoma, in 1990. "I did counterinsurgency. I think I was good at it, but even so, it was bloody, man."

"What was your particular mission?"

"We had to be able to go to a guerrilla camp, and destroy it, and leave no trace that we had ever been there."

"That would mean killing everyone."

"Ach. Yaw. Everyone. And do it alone if we lost our partner, as sometimes happened. I mean, I lost my partner, but not in the bush. He was black, a Namibian. He went to a pub to celebrate his birthday. A SWAPO informant was there and called some chaps and reported that four of our men were there. The SWAPO chaps came to the pub and started shooting. But see, the birthday party had started, and a woman there knew my partner was celebrating. She threw herself in front of him to protect him."

"Amazing."

"Yaw. But they just shot her, and shot him, and shot the others. Four dead, and they left the woman there to bleed to death."

It was a horrible story, without a moral, but after it sank in I asked Hansie what birthday his partner had been celebrating.

"That's interesting," Hansie said. "Yaw, he had seen his whole family killed by SWAPO gunmen, so he joined when he was fourteen. He was a big chap, and they have no ID cards up there, so no one knew. He was celebrating his sixteenth birthday."

"And SWAPO got into power."

"All the people we fought against are now in power — in Namibia and Zimbabwe and here." Hansie chuckled grimly. "It's crazy. They were called Communists. Well, were they? They were trained by Russians. They got their weapons from China and Cuba. They knew how to use them. And the land mines! They had a Russian land mine made of Bakelite plastic that you couldn't detect. It was really lethal. Friends of mine got blown up that way. I lost so many friends — and for what?"

After telling this sad, rambling story, Hansie was quite upset. My questions had led him too far down the bleak path of bad memories. But that was often the case in South Africa. A few idle questions inspired reminiscences, and brought back the past, and the past in South Africa was dark with martyrdom.

"Ach! If I lost one of my kids in something like that I'd go doolally," Hansie said.

The closer we got to Mala Mala Main Camp, the more chewed and trampled the trees, as though a tornado had whirled through, stripping and smashing the woods.

"Elephants," Hansie said. He explained that because of hunters, the place had been almost devoid of elephants in the 1960s. There were now more than 600 in an area that should have been supporting about 150 — thus the damage.

He pointed out a herd of browsing buffalo with oxpecker birds on them, some of them stabbing at insects, others cleaning wounds. Also a pair of warthogs. "That bigger one's injured. Probably from a leopard. Some of them get away, see." The warthogs frowned at us with knobbed tusky faces, in an appearance of indignation that was gaping animal alertness.

But I was hardly looking, scarcely listening, for I was still thinking of what Hansie had told me: *Ach, well, I wasn't prepared for killing people — I mean, killing that many people.* I heard stories of maulings and tramplings and gorings, but that "Crowbar" counterinsurgency mayhem was much, much worse. The boy who had enlisted at fourteen because he had seen his whole family murdered; his sixteenth birthday party at the pub; the snitch; the arrival of the enemy with guns blazing; the woman shielding the birthday boy; and Hansie's remorse. While "dilly" was just peculiar, "doolally" was the extremest form of military madness, from Deolalie, the name of a nineteenth-century nuthouse near Bombay.

At this stage of my trip, having seen so much of Africa, it was impossible to be heading for a safari lodge without comparing animal cunning with human savagery. I believed that I had reduced my risk in East and Central Africa by admitting that as a white stranger I was prey, and by avoiding predators — doing what animals did, moving quickly in the daytime, staying alert, and not going out at night. Predators are mainly nocturnal — lions and hyenas sleep and lollygag in the daytime. And it is a fact that except for the cheetah, all the wild predators in Africa are slower than their prey. Warier, twitchier, fleeter of foot, prey had evolved into hard-to-catch creatures.

In that same spirit, decent Africans tried to outwit the rascals, warned each other of dangers, warned strangers, too. Theft, assault, and rape were primarily nocturnal crimes, not merely because darkness helped the perpetrator in his stealth but because the thief or rapist who was caught could be blamelessly beaten to death under the terms of the unspoken African law that sanctioned rough justice.

Territory defined behavior. Different species might coexist — giraffe and zebra, warthogs and kudu. But two rhinos could not inhabit the same area, and they always battled for dominance, as the gangs did in Soweto.

Yet the bulky mammals and the decorative birds — impressive for their color and size — were predictable. They did what animals do: ate, slept, and looked for water; groomed and head-butted each other, vocalized and snorted, competed and fought; made a career out of learning how to subsist while saving their skin. But none fought so cruelly or so pointlessly as humans, and none, not even elephants in their fits of trumpeted grief, had the redeeming quality of remorse. As Professor Lee Berger had said, humans were vicious, we had invented mass slaughter, but we were also the most peaceable animal — both much better and much worse than other mammals.

◇ ◇ ◇

Of all the creatures that inhabited the forty-five thousand acres of Mala Mala — and that included the regal waterbuck and the brown snake eagle, the nimble klipspringer and the four-foot monitor lizard, as well as the majestic Big Five — the one that fascinated me most was Mike Rattray, the owner and driving force behind the reserve. When approaching from a great distance and waving his stick and vocalizing, he much resembled one of his own strutting red-wattled hornbills. But he was another species and altogether more colorful and subtle, the jolliest, the fiercest, the least predictable, the hardest to photograph, and was usually followed by his attractive mate, Norma.

Rattray was never without the stick. He used the thing to make a point or to single someone out of a crowd or, in a threat posture, as a weapon. He looked a bit like Captain Mainwaring, the same drooping cheeks and deadpan, the same drawling way of speaking, always something unexpected.

"Going to 'fight to the death,' is he?" he would say somewhat adenoidally. "Well, let me tell you, whenever someone says they are going to fight to the death, they're ready to surrender. They are dead scared.

Your move? Get a stick. Like this" — and he flailed his own. "Give them two clouts on the backside. A good hiding. 'Stop playing the fool.' They'll stop their nonsense soon enough. Know what the nyala bull does?"

I said I did not know much about this large antelope.

"The nyala bull is a very narrow animal," Rattray said, and demonstrated its narrowness by lifting his stick to a vertical position and pressing the palm of his free hand against it. "Very narrow. But when they want to frighten an enemy, they swell up" — he scowled and blew out his cheeks, to look fierce and florid and full-faced — "blow their faces up to look dangerous. It's just air!"

What had been cattle ranches and a hunting lodge and a large game reserve in the 1920s was acquired in the 1960s by Mike and his father, who had owned a ranch nearby. Rich in animals, the land had attracted hunters. As many as two hundred lions were killed in a single season, for sport and also to protect the cattle. But because of the insects and the weather, the cattle business had never been much good. When the land appeared on the market, more abutting ranches and reserves were added to the central piece. Two lodges were added to the luxurious Main Camp, an atmospheric farmhouse was improved to make Kirkman's Kamp, and the lower-priced (but pleasant) Harry's Camp was added. Altogether, Mala Mala employed 250 people. In 1993, with Mike's encouragement the many-miles-long game fence that was also an international frontier, dividing Kruger Park from Mozambique, was taken down. After that, the animals roamed freely, choosing to live nearer Rattray's watercourse, the Sand River.

Rattray, in his vigorous mid-sixties, was a horse breeder and horse racer, with a stud farm in Western Cape province. He had become an environmentalist at a time when hunters were still blasting away at anything that moved. He was a bon viveur with a knack for running hotels, a stickler for detail, something of a taskmaster, a financier of public works — his tall, Italian-made road bridge over the Sand River had withstood a ravaging flood in 1999. He was a teller of rich stories and also a fund of good ideas.

"Rhino are taking a beating, what?" he said to me in the bar one night, waving his stick for emphasis. "Being flogged something awful. And why? Because a rhino horn, retail, is worth seventy-five thousand dollars in Macau, or so I'm told. What's the answer, Paul?"

"What's the question, Mike?"

"Whither the rhinos, their fate? I say" — and he whisked his stick — "rhino farm! A farm that produces rhino horn. People groan like blazes when I mention it, but you see, a rhino horn is like a fingernail. You cut it off and it grows back. So you start a farm with white rhinos — the black ones are bolshie, never mind them — and you harvest the horns by sawing them off. That way, you cut out the poachers, cut out the middlemen, and the horn grows back in three years, ready to be trimmed again. But will anyone listen to me? No, they think I'm dilly."

I stayed in a luxurious thatched hut in Main Camp and went on game drives in an open Land Rover with a ranger before dawn until midmorning, and again at dusk, and now and then in the darkness, the time of night when the lion and the leopard were slinking in the high grass, looking for cowering impala to eat. The ranger, Chris Daphne, was young and expert. His assistant, John, who was a Zulu, sat at the rear with a rifle across his knees.

The bush was dry and dusty in the South African autumn, and on the first drive we saw buffalo, a herd of elephants, a mating pair of nyala, a bachelor herd of kudu, and some battered torchwood trees — battered because elephants loved the taste of the oily peanut-shaped fruit.

Mala Mala was not a wilderness but a reserve, and the happier for that, because the animals were not shot at. They had become so habituated to the prowling vehicles and the crowing passengers that, keeping at a humane distance, it was possible for us to see them in their unselfconscious, unthreatened natural state. The animals were generally complacent and well fed and unstressed. And the reserve was so well run that a tourist such as Margaret Thatcher or Nelson Mandela — both of whom had stayed at Mala Mala — could drop in, see some big animals, and leave, without inconvenience or discomfort.

A herd of two hundred buffalo was not unusual at Mala Mala; the sight of twenty elephants placidly chewing trees, deforesting a hillside, was not out of the ordinary. And hyenas — "The quickest of all predators to recognize weakness," Chris said; a pair of white rhino — "Did you know the rhino is related to the horse?" he asked; a tuskless elephant — "Probably more aggressive for not having tusks," he said. The birds were spectacular: the greater blue-eared glossy starling, the blacksmith plover with its characteristic *tink-tink*, the yellow-billed hornbill.

One night in the bush, on the walkie-talkie, Chris heard that a leopard had just pounced on an impala and bitten and broken its neck. We drove quickly to the spot, in time to see the leopard dragging his kill — the dead impala was the same weight as the leopard, about a hundred pounds — to a high branch thirty feet up a saffron tree, wedging it firmly into the cleft of the branch. There the leopard could devour his kill in peace, without attracting opportunistic animals. In spite of our bright flashlight, the leopard went on tearing the impala's flesh, ripping at the haunch, crunching and splintering the bones of its spine and pelvis, and by my watch gobbled the impala's entire hind leg in ten minutes.

At the same time, the guests at Mala Mala at their evening meal were sitting in a circle under the stars, gnawing on impala steaks that had just been barbecued. The eaters' canines flashed in the firelight, their fingers gleamed with meat fat, and after they swallowed they sighed with satisfaction, rejoicing in their safari.

I was late for dinner because of my leopard viewing, but I found a seat near Mike Rattray and asked him how he had gone about ending the hunting on his property.

"It was hard. The hunters were very cross. Wanted to come here and go on flogging lions," he said. He smiled, perhaps remembering the opposition, for he was a man who liked a challenge. "This was a popular hunting area. Princess Alice! Flogged a lion here, yes!"

He had foreseen the decline of game and the simple economic fact that hunting was for the few — the unspeakable in pursuit of the stuffable. In contrast, game viewing was for the many. There was more sense and more money in becoming eco-friendly. While other reserves went on hosting parties of hunters, Mala Mala eliminated hunting, practiced game management, hired university-trained rangers, and began to see a profit. And the animals thrived.

"You see, the trouble with hunters is that they take the best animals, the prize specimens," Rattray said. "They jigger the gene pool, they disturb the balance of nature. They screamed at me, but I screamed back. 'You want to hunt? By all means, hunt! But you have to take the ones with weak eyes, weak ears. Kill the weak ones — take what the carnivores take.'"

"What sort of reaction did you get?"

Even over dinner, Rattray had his stick handy for illustrating a point. He seized it and swung it. "They didn't like it. But I said, 'Don't take the clever ones.' You have to be clever to live in the bush. At the end of the drought you have the best animals. They wanted trophies — they wanted the clever ones. I said no."

It was an inspired decision. When the dominant males are killed and their heads mounted, the male cubs stay in the pride and mate with their mothers and sisters, and "jigger the gene pool." A pride without an aggressive leader becomes easy fodder for predators. In the past decade, Africa's lion population has dropped from about fifty thousand to about fifteen thousand. Botswana instituted a one-year ban on lion hunting in 2001 to determine the health and numbers of its lion population. At the same time, the Arizona-based Safari Club International — composed of millionaire big-game hunters and Republican fundraisers — intensively lobbied the Bush White House to put pressure on Botswana to reverse the ban. Botswana at first resisted, then relented. Anyone with $25,000 can play at being Hemingway's Francis Macomber and kill a lion in Botswana.

In my succeeding days at Mala Mala, driving all day in the hot bush, I saw three giraffe at a pool, their long legs widely splayed, their bodies canted and kowtowing so they could drink. A baboon with his finger in his mouth lurked behind them among some boulders in a *krans* — a cave. I saw hippos in a murky pool, wallowing and diving, peering at me, just their eyes and nostrils showing.

The T. S. Eliot poem "The Hippopotamus" contains a dozen observations about hippos, all of them mistaken, from "The broad-backed hippopotamus / Rests his belly in the mud" — something they never do — to the characterization of their gait. I saw zebra with reddish highlights in their brushy manes, a mother rhino with an eight-day-old calf, a troop of fifty baboons, and many birds — barbets, shrikes, coucals, hornbills, cormorants, kingfishers, eagles, and vultures ("The eagle's grip is much stronger than the vulture's," Chris said). I saw twelve lions, big and small, creeping through the bush just after dark, stalking a skittish herd of impala, cowering in a copse.

All of this was superb game viewing — healthy unafraid animals holding their own in a bush setting — but just as splendid and imposing was the striding potbellied figure of Michael Rattray, who was inimitable. Stories circulated about him, always admiring ones, and odd tales of life in the bush, often involving difficult guests.

There was the impossible German couple, for example, characters in a story with a tragic ending. The Herr and Frau arrived, were served a good lunch, and went on a game drive with a reliable ranger. But they complained about the food, found fault with the ranger, and were disappointed in the animals. The Herr was milder than his Frau, who loudly objected throughout the afternoon drive, hectoring the ranger. The woman was a harridan and made you think of a scolding gray-headed bush shrike, crying, "*Schlecht! Schlecht! Schlecht!*"

At dinner, Mike Rattray appeared at their table, smacking his stick against his palm. No, he didn't hit them, though he wanted to. The woman began to articulate an objection, but before she was in full cry, Rattray said, "You are not enjoying yourselves. You are complaining. There is no charge."

The couple, mollified by this apparent climb-down by the management, had returned to manipulating their forks and knives when they saw that Rattray had not moved.

"You are leaving tomorrow on the first plane," Rattray said, and quickly turned. As he walked away he could hear the woman ranting.

Before the couple left, the woman insisted that Rattray write a letter describing the circumstances of their departure and demanded that he state that they were leaving against their will.

"Absolutely not," Rattray said. He oversaw the loading of their bags into the Land Rover and turned his back on them for the last time.

Threats of a lawsuit arrived from Germany soon afterward. Many letters from German attorneys hinted at damages and expensive legal maneuvers that would bring Mala Mala to its knees. This pettifoggery went on for a month or so. Then, as quickly as the letters had started, they ended. Some months passed. The case had gone so quiet a discreet inquiry was advanced. Why the silence? The word came back: the German woman had killed herself.

The male guests at such game lodges could behave with a strange machismo, wearing shorts and knee socks. But for the visiting women the experience was either uncomfortable and insupportably buggy or else such a fantasy of khaki and muscly stud muffins and animal desire they became smitten.

In a place where stalking was a way of life for the animals, the women guests developed a stalking mentality, too, and would not be dissuaded from their hunt. I heard a number of stories of this kind of infatuation. While the husbands idled complacently in the lodge, swigging beer and staring at the elephants thrashing in the reeds in the river, the rangers received the nudges and winks or smutty suggestions of the besotted wives. And so these rangers, on a game drive for predators with an amorous client, were in the curious position of stalking stalkers while they themselves were being stalked.

"Afterwards, they write letters," a ranger told me. "They call from America or Europe. They say they want to leave their husband and move to Africa. 'I dream of Africa.' It takes a long time for some of them to give up. But it's unprofessional to have that kind of relationship with a guest."

One such stalker at Mala Mala was a woman on her honeymoon. I had the presence of mind to murmur "Shocking," but was riveted by the story of the cuckold in khaki and the new bride, two days married, who fell for the ranger. Nothing came of it, though no one held out much hope for the marriage. I regretted that the story was so short on sordid details.

Three honeymoon couples were staying at Mala Mala when I was there. They sat together in the bar. They dined together. They vied for attention by swapping stories of wedding-day foul-ups. They resembled the bush creatures that mated for life, pawed each other, and traded nuzzles, that growled amiably and were altogether feline in the shade of thorn trees throughout the hot afternoons.

As a couple, Michael and Norma Rattray were undemonstrative but affectionate. They were never apart. They had seven grown children between them and numerous grandchildren. Michael's task was management and infrastructure; Norma's brief was the lodges' decor. They conversed in animal imagery, and were delighted when one of the Mala Mala leopards appeared on the cover of *National Geographic.* The leopard was not a wayward predator that had crept darkly from the bush to wreak havoc, but a familiar creature with a pet name, like a favorite overindulged pussycat, one of the family, and as Norma said in a doting and admiring way, "rather a showoff."

"Going?" Michael said to me on the morning of my departure.

"I'm afraid so."

"Back to the States?"

"Eventually."

"God," he said. He was concentrating hard on city life. "Had some guests from New York. Friends, really. Most of our guests become friends. Chap says to us, 'Look us up if you're ever in New York. So we did. Went to the chap's house in this tall building. Couldn't believe it! He's way up here" — Rattray waved his stick, demonstrating the height of the skyscraper. "The walls were glass, windows went from floor to ceiling. Norma could hardly look down. Couldn't wait to leave."

"Like living in a tree," Norma said.

"Worse. Chap's stuck there like a gannet in a *krans!*"

His vivid image of animal horror made me laugh. I was sorry to leave; I knew I would miss him. And living in luxury in the bush was such a blissful way of passing the time — gaping at large unintimidated animals, bird watching, sipping South African wine, reading, in a cozy hut with a desk where I could sit adding pages to my erotic story. I could understand why tourists gushed: game viewing was pleasurable, it was simple and harmonious and safe; no strife, no starvation, it wasn't upsetting; not many Africans, it was hardly Africa.

21 ◈◈◈

Faith, Hope, and Charity on the Limpopo Line

BACK IN the *dorp* of Nelspruit, among the orange groves and jackfruit trees and the fields of floppy-leafed tobacco, I looked at my map and saw that I was only seventy miles from the Mozambique border — about the same distance as from Barnstable to Boston — and so I caught a cross-border bus to Maputo. I knew in advance that I would be doubling back across the border, which meant four immigration bottlenecks, two each way, and long lines. But anything was better than flying. I kept thinking of Nadine Gordimer introducing me: "He came from Cairo! On a bus!"

The bus was filled with Africans, many of whom were Mozambicans who had crossed the border to shop for items in Nelspruit that were unobtainable in Maputo. Two Indian men in skullcaps hogged the four seats in the front row of the top level. The men had pulled off their shoes and sat cross-legged, and the pong of their cheesy feet filled the upper deck. Because the bus had been advertised as a "luxury coach," a movie was shown on the overhead TV set.

The movie, *Jack*, starring Robin Williams, had seemed a facetious, thinly plotted, sentimental trifle when I first saw it in 1997. But travel-weary as I was, and with a big birthday behind me, the message of "live all you can" from the prematurely aged Jack, speaking at his high school graduation, made me absurdly emotional. A scene involving fart gas and explosive crepitation had the Indians clutching their sides in hilarity and laid one of them straight in the aisle, giggling. For a dose of reality I glanced out the window at the mud huts of the Swazi people in the direction of Piggs Peak, ruled over by the Ndlovukazi, their queen mum, the great She Elephant of Swaziland.

Across the long hills, through the stone mountains, when we came to the first shanties I knew we were at the in-between land near the border. Riffraff mostly, no one looked at home here, people newly arrived or waiting to leave. The bus stopped. We lined up and walked through the formalities. The South African officials were efficient, while the Mozambique protocols lacked substance — for example, there was hardly enough ink on the immigration officer's stamp to make an impression on my passport. About an hour and a half of this and then we were on our way, going down a good Mozambican road that the South Africans had built as a gift. We had passed Komatipoort, where there was a railway station, but no trains were running that day.

"There were floods here last year," the African next to me said. "All this was under water."

That had been in the world news, as African disasters always were — earthquakes, volcanic eruptions, massacres, famines, columns of refugees. *And these are the lucky ones.* Images of inundated fields, people clinging to treetops, and helicopter rescues had appeared on TV for a week before becoming old news. The trouble with such disasters was their unchanging imagery — viewers got bored with them for their having no silver lining and no variation. For a catastrophe to have legs, it needed to be an unfolding story, like a script with plot points, and preferably a happy ending. The ending of the Mozambique floods came with the news of cholera and poisoned water, of thousands of people who had been made homeless, and hundreds who had drowned like rats.

"And the worst was when the floods moved the land mines," the man said. "Picked them up and floated them all over the place. There was a grid saying where they had been put, but after the floods the land mines were all in different places and couldn't be located."

Ray, the land mine expert I had met in Sudan, had told me this was largely a rural myth in Africa. It was rare for whole mine fields to move like ghost landscapes. And anyway, dogs could sniff them out. I suggested this to the man in the seat next to me.

"I saw a woman chasing a pig," he said, to contradict me. "It was near my house outside Maputo. Suddenly there was a huge explosion. The woman's head was up a tree. Her arms and legs were all over the place. I mean, she stepped on a land mine in her own garden that had not been there before."

Maputo appeared as a succession of outlying shantytowns, and soon we were traveling from one district to another, with not much improvement in the look of things. Maputo was a true version of an African city, miles of slums and local markets leading to the main streets and shops in the center of town — a few tall buildings and rows of street lamps surrounded by miles of blight and danger: uncontained urbanization.

When the bus stopped and I got out, I was besieged by beggars, taxi drivers, chewing-gum hawkers, shoeshine boys, and opportunists shrieking "Meesta!" I surrendered to a taxi driver named Candido and asked him to take me to the Polana, a decayed wedding cake of a hotel on the seafront which had somehow survived from colonial days.

"Any advice?" I asked Candido.

"Don't walk at night," he said.

He explained the recent exchange rate of their devalued currency, the meticais. This ride was 60,000, a meal might be 175,000, and a bus ticket to South Africa probably 500,000. A hundred dollars was about 2,500,000 meticais. The rate had changed for the worse since my trip to Beira.

"And be careful of naughty boys" were Candido's parting words. "They will steal from you."

South Africans went to Mozambique for some of the reasons Americans went to Mexico: for "color" and a whiff of the gutter and the slum; for cheap eats, fresh tiger prawns especially; for "the real Africa," authenticity, and ugly knickknacks; also for snorkeling and swimming and whoring.

The fleshpots and other pleasures were in southern Mozambique and the coast just north of Maputo. Beira and the province of Zambezia, where I had been before entering Zimbabwe, were almost inaccessible by road from the capital. The north of Mozambique was like another country, sharing a border with Tanzania and possessing an East African culture, with remote villages inland, ancient fishing communities on the coast, and some of the best artisans and carvers in Africa, the Makonde people. No one went there.

In contrast, the deeper south of Mozambique was southern African in every respect — industrialized, detribalized, overpopulated, and crime-ridden, sharing a border with Swaziland and the South African province of KwaZulu-Natal, half a day's bus ride from the prosperous seafront city of Durban.

Maputo was much praised as a desirable destination, but it was a dreary, beat-up city of desperate people who had cowered there while war raged in the provinces for twenty-five years, destroying bridges, roads, and railways. Banks and donors and charities claimed to have had successes in Mozambique. I suspected they invented these successes to justify their existence; I saw no positive results of charitable efforts. But whenever I expressed skepticism about the economy, the unemployment, the potholes, or the petty thievery, people in Maputo said, as Africans elsewhere did, "It was much worse before." In many places, I knew, it was much better before.

It was hard to imagine how much worse a place had to be for a broken-down city like Maputo to seem like an improvement. Some hotels, villas, shops, and cafés existed from the Portuguese time, but that period had ended decades before. The grotesque fact was that from 1482, when Captain Diogo Cão planted the Portuguese flag on the coast of the Congo, the five-hundred-year history of the Portuguese in Africa was one big racket of exploitation — first the slave trade, then diamonds and oil in Angola, and agriculture in Mozambique.

Outsiders with no memory praised Maputo. Yet Maputo was a seedier version of its previous incarnation, the seedy former capital, Lourenço Marques, with higher walls around the villas and more barbed wire and much worse roads. Having seen the country's interior, I knew what lay beyond the pale: blown-up bridges, devastated towns, ridiculous roads, defunct railway lines, no lights, no water, no telephones, no public transport. Perhaps the rural poverty that I had observed accounted for the large influx of people into the cities. It was easy to see that Maputo had all the characteristics of many African cities — a sprawl of shantytowns and poor markets, idle people and lurkers, an appalling vastness and a look of desperate improvisation. Maputo was in no sense a metropolis but, like all the other African cities, a gigantic and unsustainable village.

Not heeding Candido's advice, and against my normal practice of staying inside at night, I went for a walk in Maputo to look for a place to eat. The long bus ride from Nelspruit had left me needing exercise. If I walked fast, I reasoned, my chances of being robbed would be reduced.

Like jackals, some small boys leaped from the shadows and followed close behind me, calling out, "Hungry, hungry."

I kept going, encouraged by the lighted shop fronts, the night watchmen, the busy cafés. This was the main street of the upper town. The port was down below in the commercial district. The boys, four little bony forms, smelling of the street, crowded me and snatched at my fingers. They had sad embryonic faces and small sticky hands.

"Give me money," each one said in turn.

I had prepared myself for such an encounter. My pockets were empty, I wore a cheap watch, I carried very little money. I said no and picked up my pace, but they stayed with me.

Waiting to cross the street, I flapped my hands to prevent them from being snatched. One boy, the most poised and persistent of the four, assumed a scolding tone.

"If you give me something I will leave you and you can go," the urchin said with a good command of English. "But if you don't give me money or whatnot, I will follow you and I will not leave you, and I will ask and ask."

It was an impressive piece of hectoring, and portended a great career for the boy in politics or law, but I told them all to go away. As I spoke, some better prospects appeared: two young white women carrying shoulder bags, looking bewildered and benevolent. Like gnats, the urchins whirred off to their new victims.

I found a restaurant, ordered the predictable meal — seven dollars' worth of tiger prawns — and talked to the owner, Chris, who was of Greek descent. He, like many other entrepreneurs in Mozambique, was a South African, a junk dealer by trade. The junk business had boomed in Mozambique while the various wars were being fought, producing scrap metal in the form of bombed bridge girders, blown-apart truck chassis, shattered railway cars, steel rails, iron pipes, and crashed plane fuselages.

"We made good business. Buy for forty, sell for eighty. Ship to India, Turkey, Singapore."

But destruction had waned in the country. So much had been wrecked, there was little left to destroy. Chris's father had gone back to

Greece to live in retirement, and Chris had started this restaurant, not as profitable as junk dealing, but a business with a future.

Walking back to the hotel, I saw that, as it was late, the streets and sidewalks were filled with loiterers, prostitutes, urchins, beggars, and people doing what people did in African cities at night, sleeping as though mummified in gauzy ragged blankets in the brightest doorways, for safety.

On my way to Maputo's railway station the next day, I stopped at the Natural History Museum to see what it had of ethnographic interest. The answer was not much. Among mounted creatures with their straw stuffing falling out (a toppling elephant, a mangy eland, a mildewed lion), there were some unusual Makonde carvings of figures with upraised arms, looking like stylized and pious Egyptian devotees. The rest were unremarkable spears, shields, dippers, bowls, arrows, and bangles.

No objects I had seen in any African museum (Nairobi, Kampala, Dar es Salaam, and Harare) could compare with the African objects in the museums in Berlin, Paris, or London. Of course, much of that stuff had been looted or snatched from browbeaten chiefs. And every year there were many "tribal art" auctions all over the world, and as far as I could tell this material never found its way back to Africa. With some notable exceptions, the great pieces of African art were in private collections outside Africa. Africa itself was a disappointing destination for anyone looking for good examples of African art.

In the museum, photographs of old customs of northern Mozambique showed people with tattoos and scarification, grinning boys with teeth that had been filed into sharp fangs, and naked men and women. The intention was to depict the customs as freakish, for also in the photos were shocked bystanders, Africans in mission clothes smiling in horror at the bare buttocks of their fellow Mozambicans. The pictures had been taken in the provinces north of Zambezia — in Nampula, Niassa, and Cabo Delgado — places that were easier to reach by crossing Lake Malawi or by penetrating on the back roads of southern Tanzania.

This hinterland — the largest part of Mozambique — seemed inviting to me as an enormous area without roads or commerce, where missionary planes sometimes landed but otherwise was cut off from the rest of the country. Looking at the artifacts, the photos, and a detailed map in the museum, I thought that if I ever returned to Africa I would travel to this forgotten wilderness. I had found, on my trip down the Shire River and into the Zambezi, that rural Africa was not the lost cause that the cities appeared to be. In the life of the village there was often enough of a repository of tradition for there to be remnants of the decencies that were still vaguely chivalrous.

One of the place names in that wilderness, Quionga, was chiseled in stone on a war memorial in the Praça dos Trabalhadores, the Workers Plaza, another African irony, with idle men and young layabouts all over it. The memorial, in front of Maputo's main railway station, was an odd monolith of the 1930s, a thirty-foot chunk of carved granite. It was an Art Deco representation of a big busty woman, holding a sword and flanked by a rearing serpent, and inscribed *Força* on one side, *Génio* on the other. In Portuguese on the plinth was the fond inscription *To the combatants, European and African, of the Great War, 1914–1918,* with the names of the battles, all of them buried settlements in provincial Africa, strange jungle skirmishes between the Portuguese and the Germans on the remote borders of their colonies, Quionga among them.

How like the perverse Portuguese to record Quionga as a victory. Perhaps the mention was face-saving, for it had been a humiliating defeat, one of many in Portuguese East Africa during the First World War. Portugal had only entered the war in 1916. That same year, Portuguese officers commanding an army of Africans launched an attack across the Rovuma River, on the disputed northern border of German East Africa, hoping to win Quionga back.

The Germans were ready for them, and they counterattacked, General Paul von Lettow-Vorbeck leading the charge with two thousand Africans. The Portuguese force fell back, then retreated, and kept retreating, for hundreds of miles through the bush. Lettow-Vorbeck pushed south, marauding, resupplying by plundering from settlers, putting the Portuguese to flight with his ragtag army of African warriors. By the end of the war Lettow-Vorbeck had driven halfway into Portuguese territory, almost to the Zambezi Valley.

The war in Mozambique was one of the more hideous charades of colonialism. It was easy enough to imagine a monocled and crazed Klaus Kinski with a sunburned, aquiline nose in this bush-bashing role, the aristocratic general from German East Africa, with his armed but barefoot Africans, advancing through the jungle to fight the indignant but helpless Portuguese, with their armed but barefoot Africans. All this African madness because of an insane war in Europe. The whole thing would have been comic except that at the end of the war, after the armistice, pleading for Quionga to be restored to them, the Portuguese claimed that 130,000 Africans were slaughtered fighting for Portugal in Mozambique. Thus the monument.

◈ ◈ ◈

Maputo's main railway terminal, dating from about 1910, seemed to me the most beautiful station in Africa. The station with its distinctive iron dome had been designed by Gustave Eiffel and was easily as elegant as his tower in Paris, though hardly more practical. In its shape and lines it was aesthetically satisfying, uplifting to anyone with the wit to appreciate it, but otherwise serving no purpose except to accommodate the few underpaid employees of the railway — Caminhos de Ferro Mozambique — which was slowly chugging toward obsolescence.

High and broad-shouldered, made of plaster-faced brick, painted green and cream, with a plump iron dome and a prominent clock high up on a cupola, the station was such a marvel of architectural frivolity that it was a wonder the thing had not been pulled down. Little sentimentality was shown for colonial structures in independent Africa. Since they represented the pomposity and wealth of the white rulers in the oppressive years of overlordship, they were usually the first buildings to be vandalized or defaced.

By the time Eiffel was commissioned to design the station (as well as the Iron House, near Maputo's botanical garden), he had been disgraced by his involvement in the Panama Canal scandal. Though Eiffel had joined the Panama Canal Company merely to lend his illustrious name to a troubled project, he was convicted in 1893, with Ferdinand de Lesseps and others, of misusing funds — specifically, bribing French politicians to approve a loan, in order to buy time for the failing company. His sentence was set aside. This pioneer in aerodynamics and innovator in metal — freed but shamed — took a back seat in his world famous-design firm. His masterpieces were behind him: the tower in Paris, the dome of the Nice Observatory, the Tan An Bridge in Indochina, the Bon Marché department store in Paris, the Maria Pia Bridge in Portugal, the armature for the Statue of Liberty. What had been the Lourenço Marques railway station — in a distant city, in a remote colony — even today, almost a century on, showed the hand of a master innovator in metal.

Eiffel's station was far more attractive and better preserved than any in Egypt or South Africa. Ethiopia's stations were picturesque (though its trains were grim), Kenya's were in ruins, Uganda's defunct, Tanzania's just minimalist concoctions from Maoist blueprints. Zimbabwe Railways maintained solid little brick cottages, like English country stations, but they were on the wane, like much else in that tottering nation. I found the Maputo station purely by chance, and went back on two successive days to admire its wood paneling and etched glass, its station buffet and waiting rooms. On the third day I went for a train ride.

Although no one in town seemed to know much about Mozambique Railways and hardly anyone took the trains, some trains still ran, three lines anyway, including an international express, the slow train to Komatipoort and Johannesburg. No railway timetables were published. The arrival and departure times were scribbled on pieces of paper and tacked to a notice board inside the station. I lingered over the names, loving the destination Zona Verde, and settled finally on the Limpopo Line, for the name alone.

The Limpopo Line, running northeast out of the capital to the town of Chokwe, was the embodiment of all that I loved as well as all that I despaired of in the Africa I had seen so far. The train, a solid and usable artifact, almost indestructible in its simplicity, was atmospheric but grubby, badly maintained, and poorly patronized. This working relic had been retained because the country was too impoverished to replace it or modernize it. At the height of its working life the train had carried many people comfortably into the remote bush. Such were the ambitions of Portuguese colonialism that the line had once continued through Gaza province into Central Africa, linking Mozambique with Rhodesia and Nyasaland. These places, now called Zimbabwe and Malawi, were a hundred times harder to get to by any land route than they had been forty years ago and more. One of the epiphanies of my trip was the realization that where the mode of life had changed significantly in the Africa I had known, it had changed for the worse.

The look of the train standing in the station at eight in the morning raised my hopes as much as the procedure required for buying a ticket and being allocated a seat had done. Yet the train was something of an illusion, and the ticket shuffling only an empty rigmarole. There were few people on board, the train was falling apart, and it seemed as if the gesture-conscious railway staff were just going through the motions. One purpose was served, though: the train was able to accommodate large, heavy bundles and crates. As a cargo carrier the train was indispensable, and it was a more straightforward and simple conveyance than any of the buses.

The weirdness of this old railway passing Maputo's new airport at its first stop, Mavalane, made it seem like a ghost train erupting from the past to rattle hauntingly across the present. The station names were printed on a card that was framed and fastened to the wall. Romao, Albasine, Jafar, Papucides, Marracuene, Bobole, Pategue, Manhiça — evocative names, but they were no more than muddy villages.

Manhiça was hardly fifty miles from Maputo, though it took most of the morning to get there. I thought I would get off at this station and then head for Xai-Xai up the coast, which was noted for its beaches and its natural beauty.

"The flood was here," a man said as we passed a low-lying district of shacks outside the city. He saw that I had been gaping out the window. "The people were rehoused. New people have come hoping for a new flood, so that the government will find them houses." But the government would not have paid for that housing; it would have been funded by what an American chronicler of recent history in the country called "the Donors' Republic of Mozambique."

Africans praying for a disaster so that they would be noticed seemed to me a sorry consequence of the way charities had concentrated people's minds on misfortune. But without vivid misfortune Africans were invisible to aid donors.

The train passenger explaining the huts wore a tie and importantly manipulated his cell phone; other passengers wore rags. Women nursed babies in some seats, some children frowned at me. I could not blame them, for I was the only alien on the train, or so it seemed until I went for a walk from car to car.

The ring of another cell phone caught my attention. I looked over and saw a young alien woman, head bent, talking confidentially in

Portuguese into her small receiver. I kept walking through the rattling carriages to the *ka-chink ka-chink ka-chink* of the wheels bumping over the rail joints. The train was less than half full, quite a novelty for an African conveyance. Trains and buses never seemed to travel without twice the number of passengers they had been designed for — ten in a car, twenty in a van, eighty in a bus, and Tanzanian trains were piled high with people. Here the passengers sat in postures of repose. Some slept. Others nibbled stalks of sugar cane. I counted sixty-two children. None of them was fussing; they sat in silence watching the drooping palm fronds and muddy fields and the huts passing by.

On my way back through the train I caught the eye of the white woman and said hello. She greeted me in so friendly a way that I paused and chitchatted until the swaying of the train on the curves swung me and had me grasping seat backs to keep my balance. That sudden motion was helpful, for it seemed natural for me to avoid it by sitting down across the aisle from this sweet-looking woman.

"I'm Susanna," she said.

"Paul," I said, and shook her hand.

She was young, pale, in her mid-twenties, rather thin, with such a slight figure and such a short haircut that you might at first have taken her to be a pretty boy. She wore khaki slacks and a loose sweater and no makeup, as sensible women did when they were traveling alone in Africa, so as not to call attention to themselves; but the result in her case was a look of stunning androgyny that I found compelling. She was from Ohio.

"I'm going to Manhiça."

"What a coincidence," I said. "Are you a traveler?"

"I'm on a mission."

I liked that: it meant so many things. But in her case it was a traditional use of the phrase. She was an Assembly of God missionary, who had decided one day that she was being called to Africa. She had attended Bible college in South Africa, and after having made a number of sorties into Mozambique, she had set up house in Maputo with the ambition of mass conversion — that is, gulling locals into believing in hellfire and penance. After the dusky pietists submitted, she would offer lessons from other parts of pious Africa, declaiming sermons with a Joycean text: "And thereafter in that fruitful land the broadleaved mango flourished exceedingly."

"How did you happen to decide on a mission here?"

"Because I'm a sinner saved by grace."

Sometimes people say, *I've got the answer to our parakeet problem. Let's flush it down the john and we won't have to take the messy thing to Daytona this year!* And you don't know quite how to reply.

But I said, "How's business?"

"There's so much to do here."

"I thought Jimmy Swaggart was taking care of all that." I had seen the man's books and videotapes on sale in the Maputo street markets and in Malawi, too.

Susanna said, "He's real popular. They love Jimmy Swaggart here. It's the music and the videos."

"I guess they haven't heard that he's Elmer Gantry," I said, but didn't get a rise — maybe she hadn't read Sinclair Lewis — and so I added, "A fake, a snake-oil seller, an old hypocrite."

"He's a sinner saved by grace," she said, making the phrase sound like one word. "Like me. Like you."

"Thanks, but not like me. I have my faults, but being like Jimmy Swaggart is not one of them."

"We're all sinners saved by grace."

Her calling me a sinner was not quite so offensive as it could have been, because all the while she was smiling and looking like Peter Pan. And of course the insinuation had a teasing, almost coquettish hint of naughtiness, as though she were saying *You wicked man!* So I let it pass. As far as I was concerned, this was just small talk on the Limpopo Line.

"How long do you figure you'll be on your mission?"

"The Lord guides me. The Lord sent me here. I'll stay as long as the Lord wants me."

"What does the Lord want you to do in Mozambique?"

"He wants me to tell people about Him so that they can be saved."

"What about homosexuals? Do you have any views on them?"

"Homosexuality is an abomination. It says so in Leviticus."

A Christian childhood, a lifetime of travel, of sleeping alone in hotel rooms with nothing but the Gideon Bible to read, and many years of close textual analysis to flesh out the preachers in my novels *The Mosquito Coast* and *Millroy the Magician* had given me enough experience with scripture to reply to evangelists like this, who seldom expected a rebuttal. Anyway, we were on the Limpopo Line in Mozambique with nothing else to do.

"Leviticus says a lot of things that no reasonable person can agree with," I said. "The Mosaic law is full of weird prejudices. Chapter fifteen is all about a woman being an unclean abomination when she's menstruating and how she has to sleep alone then. I wonder how many Christians obey that one? Chapter eleven says fish without fins and scales, like shark and eel, are an abomination. If you follow that logic, calamari and shrimp are out. That makes marinara sauce an abomination. Leviticus eleven-six says that rabbits are cud chewers but don't have a cloven hoof, and that's why you can't eat them. Ever hear of a rabbit chewing its cud? Later on, Leviticus says that a man can't marry a nonvirgin or a divorced woman, and that priests can't cut their beards."

Susanna was undaunted and stubborn. She said, "Not just Leviticus. In Romans, Paul says that homosexuality is a sin."

"You're wearing pants," I said. "What does Deuteronomy say about that?"

She smiled, looking gamine, perhaps knowing what was coming.

"The Bible says that women are forbidden to wear men's clothes."

"Sometimes you have to interpret scripture," Susanna said.

"I was hoping you'd say that. Deuteronomy twenty-two-five condemns a woman who wears an article of men's clothing as an abomination," I said. "You are wearing trousers. I don't have a problem with them. Moses says that the Lord does."

"I guess I just interpreted it."

"That's fine. Why don't you interpret Paul on gays?"

"I don't hate homosexuals, but they're committing a sin."

"Then why not kill them? Leviticus twenty-thirteen says that sodomites must be put to death," I said. "And if you eat shrimp and wear men's clothes, you are committing a sin, too, aren't you?"

"I know I'm a sinner," she said cheerfully. "We're all sinners saved by grace."

"Do you believe in evolution?"

"I believe the Bible."

The happy hunting ground of all minds that have lost their balance is not the works of Shakespeare (as Buck Mulligan says) but the Holy Bible.

"Adam and Eve? Garden of Eden?"

"Yes."

"How long have humans been on earth?" I asked. "You would say, what, something like four thousand years?"

"Between four thousand and six thousand years," she said.

"You know this as a scientific fact?"

"It's in the Bible."

Such people had one book in their library, containing all history, all science, all geography, all nutrition. She was not alone. She would have agreed with the absurd notion, propounded by the conflicted Philip Gosse, fanatical Christian and avid scientist, "that when the catastrophic act of creation took place, the world presented, instantly, the structural appearance of a planet on which life had long existed" — in other words (the words are those of his son, Edmund, in his 1907 chronicle of a weird childhood, *Father and Son*), "that God hid the fossils in the rocks in order to tempt geologists into infidelity."

You just wanted to weep, not for such smug, pigheaded ignorance, but for what made it worse: Susanna was here in Mozambique spreading disinformation and fear.

"Call this a feeble rational quibble," I said, "but humans have been on earth for two million years. And Mesopotamia was settled at the date you give for the Creation."

And in the year 1498, Vasco da Gama landed on Ilha de Mozambique, on the north coast of the Portuguese territory. Ten years later, priests were sent out from Lisbon and a vigorous trading center and missionary enterprise was started: Susanna's antecedents in proselytizing — five centuries of this! But from experience I knew that there was no way that I could dissuade her from her belief, no light that I could shed.

I said, "I don't want to argue. I know I will never change your mind. I simply want to tell you that I don't agree with you and that you're inconsistent. Tell me what you're doing in Mozambique."

"Teaching scripture and also trying to set up a center to get prostitutes off the street," Susanna said, an answer that also echoed over five hundred years on this coast. "Their families send girls out to make money, and people come here from Europe looking for them — Germans on sex tours get child prostitutes in Mozambique."

"How do you stop that happening?"

"We have a street mission. We pray. We help the prostitutes."

"Don't you find that men try to pick you up?"

"All the time," she said. "They say horrible things to me. But I say, 'Christ is my husband — I'm married to the Lord.'" She shrugged. "They just laugh."

"I take it your mission is mainly concerned with prostitutes, then?"

"Quite a lot," she said.

I told her what I had read in *The Road to Hell,* that men encouraging child prostitution were criminals, but from an economic point of view a woman choosing to go into prostitution was making a rational decision. It was one of the rare chances for a woman to make real money. Susanna was not impressed with this argument.

I had a job in a factory, sitting at a machine, and then I realized I was sitting on a gold mine, the prostitute says, summing up her calling. The snag with trying to persuade prostitutes of the wrongness of their profession was the crystal logic of this. Leviticus also had a great deal to say about harlotry — the women who may and may not be temple harlots, how it was forbidden to marry them, how the Lord said to Moses: "Go, take yourself a wife of harlotry and have children of harlotry."

Susanna said, "Not just prostitutes. I mean, the sex is constant. People here have sex all the time."

"Africans tend to have sex within their own age group," I said, quoting the Samburu elder I had met in Kenya.

"No," Susanna said. "Boys sleep with grannies. Girls go with men. Women commit adultery. They start having sex when they're six or eight years old."

"Maybe playing at it," I suggested. And I thought that if you were looking for graphic illustrations, it would be more satisfying to discuss sex with a Christian like Susanna than with a jaded libertine.

"No, doing it," Susanna said, her face clouding over. "I was up in Nampula, and we talked to a chief about condoms. He said, 'You don't eat sweets with the wrapper on. You don't eat candy that's in paper. You don't carry an umbrella if it's not raining.' He just laughed at us."

"I don't understand the part about the umbrella."

"Neither do I," she said. "But AIDS is a problem because no one does anything about it. Lots of people in our church have AIDS. Three of my co-workers have AIDS. It's terrible. They have sex with four-year-olds, thinking it's a cure. They pray to their ancestors!"

"I think it's good that you're concerned with AIDS, but when you condemn people for praying to their ancestors, you sound like you're condemning them as pagans. 'Destroy your heathen idols.' Isn't that what the Taliban say?"

Mozambicans were not sufficiently unhappy, not poor enough, not sick enough, not adequately deluded; they needed to feel worse, more blameworthy, more sinful, abused for merely having been born, for original sin was inescapable. And like all the other missionaries, Susanna was determined to bully Africans into abandoning their ancient pantheism, which had been inspired by the animals and flowers of the bush, by the seasons, and by their long-held hopes and fears.

So this Christ-bitten nag and every other twaddler like her sought out Africans in remote fastnesses such as Nampula, to abuse them with the notion that they were sinners, to browbeat them into arcane forms of atonement, such as screeching hymns and the dues-paying routine of tithes. The missionaries' aim was the creation of African nags and twaddlers who were morbid and sanctimonious, and whose victory was the destruction of their homegrown pieties and their ancient artifacts of veneration.

Speaking softly, I suggested these arguments to Susanna, and wanted to add, as Henry James had said in a letter to a do-gooding friend, "Only don't, I beseech you, *generalize* too much in these sympathies and tendernesses — remember that every life is a special problem which is not yours but another's, and content yourself with the terrible algebra of your own."

She held her ground, but later let slip the fact that she had once had a husband. She reluctantly disclosed that she had been married for three years and was now divorced. This I found wonderful.

"The Bible says that divorce is not an option," I said in the sort of scolding tone I imagined she would have used on a gay person. "Aren't you afraid of incurring the wrath of God?"

"My husband was abusive. I prayed. He beat me. 'I want you to worship me!' he said. He hated that I loved the Lord." Susanna looked tormented. "I didn't know what to do. I just prayed."

"I think you did the right thing by leaving this man," I said, "but a pious Christian would disagree with me. A Christian might say, 'Be a martyr for your faith! He beats you — he kills you for loving the Lord, and you go to heaven. You can't lose. The sinner will see his crime, and feel remorse, and repent. So you both end up in heaven.' I'm not saying I agree, but isn't that what's supposed to happen?"

"I still don't know if I did the right thing," she said.

"You definitely did the right thing, but it wasn't by the book," I said. "All I'm saying is that you should be as open-minded when you're dealing with gays."

She said nothing. I thought of changing my seat, but she was a compellingly decorous bigot with sex on the brain, and we had not yet reached Manhiça. I stayed put and was glad I did, for with time to kill Susanna told me how she ran a shelter in Maputo — another admirable effort. Street kids were invited to stay there, where they were given baths and food and clean clothes. She had been doing this for two years, and during that time she had gotten to know the street kids — boys mostly. One night when she was getting out of a car, some boys accosted her and begged for money and then, seeing that she was alone, slashed her bag and stole all her money. She recognized the boys as ones she had bathed, fed, and clothed at the shelter, and what's more, they recognized her as an easy target.

The shelter, too, seemed like another duff scheme, like rescuing prostitutes from the lucrative streets of Maputo, one of the few ways of making a living in Mozambique that was unconnected with weeding maize. Not for the first time I was reminded of Mrs. Jellyby and her obsessive busybody philanthropy.

We came to Manhiça. Susanna said, "I'm going to pray for you. For your happiness and health, your family, and your safe travels."

"I'm going to pray that you stop using the word 'abomination' for gay people," I said. "Also, I'm going to pray that you read a history book and a book of paleoanthropology and that you stop calling these poor people sinners. As if they haven't got enough to worry about."

We had arrived late. I had missed the bus to Xai-Xai, and there was no other way to go there except by *matatu* or by *chapa*, as the overcrowded minivans were called here. Now that I was reading the South African newspapers regularly, I kept seeing items about minivan crashes and multiple deaths, so I had sworn them off as deathtraps. I had made it safely so far; I did not want to press my luck by imperiling myself further. I ate lunch in Manhiça — caldo verde, soup with mashed potatoes and greens and garlic, the dubious culinary legacy of the colonial masters. Obscurely irritated by my to-and-fro with the missionary, who believed herself to be in sole possession of the truth, I decided to take a taxi back to Maputo.

The next day was a national holiday, Samora Machel Day. Machel had been Mozambique's president from independence in 1975 until his death in a plane crash, an event that looked like part of a sinister plot, in 1986. The holiday was the fifteenth anniversary of the crash. No one seemed to mind that Machel had been the leader of a chaotic and bankrupt country. The political and economic failure was not entirely of his own making, but he had presided over it. On posters he was depicted as a benevolent bearded figure in combat fatigues and a Fidel cap, over the slogan *Samora — Our Inspiration (Nossa Inspiraçao).*

"Machel was nobody," a sour Portuguese named Da Silva said to me at the Polana. "He was just a hospital worker. His job was to carry out corpses from the wards. I know — my wife worked in the hospital."

Da Silva could hardly be blamed for being bitter. His house in Maputo had been confiscated. He had returned to Maputo from his home in Johannesburg to try to obtain some compensation. His forcible exit from the country in 1974 had been undignified.

"They said my wife was a prostitute. They made us into refugees. We had nothing. We had to run away. I am here, but you know what? I want to cry. They have destroyed this country. The only people left are opportunists and thieves. Angola is better."

That was news to me. I had been under the impression that Angola, still divided by a civil war, was an impossible and dangerous place. Chaotic Mozambique was at least peaceful.

Da Silva said, "My son is there," and winked at me and made a finger-rubbing gesture to indicate his son was raking in the bucks.

I used the two-day Samora Machel holiday to sit on the bluff by the Indian Ocean and write. I was nearly finished with my erotic novella, well over a hundred pages. It was a pleasant task, like whittling a block of wood into a discernible shape. Then I put it aside, looked out at the Indian Ocean, and thought about my trip — how far I had come and what remained, the train trip from Johannesburg to Cape Town.

The last leg of my safari I contemplated with mixed feelings. I was eager to take this train, and I was sorry my trip was ending. This mode of travel suited my disposition. I had kept the promises I had made for my peace of mind: no deadlines, no serious appointments, no planning ahead, no business, no cell phone, no e-mail. If anyone inquired, I was unobtainable. I had remained unobtainable. No one knew I was in Mozambique. This sort of disappearance made me feel wraithlike and insubstantial, as though I had become a ghost, without the inconvenience of dying in order to achieve it.

For the exercise, I walked to the Samora Machel celebration at the Praça da Independencia, which was at the top end of Samora Machel Avenue, near the botanical garden. I passed the Iron House, the Casa de Ferro, and admired Eiffel's design. Children were running and jumping under the statue of Machel. The plaque on the statue's base had been vandalized, making the inscription indecipherable. In the plaza, soldiers danced with each other, men and women dressed the same, bopping clumsily in combat boots, laughing as they stumbled.

I left Maputo early the following morning on the good bus, hummed across the savanna, and swayed into the low hills. There were the usual snags and odd looks at the border posts, then the perverse miracle of South African freeways and beautiful houses and dismal orderly squatter settlements. I was in Johannesburg before dark.

22 ◇◇◇

The Trans-Karoo Express to Cape Town

AFTER EVEN a short spell in the warped fourth dimension of Mozambican ruin and reconstruction, it seemed odd to be back so soon in the bustle of urban South Africa. I was disconcerted by the sight of smooth streets and stoplights, of mature roadside trees and undefiled parks, and of such a novelty as a stylish babe in a new convertible, gabbing on a cell phone in Rosebank, a diamond dealer perhaps, or someone cornering the market in tanzanite. It was even stranger to hear the Johannesburgers' constant grumbling, black-and-white obliquities about their lack of prosperity, their sagging economy, how the buying power of their money had halved in only a few years.

The frequent South African remark "This is a First World country with a Third World mentality" could easily have been applied to so many countries in the world that I had seen, I did not take it seriously. The statement brought to mind not just Northern Ireland but some of the more picturesque and sullen parts of the United States and Europe — irreconcilable, like parts of South Africa.

For me, South Africa was a place where almost everything worked, even the political system. The whole huge place was accessible by train and bus. One of the consequences of the decades of white government paranoia was the ambitious road-building program, for military purposes, to keep order. This road network meant that the army could go anywhere, and now civilians could do the same. The universities were excellent, the level of public debate was impressive, and the newspapers were embattled, following crime stories and impartially assessing government policy and political scandals, which in South Africa were sometimes steamily related. Even the education system was praised for its high-mindedness.

So it seemed worrisome when a front-page headline the day after I arrived was "Gordimer 'Too Racist' for Schools"—Nadine's novel *July's People* had been stricken from the reading list by the Book Selection Committee of the Gauteng Province Education Department. Because this province included Johannesburg and Pretoria, it contained South Africa's largest concentration of classrooms, in which this plausible doomsday novel had been required reading. The book was labeled "deeply racist, superior and patronizing," and "an anachronism because it projects a South African future that has not happened," and "not acceptable as it does not encourage good grammatical practice."

The silly remarks were an excuse for me to reread *July's People*, which I did with pleasure. One morning I wrote an article for the Johannesburg *Sunday Independent*, jeering at the ignorance and philistinism of the Book Selection Committee and having a bit of fun with Nadine's chief persecutor, a commissar who rejoiced in the name Elvis Padayachee. I mentioned that the imaginative brilliance of Gordimer's work was its utter fidelity to the truth—how we behave, how we speak, how our cities look, how our marriages work, how we love, how we die—and that if someone writes truthfully, her work will always seem prophetic. Given the uncertainties and changes in South Africa, the cataclysmic events in *July's People* were still possible. Thirty years before, in *A Guest of Honour*, she had described the crisis that was being played out by rivals, land reformers, and racists in Zimbabwe today.

Nadine said, "This sort of banning reminds me of the days of the apartheid regime, when they suppressed books they didn't like. I had thought we had moved on from that."

She said the suppression was a bad sign; she didn't take it personally. But censorship in South Africa had never been simple. In the days of paranoid white rule, not only had my *Jungle Lovers* and *The Mosquito Coast* been banned, but for their seemingly racial and inflammatory titles, so had *The Return of the Native* and *Black Beauty.* On the other hand, *The Mosquito Coast* was now a required book in South African high schools, and my defense of *July's People* was prominently published. I could not think of another newspaper in Africa that would have printed my piece, because I mocked a government directive for its stupidity.

"I am much more worried about Reinie," Nadine said of her ailing husband. "He's very weak. He is my concern at the moment."

Knowing in advance that this was the last leg of my trip, and perhaps the best railroad, I dithered over boarding the train to Cape Town. I wanted to savor the anticipation of going, but I also procrastinated, because after this my safari would be at an end. I lay on my hotel bed in Johannesburg replaying my journey through the good people I had met, seeing the proud Nuba, Ramadan, driving me across the gritty wadis of the Sudanese desert; Tadelle and Wolde in box-creased newly bought clothes at our sad parting on the Ethiopian border at Moyale; Wahome, the writer and former political prisoner in Nairobi; Apolo, the unlikely prime minister, teasing me in Uganda; the hospitable captain and squiffy-eyed Alex on Lake Victoria, who was at this moment in the engine room of the *Umoja,* tinkering with the old diesel; Julius on the bush train from Mwanza; Conor and Kelli on the Kilimanjaro Express; Una Brownly, the self-effacing nurse from Livingstonia mission; my student Sam Mpechetula in Zomba; Karsten Nyachikadza, the expert paddler, in Marka village on the Shire River, smiling at life in general through a haze of blue smoke; the farmer Peter Drummond outside Norton, shrugging at the appearance of yet more invaders; all the African political prisoners; and the long-distance bus drivers and the market women, cheerful people doing their jobs against the odds. I was grateful to them for making my trip pleasant. I missed them. I wished them well.

At Park Station one morning, waiting in line to buy a train ticket, I struck up a conversation with the young African woman in front of me and told her where I was going.

She said, "I heard the other day on the radio there is a really posh train running to Cape Town. It's expensive in our money, but in your money it's probably cheap. Ach, have a safe trip."

Another kindly person, helping me on my way.

It wasn't the well-known Blue Train, and it wasn't first class; it was premier class, a new designation, on the Trans-Karoo Express. I bought a ticket and made a reservation. The fare of $140 included all meals and a private compartment. At the Park Station newsstand I bought two blank notebooks. I expected to have plenty of time to make a fair copy of my long story. It was a twenty-seven-hour trip, 850 miles from Johannesburg to Cape Town, across the high desert known as the Great Karoo, something like the distance from New York to Chicago.

I left the next day. Waiting with the other passengers on the platform for the train to arrive, I noticed the different postures of anticipation. The whites habitually stood, looking watchful, facing inward in little family groups, surrounding their luggage; the blacks lounged on the benches in pairs, looking relaxed, their legs extended; the rest — the mixed-race people, the *uitlanders,* foreigners, Indians — seemed to keep moving, circulating warily among the others.

Because of security, steel fences divided the platform, and only travelers could get past this barrier.

"Not like this in Australia," said a stocky white man hefting his bag — Bob, traveling with his wife, Sylvia, both of them about fifty and rueful. "And years ago you could see your family off. It was friendly. None of this security. None of these fences."

"Different in Australia," Sylvia said.

They were Johannesburgers born and bred, but within eight months they would be emigrating to Brisbane and planned never again to return to South Africa. "It's just too horrible what's happened here," Bob said, in that complex South African way of saying "here," *yeueah.* He was a factory worker, hoping to find employment in Australia, but would he? His trade was the fabrication of railway ties — cement and wooden "sleepers." Not much call for those in Oz.

An African approached me, singling me out of the large group of waiting travelers, and said, "Mr. Theroux?"

No one ever mispronounced my name in South Africa, because Leroux was a common name and the place was full of the descendants of French Huguenots.

"How did you know it was me?"

"I'm the steward. After a while on this job you get to know people by sight. I can usually fit a name to a face."

That was Craig. He escorted me to my compartment and explained the train's features — hot shower next door, bar in the next coach, reading area and lounge. Pinky, a Zulu woman in a smart uniform, would take my drink order. Lunch would be served in an hour in the dining car.

The train whistle blew two sour notes, and with a yank on the couplings like an anvil clang, we pulled out of the station and headed west. I sat in perfect contentment and watched the city pass the windows. The long shadows of big buildings were replaced by the brighter suburbs, the garages, the fast-food outlets, the supermarkets, the squat fenced-in bungalows, and the one-man businesses that characterized small settlements: Mohammed's Meat Market, Solly's New and Used Hardware, Dave's Deals for Wheels, Prinsloo's Panelbeating. If there were no people in sight, I would have taken these lifeless and antiquated Edwardian terraces and arcades to be Australian, for they showed the same early-1900s colonial architecture, bungalows of hot stucco with gingerbread trim and tin roofs, even the same hardy shrubbery, bright-eyed lantana bushes and peeling, droopy eucalyptus trees. Farther out, the small industries: meatpackers, tire warehouses, cement, scrap metal, soap. They actually made things here.

Sixty or so miles out of Johannesburg we passed an enormous graveyard at Tshiawelo, Avalon Cemetery. Two heroes of the struggle were buried here, Joe Slovo and Helen Joseph. But all I saw were muddy slopes and fields, without either trees or grass, just crude graves. Each grave was surrounded by an iron cage, like a baby's crib made of rusty uprights and steel mesh, to keep the digging animals out — dogs, hyenas, ferrets, whatever. In different parts of the graveyard, funerals were in progress, people praying or standing near newly dug holes, in the posture of mourners, no one standing straight, everyone somewhat crook-legged and bowed in crippled attitudes of grief.

At Roodepoort a little later, in the dining car, George, the waiter, served me pan-fried Cape salmon fillets while a whole platform of waiting, luggage-carrying Africans burdened with bales, baskets, crates, and blanket rolls looked in at me — or were they looking at the African family of four at the table behind me, being served by the jolly white waiter?

The towns here were small and orderly, most of them built in the shadow of mine workings, rows of houses on the main street, a school, a church, a rugby field, low hills and fields beyond, Mayberry in the gold fields, among mine dumps that looked like hills. Some of these towns looked as if they had been built to last. The station at Krugersdorp, with corbels and finials and severe Cape Dutch ornaments, had been built in 1899, the date carved high on its cupola. At the edge of town stood simple, solid, uncomfortable-looking miners' huts and miners' hostels, also a century old and still inhabited, and partly hidden by billboards saying *Please Condomise* and *Thank You for Condomising.*

In even the whitest town on the veldt there was a reminder of less fortunate Africa — a ragged man walking on a path, an old man riding a bike, a woman balancing a bulging bale on her head, an amazing bird on a post, African huts, barefoot kids, tin privies, squalor, corn fields. One place I took to be an armed camp — high chain-link fence, razor wire, guard dogs, floodlights on poles — turned out to be the perimeter of a country club, and an area that looked like a training ground for recruits, just a golf course.

We came to Potchefstroom. I remembered the name from a story a Venda man named William had told me in Johannesburg. He had grown up in Pietersburg, in what had been Northern Transvaal, and had gone to a black school there.

"It was just a country school," he said. "I was very young and didn't know anything. One day we took the train to Potchefstroom to play another school in football. After the game we were so hungry! We walked to a restaurant. We saw white people inside, but they wouldn't let us in. They said, 'Go to the window.' Beside the restaurant was the window where we were served."

I told him that this arrangement was common in the American South up to the 1960s.

William said, "Here it was take-away for black people and sit-down for white people. We didn't get angry. That was the situation. We got used to it, but that was my first experience of 'Go to the window.' I never sat in a restaurant. Even now — true — I don't know how to use a restaurant. You need money, yes, but you also have to know what to do when you get inside. I don't feel comfortable."

The signs saying *Slegs Blanke* (Whites Only) persisted into the late 1980s. I asked William whether he had children.

He said he did, two girls, sixteen and thirteen. "My kids know how to use restaurants. They have no idea of what life was like before. I haven't told them yet. I will tell them when they are twenty-one. But they won't believe me. They think it's nothing to go into a cinema or a restaurant or a hotel. When I was young we had no idea. We were afraid. Or white areas — we didn't go. We didn't hate whites. We were frightened of them. They were so hard."

I asked William to give me an example of this fear.

He said, "About 1981, I was still a teenager, working for Mr. Longman. I went to Durban with him, for a job. When we got there they wouldn't let me into the hotel. He was a carpenter, on a job there. I was his assistant. He said to the hotel people, 'I will pay for his room.' But they said no. They wouldn't let me in. So I slept in the car. After a few days, Mr. Longman found me a place to stay at the church. You think my kids would believe that?"

The name Potchefstroom had jogged my memory of his story.

Klerksdorp was the first big station on the line. An English-sounding man in the corridor said to me, "This is Terreblanche territory," meaning that it was fiercely white still — not just *verkrampt,* unbending, but far-right neofascist. Eugene Terreblanche, a bearded demagogue in his late fifties, was the white separatist leader of the Afrikaner Weerstands Beweging (Afrikaner Resistance Movement), a rump of unrepentantly racist Boers that was based in Ventersdorp. He was now in prison serving a sentence for assaulting (and paralyzing) a black man and the attempted murder of another. Depending on whom you asked, Terreblanche was either the Afrikaner Moses or a hard-drinking womanizer and embezzler.

The fact that on the south side of the tracks there were salubrious houses did not mean the whole of Klerksdorp was prosperous, for on the north side lay a shantytown, boxy huts made of old tin sheets, with windowless walls and flat roofs, a squatter settlement as slummy as anything I had seen in Tanzania.

Markwassie, with its crude sign *173 miles to Johannesburg,* had the look of 1930s Mississippi in the evocative Depression photos: ragged blacks, hot sun-baked fields of pale cookie-dough furrows, grease-stained train yards, rusty tin-roofed warehouses, a curving shine of parallel switching tracks. Markwassie was a railway junction where skinny black children screeched and waved at the Trans-Karoo Express.

Nothing of Africa here — this looked like hot, sad old America until, about ten miles farther up the line, I saw eland cropping grass at a game ranch. In the distance were big purple and pink clouds, intimations of sunset in the still air, and the uncertain chirps of birds at the day's end on the high plains of the Middelveld.

I used the hours of darkness to turn from the window and scratch away at my erotic story, copying and revising, and reminded myself that, however secret and forbidden, such images vitalized us and fueled the imagination. In his book on Hokusai, Edmond de Goncourt wrote, "Every Japanese painter has a body of erotic works." All the great Japanese printmakers had indulged themselves in the erotic and had devised a nice euphemism for such works, calling them *shunga*, "spring pictures."

In Johannesburg I had bought Guillaume Apollinaire's *Les Onze mille verges*, which was plainly porn, not to my taste, gothic and absurd by turns, most of it too athletic or too painful to be likely. Apollinaire, who had invented the word "surrealism," had written about the Japanese prints I had in mind. I read his book quickly, and at one point, describing the motion of a train, he alluded to the Alphonse Allais couplet

> The titillating motion of trains
> Sends desire coursing all through our veins.

The dinner gong rang. I sat at a table with a shaven-headed motorcyclist named Chris and an older English couple who seemed tetchy but perhaps were only nervous. They kept their names to themselves, but they did say that they had lived in southern Africa since 1960, and "We could never live in England now." They were going on vacation in the Cape winelands. The man said he was a train buff. "My dream is to take the Trans-Siberian. But I have health problems."

In spite of his shaved head and missing teeth and bike madness, Chris had a Zenlike view of things, and he discouraged any belittling of the state of the world, Africa included. "Yaaaw, never mind." Chris said he was half English and half Afrikaner. "So, yaaaw, I've got problems, too."

"You go on all these big holiday rides with all the bikers, I suppose," the Englishman said, as though chipping flint with his teeth.

"Oh, yaaaw. Very nice. Like flying," Chris said mildly.

"Quite a few members of the swastika brigade on those rides," the Englishman said.

"Oh, yaaaw. You get everyone," Chris said. "Women. English. African, too."

I said, "I rode a bike for a while, but I stopped. I figured I would end up an organ donor."

"Oh, yaaaw. I've got me some good organs to give away. But I smoke, so — ha ha! — not lungs."

Meanwhile, we ate the four-course meal of soup, fish, Karoo lamb, and mousse for dessert. I did not volunteer anything of my travels, and was fearful of mentioning trains to a train buff, but instead asked the Englishman how he happened to choose a life in Africa.

"I was eighteen, just out of school. I joined the Colonial Service and told my mother I would be away three years. She was so angry. She said, 'You'll never come home!'" The Englishman smiled. "And I didn't."

He had worked in Northern Rhodesia until it became Zambia, then in Southern Rhodesia until the struggle for Zimbabwe became violent, and finally had come to South Africa. To ask the question that hung in the air — was he staying? — was indelicate, even impertinent.

Anyway, he changed the subject. He said, "This is, in fact, the boat train. People sailed from Europe to the Cape and took it up to Jo'burg. And they went home that way, too."

I guessed that he was tormenting himself with thoughts of emigrating to Australia.

That night, late, we came to a station in the bleak Karoo where the line passed along the western edge of the Free State, not far from the *dorp* of Koffiefontein. This tiny farming town had been the home of the late Etienne Leroux, whose *Seven Days at the Silbersteins* appeared in Afrikaans in 1962. One of South Africa's greatest and strangest novels, it is full of Afrikaner talk, in the words of the wine baron Jock Silberstein, "about pedigrees, castration, purity and impurity, damage, divorce, primogeniture, feasts, inheritances, the intermarriage of groups belonging to different races, leprosy, marriage, murder, food, the poor, prostitution, the cultivation of beards, slave labor, theft, trustees, religion . . ."

I hopped out of the train to look up at the starry sky, the brilliance of luminous pinpricks, more stars than there was darkness around them. I saw a shooting star.

"Sometimes you can even see the Mulky Why," said a disembodied voice on the platform.

In the morning, we passed the stations of Prince Albert Road and Laingsburg, where the Great Karoo descends to the Little Karoo. The Karoo is plateau land and high desert, and rolling through it on this pleasant train I had a creeping recollection of entering Patagonia, seeing the same sorts of simple farmhouses and bushes blown sideways and flocks of sheep squinting into the wind, everything except Welsh settlers and gauchos. Even in the middle of nowhere, amid grazing land of low bush, with a horizon of low blue mountains, the settlers were house-proud.

The land was mostly prairie, some of it just scrub. Here and there sat a grove of trees, each one like a farmer's implanted flag, and at the end of a long cart track a classic white house with a Dutch façade and a white gate.

A rap on my door: the steward. He said, "We are coming to Touwsrivier and De Doorns, sir. Please make sure your windows are closed and locked. We've had thefts before. People coming through the windows."

He was right about Touwsrivier, a distressed-looking community of poor houses and ragged yellowish Africans, in the Witteberg of the Little Karoo. The people were Khoikhoin, considered "coloured," the marginalized people of the provinces. The fields were full of ostriches, some of them roosting on the ground, others prancing next to the train. Some men on the platform came to my window, pressed their faces against the glass, and pointed to a dish of chocolates wrapped in foil on a little shelf, each man's gesture indicating *I want one.*

De Doorns was partly a slum in a mountain valley, some of it looking very desperate — boxy metal huts made of roughly cut corrugated sheets and poor scrap-wood houses. On the other side of the tracks, the white side, a bigger church, better houses. From the vexed Asiatic look of the men frowsting by the tracks, I took them to be Khoikhoin, their faces feline. Some of them hoisted wooden impedimenta at the train windows, which were boxes of overripe grapes. Beyond the town were vineyards, so I took these squatter camps to be the settlements of grape pickers and winery workers.

At one time, only male workers had been allowed within these town limits. Workers' hostels and huts were the tradition, a male society of lonely and hardworking laborers. As part of his pay, on Fridays each vineyard worker got two liters of wine, a drip-feed system of alcohol that had turned many of them into winos. Perhaps this explained the squatter camps, most of which had sprung up after Mandela came to power, and which were composed of whole families. In the past, the women had been left in the villages, as Nadine Gordimer described the life in a sad but perceptive paragraph of *July's People:*

> Across the seasons was laid the diuturnal one of being without a man; it overlaid sowing and harvesting, rainy summers and dry winters, and at different times, although at roughly the same intervals for all, changed for each the short season when her man came home. For that season, although she worked and lived among the others as usual, the woman was not within the same stage of the cycle maintained for all by imperatives that outdid the authority of nature. The sun rises, the moon sets; the money must come, the man must go.

At the prosperous town of Worcester — beautiful villas and trim houses, a tall steepled church, soccer fields, tennis courts, schools, lawns, flower gardens — big pleading black men begged at the windows of first class, gesturing to their mouths and pointing to their stomachs, saying "Hungry, hungry" and asking for money.

I bumped into the English couple in the lounge. Without my asking, the man volunteered that he was not planning to emigrate.

"We're not going anywhere," he said. "We're retired."

They lived in a suburb about fifteen miles north of Johannesburg. Of course there was crime there, the man said; there was crime everywhere. He gave me an example.

"I was coming home a few years ago and stopped in my driveway. I got out of my car to open the gate and was surrounded by three chaps. They had guns. They were shouting at me — they wanted my car. My wife heard the noise. She thought I was talking to the neighbors. She came out with our two dogs."

"So you were safe?" I said.

"Not a bit. The dogs were useless. They thought we were going for a ride. They wagged their tails. My wife was pistol-whipped and I was hit hard. We both needed stitches. We lost the car. But, you see, that could have happened anywhere."

"Anywhere in South Africa."

"Quite."

The couple got off at Wellington, to head for Paarl and the wineries. Wellington was another lovely place with a huge hut settlement joined to it — acres, perhaps miles of flat-topped shanties, becoming simpler, cruder, poorer, more appalling the farther they were from town. The squatter camps seemed a weird disfigurement, but I made a note to myself to visit one when I got a chance.

For hours there had been mountains to the south of the railway line, great rocky peaks, but at Bellville I got a glimpse of a single bright plateau ahead, standing in the sunshine, and I knew we were at the city limits of Cape Town.

◇ ◇ ◇

The cold gusting wind and the frothing sea, with the sunny dazzle on Table Mountain's vertiginous bulk looming behind it, made Cape Town seem the brightest and least corrupt city I had ever seen. That was its appearance, not its reality. The high wind was unusual for the Africa I had traveled through, but not for this coast, my first glimpse of the Atlantic. The wind often blew at twenty knots, sometimes gusting to forty, enough to tear small limbs from trees and send them scraping along the pavement.

Storms were general all over the Cape. The explosive rumble and sky-cracking dazzle of Cape Town's monster thunderstorms came to the attention of James Joyce, who in 1939 toyed with the idea of relocating to South Africa from Paris. He needed a job. All his work was behind him, and the first attacks on and fairly bad reviews of *Finnegans Wake* were beginning to surface. Joyce complained to Samuel Beckett that he was running out of money. When Beckett chanced upon an ad for a job at the University of Cape Town, Joyce seriously considered moving there and teaching Italian. Then he found out about the storms. Joyce admitted he had a "dread of thunderstorms." His work is full of scary thunder. "The thunderstorm as a vehicle of divine power and wrath moved Joyce's imagination so profoundly," his biographer wrote, "that to the end of his life he trembled at the sound." So he stayed in Paris, and South Africa was denied this Irish immigrant.

Its glittering plinth of a mountain and its precipitous cliffs made Cape Town seem small and tame. Unlike Johannesburg, which had a city center of dubious-looking people whose stare said *I can fox you*, Cape Town was provincial-seeming and orderly, and the train station appeared safe. I wanted to be near the sea, so I took a taxi and found a good hotel on the waterfront.

After making the usual inquiries and receiving the usual cautions, I went for a walk along the ocean and sauntered around town and through the museums. Nearby were the Company Gardens, dating from 1652 when Jan van Riebeeck, on behalf of the Dutch East India Company, planted them with the idea of provisioning Dutch ships. On their arrival at the Cape, the Dutch had found various groups of people, Khoikhoin among them, scouring the beach for shells and edible seaweed. They called these people "beachrangers" and "Hottentots."

Yet some of the natives they met spoke broken English — ones who had been in contact with the English, who had come ashore years earlier. From the first, these "beachrangers" were put to work, as van Riebeeck wrote in a memo, "washing, scouring, fetching fuel, and doing odd jobs. Some of them have even placed their little daughters, who are now dressed after our fashion, in the service of our married people."

That had been the reason for Cape Town's existence: it had been founded as a port for supplying cattle, vegetables, and water to the ships of the Dutch fleet headed for Batavia and the Indies. After ten years at the Cape, van Riebeeck himself went to the East Indies, where he died. The interior of Africa, unknown land, had held no interest for the Dutch or anyone else. The hinterland had been called "Kaffraria," a cognate of "Quefreria," a name on a sixteenth-century Spanish map. The Spaniards had gotten this word for "infidels" ("people who live without any religious laws or sanctions") from the Muslims, who had occupied Spain. The word appears on many early maps. For example, on an eighteenth-century French map that I bought while living in Kampala, I read among the descriptions of the natives, "Peuples cruels," "Anthropophages," "Sauvages," and "Hotentots." The word "Cafrerie," printed big, covers a large blank area from the Tropic of Capricorn to the Equator. In 1936, van Riebeeck's biographer naively explained, "Today, the term kaffir, with its invidious connotation utterly forgotten, is attached solely to the Bantu, and as a matter of fact it was never colloquially applied to the Hottentots."

When the Huguenots arrived with their enological improvements and enlarged the vineyards, life was just about perfect, and it remained so, for the whites anyway — wine bibbers and wog bashers — for more than a hundred and fifty years. The Dutch were content to remain in this Mediterranean climate of the western Cape until the early nineteenth century, when the British took charge of the Cape Colony. Under pressure from the missionaries, the British abolished slavery and promoted the idea of racial equality. Feeling crowded by the British, insulted in their belief in white supremacy, and robbed of their workforce of serfs and slaves, the Boers decided to abandon their fertile farms. In 1838, in what is known as the Great Trek, the Boers headed north into the interior, across the Orange River and the Vaal, to dispossess and enslave local blacks and create their own white states. Among the ostrich-skin wallets and zebra-skin cushions in the curio shops of Cape Town were supple leather *sjamboks*. It was impossible to see these whips and not think of them as the very symbol of South African history.

What impressed me in Cape Town was its smallness, its sea glow, its fresh air; and every human face was different, everyone's story was original. No one really agreed on anything except that Cape Town, for all its heightened contradiction, was the best place to live in South Africa. No sooner had I decided the place was harmonious and tranquil than I discovered the crime statistics — carjackings, rapes, murders, and farm invasions ending in the disemboweling of the farmers. Some of the most distressed and dangerous squatter settlements of my entire trip I saw in South Africa, and among the handsomest districts I had seen in my life — Constantia comes to mind, with its mansions and gardens — I also saw in this republic of miseries and splendors.

Not long after I arrived, I called Conor and Kelli, fellow travelers whom I had last seen on the faltering Kilimanjaro Express. I used a telephone number they had given me. I was curious to know what had happened to them after I had gotten off the train at Mbeya.

"Paul, it was incredible. Come over and we'll tell you all about it," Kelli said. They were both in town, staying at the house of Kelli's mother, somewhere up the side of Table Mountain.

The house, on the slopes of Devil's Peak, was so buffeted by the powerful westerly that parked cars trembled on their tires and windowpanes distorted reflections like funhouse mirrors, because the glass was pressed and sucked by the gusts. House doors flew open and slammed, plastic bags shot through the air and snagged and whipped on tree branches, trash barrels spun from the sidewalks and banged and clattered down the street.

"Look who's here," Conor said. He was clean-shaven and tidier than he had been on the train, but otherwise his exuberant Irish self. "Oh, God, after we left you in Mbeya the whole trip went downhill."

Ursula, the Finnish woman, got sick at Kapiri Mposhi and needed to be hospitalized. They were stranded there for a few days. Then the bus that Conor and Kelli took south from Lusaka kept breaking down.

"By breaking down, I mean we hit a donkey and it flew through the windscreen and died in the driver's lap, and some Boers on the bus said, 'Aye, let's have a *braai* and grill the bastard and eat 'im.' Can you imagine?"

In Conor's Dublin brogue this was a marvelous manic lilting sentence.

Instead of barbecuing the dead donkey, they pressed on to Chinhoyi, where they got stranded again. "No one had Zim dollars, so we were really up a tree. We gave up in Harare and flew home to Cape Town, bugger the buses. How about you?"

I summarized my progress from southern Tanzania, and my conclusion, too, was bugger the buses. I said I preferred the trains, especially the Trans-Karoo Express.

"We were on the Karoo two weeks ago for a weekend," Conor said, getting up from his chair so that he could fling his illustrating arms around in precise Irish gestures. "A little hotel run by a gay couple. We reckoned on a little hiking in the hills, good food, and a bit of rest. Jaysus, it turned out to be a nightmare from the moment we arrived — Kelli, her mum, and me. I said, 'Let's watch the football in the bar.' It was one of those strange Afrikaner bars, a lot of drunken farmers on a Saturday afternoon. The barman was weird — he had been a soldier in Angola and was half mental because of it. Some blacks in the corner, looking unwelcome. Anyway, I switches on the telly and a big drunken farmer lurches over and looks me in the eye."

Imitating the lurching farmer, Conor goggled into my eye.

"'Football's a kaffir sport. Either watch the fucking rugby or turn it off! No fucking kaffir sports in this bar!'

"We'd only been there five minutes, see. Anyway, he went on yelling at us because I wouldn't turn the telly off. Then the farmer said, 'Look, he's a kaffir!' — and he hugged one of the blacks in the corner, who looked horribly embarrassed — 'though he's my friend, my kaffir friend.' He goes on, 'But these bloody people are making us suffer. Nine hundred and fifty farmers have been murdered since 'ninety-four!' As he said it, Kelli — who's pretty impatient, as you know — put her hand over her mouth and pretended to yawn.

"The Boer went ballistic! He made a lunge for Kelli, and I tried to grab him.

"Then the barman — well, the barman must have done some pretty strange things in Angola, because he was really mental, I mean, he showed us his paintings later. You should have seen them, like some Vietnam vet with post-traumatic stress. They were really upsetting. The barman starts saying, '*Nie die vrou nie! Nie die vrou nie!* She's a woman, you can't hit a woman!'

"But the crazed Afrikaner was trying to hit Kelli with a pool cue and I was trying to drag him down and me mother-in-law is screaming and the telly is too loud.

"The mental barman went ballistic too, just as one of the gay guys comes in and says, 'What is the matter?' And that was the awful part, because the Boer was bellowing in Afrikaans, 'Shit! Fuck! Kaffirs!' He swung the pool cue and missed Kelli and hit the gay guy in the face.

"The gay guy began to cry. The barman vaulted over the bar and hauled off and went *boof!* right in the Boer's chest, and down he went. As he settled on the floor, we ran upstairs."

"That's an amazing story," I said, laughing, because Conor had acted it out in the center of the parlor, with the wind snarling and pressing at the windows.

"It wasn't over," he said. "When we were in our room we heard him climbing the stairs."

Conor imitated a Frankenstein monster's stumping up the stairs and along the corridor of the inn, and the Boer's growling, "I'll kill ya! I'll kill ya!"

"I locked the door, but just to be sure I took a chair. I thought: I'll break it over his head. I heard him start to bellow, 'I know where you are!' and still he was banging all over the place. But he didn't find us.

"That was the first forty-five minutes of our weekend on the Karoo. I'll tell you the rest some other time. Have a beer. Cheers. Some people are coming. I forgot to tell you, this is our going-away party. We're leaving tomorrow."

The guests arrived for the party, multihued, a cross section of Cape Town. We drank and they told more stories. I felt I had fallen among friends. I felt close to Conor and Kelli, who knew the tortuous route through East and Central Africa. But they saw no future for themselves here. They were going back to San Francisco, where they had Green Cards and jobs.

For a few days in Cape Town I did what tourists do. I took a day trip to the winelands of Franschoek and Paarl and Stellenbosch, looked at the vineyards and the cellars, went to wine tastings. I spent a morning at Constantia and an afternoon on the eastern slopes of Table Mountain, at the national botanical garden, Kirstenbosch, a lush repository of South African plants, filled with succulents and cycads and palms, as well as the fragrant varieties of low bush called fynbos, which were native to the purple moorlands of the Cape. A boundary hedge, planted by Jan van Riebeeck in 1660, was still flourishing at the margin of Kirstenbosch.

One day, intending to take the train to Simon's Town, I went to the station but got there too late. However, I was on time for another train, to Khayelitsha. I was in the mood for any train. Unable to find Khayelitsha on my map, I went to the information counter and inquired as to its whereabouts. The clerk, a young affable man of mixed race, showed me the place on the map.

Then he leaned across the counter and smiled and said, "Don't go there."

"Why not?"

"It's too dangerous," he said. "Don't go."

"I'm just taking the train. How is that dangerous?"

"The train was stoned yesterday," he said.

"How do you know it will be stoned today?"

He had a beautiful smile. He knew he was dealing with an ignorant alien. He said, "The train is stoned every day."

"Who does it? Young kids?"

He said, "Young, old, lots of people. From the town. They're not playing. They're angry. And they do a lot of damage. How do I know? Because yesterday I was on the train to Khayelitsha. With my friend — he's the driver. We were in the driver's cab. When the stones came he was hit in the side of the face. He was all bloody. Listen, he's in the hospital. He's in tough shape. He was just doing his job."

This convinced me. I decided not to go to Khayelitsha and told him so. The clerk's name was Andy. We talked a while longer. Khayelitsha, in Xhosa, meant "Our New Home," and there were 700,000 people there, most of them living in shacks, on the Cape Flats.

While we talked another clerk, a big middle-aged African woman in a thick red sweater and a wool hat, sat rocking back in a chair with her feet propped against the counter, just out of earshot. She was staring straight ahead and fiddling absently with a scrap of paper.

"I'm not a racist," Andy said, "but the blacks in this country think they are being passed over for jobs. In places like Khayelitsha they have no jobs — no money. They thought that after apartheid they would get jobs. When it didn't happen they began to get wild."

"I wanted to see a squatter camp."

"No," Andy said, smiling, shaking his head at the madness of it, and reminding me of all the times I had heard *There are bad people there.* "Don't go to a squatter camp. Don't go to a black township. You'll get robbed, or worse."

◇ ◇ ◇

The next day I went to a squatter camp. It was called New Rest, 1,200 shacks that had been accumulating for a decade on the sandy infertile soil of Cape Flats, beside the highway that led to the airport. The 8,500 inhabitants lived mainly in squalor. It was dire but not unspeakable. There was no running water, there were no lights, nor any trees; there was only the cold wind. I never got to Cape Town International Airport, but I could imagine travelers arriving, heading up the highway, looking at this grotesque settlement from a taxi window, and saying to the driver, "Do people actually live there?"

New Rest was adjacent to an equally squalid but older settlement called Guguletu, a place of old low beat-up brick houses. Guguletu achieved notoriety in 1993 when a twenty-six-year-old Californian, Amy Biehl, was killed there. She had been a Stanford graduate, living in South Africa as a volunteer in voter registration for the following year's free election, and had driven three African friends home to the township as a favor. Seeing her white face, a mob of African boys ("dozens") screamed in eagerness, for this was a black township and she was white prey. Her car was showered with stones and stopped, and she was dragged from it. Her black women friends pleaded with the mob to spare her. "She's a comrade!" Amy herself appealed to her assailants. She was harried viciously, beaten to the ground, her head smashed with a brick, and she was stabbed in the heart — killed like an animal.

A small cross at the roadside in Guguletu by a gas station marked the spot where she was murdered. It is a main road; there must have been many people around who could have helped her. No one did. A crude signboard behind the cross was daubed *Amy Bihls Last Home Section 3 Gugs* — misspelled and so crude as to be insulting.

Defying death threats, some women in Guguletu who had witnessed the crime came forward and named Amy's killers. Four young men were convicted of the murder and sentenced to eighteen years in prison. Three years after their imprisonment these murderers appeared before the Truth and Reconciliation Commission. They had an explanation. "Their motive was political and not racial." They were members of the Pan Africanist Congress, they said, and were only carrying out the program of the party, which regarded all whites as "settlers."

Their argument was ridiculous. How this murder could have been regarded as nonracial made no sense. Mandela was out of prison, elections were scheduled, the country had been all but turned over to the African majority. The mob was of course racially motivated, for they had singled her out. Still, the murderers "regretted" what they had done; they claimed they had "remorse." They pleaded to be released under the terms of general amnesty. Everything they said seemed to me lame and without merit.

The murderers' freedom would have been impossible without the assent of Amy's parents, Peter and Linda Biehl, who attended the Truth and Reconciliation Commission and heard their testimony. Though the mother of one of the killers was so disgusted and ashamed by her son's description of what he had done to Amy she could not face him, the Biehls embraced the killers. They said that their daughter would have wanted this show of mercy, as she was "on the side of the people who killed her." The Biehls would not stand in the way of an amnesty.

So the murderers waltzed away. Astonishingly, two of them, Ntombeko Peni and Easy Nofomela, were given jobs by the Biehls. They still worked in salaried positions for the Amy Biehl Foundation, a charity started by Amy's forgiving parents in their daughter's memory. The foundation received almost two million dollars from the U.S. Agency for International Development in 1997, for being "dedicated to empowering people who are oppressed."

The details of this arrangement baffled me. As a father, the thought of losing my children this way was horrifying — I would rather die myself. What would I do in the same tragic circumstances? Well, I would want the murderers off the street, and if somehow they gained their freedom, I doubt that I would give them a job. It would enrage me to hear them whining and making excuses. I would expect deeds from them. It would pain me to have to look into their faces. Amy's parents did not share my feelings.

Later, I asked a South African journalist what she thought of the Truth and Reconciliation Commission. She said, "If it was not for the concept of forgiveness, which was a steering force of the Truth and Reconciliation Commission, I wonder where we would have been. Sometimes incredible things happened — an army general responsible for a bombing met a man blinded by the explosion and they shook hands. A torturer was forced to relive his actions. Sometimes killers asked parents for forgiveness and were accepted or rejected. Many people felt the Truth and Reconciliation Commission was a sham, but I thought the process was remarkable when it worked."

The extreme and unusual forgiveness shown by Amy Biehl's parents is often remarked upon — so often provoking debate that it almost seems that the incredible mercy they showed was provocative to a salutary degree. But much of what was said by the murderers and their supporters was just cant and empty words, for though no one in South Africa seems to remember it, at the time of the amnesty the Biehls challenged them by saying, "Are you in South Africa prepared to do your part?"

Guguletu's grimness was its history as a workers' area — men's hostels and men's huts. Male workers in South Africa had always been easier to control when they were away from their families. For one thing, they could always be sent back to their villages. The mines were notorious for their hostels, which were regulated like cellblocks. The squatter colony of New Rest that grew up beside Guguletu after 1991 was composed mainly of women who wanted to be near their husbands and boyfriends. Because it had been plopped down on forty acres of sand, there were no utilities, and as a consequence it stank and looked hideous. The huts were sheds made of ill-fitting boards, scrap lumber, bits of tin, plastic sheeting. The gaps between the boards were blasted by the gritty wind.

"I get sand and dust in my bed," said Thando, the man who showed me around.

But, unexpectedly — to me, at any rate — the place had an upbeat spirit, a vitality, and even a sense of purpose. No lights had been put in, but there were shops that sold candles for a few cents apiece, and other goods were listed in scrawls on cardboard: *Oil, Teabag, Sugar, Salt* — the basics.

I had not gone to New Rest alone. I had been told of a white couple who took interested foreigners there as a way of putting them in touch with life at the margins of Cape Town. The visitors, startled by the squalor, inevitably made contributions to a common fund. A day care center for the children of working mothers had been started with this money — probably the only clean and well-painted building in the place, where two kindly African women looked after thirty-five well-behaved children.

Most of the shacks were owned by women, and more than half the women were employed somewhere in Cape Town, as domestics or cleaners or clerks. The shops in the camp were run by women, and so were the squat little bars — known throughout South Africa as shebeens, an Irish word (originally meaning "bad ale") that had percolated into the language from soldiers' slang. I went into several of these shebeens and saw drunken boys and men sitting hunched because of the low ceilings. They were nursing bottles of Castle lager, smoking and playing pool and pawing ineffectually at fat little prostitutes.

Life could get no grimmer than this, I thought — the urban shantytown, without foliage, too sandy to grow anything but scrawny geraniums and stubbly cactus; people having to draw water into plastic buckets from standpipes and burn candles in their huts; cold in winter, sweltering in summer, very dirty, lying athwart a main highway — what was worse? Rural poverty at least had the virtue of gardens and animals and the traditional house of reliable mud and thatch. Rural poverty had its pieties, too, as well as customs and courtesies.

Thando took me to meet the New Rest committee. This too was funded by contributions from visitors. The committee was, of course, all male. And they were optimists.

"There are no drugs or gangs here," one man said. "This is a peaceful place. This is our home."

The squatters were all people from the eastern Cape, the old so-called homelands of Transkei and Ciskei, as well as the slums of East London, Port Elizabeth, and Grahamstown, industrial cities that were not faring well in the new economy.

The committee had aims. One was for roads to be made throughout the squatter colony, another was for piped water.

"We want to build houses here," a committee member explained to me.

The master plan had been outlined and blueprinted by volunteer urban planners at the University of Cape Town. Every shack had been numbered and its plot recorded. A census had been taken.

"In situ upgrade," the committee spokesman said, rolling out the plan on the table in the committee room.

The idea of transforming a squatter camp into a viable subdivision by upgrading existing dwellings had been accomplished in Brazil and India but not so far in South Africa. The goal was to replace each miserable shack with a small house or hut. The driving force behind this was the pride the people took in having found a safe place to live. The goodwill of foreign visitors also helped: they had contributed money for the day care center, for three brickmaking machines, and the establishment of a trust fund. The fund was administered on a pro bono basis by an otherwise outward-bound travel company, Wilderness Cape Safaris, which had put New Rest on its itinerary. Some children were sponsored by visitors, who sent money regularly for their clothes and education. It was a strange hand-to-mouth arrangement, but the element of self-help in it made me a well-wisher.

I asked what had been here before the squatter camp and got a surprising answer. It had been low bush with the specific function of concealing initiates (*mkweta*) in circumcision ceremonies (*ukoluka*) performed by the local Xhosa people. The deed was done with the slice of a spear (*mkonto*) on boys — men, really — aged from seventeen to twenty-five. No one could explain why circumcision was left so late, but all agreed that it was a necessary rite of passage, essential for male bonding.

"Even these days they use it," one of the committee members said. "In June and December we see them, sometimes many of them, hiding in the bush at the far side."

Though it was not bush but only scrubland that lay next to the highway and bordered large scruffy settlements, the area must have had some significance as a refuge in earlier times. Here the newly circumcised young men were rusticated for six weeks of healing, wearing only rough blankets, cooking over smoky fires, their faces painted with the white clay that designated them as initiates of the old ceremony. They remained in the background. In the foreground was Guguletu and New Rest, the squatter camp. It was filled with people so grateful, all they wished for was to make their shacks more permanent, so they could stay there for the rest of their lives.

This being South Africa, and specifically the western Cape, there was hardly any distance between this squatter camp/circumcision refuge and another kind of refuge. Twenty miles up the highway in Paarl, on the slope of Paarl Mountain and its fluted monument to the Afrikaans language, among gentle hills draped in vineyards, was a magnificent country house hotel, the Grande Roche Luxury Estate Hotel. This was an eighteenth-century manor restored to its former glory and now receiving guests. I went there for lunch. The former slave quarters had been gutted and redecorated into guest suites. Weddings were held in such a serene chapel you would hardly have known that this buffed-up and beautified place had been the slave chapel.

In every sumptuous respect it was Jock Silberstein's Welgevonden Estate, as described by Etienne Leroux. A pool, a spa, a walled herb garden, a library, and a gourmet restaurant — the Grande Roche had everything. In Bosman's, the hotel restaurant, which had achieved Relais Gourmand status, I had caesar salad with slices of Karoo lamb and the herb dressing, my entrée a red stumpnose — something like snapper — served on polenta, with baby vegetables and several glasses of Grande Roche's own sauvignon blanc. Dessert was marinated strawberries and clotted cream.

Then I sat in the sunshine on a deck chair among the blossoms of the Grande Roche rose garden, drank coffee, nibbled chocolate bon-

bons from a china saucer, and looked south to where rising smoke darkened the sky. There, under that smutty sky, on the Cape Flats, was the squatter settlement — grateful people in shacks — where I had spent the morning.

Above me, offering shade, a lovely tree bloomed with thick pendulous orange flowers.

A svelte white woman passed by me, with the pert, uplifted profile of someone breathing deeply, perhaps inhaling the aroma from the herbaceous border of the path. She wore a blue silken dress and a stylish large-brimmed white hat. Her spike-heeled shoes crunched on the gravel. She smiled at me. I said hello. We talked a little.

"What kind of tree is that?" I asked.

"That's a coral tree," she said. "A *kaffir boom,* actually — you must not say that name these days, though."

◇ ◇ ◇

My ultimate destination on this African safari had been Cape Town. But as is often the case on a long trip, I arrived here only to gain a vantage point from which to see another destination, farther ahead, tempting me onward. So I dawdled and procrastinated in this sunny windswept city, in the coziness of a clean hotel, in the only province in which Mandela's African National Congress was not in the majority — a great novelty in South Africa. The provincial government was in the hands of the Democratic Alliance, a squabbling coalition of right-wing and conservative parties, Cape Town's way of asserting that it was unlike any other place in the country. Happily for me, people spoke their mind, perhaps a reaction to so many years of whispering.

Some of the locals were so vivid as to seem caricatures. "Swanie" Swanepoel was one of them, a big pale fleshy-faced Boer with angry blue eyes, a jaw like a backhoe, thick farmer's hands, and tight suspenders stretched over his huge gut and bursting shirt, hooked to his slipping trousers. Everything about him — his voice, his eyes, his jowls, even the way he crooked his fat fingers — emphasized his sense of grievance. He had hated the way the system had changed, and his refrain was *Where is the world now?*

He was originally from Upington, an agricultural town in the northern Cape, on the upper reaches of the Orange River, a twelve-hour drive from Cape Town.

"'You don't know what it's like to be poor,' people tell me. Yes, I do! I was poor! We had nothing," he told me in his secondhand shop in Cape Town. "My mother ran a boarding house. She took in poor blacks and gave them food. For that we were known as *kaffir boeties.* But the world didn't know anything of that. The world demanded that we hand over our country. They had sanctions against us. So we had to do it. And so what happened ten years ago was a disaster. And where is the world now? You know they've been killing farmers?"

"I heard about a thousand white farmers have been killed in ten years," I said.

He howled at me, "Twice that number! The world doesn't care. I say to Jews, 'This is our holocaust. This is our genocide.' They say, 'You deserve it.' You have seen this?"

He opened *Volksmoord/Genocide,* a book of photographs of grisly dismemberments, decapitations, and maimings, the text by Hattingh Fourie, in Afrikaans and English. Not much text was needed to know that what was being depicted were the murders of white farmers by African vigilantes in the hinterland. The crime-scene photographs were so horrific I had to turn away.

"This is happening on our farms right now," Swanie said. "They think they can drive me out, but I am not going anywhere. Not to Australia, thank you very much. My people have been here for three hundred years! No one cares."

"I'm listening to you, aren't I?" I said.

"No one is writing about this," Swanie said.

"What do you want people to write about?"

"The genocide," he said, and tapped the picture of a disemboweled and headless farmer in *Volksmoord.* He gave a rueful laugh. "I know Mandela. I wanted to complain. He said, 'Call my secretary.' So I did. The secretary says, 'Who are you?' I tell her who I am, Swanepoel, such-and-such. She says, 'Where were you for twenty-seven years when we were in prison?' I says, 'Lady, what prison were you in?' She says, 'What?' I says, 'Don't *what* me!' She says, 'You Boers,' and hangs up."

"How do you know Mandela?" I asked.

"Because he was around," Swanie said. "He wasn't in prison for twenty-seven years. He was on Robben Island for nineteen and then he had a very easy time of it in Victor Verster over in Drakenstein".— I had seen Verster myself on the way back from Franschoek, a rural prison, now renamed, in the heart of the wine country. "Mandela was living in the warder's house, like a bloody summer camp. And he lied to me."

Since there was no way I could verify how well Swanie knew Nelson Mandela, I changed the subject. But he was so aggrieved, there was no subject for which he did not have a ready-made rant.

"We're blamed for everything," Swanie said. "You know about that march in Cape Town in 'ninety-two?"

I said I knew nothing of it.

"They were marching and chanting, 'One Boer, one bullet.' Mandela didn't stop them. And that woman Jabavu. You know her?"

I said I didn't. Now he was in full cry, so what I said hardly mattered.

"An Indian woman. She wrote a book saying that if a black was in line waiting to be served in a shop, and a white person entered, the black had to stand aside. She was talking about District Six, and maybe there was some truth in it. But who owned the shops? Indians! The Jabavus! The Jews! The Muslims! The Boers never owned shops. We were farmers. We were in the Karoo — in the country, on the farms."

Swanie was now so angry that he threw down *Volksmoord* and began to close his shop, slamming the burglar bars, hoisting the metal screen, setting the padlocks in their hasps.

"I fought in the war — how many of these other bloody people fought in the war?" he howled. "It's the same as always, like when we were invited to sit at Dingaan's kraal. 'Leave your weapons — we won't hurt you.' The Boers thought the Zulus were being honest, so they went along. That's what this is now. It is Dingaan's kraal. The Boers went along and they were slaughtered."

Like many another South African, his sense of history was immediate and aggrieved. To illustrate betrayal, he had plucked an episode from 1838. Dingaan was Shaka the Zulu's half-brother and successor. What Swanie did not say was that the Boers, in revenge for that bit of trickery, massacred three thousand Zulus in the Battle of Blood River — the river so named because its waters frothed incarnadine with Zulu blood.

The District Six that Swanepoel mentioned had been polyglot, multiracial, and colorful, a cultural hothouse that was a cross between Catfish Row and the French Quarter. It had occupied about forty acres near the harbor, not far from Swanie's shop. I met many people who had lived there, who regretted its passing. District Six had represented what the whole of South Africa could become without racial barriers. The big happy community had produced writing and music that were so full of vitality and a spirit of freedom that the white government had become worried.

A former resident of District Six named Hassan explained to me: "One day in 1962 we all got a letter from the government. 'This is now designated as a white area.' But there were many whites there. We all lived together happily. Malays, Indians, blacks, coloreds."

"So what happened?"

"We were relocated to the Cape Flats, and District Six was bulldozed," Hassan said. "All the houses were destroyed. They left the churches and the mosques. You can see them."

Redesignating District Six as white was such a controversial decision that the land was not built upon. Houses that were planned for whites never went up.

"We had to live in an awful place near Muizenberg — Mitchell's Plain. Hot, dusty, windy," Hassan said in his local snarl — *hoat, darsty, weendy.* "There had been prisoners there in the war. Eye-talians. We got those prisoners' barracks. We hated it."

Forty years later, Hassan still lived in Mitchell's Plain, and District Six was still unpopulated. What remained was the District Six Museum, where I learned that — such was the stupidity of the apartheid government and the irrationality of its Group Areas Act — the harmonious multiracial inhabitants of the district had been separated and dispersed. The District Sixers were sent to monochromatic communities: the coloreds like Hassan to Mitchell's Plain; the Indians to another outer suburb, Athlone; the blacks to Langa and Guguletu and Khayelitsha. By the mid-1970s most of the residents had been relocated, and District Six was renamed Zonnebloem ("Sunflower"), though the name didn't stick.

On the floor of the District Six Museum was a plan of the streets and the individual houses, with snapshots attached and scribbled over by former residents, who offered details and memories in notes and testimonials, many of them heartfelt. I was shown around the museum by Noor Ebrahim, a writer who had grown up in District Six. His grandfather had come to South Africa from Bombay in the late nineteenth century with his four wives and the money to start a ginger beer business. His father had also been in the business. Noor said they were from Gujarat.

"I'm curious. Did you speak Gujarati at home?"

"No. We spoke kitchen English."

"Not kitchen Dutch?"

"It was Dutch — sort of. But we called it *kombuis Engels.* Everyone spoke it in District Six." Noor gave me a few examples, all of them Dutch. "We spoke proper English at school."

The word *kombuis,* for "kitchen," was a curious relic. I was told by a South African linguist that the word would have been laughed at in Holland, for it referred to a ship's galley. The Dutch word for kitchen is *kuijken.* Every now and then, the linguist said, a Dutch person would be startled by something spoken in Afrikaans, like the busload of theologians who were told that their bus was slowing down on the highway so that they could pull off. The expression "pull off," *aftrek* in Afrikaans, meant "masturbate" in Dutch.

Of the paraphernalia in the District Six Museum the saddest were the signboards and warnings of an earlier era, plainly worded cautions on drinking fountains and entryways: *Vir Gebruik Van Blankes* (For Use by White Persons), *Nie Blank* (Non-White), and *Slegs Blankes* (Whites Only). The earlier era was not so long ago, for the signs had been displayed as recently as the late 1980s. Similar signs, familiar and ubiquitous in the American South, had persisted into the 1960s — *White* and *Colored* over side-by-side drinking fountains, for example. Any American who could look upon South African bigotry and feel anything but shame was a hypocrite.

◇ ◇ ◇

One hot Sunday morning, with reluctance, hating to signify the end of my safari, I set out one last time. It was a day of blue sky and brisk winds. I bought a ticket on the train to Simon's Town. Though I had varied my journey with chicken buses and cattle trucks and overcrowded minivans and *matatus,* it was possible to travel by rail from Simon's Town to Nairobi. Cecil Rhodes's plan had been to extend this line to Cairo. He had always been something of a dreamer: another of Rhodes's wishes was for Great Britain to take back the United States, so that we Americans would be ruled by the monarchy, the Union Jack flapping over Washington.

First class and third class were clearly marked on the train, yet we all sat in first regardless of our tickets, black, white, and all the other racial variations that characterized Cape Town's people. The conductor was nowhere in sight; no one punched our tickets. We sat, no one speaking, on this sunny morning.

We stopped at every station — Rosebank, Newlands, Kenilworth, Plumstead, Heathfield, but in spite of the pretty names some looked prosperous and some poor, with bungalows surrounded by shaven lawns and squatters' shacks blowing with plastic litter, graffiti everywhere. Some of these places were the addresses listed in the Adult Entertainment ads of that day's *Cape Times.* I knew who lived here: "Amy Kinky to the Extreme," "Nikki and Candy for Your Threesome," "Abigail — On My Own," "Candice — Come Bend My Fender," and the anonymous but just as promising "Bored Sexy Housewife."

Dead silence in the swaying train, people reading the papers, children kicking the seats, the great yawning torpor of a hot Sunday morning. We stopped in the glare of roofless platforms and then carried on. Soon we were at the shore, passing the wind-driven waves at False Bay and Muizenberg, a very stiff southeasterly with a wicked chop driving the greasy lengths of black kelp, so thick you'd take it for a hacked-up ship's hawser. It was strewn in such profusion that it obstructed surfers from paddling out to the breaks.

Just after Fishhoek I saw a strange thing. Out the window about sixty feet from shore, sticking straight out of the sea, was a great flapping whale's tail. It was so near, a swimmer could easily have slapped it. The tail was upright and symmetrical, like a big black rubber thing swaying above the water.

A whale standing on its head? I looked around. The adults dozed and the children seemed to take it as a normal occurrence, a whale's headstand in shallow water, an enormous creature's vertical tail glistening in the sunlight, remaining upright for so long it was still there after the train passed.

"They do that all the time," a man in the next car said, when I noticed that he had seen the whale, and I asked him about it. "That was a southern right whale. It's known as 'sailing.' No one knows why they do it."

At Simon's Town, the end of the line, I walked out of the small white station into the high road. This could have been the high road of any English coastal town, with greengrocers and chemists' shops and lime-washed bombproof-looking brick houses named Belmont and Belvedere and The Pines. The arcades and shop terraces were dated 1901 and 1910, and the coast itself looked English — Cornish to be exact, rocky and wind-flattened, as though Penzance might be down the road.

The naval station was the reason for Simon's Town's existence, so it was not odd to find fish-and-chip shops and pubs advertising "Traditional Roast Beef and Yorkshire Pud." Captain Cook, Charles Darwin, Scott of the Antarctic, Rudyard Kipling, Mark Twain, and many others who had rounded the Cape of Good Hope had stopped in this beautiful harbor. The funny old self-conscious time warp, with cottages and villas and little chalets on the bluff above the road, and even the bus shelters and telephone booths mimicked those in the blustery harbor villages of the kingdom by the sea.

I walked to Boulders Beach to see the colony of jackass penguins. Unperturbed by the nearness of bungalows and spectators, they nested on eggs, frolicked in the surf, and wobbled up and down the strand like perplexed nuns.

On the coast road at one of the Simon's Town bus shelters I waited for a bus to take me to Cape Peninsula National Park. All the difficulty was behind me. I was just sitting on a bench, waiting to board a bus for the short ride to Cape Point, the end of my trip. A man on a bench opposite me was smoking a cigarette and reading a copy of that day's Johannesburg *Star*. Some words caught my eye. Flagged on the top of the front page was the teasing headline "Pessimistic Globetrotter Wins Nobel Prize."

"Looks like I've got the big one," I murmured, and leaned closer to give this stranger some news that would amaze him.

He hadn't heard me speak, nor did he hear me sigh. The feeling came and went, like the overhead drone of one of those search and rescue planes that misses the castaway adrift in a rubber dinghy: just the briefest flutter of hope. But no one actually loses, because there is only one winner in the Swedish lottery.

The man engrossed in the newspaper was fleeing his home in England, so he told me. I found it hard to concentrate after the vision I had just had. His name was Trevor. We sat together on the bus and he related his sad story. Trevor had been a crewman on a merchant vessel carrying ammo during the Falklands War. The ship had come under fire, days of shelling.

"The net result was the skipper lost it — went round the bend, wouldn't leave his cabin, had to be dragged onshore, was invalided out. But that wasn't the worst, was it?"

"What was the worst of it?" Still I saw the words "Pessimistic Globe-trotter," but I took pleasure in the way Trevor, concentrating on his story, dealt with his newspaper by folding it in quarters and tucking it under his bottom, the teasing headline pressed beneath one buttock.

"Went ashore for the post, didn't I? Was a Dear John letter, wasn't it? And they thought I'd go mental like the skipper, so they discharged me before I could take a header off the ship. Called me wife, didn't I? She says, 'There's nothing to discuss, Trevor' and 'Why are you shouting?' And she bloody hangs up on me, doesn't she? So I went home and we split up. It was horrible. Now her boyfriend goes around saying, 'Trevor refuses to have a drink with me.'"

Trevor's story and the *Star* headline somewhat colored my view of the Cape Peninsula. We crossed a great empty herbaceous moorland of purple-blue fynbos, low bushes shaking in the wind, as aromatic as the maquis in Corsica, miles of trembling herbs. Some wild things roamed here — eland and ostrich, children on school outings, baboons, tourists.

"*Tutta la famiglia!*" an Italian woman on the bus screeched, seeing some peevish baboons by the roadside baring their teeth at her.

When the bus stopped at this, the uttermost end of Africa, I got out. Trevor followed along. He lingered to buy a souvenir baseball cap lettered *Cape Point* on the crown. I kept walking, to the lookout, down to the sloping trail, to the narrow path in the bright afternoon, through the gusting wind. On my left, the cliff dropped away two hundred feet to frothy ocean. I walked to Dias Point — Bartolomeu Dias was here in 1488 — and farther on, to Cape Point itself, jutting like the prow of a ship over the bright sea, until I reached the last of the warnings, *No Access Beyond this Point,* and *Do Not Throw Stones,* and *End of Trail.*

23 ◈◈◈

Blue Train Blues

THE BLUE TRAIN that ran every few weeks between Cape Town and Pretoria was described in its brochure as "the world's most luxurious train." I returned to Johannesburg on it. The superlative was perhaps true, but even more amazing, this luxury train was operated by the South African government, the same department that ran the Trans-Karoo Express, the dusty Trans-Oranjie to Durban, and the littered, halting choo-choo to Simon's Town. Butlers in zebra-striped shirts met me at Cape Town Station and served snacks, looking disappointed at my small scuffed bag. How were they to know that it contained some lovely Chokwe carvings, my expensive watch, my spare cash, and tanzanite baubles to propitiate my wife in her enduring my long absence?

A tour group of twenty Japanese men and women scuttled ahead to board the train. And then I was shown to my wood-paneled compartment, where there was a phone and a fax machine. I winced, imagining that they would disturb my solitude, but they never rang for me.

"I am Dalton, your butler."

He brought me champagne. I sat with a book and sipped wine and read. Even from the best train across the Karoo, the scenery was the same: the great blue hills, the vineyards, the grassland, the startled ostriches, boozers under bridges, bright lime-washed bungalows blazing in the stony desert, the sight of shantytowns and squatter camps and magnificent mountains.

My book was a small Penguin paperback of Montaigne's essays, which I kept for emergencies, when I had nothing else to read; it was my bedside book, my solace. I had finished recopying the erotic story, my notes were done, so I reread "On the Cannibals." This short essay was to me like a sacred text, for in it Montaigne discussed the hypocrisy of seeing strangers as savage: "every man calls barbarous the thing he is not accustomed to." Cannibalism Montaigne regarded as less offensive than the many French cruelties. The wider world was unknown. "What we need is topographers who would make detailed accounts of the places they had actually been to." At the end he recalled his encounter, in Rouen in 1562, with three self-possessed Brazilian natives, cannibals perhaps, remembering their sense of honor, their courage in battle, their dignity as leaders, and their bare asses.

"Not at all bad, that. Ah! But they wear no breeches . . ."

My berth on the Blue Train was the softest bed of my entire trip, the dining car food the most delicious, the comfort incomparable. This comfort gave me a keener eye for seeing Africans toiling in the fields out the window: an old woman carrying two battered suitcases along a hot dry road, walking away from the tracks toward a distant hill; a man in blue overalls bent double under a mealie sack, his month's food slung over his shoulder; a child standing bare-assed in a filthy yard.

At Laingsburg a well-heeled couple on the train tossed apples from their crystal fruit bowl to children panhandling by the tracks. At Leeu-Gamka a skinny girl of about ten or eleven pleaded with me for food, murmuring in the shy prayerful way of a child softly begging. She was so thin and curveless her blue dress hung straight down from her shoulders to her knees like a faded flag of defeat. I could not bring myself to toss food to her. She ducked out of sight, and after we started up she reappeared, fierce-faced, and flung a small stone through the window, just missing my head. A few more small stones clattered into my sumptuous compartment, plopping on the cushions and smacking the wall — not serious, but meaningful; a symbolic stoning.

The Blue Train cut through the late afternoon, its wide black shadow lying flat and hurrying next to it. At dusk a great watery darkness descended, dissolving the light, the high plains going purple then blue then black, with a flattening orange stripe of sunset in the sky that made the landscape blacker.

The next day we stopped at Kimberly, a dust-blown mining town, slummy at the edges with a huge pit in the middle, "the biggest man-made hole in the world." Billions of dollars' worth of gems had been scooped from this pit, yet the town was just a dreary *dorp* of waste dumps and hills of gravel, and bungalows with tin roofs, video parlors and fried-chicken restaurants and burger joints and used car lots and a hideous desert climate with fierce summer heat and wicked winter frosts, nothing to do in the *dorp* except dig and sift and pick through the dirt for baubles. All this visible tedium and poorly paid labor was the reality behind the wickedest confidence trick in the world, the diamond trade.

Back on the train: ostrich carpaccio, followed by a choice of honey-glazed breast of duck, ostrich Wellington, or baked kingklip (a kind of eel), and dessert of chocolate mousse. I ate and watched the settlements pass, some very grand, and also some squatter colonies of tin-roofed shacks, and in some places drunks on benches, guzzling their free ration of wine at nine in the morning.

The train was almost heartbreaking for being so pleasant, for offering this view of South Africa, the same misery, the same splendor. But my work was done, my safari finished. This trip was just a dying fall; I was clinging to Africa because I had not wanted it to end.

◈ ◈ ◈

Huck never returned from "the Territory," as far as we know. Yet Captain Gulliver went home, wiser but also alienated and revolted, not by the trip but by the domestic scene. Unable to stand the Yahoo smell that adhered to his wife and the sight of his savage-looking family, he comforted himself by talking to his horse and finding companionship in the stable. Travel had changed him. You go away for a long time and return a different person — you never come all the way back. Like Rimbaud, you think, *I is someone else.*

Several occurrences in South Africa helped me find a sense of proportion. Just before I left Johannesburg, I left my locked bag and every expensive thing I owned in the safekeeping of a hotel's padlocked strong room. I took a short trip to the coast, carrying only a briefcase, my notes, my story, and a change of clothes. I did not want to be burdened by a bag or any valuables. I returned to the hotel four days later and handed over my claim check to an uncertain bellhop.

"We cannot find your bag, sir."

The thing had been stolen. And so I lost everything I had brought to Africa: watch, wallet, cash, air tickets, as well as artifacts and treasures I had bought along the way, everything except my briefcase and its rattling contents. I still had my house keys, the selection of Montaigne's *Essays,* the fair copy of my erotic story, a change of clothes, a small Congolese fetish of wood and beads, which was a remedy against thunder, and — a miracle — all the notes I had taken to inform the writing of this book.

"That's very Janiceburg," a Johannesburger said to me of the theft. "Very Jozi."

Not long after that, while I was still cursing my loss, Nadine's husband, Reinhold, died. The funeral took place on a lovely day, fragrant with sun-warmed yew trees, at Braamfontein Crematorium, an old stone building in the middle of a wooded walled-in cemetery. Among the hundred or so mourners were former political prisoners, civil rights lawyers, poets, novelists, journalists, activists, family friends.

Nadine's son, Hugo, spoke tenderly of his father. Others apostrophized him. And in the course of the service I got better acquainted with this remarkable man, Reinhold Cassirer — art connoisseur, humanist, businessman, wine expert, philanthropist, horseman, raconteur, great friend, loving husband.

Petite yet strong, sure of herself, and witty even on this occasion, Nadine spoke of her love for her husband.

"The first time I met him I asked him for a whiskey. He said disapprovingly, 'A woman doesn't drink whiskey at lunch.' But I did. And he brought me whiskey for the next forty-eight years. I wanted a son and a bulldog. He gave me both. He was my lover, my friend, my supporter. He had a wonderful respect for the privacy of my work. We shared a strong political commitment against racism and apartheid. When the first free elections were held, we went together and voted."

A measure of how the struggle for political freedom had penetrated people's lives was Nadine's speaking of how the act of voting freely together could be one of the tenderest memories of a South African marriage.

"Attending funerals has become a way of life in the townships," one of the African speakers said. "I have attended a lot of funerals lately."

"We felt we were part of the family," another man said.

That was how this funeral seemed, like a family affair. The long political struggle had made a family of all South Africans — a forgiving if a sometimes unruly family. The mourners were all sorts, every color, all ages, rich and poor, listening to Mozart during the interludes.

Nadine invited everyone back to her house for lunch, so later that morning I was standing in her garden, drinking wine among the mourners, part of the family. Some people commiserated with me about my theft, even Nadine. "I'm so sorry about your bag." But the funeral of this much-loved man, at which everyone was so gracious and philosophical, had shown me that the loss of my possessions was insignificant.

Traveling light, I thought I was returning home with nothing but my notes. I stopped in Ethiopia to break up the long return journey, and in those few days I ate something poisonous. The morning I left Addis Ababa my bowels exploded, not simple squitters but an infestation. And so I arrived home Africanized — robbed and diseased.

"Parasites," my doctor said. And, "Let's treat them empirically." For months, nothing seemed to work on easing my aching guts. I was inert, weak, with the odd debauched nausea of an extravagant illness. I felt like the cursed explorer in Edmund Lucas White's horror story "Lukundoo," who falls ill in Africa and breaks out in carbuncles, each septic bulge containing a plum-sized African head, "hideous, gibbering," with "wicked wee eyes." Throughout the writing of this book I have had the reminding motion and gassy gurgle of parasites — Africa stirring inside me for almost as many months as I was astir in Africa.

It is so much worse for Africans. The most civilized ones I met never used the word "civilization." The wickedest believed themselves to be anointed leaders for life, and wouldn't let go of their delusion. The worst of them stole from foreign donors and their own people, like the lowest thieves who rob the church's poor boxes. The kindest Africans had not changed at all, and even after all these years the best of them are bare-assed.

Postscript

THE JOURNEY ENDS, the traveler goes home, the book gets written. The result, the travel narrative, implies that it has fixed the place forever. But that is a meaningless conceit, for time passes, the written-about place keeps changing. All you do as a note-taking traveler is nail down your own vagrant mood on a particular trip. The traveling writer can do no more than approximate a country.

I was sorry when my trip ended; I had felt liberated and uplifted by the journey. Joseph Conrad once wrote, "Before the Congo I was a mere animal." I could say the same about my own experience of Africa. It made me curious again, and thinking about Africa once more I yearned to go back.

I love the African bush — I missed it; but I hate African cities. I swore that I would never return to the stinking buses, the city streets reeking of piss, the lying politicians, the schemers, the twaddlers, the crooks, the moneychangers taking advantage of weak currency and gullible people, the American God-botherers and evangelists demanding baptisms and screaming "Sinners!" — and forty years of virtue-industry CEOs faffing around with other people's money and getting no results, except Africans asking for more.

Then a friend of mine in Zimbabwe told me that since I had visited there was apparently more misery than ever: food shortages, no fuel, no hard currency, and the highest rate of inflation in the world, now at 400 percent and rising fast, the economy in such a dire state that the government could not afford to buy the German ink and paper necessary to print bills at its own mint in Bulawayo. No one could collect a salary because the banks had run out of folding money. As for the farm invasions: "Much worse. You wouldn't believe them."

He told me in detail about the blatant seizure of a farm. In July 2002 a commercial farmer in Zimbabwe — I shall call him Jones — was phoned late at night and told in a menacing voice, "You have fifteen minutes to leave your farm or you will be killed." Jones took the threat seriously, for a few months earlier his closest neighbor had been murdered by a mob for refusing to vacate his farm.

Jones, whose ancestors had come to this part of Africa over a century ago, had bought the land in 1981, a year after Zimbabwe's independence. No one wanted the tract; it was small, the ground was stony and unpromising. For a decade, Jones and his wife lived in a round makeshift hut called a rondavel, borrowed money, dug wells, put in irrigation, used fertilizer, and plowed organic matter into the sandy soil. Nearly all the commercial farmers in Zimbabwe have done this at one time or another, for the land is not inherently fertile; it is granitic sand that does not retain water. Farmed incorrectly, the soil turns into desert overnight.

Jones labored for several years to prepare the ground, and then he planted tobacco and roses — the latter he exported to Holland. He also grew seed maize and raised chickens and hogs. He transformed his small farm into a successful operation. He planted shade trees, upgraded his farm equipment, and began to pay off his bank loans. In 1992, in a final flourish of ownership, Jones designed and built a lovely farmhouse.

The house was his undoing. The elegant roof could be seen from the dirt road that ran past his fields. A prominent Zimbabwean with government connections noticed the house one day and decided he wanted it. It was he who arranged the menacing phone call. Before Jones could pack, a large mob showed up, men screaming threats. He and his wife were forced to run a gauntlet of abusive men, to sing the songs of the ruling party — ZANU-PF — and to praise Robert Mugabe, the president and the man who instigated such illegal farm invasions.

The intruder, an intimate of one of Mugabe's ministers, moved into the house, ate off Jones's crockery, sat in Jones's chairs, slept in Jones's bed, and told Jones to stay away. He fired Jones's forty farm workers and hired ten of his own at lower salaries. He harvested the tobacco and made plans to auction it. Jones, dispossessed of everything he owned, fled to Harare and began filing appeals for the return of his farm, his crops, his household goods.

The man who told me this story said, "All this happened lately. Since you were last here, more than two thousand farms have been seized. The whole situation is desperate."

Another friend of mine, this one in Malawi, a long-term expatriate my exact age, with my predilection for the bush — the exile I might have been had I stayed forty years in the African hinterland with little else to do except drink beer and chase girls and watch my bananas ripen — this friend wrote me saying, "You missed the vampires. There was a hell of a panic about bloodsuckers and some grisly murders a few months ago." He followed this with a story about a monstrous animal that had terrorized Malawi's central region. And more: people were being abducted "for their body parts."

There were other messages too, from people I had met on my trip, urging me, in the hospitable African way, to come back. No one mentioned acts of God, no one complained of bad weather. The harvests had been better than expected. The few famines had been regional and political — the governments withholding food aid, a settling of scores with disaffected people or the opposition or one of the more despised tribes. Some rigged elections, some massacres. Like most African events they went unnoticed or underreported. The outraged headline "Israeli Child Killed in Bombing" occurs often in American newspapers, but you never see the headline "African Child Killed in Bombing," for the death of one African child, or even a hundred, is not news.

So, exactly two years after finishing my long trip in Africa, goaded by friends and provoked by stories from friendly correspondents, I decided to return. I wondered what had happened in my absence. And, also, did he say *vampires?*

On my first trip through Malawi, an American diplomat had agreed with me that the country was in a dire state economically and riddled with AIDS, "but they're getting cell phones, that's positive." I had jeered at him: "Cell phones! They'll play with them like toys."

One of the first things I saw on my return to Blantyre was three Malawians, two women and a man, in the garden of a hotel, giggling at a cell phone on their table that had been switched to Speaker as a crackling voice chattered like a lost soul in a very badly rigged séance. Everyone had a cell phone. Business was worse than ever.

The Danish government had cut off all aid when they had learned that the Poverty Alleviation Fund had been used to buy brand-new Mercedes-Benzes for government ministers. The Dutch had curtailed aid because of the country's abysmal human rights record. Malawi's president, Bakili Muluzi, a Muslim, had hoped to make a friend of Saddam Hussein, and indeed a few months before the Iraq war had planned a state visit to Baghdad, bringing bags of rice and schoolbooks. When it was pointed out to President Muluzi that Malawi had no spare rice or schoolbooks and that donor countries might take a dim view of this self-serving visit, it was canceled. But Muluzi had found an ally in Libya's Muammar Qaddafi, who had sent him helicopters as well as money to set up madrassas and Islamic study centers. As a result, Malawi had become a haven for dissident Muslims. "All Taliban over there," a Malawian said to me, and on June 26, 2003, four Al Qaeda operatives were picked up and whisked out of the country to be interrogated by the CIA.

The roads I had seen under construction in 2001 were still unfinished. The schools were in worse shape than ever. The highest-paid teachers earned the equivalent of $36 a month and complained to me that they could not live on it. There were many more hookers on the streets and in bars, the HIV/AIDS statistics were higher, the coffee and tobacco prices much lower.

Most people I spoke to hankered for the days of the previous dictator, Hastings Banda, who had remained in power for more than thirty years and run Malawi as though it were his personal estate.

"We had no idea that democracy was such a mess," another Malawian who resigned from the government told me. "And no one wants to help us. They don't trust us, because we have wasted donors' money."

Out of this desperate recrimination, self-pity, poverty, and paranoia came phantoms, some real, some imagined.

The monster that appeared one midnight in the spring of 2003 was real enough, but it was unlike any beast anyone had ever seen. It was a zombie, "a human creation," the papers said, as if from the island of Dr. Moreau. Huge and hairy, it became a regular visitor, pouncing on people and "removing legs, noses, arms, and private parts." Sixteen people were maimed in one week. Whole villages fled in panic, and soon three thousand people were homeless, cowering from the beast.

Two magicians asked to be allowed to kill the beast using juju. The district commissioner protested: "The government does not recognize magic."

After months more of beast sightings and deaths and maimings, the creature was killed by villagers "using traditional methods" — not guns.

The beast was stoned, then beaten to death with sticks. Yet "its appearance still baffles people."

"It is a resurrected human being," one villager said.

But the strange beast was a hyena. In Malawi many hyenas had lost their habitats. This one, larger than normal, was starving and desperate; it had not eaten for weeks. And for the months that it lurked in the central region, the months before the harvest, a drama was enacted in which the villagers had found a target for their own anxiety and frustration and hunger.

The vampires were a greater scare. A few months before the beast's appearance, the president of Malawi formally denied that his government was "sucking people's blood in exchange for maize donations from abroad." The mention of bloodsucking was not a euphemism. Vampires had already attacked a woman and her son and tried to extract their blood. There were "bloodsucker scares" in Blantyre, the country's largest town — people blowing whistles and beating drums at night to alert the community that blood hunters were near. A provincial governor was attacked and stoned for being suspected of "harboring bloodsuckers." A reporter for the local newspaper was arrested for writing an untrue story about bloodsuckers and for "causing fear and alarm."

The president, on a private visit to Britain, said the stories embarrassed him and were "destroying the country's image." Within a day, three Catholic priests were attacked. They were suspected of being involved in bloodsucking.

Like the beast, this bloodsucking episode seemed like another metaphor for African distress. We are being eaten alive, we are losing our life's blood, and somehow the government is at fault — its denials are proof of it. In Africa, an official denial is like an admission of truth.

The Body Parts Killings were not a figment of the public imagination. Six people had been found dead, with lips, eyes, tongues, breasts, and buttocks removed from the corpses. All the victims were women. Soon there were thirteen more victims, mutilated in the same way. Some were eviscerated: lungs, livers, and intestines removed.

"These body parts are being sold to Mozambique," the president said.

No one asked why. Everyone knew that human body parts were essential to the best *mankhwala*, medicine: good for what ails you. Nineteen men were arrested for these murders. But in the end only one man was convicted of the crimes. His name was Thomson Bokhobokho. He was remorseful, confessing that he ate some of the body parts and sold the others. When asked his reason for the killings, he said, "Poverty."

There were now cell phones in Malawi, but little else had changed. I was discussing this with some friends in Blantyre when one of them pointed to some people carrying sacks of flour and jugs of cooking oil.

"They are from Zimbabwe?" one man said. "Ha! We're better off than they are!"

What could be worse than Malawi, I was wondering. Then I remembered what I had heard of Jones, the man who lost his farm to a party man who had taken a liking to it. What did a country like Zimbabwe look like with farms still under siege and limited amounts of folding money and hyperinflation? How do you run a country with no fuel at all?

In a sort of dystopian tableau, at the edge of the new, empty Harare airport, women and girls were gathering firewood and carrying it on their heads along the highway to their huts. No traffic. Cars and vans sat abandoned by the roadside. Desperate doomsday vignettes like this were frequent in Zimbabwe: people scavenging for food and fuel on well-made roads amid modern but empty buildings.

Long lines of people waited at banks; long lines of cars and minibuses at gas stations — more than three hundred at one station, most of them being minded by urchins — because the stations had no fuel. There were no tourists, of course. The hotels were empty. The shops were empty. I bought two crocodile belts for Z$70,000 (the black market equivalent of $40) and had to carry the weighty stack of small bills in a shopping bag. (Harare headline: "Pickpockets Turn to Targeting People with Bulging Plastic Bags.") I could not carry any more than the equivalent of about ten U.S. dollars in my pocket; the wad was too fat to fold. "The money is like bog roll," the salesclerk said to me, and she pointed out that a ten-dollar bill had the same value and the same surface area as one square of toilet paper. "But is useless, is rougher."

The U.S. State Department report on "Human Rights Practices in Zimbabwe" (March 2003) contained thirty-nine pages of murder, abduction, beatings, torture, rape, home invasion, "trafficking in people (slavery, child prostitution, forced labor)," and "killing of children for body parts." The sale of body parts to South African witch doctors for traditional medicine was one of Zimbabwe's few verifiable exports.

"Who are you?" a policeman demanded when I turned up at the Norton police station.

The farming town of Norton, sixty miles west of Harare, was the scene, some months before, of the brutal murder of a commercial farmer named Terry Ford. Ford had been beaten, shot six times, and his corpse mutilated by a mob of twenty-seven thugs, acting for a party man who wanted the farm. Soon after the murder, other farms in the district had been *chambanji'*d — mobbed and invaded — and seized by friends of Mugabe. The Norton police were summoned. But they had refused to show up, saying, "This is a political matter."

"I'm just an observer," I said to the Norton police chief. I wanted him to comment on the illegality of the evictions. In the past two years, two hundred policemen had left the Zimbabwe police force because of their disgust with human rights abuses. "I'm a foreigner observer."

"Go away." The man in charge was out of uniform, wearing a dirty jacket, and he shuffled toward me in broken-down shoes. He faced me, looking fierce, with bloodshot eyes and large ill-fitting teeth. "We don't want you here."

Harare with no fuel and no folding money looked very quiet, though it was full of pedestrians and milling crowds — no work, no school, an imploding economy, no rule of law, the leader of the opposition under arrest on a trumped-up charge of treason, the government a defiant kleptocracy with neither international friends nor local well-wishers. I did not meet a single person who supported the government. Yet apart from occasional work stoppages, there was no rebellion.

"It is not in our nature to be rebellious," an African writer told me. Another man said, "We don't have a culture of mass protest." A white woman, a farmer's wife, chain-smoking and furious, was more direct. "It's an arse-creeping culture. A slave mentality."

A year of fuel shortages had produced several "stayaways," one-day general strikes in which urban centers had been shut down and no business transacted. But after a day or so commerce resumed, after a fashion.

"Everyone is hungry," a teacher said. He added that there was food, but no money to buy it with.

A whole country running on fumes. Every queue was a mob, but a passive one. I was fascinated by the visible decay, the indifference of the government, the extraordinary decrepitude. I had never in my life seen such a well-developed place that was so obviously falling apart. Unable to travel home, many people from the rural areas lived like trolls in the alleys behind the banks and shops and grander buildings in Harare.

Two years before, by chance I had met Peter Drummond, the chicken farmer who also raised cattle and pigs and grew seed maize on seven thousand acres some distance from Harare. Back then, Drummond had been threatened with eviction, invaded by people demanding land. To intimidate him, the squatters had cut down shade trees near his house. I had met one of the invaders, a man who called himself Reywa, who had seized fifty acres and complained that his crops had failed because Drummond — the man he had victimized — had not helped him plant them. Two years ago I had jeered at this whining intruder (but had minimized the amount of land he had taken). He had muttered, "Drummond must plow for me, he must give me seeds and fertilizer."

I asked whether this had happened. And Drummond, who had a sense of humor, said, "Yes, I helped him. I plowed his fields. He's become a sort of friend." Drummond still hung on to his farm, but business was bad. In two years his chicken production had halved, and the fuel shortage was forcing him to cut back further.

Mugabe spent a great deal of time attacking whites and trying to make Zimbabwe's failure into a racial issue, but in fact black Zimbabweans accounted for most of the victims of human rights abuse — the government-sanctioned torture and murder, the electric shocks and beatings in police stations.

According to a recent survey by the Zimbabwe watchdog group Justice for Agriculture (JAG), 98 percent of all commercial farms — approximately four thousand farmers — were scheduled for seizure.

A model of efficiency, with a detailed database of farmers who have been evicted from their land, JAG is run by a group of volunteers and funded by donations. The spokesman and organizer is a bluff, portly, khaki-clad chain smoker named John Worsley-Worswick, who had recently lost his farm. "Obviously we can't go back to what we had, but we need meaningful land reform. Respect for property rights as decided in the courts," Worsley-Worswick told me. "The breakdown in the rule of law has been state-inspired and state-sponsored."

In my peregrinations I met farmer Jones, whose eviction story had stimulated my interest in returning to Zimbabwe. Like almost every other farmer I met here, white or black, he looked much older than his years. He was fifty-one but could have passed for sixty-five. Strangely, he was upbeat. "We're fighting this in court. Everything I have in the world has been taken from me. The thing I most regret is that I can't plant now, so we won't have a summer crop."

We were eating lunch at a restaurant, and this being Harare, only two other tables (of about thirty-five) were occupied by diners.

Jones said, "Have you seen the north — Chinhoyi and Karoi? Virtually all the farms there are gone."

I said I hadn't seen much of the hinterland because of the fuel shortage. There were no vehicles.

Jones said, "You have to see what has happened. We're going up this weekend. You can come along."

"When were you planning to leave?"

"In about twenty minutes."

So, less than an hour after I met him, I had agreed to a sudden departure on a two-day trip through farmland and bush, to Kariba and across the Zambezi River into Zambia. He would drop me off in Lusaka. We picked up Mrs. Jones, who was good-humored as well as shrewd and capable. Her folks, too, had recently lost their farm.

There had been an exodus to Zambia by evicted farmers, who hoped that by staying close to Zimbabwe they would be able to resume farming when Mugabe was out of power and the situation was reversed; either the farms would be returned to their rightful owners or compensation would be offered. About a fifth of Zimbabwe's commercial farmers had left for Australia or New Zealand, to begin new lives and even to farm, but to Jones this represented a surrender mentality.

And there was something else, verging on betrayal. Not just running from the injustice, but abandoning the country they loved. All the farmers I met in Zimbabwe loved the land, and though they tended to disparage urban clerks as paper-chewers, and politicians as parasites, they praised their workers and were proud of their labors. They knew the most intimate moods of the climate, the soil, the animals, the birds, the flora, the bush.

"We'll see elephants," Jones said as we headed north. "Look, there's a go-away bird. But I'm not going."

We drove to Chinhoyi, a small farming town of idle people and empty roads, where no one was farming and the lines at gas stations were three abreast and motionless. The bakeries had run out of flour, the shops had run out of cooking oil; there were mealies in the market for the local starch, sadza, but the price had increased tenfold. Some foreign charities, including the U.N. World Food Programme and an

Irish NGO called GOAL, were distributing food by giving it to the "war veterans," Mugabe's heavies, and asking them to hand it out in the rural areas.

"Food aid is politicized," a white Zimbabwean had told me in Harare. "Our greatest fear is that the NGOs will dig in and undermine agricultural production and make a niche for themselves in perpetuity."

"This was all farms once," Jones said from time to time, as he continued to Karoi. The gates and fences of large estates were broken, the fields were weed-choked and unplowed.

"No crops," Jones said. "This should be under winter wheat. There's good irrigation here, but look at the fields — nothing."

All we saw for the next fifty miles was one farm that seemed operational. Jones knew the man.

"They usually leave one farmer in place, but it's hell for him, because he's the man they turn to when they need a tractor or fuel or spare parts or money. And if he doesn't play ball they'll shut him down."

Not all the rolling hills in this part of Zimbabwe had been farmed. Old Africa still existed in thicknesses of trees and crumbled cliffs, vividly colored in twilight, the steep outcrops that signaled the beginning of the escarpment that banked down to the Zambezi, Zimbabwe's frontier with Zambia, home to a million animals large and small.

Dusk was casting a long shadow over these derelict farms and wooded hills, and night came on so quickly that before I knew it we were traveling in darkness.

At Makuti, just a wide place in the road where there was a turnoff to Kariba, Jones slowed his vehicle and said, "Look." A slender leopard crept out of the grass onto the shoulder, then crossed the road in our headlights, keeping low, its spots bright in the high beams. It penetrated the grass at the far side, its stiff tail bobbing.

"We need fuel," Jones said. "I know a chap in Kariba."

We drove slowly in the darkness for another hour or so.

Jones said, "Look."

Ahead, an elephant was loping down the road, looking bulky, its hindquarters looming. The animal did not turn toward us, did not speed up, did not do anything except continue to tread the white line in the middle of the road with its big flat feet, taking its time, making us follow at a decent distance. Finally, still without glancing back, he turned toward a big night-black thicket and paused, then crashed through the trees, shouldering the boughs apart.

"How could we leave this?" Jones said.

Twenty miles ahead was the tourist town of Kariba. In better times Kariba had been full of small hotels and bars, houseboats on the lake, good restaurants, suppliers and provisioners. Now not one hotel was occupied or even open, the bars were closed, and as we arrived at night no one was out. The town was in darkness.

Jones found his friend, the man with the diesel fuel, and filled his tank.

"We'll have to stay here," he said. "The border's closed."

"The hotels are shut," I said.

"I know a chap. He's not here — his house is empty. There's a key in a hiding place."

We went to the house, which was on the side of a hill overlooking the big inky lake, and it seemed that no sooner had I fallen asleep than Jones was clapping his hands in the darkness. "Up, up, up!" It was four-thirty, he said, and he wanted to be first in line at the frontier.

The Zambian side of the border was dense bush and savanna, scattered with small villages and mud huts and tiny garden plots, small granaries of woven twigs, and women pounding maize in mortars.

"Zim used to look like this," Mrs. Jones said, "years ago."

Past Kafue we crossed the railway that went on to Livingstone and Victoria Falls. One station was crowded with people sitting on bundles, sleeping in the shade of the platform, and stretched out on the tracks.

We stopped at a farm that was owned by a man who had lost his land in Zimbabwe.

Jones said, "We're headed to Lusaka. Just looking around. Anything happening?"

"The big social thing here is polo," the exiled farmer said. "I'm not that keen, but there's nothing else to do. There's a tournament this weekend."

"These Zimbos used to laugh at us," an elderly businessman told me at the polo match, pointing out the newcomers, the migrants, the exiles, the recent settlers and planters from Zimbabwe. "They said Zambia was backward, undeveloped, and so forth. Now they're here, and I can tell you we're not that happy about it."

The white Zambians I met at the polo match introduced me to several black Zambians. After the circumspection and gloom of Zimbabwe, Zambian frankness was a treat. Rodger Chongwe, who had been appointed Zambia's minister of justice and legal affairs in in 1991, said that he had resigned in 1995 "because I couldn't sit at the same table with thieves and drug dealers — my fellow ministers, of course." When he had begun speaking out, he had received death threats, and at a political rally in 1997 he was shot at and seriously wounded. He took the hint and escaped to Australia, and had just returned after five years. He said the former president, Frederick Chiluba, had encouraged the assassination attempt.

"What was he afraid of?"

"Of losing power. And he was a thief."

"How much had he stolen?"

"Four hundred million U.S. dollars."

I said that I had read that an elementary school in Hawaii regularly sent money to a school in Zambia so that the schoolchildren could have hot breakfasts.

"Politicians like Chiluba are laughing at those American kids for sending money."

This brought us to the subject of aid. Chongwe said, "The donors are making us lazy. The Japanese volunteers are doing what the city council used to do — mending potholes. It is better for us to have potholes. We would be forced to do something about them. We'd have to think for ourselves."

Another former member of parliament I met was Rolf Shenton. He was forty-one, born in Zambia. When he wasn't politicking he was a mechanic, with a garage in Lusaka. He said, "I get these aid guys at my workshop. I fix their vehicles. Yesterday it was the World Vision Land Rover. They're entrenched. Charity is a business. They don't even think about leaving. They've created imbalances in food, artificial shortages, sudden surpluses from abroad that undercut the local farmers. They make more problems than they solve."

"What's the answer?"

"We need to break the cycle. They send us doctors. Two thousand doctors have been trained by the University of Zambia Medical School. Fewer than one hundred and eighty have remained in the country. Does that make sense?"

"What about forgiving the debt?"

"Forgiving the debt is not going to solve the problem. What we need is noncorrupt government. There has not been a free election here since the 1960s."

Donors should be more interested in fair elections, Rodger Chongwe had said to me. Donors lived here, so they knew about the corruption. Donors shielded government thieves because they could tell them what to do. I asked Shenton what he thought of this.

"The donors must fuck off," he said. "Write that down! Use my name!"

I went back to Zimbabwe. The exchange rate had risen 20 percent in a week. The opposition party leader, Morgan Tsvangirai, was calling for a nationwide general strike.

The next day another Zimbabwean said, "If you don't leave now you might not make it," because the mass action would surely happen. There would be roadblocks, police cordons, Green Bombers (government-sponsored thugs). Mugabe's men would be out, and Mugabe's men would beat anyone who was demonstrating. They also hated whites. I would be beaten if I was seen outdoors. All shops would be closed. No planes would fly. The country would shut down.

So I left. People say, Nothing happens on time in Africa. Nothing will change in Zimbabwe. But, right on schedule, starting the following Monday, as promised, there was a week of protest, roadblocks, stoppages, and beatings. Whites were assaulted in Harare, and Morgan Tsvangirai was arrested. Mugabe proved that he had the loyalty of the police and the army and his thugs.

Ten days later the shops reopened and life, such as it was, resumed. There was some good news in late June. Zimbabwe, facing a serious shortfall in food, had found a new source in Zambia and was planning to import thirty thousand tons of maize, as well as soybeans and wheat, and twelve thousand tons of seed maize. All this from the bumper crop produced by the Zimbabwe farmers whose land had been taken from them, and who had begun farming over the border in Zambia.

January 2004

Dark Star Safari: Overland from Cairo to Cape Town

"Impossible to resist."—San Francisco Chronicle Book Review

Theroux takes us the length of Africa by rattletrap bus, forgotten train, and puffing steamer, confronting delay, discomfort, bullets, and bad food.

ISBN-13: 978-0-618-44687-2 / ISBN-10: 0-618-44687-7

Fresh Air Fiend: Travel Writings

"The ultimate good read for anyone fascinated by travel."—Miami Herald

From the crisp quiet of the Maine woods to the chaos of Hong Kong, Theroux journeys to remote hinterlands and crowded foreign capitals in this collection of essays.

ISBN-13: 978-0-618-12693-4 / ISBN-10: 0-618-12693-7

The Great Railway Bazaar: By Train Through Asia *"Compulsive reading."*—Graham Greene

Now a classic of the genre, Theroux's exhilarating first travel narrative chronicles his adventures by rail from Victoria Station in London to Tokyo Central.

ISBN-13: 978-0-618-65894-7 / ISBN-10: 0-618-65894-7

The Happy Isles of Oceania: Paddling the Pacific

"Perceptive, terribly readable, and wickedly funny."—Los Angeles Times Book Review

Theroux takes a trip in and around fifty-one Pacific islands, from New Zealand's rain forests to crocodile-infested New Guinea.

ISBN-13: 978-0-618-65898-5 / ISBN-10: 0-618-65898-X

The Kingdom by the Sea: A Journey Around the Coast of Great Britain

"A stimulating book."—New York Times

Theroux set out to uncover what the British were really like; the result is this perceptive, hilarious record of the journey. ISBN-13: 978-0-618-65895-4 / ISBN-10: 0-618-65895-5

The Old Patagonian Express: By Train Through the Americas

"Surely . . . the best book of train travel ever written."—Jan Morris

Theroux travels from New England to Argentina, ending his journey on the wandering Old Patagonian Express steam engine.

ISBN-13: 978-0-395-52105-2 / ISBN-10: 0-395-52105-X

Riding the Iron Rooster: By Train Through China *"Superb."*—Chicago Tribune

Here is China by rail, as seen and heard through the eyes and ears of one of the most intrepid and insightful travel writers of our time.

ISBN-13: 978-0-618-65897-8 / ISBN-10: 0-618-65897-1

Sir Vidia's Shadow: A Friendship Across Five Continents

"Both unputdownable and utterly engaging."—Jonathan Raban

This heartfelt and revealing account of Theroux's thirty-year friendship with the legendary V. S. Naipaul is an intimate record of a literary mentorship.

ISBN-13: 978-0-618-00199-6 / ISBN-10: 0-618-00199-9

Sunrise with Seamonsters: A Paul Theroux Reader

"A steamer trunk full of delights."—Chicago Sun-Times

This collection of decidedly opinionated articles, essays, and ruminations transports the reader to exotic, unexpected places in the world.

BN-13: 978-0-395-41501-6 / ISBN-10: 0-395-41501-2